The Indian World
of George Washington

The Indian World of George Washington

THE FIRST PRESIDENT, THE FIRST
AMERICANS, AND THE BIRTH OF THE NATION

Colin G. Calloway

OXFORD
UNIVERSITY PRESS

OXFORD
UNIVERSITY PRESS

Oxford University Press is a department of the University of Oxford.
It furthers the University's objective of excellence in research, scholarship,
and education by publishing worldwide. Oxford is a registered trade mark of
Oxford University Press in the UK and certain other countries.

Published in the United States of America by Oxford University Press
198 Madison Avenue, New York, NY 10016, United States of America.

Library of Congress Cataloging-in-Publication Data
Names: Calloway, Colin G. (Colin Gordon), 1953– author.
Title: The Indian world of George Washington: the first president, the first Americans,
and the birth of the nation / Colin G. Calloway.
Description: New York, NY: Oxford University Press, [2018] |
Includes bibliographical references and index.
Identifiers: LCCN 2017028686 | ISBN 9780190652166 (hardback: alk. paper)
Subjects: LCSH: Washington, George, 1732–1799—Relations with Indians. |
Indians of North America—Government relations. | Indians of North America—
Wars—1750–1815. | Indians of North America—History—18th century. |
United States—History—French and Indian War, 1754–1763. |
United States—History—Revolution, 1775–1783.
Classification: LCC E312.17 .C17 2018 | DDC 323.1197090/33—dc23
LC record available at https://lccn.loc.gov/2017028686

1 3 5 7 9 8 6 4 2
Printed by Edwards Brothers Malloy, United States of America

To Marcia, Graeme, and Meg

CONTENTS

List of Illustrations   ix

Individual Native Americans in the George Washington Story   xi

Author's Note   xv

Acknowledgments   xvii

Introduction   1

ONE: LEARNING CURVES

CHAPTER 1: Virginia's Indian Country   19

CHAPTER 2: The Ohio Company and the Ohio Country   45

CHAPTER 3: Into Tanaghrisson's World   66

CHAPTER 4: Tanaghrisson's War   84

CHAPTER 5: Braddock and the Limits of Empire   102

CHAPTER 6: Frontier Defense and a Cherokee Alliance   124

CHAPTER 7: Frontier Advance and a Cherokee War   148

TWO: THE OTHER REVOLUTION

CHAPTER 8: Confronting the Indian Boundary   171

CHAPTER 9: "A good deal of Land"   191

CHAPTER 10: The Question of Indian Allies   215

CHAPTER 11: Town Destroyer   235

CHAPTER 12: Killing Crawford   260

CHAPTER 13: Building a Nation on Indian Land   283

THREE: THE FIRST PRESIDENT AND THE FIRST AMERICANS

CHAPTER 14: An Indian Policy for the New Nation   321

CHAPTER 15: Courting McGillivray   346

CHAPTER 16: The Greatest Indian Victory   378

CHAPTER 17: Philadelphia Indian Diplomacy   397

CHAPTER 18: Achieving Empire   422

CHAPTER 19: Transforming Indian Lives   451

CHAPTER 20: A Death and a Non-Death   477

Abbreviations   493

Notes   497

Index   581

LIST OF ILLUSTRATIONS

FIGURES

1. Map published to accompany Washington's Ohio journal, showing the extent of Virginia's western claims, 1754   35

2. George Washington's map, accompanying his "journal to the Ohio," 1754   82

3. Washington Peace Medal, 1792   332

4. Hoboithle Mico. *Hopothle Mico, or the Talassee King of the Creeks,* by John Trumbull, 1790   352

5. Little Turtle, 1797   382

6. Silas Dinsmoor   464

7. Benjamin Hawkins   469

COLOR PHOTO INSERT (PLATES)

1. George Washington, by Charles Willson Peale, 1772

2. Ostenaco (*Scyacust Ukah*), by Sir Joshua Reynolds, 1762

3. *The Death of General Montgomery in the Attack on Quebec,* by John Trumbull, 1786

4. Louis Cook, by John Trumbull, c. 1786

5. Joseph Brant (Thayendanegea), by Gilbert Stuart, 1786

6. Cornplanter. *Portrait of Ki-on-twog-ky,* by F. Bartoli, 1796

7. Henry Knox, by Charles Willson Peale, c. 1784

8. Good Peter, by John Trumbull, 1792

9. Arthur St. Clair, by Charles Willson Peale, 1782

10. Timothy Pickering, by Charles Willson Peale, c. 1792

11. Indian delegation in Philadelphia, c. 1800

12. Red Jacket, after a portrait by Charles Bird King, c. 1828

13. *Apotheosis of Washington* or *Commemoration of Washington,* by John James Barralet, 1802

MAPS

1. Eastern North America at the Time of Washington's Birth   21

2. Washington's Western Lands   39

3. Washington's Ohio Country, 1744–1758   46

4. Shifting Boundaries and Land Cessions, 1763–1775   186

5. Washington's Invasion of Iroquoia, 1779   252

6. Washington's Western Journey, 1784   296

7. The Native American South   349

8. Washington's War against the Northwestern Confederacy, 1790–1794   379

INDIVIDUAL NATIVE AMERICANS
IN THE GEORGE WASHINGTON STORY

Ackawonothio (Shawnee or western Delaware chief)

Aliquippa; Queen Allaquippa (Seneca woman chief, d. 1754)

Aroas: see Silver Heels

Atiatoharongwen: see Cook, Louis

Attakullakulla; Ada-gal'kala; Ouconecaw; Little Carpenter (Overhill Cherokee chief, c. 1705–1779 or 1780)

Aupaumut, Hendrick (Stockbridge Mahican, 1757–1830)

Beaver: see Tamaqua

Belt of Wampum; the Belt; Kaghswaghtaniunt; Tohashwughtonionty; White Thunder (Seneca, d. by 1762)

Big Tree; Great Tree; Karontowanen; Kiandochgowa (Seneca, d. 1792)

Black Hoof; Catahecassa (Shawnee, c. 1740–1832)

Bloody Fellow; Nenetuah; Nenetooyah; Washington gave him the name General Eskaqua or Iskagua, meaning "Clear Sky" (Cherokee, d. c. 1800)

Blue Jacket; Waweyapiersenwaw (Pekowi Shawnee war chief, c. 1743–1808)

Brant, Joseph; Thayendanegea (Mohawk war chief, 1743–1807)

Brown, John (Chickasaw chief)

Buckongahelas; Pachgantschihilas (Delaware chief, c. 1720–1804/5)

Bullen, Captain James; Jimmy Bullen (Catawba chief, d. 1758)

Canasatego (Onondaga, d. 1750 or 1760)

Captain Jacobs; Tewea (Delaware war chief, d. 1756)

Captain Pipe: see Hopocan

Chutloh; Tsu-la; Kingfisher (Cherokee)

Colbert, George; Tootematubbe (Chickasaw chief, 1764–1839?)

Colbert, William; Cooshemataha (Chickasaw chief, d. c. 1835)

Conoghquieson; Kanaghquaesa (Oneida sachem, d. 1776 or 1777)

Cook, Louis or Lewis; Colonel Louis; Atiatoharongwen; Akiatonharónkwen; Atayatagh-ronghta (Abenaki–African American–Kahnawake Mohawk, 1740–1814)

Cooper, Polly (Oneida)

Cornplanter; Kayenthwahkeh; Ki-on-twog-ky; sometimes called Obeal or Captain Abeel (Allegheny Seneca war chief, 1740s or 1752/53–1836)

Cornstalk; Colesquo (Mekoche Shawnee chief, c. 1720–1777)

Corn Tassel; Tassel; Old Tassel; Utsi'dsata (Cherokee, d. 1788)

Cussetah Mico; Cussetah King; Cussitah King (Creek chief): see Eneah Mico

Custaloga (Delaware chief, d. 1776)

Delaware George; Nenatcheehunt; Nenatchehan (Delaware, d. c. 1763)

Doublehead; Chequalaga; Chuquilatague (Cherokee, 1744–1807); brother of Corn Tassel

Dragging Canoe; Tsí-yu-gûnsí-ni; Tsi'yu-gûnsi'ni; Chincanacina (Overhill Cherokee; head warrior of Malaquo, or Great Island and Chickamauga chief, c. 1730–1792)

DuCoigne, Jean Baptiste (Kaskaskia chief, 1750–1811)

Efau Hadjo; Mad Dog (Creek chief of Tuckabatchee)

Eneah Mico; Neah Mico; Cussetah Mico; Cussetah King; Cussitah King; the Fat King; Fat King of Cussitah (Creek chief)

Egushawa; Egushewa; Agushaway; Agashawa; Negushwa (Ottawa war chief, c. 1730– c. 1796/1800)

Farmer's Brother; Honanyawas; Honeyewus; Ogh-ne-wi-ge-was (Buffalo Creek Seneca chief, c. 1725–1815)

Franchimastabé (Choctaw chief, d. c. 1801)

Fusatchee Mico; White Bird King; Bird Tail King (Creek chief of Cussetah)

Gill, Joseph Louis (Abenaki chief at Odanak, 1719–1798)

Good Peter; Agwerondongwas; Agwrondougwas; Gwedelhes (Oneida chief of the Eel clan, d. 1793)

Guyasuta; Kayashuta; Kayasota (Allegheny Seneca chief, c. 1725–1794 or 1795)

Hagler; King Hagler; Nopkehe (Catawba chief, c. 1690/1700–1763)

Half King: see Tanaghrisson

Half Town; Gahgeote; Achiout (Seneca)

Hallowing King (Creek chief of Coweta)

Handsome Lake; Ganiodaio (Seneca, c. 1735–1815)

Hanging Maw; Uskwa'li-gu'ta; Scolaguta (Cherokee chief, d. 1798)

Hendrick, Theyanoguin (Mohawk, c. 1680–1755)

Hendricks, Captain Solomon (Stockbridge)

Hoboithle Mico; Hopoithle Mico; Opothle Mico; the Tame King; Tallassee King; Good Child King (Creek chief of Tallassee, d. 1813)

Hopocan; Hobocan; Pipe; Captain Pipe (Delaware chief of the Wolf clan, c. 1725–1794)

Jeskakake; known to the French as Déjiquéqué (Cayuga chief)

Judd's Friend: see Ostenaco

Kanuksusy; Canachquasy; Cassiowea; Newcastle; Washington gave him the name Fairfax (Seneca, d. 1756)

Keekyuscung; Ketiuscund (Delaware chief)

Keenaguna; Lying Fawn (Cherokee)

Keehteetah; Keenettehet; Kenotetah: see Rising Fawn (Cherokee)

Killbuck; John Killbuck; Gelemend; Kaylelamund (Delaware chief of the Turtle
    clan, c. 1722–1811)
Killbuck, John, Jr. (Delaware); son of John
Killbuck, Thomas (Delaware); son of John
Kithagusta; Ketagusta; Kitegisky; Keetakeuskah; the Prince (Cherokee); brother of
    Oconoosta
Kunoskeskie: see Watts, John
Little Turkey; Kanitta; Kanagita (Cherokee chief, d. 1802)
Little Turtle; Mishikinaakwa (Miami war chief, 1752–1812)
Logan; John Logan; Tachnechdorus (Mingo, 1725–1780)
McGillivray, Alexander (Creek chief, 1759–1793)
Mad Dog: see Efau Hadjo
Memeskia; Old Briton (Piankeshaw Miami, d. 1752)
Moluntha; Melonthe (Mekoche Shawnee chief, d. 1786)
Montour, Andrew; Satellihu; Eghnisara (Oneida-French intermediary)
Neetotehelemy; Netawatwees; Newcomer (Delaware chief, d. 1776)
New Arrow (Seneca)
Nimham, Abraham (Stockbridge, d. 1778)
Nontuaka; the Northward; the North Nation (Cherokee)
Neolin (Delaware prophet, fl. 1750s–1760s)
Occom, Samson (Mohegan preacher, 1723–1792)
Oconostota (Cherokee chief; First Warrior of the Overhill Cherokees and Great
    Warrior of the Cherokees, c. 1712–1782)
Ogaghsagighte; Jean Baptiste (Kahnawake Mohawk)
Opechancanough (Powhatan chief, 1545–1644)
Orono, Joseph (Penobscot chief, 1688?–1801)
Ostenaco; Ustenaka; Judd's Friend; also known by his war title Outacite, Outacity,
    Outassite, Skiagusta, or Mankiller of Keowee (Cherokee chief; Second Warrior
    of the Overhill Cherokees, c. 1703–c. 1780)
Otsequette; Otsiquette, Peter; Ojekheta; Otchikeita (Oneida, d. 1792); adopted son
    of the marquis de Lafayette
Painted Pole; Red Pole; Messquakenoe (Shawnee, d. 1797)
Paxinosa; Bucksinosa (eastern Shawnee chief)
Pisquetomen (Delaware, d. c. 1763), brother of Shingas and Tamaqua
Piominko; Piomingo; Opoia Mutaha; Mountain Leader (Chickasaw chief,
    c. 1750–1798)
Powhatan; Wahunsonacock (Powhatan chief, c. 1547–1618)
Pontiac (Ottawa war chief, c. 1720–1769)
Raven: (Cherokee) war title of Chota, or Colonah; the Raven of Chota at the time
    was Savanukah, nephew of Oconostota
Raven Warrior: (Cherokee) war title of Hiwassee
Red Jacket; Sagoyewatha, "Keeps Them Awake"; Cowkiller (Seneca, c. 1758–1830)

Rising Fawn; Keehteetah; Keenettehet; Kenotetah (Cherokee from Hiwassee)

Saint-Aubin, Ambroise (Maliseet chief, d. 1780)

Sayengeraghta; Sayenqueraghta; Kayenquarachton; Kayinguaraghtoh; Old Smoke; Vanishing Smoke; the Seneca King (Seneca chief, d. 1786)

Scarouady; Scaroyady; Monacatootha; Monacatoocha (Oneida half king, fl. 1751–1756)

Shingas (Delaware war chief, fl. 1740–1763)

Silver Heels; Aroas (Seneca messenger); son-in-law of Belt of Wampum

Skenandoah; John Skenandon (Oneida, d. 1816)

Swashan (Abenaki chief)

Taboca (Choctaw chief)

Tamaqua; the Beaver; King Beaver (Delaware chief, d. c. 1770)

Tanaghrisson; Tanachrisson; Thanayieson; Johonerissa; Deanaghrison; the Half King (Seneca, c. 1700–1754)

Tarhe; the Crane (Wyandot chief, 1742–1818)

Teedyuscung; baptized as Gideon (eastern Delaware chief, 1700–1763)

Tekakiska; Tekakisskee; Taken Out of the Water (Cherokee)

Teesteke; Toostaka; Common Disturber; the Waker (Cherokee)

Thaosagwat, Hanyerry or Hanyost (Oneida, d. 1779)

Tomah, Pierre (Maliseet chief, fl. 1775–1780)

Ucahula (Cherokee warrior)

Uhhaunauwaunmut, Captain Solomon (Stockbridge)

Ugulayacabe; Wolf's Friend (Chickasaw, fl. 1780s–1799, d. by 1805)

Vincent, Captain John (Kahnawake Mohawk)

Vincent, Lewis; Louis Vincent; Captain Lewis; Sawantanan; Sawatanen (Huron from Lorette; Dartmouth graduate)

Wawhatchee (Cherokee, head warrior of Keowee)

Watts, John; Kunoskeskie; Young Tassel (Chickamauga Cherokee chief, d. 1802)

White Bird King; Fusatchee Mico (Creek chief)

White Eyes; Quequedegatha; Koquethagechton (Delaware war chief of the Turtle clan, c. 1730–1778)

White Eyes, George Morgan; son of White Eyes

White Lieutenant (Creek war chief of Okfuskee, d. 1799) [There was also a White Lieutenant of Coushatta and of Oakchoy]

White Mingo; Kanaghorait (Seneca chief, d. by 1777)

Wingenund (Delaware chief)

AUTHOR'S NOTE

THERE IS NO GENERAL agreement about the appropriate collective term to apply to the indigenous peoples of North America. Although I occasionally use Native, Native American, indigenous, or, as in the title, First Americans, I most often use Indians or Indian people, which was the term most commonly used at the time. In writing a book aimed at a broad readership, I have used the names for Indian nations that seem to be the most readily recognizable to the most people: Iroquois rather than Haudenosaunee; Mohawks rather than Kanienkehaka; Delawares rather than Lenni Lenapee; and Cherokee, which derives from other people's name for them, rather than how Cherokees referred to themselves, *Ani-Yunwiya,* "the principal people." Applying the same criteria to individuals necessarily involves some inconsistencies, such as Joseph Brant rather than Thayendanegea and White Eyes instead of Quequedegatha or Koquethagechton, but Attakullakulla rather than Little Carpenter and Piominko rather than Mountain Leader.

ACKNOWLEDGMENTS

I HAVE ACCUMULATED MANY debts in the course of researching and writing this book. My notes cite the many scholars of Native American history and of George Washington whose work has guided and informed me. A glance at the number of times *PGW* appears in the notes will convey a sense of how much I have relied upon and benefited from the dedicated and meticulous work of the teams of scholars who have compiled, edited, and made accessible the *Papers of George Washington.*

Dartmouth College supported my work with sabbatical leave and the award of a senior faculty fellowship. Years of teaching at a college where I have Native and non-Native students in every class has been invaluable preparation for writing a book like this for a broad spectrum of readers, some of whom may see themselves on opposing sides of the country's history. Macy Ferguson and Presidential Scholars Theresa Smith and Kevin Schorr all assisted early in the project by gathering material from the *Washington Papers*; Theresa continued to contribute with sustained interest and some excellent research of her own.

For encouragement, conversations, suggestions, interest, and support at different times along the way, and in some cases all along the way, I am grateful to Douglas Bradburn, Timothy Breen, Catherine Brekus, Stephen Brumwell, Ric Burns, the late Drew Cayton, Jay Hull, David Hildebrand, N. Bruce Duthu, Dan Gerstle, Patrick Griffin, Ed Hamilton, Fred Hoxie, Tsianina Lomawaima, Michael McDonnell, Alyssa Mt. Pleasant, Kristofer Ray, James C. Rice, Chris

Rogers, Mark Sampson-Vos, Elliott West, David Silverman, Rick Thompson, Paul Williams, and Jace Weaver. Thomas Agostino, Kris Ray, and James Rice read and provided feedback on selected chapters from an early draft of the manuscript; Stephen Brumwell, Michael McDonnell, and David Silverman read the whole thing.

I am deeply grateful to the staffs of the Baker-Berry Library and Rauner Library at Dartmouth College; the New York Public Library, Manuscripts and Archives Division; the Massachusetts Historical Society; and Meg McSweeney and the David Library of the American Revolution at Washington Crossing, Pennsylvania. Having spent a quarter of a century working in a Native American Studies program, I wanted to complete this book at George Washington's Mount Vernon in Virginia. The Fred W. Smith National Library for the Study of George Washington awarded me a fellowship that allowed me to do so. Doug Bradburn, Stephen McLeod, Mark Santangelo, Mary Jongema, Emily Rosa, and all their colleagues and staff at Mount Vernon made the experience pleasant and productive beyond all my expectations.

I have presented parts of the material in this book at the Native American and Indigenous Studies Association conferences in Austin, Texas, and in Washington, DC; the Boston Athenaeum; the Huntington Library in San Marino, California; George Washington's Mount Vernon; the David Library of the American Revolution; the University of Georgia; George Washington University; the Norwich, Vermont, Historical Society; the Vermont Humanities Council; and Yale University.

At Oxford University Press, I have benefited from the support, professionalism, and expertise of many people. Timothy Bent and Niko Pfund demonstrated early enthusiasm and sustained commitment to the project. Tim's expert editing helped tighten the book and saved readers from my fondness for too many overlong quotations. Alyssa O'Connell was enormously helpful in the early stages of securing permissions; Mariah White picked up where Alyssa left off and saw the manuscript into production; and production editor Janet Foxman steered it expertly to completion. In addition, I am grateful to India Cooper for her careful and thoughtful copy editing, to Jeffrey Ward for his excellent maps, and to Meg for her help with the jacket design.

Of course, any errors, omissions, or misstatements are nobody's fault but my own.

Book dedications expressing love and gratitude to my family have become routine, and I would not have it any other way. Marcia has been there since my very first book; Graeme and Meg grew up with me writing books. Having these three people as my world makes me think I have been rather more fortunate than anyone deserves to be.

Introduction

ON MONDAY AFTERNOON, FEBRUARY 4, 1793, President George Washington sat down to dinner at his official home on Market Street in Philadelphia. Washington's dinners were often elaborate affairs, with numerous guests, liveried servants, and plenty of food and wine. On this occasion Secretary of State Thomas Jefferson, Secretary of War Henry Knox, Attorney General Edmund Randolph, Governor of the Northwest Territory Arthur St. Clair, and "the Gentlemen of the President's family" dined with him because they were hosting an official delegation. Six Indian men, two Indian women, and two interpreters, representing the Kaskaskia, Peoria, Piankashaw, Potawatomi, and Mascouten Nations, had traveled more than eight hundred miles from the Wabash and Illinois country to see the president. Before dining, they made speeches and presented Washington with a calumet pipe of peace and strings of wampum. Thomas Jefferson took notes.[1]

Just one week later, Monday, February 11, Washington's dinner guests included several chiefs from the Six Nations—the Haudenosaunee or Iroquois—a Christian Mahican named Hendrick Aupaumut, and Akiatonharónkwen or Atiatoharongwen, the son of an Abenaki mother and an African American father, who had been adopted by Mohawks but now lived in Oneida country, and who was usually called "Colonel Louis Cook" after Washington approved his commission for services during the Revolution. Before dinner the president thanked his Indian guests for their diplomatic efforts in carrying messages to tribes in the West.[2]

Indian visits halted when yellow fever broke out in Philadelphia in the summer of 1793. Five thousand people died, and twenty thousand fled the city, including, for a time, Washington, Jefferson, Knox, and Secretary of the Treasury Alexander Hamilton, who survived a bout of the fever. A Chickasaw delegation on its way to see the president turned back on hearing of the epidemic in the fall.³ But the visits resumed the next year. On Saturday afternoon, June 14, 1794, Washington welcomed a delegation of thirteen Cherokee chiefs to his Market Street home in Philadelphia. They were in the city to conduct treaty negotiations, and the members of Washington's cabinet—Jefferson, Hamilton, Knox, and Colonel Timothy Pickering—were also present. In accordance with Native American diplomatic protocol, everyone present smoked and passed around the long-stemmed pipe, in ritual preparation for good talks and in a sacred commitment to speak truth and honor pledges made. The president delivered a speech that had been written in advance. Several of the Cherokee chiefs spoke. Everyone ate and drank "plentifully of Cake & wine," and the chiefs left "seemingly well pleased."⁴ Four weeks later, Washington met with a delegation of Chickasaws he had invited to Philadelphia. He delivered a short speech, expressing his love for the Chickasaws and his gratitude for their assistance as scouts on American campaigns against the tribes north of the Ohio, and referred them to Henry Knox for other business. As usual, he puffed on the pipe, ate, and drank with them.⁵

The image of Washington smoking and dining with Indian chiefs does not mesh with depictions of the Father of the Nation as stiff, formal, and aloof, but it reminds us that in Washington's day the government dealt with Indians as foreign nations rather than domestic subjects. The still-precarious republic dared not ignore the still-powerful Indian nations on its frontiers. In dealing with the Indians, Henry Knox advised the new president, "every proper expedient that can be devised to gain their affections, and attach them to the interest of the Union, should be adopted."⁶ Deeply conscious of how he performed in his role as the first president, and an accomplished political actor, Washington engaged in the performative aspects of Indian diplomacy, sharing the calumet pipe and exchanging strings and belts of wampum—purple and white beads made from marine shells and woven into geometric patterns that reinforced and recorded the speaker's words. New York Indian commissioners explained it was Indian custom when meeting in council to "smoke their Pipes together, and to open their Minds to each other."⁷ The most powerful man in the United States followed the custom of his Indian visitors.

These Indian visits were not isolated events, and the Indians were not unwelcome dinner guests. Tribal delegations were a regular sight on the streets of Philadelphia and other colonial cities before the Revolution, and they continued to visit the new nation's new capital in order to conduct diplomacy or just, as the missionary Rev. Samuel Kirkland put it, "to get a peep at the great American Chief."[8] Formal dinners were not just an occasion to share a meal but a form of political theater essential to establishing relationships between hosts and guests, providing an opportunity for the host to demonstrate hospitality, display wealth, and assert status through food and wine, seating arrangements and manners, and the meanings attached to all those things.[9] In his first term in office, Washington dined, often more than once, with Mohawks, Senecas, Oneidas, Cherokees, Chickasaws, and Creeks. In some cases, they came to Philadelphia because he had personally invited them. In later years, Washington occasionally hosted Indian dinner guests at Mount Vernon, and he continued to dine with Indian delegates to the very end of his presidency: in the last week of November 1796, he dined with four groups of Indians on four different days.[10]

Washington's entire Indian policy and his vision for the nation depended on the acquisition of Indian territory, but in 1793–94 he insisted that no one talk to the visiting Indians about buying their lands.[11] These were perilous years for the young nation: hostile foreign powers, Britain in the North and Spain in the South, threatened American borders and interests; a powerful Indian confederacy north of the Ohio River had defeated one American army, destroyed another, and remained defiant; and what Washington called "the momentous occurrences in Europe" threatened to embroil the United States in conflict between Britain and Revolutionary France.[12] Washington knew that Indian lands were vital to the future growth of the United States, but, as his gag order on talk of buying land illustrates, he also knew that Indians were vital to the national security, and on occasion the very survival, of the fragile republic.

American history has largely forgotten what Washington knew. Narratives of national expansion and Indian conquest often neglect the complexity of Indian relations and ignore the reality of Indian power in the very formative years of the nation. Historians of the early Republic who focus on creating a new nation, the rivalry between Hamilton and Jefferson, and the challenges posed by relations with Britain and Revolutionary France often treat Indian affairs as tangential or even irrelevant.[13] In fact, federal officials devoted much time, attention, and ink to conducting diplomatic relations with

Indian politicians who, as the Moravian Rev. John Heckewelder observed, "display[ed] as much skill and dexterity, perhaps, as any people upon earth" in "the management of their national affairs."[14] Indian nations figured alongside European nations in the founding fathers' thinking about the current and future state of the union. Indian leaders were adept at playing on American fears of British and Spanish backing for Indian resistance. Debates over the sovereignty of the United States and struggles over the extent and limits of federal authority and states' rights centered on Indian treaties, and Indian issues, wars, and land policies were critical in developing a strong central government.[15]

Multiple books tell us how Washington forged the nation, and how he handled partnerships and rivalries between various founding fathers, but nothing was more central than the relationship between the first president and the first Americans. From cradle to grave Washington inhabited a world built on the labor of African people and on the land of dispossessed Indian people. Indian people were not as ubiquitous in his daily life as the enslaved men, women, and children who planted, tended, and harvested his crops, cut his wood, prepared and served his food, washed his laundry, cleaned his house, and attended to his every need. Nevertheless, Indian people and Indian country loomed large in Washington's world. His life intersected constantly with them, and events in Native America shaped the direction his life took, even if they occurred "offstage." Indian land dominated his thinking and his vision for the future. Indian nations challenged the growth of his nation. A thick Indian strand runs through the life of George Washington as surely as it runs through the history of early America.

Probably more books have been written about Washington than about any other American, but few of them pay much attention to Indians, let alone consider the role they played in his life. Certainly none of Washington's biographers have shown any particular interest or expertise in Indian history. It would command more attention if biographers recounting Washington's schemes to acquire and develop territory beyond the Appalachians replaced the term "western land"—which implies that it was an unclaimed resource—with "Indian land"—which acknowledges that it was someone's homeland. Washington spent much of his adult life surveying and speculating in Indian lands. The Virginia of his youth was very much a British colony—linked to the mother country across the Atlantic by ties of loyalty, taste, and economy—but Virginians who ventured a hundred miles or so into the interior of the continent quickly found themselves in Indian territory. Virginia was at the forefront of colonial expansion westward, and Washington was at the forefront of Virginian expansion. Washington was ambitious, for himself and for his nation.[16] His ambition led him down many paths, but it always led him back to Indian country.

Washington's first trips westward were as a surveyor, and he looked on Indian lands with a surveyor's eye for the rest of his life. Surveyors transformed "wilderness" that disoriented and threatened settler colonists into an ordered landscape they could understand and utilize. In colonial Virginia surveyors enjoyed status; in Indian country they met with suspicion if not outright hostility. Armed with compass, chains, and logbooks, surveyors were the outriders of an advancing settler society intent on turning Indian homelands and hunting territories into a commodity that could be measured and bounded, bought and sold, and Indians knew it. When the frontier trader Christopher Gist did some surveying near the Delaware town of Shannopin, on the southeast side of the Allegheny River, in the fall of 1750, he did so on the quiet: "I...set my Compass privately, & took the Distance across the River, for I understood it was dangerous to let a Compass be seen among these Indians."[17]

Washington and his fellow Virginians speculated, surveyed, and encroached upon western lands on the assumption that permission from a king, governor, or council gave them the right to do so, and they often acted as though any Indians could cede the land of all Indians. But Indian people had something to say about it, and were intent on defending their rights and the territory that colonial governments and land companies carved up so cavalierly. "That it is a difficult matter to discover the true owner of any lands among the Indians is a gross error, which must arise from ignorance of the matter or from a cause which does not require explanation," Sir William Johnson, the British superintendent of Indian affairs in the North, observed to the Lords of Trade in 1764. "Each nation is perfectly well acquainted with its exact original bounds."[18] Indian country was a mosaic of tribal homelands and hunting territories, where individual nations guarding their own interests created a complicated landscape of multiple foreign policies, competing agendas, and shifting strategies. Speculating, surveying, and making land deals in Indian country required knowledge, quick learning, and fast footwork. It was no place for a novice.

As a novice in Indian country, Washington misread situations and mishandled Indian allies, and in the process sparked a war that in turn set in motion developments that led directly to the American

Revolution. Blessed and blinkered by hindsight and Washington's future role, historians of earlier generations often put the best face on his diplomatic and military expeditions into the Ohio country in 1753 and 1754, respectively. One described Washington's journal of the first expedition, which he hurriedly wrote on his return and which was widely published, as "a testimonial to his maturity and capacity for leadership."[19] Another, glossing over the debacle of the second expedition, pronounced: "It is thus obvious that Washington was already demonstrating those qualities of courage and leadership indicative of his future greatness."[20] In reality, young Washington found himself out of his depth in a complex world of rumors, wampum belts, and tribal agendas. As events spiraled out of his control, he received a crash course in Indian diplomacy, intertribal politics, and frontier conflict under the tutelage of a formidable Seneca named Tanaghrisson.

During the French and Indian War, Washington participated in two British military campaigns to take the strategically crucial Forks of the Ohio from the French. The first, in which he gave General Edward Braddock bad advice, was a disaster; the second, in which he predicted failure and tried to undermine General John Forbes, succeeded. Indians determined the outcome of both.

For Washington the so-called French and Indian War was primarily a war against Indians. As commander of the Virginia Regiment defending western areas of the colony against Indian raids, he learned much about frontier warfare, and about fighting with limited means. Indian diplomacy helped end the fighting in Washington's theater of operations. Indian actions at the close of the war shaped Crown policies that set the American colonies on the road to revolution and helped push Washington's personal break with Britain. The Anglo-Cherokee War and the multitribal resistance movement known as Pontiac's War prompted the British government to take two crucial steps: impose a limit on westward expansion, which threatened Washington's investments in Indian land, and keep a standing army in America, which required taxing the colonies to pay for it. For Americans the Revolution was a war for independence, and it was also a war for Indian land; for Indians, the Revolution was a war for their land, and it was also a war for their independence. The Indians' fight, which for many tribes meant allegiance to the British, provided patriots with an important unifying cause.[21]

Washington never moved west himself, but the West beckoned him and the nation he led. His long association with the region as surveyor, speculator, soldier, landowner, and politician shaped his career and his vision of America's future tied to western development. As a young man, he pursued wealth in land and a military reputation in the West; in his later years, the West became a key to building national unity.[22] By the end of his life, according to one of the editors of the monumental *Papers of George Washington,* he probably knew more than any other man in America about the frontier and its significance to the future of his country.[23] He had also accumulated more than 45,000 acres of prime real estate in present-day Kentucky, Ohio, Pennsylvania, the Shenandoah Valley, and West Virginia.[24] It was the West, says another of his editors, that "made the Virginia farmer lift his eyes to prospects beyond his own fields and his native Virginia"; the West that "stretched his mind" to embrace an expansive vision of a republican empire; the West that, more than anything else except the Revolutionary War, prepared him for his role as nation builder.[25]

Washington knew that the frontier was Indian country and that the future he envisioned would be realized at the expense of the people who lived there. He presided over and participated in their dispossession. He dispatched armies into Indian country; he lost an army in Indian country. The bulk of the federal budget during his presidency was spent in wars against Indians, and their affairs figured regularly and prominently in the president's conferences with his heads of departments.[26] He promoted policies that divested Indians of millions of acres; he sent treaty commissioners into Indian country and signed the treaties they made, even as he sometimes studiously avoided conversations about purchasing land with Indian delegates who came to the capital. His conduct of Indian affairs shaped the authority of the president in war and diplomacy. He participated in, indeed insisted on, the transformation of Indian life and culture. In the course of his life, he met many of the most prominent Native Americans of his day: Shingas, Tanaghrisson, Scarouady, Guyasuta, Attakullakulla, Bloody Fellow, Joseph Brant, Cornplanter, Red Jacket, Jean Baptiste DuCoigne, Alexander McGillivray, Little Turtle, Blue Jacket, Piominko. He also met many lesser-known individuals, who cropped up time and again in dealings between Indians and colonists, men like the Seneca messenger Aroas or Silver Heels, the Oneida-French intermediary Andrew Montour, and the Seneca Kanuksusy, who appeared in colonial negotiations under his English name, Newcastle. Having more than one name was not uncommon. Washington himself was given or assumed an Indian name, Conotocarious, meaning "Town Destroyer" or "Devourer of Villages," and an Indian messenger who arrived at Fort Harmar in July 1788 was identified as "George Washington, a Delaware."[27] He was not the only Indian to bear Washington's name.

Washington knew and associated with men who knew and associated with Indians: soldiers who fought against Indians; merchants who traded with Indians; interpreters who moved back and forth to Indian country; agents who implemented his policies there; missionaries who lived and prayed with Indians; men who hunted, traveled, ate, and drank with Indians; men who shared lodges, beds, and relatives with Indians; western politicians who built their political reputations fighting and dealing with Indians; speculators who, like Washington himself, acquired large amounts of Indian land as a way of elevating their status in society. Washington's world was one where eastern elites as well as frontier folk were steeped in Indian affairs.[28] Charles Thomson, secretary of the Continental and Confederation Congresses from 1774 to 1789, brought Washington word of his election to the presidency and traveled with him to the inauguration. Thomson was an adopted Delaware. As a young man, before he shifted his attention to business and politics, he had immersed himself in Indian affairs: a Latin tutor at the Quaker school in Philadelphia, he served as a clerk and copyist for the Delaware chief Teedyuscung, acted as secretary at the Treaty of Easton in 1757, and wrote a tract blaming Indian support for the French on Pennsylvania's record of unscrupulous treaty practices—in which he also criticized Washington's conduct in dealing with the Indians in the Ohio country.[29] Charles Lee, one of Washington's generals in the Revolution, claimed to have married an Iroquois woman, was adopted by the Iroquois, and had an Iroquois son. (The child inherited his clan and tribal identity from his mother).[30] Benjamin Hawkins, whom Washington appointed superintendent of the southern Indians, spoke Muskogee, was adopted by the Creeks, and had seven children with his common-law wife, Lavinia Downs, said by some to be a Creek woman. The Irishman Richard Butler, appointed superintendent of Indian affairs after the Revolution, traded with the Shawnees, had a Shawnee wife, sent Washington a Shawnee vocabulary when Catherine the Great of Russia asked the president for information on Indian languages, and died with a Shawnee tomahawk in his skull. Washington moved among networks of men who were deeply interested in Indian affairs and were sometimes intimately acquainted with individual Indians. For many of these men, acquiring Indian lands seemed as natural as breathing. Some swindled each other out of land with as few qualms as they swindled Indians out of land.

Indians were of central importance in Washington's world, but for most of his life he operated on the peripheries of theirs. When he speculated in Indian lands, fought Indian enemies, and exchanged wampum belts with Indian chiefs, he touched the edges of an indigenous continent crisscrossed by networks of kinship, exchange, and alliance among multiple nations. For most of his life, several colonial powers competed for that continent but none controlled it, and indigenous power in the interior affected and limited imperial ambitions.[31] In Washington's administration, the process of creating the "United States" occurred "in dialogue with other nations," including Native nations. Establishing the sovereignty of the United States required wrestling with the sovereignty of Indian nations and their place in American society.[32] By the time Washington died, Indian power remained formidable in many areas of the continent, and American sovereignty remained contested in many spaces, but the United States had become a central presence in the world of all Indian peoples east of the Mississippi, and American expansion into Indian country was well under way. Washington, in association with men like Henry Knox, developed and articulated policies designed to divest Indians of their cultures as well as their lands and that would shape US-Indian relations for more than a century..

Washington's paths through Indian country connected his story to indigenous peoples who told their own stories, organized and lived their lives in distinct ways, and had different visions of America and its possibilities. But theirs was not the Indian world Washington saw and knew; the Indian world he saw was the world most Americans saw. He found little to admire in Indian life. Few of its ways of living or thinking rubbed off on him. No gallery of Native American artifacts graced Mount Vernon as it did Monticello. When Washington looked at Indian country, he saw colonial space temporarily inhabited by Indian people. What he regarded as new lands were in fact quite ancient, but he showed little awareness that the ancestors of Shawnees and Cherokees had walked those lands for thousands of years before he set foot or his surveyor's gaze on them. Jefferson was interested in the ancient petroglyphs on the banks of the Kanawha River;[33] Washington was more interested in the extent and fertility of his lands on those riverbanks. When he looked at Indian people, he saw either actual or potential enemies or allies. They and their lands feature recurrently and prominently in Washington's correspondence, and on occasion he expressed sympathy for Indian people. But his writings tell us little or nothing about Indians' family life, clan affiliations, kinship networks, gender relations, languages, subsistence strategies, changing economic patterns, consensus politics, traditional religious beliefs and ceremonial cycles, distinctive Christianity, or social ethics. There was much he did not see or understand. He did not— could not—comprehend how mythic stories, clan histories, and spiritual forces shaped how Indian people perceived their world. He did not understand many of the words and sounds he heard in Indian country. Rarely if ever did he show any appreciation that the societies there functioned according to their own rules, rhythms, beliefs, and values. He demonstrated no understanding of the roles of women in Native society, beyond being farmers, and he wished to see Indian men take over that role. In all of that, he was not much different from most of his contemporaries.

Indian country was not exclusively Indian, and had not been for a long time. It was a porous world undergoing profound and far-reaching changes. Imported diseases had scythed through populations and continued to wreak demographic havoc; imported animals, crops, and plants had altered the environment; new religions, ideas, and influences had infiltrated and sometimes divided Indian societies; imperial rivalries intruded into tribal politics; goods manufactured in European mills tied Indian communities to an Atlantic world and an emerging global trade system. By the time Washington encountered Cherokees, Iroquois, or Delawares, he met men who wore deerskin leggings and moccasins and displayed body and facial tattoos but who also often wore linen shirts and wool coats, and even the occasional three-cornered hat. He spoke with chiefs who wore armbands of trade silver and displayed European symbols of distinction like the officer's crescent-shaped silver gorget he himself wore around his neck when he posed for his portrait by Charles Willson Peale in 1772 (see plate 1). He would have seen women who wore calico blouses and kept their children warm with blankets of red-and-blue stroud, a durable woolen cloth produced in England's Cotswolds. Some of the Catholic Indians Washington encountered from the St. Lawrence or the Great Lakes wore crucifixes, spoke French, and had French names. Like anyone else who spent much time on the eighteenth-century frontier, he would also have met white men who wore breechcloths, moccasins, and hunting shirts and bore facial tattoos.[34] Constantly pressing the edges of Indian country were Scots-Irish, Anglo-American, and German settlers, the kind of people that Washington and his kind of people—Tidewater planters and gentlemen—characterized as more savage than savages. He might have seen black faces; at a time when buying and selling people was as common as buying and selling land, traders, Indian agents, army officers, and settler colonists took African slaves with them when they crossed the Appalachians. Indians also sometimes owned and trafficked in African slaves and harbored runaways. Some of the chiefs who ate dinner with Washington in New York or Philadelphia would not have been surprised to be waited on by black slaves; like Washington, they were slaveholders.

Washington sometimes spent days at a time in Indian villages. He would have seen cows, pigs, and chickens: Indians got pigs from Swedish settlers in the Delaware Valley in the seventeenth century, and Delaware people called chickens *tipas*, mimicking the sound Swedish settlers used to call poultry.[35] If he entered Indian lodges he would have seen many familiar objects: brass kettles, copper pots, candles, looking glasses, awls, needles, and threads. If he shared a meal, he would have eaten indigenous food—corn, beans, squash, pumpkin, venison, elk, bear's meat, fish, hominy cakes, berries, nuts, acorns, wild onions, maple sugar—perhaps supplemented by beef, chicken, pork, milk, apples, peaches, watermelon, turnips, peas, potatoes, honey, and many European imports that Indians had added to their diets.[36] He might have met Indian people who had developed a taste for tea and sugar; he certainly met people with a taste for rum. He would have spoken with Native people who could speak English and who, their own languages lacking profanity, had learned to swear in it.[37] (A British officer traveling in the Wabash country in the 1760s was called a "D—d son of a b—ch" by one Indian and given a copy of Shakespeare's *Antony and Cleopatra* by another.[38]) Washington also saw people whose faces, like his own, were marked by smallpox. Even the landscape Washington coveted bore evidence of change. Invasive weeds and grasses from Europe altered the meadows he found so attractive. By the time Virginians crossed the Appalachian Mountains into Kentucky, bluegrass and white clover, initially brought from England as fodder and in the dung of the animals that ate them, had spread ahead of them and taken root as "Kentucky bluegrass." European birds, bugs, seeds, and weeds had transformed the lands Washington viewed as "wilderness."[39]

Washington lived in, shaped, and eventually presided over a colonial world. At the same time, he lived his life in a world of Indian omnipresence, enduring power, and recurrent encounter, where Indian people acted as well as were acted upon and changed the societies that changed them. As happened elsewhere in the world, the colonized affected the colonizers, and cultural interactions produced new hybrid societies. Like slavery, some aspects of Native

America were so commonplace in Washington's world that they hardly merited mention in his writings: he does not tell us, but we know, that indigenous foods formed part of his—and his slaves'— diet, that Native herbal medicines were part of the colonial medicine cabinet, and that when he traveled the country before the Revolution, which he did more often and more extensively than almost any other colonial American, he generally followed Indian trails.[40]

Indian people and Indian lands affected key developments in Washington's life and the emerging American nation he helped to create. Indian relations were interwoven with questions of empire (whether European or American). Indians' actions contributed to the outbreak and course of the French and Indian War, and their reactions to its outcome prompted British policies that turned Washington and other Americans to revolution and independence. Indian lands furnished the territorial and philosophical foundations for the new expansionist republic that emerged. At the same time, the power Natives wielded, the resistance they mounted, and the diplomatic influence they exerted exposed the limits of federal power, aggravated tensions between federal and state governments, fueled divisions between East and West, and threatened to fragment the nation Washington was building.[41] Washington and the new government interpreted and applied the Constitution to establish nation-to-nation relationships with Indians conducted through war and treaty, but Indians preexisted the United States and its Constitution and conducted their own relations in their own way, and for a long time the United States lacked the power to make them do otherwise. Fighting, fearing, and hating Indians had helped forge a common identity among white peoples before; now the shared experience of Scots, Irish, Germans, English, and others in fighting and dispossessing Indians helped forge a common bond as Americans. Washington disparaged unruly frontier folk as disturbers of order and tranquility, but by harnessing their aggressive expansionism the government created a new, racially defined empire and a nation of free white citizens that excluded Native Americans as it also excluded African Americans. It was the national identity of a nation built on Indian land.[42]

The Indian world Washington knew was very different when he died in December 1799 than it had been at his birth in 1732. His life spanned most of the eighteenth century, an era of momentous change in North America when, as the historian James Merrell puts it, "the balance tipped irrevocably away from the Indians."[43] Washington, more than most, had a hand on the scales and was instrumental in the dispossession, defeat, exploitation, and marginalization of Indian peoples. He rarely used the term "Indian country"—he called it "wilderness," "the frontier," "the Ohio country," "the West"—but he lived his whole life with one eye on it and one foot in it. Neither his life nor that of his nation would have developed the way it did without his involvement and experiences in Indian country. Washington may not have been personally affected by his own interactions with its inhabitants, but the Indian world that he changed and his nation eventually displaced was also the world that, in many important and overlooked ways, shaped Washington and the nation he led.

Scholars of Washington's life and times owe an incredible debt to the teams of editors who have collected, meticulously edited, published, and digitized the voluminous papers of the first president. Their endeavors provide an invaluable and accessible resource, and one that makes it impossible to deny that Indian America mattered in Washington's day. The editors note, however, that some of the papers have been previously edited—by Washington himself. Washington kept letter books during his service on Braddock's campaign in 1755 and three years subsequently as colonel of the Virginia Regiment. In the 1770s and probably later, he made major revisions to these manuscripts "not once but at least twice." He made most of his revisions by striking out words, lines, or sentences and inserting new ones. But sometimes "he carefully scraped the original ink off the paper with a knife and then wrote his changes there." For the most part, the alterations and insertions did not produce important differences, but they do reveal Washington as someone concerned with his reputation.[44] In Indian country, he had good reason to be.

Washington is the "father of the nation," and he assumed the role of "great father" to Indian people as well. Yet the Iroquois called him "Town Destroyer," and with justification. This book acknowledges these contradictions, but its goal is neither to demonize Washington nor to debunk him as an icon of republican virtue.[45] Washington's dealings with Indian people and their land do him little credit, but on the other hand his achievement in creating a nation from a fragile union of states is more impressive when we appreciate the power and challenges his Indian world presented. The purpose is to show how Washington's life, like the lives of so many of his contemporaries, was inextricably linked to Native America, a reality we have forgotten as our historical hindsight has separated Indians and early Americans so sharply, and prematurely, into winners and losers.

George Washington dominates the formative events of American nation-building like no one else. He commanded the Continental

Army that secured American independence, he presided over the convention that framed the Constitution of the United States, and he was the nation's first president, serving two terms and setting the bar by which all subsequent presidents have been measured in terms of moral character and political wisdom.[46] Ignoring or excluding Native America from Washington's life, like excluding it from the early history of the nation, contributes to the erasure of Indians from America's past and America's memory. It also diminishes our understanding of Washington and his world. Restoring Indian people and Indian lands to the story of Washington goes a long way toward restoring them to their proper place in America's story.

With the exception of his expeditions in the Ohio Valley during the French and Indian War, the key events of Washington's life occur in the East—Mount Vernon, Philadelphia, Yorktown. But Washington's involvement with the West was lifelong, and he consistently looked to western land for his own personal fortune and for the nation's future. Securing Indian country as a national resource was essential to national consolidation and expansion, and few people knew more about securing Indian land than he did.

In one of the most iconic images in American history, Washington stands resolutely in the prow of a boat facing east. Emanuel Leutze's epic 1851 painting, *Washington Crossing the Delaware*, captures a pivotal moment during the War of Independence. After a string of demoralizing defeats and with the rebel army on the verge of disintegration, the Revolution faced its darkest hour. Then, on Christmas night 1776, Washington led what was left of his army in a daring and desperate attack. In the teeth of a storm, they crossed the ice-clogged Delaware River from Pennsylvania to New Jersey and roundly defeated a garrison of Hessian soldiers at Trenton. A week later, they defeated a British force at Princeton. The Revolution, for the moment, was saved, and the twin victories breathed life into a cause that had seemed lost.[47] After he died, Washington achieved almost godlike status as the savior of the Revolution and the father of the Republic.

But the Revolution was not only a war for independence and a new political order; it was also a war for the North American continent. Washington and the emerging nation faced west as well as east. If Washington did resemble a god, he perhaps most resembled the Roman Janus. Depicted with two faces, looking in opposite directions, Janus was not "two-faced" in the modern, negative sense of the term as duplicitous. As the god of passages and transitions, beginnings and endings, he looked simultaneously to the past and to the future. As America's god of the passage from colony to nation,

Washington looked east to the past and west to the future. And when he faced west, he faced Indian country.

This is not another biography of Washington, but it employs a biographical framework to show how Native America shaped the life of the man who shaped the nation. Tracing Washington's life through the Indian world of his time, and revealing the multiple points where his life intersected with, affected, and was affected by Indian people, Indian lands, and Indian affairs, offers an unfamiliar but more complete telling of what some would say is *the* American story.

PART ONE

Learning Curves

CHAPTER 1

Virginia's Indian Country

I N *NOTES ON THE STATE OF VIRGINIA*, published in 1787, Thomas Jefferson portrayed the colony at the time of first English settlement 180 years before as a country full of Indians. About forty different tribes occupied the region, the most powerful being the Powhatans, Mannahoacs, and Monacans. The Powhatan chiefdom south of the Potomac River consisted of at least thirty tribes and covered about eight thousand square miles. Jefferson calculated their population to have been about 8,000 people, of whom 2,400 were warriors. In characteristic Jefferson fashion, he listed the various tribes in a table, arranged by confederacy and geographic region. He provided population estimates when the English first arrived and again in 1669, when the Virginia Assembly attempted a head count. By then "spirituous liquors, the small pox, war, and an abridgment of territory...had committed terrible havoc among them," cutting their numbers by two-thirds. (Other estimates suggest that war, diseases, and migrations produced population collapses of 80 percent in some areas, from perhaps 20,000 to about 1,800.[1]) Their subsequent history was one of further rapid declension, as Chickahominies, Mattaponis, Pamunkeys, Nottaways, and other peoples were reduced to handfuls or migrated to the Susquehanna Valley or southern Piedmont.[2] For Jefferson, who was primarily interested in Indian land, languages, and antiquities, the indigenous inhabitants of Virginia were a memory, Virginia's Indian country a thing of the past.

In fact, there were multiple dimensions to Virginia's Indian world. By the time Washington was born in 1732, the colony recognized and dealt with three broad categories of Indian people. The first comprised Indians in the Tidewater region, who were few in number, no longer lived in tribal communities, and were increasingly swallowed up in the sea of black faces that constituted the lowest echelon of Virginian society. They lived and worked in colonial society as servants, slaves, or free persons, and came under the colony's jurisdiction often without being specifically identified as Indians. Surviving enclaves of tribes that had been defeated in the wars of the previous century constituted a second category of "tributary Indians" living under colonial jurisdiction. They made annual tributes of furs and skins, while the colony appointed their leaders and passed laws that curtailed their lives and defined their status, sometimes lumping them together with blacks and mulattoes. These tributary groups, said the governor of Virginia half a dozen years before Washington was born, were "inconsiderable, and withal so divided among themselves that they seem rather to want our protection, than to seek to give us any umbrage."[3]

That was not the case with the more distant groups, a third category Virginians called "foreign Indians."[4] Virginians who pushed beyond the Appalachian Mountains entered an Indian world where the Haudenosaunee or Iroquois, Shawnees, Cherokees, and others presented a varied and formidable array of indigenous power. Virginia by 1732 had defeated and dispossessed the Indian inhabitants to secure its hold on the Tidewater region, but like other European colonies it existed on the outskirts of a vast Indian continent. It would take most of Washington's lifetime for Virginia and then the United States to secure the western territories Virginia claimed by virtue of its colonial charter. The still-powerful "foreign nations" were the Indian peoples who most affected Washington's life.

LIKE OTHER ENGLISH COLONIES in North America, Virginia was established and built on Indian land. Simply put, the king of England claimed the land by right of discovery and granted an enormous swath of territory to the colony—actually as far as the "California Sea," although no one quite knew where that was. The colonial government then doled out grants of land, which speculators, surveyors, and settlers divided into parcels and property. Indian people were dispossessed and their rights of occupancy extinguished by war, deeds, and treaties.[5] The process of converting Indian homelands into Virginian real estate was well under way by the time of Washington's birth.

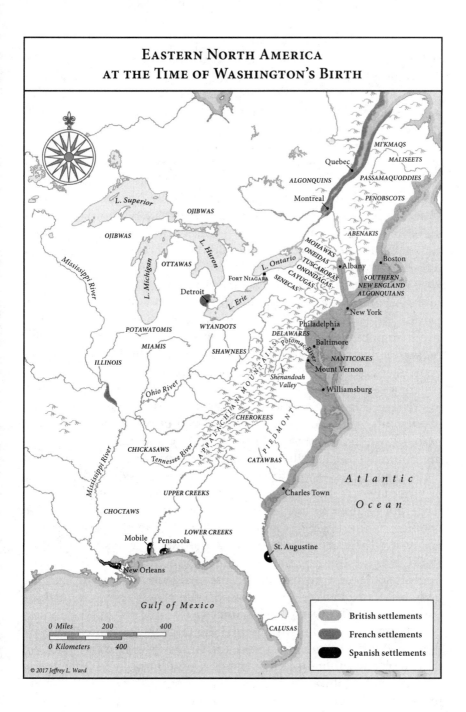

EASTERN NORTH AMERICA
AT THE TIME OF WASHINGTON'S BIRTH

MI'KMAQS

MALISEETS

Quebec

PASSAMAQUODDIES

ALGONQUINS

PENOBSCOTS

Montreal

L. Superior

OJIBWAS

ABENAKIS

OJIBWAS

MOHAWKS
ONEIDAS
TUSCARORAS
ONONDAGAS
CAYUGAS

Boston

Albany

OTTAWAS

L. Huron

L. Ontario

FORT NIAGARA

SENECAS

SOUTHERN
NEW ENGLAND
ALGONQUIANS

Mississippi River

L. Michigan

Detroit

L. Erie

New York

POTAWATOMIS

WYANDOTS

Philadelphia

DELAWARES

MIAMIS

SHAWNEES

Potomac River

Baltimore

ILLINOIS

Ohio River

Shenandoah
Valley

NANTICOKES

Mount Vernon

Williamsburg

CHEROKEES

PIEDMONT

CHICKASAWS

Tennessee River

APPALACHIAN MOUNTAINS

CATAWBAS

Mississippi River

UPPER CREEKS

Charles Town

Atlantic

Ocean

CHOCTAWS

LOWER CREEKS

Mobile   Pensacola

St. Augustine

New Orleans

Gulf of Mexico

0 Miles   200   400

CALUSAS

0 Kilometers   400

British settlements

French settlements

Spanish settlements

© 2017 Jeffrey L. Ward

In 1607 the Virginia Company, a private enterprise chartered by King James I to establish "a Colonie of sondrie of our people into that parte of America commonly called Virginia," built a small outpost on the James River, then known as the Powhatan River.[6] The company expected to generate profits for its investors, but the colonists, arriving in a period of severe drought, suffered from hunger, malnutrition, and typhus. Half died in the first winter, about 80 percent in the next winter; some of those who survived, we now know, did so by resorting to cannibalism. The rest depended on the local Indians and their food. In *The History and Present State of Virginia*, printed in 1705, the historian Robert Beverley described the bounty of resources the Indian inhabitants enjoyed "without the Curse of Industry" before English settlement diminished their land and restricted their subsistence. They hunted deer, elk, buffalo, turkeys, ducks, and other fowl; gathered fruits and nuts; harvested vast quantities of fish with ease; and grew watermelons, pumpkins, winter and summer squash, gourds, peas, beans, potatoes (which were "nothing like" English and Irish potatoes in shape, color, or taste), tobacco, and corn. "This *Indian Corn* was the Staff of Food, upon which the Indians did ever depend."[7] English colonists came to depend on it as well.

The tiny English settlement nestled on the edge of an Indian world. The Algonquian-speaking Powhatans dominated the coastal plain south of the Potomac River. A dozen or more Indian nations, perhaps five thousand to seven thousand people, lined the banks of the Potomac and its tributaries, and the area from the Potomac to the Rappahannock—what became known later as the Northern Neck of Virginia—was the most heavily populated area of the Chesapeake Bay. North of the Potomac lived the Piscataways and other Alqonquian peoples; at the head of Chesapeake Bay and in the Susquehanna Valley lived the Iroquoian-speaking Susquehannocks. The Indian world shaped the colonial Virginia world that replaced it. The English settled where Indians had settled, operated along existing patterns of exchange, and followed indigenous routes in making connections with other parts of America.[8]

At first the Powhatans watched the English and waited. Despite their firearms and metal weapons, the strangers were clearly inept in their new environment and seemed to pose little threat. The paramount chief, Wahunsonacock, whom the English called Powhatan, presided over thirty-two lesser chiefdoms, about 150 towns, and a population of some fourteen thousand.[9] He commanded tribute from subordinate tribes, controlled the distribution of sources, conducted foreign policy, and enjoyed revered status as an intermediary with the spirit world. Powhatan saw the newcomers as potential allies and extended gifts of corn to them. He appears to have attempted to bring the English leader Captain John Smith under his wing as another *werowance* (subordinate chieftain), even as Smith presumed to make Powhatan a subject of King James I. During the early years of the colony, the Powhatans and the English adjusted to each other's presence, and each made efforts to impose their ways on the other.[10] Tensions increased as the colonists secured their toehold and flexed their muscles. Sporadic fighting broke out when the English began to push up the James River, took hostages, and seized supplies of corn. Some Indians believed they were "a people come from under the world to take their world from them," one chief told Smith. "We perceive and well know that you intend to destroy us."[11]

Conflict between Europeans and Indians is often depicted as a clash between farmers and hunters, but in the Potomac Valley, as in many other areas, it was a clash between farmers and farmers. The English grew many of the same crops as their Indian neighbors, adopted similar agricultural techniques, preferred the same soils, and grazed their livestock where Indians hunted deer and other game. But, unlike Indians, English farmers sought to transform the environment into a world of fields and fences.[12] It was a transformation that left little space for Indian subsistence cycles and seasonal mobility or, ultimately, for Indian people. The intermediary efforts of Powhatan's famous daughter, Pocahontas—who married the colonist John Rolfe and traveled to England, where she died in 1617— could not avert a collision between two cultures competing for the same fertile lands. In 1618 there were 400 English people in Virginia; four years later there were about 1,240. They needed the Indians' lands, and, since most opted to plant tobacco for profit rather than plant enough corn for food, they continued to depend on Indians' corn, acquired through trade or force if necessary.[13] As Englishmen endeavored to establish dominion in Virginia, they not only claimed Indian lands for the Crown but also attempted to impose their Christianity and forms of property, gender, and social organization on Indian peoples. They invoked the Indians' cultural resistance as justification for dispossession: people who refused religion and civilization had no right to the land.[14] It was a policy and a mindset not unlike that which a future first president and a new nation would adopt.

Powhatan died in 1618. In 1622 his brother Opechancanough led a brutal war against the aggressive infant colony. Early one spring morning, Indians attacked English settlements along the banks of the James River, killing people, burning houses, and destroying live-stock. At least a quarter of the English colonists died. The colonists responded with scorched-earth tactics, and the conflict dragged on for years. But whereas Virginia became a royal colony and continued to grow in the 1620s and 1630s, war and disease took their toll on the Indians. By 1640 the English population had passed eight thousand; the Indian population had probably dropped below five thousand.[15]

After the war of 1622, a new class of leaders came to dominate the colony. Under Governor Sir Francis Wyatt, they dominated the Council of State at Jamestown, replaced the stockholders of the Virginia Company as the major policy makers, and developed aggressive new policies for dealing with Indians, warring against those they perceived as enemies, trading with those they saw as allies. "In so doing," observes the historian J. Frederick Fausz with a glance ahead to George Washington's eventual leadership style, "they established the earliest model of the frontier elite—high status gentlemen who combined military, political, social, and economic leadership, merged public service with profitable private interests, and integrated aristocratic formality with popular familiarity." And their brutal campaigns against Indians earned them respect and following among the "lower-born." After the founding of Maryland in 1634, Virginians competed with their colonial rivals to the north for control of the Indian trade, and some of the first men to settle along the Northern Neck of Virginia did so in order to trade with the Susquehannock Indians.[16]

The Powhatans lost territory steadily. Opechancanough's second assault on Virginia in 1644 killed more than four hundred colonists, but it was a final act of defiant desperation. The English regrouped and retaliated. The aged and feeble Opechancanough was taken as a prisoner to Jamestown, where an English soldier killed him. The Indians sued for peace in 1646, and the subsequent treaty reduced the surviving members of the Powhatan chiefdom to tributary status. They agreed to pay the governor "twenty beaver skins att the going away of Geese yearly" as tribute. Their leaders had to be approved by English officials, and they were to serve as scouts and allies if needed. Now firmly in possession of coastal Virginia, the English expelled Indians from colonial settlements. They established a boundary around the perimeter of the colonies that Indians were forbidden to cross unless they wore passport badges or special striped clothing to identify them as messengers. In a pattern Washington would see repeated many times, however, colonial settlers crossed boundary lines and moved onto Indian lands.[17] Small reservations—the first in the country—were established at Pamunkey, Mattaponi, and other places. Scores of Indian captives were enslaved.

After the final defeat of the Powhatan chiefdom, Virginians began shifting from an economy based on frontier trade to one dependent on agriculture, while at the same time they now had access to the extensive trade of the interior, a trade in both skins and slaves that would play a key part in Virginia's economy and in building the fortunes of families like the Byrds of Westover.[18] John Washington, the future president's great-grandfather, entered this world in 1657. Sailing from England, he settled near the Potomac River and made a place for himself in the rough-and-tumble of his new environment, fighting Indians and acquiring land. In 1674 he patented 5,000 acres in what was the traditional homeland of the Doeg Indians. But conflicts between colonists and Doegs threatened his grant: he risked forfeiture if he did not plant and settle it within two years. Like his great-grandson, Washington, a colonel in the Westmoreland County militia, went to war to defend his country and advance his own interests. He was joined by other Virginian militia units under Colonel George Mason, Major Isaac Allerton, Major Richard Lee, and Captain Giles Brent (who was part Indian)—founders of Northern Neck dynasties—and by Maryland troops under Major Thomas Truman. This intercolonial force turned from hunting down Doeg Indians and laid siege to a town of friendly Susquehannock Indians on Piscataway Creek in Maryland, roughly across the Potomac from the land that would later become the Mount Vernon estate. When five Susquehannock chiefs emerged to parley, the militia commanders had them seized, bound, and murdered. Maryland officials later impeached and fined Truman for this "barbarous cruelty"; Governor William Berkeley of Virginia gave Washington a stiff rebuke. The Susquehannocks began calling Washington Conotocarious, meaning "Devourer of Villages" in their Iroquoian language. It was a name his great-grandson would inherit—or at least claim—and then earn in his own right.[19]

The Susquehannocks were a much more formidable opponent than the Doegs. Susquehannock retaliations helped arouse popular support for Nathaniel Bacon's rebellion against Governor Berkeley. Frontier inhabitants complained that the governor did not prosecute the war with sufficient vigor. Instead, he established a line of forts that proved inadequate to the task of stemming Indian attacks, a problem George Washington would encounter eighty years later.[20] Bacon urged a war of extermination against all Indians, "whether

Friends or Foes." According to Robert Beverley, people were "ready to vent all their Resentment against the poor Indians."[21] When Bacon and his followers started killing Indians, Berkeley outlawed him for waging war without the approval of the Virginia Assembly. Bacon promptly turned on the government, harnessing widespread resentment against a body that awarded generous land grants to eastern elites but extended inadequate protection to frontier settlers. By the time social order was restored, the English had driven Indian peoples from Tidewater Virginia, driven them underground, or driven them into slavery. Many surviving Indians left the region for the Susquehanna Valley, leaving only four tributary communities in the colony.[22] The war removed Indians as a threat and as a dominant presence in the Tidewater. Virginia would not fight another Indian war for nearly eighty years.

After three marriages, John Washington died in 1677 at forty-six, probably of typhoid fever. His eldest son, Lawrence, died in 1698 at thirty-eight. Lawrence's second son, Augustine, known as a tough businessman, increased his landholdings from 1,100 acres to 2,850 by marrying Jane Butler. She bore him three children: Lawrence, Augustine Jr., and Jane. When his first wife died, Augustine married Mary Ball. Their first child, George, was born on February 11, 1732, adjusted according to the new Gregorian calendar to February 22.[23] His birthplace at Wakefield on Pope's Creek, like much of his father's property and George's boyhood home, lay on sites Indians had occupied and farmed for generations.[24]

Confined to bounded and diminishing enclaves within their homeland, Virginian Indians endured continued land loss, population decline, poverty, and lack of legal protection for their lands and persons. Many found employment as guides, laborers, and servants and earned cash by selling baskets, pottery, mats, tanned deerskins, and other goods in English settlements. As Virginia planters began to build fortunes harvesting and marketing a Native plant on Native lands, many Indian people became slaves in their expanding tobacco fields, servants in their growing households, and wage laborers in the colonial economy. Virginians took captives in their wars against local Indians, kidnapped and indentured the children of tributary Indians, and imported and enslaved "foreign" Indians taken captive by other Indians. The Virginia Assembly attempted to regulate Indian slavery, waffled on whether to allow it or outlaw it, but effectively legalized it in 1682. They shipped some Indian slaves to the Caribbean and to other colonies. Other Indian slaves toiled alongside African slaves on Chesapeake tobacco plantations, although they were valued less highly than the African slaves.[25]

Virginians began trading for Indian slaves in the 1650s. Around 1656 they first encountered the Westos, whom they called "Stranger Indians." A group of Eries who had fled Iroquois attacks in the north and migrated to the James River, the Westos became Indian slavers. Together with Occaneechis from the Piedmont area, and armed with English guns, they raided farther south and deep into the interior, bringing captives to slave traders in Virginia and Carolina. Then, having dominated the southeastern slave trade for thirty years, the Westos became its victims when migrant Shawnees in the pay of Carolina destroyed them. After the 1670s traders from Carolina developed more extensive slave-trading networks. Indians traded deerskins for English guns and then turned their guns on less-well-armed neighbors to acquire captives to sell to the English as slaves. Virginian traders led packhorse trains over the mountains to Cherokee towns, and Cherokees armed with Virginian guns pushed Muskogean peoples out of eastern Tennessee and into what is now Alabama and Georgia. By the 1690s English traders had reached the Chickasaws in the Mississippi Valley, and Chickasaws were raiding across the great river for captives, whom they traded to Virginia and Carolina. Trade paths and slave raiding brought Indians from far beyond the Tidewater regions into contact and commerce with the Atlantic world, and the repercussions reverberated deep into the interior. Guns and slave raids generated unprecedented levels of violence, upheaval, and migration and created conditions and routes that allowed epidemic diseases to spread like wildfire. In 1696 smallpox arrived in Virginia, probably on board African slave ships. From there it traveled south along the coast and into the Carolina Piedmont. It devastated the remaining Indian peoples of the Tidewater region who lived closest to the English, and once it penetrated the slave-raiding-and-gun-trading networks it swept the Southeast on a four-year rampage. Emerging from the chaos, peoples from different groups, languages, and cultures, who lived more distantly from the English and suffered less severe mortality rates, coalesced to form new polities.[26] The combined effects of gun violence, slave wars, and smallpox sent populations plummeting. By one estimate, the Indian population of the Southeast fell by two-thirds in the roughly half a century before Washington was born, from approximately two hundred thousand in 1685 to fewer than sixty-seven thousand in 1730.[27]

As Virginia Indians struggled to adjust to the new world that English invasion and colonialism had created, the English increasingly consigned them to a separate world reserved for inferior races.[28] In 1691 the Virginia Assembly passed a law forbidding white people to marry "Negroes, Mulattoes and Indians" on pain of expulsion from the colony. Apparently it had the desired effect: unlike the French, said Alexander Spotswood, lieutenant governor from 1710 to 1722, Virginians had no interest in "beginning a nearer friendship by intermarriage,...for notwithstanding the long intercourse between ye Inhabitants of this Country and ye Indians, and their living amongst one another for so many Years, I cannot find one Englishman that has an Indian Wife, or an Indian married to a white woman."[29] Pocahontas and John Rolfe were the exception, not the rule. The College of William and Mary, chartered in 1693, was partly dedicated to educating Indian students but had few or no pupils until the eighteenth century. (Then enrollment may have varied from as few as one or two to as many as two dozen. In 1723 the college established a separate building, the Brafferton School, where Indian students were taught the rudiments of reading and writing and in theory trained as missionaries.[30]) In 1705 Virginia declared Indian slaves, along with black and mulatto slaves, to be "real estate" and forbade them, as it did blacks, to hold office, testify in court, sue white people, or strike a white person, even in self-defense. Eighteenth-century Virginians recognized different categories of Indians: black Indians, colored persons of Indian descent, white Indians, and mulatto Indians. Colonial constructions of race that identified "mixed" Indians as blacks segregated Indian people from settler society and increased the servile labor force while at the same time reducing the number of people with a rival claim to the land.[31] In 1711 the Executive Council required tributary and other friendly Indians to wear badges of copper and pewter, respectively, and not "to hunt or come among the Inhabitants of this colony" without them.[32]

By 1700 war, disease, land loss, and the destructive conditions created by colonialism had reduced Tidewater Virginia's Indian population to perhaps 10 percent of what it had been in 1600. Thirty years later, fewer than 1,000 Indians may have survived in Virginia east of the mountains, amid a sea of white (103,000) and black (almost 50,000) faces.[33] According to Robert Beverley, the Indians were "almost wasted"; the Virginia militia kept "the *Indians* round about in Subjection, and have no sort of Apprehension from them."[34] Andrew Burnaby, a young Englishman who visited Washington at Mount Vernon during his travels in 1759, passed by a Pamunkey town where the remnants of the tribe lived, "the rest having dwindled away through intemperance and disease." Inhabiting about 2,000 acres on the Pamunkey River, they were chiefly employed hunting or fishing for the local gentry. "They commonly dress like the Virginians, and I have sometimes mistaken them for the lower sort of that people," wrote Burnaby.[35] Washington grew up in a world where his few Indian neighbors eked out an existence by fishing and hunting or worked as farmhands, servants, and slaves. Virginians treated them as dependent people, not independent nations.

Things were different beyond the mountains.

HAVING REDUCED THE NEIGHBORING TRIBES to tributary status and pushed to the Fall Line (the edge of the Piedmont and the Coastal Plain), Virginians began extending their settlements westward and funneling through gaps in the Blue Ridge Mountains. Young planters moving west into the rich lands of the Shenandoah Valley met growing numbers of immigrants moving southwest from Pennsylvania, following natural corridors and pushing deep into Indian country.[36] The majority of migrants to Virginia in the seventeenth century had come from the South and West of England. They brought their regional folkways with them, and the great planter families set the model for a society ordered around property, wealth, and rank. Many of the emigrants pushing down the Shenandoah were German-speaking people, who had a reputation for being orderly and industrious. But many more were from northern Britain, and most were Scotch-Irish Presbyterians. They brought with them a long history of borderland violence and built communities that struck contemporaries as mobile, disorderly, and militant. Descendants of Scots transplanted to Ulster in the early seventeenth century to create a buffer against the Catholic Irish, they again served British imperial policy by creating a buffer against the French and the Indians. In fact, they often spearheaded the invasion of Indian country, squatting wherever they found vacant land and flouting any attempts to regulate or restrain them. James Logan, provincial secretary of Pennsylvania, declared them "troublesome settlers to the government and hard neighbors to the Indians."[37] Settlers from Maryland and Pennsylvania migrated southward into Virginia in such numbers that William Byrd II said they "swarm[ed] lik the Goths and vandals of old."[38] But Byrd was happy to settle the newcomers—especially industrious Swiss immigrants—on the frontiers to guard against Indian attacks. The Virginia gentry learned that it paid to share the western lands with newcomers, so long as they kept the best for themselves.[39] It was a lesson Washington would learn well and a policy he would perpetuate.

Virginia's westward orientation took it across old paths that connected the Iroquois in the north to the Indian peoples of the

Chesapeake and, farther south, to the Cherokees and Catawbas. Virginians who pushed over the Blue Ridge Mountains came into the orbit of the Haudenosaunee, the Five Nations of the Iroquois in what is now upstate New York. The Mohawks, Oneidas, Onondagas, Cayugas, and Senecas had united in a league of peace long before Europeans arrived. Virginia first established relations with them in 1677, when it joined the Covenant Chain, a series of alliances that developed in the seventeenth century between the Five Nations and their Native allies and the English colonies. Virginia began sending diplomatic missions to negotiate with the Iroquois, usually working in conjunction with the governor and council of New York in Albany. (At one such meeting, the Iroquois gave Governor Howard Effingham the name Assarigoa; they may have been referring to the sword he wore as part of his formal attire, but to Mohawk ears the name Howard, translated via Dutch interpreters, sounded like *assarakowa*, meaning "long knife." The Iroquois addressed all subsequent governors of Virginia by this title. With more sinister connotations Indians called first Virginians and then all American frontiersmen "long knives.") By joining the Covenant Chain, Virginia entered a new area of Indian country and a new era of Indian relations.[40]

The Iroquois were rebuilding. Recognizing that entanglement in imperial conflicts between England and France had sent their population into a downward spiral, Iroquois diplomats pulled out of the decline by pulling out of the conflicts. They negotiated treaties with the French and their Indian allies at Montreal and with the English at Albany in 1701, charted a new foreign policy of neutrality, and practiced a diplomatic balancing act that allowed them to steer clear of imperial wars and regain their strength. They took smaller nations, including refugees from Virginia and Maryland, under their protection as "props" to their league and, on the basis of past wars, claimed dominion over large areas they did not occupy.

Iroquois warriors resumed, or continued, raiding Catawbas, Cherokees, and Saponis, as well as Virginia's tributary tribes. They waged "mourning wars" in which killing or capturing enemies helped to appease the spirits of deceased relatives (and offset population losses at home). Catawbas and Cherokees reciprocated.[41] War parties followed the Warriors' Path, also known as the Great Indian Warpath, through the Shenandoah Valley, and sometimes threatened Virginian settlements. In 1716 Governor Spotswood led an expedition of sixty-three gentlemen and adventurers across the Blue Ridge Mountains and into the Shenandoah Valley, where he acquired more than 85,000 acres of land in the next six years. But Spotswood's western land ambitions collided with the Iroquois, who claimed the Piedmont as hunting territory and a right-of-way for their war parties. The governor needed Iroquois cooperation, or at least acquiescence, in his schemes for western settlement. In 1722 he traveled almost six hundred miles to attend a treaty negotiation with the Five Nations in Albany, where he secured their agreement to give up the Piedmont as hunting ground and stay west of the Blue Ridge Mountains. The Piedmont—including the future sites of Thomas Jefferson's birthplace and Monticello—was open to English colonization. Nevertheless, conflicting claims and disputed boundaries among Indian nations, colonial governments, and private interests continued to check Virginian expansion.[42]

The governor and Royal Council of Virginia had to approve land grants, but most grants went to the families who dominated the council. In essence, gentry sitting in the Assembly or House of Burgesses made huge grants of lands for small sums of money to gentry who promised to settle farmers. Between 1728 and 1732, Lieutenant Governor William Gooch and his council issued ten land orders for more than 360,000 acres in the Shenandoah Valley, 125,000 acres in 1732 alone. The terms encouraged rapid settlement: those individuals or groups to whom the land was granted had two years in which to settle one family for every 1,000 acres; each family had to "improve" 3 of every 50 acres granted within three years. A few colonists made their way into the Shenandoah Valley in the late 1720s, but the first substantial migration occurred in 1732. Meanwhile, Lord Thomas Fairfax's agent, Robert "King" Carter, was granting large areas in the northern Shenandoah Valley to prominent Tidewater families. Fairfax, who had left his ancestral estate at Leeds Castle in Kent and settled at Belvoir on the Potomac, had inherited a royal grant, made by Charles II to Royalists in 1649, of more than 5 million acres between the Potomac and Rappahannock Rivers and reaching across the Alleghenies. He would later move west himself into the Shenandoah Valley. Virginia's liberal land policies created a lucrative market for ambitious men with capital to invest.[43]

By the time Washington was born, then, Virginian traders had penetrated Indian country, tobacco planters from the Tidewater were moving west, and livestock farmers from Pennsylvania were moving south into the Shenandoah Valley and parts of the Piedmont. They caused far-reaching changes in the lands they occupied. Indian women typically planted their fields with corn, beans, and squash and left them fallow in a cycle that allowed the soil to regenerate and replenish. Virginia tobacco planters practiced single-crop agriculture

that drained the soil of nutrients until the land was exhausted, sometimes after three or four years. They then cleared new plots of land
and let the depleted ground lie fallow. But it took about twenty years
for fallow fields to recover and again become suitable for tobacco,
and a planter needed roughly twenty acres for each laborer he used
to grow tobacco. With additional acreage to graze livestock, grow
corn, and harvest wood for burning and building, the system of shifting agriculture that planters used to avert chronic soil exhaustion
required huge amounts of land.[44] As happened elsewhere, when
planters and their laborers spread inland, they altered landscapes
and ecosystems. They cut into forests; spread invasive grasses, weeds,
parasites, and pests; and brought in cattle, pigs, and other domesticated livestock that grazed and trampled indigenous fauna and
Indian fields and drove away deer.[45]

Many gentlemen planters, like Washington's father, added new
lands to their estates and invested in western lands whose values
would increase as soil fertility in the older, more settled areas of the
colony decreased under the exhaustive impact of tobacco cultivation.
As population grew and young men moved west to establish their
own households and start small plantations, planters supplemented
their income from tobacco cultivation by selling or renting lands to
tenants who would occupy and improve them. Tobacco cultivation
entered a period of growth that, though interrupted by bouts of
international war, held for more than thirty years, producing a
"golden age" for Chesapeake planters. Tobacco imports to Britain
rose from 41 million pounds in 1730 to 85 million pounds in 1753,
declined during the Seven Years' War, then resumed their climb to
98 million pounds in 1763.[46]

Western lands offered Virginia's planters new opportunities but
also rendered them increasingly dependent on tobacco cultivation
and the labor system on which in turn it depended. African slaves
made up 30 percent of Virginia's population, and race and rank
divided Virginian society. Every individual occupied a recognized
place in the social order. An individual like Washington, born into a
family that stood outside the first rank of gentry planters like the
Carter, Fairfax, and Lee families, was anxious to cement his place
and advance his wealth and status.[47] Indian lands across the mountains offered the opportunity to increase wealth; fashionable clothing, furniture, and other manufactured goods from across the
Atlantic offered the means to display the status wealth brought.

Virginia tobacco planters participated in an Atlantic exchange
system that rendered them dependent on English merchants, and

their fortunes were inextricably tied to European markets for their addictive crop.[48] Great planters since the seventeenth century had relied on the consignment system: they shipped their tobacco to a merchant in England, who then sold the cargo on the planter's account and purchased goods for the planter, charged to the account against the anticipated profits from the sale of tobacco. By the time young Washington was growing up and tobacco production was extending westward, Scots were getting in on the tobacco trade and changing the way business was done. Advantageously located for transatlantic trade on the west coast of Scotland, Glasgow merchants introduced direct trade: agents of the company purchased tobacco direct from the growers and then shipped it to Britain, where it was sold on the reexport market. The Glasgow firms established stores in Virginia, where planters could purchase goods with tobacco or on credit. The great Tidewater planters continued to operate on the consignment system to sell their large crops and to acquire the goods that marked their status, as well as the clothing, tools, and other supplies they furnished their slave labor force, but the direct-trade system suited smaller planters and farmers who were operating in the interior, and it came to dominate the tobacco industry as it extended westward.[49]

An indigenous plant from the Americas helped transform Glasgow from an old cathedral market town into an international financial and commercial center, and indeed an imperial city. It created a wealthy class of "tobacco lords." Like Virginia planters, Glasgow tobacco lords were closely connected by marriage and kinship. Like George Washington, most bought landed estates, albeit in Scotland rather than the colonies, to give them economic security and entry into the lifestyle of the political and economic elite. One, George Buchanan, built "Virginia Mansion" on Virginia Street and purchased an estate in Lanarkshire called Mount Vernon.[50]

As Virginians negotiated deals with merchants across the Atlantic, they also had to negotiate with the Iroquois over the Blue Ridge Mountains. Surveyors and settlers in the Shenandoah Valley clashed with the Iroquois, whose right to travel west of the Blue Ridge had been confirmed at the Treaty of Albany in 1722. Lieutenant Governor Gooch continued diplomatic efforts to bring the Iroquois "to a nearer Correspondence, and a stricter alliance with this Country."[51] After a series of skirmishes threatened to produce open war, Virginia and the Six Nations (the Tuscaroras having joined the Iroquois League in 1722) met to resolve their issues in June and July 1744. Two hundred and fifty Iroquois men, women, and children traveled to the frontier town of Lancaster, Pennsylvania, to meet with commissioners William Beverley and Thomas Lee from Virginia, as well as representatives from Maryland and Pennsylvania. It was the first time the English held a major meeting with the Iroquois away from Albany.[52] Six Nations chiefs and colonial officials discussed land disputes, frontier violence, and strengthening their relations. An Onondaga, Tachanoontia, announced: "All the World knows we conquered the several Nations living on Sasquehanna, Cohongoronta [the Potomac], and on the Back of the Great Mountains in Virginia." By claiming dominion where their war parties had once ranged, the Iroquois created a fiction of conquest that the British readily embraced in their conduct of Indian affairs and their efforts to acquire other peoples' lands. The Iroquois left Lancaster with £400 in goods and cash and assurances that they could travel unimpeded through Virginia into Catawba country. In return, they had signed a treaty that, on the basis of a dubious claim that they had conquered the original inhabitants of the area, ceded their claims to the Shenandoah Valley and the claims of other tribes for whom they claimed to speak. Or so they believed. The Virginians at the treaty had neglected to mention that the original royal charter granted the colony land "from sea to sea" and that the northern limits of the colony extended northwest from the Potomac River as far as Canada. As the Treaty of Lancaster was worded, the Iroquois actually handed over the entire Ohio country and much more. The treaty unleashed a flurry of land speculation in the Shenandoah Valley and beyond.[53] George Washington was only twelve years old, but the Iroquois cession of other peoples' lands at the Treaty of Lancaster pointed Virginia west, turned the Ohio country into a bitterly contested borderland, and set a stage that would shape his formative years and his thinking about the West for the rest of his life (see figure 1).

VIRGINIANS ALWAYS LOOKED WEST.[54] Four large rivers running from the west and their fertile lands beckoned colonial settlers and gave them access to more lands in the interior of the continent. More than 380 miles in length, the Potomac River linked up with other river systems and connected the Chesapeake Bay to the Ohio and Mississippi Valleys.[55] Washington was born and lived most of his life in the region between the Potomac and Rappahannock known as the Northern Neck. Even among land-hungry Virginians, Northern Neck planters were notorious land speculators and developers. Great families like the Carters, Lees, and Fitzhughs, who held leadership

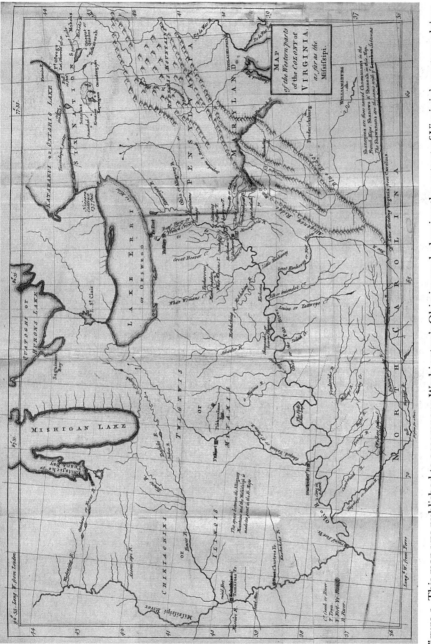

Figure 1 This map was published to accompany Washington's Ohio journal, showing the extent of Virginia's western claims.

positions in the House of Burgesses and dominated the social and political life in the older, settled areas of the region, took the lead in acquiring new lands for settlement. Robert "King" Carter built a fortune and a family dynasty on the ruthless acquisition of land and slaves: when he died he passed on to his descendants 333,000 acres of land and 829 slaves. For Northern Neck planters, and for Washington in particular, the West was not just an arena for speculation; it was key to the agricultural and commercial development of the Potomac River, which connected Virginia to the Ohio country.[56] Virginian land dealers and settlers pushed west beyond the Blue Ridge Mountains, spreading along the Shenandoah Valley and then across the Allegheny Mountains. In the span of a generation, between 1720 and 1754, most of the Piedmont and part of the valley was surveyed and twenty-five new counties formed. In an age of rampant territorial expansion, Virginia's surveyors held the keys—or rather the chains and compasses—to convert public land to private property.[57]

Surveying and speculating went hand in hand. In Europe, surveyors mainly measured and mapped existing properties and verified earlier records; in America, they carved up Indian country and remade indigenous space to create extensive new properties. Surveyors used Gunter's chain, designed in 1620 by an English clergyman and mathematician named Edmund Gunter, as the standard instrument for measuring distance. The 66-foot chain had 100 links. Ten chains measured 1 furlong; 80 chains equaled 1 mile. Ten square chains equaled 1 acre. Once planters and settlers had chosen their claims, surveyors roughly measured lengths of chains and links to gauge acreages of 50 acres or multiples thereof. A measurement of 6 chains and 25 links on a property running for 1 mile from a riverbank gave a total of 242,000 square yards, or 50 acres. "This was frontier math," wrote the late Andro Linklater, author of *Measuring America*, "and it became second nature to anyone who wanted to own land."[58]

Surveyors located good lands and helped establish clear title. They measured and staked out parcels of land with chains and pins and then produced a written report and a plat (a map of the property), which, duly recorded, gave their clients' claims legal backing against squatters and rival claimants. All grants and purchases of land had to be platted by a licensed surveyor before the claims could be entered on the land registry and patented, so there was plenty of work for surveyors. County surveyors were responsible for carrying out work within their county borders, and each surveyor owed his appointment to the surveyor general of the colony, whose office in turn was a privilege of the College of William and Mary. The college did little or nothing to train, certify, and select surveyors; it simply received a portion of their fees. Because land ownership conveyed civil power in Virginia, surveyors and the property lines they ran could shape the contours of colonial politics, and surveyors often represented large landowners and large land companies. And because the surveyors were the first to venture out onto the new territory, they had the opportunity to identify and acquire the best lands for themselves. In colonial Virginia, surveying was a lucrative and respectable occupation. In the Shenandoah Valley, Indians called a surveyor's compass the "land stealer."[59]

Simple descriptions of American territorial expansion depict families of settlers moving west to build new homes and new lives. However, in the early eighteenth century, wealthy speculators and surveyors often operated in advance of settlers and sometimes worked against them as planters. Large planters, or at least the agents and surveyors they deployed, often established their legal right to frontier property with a paper trail of surveys, plats, grants, deeds, and warrants before small farmers arrived on the scene. Settlers sought land for residence and subsistence; speculators and surveyors sought land for profits. They would realize those profits by selling or renting to settlers at some future date when the value of the lands had increased. Until then, their goal was often to *exclude* settlers. Close-knit networks of speculators and surveyors did much of the work of transforming Indian lands into real estate.[60]

From a young age and for the rest of his life, George Washington immersed himself in the land business. As a teenager he cut his teeth as a surveyor and caught the fever for speculating in western land. Applying Anglo-Virginian ideas of land ownership, he would worry little about Indian rights of occupancy and much about establishing his paper rights as he scrambled to amass a personal fortune.

Washington's father had been a surveyor, and Washington received some rudimentary education in surveying as a youth. His first practical experience in backcountry surveying came in the spring of 1748.[61] The sixteen-year-old was invited to tag along with a surveying party as a traveling companion for his friend and neighbor George William Fairfax, the twenty-four-year-old nephew of Lord Thomas Fairfax. Some ten thousand settlers, including Germans from Pennsylvania, were living in the Shenandoah Valley by this time, and the surveying party headed west to pin down boundaries where they were beginning to settle on his lordship's lands. Washington's journal of his trip to the Blue Ridge Mountains and beyond to the

Shenandoah records his first experience roughing it on the frontier—
he complained about the dirt and discomfort he had to endure—
and marks the beginning of a lifelong obsession with western land.[62]

He also met his first "wild" Indians. At the mouth of the south
branch of the Potomac in Maryland, the surveying party stopped at
the trading post of one Thomas Cresap. Born in Skipton in Yorkshire
in 1702, Cresap had migrated to America when he was fifteen and
established himself as a frontier trader and land speculator. When
"thirty odd Indians coming from war" arrived at the post, Washington
penned a description of them in his diary. The surveyors gave the
Indians liquor to encourage them to perform a "war dance," and
Washington described that as well. But he was not interested in them:
"Nothing remarkable on Thursday but only being with the Indians
all day so shall slip [sic] it." He was not impressed by the Indians or
by the German settlers he met, calling the latter "as Ignorant a Set of
People as the Indians."[63] The young Virginian seemed to hold in
equal disdain the people whose lands he would take and the people
he would recruit to rent those lands. It was an attitude he would find
difficult to shake; as president, in addition to regarding frontier settlers as no better than Indians, he would frequently blame them for
his real estate troubles and the nation's Indian wars.[64]

After his first trip into the Virginia backcountry, Washington
returned as a surveyor four times in the next five years.[65] In the spring
of 1749 (by which time he had evidently fallen in love with Sally
Fairfax, who had married his friend George William in December),
Washington helped survey the new port town of Alexandria on the
Potomac. In July he was appointed surveyor of the newly formed
Culpeper County. The appointment of a seventeen-year-old owed
more to his connection to Lord Fairfax than to his experience in the
field. Washington spent less than a year as county surveyor and carried out only one survey. Then he turned his attention west of the
Blue Ridge Mountains, where Lord Fairfax gave him steady work
and more profitable opportunities surveying parcels of land for sale
and settlement.[66]

In the spring of 1750, he was surveying in the Shenandoah
Valley again. By October he had made enough money to buy 1,459
acres in the valley, most of it along Bullskin Creek in Frederick
County. He was eighteen. It was the beginning of a career in land
dealing and the first in a lifetime of land investments.[67] In all,
Washington conducted forty-five surveys west of the Blue Ridge.[68] In
three years he earned about £400 from surveying fees and took
advantage of his position to acquire 2,315 acres of prime land in the

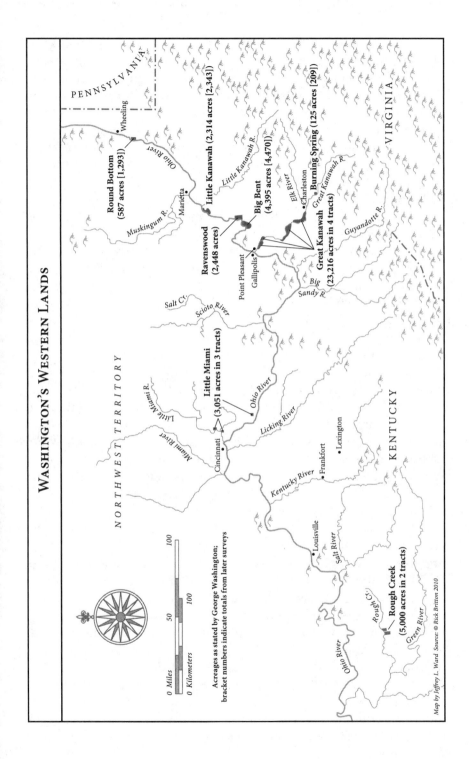

WASHINGTON'S WESTERN LANDS

PENNSYLVANIA

VIRGINIA

NORTHWEST TERRITORY

KENTUCKY

Round Bottom
(587 acres [1,293])

Little Kanawah (2,314 acres [2,343])

Big Bent
(4,395 acres [4,470])

Burning Spring (125 acres [209])

Ravenswood
(2,448 acres)

Great Kanawah
(23,216 acres in 4 tracts)

Little Miami
(3,051 acres in 3 tracts)

Rough Creek
(5,000 acres in 2 tracts)

Wheeling

Marietta

Point Pleasant

Gallipolis

Charleston

Cincinnati

Frankfort

Lexington

Louisville

Ohio River

Muskingum R.

Little Kanawah R.

Elk River

Great Kanawah R.

Guyandotte R.

Big Sandy R.

Salt C.⁎

Scioto River

Ohio River

Little Miami R.

Miami River

Licking River

Kentucky River

Salt River

Rough C.⁎

Green River

Ohio River

Acreages as stated by George Washington;
bracket numbers indicate totals from later surveys

0 Miles   50   100

0 Kilometers   100

Map by Jeffrey L. Ward Source: © Rick Britton 2010

Shenandoah Valley.[69] He did not survey professionally again, but he used his surveying skills for the rest of his life, even as president, acquiring new lands for himself by purchase or grant, defining and defending the boundaries of his holdings, and dividing them into profitable lots. Between 1747 and 1799 Washington surveyed or had surveyed more than two hundred tracts of land, and he acquired title to more than 65,000 acres in thirty-seven different locations. By the time he died, he owned more than 52,000 acres spread across Virginia, Pennsylvania, Maryland, Kentucky, New York, and the Ohio Valley, in addition to lots in Virginian towns and Washington City.[70]

Taking a break from accumulating money and land, Washington accompanied his half brother Lawrence to Barbados in 1751 on what was supposed to be a recuperative trip for Lawrence's tuberculosis. While there, George succumbed to smallpox, a disease since eradicated but still a dread killer in the eighteenth century. Fortunately, it was a mild case; he survived, pockmarked but immune for the rest of his life, and was back home in Virginia before Christmas. Lawrence was not so lucky; his health continued to deteriorate, and he returned home to die the next year.

When his father died in 1743, eleven-year-old George Washington inherited Ferry Farm on the Rappahannock River, where he lived with his mother and siblings.[71] Lawrence, the eldest son, inherited the much larger farm on the Potomac, which he renamed Mount Vernon after the British admiral under whom he had served. When Lawrence died in 1752, Mount Vernon passed to his daughter, Sarah. When she died young two years later, George began to rent the estate from his brother's widow, Ann, who had remarried and moved away. When Ann died in 1761, he inherited Mount Vernon outright.

Lawrence's death also left vacant his position of adjutant general, which carried the rank of major and responsibility for raising, organizing, and training the local militia when called up by the colonial government. Washington took the moment to step into a military career. When the governor and council divided the adjutancy into four districts, Washington applied for the Northern Neck, where he lived. That post went to William Fitzhugh, and Washington was awarded the Southern District instead. In February 1753, just before his twenty-first birthday, he took the oath of office and the military title that went with it. When Fitzhugh resigned after just a few months, Washington successfully lobbied Lieutenant Governor Robert Dinwiddie and the Virginia Council to secure the vacant Northern Neck adjutancy.[72] With no military experience whatsoever, he was now a soldier as well as a land speculator.

BOTH CAREER PATHS LED TO the Ohio country. Virginians like Washington who ventured there were like blind men feeling an elephant: they touched the edges of an Indian world they could barely imagine, a continent inhabited by countless Indian nations, confederacies, villages, bands, and clans that built and sustained relations with one other; that faced west, north, and south as much as they faced east to confront a growing English presence; and that conducted their own foreign policies in a kaleidoscope of shifting positions. Political power was diffused; communities were generally autonomous, and they reached decisions by consensus. Individuals were expected to subordinate their own interests and ambitions to the good of the community. Unlike elite Virginians, Indian leaders reckoned wealth in relatives rather than in land, slaves, and money, but like Virginians, they measured their influence in the extent, and status, of personal connections—in their relatives and the followers who gave them their allegiance. Communities maintained order by custom, clan obligations, and the force of public opinion. Throughout the eastern woodlands, in villages nestled in fertile river bottoms, people sustained balanced economies based on extensive cornfields, hunting, and trade. A communal ethic of sharing and a moral economy of reciprocity provided practical ways of dealing with periods of plenty and scarcity. Clan law prohibited incest—marrying a member of the same clan—and regulated homicide: a killing, whether by a member of the community or an outsider, demanded a killing to balance the death and restore order. People kept the world in balance by prayer, ritual, and ceremony, and kinship with the spirit world. Spiritual forces permeated everyday lives and possessed and exerted power. Access to spiritual power required observing proper rituals, conducting appropriate ceremonies, and behaving in respectful ways—with other people, with animals, with the natural environment. In the absence of centralized government, written laws, courts, police or penal systems, or churches, Virginians regarded Indian societies and ways of life as wild and disorderly; they did not and could not see that Indian beliefs, ethics, and obligations gave their lives and their world meaning, order, and cohesion.[73] Yet Washington and his fellow Virginians also saw things and ways of ordering the world that Indians did not see: invisible lines on the landscape drawn on surveyors' plats and in deed books, and a future of fields, pastures, and meadows.[74]

In part, Virginians failed to see order in Indian country because their very presence made things increasingly disorderly. What the Lakota writer Luther Standing Bear said about the trans-Mississippi

West in the nineteenth century was equally true of the trans-
Appalachian West in the eighteenth: it only became wild when white
men arrived. Escalating conflict, epidemic diseases, and entanglement
in Atlantic trade networks brought change, chaos, and catastrophe
to societies that strove for continuity and harmony. Widening imperial and tribal contests made war a way of life for many communities,
demanding and diverting more of their energies and resources, and
upsetting balances between generations, between genders, and
between civil chiefs and war chiefs that had helped curtail violence
in the past. The Cherokees in the southern Appalachians may have
numbered about twenty thousand people when Washington was
born; six years later smallpox struck. The trader James Adair said it
cut their population in half. He probably exaggerated, but the epidemic was devastating enough.[75] Meanwhile, Cherokee and other
southeastern hunters armed with guns killed more and more deer
and exchanged thousands of deerskins to English traders. By the late
1750s Savannah, Georgia, was annually exporting more than 200,000
pounds of deerskins to England; Charleston, South Carolina, more
than 355,000 pounds. The English tanning and leather-dressing
industry converted them into fine-quality gloves, shoes, hats, and
buckskins. English traders brought pack trains carrying cloth, guns,
powder and shot, metal pots, iron axe heads, steel knives, traps, tools,
and rum to Cherokee towns and furnished goods on credit charged
against a hunter's anticipated take of deerskins. Like Virginia planters, Cherokee hunters became dependent on manufactured goods
acquired via the Atlantic trade. Cherokees could not "live independent of the English," said one chief in 1750. "The Cloathes we wear,
we cannot make ourselves, they are made for us. We use their
Ammunition with which we kill Deer. We cannot make our Guns,
they are made to us. Every necessary Thing in Life we must have
from the white People."[76]

Virginia and South Carolina competed for their business. In his
History of the Dividing Line betwixt Virginia and North Carolina, written
in 1728 (although not published until 1841), William Byrd II
asserted that Virginians had been trading with the Cherokees before
the colony of Georgia "was thought of." South Carolina, however,
being closer to the Cherokee towns, quickly assumed the lion's share
of the business and attempted to monopolize it. Virginia tried to
insert itself into the Cherokee trade, and Cherokees looked to
Virginia to provide more trade options and better terms than they
got from South Carolina. Prompted in part by disputes with South
Carolinian traders, Cherokees sent a message to Virginia in 1734

asking for trade. The Overhill Cherokee chief Attakullakulla or Little Carpenter, who as a youth had accompanied a Cherokee delegation to London in 1730, led a delegation to Williamsburg in 1751 to pursue closer commercial and diplomatic ties with Virginia. The move drew protests from Governor James Glen of South Carolina, which jealously guarded its Cherokee trade. "It is absolutely necessary for us to be in friendship with the Cherokees," wrote Glen. He estimated the Cherokees "to be about 3,000 Gunmen, the greatest Nation that we now have in America, except the Chactaws. And while we can call them Friends they may be considered as a Bulwark at our Backs, for such Numbers will allways secure us on that Quarter from the attempts of the French." Glen realized that he could not keep the Cherokees in line by threatening to cut off trade, as that might push them into the arms of the French.[77] Cherokees may have depended on European goods, but they were not politically dependent on any one of the European powers that competed for their trade and allegiance. As W. Stitt Robinson concluded more than half a century ago from his review of the intercolonial contest for their trade, Cherokees were more influential in shaping Virginian Indian policy than Virginians were in influencing Cherokee politics.[78]

Indian people responded to the presence and pressures of colonial settlers, traders, missionaries, and imperial rivals in various ways. Sometimes they adapted to new situations without abandoning old values and managed to strengthen rather than weaken their communities, cultures, and chances of survival. Nevertheless, new demands, new opportunities, and new threats produced tensions and divisions between and within communities. Indian people were always in motion, but now Indian country was a world of perpetual movement. People trying to escape violence, slave raids, disease, and the pressures of settler colonialism took refuge in other areas and in other communities. People in search of richer hunting territories moved away from colonial settlers; people seeking access to guns, gunpowder, and goods moved toward colonial traders and took advantage of new economic opportunities. The "tribal" map broke down where groups, families, and individuals moved and merged with other peoples, creating composite communities and multitribal collections of villages. In the lower Susquehanna Valley, for example, Shawnee, Delaware, Nanticoke, and Conoy migrants joined Susquehannocks and other peoples who had taken refuge in the area after Bacon's Rebellion. Then, when colonial settlement began to crowd the valley, they left the Susquehanna and headed west across the Allegheny Mountains. Tuscaroras migrated from North Carolina and joined the Iroquois; other peoples moved away from Iroquois domination. Virginians struggled to control the traffic of raiding parties on the Warriors' Path and prevent Indians from crossing the Potomac. For the Shawnees, described by one trader as "the Greatest Travellers in America," recurrent movement became almost a way of life and a marker of identity.[79] Indian leaders covered great distances to visit colonial capitals; colonial governments struggled to keep up with the "who's who" of Indian country in a constantly shifting political landscape.

Upheaval and catastrophe reflected loss of spiritual power that could be explained as a result of weakened traditional culture and declining observance of necessary rituals. In Washington's lifetime, Indian peoples periodically sought to revive their spiritual power in movements of cultural rejuvenation that grew into or merged with political movements to throw off colonial control. If Washington heard of such developments in Indian country, like most of his contemporaries he little understood them; yet they would profoundly affect the course of his life and that of the country he would lead.[80]

CHAPTER 2

The Ohio Company and the Ohio Country

I N MANY WAYS AND for most of his life, George Washington's Indian world *was* the Ohio country. Virginia's expansion and his ambitions led there, his formative experiences with Indians occurred there, and his vision for personal fortune and the nation's future focused there. His actions, campaigns, and policies would help transform the Ohio country from a Native American world to an Anglo-American world. To the English, the Ohio country seemed a wild place that needed the tending hand of settlers and civilization to cultivate its bounty. But the Ohio country already had its own settlers and civilizations. Ohio Indians saw the Appalachian Mountains as a buffer against English encroachment, and they knew that the forces unleashed by colonial intrusion and the actions of surveyors, speculators, and empire builders—men like Washington—were what made the Ohio country a wild and volatile place.

International, intercolonial, intertribal, and private competition destabilized the region years before Washington appeared on the scene. Virginia considered the Ohio country to be within its boundaries as set by royal charter and believed that Treaty of Lancaster made with the Iroquois in 1744 confirmed and guaranteed its right to the area. But Pennsylvania, France, and multiple Indian nations all had something to say about that. Prior to the Lancaster Treaty, Pennsylvanians dominated the Indian trade in the Ohio Valley; most Virginians followed the valleys that led to the southwest to trade with the Cherokees and other nations.[1] But when Thomas Lee and William Beverley returned from Lancaster with a massive

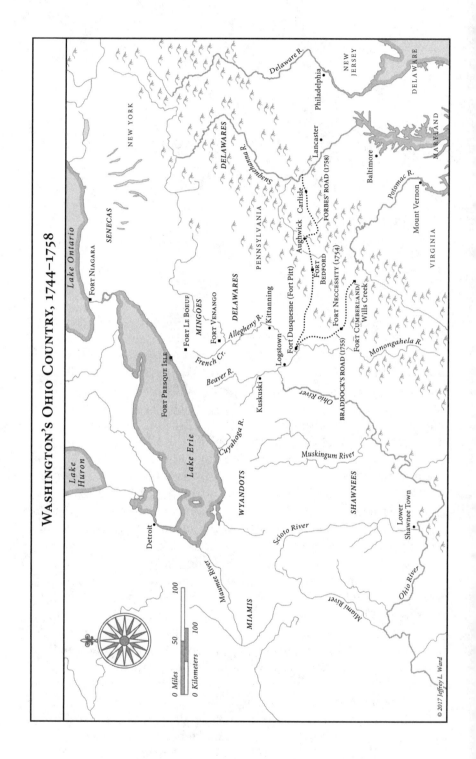

WASHINGTON'S OHIO COUNTRY, 1744–1758

© 2017 Jeffrey L. Ward

cession of Indian territory, land fever infected the Virginia elite. The gentry who dominated the government granted millions of acres west of the Appalachians to the gentry who owned the land companies. In the first session of the Virginia Assembly after the Treaty of Lancaster, Lieutenant Governor William Gooch approved a grant of 100,000 acres on the Greenbrier River in present-day West Virginia to the Greenbrier Company, a syndicate headed by John Robinson Sr., Speaker of the House of Burgesses, and 100,000 acres on the Kanawha River to the Wood's River Company, headed by James Patton, commander of the Augusta County militia. In the next nine years the governor and council authorized thirty-six grants west of the Alleghenies.[2]

In 1747 Thomas Lee and a group of influential men from the Northern Neck formed the Ohio Company of Virginia, setting events in motion that would shape Washington's first experiences in Indian country. The company petitioned Lieutenant Governor Gooch and the council for a grant of lands in the territory allegedly ceded by the Iroquois at Lancaster. To advance its case the company promised to open trade with the various Indian nations, settle a given number of people on their lands, and build forts to protect them. The company's membership changed over time but consistently included leaders of Virginia's aristocracy, men closely related by family ties as well as business, political, and social connections.[3] Thomas Lee was a member of the council. The thirteen original members included Lee, his three sons and a son-in-law, Lawrence and Augustine Washington Jr. (whose daughter married one of Lee's sons), and the frontier trader Thomas Cresap. Lawrence Washington was the first chairman of the company. Cresap lobbied for the petition in Williamsburg and presented it to the governor and his council. When Gooch postponed action on the petition and referred it to the Board of Trade, the company secured the services of John Hanbury, a well-connected London merchant, to lobby on their behalf and use his political influence to present the petition directly to the Privy Council. Hanbury was offered a share in the company and became its fourteenth member and main promoter in London.[4]

Hanbury secured an audience with King George II and submitted a petition that was a mixture of half-truths, wishful thinking, and grandiose ambition. It asked for a grant of 200,000 acres near the Forks of the Ohio, and an additional 300,000 acres once the company met the terms of the original grant by settling one hundred families on the land and building a fort to protect the settlement. The grant would encompass parts of Virginia and parts of Maryland, almost all of what is now western Virginia, and southwestern

Pennsylvania. The petition conveyed the kind of assumptions and agendas that influenced Washington at an early age and shaped his personal and public plans for Indian country.

The Ohio Company derived its claim from the Six Nations, who claimed all the lands west of Virginia by right of conquest. At the Treaty of Lancaster the Six Nations had ceded "all the said Lands west of Virginia with all the right thereto, so far as your Majesty should at any time thereafter be pleased to extend the said colony." Since most of the Indian nations in the Ohio country were allies of the Six Nations and the British, and had requested trade from Virginia, the company was ready and willing to seize the opportunity. Conveying goods by easy passage and at little expense from the Potomac to the Ohio country, it would establish trading relations with the Indians so "they may be forever fixed in the British Interest and the prosperity and safety of the British Colonies be effectually secured." Establishing a fort and settlements would strengthen the frontier and dramatically increase Britain's share of the fur trade. At the same time, it would promote the consumption of British manufactures, expand commerce, increase shipping and navigation, "and extend your Majestys Empire in America."[5] In other words, the Ohio Company advanced the Crown's imperial interest by pursuing its own self-interest. The Board of Trade and Privy Council agreed and recommended granting the petition. The king signed the instructions empowering Gooch to make the grant. In July 1749 Gooch and his council granted the company permission to take up 200,000 acres in the unsettled parts of Virginia beyond the Alleghenies, in the vicinity of the forks of the Ohio.[6]

Thomas Lee sent George Washington in 1749 to survey lands for the company in the region where Fifteen Mile Creek joins the Potomac and on the Great and Little Capon, and sent the Maryland trader Hugh Parker and Thomas Cresap to survey the Ohio country.[7] They had to be discreet. When Indians saw surveyors, they knew the Ohio Company was after their land—knowledge that might well push them into the arms of the French, which was exactly what the Crown hoped to avoid.

As the Ohio Company saw it, the country was a land speculator's dream. Company resolutions described rivers stocked with fish and wild fowl; woods abounding with buffalo, elk, deer, wild turkey, and other game; and fertile lands "far exceeding any Lands to the East of the great Mountains," containing "Timbers of all kinds and Stone for building, Slate, Limestone Coal, Salt Springs and various Minerals." It was, in short, "a Countrey that wants nothing but

Inhabitants to render it one of the most delightful and valuable Settlements of all his Majesties plantations in America."[8]

But the Ohio country had multiple claimants, and Virginia had more than one land company. The same day the Ohio Company received its 200,000-acre land grant, Gooch's council granted the Loyal Land Company—organized by Dr. Thomas Walker, Peter Jefferson, Colonel Joshua Fry, and other speculators—800,000 acres along the boundary between Virginia and North Carolina west of the Blue Ridge Mountains in the Ohio Valley. Walker headed west on a four-month expedition to survey the territory. He renamed the Shawnee River in honor of the Duke of Cumberland, who three years earlier had brutally suppressed the Jacobite Rebellion in Scotland, and passed through what became known as the Cumberland Gap into what became known as Kentucky.[9]

Traders from Pennsylvania who had followed their Indian customers west were already active in the Ohio country. Virginians who wanted Indian land more than they wanted Indian trade faced a tough challenge in dislodging them. Pennsylvania traders warned Ohio Indians that if the Ohio Company built a road across the mountains, the Catawbas would use it to raid them and that a settlement would drive away game. Thomas Lee complained to the Board of Trade in October 1749 that so many Indians had been led to suspect the company's goal was to ruin them, not trade with them, that "without a treaty and presents we shall not be able to do anything with them." A month later, he complained to Deputy Governor James Hamilton that his Pennsylvanian traders had rendered execution of the king's grant impracticable by convincing the Ohio Indians that the fort was "to be a bridle for them" and that the real purpose of roads the company planned to make was to bring the Catawbas down on them. "Yet," Lee asserted, "these are the lands purchased of the Six Nations by the treaty of Lancaster." The western boundary of Pennsylvania, and the question as to whether the Forks of the Ohio fell within Virginia or Pennsylvania, remained in dispute for years.[10]

Like Virginia and Pennsylvania, France felt it had a legitimate claim to the Ohio country, dating back to 1682, when René-Robert Cavelier, sieur de La Salle, claimed the entire Mississippi River drainage basin by right of discovery and named it Louisiana. French officials saw the Ohio River as the vital link between their colonies in Canada and the lower Mississippi Valley. In 1749, alarmed by the activities of British traders in the region, the comte de La Galissonière, the governor of New France, dispatched Captain Pierre-Joseph de Céloron de Blainville from Montreal with more than two hundred

Canadians and thirty Indians into the Ohio country. Céloron was to reassert France's claim—which he did by nailing to trees a series of tin or copper plaques bearing the French royal arms and burying in the ground below lead plates inscribed with the French claim—impress the Indians with his show of military force, and assess the growing English threat.[11] The French dismissed English attempts to justify their pretensions on the basis that the Iroquois had rights to the country and the Iroquois were subject to the British crown: just having set foot on a territory did not give the Iroquois title to it, they said, and as for the Iroquois being British subjects, it was well known they refused to acknowledge any sovereign.[12]

Gooch resigned and returned to England in 1749. Thomas Lee, as president of the Virginia Council, took over as acting lieutenant governor, and in that position advanced the interests of the Ohio Company, of which he was also, of course, acting president. When Lee died in November 1750, Lawrence Washington took over as head of the company until his death; he willed his shares to his younger brother George. Interim lieutenant governor Lewis Burwell was not particularly accommodating to the company's plans, fearing that its expansion into the Ohio country would spark French and Indian hostility. Consequently, even before Robert Dinwiddie arrived as the new lieutenant governor in November 1751, the Ohio Company made him a shareholder and secured his support. As both lieutenant governor of the colony and a major stakeholder in the company, Dinwiddie was determined that Virginia should play a leading role in the expansion of the British Empire in America. He aggressively asserted Virginia's claims to the Ohio country against those of Pennsylvania and pushed forward plans to help the Ohio Company plant a settlement at the Forks of the Ohio.[13]

The Ohio Company now had the green light from the home government to begin developing and securing the region for the empire. In the bitterly contested Ohio country, however, government approval even at the highest level was only a first step toward making good on a claim. The company's plans would come to nothing without the consent and cooperation of the Ohio Indians themselves.

Native people inhabited the Ohio country for at least ten thousand years before George Washington set foot in it, and they had seen their share of conflict. By the middle of the eighteenth century, the region had become a refuge for displaced peoples and a crossroads of cultures. The Shawnees seem to have originated in the Ohio Valley. They may have descended, at least in part, from a people known to archaeologists as the Fort Ancient Culture, who lived from about 1400 to 1650 in an area that embraced southern Ohio, southern Indiana, western Virginia, and northern Kentucky. Shawnees left to escape the reverberations of war and disease in the mid-seventeenth century but returned in the early eighteenth century and settled in the Scioto and Miami Valleys. The Shawnees traditionally comprised five divisions, or society clans, each with its own area of responsibility for the welfare of the tribe. The Chillicothe and Thawekila divisions took care of political matters and generally supplied tribal political leaders; the Mekoches were concerned with health and medicine and provided healers and counselors; the Pekowis were responsible for religion and ritual; the Kispokos generally took the lead in preparing and training for war and supplying war chiefs. These divisions were semiautonomous, had their own chiefs, occupied particular towns (often named after the division), and sometimes conducted their own foreign policies with other tribes.[14]

Pushed out of eastern Pennsylvania by English pressure, some Delawares migrated to the Susquehanna Valley. Others moved west and settled along the Allegheny River and its tributaries, establishing villages at Kittanning, Venango, and Kuskuski, formerly an Iroquois settlement, on Beaver Creek and the Shenango River near present-day New Castle, Pennsylvania. Some moved farther west to the upper Muskingum Valley. Wyandots or Wendats, remnants of the once-powerful Huron confederacy, had established communities near Detroit and Sandusky. Splinter groups from the Iroquois confederacy—primarily Senecas and Cayugas—migrated west and settled in the area between Lake Erie and the Allegheny River, where they became known to the English as Mingoes, derived from the Delaware word for them, *Mingwe*. When Shawnees and other peoples began returning to the Ohio country in the early eighteenth century, the Iroquois claimed they were their dependents. Miamis, Weas, and Piankashaws relocated to the Wabash Valley from Michigan, as did Kickapoos and Mascoutens from the Illinois Country. The roughly two thousand people clustered around the mouth of the Cuyahoga River (present-day Cleveland) in 1742 included Senecas, Cayugas, Onondagas, Oneidas, Mohawks, Mahicans, Ottawas, Ojibwas, and Abenakis from northern New England and Quebec. The Ohio Valley, said one Cayuga, was "a Republic composed of all sorts of Nations."[15]

The French, the British, and the Iroquois all claimed to control the region, but none did. France and Britain both knew they could only exercise sovereignty there through Indian proxies. Ohio Indians increasingly sought to assert their independence from the Iroquois, as well as to preserve their land and independence from both the French and the English, often by playing one against the other. Noting how few Shawnees had attended the Treaty of Lancaster, Deputy Governor George Thomas of Pennsylvania observed "that the closer our union has been with the Six Nations, the greater distance they have kept from us."[16]

In the looming imperial contest, the central council of the Iroquois Confederacy, located at Onondaga near present-day Syracuse, New York, continued to pursue the strategy of neutrality its diplomats had initiated in 1701 at the Treaty of Montreal with the French and the Treaty of Albany with the English. But Onondaga's authority petered out west of the Alleghenies, and Ohio Indians sometimes had other ideas. In November 1747, during the Anglo-French conflict known in America as King George's War, a delegation of ten Indian warriors from the Ohio traveled to Philadelphia and met the provincial council, which advised the governor and acted as the upper legislature. It was unusual for warriors to take such a step, and they explained their reasons. They were "of the Six Nations," they said, meaning they were Mingoes, but they were breaking with Iroquois policy. Despite repeated English requests to join them in fighting the French, the "old Men at the Fire at Onondaga" had stuck to their policy of neutrality. Finally, said the warriors, the young men and the war chiefs "consulted together & resolved to take up the English Hatchet against the will of their old People, and to lay their old People aside as of no use but in time of Peace." They asked Pennsylvania to furnish them with better weapons—wooden clubs were of little use "against the hard Heads of the French," they said— and left armed with guns, powder, lead, steel knives, and tomahawks.[17] Deputy Governor Hamilton of Pennsylvania put his finger on what had happened: "by suffering their young Indians to go and settle" in the Ohio country, the Six Nations had helped to generate a "new interest" that challenged the Confederacy's claims to hegemony over the region.[18]

Onondaga designated emissaries—the English called them "half kings"—to represent its interests in Indian towns outside Iroquoia. Half kings could speak and negotiate for the Confederacy but could not make binding decisions without approval from Onondaga. In the Ohio country, where Onondaga was trying to maintain its waning influence over nations that were trying to maneuver their own course among the English, French, and Iroquois, half kings had to bolster an appearance of authority with large doses of diplomatic ability. Their authority in the region rested in large measure on how well they represented Ohio Indians' interests. They were also prepared to bypass Onondaga and open direct relations with the English colonies when they saw the interests of the Iroquois in Ohio diverge from those of the Iroquois in New York. "It is not at all clear," notes the historian Richard White, that the half kings "obeyed any instructions from Onondaga that they did not want to obey."[19]

One half king exerted enormous influence on the life of George Washington. Tanaghrisson seems to have been Catawba by birth, captured with his mother in an Iroquois raid. As was common practice to bolster falling populations and replace lost kin, a Seneca family adopted him, at which point he became a Seneca. He did not appear in the written records until quite late in his life. He and an Oneida chief named Scarouady were appointed half kings to the Ohio country sometime before September 1748, when they told Pennsylvania's interpreter Conrad Weiser they "had nothing in their Council Bag, as they were new beginners" and asked him for gifts because "they often must send Messengers to Indian Towns & Nations, & either to recompense a Messenger or to get Wampum to do the business."[20] Scarouady, also called Monacatootha, was known as "a Person of great Weight" in Indian affairs and functioned as the half king for the Shawnees.[21] Tanaghrisson was half king for the Ohio Delawares and Mingoes and the resident delegate at Logstown.

→ Located near present-day Ambridge, Pennsylvania, Logstown was a multitribal village and an important trade center. It also functioned as a council fire—a designated meeting place—for the Indian peoples living in the upper Ohio Valley and was fast surpassing Onondaga in regional importance. It was here that Indians from throughout the Ohio country met in council and then sent ten warriors to Philadelphia to inform the government of Pennsylvania that they would no longer swallow Onondaga's policy of neutrality. Logstown served as headquarters for many English traders who exchanged merchandise and developed personal ties with the Indians living there, and it was a center of anti-French sentiment.[22] Captain Pierre-Joseph Céloron de Blainville stopped at Logstown during his expedition to assert French sovereignty in the Ohio country. He found the village inhabited by Iroquois, Shawnees, and Delawares, as well as some Mohawks from Kahnawake and Lake of the Two Mountains (present-day Oka), Abenakis, Nipissings, and Ottawas. Céloron also found they had their own ideas about sovereignty. Four flags—three French and one English—flew above the village. Either different groups within the village were displaying their allegiances or the villagers were hedging their bets. They evaded Céloron's requests to oust English traders by claiming the chiefs who could make such a decision were absent, which they may well have been, and deliberately so. Céloron described it as "a bad village," which the English had turned against the French with "cheap merchandise."[23]

Virginia lieutenant governor Dinwiddie and the Ohio Company knew they would have to deal with Logstown. To secure their claims to territory in the Ohio country, they needed to establish alliances with Indian nations to expel the French, secure confirmation of the Lancaster Treaty by chiefs who were not present at the treaty and would not have ceded their territory if they had been, and obtain consent to building a trading house on the claimed lands. Ohio Indians told George Croghan, a Pennsylvania trader and Indian agent, that they did "nott Like to hear of there Lands being Setled over the Allegany Mountain, and in particular by the Virginians."[24] As at the Treaty of Lancaster, the Virginians chose to deal with the Iroquois, but representatives from Onondaga could not be prevailed upon to travel to Virginia. (Iroquois chiefs who declined an invitation to visit Virginia in 1750 said that they lost so many men every time they traveled to Philadelphia that it seemed "the evil Spirits that Dwell among the White People are against us and kill us," and they could only assume that traveling deeper into the colonial settlements would be even more dangerous.[25]) With the French increasing pressure, time was of the essence. Dinwiddie and company chose the expedient of dealing with the Six Nations representative in the Ohio country. That meant negotiating with Tanaghrisson at Logstown.

To further its plans of opening a route from the Potomac and establishing trade with the Ohio Indians, the Ohio Company first built a storehouse at the head of canoe navigation at the mouth of Wills Creek, near present-day Cumberland, Maryland, where the Warriors' Path between the Iroquois and the southern Indians crossed other paths that led to the Ohio country. The company instructed Thomas Cresap to blaze a trail from Wills Creek to Redstone Creek, a tributary of the Monongahela River, which he did with the help of a Delaware guide named Namacolin. The Pennsylvania trader William Trent built a storehouse at the confluence of the Redstone and Monongahela. Located near the site of a massive pre-Columbian earthwork, Redstone became the strategic center for Virginia's trading operations into the Ohio Valley.[26]

The Ohio Company dispatched Christopher Gist on two expeditions to explore the territory, select the land to be included in the grant, and gain the support, or at least assuage the concerns, of the Indians. Before Thomas Lee died in 1750, the company instructed

Gist to take a party of men "as soon as possible to the Westward of the great Mountains...in Order to search out and discover the Lands upon the River Ohio, & other adjoining Branches of the Mississippi down as low as the great Falls thereof," at present-day Louisville, Kentucky. Gist was to note the passes through the mountains and the width and depth of the rivers, "take an exact Account of the Soil, Quality, & Product of the Land," survey the stretches of good level land he found, and make a map of the country he passed through. In addition, he was to observe what Indian nations lived there, their numbers, whom they traded with, and what they traded for.[27]

Gist set out on the last day of October 1750, following an old Indian trail up to the Juniata and then across the Allegheny. Delayed by sickness and snow, he took refuge in Indian camps, and at one point when he was very sick "sweated myself according to the Indian Custom in a Sweat House, which gave Me Ease and my Fever abated." At the Delaware town of Shannopin, near modern Pittsburgh, while he recovered and his party rested and fed their horses, Gist did some surreptitious surveying. At Logstown a few days later, the people "began to enquire my Business, and because I did not readily inform them, they began to suspect me, and said, I was come to settle the Indian's Land, and they knew I should never go Home again safe."[28]

At Logstown Gist teamed up with George Croghan and an interpreter, Andrew Montour. Montour, known to the Indians as Satellihu or Eghnisara, was the son of an Oneida war chief and Isabelle Montour, a French-Indian interpreter and culture broker known as "Madame" Montour. He had grown up among the Oneidas in New York and the Delawares and Shawnees on the Susquehanna River, and lived among the Six Nations in the country between Lake Erie and the Ohio. He spoke French, English, Mohawk, Oneida, Wyandot, Delaware, Miami, and Shawnee. He worked as agent and interpreter for Pennsylvania, and Tanaghrisson said the Iroquois were pleased to have him as an interpreter because he was "one of our own People" and they could be "sure our Business will go on well & Justice be done on both Sides." Montour dressed the part: he favored elaborate European clothes while wearing Indian face paint, applied with bear's grease, and brass pendants hanging from his ears.[29] Individuals like Montour who moved easily between Indian and colonial society often aroused English suspicions, but men like Croghan, Conrad Weiser, and Thomas Cresap who worked with him generally trusted him and vouched for his honesty and integrity as well as his ability.[30]

Leaving Logstown, the trio traveled deep into Indian country, holding councils and gathering information on the dispositions of the different tribes for Lieutenant Governor Dinwiddie. The Wyandots were divided between French and English factions and warned Gist to stay away from the Ottawas, "a nation of French Indians."[31] The Delawares, on the other hand, consisted of "about five hundred fighting Men all firmly attached to the English Interest." They were "not properly Part of the Six Nations but are scattered about, among most of the Indians upon the Ohio, and some of them among the six Nations, from whom they have Leave to hunt upon their Lands."[32] At Lower Shawnee Town, a community of three hundred warriors and 140 houses at the confluence of the Scioto and Ohio Rivers near present-day Portsmouth, Ohio, Gist, Groghan, and Montour met the Shawnees in "a Kind of State-House of about 90 Feet long, with a light cover of Bark." The Shawnees had been "formerly at variance" with the Six Nations but were "now reconciled," and good friends to the English. Distant enough from Europeans to safeguard their autonomy, they permitted Pennsylvania traders to establish trading houses.[33] When Gist reached the Miami towns, he was at the far western edge of British contact with the Indian world. The Miamis, he reported, were "accounted the most powerful People to the Westward of the English Settlements, & much superior to the six Nations with whom they are now in Amity: their Strength and Numbers are not thoroughly known, as they have but lately traded with the English." Other tribes farther to the west regularly came to the Miami villages, "& 'tis thought their Power and Interest reaches to the Westward of the Mississippi, if not across the Continent." Although Gist exaggerated the extent of the Miamis' power, he thought they were well disposed to the English and favored an alliance with them.[34] They wanted to increase their English trade. Gist, Croghan, and Montour held councils with them to promote an alliance and counteract French influence. As he traveled, Gist also made note of areas of land that were level, well watered, well timbered, rich in game, and "full of beautiful natural Meadows." "In short," he wrote of one area, "it wants Nothing but Cultivation to make a most delightful Country."[35]

Croghan and Montour were back at Logstown in May 1751, representing Pennsylvania's interests. The resident Six Nations, Delawares, and Shawnees welcomed them "by firing Guns and Hoisting the English Colours." Two days later, forty Iroquois warriors from the headwaters of the Ohio arrived with Captain Philippe-Thomas Chabert de Joncaire, who was the son of a French father and a Seneca mother. Joncaire requested an answer to the speech Céloron had made two years before, demanding that the Indians turn away the English traders. Following Indian protocol, he presented a large belt of wampum. One of the Six Nations chiefs, who would likely have been Tanaghrisson as the ranking half king at Logstown, answered that the Indians had no intention of turning away the traders. "Go and tell your Governor to ask the Onondaga Council If I don't speak the minds of all the Six Nations," he said, and returned Joncaire's wampum belt. Croghan urged the Indians to renew their friendship with the English and continue doing business with Pennsylvania traders. He gave them gifts from the governor of Pennsylvania to help seal the deal. The Indians received Croghan's wampum belts "with the Yo-hah," or shout of approval. Finally, in open council, the Six Nations chief spoke to Joncaire "very quick and sharp with the Air of a Warrior." Why were the French disturbing the peace? he asked. What right did Onontio, the governor of New France, have to their lands? "Is it not our Land?" he demanded, "Stamping on the Ground and putting his Finger to John Coeur's Nose." Joncaire should go home and tell Onontio that the Six Nations would not put up with it. The chief said he expressed "the Sentiments of all our Nations" and emphasized his statements by handing Joncaire four strings of black wampum.[36] Croghan maintained that Tanaghrisson, Scarouady, and an Iroquois chief called Kaghswaghtaniunt or Tohashwughtonionty, also known as Belt of Wampum or just the Belt, all told him in Montour's presence that they and Onondaga agreed to permit a trading house.[37]

Gist returned from his first expedition in the spring of 1751. He set out on his second the same year. Departing from Wills Creek the first week of November, he crossed the mountains through Sandy Gap. Again he was looking for good land, but this time also collecting samples of minerals. Again the Indians were suspicious. On his return journey a Delaware who spoke good English told him that their chiefs the Beaver (Tamaqua) and Captain Oppamylucah "desired to know where the Indian's Land lay, for that the French claimed all the Land on one Side the River Ohio & the English on the other Side." Oppamylucah had asked Gist the same question when he had stopped at his camp on the first leg of the journey. "I was at a Loss to answer Him as I now also was," Gist confessed.[38]

The Ohio Company was satisfied that Gist's journeys had dispelled the prejudices against Virginia that Pennsylvania's traders, if not its government, had "artfully propagated" among the Indians. The Indians saw they could trade with the company on more favorable terms than with Pennsylvania traders, but since Gist had not obtained the Indians' approval for building a settlement on the Ohio, that issue remained to be dealt with the following spring.[39]

Gist, Croghan, and Montour had persuaded the tribes to meet Virginian commissioners and make a treaty at Logstown.

It was a significant step. Previously, the Six Nations had monopolized colonial relations with the supposedly subordinate tribes of the Confederacy. The Ohio Indians were "but Hunters and no Counsellors or Chief Men," the Iroquois said, and "had no right to receive Presents that was due to the Six Nations."[40] In other words, diplomacy and gifts went through the Six Nations at Onondaga. By dealing directly with the Ohio Indians at Logstown, Virginia initiated, or recognized, a shift in Indian relations that diverted influence away from the Iroquois. Virginia officials may not have fully grasped the significance of the departure from established protocol, but seasoned operators in Indian country like Montour and Croghan surely did. The Ohio Indians now occupied the pivotal position in the Anglo-French rivalry for continental supremacy. Tanaghrisson and Scarouady took advantage of the new situation to make themselves indispensible intermediaries between the English and the Ohio Indians. They claimed authority over the Ohio tribes as representatives of the Six Nations but increasingly functioned as an alternative source of leadership for the Ohio Indians in dealing with the Six Nations. The Ohio nations took advantage of the widening fissure between the half kings and the Six Nations as they distanced themselves from Onondaga.[41]

Dinwiddie appointed Joshua Fry, Lunford Lomax, and James Patton as treaty commissioners. Educated at Oxford, Fry had migrated to Virginia, where he became a professor of mathematics at the College of William and Mary and a surveyor; in partnership with Peter Jefferson, the future president's father, he prepared a map of Virginia. Lomax, like Fry, was a member of the House of Burgesses. The Irish-born Patton was a militia colonel and land speculator.[42] Montour attended as interpreter; Croghan offered his services in the hope that Virginia would give him what Pennsylvania would not: recognition of a dubious grant from the Indians of 200,000 acres near the Forks of the Ohio.[43] Dinwiddie knew the Ohio Indians had objections to the Treaty of Lancaster: "They say they do not understand Pen and Ink work, and that their Interpreter did not do them Justice." Nevertheless, he instructed the commissioners to insist on implementing that treaty and establishing a settlement on the Ohio.[44] In May 1752 Gist led the commissioners to Logstown.

Several days after the commissioners arrived, they reported in their journal of the treaty, Tanaghrisson and other chiefs "came down the River with English Colours flying." They then spent almost a week "employed in their own Business" (read: kept the commissioners waiting) before the council began.[45]

The Virginians produced a copy of the Treaty of Lancaster, in which the Iroquois had ostensibly recognized "the King's Right to all the Lands in Virginia as it was then peopled, or hereafter should be peopled, or bounded by the King." They requested confirmation of the deed and approval for building a settlement on the southeast bank of the Ohio River. Gist assured the Indians that in making a settlement the British intended to establish ties of friendship and provide goods to the Indians at much cheaper rates; "the King, our father, by purchasing your Lands, had never any Intention of *takeing them from you*, but that we might live together as one People, & *keep them from the French*, who wou'd be bad Neighbours." The Shawnees and Delawares were not fooled. They refused to recognize the Iroquois' cession at Lancaster and agreed only to a trading house at the Forks, not a settlement.[46]

The commissioners dispatched Montour "to confer with his Brethren, the other Sachems, in private" and persuade them of the benefits of a settlement to their trade and security. Gist, Croghan, and Montour met with Tanaghrisson in private one evening at Croghan's house—a meeting the historian Francis Jennings characterized as "the boys in the back room." What was said there is unclear, but Tanaghrisson secretly confirmed the Lancaster Treaty. He encouraged the Virginians to build "a Strong House" at the Forks, and the Pennsylvanians to build another somewhere on the river, to act as a bulwark against the French and keep the Indians supplied with the guns, ammunition, and other commodities they needed.[47]

Tanaghrisson was playing the angles. He was not about to acknowledge in open council that the Iroquois had ceded the Ohio country to Virginia. "We are willing to confirm any Thing our Council has done in Regard to the Land," he explained, "but we never understood, before you told us Yesterday, that the Lands then sold were to extend further to the Sun setting than the Hill on the other Side of the Allegany Hill [in other words, the crest of the Appalachians], so that we can't give you a further Answer now." He would have to defer to Onondaga to confirm the cession. Carefully evading the thorny issue that was the crux of the meeting, Tanaghrisson managed to present himself as a friend to the English, a loyal representative of Onondaga, and a defender of Ohio Indian rights and lands.[48] He also had to ensure that the Virginians did not bypass him and deal directly with the Shawnees and Delawares as those tribes asserted their growing independence from the Six Nations.

The Six Nations and Delawares had a complicated history. The Iroquois claimed dominance over the Delawares, ritually making them metaphorical "women" by denying them authority to make war without Iroquois approval. The Delawares acknowledged themselves under Iroquois protection and agreed not to wage war without Iroquois approval, focusing instead on making and maintaining peace, a role they had traditionally exercised among eastern tribes and for which women held great responsibility in Iroquois society. Calling the Delawares "women" defined the symbolic relationship. But the meaning attached to the Delawares' metaphorical womanhood shifted. Europeans misread it as demeaning. In time, as Iroquois sold Delaware lands without consulting them, Delawares found it demeaning as well.[49] The Iroquois browbeat the Delawares into acquiescing in colonial land thefts such as the notorious Walking Purchase in 1737, when Pennsylvanians defrauded the tribe of lands in the Lehigh and Delaware Valleys.

At the Logstown conference, Tanaghrisson acted as if the Iroquois still had authority over the Delawares, but it was little more than an act. Colonial powers always struggled with the decentralized and diffused political structures of Native societies and adopted a "take me to your leader" approach when doing business in Indian country. They appointed certain Native leaders to act as brokers and called them "kings," although they were never that. As William Penn observed, so-called Delaware kings exerted significant influence, but in a society that operated by consensus, "they move[d] by the Breath of their People." Their powers were "rather persuasive than coercive," noted an English traveler, and the Moravian missionary David Zeisberger explained that a Delaware chief "may not presume to rule over the people, as in that case he would immediately be forsaken by the whole tribes, and his counselors would refuse to assist him."[50]

The previous Delaware "king," Alumapees, had died in 1747. Who would now speak for the Delawares? The commissioners noted in their journal: "At this Time the Delawares had no King, but were headed by two Brothers, named Shingas & the Beaver, who were Dress'd after the English Fashion, & had Silver Breast Plates [gorgets] & a great deal of Wampum about them."[51] In the course of the treaty Tanaghrisson performed his role as the Six Nations representative and designated Shingas as "king" of the Delawares, "with whom all public business must be transacted between you and your brethren the English." In Shingas's absence, his brother Tamaqua (the Beaver) stood proxy for him. Tanaghrisson placed a laced hat on his head and presented him with "a rich jacket & suit of English Colours," which the commissioners had given him "for that Purpose."[52] In reality, Tanaghrisson may have done little more than confirm the Delawares' choice, although Delaware people later insisted that the Virginians, not the Indians, made Tamaqua "king" and that the real leader was a chief named Neetotehelemy or Netawatwees, also known as Newcomer.[53] As for Shingas, his subsequent actions would demonstrate that he was neither an Iroquois puppet nor Tanaghrisson's "man."

Disaster struck a week or so after the Logstown conference ended. In June 1752 a French-Ottawa officer named Charles-Michel Mouet de Langlade, along with about 240 Ottawa, Ojibwa, and Potawatomi warriors, attacked and destroyed the Miami town of Pickawillany, where Pennsylvanians operated the largest trading post west of the Appalachians. The Miami (Piankashaw) chief Memeskia, also known as Old Briton for his attachment to the English, had told Céloron to leave the country in 1749.[54] Now, Langlade's warriors killed Memeskia, boiled and ritually ate his body in front of his people, and drove the English traders back across the mountains.[55] The raid sent shock waves through Indian country. Runners carried wampum belts and speeches as the Miamis, Shawnees, and Delawares looked to the Iroquois and English to meet their obligations as allies in the Covenant Chain and provide support and protection.[56]

Meanwhile, alarmed by the activities of Virginian and Pennsylvanian traders and land speculators in the region, the French decided to build a chain of forts to protect the water route along the Allegheny and Ohio Rivers. Ange de Menneville, marquis Duquesne, the governor of New France, dispatched the sixty-year-old veteran Pierre Paul de la Malgue, sieur de Marin, with two thousand men to carry out the fort-building campaign. Claude-Pierre Pécaudy de Contrecoeur, who had served as second-in-command in Céloron's expedition in 1749, was placed in command of Fort Niagara on the southern edge of Lake Ontario, by way of which men, supplies, and equipment for the new forts were moved into the Ohio country. The first fort, Presque Isle at present-day Erie, Pennsylvania, was completed by May 1753. An Indian who came to Logstown from Montreal reported that the French troops marching toward the Ohio set the whole earth trembling.[57] Indian messengers brought word that the French were building canoes and coming to expel the English traders. The British commander at Fort Oswego, hearing inflated reports of the size of the French and Indian force heading south to build forts, warned that if the English did nothing to stop it, they could "bid adieu to the Indians on the Continent," as the French would "be Masters of them all" and extend their dominions throughout in America.[58] For generations,

the French had cultivated and maintained alliances in Indian country through accommodation, ritual, gift exchange, and kinship ties.
Now they sought to assert control over the Ohio country by force
rather than diplomacy.[59]

In February 1752 Shawnee Indians had sent a message and six
strings of wampum to the governor of Pennsylvania. "All the Nations
settled on this River Ohio and on this side [of] the Lakes are in
Friendship and live as one People," they said, "but the French, who
are directed by the Evil Spirit and not God, trouble us much." They
cheated and threatened the Indians and had recently killed "thirty
of our Brothers the Twightwees" or Miamis. Now the Shawnees were
preparing to strike back and requesting assistance. But Pennsylvania's
Quaker-dominated assembly could offer no help, "because you well
know the Principles of the People here who have the disposition of
the Publick Money are entirely averse to any such measures," Deputy
Governor Hamilton explained to Croghan.[60] And Virginians were
more interested in acquiring the Ohio country than in helping the
Indians defend it against the French.[61]

In May 1753 Croghan, his brother-in-law and former business
partner William Trent, and several other traders met with the Indians
at Pine Creek, about twenty miles above Logstown. They wanted to
know if the Indians would oppose the French and if it was safe for
traders to remain among them. The Indians wanted to know if the
English would help them defend their lands against the French or if
they just wanted the lands for themselves. Trent assured Tanaghrisson
that Virginia regarded the Ohio country as belonging to the Indians
and would supply them with arms and ammunition if the French
attempted to settle or build forts there. The Indians said "it was an
affair of great Consequence" that required careful consideration.
After counseling with his fellow chiefs through the night and into
the early afternoon, Tanaghrisson gave Trent a carefully worded reply:
if the French came peacefully, the Indians "would receive them as
Friends, but if they came as Enemies they would treat them as such."[62]

A month later, however, Tanaghrisson and Scarouady sent
another message to the governor of Virginia, saying, "We do not want
the French to come amongst Us at all, but very much want our good
Brothers the English to be with us, to whom our Hearts are good and
shall ever continue to be so."[63] At another council at Logstown in July
and August, called by Trent to strengthen the chain of friendship,
assert Virginia's intention to build a trading house on the Ohio, and
urge the tribes to unite in the face of the French threat, Tanaghrisson and Scarouady declared "that the Half King shall go and

warn the French off our Land."[64] The Delawares had warned the French at Niagara not to come farther into the Ohio country; when the French ignored that warning, a council at Logstown had sent another. This would be the third. Iroquois protocol required giving three warnings before going to war.[65]

Onondaga watched developments in the Ohio country with concern. Returning from Onondaga to Pennsylvania in the spring of 1753, Montour reported that the Six Nations chiefs urged the governor of Virginia to use his influence to prevent war, especially in the Ohio country, which was their best hunting ground. They "were against both the English and French building Forts and settling Lands at Ohio, and desired they might both quit that Country, and only send a few Traders with Goods sufficient to supply the wants of their Hunters." What was more, the chiefs at Onondaga "did not like the Virginians and Pennsylvanians making Treaties with these Indians, whom they called Hunters, and young and giddy Men and Children; that they were their Fathers, and if the English wanted anything from these childish People they must first speak to their Fathers."[66] The Six Nations exaggerated their authority over the Indians of the Ohio country.

The French pushed a road south and built a second post at Fort LeBoeuf, on a branch of French Creek (present-day Waterford, Pennsylvania) in July. At the Indian village of Venango on the Allegheny River (present-day Franklin, Pennsylvania), they ousted the resident trader and gunsmith, John Fraser or Frazier, fortified his trading post, and began construction of Fort Machault. In the face of this intrusion, and amid Indian fears that the French and English were in cahoots to divide the land between them, Tanaghrisson and Scarouady fashioned a strategy for keeping both out of the Ohio country. They did not want to hand control of the region to Britain; rather, they wanted British allies and trading partners to counterbalance French influence, which threatened both Onondaga's and their own influence among the resident tribes.[67] The Indians needed European traders, not European garrisons and settlements.

While Tanaghrisson went to warn off the French, Scarouady headed east to persuade the Pennsylvanians and Virginians to stay away. Tanaghrisson traveled north to Fort Presque Isle and warned the commander, the sieur de Marin, to advance no farther toward "the Beautiful River," the Ohio. At the Logstown conference Tanaghrisson had told the English that he could make no decision without consulting the Onondaga council; now he told the French that he and the Ohio Indians would act independently of Onondaga:

"The river where we are belongs to us warriors. The chiefs who look after affairs [i.e., the Onondaga council] are not its masters. It is a good road for warriors and not for their chiefs." Implicitly denying the authority of the Six Nations in the Ohio country, and claiming to speak "in the name of all the warriors who inhabit the Belle Rivière," he said he had come to find out the French intentions "so that we can calm down our wives." The Indians had told the English to withdraw, and they were telling the French to do the same. "We shall be on the side of those who take pity on us and who listen to us." Handing Marin a wampum belt to halt their progress and cease construction of the forts, he declared: "This is the first and last demand we shall make of you, and I shall strike at whoever does not listen to us."[68]

Marin was not intimidated. He dismissed Tanaghrisson's threat, refused to accept his wampum belt, and responded with threats of his own. "You seem to have lost your minds," he retorted. As for Tanaghrisson's demands and his claims to speak for all the tribes of the Ohio, "I despise all the stupid things you said. I know that they come only from you, and that all the warriors and chiefs of the Belle Rivière think better than you, and take pity on their women and children." Marin had no intention of disturbing the Indians, but he had every intention of carrying out the king's instructions and would crush anyone who stood in his way. Although Tanaghrisson reasserted that he was sent by the Ohio nations and that it would be up to them to decide what they would do, Marin may have not have been far off the mark in his assessment of Tanaghrisson's standing: when Shawnee delegates spoke to the French the next day, they distanced themselves from the half king and his hard line, and the Onondaga council did not countenance his position.[69]

Tanaghrisson had delivered the final warning. "This is the third refusal you have given me," he reminded Marin. It was an ominous statement, implying there could be no turning back. "The great Being who lives above, has ordered Us to send Three Messages of Peace before We make War," Scarouady explained to the Pennsylvanians. "And as the Half King has before this Time delivered the third and last Message, we have nothing now to do but to strike the French."[70] Tanaghrisson's bold front was more bluff than reality, however. According to one report, he returned from his confrontation with the French commander with tears in his eyes, but they were likely tears of frustration rather than of anguish at impending war. Another said, "This Chief who went like a Lyon roaring out destruction, came back like a Lamb." Tanaghrisson did not speak for the Six Nations, who wanted to remain neutral, or for Delawares, whose villages lay in the path of the French invasion and perhaps favored accommodation over defiance. As evidenced by the Shawnees' repudiation of him, the tribes for whom he claimed to speak were far from united behind him. There would be more warnings and wampum belts before diplomacy gave way to war.[71]

Dinwiddie wrote alarming reports to fellow colonial governors and dispatched messengers to the Catawbas, Cherokees, and Six Nations, urging them to make common cause with the English against cunning enemies who pretended to embrace them "but mean to squeeze You to Death." He invited Miamis, Mingoes, Shawnees, and Delawares to Winchester, Virginia, in September 1753, where they were urged to mend their differences with the southern tribes and unite in face of French aggression. He tried to work with Governor James Glen of South Carolina to recruit allies from the Catawbas and Cherokees. But Glen suspected Dinwiddie of pushing the Ohio Company's agenda and was intent on maintaining control over negotiations with the tribes; when Dinwiddie asked for help, Glen and his council refused, and relations between the two governors continued fractious.[72]

In October 1753 the French were reported to be on the move, in two hundred canoes, to build their final fort in the system at the Forks of the Ohio.[73] Marin fell ill and died that month, and the fort-building campaign halted for more than half a year. Disease, drought, and fatigue, rather than Tanaghrisson's threats, caused the delay, giving the English time to mount a response.

Ohio Indians watched to see how they would respond: "The Eyes of all the Indians are fixed upon you," William Trent advised Dinwiddie in August 1753. What he did now would determine whether the Indians joined the English against the French or the French against the English.[74] Although Scarouady was unable to get Virginia or Pennsylvania to hold back their settlements in the Ohio country, the English seemed to pose less of a threat than the French. But the Indians needed guns, ammunition, and assistance if they were to mount effective resistance to the French invasion. In October they sent a speech written by a Mohawk named Jonathan Cayenquerigo, along with a wampum belt "dyed a bloody Colour," to the governor of Pennsylvania, asking that he and the governor of Virginia take hold of it and come to their assistance.[75] Pennsylvania's governor failed to respond.[76] Lieutenant Governor Dinwiddie's response was not exactly the demonstration of English support Tanaghrisson was looking for. The French and British had each signaled their intention to assert control of the Ohio country. The French sent a war party that killed and ate a Miami chief, and an army that built a string of forts. Virginia sent a messenger boy to ask that the French withdraw.

CHAPTER 3

Into Tanaghrisson's World

A S A SERVANT OF THE BRITISH EMPIRE and a shareholder in the Ohio Company, Lieutenant Governor Robert
Dinwiddie peppered the home government and his fellow
colonial governors with warnings that France was gearing up to seize
the Ohio country, and he requested permission to build a fort there.
In August 1753 the government ordered him to demand the withdrawal of French fortifications and begin construction of British fortifications. Dinwiddie wrote a letter, formally demanding that France
abandon its forts and claims in the Ohio country, and looked for
someone to deliver it to the French commander in the region.
Twenty-one-year-old George Washington rode to the governor's
palace in Williamsburg and put himself forward for the mission.

Young Washington had few qualifications for an assignment of
that magnitude and no experience in Indian country. He would have
found himself a novice in the geopolitics and Indian diplomacy of
the Ohio Valley at any time. He entered the region at a moment
when multiple agendas and ambitions among empires, colonies,
tribes, and individuals generated a kaleidoscope of competition that
challenged the knowledge and skills of even seasoned frontier operators. Men like Christopher Gist, Thomas Cresap, or George Croghan
had the experience and contacts to operate in Indian country but
lacked the gentry status necessary to represent Virginia in a formal
diplomatic mission to a European power.[1] Washington had the necessary status and was eager to go. Dinwiddie entrusted him with the
mission.[2]

His instructions were to travel northward to the Ohio, gather information about the French forts and forces in the Ohio country along the way, and then deliver Dinwiddie's letter to the French officer commanding at Fort LeBoeuf. "The Lands upon the River *Ohio*, in the Western Parts of the Colony of *Virginia*, are so notoriously known to be the Property of the Crown of *Great-Britain*," the letter declared, "that it is a Matter of equal Concern and Surprize to me, to hear that a Body of *French* forces are erecting Fortresses, and making Settlements upon that River, within his Majesty's Dominions." By what authority did the French invade British territory? Dinwiddie asked. It was his duty to demand that they depart peacefully and not interrupt the harmony that King George wished to maintain with King Louis. Dinwiddie trusted the French commander would receive Major Washington "with the Candour and Politeness natural to your Nation" and send him back "with an Answer suitable to my Wishes for a very long and lasting Peace between us."[3]

Washington left Williamsburg on the last day of October 1753. At Fredericksburg he engaged as his French interpreter Jacob Van Braam, a Dutch friend of the family who had once taught him fencing. At Alexandria and Winchester he acquired supplies, horses, and baggage. Traveling north to Wills Creek, he hired Christopher Gist as his guide, John Davison as Indian interpreter, Barnaby Currin (an Ohio Company employee and former Indian trader), and three others: John MacQuire, Henry Steward, and William Jenkins. Washington was a young man in a hurry; he wanted to take the most direct route, get the job done, and return home, mission accomplished. But diplomacy in Indian country was a slow and deliberate process, hedged about by time-consuming rituals and protocols. Emissaries did not always follow the most direct path: different paths could have different purposes; a peace mission would not travel a warpath, and attending to social, political, and ceremonial obligations sometimes involved diversions. Travel, like so much else in Indian country, was governed by relationships, not just weather and terrain.[4]

According to Dinwiddie's instructions, Washington was to proceed to Logstown, inform the resident half king Tanaghrisson, Scarouady, and other prominent chiefs of his errand, and get them to furnish warriors as an escort.[5] Gist knew where to go and whom to meet. The group crossed the Allegheny River and proceeded to a spot on the Ohio where the Ohio Company had planned to build a fort, a site that Washington correctly assessed as less well situated than the Forks of the Ohio, where the French intended to build. More important, for the moment, was that it was also the home of

Shingas, the noted chief of the Turkey or Unalachtigo division of the Delawares. Gist knew it would be important to have Shingas accompany them to Logstown as a representative of the Delawares and as an interpreter, so he and Washington called on the chief and invited him to a council there.[6] Shingas agreed and went with Washington to Logstown, some forty miles farther on.

Twenty-five days after leaving Williamsburg, Washington arrived at Logstown, only to learn that Tanaghrisson was at his hunting cabin some fifteen miles away. So Washington met with Scarouady and some other chiefs and informed them of his mission. Scarouady was a veteran Oneida war chief, whom Washington later described as "a man of Sense and Experience & a great friend to the English."[7] Like any other colonist embarking on diplomacy in Indian country, Washington had a rudimentary understanding of the role of tobacco as a gift and wampum as a means of communication and establishing trust. He gave Scarouady a string of wampum and a twist of tobacco and asked him to send for Tanaghrisson, which Scarouady promised to do by a runner in the morning.[8]

The next morning four French deserters arrived in camp. Washington took the opportunity to quiz them about the disposition of French forces and the location of their forts. He learned the French had not completed their fort-building program that year because of the sieur de Marin's death and sickness among the troops. The race for the Forks of the Ohio was still on.

Tanaghrisson arrived at three in the afternoon. Taking Davison with him as interpreter, Washington immediately invited the chief to a private meeting in his tent. Although in his fifties and past the prime of life, Tanaghrisson would have been an impressive figure. An experienced warrior and diplomat, with tattoos on his face, chest, and arms, and probably wearing a mixture of Native and European clothing, he represented and juggled the overlapping and sometimes competing interests and agendas of the multiple nations in Ohio, the Iroquois League, and himself. Representing British and Virginian interests and perspectives, Washington could have had little understanding of the stakes and complexities of Indian diplomacy as practiced by Tanaghrisson.[9]

Washington asked Tanaghrisson about his journey to speak with the now-dead sieur de Marin and the best route to take. Tanaghrisson recommended going by way of the Indian town at Venango and said that it would take five or six days' hard travel. He then proceeded to give Washington his version of the meeting with Marin, who had received him "in a very stern Manner." According to Tanaghrisson, he had told Marin the French were "the Disturbers in this Land." The Indians would not have opposed them if the French had come as traders like the English, but they would not submit to armed invaders building forts. Tanaghrisson then laid out the Ohio Indians' position and policy, and recited his statement clearly for Washington's ears and Virginia's benefit:

> Fathers, Both you and the English are white, we live in a Country between; therefore the Land belongs to neither one nor t'other: But the Great Being above allowed it to be a Place of Residence for us; so Fathers, I desire you to withdraw, as I have done our Brothers the English; for I will keep you at Arms length: I lay this down as a Trial for both, to see which will have the greatest Regard to it, and that Side we will stand by, and make equal sharers with us. Our Brothers the English have heard this, and I come now to tell it to you, for I am not afraid to discharge you off this Land.[10]

(When Dinwiddie read the account of Tanaghrisson's speech, he thought it remarkable that he should have insisted that the land belonged to the Indians after having agreed at the Treaty of Logstown to let the English settle and build a fort there.[11]) Whether or not Tanaghrisson delivered his statement as boldly to a French commander in a French fort as he did to an impressionable young Virginian in his own village, he certainly conveyed the tone of the French response. "Child, you talk foolish [when] you say this Land belongs to you," Marin told Tanaghrisson. "It is my Land, and I will have it." He rejected Tanaghrisson's speech and the wampum belt that accompanied it ("here is your Wampum, I fling it at you"), he dismissed the Indians as "Flies, or Musquitos," and he repeated his determination to advance down the Ohio and sweep aside any opposition. His troops were as numerous "as the Sand upon the Sea Shoar," he boasted.[12]

More than thirty years later, preparing some "remarks" for his potential biographer David Humphreys, Washington said it was on this occasion that Tanaghrisson gave him the same name that Indians had given his great-grandfather, Conotocarious, which name "being registered in their Manner and communicated to other Nations of Indians, has been remembered by them ever since in all their transactions with him during the late war." Why a Seneca in the 1750s should have remembered a name given first to John Washington by the Susquehannocks in the 1670s, or even have made the family connection, is unclear. It seems more likely that Washington remembered the name from family lore and took it for himself, a young man's act of bravado. Despite its hostile connotations, Washington took pride in the name. He signed his message to Tanaghrisson "Washington or

Conotocarious," and he used the name writing to Andrew Montour two years later.[13] It was not uncommon for Indian people to bestow names as a mark of respect, but doing so often carried obligations on the part of the recipient.[14] Simply assuming his great-grandfather's name—if that is what Washington did—presumably carried less significance. However, by the time Washington penned his remarks for Humphreys, "the late war" referred to the Revolution, when the Iroquois did indeed refer to him as the "Town Destroyer."

Washington and Tanaghrisson met again the next day in the village longhouse, accompanied by Gist, Scarouady, and other chiefs. With Davison interpreting, Washington informed the chiefs of his mission and asked their advice and assistance in continuing his journey. Lieutenant Governor Dinwiddie esteemed them as friends and allies, and "desired me to apply to you for some of your young Men to conduct and provide Provisions for us on our Way, and be a safeguard against those *French Indians* who have taken up the Hatchet against us," Washington said, confirming his words with a string of wampum. After the chiefs consulted, Tanaghrisson stood up and gave a guarded response. "We shall put Heart in Hand and speak to our Fathers, the *French,* concerning the Speech they made to me, and you may depend that we will endeavour to be your Guard," he assured Washington. He intended to send an escort of Mingoes, Shawnees, and Delawares, he said. But he was not about to be rushed into an English alliance that might mean conflict with the Ojibwa, Ottawa, and Huron allies of the French. "Brother, as you have asked my Advice, I hope you will be ruled by it, and stay until I can provide a Company to go with you." Protocol demanded that Tanaghrisson retrieve the wampum belt that symbolized friendship with the French and return it to them and he wanted to get the Delawares and Shawnees to do the same with the belts the French had given them. That would take some time. "The French Speech-Belt is not here, I have to go for it to my hunting-Cabbin; likewise, the people which I have ordered in are not yet come, nor cannot till the third Night from this; till which Time, Brother, I must beg you to stay." Washington was anxious to be on his way and protested that his "business required the greatest expedition," but there was little he could do. "As I found it was impossible to get off without affronting them in the most egregious Manner," he noted in his diary, "I consented to stay." Things would proceed according to Tanaghrisson's timetable, not Washington's.[15]

Early the next morning, November 27, Tanaghrisson set off for his cabin on Beaver Creek. Before he left he dispatched runners to the Shawnee chiefs and sent for Shingas to bring the Delaware wampum belt. He returned the following evening and came with Scarouady and two other chiefs to Washington's tent. They asked "to know on what Business we were going to the French." Washington had expected the question and, especially after hearing Tanaghrisson's forceful speech that the Ohio country belonged to nether Britain nor France, knew better than to announce he was carrying a letter asserting Britain's claim to the region. Instead, he gave "as satisfactory Answers" as possible. His answers "allayed their Curiosity a little" but may also help explain the subsequent lack of enthusiasm for assisting his mission. Scarouady then divulged that an Indian had brought news a few days ago that the French had held a council with the Mingoes, Delawares, and other nations at Venango. Captain Philippe-Thomas Chabert de Joncaire, "their Interpreter in Chief, living at *Venango*, and a Man of Note in the Army," told them the French soldiers had intended to come down this river this fall but, the waters growing cold, had gone into winter quarters instead. However, the Indians should expect them in the spring and had better not interfere "unless they had a Mind to draw all their Force upon them." The French expected that it would take three years to defeat the English, but if the English proved equally strong the two powers would join forces against the Indians "to cut them all off, and divide the Land between them." The French had lost a few soldiers but had enough reinforcements to make them "Masters of the Ohio."[16]

Tanaghrisson and Scarouady came early the next morning and requested another day's delay. The Shawnee chiefs had not brought their wampum belt, and no renunciation of their French alliance would be valid without it, Tanaghrisson explained. But the belt would certainly arrive tonight. Recognizing that returning the wampum was essential to "shaking of[f] all Dependence upon the French," Washington agreed to stay, "as I believed an Offense offered at this Crisis, might be attended with greater ill Consequence, than another Day's Delay." Tanaghrisson explained that the Delawares did not have their wampum belt at Logstown either; it was in the hands of Custaloga, a chief at Venango. And Shingas would not be able to accompany the Virginians on their mission. He said his wife was ill, but Washington believed the real reason was "Fear of the French."[17] Washington must have suspected that he was getting the runaround. His diplomatic mission could not proceed without the appropriate wampum belts, but clearly the Delawares and Shawnees were dragging their feet and in no hurry to return their belts and sever diplomatic relations with the French. In this instance, the affair of the wampum belts was, literally, a shell game.

Washington had his eyes on the French and what they were doing—or at least, prompted by Tanaghrisson, what he *thought* they were doing. The Shawnees, Delawares, and other Ohio nations had their eyes on the both the French and the English. They were also watching the Iroquois, who, they assumed, would follow their own interests and sacrifice theirs as they had in the past. They were also taking note of developments to the north, an area barely on Washington's radar. There, many Anishinaabeg—Ojibwas, Ottawas, and Potawatomis—and other Great Lakes Indians were tied to the French by bonds of marriage and trade and, as they had demonstrated when they destroyed the Miami village at Pickawillany, increasingly hostile to the English. The Iroquois, Shawnees, and Delawares had no wish to come to blows with the Anishinaabeg. The Shawnees also were angry and distrustful of the English after South Carolinians in the spring of 1753 captured and held hostage half a dozen Shawnee warriors on their way to raid the Catawbas.[18] Delawares had tolerated their position as "women" in the Iroquois Confederacy so long as the Six Nations and their British backers offered them military protection and access to trade goods. Now, with the French and their Indian allies invading the Ohio country, and Onondaga clinging to a precarious neutrality, western Delawares were reassessing their relationship with both the Iroquois League and the British, neither of whom displayed much evidence of being able to protect them.[19] It is unlikely Washington knew much about these shifting dynamics.

By late evening the Shawnees still had not turned up, but now, Tanaghrisson said, it should not delay their journey. In Washington's hearing, he recited the speeches that were to be repeated by an elderly Cayuga chief named Jeskakake when he gave up the belt and terminated their alliance to the French. He also handed Jeskakake a string of wampum that Shingas had sent for Custaloga to take and give back to the French. He then gave another "very large String of black [purple] and white Wampum, which was to be sent immediately to the Six Nations, if the French refused to quit the Land at this Warning; which was the third and last Time, and was the Right of this *Jeskakake* to deliver." In other words, if the French failed to heed the traditional third warning to abandon their posts and leave the Ohio country, Jeskakake would carry the belt to Onondaga so the council could issue a declaration of war. Presumably, Gist was kept busy explaining to his young charge the different purposes of the different belts and the diplomatic intricacies that determined who delivered what wampum to whom and with what meaning.[20] This was a world where wampum spoke louder than words, and words carried no weight unless accompanied by wampum. Washington needed to learn the language of the belts.[21]

The chiefs assembled in their council house that night—without Washington and Gist—to consider how many men should escort the Virginians on their journey. After the forceful declarations he had heard from Tanaghrisson, Washington must have been bitterly disappointed that instead of sending a force of warriors, the council decided "only three of their Chiefs, with one of their best Hunters, should be our Convoy." Not a single Shawnee or Delaware went along. The reason the Indians gave for not sending more was "that a greater Number might give the *French* Suspicions of some bad Design, and cause them to be treated rudely." Washington was right to be skeptical but probably naïve in thinking the real reason was that "they could not get their Hunters in." The historian Francis Jennings blamed Washington himself, who "by personality or purpose...seems to have stirred instant dislike" among the Ohio Indians, but the causes of the Indians' ambivalence ran deeper than that. They suspected English intentions as much as they did French and were not ready to play their hands. When Washington finally departed Logstown on the morning of November 30, the only Indians in his party were Tanaghrisson, Jeskakake, a chief named White Thunder, and a young man Washington knew only as the Hunter. White Thunder was the Iroquois known as Belt of Wampum. Conrad Weiser described him as "a man of very good understanding, has a good countenance, speaks well, and is reckoned among the greatest Warriors among the Six Nations. I esteem him very much." The Hunter was a Seneca warrior called Guyasuta, who would feature prominently in the affairs of the Ohio country for the next forty years.[22]

Following their Indian guides through freezing rain, Washington and his party made their way along the forest trails of western Pennsylvania, then north from the Forks of the Ohio to the Indian town and French outpost at Venango, a distance Washington estimated as about sixty miles from Logstown, but more than seventy miles the way they traveled.[23] They reached Venango on December 4. Washington immediately went to the house of John Fraser, which the French had commandeered and over which the French colors now flew. Captain Joncaire received Washington and Gist but explained that he was not the appropriate person to accept Virginia's petition: Washington would have to take it on to Fort LeBoeuf. Having dispensed with that business, Joncaire invited them to dinner and, Washington remembered, "treated us with the greatest Complaisance." The wine flowed freely, and the French officers became less restrained in their talk, telling Washington "that it was their absolute Design to take Possession of the Ohio, and by G—— they would do it." France claimed the Ohio by right of discovery by La Salle sixty years earlier, and the purpose of the French expedition now was to prevent the English settling there.[24] Washington gave the impression in his diary that he remained in control of the situation, sipping from his glass but listening through an interpreter and observing while the French officers in true Gallic fashion allowed too much wine to loosen their lips. But forty-six-year-old Joncaire was no fool; at an outpost where everything, including wine, was probably in short supply, his hospitality more likely was designed to get Washington to divulge information, or to provide the occasion for an informal but clear assertion of French rights to the Ohio.

Pouring rain all day on the fifth prevented Washington's party from traveling on. Although not mentioned in Washington's journal, Gist recorded that "Our Indians" met in council with the Delawares and told them to hand back their wampum belt to the French, as Shingas desired. The Delawares refused.[25]

Hearing that Tanaghrisson was with the group, and knowing full well how important he was to maintaining relations with both the Six Nations and the Ohio Indians, Joncaire made a show of being concerned that Washington had not brought the Half King with him the day before. Washington made the best excuses he could, claiming he had heard Joncaire say "a good deal in Dispraise of *Indians* in general" and did not think Tanaghrisson would be welcome. He confessed to the real reason in his journal: "I knew that he [Joncaire] was Interpreter, and a Person of very great Influence among the *Indians*, and had lately used all possible Means to draw them over to their interest; therefore I was desirous of giving no Opportunity that could be avoided." Joncaire indeed possessed fluency in Seneca, experience in Iroquoia, and connections in Indian country—all things that Washington lacked. But there was nothing Washington could do when Joncaire invited Tanaghrisson and the other chiefs to join him and Washington in his cabin. Joncaire greeted the Indians like old friends and proceeded to ply them with liquor, "so fast," complained Washington, "that they were soon render'd incapable of the Business they came about."[26]

Nonetheless, Tanaghrisson was quite sober when he turned up at Washington's tent the next day. He insisted that Washington wait and hear what he had to say to the French. He intended to deliver his message and return the wampum with the appropriate formality and protocol. Washington was against it. He was anxious to be on his way to Fort LeBoeuf and did not want Tanaghrisson speaking to anyone until he addressed the French commandant there. Tanaghrisson insisted, however, that Venango was the place "where all their Business with these People was to be transacted" and Joncaire was the officer responsible for Indian affairs. Tanaghrisson had to deliver his warning at Venango, and Washington had to stay and see the outcome. He sent some of the party and the horses farther up French Creek, ready for departure as soon as the business was finished. When Tanaghrisson and Joncaire met in council, Washington, as Virginia's envoy, could only watch as the Seneca chief and the French officer acted out their prescribed roles in a scene of political theater. Tanaghrisson stood and "spoke much the same as he had before done to the General" and offered Joncaire the French speech belt. Joncaire, who knew the belt was coming, refused to accept it, as Tanaghrisson knew he would. The appropriate person to receive such a belt, Joncaire explained, was Jacques Legardeur de Saint-Pierre, who had taken over as the French commander at Fort LeBoeuf on the death of the sieur de Marin. Joncaire would furnish an escort of four French officers, something Washington would rather have done without.[27]

And still Washington could not get on his way. "We found it extremely difficult getting the Indians off To-day," he wrote on December 7, "as every Stratagem had been used to prevent their going up with me." He had left the interpreter John Davison with them during the night with strict instructions not to let them out of his sight, "as I could not get them over to my Tent (they having some Business with *Custaloga*, to know the Reason why he did not deliver up the *French* Belt which he had in Keeping)." Finally, Washington sent Gist to get the Indians moving, "which he did with much Persuasion."[28] It was a tug-of-war: Joncaire did everything he could to get the Indians to stay behind, and Gist "took all care to have them along with us."[29]

Leaving Venango late in the morning on the seventh, Washington's party was slowed by heavy rain, snow, and hard traveling. Unable to cross French Creek, which was in flood, they had to make their way through many mires and swamps. Nevertheless, Washington the surveyor made note of "much good Land" and "Several extensive and very rich Meadows," one of them almost four miles long.[30] As he would throughout his life, Washington identified lands for future development without considering the possibility that they had been previously cleared and managed by Indian people.

Venango was little more than a trader's house with a stockade around it. Fort LeBoeuf was a much more formidable frontier outpost, and Washington duly took notes on its fortifications. He had time to do so because he was kept waiting again. On the twelfth Legardeur de Saint-Pierre, who had arrived as commandant only a week before Washington, gave him an audience. Washington described him as "an elderly Gentleman, and has much the Air of a Soldier." At fifty-two, Saint-Pierre was a seasoned campaigner. In his thirty years of military service he had accumulated extensive experience in Indian country that included campaigning against the Chickasaws and dealing with Abenakis, Assiniboines, Choctaws, Crees, Mohawks, and Sioux. Just the year before he had traveled hundreds of miles to the Red and Winnipeg Rivers, exploring the Canadian prairies in search of the western sea. He would not have been unduly impressed with Washington's trek from Virginia. He was also, needless to say, more than a match for a young Virginian who wanted very much to have "the Air of a Soldier" himself. Saint-Pierre informed Washington that they must wait for Pierre Legardeur de Repentigny (Washington called him "Reparti"), the commander at Fort Presque Isle, who had been sent for because he spoke a little English. Only then could Washington present Dinwiddie's letter. When Repentigny arrived and Washington handed over the letter, Saint-Pierre and his officers retired into a private room to translate the document, then asked Washington to come in with his interpreter Van Braam to look over it and make corrections. The French officers then held another council to discuss the letter on December 13. Washington took the opportunity to take note of the fort's dimensions and make whatever observations he could, and instructed his party to compile a tally of the men and canoes at the fort.[31]

The next day, snow was falling fast. With the horses growing weaker, Washington sent Barnaby Currin and two others to take them without loads to Venango and wait there if there was a prospect of the river freezing, and, if not, to continue back down to the Forks of the Ohio. Waiting for the French to respond, Washington fretted about what they were up to with his Indian allies. "As I found many Plots concerted to retard the *Indians* Business, and prevent their returning with me; I endeavour'd all that lay in my Power to frustrate their Schemes." Tanaghrisson met privately with Saint-Pierre and a couple of officers and presented him with the wampum belt, as he was supposed to do. But Saint-Pierre understood that accepting the belt meant severing diplomatic relations. Instead, Tanaghrisson told Washington, "he evaded taking it, and made many fair Promises of Love and Friendship; said he wanted to live in Peace, and trade amicably with them, as a Proof of which he would send some Goods immediately down to the Loggs-Town for them." Rather than let Tanaghrisson terminate his allegiance and commitments to the French, Saint-Pierre was trying to pry him away from his allegiance and commitments to the English.[32]

Finally, after keeping Washington waiting all day, Saint-Pierre delivered his answer on the evening of the fourteenth. It was hardly the diplomatic confrontation Washington expected. Instead, Saint-Pierre simply and cordially handed Washington a sealed letter to be delivered with all expediency to Lieutenant Governor Dinwiddie and offered to provide whatever supplies he needed for the return journey. Saint-Pierre was killed two years later at the Battle of Lake George, but he had quietly won this opening encounter. He had effectively reduced Washington to an errand boy.

The next morning Saint-Pierre ordered provisions and liquor to be loaded into Washington's canoe and behaved very amicably. While he was doing all he could to help the Virginians on their way, however, he was also doing all he could to get the Indians to stay. "Every Stratagem that the most fruitful Brain could invent, was practiced, to win the Half King to their Interest," Washington fumed. He feared that leaving Tanaghrisson behind would give the French the opportunity to do just that. He was on the verge of losing his Iroquois allies. "I can't say that ever in my Life I suffer'd so much Anxiety as I did in this Affair," he wrote. When he pressed Tanaghrisson "in the strongest Terms to go," Tanaghrisson replied that Saint-Pierre "would not discharge him until the morning." Washington promptly marched over to the commandant and complained that by detaining the Indians, Saint-Pierre, contrary to his promises, was detaining him, too. Saint-Pierre denied it and professed not to know why the Indians were staying, but Washington found out he had promised them guns and ammunition if they waited until the next morning. Tanaghrisson wanted to stay and receive the gifts, and Washington was forced to delay once again: he dared not depart and leave the Indians alone with the French. He agreed to wait another night, on the promise that nothing would hold up the Indians in the morning. Even then, Washington complained, the French "were not slack in their Inventions to keep the Indians this Day also." They gave the gifts they had promised but "then endeavoured to try the Power of Liquor, which I doubt not would have prevailed at any other Time than this."

Washington insisted so adamantly that Tanaghrisson keep his word "that he refrained, and set off with us as he had engaged."[33]

With the sealed letter to Dinwiddie in his pack, Washington and his companions paddled their canoes down the rock-filled and ice-choked creek back to Venango. They reached it on the twenty-second after a meandering and exhausting journey that Washington estimated at 130 miles.[34] After a night's rest, Washington was ready to be off again. He asked Tanaghrisson whether he intended to travel with them or continue by water. Tanaghrisson replied that White Thunder had hurt himself and was sick and in no shape to travel, so he would have to carry him down by canoe. Washington remained unsure of his Indian allies so long as the French were around: "As I found he intended to stay here a Day or two, and know that Monsieur Joncaire would employ every scheme to set him against the English as he had done before; I told him I hoped he would guard against his Flattery, and let no fine Speeches influence him in their Favour." Tanaghrisson told him not to be concerned, "for he knew the *French* too well, for any Thing to engage him on their Behalf." He offered to send the young hunter Guyasuta to accompany Washington.[35]

Leaving their Indian allies behind, the Virginians pushed on south. Washington abandoned his militia uniform and "put myself in an Indian walking Dress"—buckskins and moccasins—for the journey. For three days—including Christmas Day—they plodded through woods and deep snow, walking their emaciated horses. On the twenty-sixth, their mounts finally gave out, and Washington decided to carry on with Gist while the rest of the party found refuge from the storm for themselves and the horses. "I took my necessary Papers, pulled off my Cloaths; tied myself up in a Match Coat [usually made of coarse woolen cloth]; and with my Pack at my Back with my Papers and Provisions in it, and a Gun, set out with Mr. *Gist*, fitted in the same Manner."[36]

The next day, the twenty-seventh, they arrived at an Indian village ominously known as Murdering Town, presumably in memory of some dark deed. An Indian, whom Gist recognized from their talks with Joncaire at Venango, came over to speak with them. Addressing Gist by his Indian name, Annosanah, he offered to guide them to the Forks of the Ohio. Washington accepted; Gist was skeptical. His doubts increased as the Indian seemed to be leading them to the northeast, away from the Forks. Then the Indian suddenly turned, dropped to one knee, and fired his musket at them. Gist overpowered him before he could reload and was ready to kill him. Instead, at Washington's insistence, they kept him prisoner until about nine in the evening and then released him. They hurried on through the rest of the night to put as much distance as possible between themselves and their enemies, who they assumed would come after them as soon as it was light enough to follow their tracks. They kept traveling the next day until dark before they felt safe enough to sleep.[37]

The weather was so cold they had expected to find the Allegheny frozen. Instead, great chunks of ice flowed downriver. There was no way to cross it except by raft. With just "one poor Hatchet" between them, they spent an entire day building a makeshift raft. Just after sunset, they launched it, hoping to make their way down to Shannopin's Town. Halfway across the river they became trapped in ice. When Washington tried to push the ice away with his pole, the current caught it with such force that he was thrown into the river. Thrashing about in the frozen waters, he managed to grab the corner of the raft, and Gist pulled him aboard. Gist steered the raft to a small island, where, his own fingers and some of his toes frostbitten, he built a fire and got Washington out of his wet Indian clothes and back into his dry uniform, to stave off hypothermia. The site of the near-fatal accident, now named Washington's Crossing, is beneath Pittsburgh's Fortieth Street Bridge. The severe cold that almost killed Washington froze the river that night. The two men walked to shore in the morning.[38]

They made their way to Fraser's cabin. There they encountered a war party of twenty warriors who had been heading south, presumably to raid the Cherokees or Catawbas, but had turned back. At the head of the Great Kanawha River the Indians had come across seven bodies scattered around a cabin. They had been scalped, "all but one Woman with very light Hair," and some had been "much torn and eaten by Hogs." The war party hurried away "for Fear the Inhabitants should rise and take them as the Authors of the Murder." From the marks that were left, they said, the killers were "*French* Indians of the Ottoway Nation."[39] Events were overtaking Washington even as he hurried to get the French message to Dinwiddie.

While he waited at Fraser's for horses, Washington took the opportunity on New Year's Eve to travel three miles to the mouth of the Youghiogheny River to visit Queen Aliquippa, a Seneca clan mother of considerable influence in the region, "who had expressed great Concern that we passed her in going to the Fort." Conrad Weiser described her in 1748 as an old woman who wielded "great authority"; Céloron de Blainville said in 1749 that she regarded herself "as a queen" and was devoted to the English. Her son, Canachquasy or Kanuksusy, had been the spokesman for the ten warriors who traveled from the Ohio to Philadelphia in 1747, asserting their independence from Onondaga's neutral stance and requesting arms to fight the French. On their way to the Treaty of Logstown in 1752, the Virginia commissioners exchanged a gun salute when they reached Aliquippa's town, then "went on Shore to wait on the Queen, who welcomed them & presented them with a String of Wampum to clear their Way to Loggs Town." She gave the commissioners a meal and food for their journey; they gave her a brass kettle, tobacco, and other small gifts.⁴⁰ Thinking of diplomacy as business conducted exclusively by men, Washington had committed a faux pas by not paying his respects to her on the outward journey. Letting him know it, she gave him the opportunity to make amends. Washington gave her a match coat and a bottle of rum, the latter of which, he wrote dismissively, "was thought the best Present of the two." He underestimated whom he was dealing with. Aliquippa wanted more than a courtesy call and a bottle of rum. She wanted information, she wanted to impress on him the need to erect a Virginian post in the area, and she knew what was at stake.⁴¹

DINWIDDIE DID NOT WAIT for Washington's return with the French response before pressing his claim to the Ohio country. As Washington made his way to Wills Creek, he encountered a pack train of seventeen horses loaded with supplies and materials for building a fort at the Forks of Ohio and, the following day, some families going out to settle.⁴² Occupying the Forks region would protect British interests against the French and bolster Ohio Company claims against Pennsylvania and rival land speculators in Virginia.⁴³

Washington reached Wills Creek "after as fatiguing a Journey as it is possible to conceive, rendered so by excessive bad weather." He was back at Belvoir, the home of George William Fairfax and, of more interest, his wife, Sally, by January 11. After a day's rest, he set out for Williamsburg and delivered Saint-Pierre's letter to Dinwiddie. It would have been better, Saint-Pierre wrote, if Washington had been ordered to proceed to Canada to see the governor, the marquis Duquesne, who was the more appropriate person "to set forth the Evidence and Reality of the Rights of the King, my Master, upon the Lands situated along the River *Ohio*, and to contest the Pretensions of the King of *Great-Britain* thereto." He would forward Dinwiddie's letter to Duquesne, and "his Answer will be a Law to me." As for Dinwiddie's summons to retreat, Saint-Pierre did not think himself obliged to obey it; he had his orders to be there, and Dinwiddie should not doubt for a moment that he was determined to carry them out. "I made it my particular Care," ended Saint-Pierre, "to receive Mr. Washington, with a Distinction suitable to your Dignity, and his Quality and great Merit." Dinwiddie communicated the letter to the Virginia Council.[44]

Dinwiddie was surely not surprised by Saint-Pierre's response. He had dispatched Washington to satisfy diplomatic protocol and gather information rather than with any realistic expectation that the French would tamely abandon the Ohio country. Dinwiddie immediately ordered Washington to write up the notes in his diary as a report he could present as evidence of the growing French and Indian threat. Washington completed the task overnight, and the governor had the report printed, together with Washington's map of the Ohio country (see figure 2). He used it to impress upon the House of Burgesses the need for urgent action and to leverage money.[45] The Assembly had hitherto proved reluctant to finance the schemes of a governor so clearly tied to the Ohio Company; "it was yet thought a Fiction; and Scheme to promote the Interest of a private Company," noted Washington.[46] Now it duly expressed its outrage at the encroachments of the French and their Indian allies and awarded Washington £50 as testimony of its approval of his service.[47]

As confirmation of the French threat, Dinwiddie forwarded Washington's instructions, his journal, and the letters exchanged to the Lords of Trade.[48] He also ordered Captain William Trent to raise up to one hundred men and build a fort at the confluence of the three rivers. With assistance from "our good and faithful friends and Allies the Indians of the six Nations and such others as are in Amity with them," the garrison would defend the king's lands in the Ohio Valley against the illegal invasion by "persons pretending to be the Subjects of his most Christian Majesty the King of France."[49]

Dinwiddie ordered Washington to raise one hundred militia from Augusta and Frederick Counties, but no one showed up to respond to his summons. In February the House of Burgesses voted £10,000 for frontier defense, and in place of the ineffective militia system Dinwiddie raised a new Virginia Regiment of three hundred volunteers in six companies of fifty each. The provincial troops, as the men of the Virginia Regiment were called, stood somewhere between British regulars and colonial militia in terms of employment, organization, and service.[50] Colonel Joshua Fry was to command the regiment and lead an expedition to secure the Forks of the Ohio. Fry had drafted a map of Virginia's western territories with Peter Jefferson,

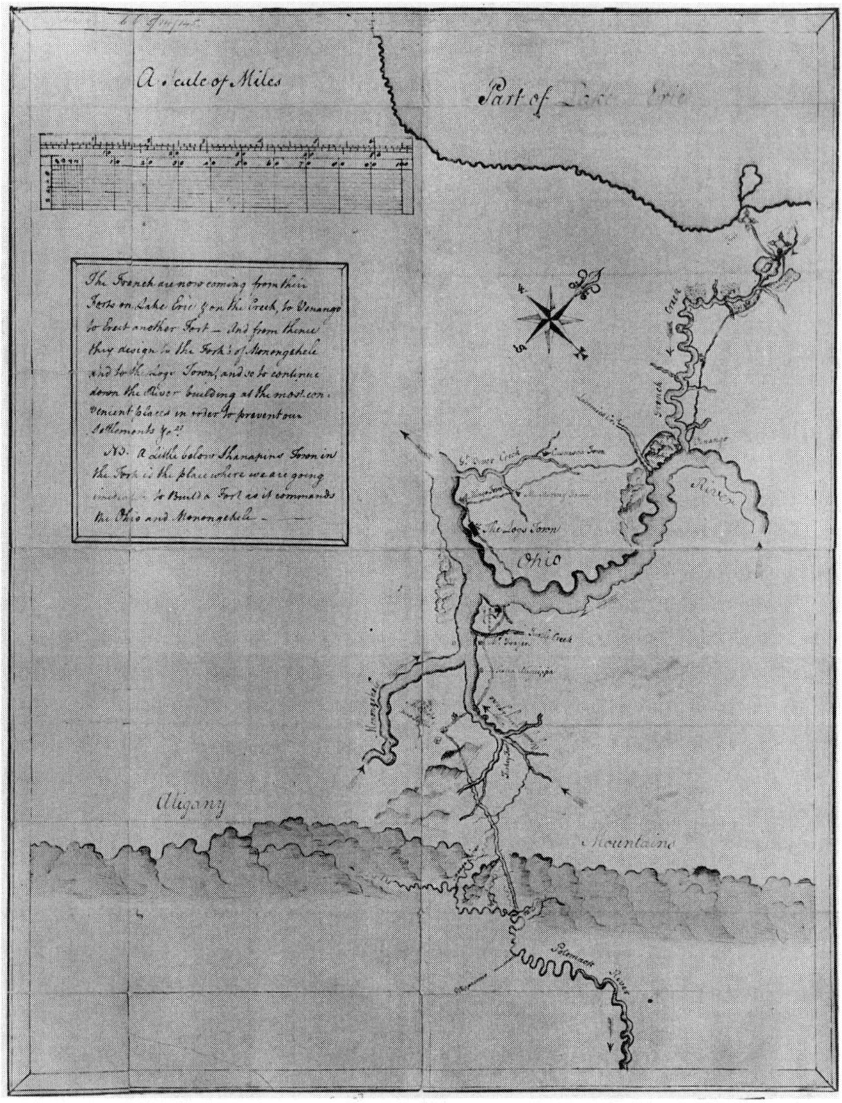

Figure 2 Washington drew this map after his journey to the Ohio in 1753. In addition to charting the geography, he provided notes regarding French plans to occupy the strategically crucial Forks of the Ohio, where the Allegheny and Monongahela Rivers meet. The map, published first in Williamsburg and then in London, helped galvanize the British into action.

Lawrence Martin, *The George Washington Atlas* (Washington, DC: United States George Washington Bicentennial Commission, 1932), plate 11. Library of Congress.

attended the Treaty of Logstown, and commanded militia, but he had never seen combat. Washington, not yet twenty-two but suddenly famous, requested and was appointed second-in-command, at the rank of lieutenant colonel. As added incentive for raising troops who received meager pay, Dinwiddie promised that after the war a grant of 200,000 acres on the Ohio River would be divided, according to rank, among the veterans. The expedition seemed tailor-made for a young man intent on making his reputation in the military and his fortune in Indian land.[51]

Many Virginians, however, saw no need to fight a war to further the schemes of the Ohio Company in distant lands, and Washington had a hard time filling his ranks. Militiamen with homes and livelihoods to protect preferred to stay home, leaving the defense of Virginia's frontier to the "lesser sort," men from the lower ranks of society, who signed up in expectation of being paid for their service.[52] Washington complained about his own pay and about the "loose, Idle," and "ungovernable" men who volunteered. Writing to Dinwiddie from the comfort of Belvoir in early March 1754, to request smart red uniforms for his troops, he supported his request with a description of Indian temperament. "It is the Nature of Indians to be struck with, and taken by show and this will give them a much higher Conception of our Power and greatness and I verily believe fix in our Interest many that are now wavering and undetermin'd whose Cause to Espouse." Even a red coat of the coarsest cloth would answer the purpose, because red was the color of blood and viewed "as the distinguishing marks of Warriours and great Men." By contrast, "the shabby and ragged appearance the French common Soldiers make affords great matter for ridicule amongst the Indians and I really believe is the chief motive why they hate and despise them as they do. If these are the Effects, the Cause may be easily, and timely remedied." Washington hoped the governor would forgive his taking the liberty to impart the information; he did so with good intentions. "It is," he added, "my acquaintance with these Indians, and a Study of their Tempers that has in some measure let me into their Customs and dispositions." Dinwiddie replied that he had no objections to Washington's troops being in uniform dress but suggested that the young officer had more pressing matters to attend to than waiting for uniforms to be made.[53] Washington evidently thought himself something of an expert in Indian affairs already. The next year would reveal how much he had to learn.

CHAPTER 4

Tanaghrisson's War

ANAGHRISSON AND SCAROUADY HAD asked Virginia to build a strong house at the Forks of the Ohio, and Pennsylvania another elsewhere on the river, or at least they had agreed to permit it.[1] Now, early in 1754, with a delegation of Ohio Indians, they were at the Forks to meet the Virginians. Tanaghrisson was given the honor of laying the first log. As he did so he announced that the fort "belonged to the English and them and whoever offered to prevent the building of it they the Indians would make war against them." But the Seneca half king was embracing an English alliance and defying the French with a level of commitment many other Ohio Indians did not share. Some were suspicious of British intentions in building an outpost in the heart of their country; others were concerned that the action might precipitate a war with the French that would be fought in their country. The local Delawares refused to provide the construction crew with meat.[2] George Croghan, who knew the Ohio country as well as any European, explained the situation to the governor of Pennsylvania: "The whole of ye Ohio Indians Dose Nott No what to think, they Imagine by this Government Doing Nothing towards the Expedition that the Verginians and the French Intend to Divide the Land of Ohio between them." It was clear the Six Nations were not about to risk attacking the French, which left them, and Tanaghrisson, with little leverage over the Shawnees and Delawares. The Ohio Indians, Croghan assured the governor, "will act for themselves att this time without Consulting ye Onondago Councel."[3]

Tanaghrisson's bluff was quickly called. The French had targeted the Forks of the Ohio as the site for the last fort in their chain,
and despite delays it was scheduled for construction in 1754.[4] William
Trent and his second-in-command, Edward Ward, began building
their fort on February 17. No sooner was it completed than on April
17 Captain Claude-Pierre Pécaudy de Contrecoeur, who had replaced
Saint-Pierre as commandant of the Ohio country, arrived with five
hundred French troops and eighteen cannon. He demanded that
Ward surrender the fort and return to Virginia. Trent was away gathering provisions, and Ward had little choice. As the Virginians
departed, Tanaghrisson shouted in defiance and frustration to the
French that it was he who had ordered the fort to be built and laid
the first log. The expulsion was a blow to Tanaghrisson's standing in
Indian country as well as to Virginia's ambitions on the Ohio. The
French dismantled Virginia's little outpost and built their own. Fort
Duquesne was a formidable structure, with four bastions, two rave-
lins or outworks, a dry moat, log and earth walls, officers' quarters,
powder magazines and storehouses, a blacksmith shop, a bakery, and
a hospital. It became France's center of operations and Indian relations in the region.[5]

As Ward and his crew slogged back to Wills Creek, they met
George Washington and 186 men on their way to garrison the fort
they had just surrendered. Dinwiddie had sent Washington ahead as
an advance force; Colonel Joshua Fry was to follow with the rest of
the Virginia Regiment, and additional troops from Virginia, North
and South Carolina, Maryland, and New York were to reinforce them
and expel the French from Virginia's Ohio country. Three Scots who
would feature prominently in Washington's life accompanied him:
Captains Peter Hoag and Adam Stephen and the expedition surgeon, James Craik.[6]

Rather than continue to the Forks with so small a force,
Washington marched to Redstone Creek, about thirty-seven miles
from the fort, to await Fry and the main body of the regiment.
Tanaghrisson sent two young runners to ascertain that the Virginians
were on the march, along with a speech, accompanied by a wampum
string, which Washington noted in his journal was "addressed... to
me personally." The Indians had been expecting a French attack,
and now it was coming, Tanaghrisson said. "We are now ready to
attack them, and are waiting only for your aid. Take courage and
come as soon as possible, and you will find us as ready to fight them
as you are yourselves.... If you do not come to our aid soon, it is all
over with us, and I think that we shall never be able to meet together

again. I say this with the greatest sorrow in my heart."[7] Washington was quick to reassure Tanaghrisson that he was on his way with "a small part of our army, ... clearing the roads for a large number of our warriors, who are ready to follow us, with our large artillery, our munitions, and our supplies." He used his Indian name, Conotocarious.[8] The Seneca half king and the Virginian colonel both spoke with a bombast and confidence of power behind them that the realities of their respective situations scarcely merited. A week later Washington wrote Dinwiddie, requesting the artillery of which he had boasted. He also suggested enlisting the assistance of the Cherokees, Catawbas, and Chickasaws, since he had heard that six hundred Ojibwas and Ottawas were heading down the Scioto River to join the French. If the southern Indians did come, peace would first have to be mediated between them and the Six Nations because, as Washington was told, there was "no good harmony subsisting betwixt them."[9] Dinwiddie was already working on it.[10]

Back in Williamsburg, Ward appeared in the Council Chamber on May 4, accompanied by an Indian and an interpreter. He produced the French summons to surrender, along with a speech from Tanaghrisson to Dinwiddie "desiring to know where we were, what was our Strength, and the Time they might Expect our Forces to join them." With the council's approval, Dinwiddie sent word assuring Tanaghrisson that help was on the way.[11]

Washington kept in communication with Tanaghrisson as he advanced toward the Monongahela River. Traders brought Washington daily news: one reported that Tanaghrisson had sent fifty warriors to meet Washington.[12] Washington sent Tanaghrisson updates on his progress; Tanaghrisson sent news about the French. On May 19 Washington sent Tanaghrisson a note urging his Indian brothers to have courage and "march quickly toward your brother the English; for new forces are joining him which will protect you against your *perfidious enemy* the French."[13] Five days later a messenger arrived from Tanaghrisson with word that a French army was on the move against Washington "resolved to strike the first English they meet."[14]

Washington was also communicating developments to Dinwiddie and Fry, asking Dinwiddie for ample supplies of wampum and treaty goods to compete with the French and urging Fry to request treaty goods "in the strongest possible terms." "Nothing can be done without them," he said. "All the Indians that come expect presents." Indians were a mercenary bunch, Washington declared in what would become a recurrent refrain; if you wanted them to scout, hunt, or carry out any other service, you had to pay for it, "and that, I believe, every person, who is acquainted with the nature of Indians, knows."[15] Washington evidently saw no irony in his own complaints that he was not paid enough, complaints that Dinwiddie advised him were ill timed.[16]

At Fort Duquesne, Contrecoeur was getting his own Indian reports of the advancing Virginian force. On May 23 he dispatched Ensign Joseph Coulon de Villiers, sieur de Jumonville, and thirty-five soldiers to see what the Virginians were up to and to demand they withdraw from King Louis's territory, much as Dinwiddie had dispatched Washington to demand the French do in the fall. On May 24 Washington reached a place known as Great Meadows and halted to establish a base camp before pushing on against Fort Duquesne. He then dispatched runners asking Scarouady and Tanaghrisson to meet him.[17] On the twenty-seventh Christopher Gist arrived in camp, reporting that the French had been making inquiries about Tanaghrisson. Washington shared the information with the young Indians in the camp and distorted it. "*I wanted them to understand*," he emphasized in his journal, "*that* the French intended to kill the Half King." It had the desired effect: the Indians "offered to accompany our People and go after the *French*," and said that if Tanaghrisson had been killed or even insulted they would send word to the Mingoes "to incite their Warriors to fall upon them." Edward Lengel, former editor in chief of the *George Washington Papers*, says quite simply that it was a lie and "Washington *wanted* a fight."[18]

That evening, a Seneca runner named Silver Heels, also known as Aroas, arrived from Tanaghrisson with a message. Washington would encounter the runner many times in his life. Translated and badly written by his interpreter John Davison, the message warned that a party of fifty French soldiers was in the area and Washington should come quickly. Washington selected forty men and, following Silver Heels, hurried off in "a heavy rain, with the night as black as pitch and by a path scarcely wide enough for a man." They reached Tanaghrisson's camp just about dawn and immediately conferred on what to do next. "We decided to strike jointly," wrote Washington, and set off "in Indian fashion, one after the other." Each was likely disappointed by the other's force. Instead of a contingent of Ohio tribes ready to fight with Washington's soldiers, Tanaghrisson had fewer than a dozen warriors. Tanaghrisson knew Washington was young and untested. James Smith, who spent several years as an Indian captive, said Indians would think it "a most ridiculous thing to see a man lead off a company of warriors, as an officer, who had never been in a battle in his life: even in case of merit, they are slow

in advancing any one, until they arrive at or near middle-age."[19]
Tanaghrisson clearly "outranked" Washington. He knew the location
of the French and said it would be easy to surround and surprise
them. The French had made clear their determination to defend the
Ohio country against British invasions or assault, and there were
other reports of French activity in the area, but the only information
Washington had that the French soldiers were actually coming to
attack him came from Tanaghrisson.[20]

Pushing on through the woods and through the night,
Washington and Tanaghrisson found the French camp at dawn in a
ravine at the base of a rocky cliff. It was Jumonville's detachment.
What happened next has always been a matter of dispute. Washington,
who often wrote detailed and meticulous entries in his diaries, kept
this journal entry and his report to Dinwiddie deliberately brief.
When the French discovered them he ordered his men to open fire.
"We killed M. de Jumonville, commanding this party, with nine
others; we wounded one and made 21 prisoners," he wrote. "The
Indians scalped the dead, and took most of their arms." The entire
skirmish was over in fifteen minutes.[21] Thirty-three years later, preparing remarks for his would-be biographer David Humphreys, his
usual memory for detail failed him and he glossed over the event in
a single sentence.[22]

An Ohio Iroquois who participated in the ambush said Tanaghrisson and Scarouady and their warriors circled left and right to
cut off escape and "directed Col Washington with his men to go up
to the Hill," and Washington himself fired the first shot.[23] It seems that
the French soldiers, surprised by the Virginians firing down on them,
broke and ran. Tanaghrisson's warriors cut off their escape. A French
survivor said the Indians did not fire and the English did all the killing,
but Davison, who was at the fight, said that although there were only
eight Indians they did most of the execution. When the English fired,
"which they did in great Confusion, the Indians came out of their
Cover and closed with the French and killed them with their
Tomahawks, on which the French surrendered." The Ohio Iroquois
informant said eight of the French soldiers "met with their Destiny
by the Indian Tomayhawks." Scarouady also said that the Indians did
most of the fighting and most of the damage. They killed ten
Frenchmen and delivered twenty-one prisoners to Washington, "telling him we had blooded the Edge of his Hatchet a little." The
Pennsylvania Gazette also reported that the French "took to their Heels,"
but Half King and his warriors lay in ambush and fell on them. Given
the confusion of combat and the inaccuracy of eighteenth-century

firearms, it is unlikely that the Virginians killed ten French soldiers while wounding only one; the casualty ratio is more indicative of Indian tomahawks wielded at close range than muskets fired downhill.[24]

The French prisoners insisted they had been sent by Contrecoeur to present Washington with a summons to withdraw or bear the blame for any hostilities that followed. Jumonville had held up papers, calling for a ceasefire, and the only French soldier to escape back to Fort Duquesne said the ensign was killed as he tried to read aloud the summons to the Virginians.[25] Washington devoted much more space to refuting the French claim that this was an embassy than he did to recounting the fight. They were spies, he said, and it was not true that they called out to their attackers when the fighting began. What was more, "the Half King's opinion in this case is that they had evil designs, and that it was a mere pretext; that they had never intended to come to us as anything but enemies, and that if we had ever been so foolish as to let them go, he would never help us to capture other Frenchmen." Before the day was over, Washington sent Dinwiddie a second letter, repeating that the French were spies and denying that they had called out not to fire. He urged Dinwiddie to disregard anything the French prisoners might say to the contrary (which Dinwiddie did).[26] Dinwiddie congratulated Washington on his success, which would show the Indians that the French were not invincible "when fairly engaged with the English."[27] Washington and Tanaghrisson both protested too much.

Most accounts indicate that Tanaghrisson killed Jumonville in cold blood. John Shaw, a twenty-year-old Irish soldier in the Virginia Regiment who did not take part in the fight himself but spoke with others who did, testified later that when the French found their escape route cut off by the Indians, they ran back to the Virginians asking for quarter. "Some Time after the Indians came up the Half King took his Tomahawk and split the head of the French Captain haveing first asked if he was an Englishman and haveing been told that he was a French Man. He then took out his Brains and washed his Hands with them and then Scalped him."[28] Another account, this one given to Contrecoeur by a deserter from the English camp who may have been an Iroquois, reported that Tanaghrisson came up to the wounded Jumonville and said, "Thou art not yet dead, my father," and then tomahawked him. For Tanaghrisson to address the young officer as "father" might seem strange, but if true, Fred Anderson observes, "the last words Jumonville heard on earth were spoken in the language of ritual and diplomacy, which cast the French father (Onontio) as the mediator, gift-giver, and alliance-maker among

Indian peoples. Tanaghrisson's metaphorical words, followed by his literal killing of the father, explicitly denied French authority and testified to the premeditation of his act."[29]

Tanaghrisson's action, therefore, was more than a grisly atrocity in the heat of combat; the Half King publicly and dramatically severed the peace that had existed between the Ohio tribes and their French father and washed his hands of the French alliance as he washed his hands in Jumonville's brains. Tanaghrisson said he must send the French scalps to the other Ohio nations, inviting them to take up the hatchet, and he promptly dispatched a runner to carry a hatchet and a black wampum belt to Shingas and the Delawares. He also reaffirmed the Ohio Indians' determination to act independently of the Onondaga Council. Claiming to speak for the Ohio nations, Tanaghrisson had warned the French to stop their advance into the Ohio country. When the French ignored his warnings, and the Ohio Indians' resolve began to waver in the face of the invasion, Tanaghrisson tried to save face and regain the initiative by pushing both the Indians and the British into more decisive action. When Jumonville began to read his document, Tanaghrisson, who understood French, which Washington did not, literally cut him off. "It was Tanaghrisson who goaded young Washington into the fateful encounter at what became known as the Battle of Jumonville Glen," wrote the late historian David Dixon, "and, it was Tanaghrisson who ended any chance of reconciliation between the two European adversaries by killing the hapless Ensign Jumonville." Because Washington was nominally in command in the opening clash of what became the global conflict known as the Seven Years' War, he is often credited with starting it. "In reality," concluded Dixon, "it was an aged Seneca sachem who began the first of the World Wars."[30]

News of the skirmish reverberated around the colonies and across the Atlantic. When the news reached Albany, where Benjamin Franklin and other colonists were negotiating with the Iroquois, the Mohawk chief Hendrick said "if it be a Fact that the Half-King be engaged in blood, 'tis of more consequence to ye English than twenty such Treaties."[31] The governors of Virginia and of New France both blamed Tanaghrisson. "This little skirmish was by the Half King and their Indians," Dinwiddie emphasized in his report to the Board of Trade. "We were as auxiliaries to them, as my orders to the Commander of our Forces was to be on the defensive."[32] Dinwiddie was on the defensive himself, but his characterization of the action as one in which the Indians called the shots may not be far off the mark. Governor Duquesne ordered Contrecoeur to find a way to have Tanaghrisson killed by Indians so that the French would not be implicated in the assassination.[33] The Versailles government, finding it difficult to believe that the English king who had so often expressed his desire for peace could have authorized the actions, demanded an explanation from the British court. In the meantime, Duquesne was ordered to assume a defensive posture and repel force if necessary. King Louis wished to avoid bloodshed and would approve Indian attacks on the English only if they were essential for the safety of the colony.[34]

In an often-quoted letter to his younger brother Jack after the fight, Washington said he had heard the bullets whistling by—a favorite chapter title for Washington biographers—and found "something charming in the sound." (When George II, the last British monarch to lead an army into battle and a veteran of European bloodbaths, read of it in the *London Magazine,* he suggested the young man might not find the sound so charming had he heard it more often).[35] But Washington's bravado after the event surely masked his emotions and reactions just as his accounts tried to conceal what really happened. And that was that Tanaghrisson had maneuvered the inexperienced Washington into attacking an enemy that was not looking for a fight—that was not, officially at least, even an enemy. The young colonel then stood by helplessly as his first action spiraled out of his control, surely unnerved by Tanaghrisson's bloody deed and no doubt stunned by the likely repercussions of what had happened.[36] Tanaghrisson's gamble was Washington's debacle.

The gamble did not pay off. Anticipating a French counterattack, Washington had his men build a fort "with a little palisade" in Great Meadows, about five miles southeast of Jumonville Glen; Washington called this circular stockade surrounded by entrenchments Fort Necessity. He had no experience building fortifications, and it showed. In a depression, overlooked by hills, and with forest cover within firing range, the fort was so poorly situated and constructed that "only an amateur or a fool would have thought it defensible." Washington said it would withstand an attack by five hundred men.[37] He also thought that he could still march on Fort Duquesne but turned back as reality began to sink in.

On the evening of June 1, Tanaghrisson, Queen Aliquippa, and twenty-five or thirty families arrived—between eighty and a hundred people, but few of them warriors. Tanaghrisson had sent Scarouady to Logstown with a belt of wampum and four French scalps to be forwarded to the Six Nations and other tribes, telling what had happened and asking for their assistance "to uphold this first blow." Tanaghrisson said he had more to say in council that would wait until the Shawnees arrived in the morning, but the next day only two or three families of Shawnees and Delawares drifted in.[38] Washington held a ceremony in which he presented Tanaghrisson with a silver gorget of George II and bestowed on him the name Dinwiddie, which he said meant "the Head of Everything." Aliquippa asked that her son, Kanuksusy, "might be taken into Council, as She was declining and unfit for Business and have an English Name given him." On Tanaghrisson's advice, Washington called the Indians together, presented Kanuksusy with a medal to wear "in remembrance of his g[rea]t Father the King of England," and gave him the name Fairfax, saying it meant "First of the Council." Bestowing honorary names was common practice in Indian country. Scarouady's only son was also baptized Dinwiddie, and other Indians had the name as well. Washington gave his own name to Scarouady.[39]

It would take more than high-sounding names to maintain the Indians' allegiance. Washington knew he was out of his depth and asked for help. Andrew "Montour would be of singular use to me here at this present, in conversing with the Indians," he wrote to Dinwiddie in early June, "for I have no Person's that I can put dependence in: I make use of all the influence I can to engage them warmly on our side, and flatter myself that I am not unsuccessful, but for want of a better acquaintance with their Customs I am often at a loss how to behave and should be reliev'd from many anxious fear's of offending them if Montour was here to assist me." In fact, Dinwiddie had already dispatched Montour with a wampum belt for Tanaghrisson and a supply of "4000 Black & 4000 white Wampum" for Washington to use when he had to make speeches. He also sent Croghan to serve as interpreter, and more medals for Washington to hand out to the chiefs. Washington, who had lectured Dinwiddie on Indians just three months before, now assured him he would turn to Croghan and Montour for guidance "in all Indian affairs agreeable to your Honour's directions."[40]

On May 31 Colonel Joshua Fry died after falling from his horse. Washington took command of the Virginia Regiment.[41] Reinforcements arrived in mid-June: almost two hundred troops from Virginia (including Captain Andrew Lewis and Lieutenant George Mercer) and a South Carolina independent company of one hundred British regulars under Captain James Mackay, who, as an officer commissioned by the king, refused to place himself under the command of a colonial officer appointed by a governor. Even with his force increased to almost four hundred men, Washington realized that without Indian allies he was in trouble.

The Ohio Indians were skeptical about throwing in with the British and suspicious of their intentions. Washington invited them to meet him at Gist's settlement, a dozen miles away on Chestnut Ridge near present-day Braddock, Pennsylvania. About forty Delaware, Shawnee, and Iroquois delegates arrived and expressed their reservations in a council with him on June 18. They had been told the Virginians intended to destroy any Indians who did not join them, "wherefore we who keep in our Towns, expect every Day to be cut in pieces by you." The English had no intention of hurting them, Washington replied; the rumor must have been invented by the French to deceive them. The Frenchman made beautiful speeches and promised great things, "but all this is from the lips only, while in his heart there is only corruption and poison." The English were the Indians' true friends, Washington said, and then he lied: his army was there "to maintain your rights, to restore you to possession of your lands and to guard your women and children." The Indians should sharpen their hatchets and unite with their English brothers who had "taken up the sword in your defense and in your cause." He would provide sanctuary, food, and clothing to their women and children while the warriors were away fighting the French.[42] Washington's meager and ill-supplied force hardly added weight to his arguments and promises to Indians who showed no inclination to join the impending fight, and the council broke up. Shingas agreed to keep scouts along the river to warn of any French activities and gave assurances of assistance, but he refused to bring his people to Washington's camp for fear, he said, of offending Onondaga. He advised Washington to send a war belt to invite warriors "to act independently of their King and council"—in other words, circumvent the Half King and Onondaga and deal directly with Shawnees and Delawares—and "promised to take privately the most subtil Methods to make the Affair succeed, though he did not dare do it openly." Then Shingas and the rest of the Indians left. They had little reason to throw themselves into a war between colonial powers that would be fought in their own country and little reason to think the British would win it. Tanaghrisson, whose actions and miscalculations had led to the situation, recognized it was hopeless, and left. He may also have been affronted by Washington's dealings with Shingas.[43] Whatever the reasons, Washington was left without Indian allies to face the impending French retaliation.

Receiving word that a French army was on the march, Washington's little army retreated to their hastily built stockade and prepared for the assault. Captain Louis Coulon de Villiers, brother of the murdered Ensign Jumonville, who had recently arrived at Fort Duquesne with a reinforcement of twenty soldiers and 130 Indians, begged Contrecoeur to let him command the expedition to avenge his brother's death. Contrecoeur sent him off with orders to find and destroy the English army "in order to punish them for the murder that they inflicted on us in violating the most sacred rights of Civilized Nations." Villiers's force consisted of six hundred French and Canadian soldiers and about one hundred Indians—Abenakis, Algonquins, Hurons, Nipissings, and Ottawas, and Iroquois from villages on the St. Lawrence, some of whom were ambivalent about fighting in the Ohio country, where they had friends and relatives.⁴⁴ A handful of Ohio Indians tagged along but showed no more inclination to fight for the French than for the British. They provided indifferent service as scouts, and may even have provided misinformation in a vain attempt to divert the French from attacking Washington.⁴⁵

Villiers reached Great Meadows on July 3 and began his assault. The fort afforded little protection against the French gunfire from the woods, and torrential rain flooded the defenders' ditches and soaked their powder. By night, Washington's command had suffered thirty killed and more than twice as many wounded. "Our men behaved with singular Intrepidity, and we determined not to ask for Quarter but with our Bayonets screw'd, to sell our Lives as dearly as possibly we could," Washington claimed later, but it is doubtful that many of them shared his expressed resolve. Discipline started to unravel, and some of the men broke into the storehouses and began getting drunk on rum. It was only a matter of time before the French and their Indian allies closed in for the kill.⁴⁶

Then, with his brother's killers within his grasp, Villiers offered to parley and proposed terms of surrender. He said his men were tired and wet, and the Indians were fed up and leaving the next day. But Washington's men were more tired and wet, and Villiers could have crushed the Virginians with or without Indian help. Villiers wanted to wrap up the siege in a hurry because he believed Washington was about to be reinforced; "it was repeated continuously that drum beats or cannon fire were heard in the distance," he wrote. Since the Ohio Indians who had attached themselves to his command were likely to be the ones ranging through the forests, they were the likely source of the misinformation. They had abandoned Washington's little army, but in David Dixon's view, they recognized it was the only countervailing force to French power in their country and did not want the French to destroy it.⁴⁷ If this interpretation of their actions and motivations is correct—and it is plausible—then an

Ohio Indian got Washington into the mess at Great Meadows, and
Ohio Indians got him out of it.

Villiers sent Washington word that since France and England
were not at war he was willing to spare the defenders from "the cruelty from the Indians to which they were Exposed." The French had
come only to avenge Jumonville's murder and to remove the Virginians
from the French king's land. They would allow them to go home in
peace with full military honors. Around eight o'clock in the evening,
Villiers, Washington, and Mackay signed the rain-soaked document
laying out the terms of surrender. Both the preamble and the final
article referred to Jumonville's death as "assassination" or "murder."[48]
Washington's admission gave the French an enormous propaganda
asset.[49] The articles of capitulation were published in the colonial
newspapers.[50] One English writer denounced the surrender document as "the most infamous a British subject ever put his hand to."[51]
Washington claimed he did not know what he signed because Van
Braam did not translate it accurately.[52]

Washington's journal of the expedition, left behind in the hurried evacuation, fell into French hands. It was translated in Montreal
and parts of it published in Paris in 1756; a retranslation was published in London and New York a year later. (The original has been
lost, although another, more reliable version turned up in Contrecoeur's papers.) Washington said the publication contained heavy
editorializing, significant omissions, "and many things added that
never were thought of." Governor Duquesne said Washington's journal revealed him to be "the most impertinent of men, but that he is
as clever as he is crafty with credulous Indians. Besides, he lies a great
deal in order to justify the assassination of Sieur de Jumonville, which
has recoiled upon him, and which he was stupid enough to admit in
his capitulation."[53] William Johnson, the British superintendent of
Indian affairs for the North, wished Washington "had acted with prudence and circumspection requisite in an officer of rank"; he suspected he had been too hungry for glory.[54] Lieutenant Governor
James DeLancey of New York reported the news of Washington's
defeat to the Lords of Trade; the particulars were not exact, he said, but
there was no doubt about "the truth of the disaster."[55] Washington's
bungling fueled British attitudes about the incompetence of colonial militia and convinced the government in London that it needed
to dispatch regular troops under centralized command to oust the
French from the Forks.[56]

Three years later, when Fort William Henry surrendered to the
French, the marquis de Montcalm's Indian allies fell on the departing

garrison and perpetrated the massacre made infamous by James Fenimore Cooper's *The Last of the Mohicans.* With the exception of some routine plundering, no such atrocities occurred at Fort Necessity. As Washington and what was left of his army filed out of what was left of the fort on the morning of July 4, they saw "many of our Friend Indians" with the French, some of whom they recognized by name. Several came and spoke to the soldiers, "told them they were their Brothers, and asked them how they did." Yet, said Washington, "we had not one Indian to assist when the Action commenced or ended."[57] He saw their presence as open-faced betrayal, but he had consistently misread the motives and actions of the Ohio Indians who wanted to maintain a balance of power in the region and hesitated to take part in Tanaghrisson's war, on either side. Dinwiddie was perhaps closer to the mark, although he echoed the view of Indian unreliability: "Mr. Washington had many of the Indians with him, but I observe these People remain inactive till they see how Affairs go, and, generally speaking, side with the Conquerors," he wrote; "in my private Opinion, little dependence is to be put to them."[58] In accordance with the French terms for surrender, Washington provided two hostages, Van Braam and Captain Robert Stobo, who were taken to Fort Duquesne. Stobo managed to smuggle out information and a plan of the fort via two Delaware visitors; they passed it on to George Croghan, who took it to Philadelphia. The Delawares were Shingas and Delaware George. "Neither had lifted a finger to help Washington," the historian Francis Jennings noted, but the English "were wrong about them being pro-French. They were pro-Delaware."[59]

With Fort Necessity burning behind them, Washington and his demoralized troops withdrew to Fort Cumberland at Wills Creek. En route, the Virginia Regiment began to disintegrate: men deserted, and Washington was helpless to stop them. In Edward Lengel's assessment, "his command had completely fallen apart. His humiliation was complete."[60] From Wills Creek, Washington traveled by canoe about 170 miles down the Potomac River to Great Falls (about 14 miles above present-day Georgetown). He was exploring the possibility of using the Potomac as a supply route to the Ohio country. For the next forty-five years, he would promote developing the Potomac into a navigable waterway that would boost western expansion and link western settlement to eastern markets.[61]

Once safely back in Virginia, Washington explained his failure to attract more Indian allies (never more than thirty, he said) by blaming Montour and Croghan for boasting that they had far more influence over the Indians than was actually the case and by complaining that he had not been adequately supplied. The only reason the Indians supported the French was that the French had more goods to give them; Washington had so few goods and provisions that the Indians asked, "when they were to join us, if we meant to starve them to death as well as ourselves."[62] Washington's understanding of Indian motivations and the significance attached to gifts, like his understanding of Indian character, remained one-dimensional. Indians who had been ambivalent before now had few doubts about where their best interests lay.

After Washington's defeat, Tanaghrisson abandoned Logstown. He and Scarouady went east with their followers to Aughwick, on the Juanita River near present-day Shirleysburg, where Croghan ran a trading post, and where they were supported by funds from the government of Pennsylvania. Shawnees and Delawares who arrived in August asked if the English were making any preparations to fight the French, which they thought would not be difficult to do in the fall but would be very difficult to do if deferred to the spring. Tanaghrisson sent runners to bring Shingas and the Delawares and Shawnees for a council. The Delawares and Shawnees were unimpressed by Britain's response to the French invasion and feared that if the English did nothing in the autumn, the Ohio country would fall to the French.[63] Deputy Governor Hamilton of Pennsylvania dispatched the interpreter Conrad Weiser to work with Croghan at the upcoming conference. Since the Pennsylvania Assembly continued to insist on frugality and Hamilton was waiting to be replaced in office by Robert Hunter Morris, Croghan and Weiser were instructed to spend no more than was necessary and to have the Indians sit tight for the moment—at the same time, they were to assure them the English had every intention of striking back at the French. It was a difficult task to provision more than two hundred Indians and stay within Hamilton's budget; it was a tougher job to convince the Indians that the parsimonious and dilatory English had the power and determination to oppose and repel the French. Weiser confided to Tanaghrisson and Scarouady before the council that it would be "better not to mention any thing about the Virginians striking the French this Fall."[64]

Things had not worked out as Tanaghrisson had planned. He had encouraged Washington to fight the French and had encouraged the Shawnees and Delawares to assist him. The capitulation at Fort Necessity was a blow to Tanaghrisson's standing and to Iroquois authority over the Ohio Indians.[65] Like Washington, Tanaghrisson was quick to place the blame elsewhere. On his way to the council with Weiser and Montour, the old chief "complained very much of the Behavior of Col. Washington to him (tho' in a very moderate way, saying the Col. was a good-natured man but had no Experience)." Washington tried to command Indians as he did his slaves, had them out scouting every day, and would never take advice from them. He made no fortifications except "that little thing upon the Meadow," and expected the French to attack across open ground. Had he listened to Tanaghrisson and made the kind of defenses he advised, Washington would have been able to repulse the French, who had fought like cowards while the English fought like fools. Like the other Indians, Tanaghrisson left before the battle began "because Col. Washington would never listen to them, but was always driving them on to fight by his Directions."[66] At the same council, Delaware and Shawnee chiefs assured Tanaghrisson and the British they had not gone over to the French and had not fought at Fort Necessity. Tamaqua told Tanaghrisson they had done their best not to interfere in war, but their stance was increasingly difficult to maintain; "now Things seem to take another turn, and a high Wind is rising," he warned.[67]

The Ohio Iroquois who gave the account of the Jumonville fight also blamed Washington for the Indians' ambivalence and hesitation in coming forward. After the Indians had guided him on his mission to the French fort in 1753, Washington "never thought it worth his while" to inform them what happened in his talks with the French, as he had promised to do. After the ambush on Jumonville, he never consulted with them or took their advice, and he did not believe them when they warned him of French numbers prior to the fight at Fort Necessity. The Indians never knew what transpired when Washington surrendered and could not understand why he totally abandoned the country afterward. Washington's conduct in war and diplomacy lent weight to French warnings that the British were untrustworthy allies, concluded the Iroquois.[68]

Relations between the British and the Indians were at a crisis point. The Mohawk chief, Theyanoguin or Hendrick, declared the Covenant Chain broken. The British and Iroquois met at Albany in June and July 1754 to mend their fences and repair the chain. In addition, the colonial delegates at the Albany Congress discussed joint defensive measures against the French, although Pennsylvania's delegate, Benjamin Franklin, went further and tried to advance a plan of colonial union. Franklin saw the Albany Plan as a blueprint for western expansion with a central government that would have control over Indian affairs, including the power to make war and peace, make treaties, regulate trade, purchase land that was not within the boundaries of any one colony, grant land, and make laws for new settlements. Many of the provisions would reappear in the US Constitution, but in 1754 colonial assemblies rejected the plan. Dinwiddie did not attend the Albany Congress. He maintained that he was too busy trying to build support among the southern tribes. Hendrick suspected he was too busy coveting Indian land. The governors of Virginia and Canada were "both quarrelling about lands which belong to us, and such a quarrel as this may end in our destruction," he told the Albany delegates. Hendrick himself was involved in selling Indian lands. Two days after Washington surrendered Fort Necessity, Hendrick and twenty-two other Iroquois signed a deed conveying to Pennsylvania lands west of the Susquehanna River. Before the Albany Congress was over, the unscrupulous trader Henry Lydius had also acquired a dubious deed to the Wyoming Valley and part of northwestern Pennsylvania. Once again, the sales were based on the notion that the Six Nations could sell lands they claimed by right of conquest. The Delawares and Shawnees who lived on those lands would soon be fighting to defend them.[69]

Rumors and reports from Indian country persisted throughout the summer of 1754: the French were stepping up preparations, and their troops were on the move; Indian anxieties were growing, and people were relocating out of harm's way. Daniel Claus, a British agent among the Mohawks, reported that about one hundred Iroquois had gone to Canada. People thought it was out of fear of the French; "they say there never was the like seen how quick the said Nations turned after Col. Washington's defeat." Some Ohio Indians joined the French.[70] Tanaghrisson remained steadfast, however, declaring he would "live and die with the English." He did the latter. On October 1 Scarouady and some other Six Nations chiefs arrived at the house of the trader John Harris, bringing Tanaghrisson and his family with them. Tanaghrisson was "in a very low Condition" and died a few days later, probably of pneumonia. Croghan said all the Indians mourned his passing. The *Virginia Gazette* gave it front-page notice. Dinwiddie said Britain had lost a brave and steady friend. Croghan gave a condolence speech and presents to cover Tanaghrisson's grave, as the Indians could "not see the Road nor hear what the Governor of Virginia had to say to them till that Ceremony had been done."[71] Some of Tanaghrisson's followers attributed his death to witchcraft. Scarouady, who took over his duties, said, "The French joked with Us on the Death of the Half King, and laughed, but we shall make them cry before We have done with them."[72]

Scarouady remained firm in his allegiance to the English and continued to try to fan the flames of the conflict he and Tanghrisson had engineered. Richard Peters, a member of the Pennsylvania governor's council and a delegate to the Albany Congress in 1754, believed he had "an aversion to the French, and wants without any good Reason to strike them." Scarouady agreed to carry a message from the governor of Virginia to Onondaga, inviting the Six Nations to come to Winchester in the spring. Maryland and Pennsylvania added their own belt to reinforce the invitation. On Christmas Day 1754, Scarouady set out from Philadelphia. Such an errand trod on the toes of William Johnson, who jealously guarded his role as the liaison between the British and the Six Nations, and Peters warned him that, whatever the public face of the errand, Scarouady might have his own agenda and secretly try to incite the Six Nations to war. Scarouady carried a large black belt of fourteen rows, which was inappropriate for a peaceful invitation, and Peters feared the Six Nations would interpret it as a message of war. He did not buy Scarouady's explanation that its color had no significance, as there was no hatchet on it, and that he would not use it to talk of war. The governor asked Peters to forewarn Johnson and Hendrick so "that all Mistakes may be prevented and no bad Consequences ensue."[73] Meanwhile, the government of Pennsylvania fed the Indians who remained at Aughwick throughout the winter. Queen Aliquippa died there in December 1754.[74]

The House of Burgesses conveyed its formal thanks to Washington and his officers for their conduct at Fort Necessity, which gave Washington great "satisfaction."[75] Dinwiddie, however, described Washington's conduct as wrong in many respects. If he had followed Dinwiddie's orders, he would not have engaged the enemy before reinforcements arrived.[76] Dinwiddie broke the Virginia Regiment into several companies, with no officer holding a rank higher than captain. "This was too degrading for G. W. to submit to," Washington wrote years later, referring to himself in the third person. Rather than accept a reduction in rank, he resigned and returned to private life.[77]

For a crucial moment, Tanaghrisson had dominated Washington's relations with the Indians and the French in the Ohio country. Like Macbeth's poor player, he had strutted and fretted his hour upon the stage, and at times he had been full of sound and fury that did not signify very much. Now he had left the stage, but he had set it for the first truly global conflict. As Robert Hunter Morris, the new deputy governor, told the Pennsylvania Assembly, "the Eyes of Europe" were now turned "to this Quarter of the World."[78] Tanaghrisson did not live to see the storm he had unleashed, but it caught Washington in its path and changed the course of American history.

CHAPTER 5

Braddock and the Limits of Empire

I N MARCH 1755, after fifty-six days crossing the stormy Atlantic, the largest British army that had been sent to America landed in Virginia. Its commander in chief, General Edward Braddock, had arrived on February 20. The army consisted of two regiments dispatched from garrison duty in Ireland—the 44th, commanded by Colonel Sir Peter Halkett, and the 48th, commanded by Colonel Thomas Dunbar. Other officers included Lieutenant Colonel Thomas Gage (who twenty years later commanded the British forces at Lexington and Concord) and Lieutenant Colonel Horatio Gates (who twenty-two years later defeated a British army at Saratoga). Braddock was to raise two more regiments of volunteers in the colonies. His goal was to take the French forts at the Forks of the Ohio and Niagara, while other expeditions took the forts at Crown Point on the southwestern shore of Lake Champlain and Beauséjour in Nova Scotia.[1] Lieutenant Governor Dinwiddie assured Braddock in June, "I have no doubt the Fr. Will surrender on Sight of y'r Forces." Like his superiors in London, Dinwiddie misjudged the realities of power in the Ohio country, where Indian power and indigenous foreign policies trumped imperial ambitions. Six months later, he was struggling to comprehend what happened to Braddock's grand army, which, he wrote, "appears to me as a dream."[2]

In order to launch his campaign, Braddock had to deal with colonial assemblies that were supposed to provide money and manpower, and with Indians who were to provide the scouts and allies he needed to operate effectively in Indian country. Braddock's strategy and route had been decided for him in London, based on political rather than logistical or tactical considerations. Instead of attacking Fort Niagara first, which would have allowed him to transport troops and supplies across the Great Lakes and cut off Fort Duquesne from its supply line, the Duke of Cumberland ordered Braddock to assault Fort Duquesne from Virginia and then head north to take Niagara. Virginia was not the best place to supply or provide transportation for an army. Dinwiddie threw his support behind Braddock, but in a pattern that was to be repeated throughout the Seven Years' War, colonial noncooperation, parsimony and profiteering, inadequate and insufficient recruits, and a lack of horses and wagons frustrated and infuriated the general, who in turn alienated colonial assemblies and citizens with his high-handed and disdainful attitude. His argumentative and overbearing quartermaster, Sir John St. Clair, made matters worse.[3]

Pennsylvania boasted the largest city in British North America, better roads, and more horses and wagons, but Braddock fared little better there than in Virginia. "I cannot help expressing the greatest Surprise to find such pusillanimous and improper Behaviour in your Assembly," he told Deputy Governor Robert Hunter Morris, "and an absolute Refusal to supply either Men, Money, or Provision for their own Defense."[4] Dinwiddie voiced similar complaints about Pennsylvania. Morris blamed the failure to supply funds on the Quaker Assembly, when in fact Morris himself was vetoing grants in accordance with instructions from Thomas Penn, the proprietor of the colony, who was out to discredit the Assembly. It took sterling efforts by Benjamin Franklin to come up with the wagons Braddock needed to get his campaign on the road.[5]

Washington had resigned his command in a huff.[6] But Braddock's expedition offered an opportunity to restore his reputation after the disaster at Fort Necessity and revived his interest in a military career.[7] Washington wanted a place in Braddock's expedition and made inquiries through friends and contacts. A regular commission in the British army, usually purchased by members of the aristocracy, was beyond his reach, and he had done nothing so far to earn advancement on the basis of his military merit. He could volunteer as an aide and hope to obtain a commission that way. "Conceiving, I suppose, that the small knowledge I have had an opportunity of acquiring of the Country, Indians, &c was worthy of his notice; and might be useful to him in the progress of this Expedition," Washington approached Braddock through his aide Robert Orme, importuning to join the campaign as a member of the general's staff or military family. Orme replied that Braddock understood Washington's concerns about issues of command and would "be very glad of your company in his family by which all inconveniences of that kind will be obviated."[8]

Technically violating the terms of his surrender at Fort Necessity, when he pledged not to return to the Ohio country for a year, Washington set off to join Braddock. He did so, he told William Byrd III of Westover, with no other goal than "serving my country without fee or reward."[9] Leaving management of Mount Vernon to his younger brother Jack, and over his mother's objections, he joined the army at Frederick in early May. He was appointed to the general's family as an aide-de-camp, which meant, he told Jack, he was "freed from all command but his, and give his Orders to all." He recognized he had an opportunity to make "an acquaintance, which may be serviceable hereafter, if I can find it worth while pushing my Fortune in the Military way," and he was not going to waste it. He expected to advance his career and his fortune by participating in an easy victory: "As to any danger from the Enemy," he reassured his brother, "I look upon it as trifling, for I believe they will be oblig'd to exert their utmost Force to repel the attacks to the Northward."[10] Braddock may not have shared his confidence, at least in private—he confided to a former mistress before he left England that his army was being "sent like sacrifices to the altar."[11]

Having inherited his brother Lawrence's shares in the Ohio Company, Washington had a personal stake in securing the Forks of the Ohio and in where the road was built to do so. Braddock was to follow roughly the same route Washington had traveled the previous year to Fort Necessity, across enormously difficult terrain. The Duke of Cumberland may have been influenced by the Ohio Company, in particular by John Hanbury, who was one of the people consulted for advice and who not surprisingly recommended centering operations in Virginia. Cumberland was certainly misinformed about the geography and topography: the maps available to him showed Fort Duquesne to be just 15 miles from the British outpost at Wills Creek; the actual distance was about 120 miles.[12] Washington and other members of the company exerted their influence to make sure Braddock selected a route that ran through northwest Virginia to the company storehouse at Redstone Creek and on to the Forks, rather than one that cut through Pennsylvania. Company agents also supplied Braddock's army.[13] Despite the protestations of disinterested service he had made to William Byrd, Washington was still a young man on the make.

When Washington arrived at Fort Cumberland, there were about one hundred Indian men, women, and children there, with

George Croghan and Andrew Montour. Dinwiddie had tried without success to recruit Catawba and Cherokee warriors to join Braddock's army; these Indians were mainly Mingoes under Scarouady who had accompanied Croghan from Aughwick.[14] They were not there as idle spectators; Scarouady and Tanaghrisson had pleaded with the British to expel the French from the Ohio country, and now it seemed to be happening. A British sailor—from a Royal Navy detachment that accompanied the army to move the cannons by block and tackle—said the Indians were surprised at the numbers of soldiers and their regular way of marching. He also recorded his initial impressions of the Natives. "The men are tall, well made, and active, but not strong, but very dexterous with rifle barreled gun, and their tomahawk, which they will throw with great dexterity at any mark and at a great distance." He thought the women were well made and had many children—but that they had "had many more before spirits were introduced to them"—and he described how they carried their babies on cradleboards. "They paint themselves in an odd manner, red, yellow, and black intermixed. And the men have the outer rim of their ears cut, which only hangs by a bit top and bottom, and have a tuft of hair left at the top of their heads, which is dressed with feathers." Most wore a blanket and deerskin moccasins. Like many other Europeans who saw no churches or organized services in Indian communities, the sailor assumed the Indians had "no notion of religion, or of any sort of Superior being." He thought them "the most ignorant people as to the knowledge of the world and other things" and complained that their dancing and war songs made "a horrible noise." Braddock gave strict orders that the soldiers stay away from them and not speak to them lest they should give offense.[15]

Most of the army likely shared the sailor's attitudes and antipathy toward their Indian allies. Relations were not good and were about to get worse. Soldiers enticed Indian women into camp with liquor and then seduced or raped them. Braddock responded with floggings—as many as nine hundred lashes, a nearly fatal punishment—for selling liquor to the Indians and ordered the Indians to send their women and children back to Aughwick. The Indians were appalled by that kind of punishment and offended by that kind of order. Many of them left with their women.[16]

Scarouady, Shingas, and several other sachems wanted assurances that if they helped the redcoats the British would not steal their land once the war was over. Braddock, so the story goes, would have none of it. According to Charles Stuart, who was captured in an Indian raid in Pennsylvania in the fall of 1755, Shingas told his prisoners he regretted what had happened but that the English, not the Indians, had caused the war. Recalling the council held at Fort Cumberland, Shingas said he had asked what the general intended to do with the land if and when he drove out the French and their Indian allies. Braddock replied "the English Should Inhabit & Inherit the Land." Would not their Indian allies be allowed to live and trade among them and have enough hunting ground to support their families? Shingas queried; otherwise they would have nowhere to go but the lands of the French and their Indian allies, who were Shingas's enemies. Braddock replied disdainfully that "no Savage Should Inherit the Land." Shingas and the other chiefs conveyed Braddock's answer to their people that night. In the morning they returned to Braddock with the same question, hoping he might have changed his position. Braddock gave the same answer as before. The chiefs replied that "if they might not have Liberty To Live on the Land they would not Fight for it." Braddock retorted he did not need their help to drive out the French and their Indians. When the chiefs related the conversation, their people "were very much Enraged," and some immediately went and joined the French. But most remained neutral, waiting to see how things would turn out when Braddock and the French met in battle. Braddock was left with only a handful of Indian allies. Even then, Shingas said, most of the Indians hoped the English would prevail, but once Braddock's army was destroyed they had no choice but to join the French "for their own safety."[17]

Stuart made a statement of his captivity experiences for the military authorities, and historians have usually accepted his account of Shingas's account—in other words, hearsay evidence—and pinned the blame for Braddock's poor showing with the Indians on this incident. Contemporaries, too, reported he mishandled his allies. Dinwiddie said, "I fear Gen'l Braddock despis'd them too much." Benjamin Franklin said, "He slighted & neglected them, and they gradually left him." When Franklin brought up the danger of Indian ambush, Braddock only "smil'd at my Ignorance, & reply'd, 'These Savages may indeed be a formidable Enemy to your raw American Militia, but, upon the King's regular & disciplin'd Troops, Sir, it is impossible they should make any Impression.'"[18] Yet despite his enduring image as arrogant, ignorant, and stubborn, Braddock attempted to cultivate Indian allies with gifts, followed the rituals of wampum diplomacy, and assured them he would restore their lands to them if they would assist him in defeating the French.[19] George Croghan, head of the Indian scouts, was not a man to mince words when he saw superiors mishandling Indian allies, but Braddock, he said, behaved "as kindly as he possibly could" when he met with the Indians and ordered that they should "want for nothing." The Delawares promised to join the army on its march but failed to show up: whether deterred by previous English breaches of faith or biding their time to see how Braddock fared against the French, Croghan could not tell.[20]

The Indians' aversion to supporting Braddock's army stemmed from deeper issues than the general's supposed arrogance and cultural insensitivity. Shingas's pointed questions reflected ongoing concerns about British intentions. The recent cession of lands at the Albany Congress rankled. Having been pushed west repeatedly, Shingas and the western Delawares were determined not to have to migrate again. They were concerned by the French invasion, which threatened their territorial security and violated their sovereignty, but they also resented the intrusions of Pennsylvania traders and Virginia speculators. They waited to see what the outcome of Braddock's expedition would be.[21] What influence Washington's earlier poor showing may have had on their decision is difficult to assess. Sir William Johnson told Braddock the principal factors governing Indian actions were, first, fear of the French "& the shameful hand we have always made of our former Expeditions" and, second, that many of the chiefs were attached to the French by kinship and other ties. Unfortunately, by the time Johnson wrote this, Braddock was dead.[22]

Customarily attributed to British high-handedness and ineptitude, Braddock's eventual defeat at the Battle of the Monongahela is better understood as an Indian victory: a multinational assemblage of Native warriors, supported and directed by French Canadian officers who were experienced in fighting and leading Indians, brought their mobility, firepower, and marksmanship to bear on inadequately trained troops in a situation where conventional tactics proved disastrous.[23] Hundreds of Indians rallied to the French at Fort Duquesne for a variety of reasons that included fear of English encroachment but also economic and kinship ties with the French. Many came from the upper Great Lakes, the Mississippi, or mission villages on the St. Lawrence, and would not have been particularly concerned about the threat to Ohio Valley lands. One of the warriors who had answered the French call for help and traveled to Fort Duquesne that summer was a teenager called Atiatoharongwen or Atayataghronghta. Born in Saratoga in 1740 to an African American father and an Abenaki mother from Odanak, he had been captured as a child during a French and Indian raid on the town, adopted by Mohawks, and grew up as a French Catholic Mohawk at Kahnawake. Twenty years later, Washington would come to know him as Louis Cook.[24]

In contrast with the Indian allies the French mustered, Brad-dock's Native contingent was tiny. Only eight Ohio Iroquois warriors accompanied his army (although sixteen others joined after the battle). Washington already knew most of them. Scarouady had little choice but to stick with Braddock. Like Tanaghrisson, he clung to the hope that allying with the British to expel the French would con-firm Iroquois dominance and restore Indian autonomy in the Ohio country. It was, says Fred Anderson, "a vision shared by almost no one else."[25] The others were Scarouady's son; Kanuksusy, the son of Queen Aliquippa, whom Washington had met in 1753 and, as we've seen, given the name Fairfax (and to whom the governor of Pennsylvania gave a new name, Newcastle, after the battle); White Thunder or Belt of Wampum, who had been one of Washington's escorts; his son-in-law Silver Heels; Tanaghrisson's son, Gahickdodon, whom the English sometimes called Johnny; and another Indian, Skowonidous, whom they called Jerry. Jerry later deserted, and Scarouady's son was killed by friendly fire, leaving Braddock with just six Indian allies—less than 1 percent of the number aligned with the French—by the time of the battle.[26]

Washington would soon learn the importance of having Indian allies, but, as Fred Anderson points out, at this point he saw little role for them in his conventionally European view of warfare, and he also had his own reasons for shunning them. Indians delayed the settle-ment of the Ohio Valley that Washington and his Ohio Company friends needed to promote, and one way or another, Indian actions had contributed to his military setbacks. He had good reason to want Indians driven from the Ohio Valley along with the French.[27]

In mid-May, with his army running short of supplies and awash in logistical difficulties, Braddock sent Washington to Hampton to draw £4,000 from the army's paymaster, and to tell the paymaster to deliver an additional £10,000 to Fort Cumberland within two months. Braddock was in a hurry, but Washington took his time. He made a side trip to Mount Vernon; went shopping in Williamsburg, where he bought gloves, stockings, toothbrushes, and other items; and tested the political waters for running for a seat in the House of Burgesses. By the time he returned to camp at the end of the month, Braddock was almost ready to march.[28]

A road had to be cleared through the forest before the army could advance, however, and it was another week before it set out. The two royal regiments went first, with three independent compa-nies of provincials, and eleven companies of volunteers (nine from Virginia, one each from North Carolina and Maryland) brought up the rear with the artillery. Dr. Thomas Walker was commissary to the Virginia troops. Daniel Morgan and twenty-year-old Daniel Boone served as teamsters. Discipline was harsh, drunkenness and desertion were common, and morale was low. Hacking out a road as it went, and hauling wagons and artillery, the army inched its way through dense forest and across mountainous terrain. Heavy rain, mosquitos, accidents, desertions, and disease further impeded progress. Acrimonious quarrels between the officers didn't help; most of them hated Robert Orme, who had made himself Braddock's favorite.

Washington's experience in transporting supplies along forest and mountain trails was limited to packhorses. He fretted as two thousand soldiers lugged their equipment and maneuvered heavy artillery and wagons over mountains and through forests; instead of pushing on with vigor, he wrote in private to his brother, they stopped to level every molehill and build bridges over every creek. It took four days to travel twelve miles.[29] After more than two weeks of snail's progress, Washington said, Braddock asked his advice on how to proceed, since he had been in this country before. Although we have only Washington's word for it, he urged his commander "in the warmest terms I was master of" to press on against Fort Duquesne with a flying column supported by artillery, leaving the heavier material to follow at a slower pace. On June 17 Braddock divided his army, forging ahead with eight hundred soldiers, eight artillery pieces, and thirty wagons; Colonel Thomas Dunbar was to bring up the rest of the troops and the baggage. It was a decision some historians think contributed to the disaster that followed.[30]

As the flying column pushed on, Indians increasingly sniped at the edges, took the occasional captive or scalp, and left grisly evidence of the fate awaiting anyone who fell into their hands. Washington was certain they lacked the strength to mount a serious assault, but their use of psychological terror further eroded the morale of soldiers already out of their element in a strange and threatening environment.[31] Nervous soldiers shot and killed Scarouady's son when the Indian guides were coming to their assistance against enemies lurking in the woods. Braddock offered condolences to the grief-stricken father and ordered a full military funeral.[32]

Like many others, Washington came down with the "bloody flux," the contemporary term for dysentery. His condition became so severe he could not ride a horse and was confined to a cot in the rear of the army. Craik, the army physician, prescribed Dr. Robert James's fever powder, a medication used for a variety of maladies in the eighteenth century, and that eased his distress somewhat. Sitting astride his horse on cushions, Washington rejoined the column in time to cross the Monongahela River, the final obstacle before Fort Duquesne.[33] On July 9 Braddock ordered Lieutenant Colonel Thomas Gage to advance with three hundred regulars and make the crossing. Croghan and Scarouady led the way. Braddock had achieved an impressive military feat: he had assembled an expedition, constructed 150 miles of new road over the Allegheny Mountains, marched some 250 miles in less than three months, and arrived at the Monongahela with the means to lay siege and take Fort Duquesne.[34] Gage crossed the river unopposed.

Meanwhile, forty-four-year-old Captain Daniel-Hyacinthe-Marie Liénard de Beaujeu was hurrying toward the river with about 250 French and 650 Indians. Most of the Indians were Ottawas, Ojibwas, and Wyandots from the Great Lakes, although some Shawnees, a few Delawares and Mingoes, and even some Otos and Osages from beyond the Mississippi were present. Just the day before, according to a French account, the Iroquois and Shawnees inhabiting the area around Fort Duquesne, who hitherto had remained neutral, had come to join Beaujeu. A Delaware Indian eight years later said there were no Delawares at Braddock's defeat, and only three Shawnees and four Mingoes, all the rest being northern Indians.[35] Intending to set an ambush at the Monongahela, the French and Indians had to improvise and attack the British advance column that had crossed the river before they reached it. In the opening exchange of shots, a British musket ball killed Beaujeu. Gage opened fire with his artillery, and it looked for a moment as if the redcoats would swat aside the opposition. But the Indians begin to enfilade the British column and, firing from behind trees, picked off the gun crews and officers. Trained to hold their ranks under fire, the redcoats made easy targets for unseen enemies pouring fire into them. Packed in a killing pen with their officers dropping around them, they began to fall back. In doing so, they collided with the main body that Braddock had ordered forward to support Gage, generating more confusion.[36]

According to Orme, who was severely wounded in the thigh, the officers "were absolutely sacrificed by their unparalleled good Behaviour" as they tried in vain to rally their troops. Braddock had five horses killed under him before a bullet passed through his right arm into his lungs. Sir Peter Halkett was killed instantly. His son, a lieutenant in the 44th, was killed as he knelt over his stricken father. "Poor Shirley"—Braddock's secretary and the son of General William Shirley—"was shot thro' the Head." Washington, said Orme, behaved "the whole Time with the greatest Courage and Resolution."[37]

Washington escaped without injury, although he told his mother and brother he had two horses shot under him and four bullets through his coat.[38]

Later traditions attributed to Indians the prophecy that the "Great Spirit" shielded Washington from harm in the battle to fulfill his greater destiny as "the chief of nations" and "founder of a mighty empire." According to Osage tribal tradition, their warriors at the battle remembered a tall man who rode "toward the guns and arrows of the Heavy Eyebrows [the French] and the Indians." After his first horse fell with bullets and arrows in its neck, he mounted another, which fell in the same way, but the rider escaped untouched. The Osage warriors said "they shot at him with arrows, and for some reason the arrows seemed to miss him. Later they said they curved around him." They said "this tall, brave Long Knife" was George Washington, "and he was spared to become the father of his country because of his strong medicine." Reviewing the tradition in the twentieth century, the Osage tribal historian and writer John Joseph Matthews pointed out that the Osages knew nothing about Washington until many years later.[39] Indian warriors who witnessed Washington's escape from death likely would have attributed it to spiritual protection, just as Washington and his contemporaries attributed it to "providence." The notion that he was spared for some future, higher purpose came much later, however.

Washington extolled the bravery of the officers and of his Virginian troops, who "behav'd like Men, and died like Soldiers," breaking for the trees and fighting the Indians with their own style of warfare. The behavior of the redcoats, on the other hand, was "dastardly"; they "were immediately struck with such a deadly Panick, that nothing but confusion and disobedience of order's prevail'd amongst them." Ignoring the officers' efforts to stop them, they "broke and run like Sheep before the Hounds," throwing aside equipment and abandoning wounded comrades to the enemy. The officers had no more chance of rallying them than "if we had attempted to have stopd the wild Bears of the Mountains."[40] Everyone agreed the officers conducted themselves well, but not all officers agreed that the rank and file deserved all the blame: "I Can't help thinking their misbehavior is exaggerated," wrote one, "in order to palliate the Blunders made by those in the direction, as they make no allowance for regular Troops being surprised, as was manifestly the Case here, and no manner of disposition made—but one of Certain destruction."[41] Quartermaster John St. Clair, not known for generosity to his fellow man, likewise came to the defense of the

British troops, observing that "something besides Cowardice must be Attributed to a Body of men" who suffered 50 percent casualties before they retreated.[42]

In fact, the British stood their ground for almost three hours before their lines crumpled and broke. Among the first to run were wagon drivers at the rear of the column who unhitched their teams and rode for safety, among them Daniel Boone and Daniel Morgan, who took a bullet in the mouth.[43] In the rout that ensued, Indian warriors butchered soldiers and civilians running for their lives and scrambling back across the Monongahela. The disintegrating army abandoned weapons, wagons, supplies, and horses. According to tribal tradition, Potawatomis and Hurons (Wyandots) acquired their first horses at Braddock's defeat.[44]

Years later Washington claimed that "before it was *too late*" he had offered in vain to lead the provincials and fight the enemy "in their own way." He presumably wanted to absolve himself of any responsibility for the disaster and demonstrate his early mastery of American-style warfare, but neither his own letters immediately after the battle nor other contemporary sources corroborate his statement. Just which of his previous experiences fighting in Indian country would have given him the confidence to make such an offer is not clear.[45]

He did, however, perform heroic service in defeat. He escorted the mortally wounded Braddock from the field with the straggling remnants of the army. At Braddock's order, he rode back through thick woods and darkness to tell Colonel Dunbar to hurry forward with food and medical supplies. "The shocking Scenes which presented themselves in this Night's March" haunted Washington for years. "The dead—the dying—the groans—lamentations—and crys along the Road of the wounded for help," he recalled, "were enough to pierce a heart."[46] Braddock breathed his last at Great Meadows. Washington and other surviving officers buried him in the road, and the troops marched over the grave to conceal it from the Indians. Washington remained loyal to his dead commander: Braddock lacked tact and was "blunt in his manner even to rudeness," he wrote, but he was "brave even to a fault and in regular Service would have done honor to his profession."[47]

Others were not so forgiving. When Robert Hunter Morris sent General Shirley reports of the defeat—and of the death of Shirley's son—he pinned the blame on the commanders who had been overconfident, lacked caution, "and held in too great Contempt the Indian Manner of Fighting." They had let themselves fall into an ambush where they were exposed to the enemy's fire from all sides and, unable to see them, "could only fire at their Smoak." Keeping the soldiers in ranks and firing in platoons gave every advantage to enemies concealed behind logs and trees, and the resulting confusion made the slaughter more terrible. In such a situation, the soldiers' panic was "not so much to be wondered at." It was, said Morris, "the most shameful blow that ever English troops received."[48]

Colonel Dunbar marched what was left of his army to winter quarters near Philadelphia in the middle of summer. His retreat left the road to the Ohio open to enemy invasion and left backcountry settlers in "imminent Peril of being inhumanely Butchered by our Savage neighbours." It also left Dinwiddie fuming in letter after letter.[49] Dunbar and his officers wrote General Shirley explaining why they felt it was impossible for them to mount an expedition against Fort Duquesne. In addition to lack of artillery, the lateness of the season, and the condition of the troops, they now had no Indian allies, and "nor do we hear of any Measures having been taken to get any."[50]

The Indian allies were not completely lost—yet. Scarouady and several others who had fought with Braddock were meeting with Deputy Governor Morris and members of the Provincial Council in Philadelphia even as Dunbar wrote his letter to Shirley. Braddock's pride and arrogance caused most of the Indians to leave him before the battle, Scarouady explained: "he looked upon us as dogs; would never hear anything that was said to him," and refused to heed their warnings. Even so, Scarouady offered to gather Indian allies to assist the English in another expedition. "One word of Yours will bring the Delawares to join You," he said; "if you will but Exert Yourselves we can beat and humble the French." He gave them a wampum belt "to admonish You to exert yourselves." Instead, Morris and the council thanked the Delawares for their assurances of friendship and asked them to wait until the Six Nations reached a decision. Conscious of the growing power of the French and their Indian allies following Braddock's defeat, the Delawares were in no mood and no position to wait and see what Onondaga would do. Returning from Philadelphia with no prospect of timely support, Shingas, Captain Jacobs, and other chiefs "agreed To Come out with the French and their Indians in Parties To Destroy the English Settlements."[51] Sent by Morris to gain information at the Indian towns on the Susquehanna in November 1755, Silver Heels returned with dire news: the French had persuaded the Delawares and Shawnees on the Ohio to strike the English, and had put the hatchet into the hands of the Susquehanna Indians, "a great many of whom had taken it greedily" and were preparing to go to war against the people of Pennsylvania.[52] By then Shingas and a war party of 150 warriors had already crossed the mountains and were raiding settlements in Virginia and Pennsylvania. Since the British had refused to put the hatchet into the Delawares' hands to let them defend their homeland against the French and their Indian allies, the Delawares now took up the hatchet themselves to defend their homeland against the English. No longer willing to act as "women" or Iroquois subordinates, they ritually threw off the military restraints imposed on them by the Iroquois, abandoned their traditional practice of diplomacy, and turned to violence to achieve their goals. For Delawares, the so-called French and Indian War was a war of independence.[53]

WASHINGTON COMPLAINED IN 1755 that his services in the Ohio country over the previous two years had been at considerable personal expense and had gained him nothing.[54] Nevertheless, he emerged from the slaughter on the Monongahela not only unscathed but with his reputation considerably enhanced. His military experiences in Indian country amounted to one debacle and two disastrous defeats, the Jumonville affair followed by Fort Necessity and the rout at the Monongahela, but reports of his remarkable escapes from death in the battle, his undoubted courage, and his resilience in the face of defeat elevated Washington to hero status. Virginians were hungry for a hero amid so many setbacks, while in Pennsylvania, Christopher Gist wrote him, people talked of Washington more than any other officer in the army and would be willing to serve under his command as irregulars, "for all their Talk is of fighting in the Indian way."[55] Washington made it known that he wanted to command Virginia's next campaign, and lobbied influential contacts. When the House of Burgesses voted to raise twelve hundred men organized in sixteen companies and offered him the command, he protested that he lacked the experience and could not accept; he accepted when the Assembly improved the terms of the offer. In August 1755 Washington was appointed colonel of the Virginia Regiment and commander in chief of all Virginia's forces with a salary of thirty shillings a day, an expense account of £100 per year, and 2 percent commission on all official purchases he made. He immediately designed a uniform for himself and his officers (blue coat, with scarlet cuffs and facings, blue breeches, and a silver-laced hat).[56] Knowing his mother's feelings on the subject, Washington wrote her: "If it is in my power to avoid going to the Ohio again, I shall, but if the Command is press'd upon me by the genl voice of the Country, and offed upon such terms as can't be objected against, it woud reflect dishonor upon me to refuse it."[57] In another age, he might have been called "the Comeback Kid."

Washington made his headquarters and center of operations for organizing the defense of the Shenandoah Valley at Winchester, a town of some sixty log cabins close to passes through the Blue Ridge Mountains and a major stopping point for Iroquois and Cherokees traveling the Warriors' Path.[58] He appointed Adam Stephen, his companion from the Fort Necessity and Fort Duquesne campaigns, lieutenant colonel in command of the Virginia Regiment at Fort Cumberland, to block a pass that led to Virginia; made George Mercer his aide-de-camp; appointed Peter Hoag captain of the Virginia Regiment; and promoted his cousin Andrew Lewis to major, in command of the new companies of recruits as they arrived at Winchester.[59] The officers were to raise the enlisted men for the new regiment. Washington wanted another campaign against Fort Duquesne, but it was all he could do to cobble together a defense of Virginia's 350-mile western frontier.

By the 1750s Virginians had pushed across the Potomac watershed and into the Alleghenies. Their settlements were dispersed farms in valleys, exposed, and difficult to defend.[60] Pennsylvania, with a pacifist Quaker assembly, had no militia force to defend its frontier settlers. Maryland pulled its defenses back to Fort Frederick, a mere forty-five miles from Baltimore. The Virginia Assembly ordered construction of a line of forts as a defensive cordon on the colony's western frontier. Eventually a chain of small forts, some of them no more than "log pens" or garrison houses, stretched at roughly twenty-mile intervals across almost four hundred miles of mountainous terrain stretching from the Potomac through the Alleghany Mountains to the borders of North Carolina. Mobile woodland warriors, who had little to fear from colonial soldiers cooped up in blockhouses, skirted around them with ease, but the forts did provide refuge for frontier families.[61] Stephen lacked the men and resources to defend backcountry settlers against Indian attacks and atrocities: conditions at Fort Cumberland, he told Washington, were deplorable.[62] Washington, meanwhile, "made himself very comfortable in Winchester," where he rented a house, "entertained in style," and kept an eye on his business affairs.[63]

Indian raids were a central part of the French war effort. Governor Pierre de Rigaud de Vaudreuil de Cavagnial of New France appreciated the need to treat Indian allies as equals, keep them well supplied, and shape his tactics to suit their ways of fighting, lessons

Washington and the British had still to learn. Undersupplied and vastly outnumbered by the British—about twenty to one—the French kept the bulk of their regular military forces on the New York frontier and the St. Lawrence to protect Canada from invasion. At the same time, they encouraged and equipped their Indian allies waging guerrilla warfare on the western frontiers of the British colonies in an effort to divert British energies and resources from the North and demoralize the backcountry inhabitants to the point they would seek peace. "Nothing is more calculated to disgust the people of those Colonies and to make them desire the return of peace," Vaudreuil told Versailles. François-Marie Le Marchand de Lignery, the French commander in the Ohio country after 1756, was a veteran of France's wars against the Mesquakie (Fox) and Chickasaw in the 1730s and had fought at Braddock's defeat. He made Fort Duquesne the base for Indian raids against Virginia and Pennsylvania. Indian raiders targeted vulnerable groups and employed terror tactics and psychological warfare. Scalping, torture, and mutilations generated fear, destroyed morale, and spread panic that rolled back the frontier. "You cannot conceive what a vast Tract of Country has been depopulated by these merciless Savages," Pennsylvania's deputy governor wrote in November 1755. Raids that devastated one region often propelled settlers to abandon a neighboring area; Indians would then raid farther east, target another region, and generate another round of flights. People who did not flee "forted up" in makeshift stockades. With their economies and populations disrupted by war, Indian raiders carried home much-needed plunder, as well as captives who might be adopted to take the place of deceased relatives. Shingas led raids that penetrated as far as the south branch of the Potomac and into Cumberland County, Pennsylvania. The man Washington had thought fearful of the French two years before now earned the sobriquet "Shingas the Terrible."[64]

For more than three years following Braddock's defeat, raiding parties from the Ohio ravaged the backcountry of Virginia and Pennsylvania. Delawares and Shawnees made common cause with the French, along with Wyandots, Miamis, Ottawas, Ojibwas, Potawatomis, and other Great Lakes allies of the French, some of whom had made their homes in the Ohio country. But the Indians did not wage a united war. Different tribes, and even groups within tribes, fought their own parallel wars. Delawares and Shawnees fought for Delaware and Shawnee reasons, not for those of their French or Indian allies. Not all Delawares and Shawnees went to war. Delaware converts in Moravian mission villages took no part, Delawares on the Susquehanna fought for different purposes than Delawares in the Ohio country, and one group of Shawnees, under Paxinosa or Bucksinosa, remained friendly to the English. Other Shawnees, rather than serving as French auxiliaries or giving vent to general anger against English encroachment, as the French realized but the British did not, went to war in large part because they were outraged at the imprisonment in South Carolina by the English of six of their warriors, one of whom died in captivity.[65]

Yet there were common grievances. Delawares in the Wyoming Valley cited years of trade abuse, land theft, and unpunished murders that cried for revenge; the English "used us like Dogs," they said, and "would make Slaves of us" if they let things go on as they had. Teedyuscung, an eastern Delaware with a reputation for hard drinking and big talking, said the French and English were both trying to "coop us up, as if in a Pen," but the English need only look into their hearts to understand why the Indians struck them harder than the French.[66] "Why can't you get sober and once think impartially?" an Ohio chief named Ackawonothio later asked the English; it was no wonder the Indians joined the French. They were doing what any people would—defending their lives, their women and children, their land and their freedom. God had made Indian country for the Indians, not for white people, but Pennsylvanians kept encroaching (and "where one of those People settled, like Pidgeons, a thousand more would settle"), and "a Company of Wicked Men in Virginia" had tried to build a fort, no doubt intending to take over the land and make slaves of the Indians. The tribes had no love for the French but fought with them to hold back the English, who were as numerous "as Musketoes and Nitts in the Woods."[67] The consistent goal of the Indians in the Ohio country was to keep their country free of European settlement. Any peace must include a guarantee of their territorial autonomy.[68]

The Six Nations' consistent goal was to limit their involvement in the conflict and minimize the war's impact on their league and their communities.[69] Iroquois efforts to restrain the Delawares and Shawnees fell on deaf ears, however. Scarouady offered the Wyoming Valley Delawares a wampum belt to dissuade them from going to war against the English, but they refused even to accept it, pushing it aside with a stick "in a contemptuous Manner," and "gave him ill Language." Mohawks sent messengers charging the Delaware warriors "to get sober, as we look upon their Actions as the Actions of drunken Men." But the Delawares and Shawnees refused to be governed any longer by people who had sold their lands from under them at the Albany Congress, and by going to war themselves showed they were no longer "women" under Iroquois control: "We are Men, and are determined to cut off all the *English*," Delawares declared; "so say no more to us on that Head, lest we cut off your private Parts, and make Women of you, as you have done of us."[70]

To the people who suffered them, and the colonial governments and troops that struggled to contain them, Indian raids seemed like unpredictable outbreaks of savagery and a wave of mindless violence. Pennsylvanians who formerly lived alongside and traded with Delawares now demonized them as the war severed decades of face-to-face interaction, cautious coexistence, and human ties. Indian warriors often attacked places from which they had been displaced, targeted communities on disputed land, and settled old scores with people they knew. The Delawares, according to one British account, "did us the greatest Mischief" because they knew the location of almost every settlement on the frontier and acted as guides for the French Indians. Shawnee raiders killed Colonel James Patton of the Augusta County militia. Patton had been one of the commissioners at the Logstown Treaty in 1752 and was now a member of the Virginia House of Burgesses with extensive landholdings. Sometimes Indian raiders addressed their victims in English or German; sometimes captives recognized their captors.[71] Shingas the Terrible spared the life of Charles Stuart and adopted him into his family because Stuart had shown Delaware people generosity and hospitality before the war.[72]

Stuart was one of hundreds of people taken captive. For all the horrors of Indian warfare, Indians were far more likely than British or colonial soldiers to spare the lives of their enemies. They traditionally took captives in war. Iroquois and Shawnees returning along the Warriors' Path often brought captives from raids in Cherokee or Catawba country. In this war, Shawnees and Delawares captured hundreds of people, mainly women and children. Levels of violence varied according to time and circumstance, and Indians were much more likely to kill soldiers and militiamen, but in five years of attacks on settlers, they captured more (perhaps as many as 822) than they killed (765). Indians, by comparison, were seven times more likely to be killed than captured. Shawnees, who spearheaded the attacks on Virginia and earned a reputation for ferocity, took three times as many people captive as they killed in the years 1745–64. They added at least 327 captives and converts to their communities, and although most were eventually returned, more than a hundred may have remained and lived out their lives with the Shawnees. Mary Jemison, for one, was captured as a teenager by Shawnees in western Pennsylvania in 1758 and adopted by two Seneca women in place of a brother killed in the war. She married, raised a family, and lived the rest of her life as a Seneca.[73]

Captives' fates and experiences varied, depending on circumstances, the character of their captors, the decisions of bereaved relatives back in the villages, and even chance happenings. Adult males, older people, and crying infants might be tomahawked and left for dead on the trail, and other captives might be ritually tortured once they reached the village. On the other hand, Indians often displayed considerable—and considered—kindness to those, mainly women and children, they targeted for adoption into their community and conversion to their way of life. Even the notorious running of the gauntlet sometimes turned out to be a symbolic event. Marie le Roy and Barbara Leininger, taken captive in the fall of 1755, arrived in December at the Delaware town of Kittanning, where they "received [a] welcome, according to the Indian custom." Instead of being severely beaten, however, they each received three blows on the back, "administered with great mercy." The captive girls "concluded that we were beaten merely in order to keep up an ancient usage, and not with the intention of injuring us."[74] Horror stories of the treatment white women could expect if they fell into Indian hands had circulated since Puritan times in New England, and they added to the terror now, although fueled by rumor more than reality. Indian men whose ritual preparations for war included sexual abstinence and whose captives might be adopted as clan relatives were unlikely to risk compromising their war medicine or infringing incest taboos by forcing themselves on female captives. The Indians "are said not to have deflowered any of our young women they captivated, while at war with us," explained the trader James Adair; "they would think such actions defiling, and what must bring fatal consequences on their own heads." According to one escaped captive "even that blood-thirsty villain, Capt. Jacob, did not attempt the virtue of his female captives."[75]

Even so, the raids took a heavy toll. By the end of 1756, Indian raiders had killed more than one thousand colonial settlers and soldiers. One-third of the men in Virginia's army were lost during Washington's first eighteen months back in command. Refugees flooded into Winchester, where Washington tried to stem the tide, and the Pennsylvania frontier recoiled to Carlisle. Colonists abandoned more than nine hundred farms and evacuated a swath of territory from fifty to two hundred miles wide, almost thirty thousand square miles.[76]

Even some Christian Delawares, who had adopted the Moravian faith, joined the exodus after a war party attacked one of their mission villages. Pennsylvania, a colony once defined by peace, was transformed into a frontier war zone.[77] James Smith, who had been captured during Braddock's expedition, said the Indians boasted they had driven the English out of the mountains; laid waste much of the best land in Virginia, Maryland, and Pennsylvania; and hoped to push the Virginians back to the sea. "The white people appeared to them like fools," they said; "they could neither guard against surprise, run or fight."[78]

After Braddock's defeat, the main focus of the war, and of British regular forces, shifted to the North. Virginia was left to defend its own frontiers. Neither Virginia nor Pennsylvania was equipped to wage this kind of warfare. Unlike New England, where the colonists had experienced recurrent conflicts with the French and Indians, Virginia and Pennsylvania had enjoyed long years of peace. Neither had developed a tradition of militia defense. The militia had been Virginia's principal defense in the seventeenth century, but by the middle of the eighteenth century it had become more of a social institution. Washington in January 1757 described Virginia as "a Country young in War," which "Untill the breaking out of these Disturbances has Lived in the most profound, and Tranquil Peace; never studying War or Warfare. It is not therefore to be imagined She can fall into proper Measures at once."[79] In later years he recalled he could do no more than distribute troops along the frontiers in stockade forts, "more with a view to quiet the fears of the Inhabitants than from any expectation of giving security on so extensive a line to the settlements."[80]

In addition to death and misery, the raids created tensions and opened deep rifts within society. Most Virginians had little interest in Ohio lands and Ohio Company schemes, and they resented being called upon to supply men and money for a rich man's fight. Dinwiddie complained loudly about the spineless and parsimonious character of the populace, who neither rallied to defend the colony themselves nor voted sufficient money to keep the militia in good shape. "They seem to be seiz'd with a Panick at the approach of a few Fr. And Ind's," he told Lord Fairfax.[81] What was more, Dinwiddie had to keep part of his forces close to home to guard against unrest among African slaves, who had been "very audacious" since Braddock's defeat.[82] Backcountry folk who bore the burden of the raids resented eastern elites who were supposed to organize defense; backcountry elites clashed with colonial authorities in Williamsburg and

London. Gentlemen officers fumed about rank-and-file militiamen who were willing to defend their own homes against immediate threats but refused to serve for prolonged periods away from their fields and families. Farmers who had abandoned lands resented other farmers who coveted those lands. Divisions widened between Germans and Scotch-Irish on the frontier, and between pacifist Quakers and Presbyterians in Pennsylvania.[83] Faced with an unpopular war and wary of the threat of slave revolt, Virginia's political leaders tried conscription. In effect, this meant that the "better sort," who ran the colony, and the "middling sort," who usually served in the militia, left frontier defense to the "lesser sort," who were conscripted to fill the ranks of the Virginia Regiment. The poor resisted conscription and evaded draft laws, and those in the ranks gave halfhearted service and often deserted, compelling Virginia to abandon conscription and introduce an enlistment bounty in 1758.[84]

It is often said that the disaster on the Monongahela convinced Americans in general, and Washington in particular, to break with conventional British tactics and employ their own, American, way of war. Looking back on the battle several years after the Revolution, Washington wrote: "The folly & consequence of opposing compact bodies to the spare manner of Indian fighting, in woods, which had in a manner been predicted, was now so clearly verified that from hence forward another mode obtained in all future operations."[85] The French Troupes de la Marine serving in Indian country commonly modified their uniforms with Indian moccasins, leggings, and loincloths, and English colonial forces, too, had long included ranger units that incorporated Indians and Indian ways of fighting. Nevertheless, Braddock's defeat drove home the limitations of conventional modes of warfare in frontier fighting. When Major General James Abercromby arrived in America in the spring of 1756, Dinwiddie warned him that he was coming to a country covered with woods and inaccessible mountains where there was no place for conventional European ways of war. "The Indian Method is bush fighting and watching every Opp'ty to destroy their Enemys." However distasteful Abercromby might find Indian allies, they were "absolutely necessary to attack the Enemy's Indians in their way of fighting and scowering the Woods before an Army."[86] British commanders modified their tactics to help them win the war in America. Washington trained his men in Indian ways of warfare, and Dinwiddie ordered other officers to do the same.[87] However, it took time to retrain and reequip troops, and even as Washington came to recognize the effectiveness of the Indians' tactics, he despaired of being able to match them.[88]

Benjamin Franklin said Braddock's defeat and Dunbar's subsequent inaction showed Americans for the first time that the British regulars' reputation for military prowess was exaggerated.[89] In some accounts, Washington learned from the experience how to beat the British in the Revolution by having his men fight Indian fashion, shooting down ranks of redcoats from behind trees. Washington did apply elements of irregular warfare, but he remained committed to regular war waged by a regular army and did not abandon British methods. He trained his troops to fight from cover when necessary but continued to rely on regular soldiers and tried to build a conventional army. He did his best to emulate British standards of discipline: his complaints about the redcoats at the Monongahela focused on the breakdown of their discipline in the face of Indian assault, and he constantly complained about the lack of discipline in his own militia. For British and Americans alike, war in America involved "irregular," guerrilla warfare punctuated by "conventional" campaigns and battles. Rather than cause Washington to fight like an Indian, Braddock's defeat convinced him that effective campaign management, efficient transportation and supply systems, rigorous training, and strict discipline were fundamental to military success.[90]

In that area, Washington met recurrent frustrations. Men deserted; officers quarreled; supplies were embezzled. He complained about local militia and about backcountry settlers who subverted his authority, denied him appropriate deference, withheld provisions, undermined the discipline of his troops by peddling liquor, and fled at the first rumor of Indians.[91] The Virginia backcountry was a very different world from that of the Chesapeake tobacco planter. The Indian raids brought him face-to-face with the sufferings of people who frustrated and angered him, but defending those people, the historian Warren Hofstra suggests, also brought him "face to face with the essence of republican politics"—the need to promote the welfare and win the support of citizens he neither understood nor liked. "Mastering his revulsion for the people for the sake of the success he coveted would ultimately compel him to see himself as the virtuous leader who could place the public welfare before self-interest."[92]

That meant he must defend the public against its own fears and control the rumors that flew through the backcountry settlements, fabricating impending attacks, magnifying the size of war parties, and amplifying the psychological impact of actual raids. "The Inhabitants of Pennsylvania are more scared than hurt," wrote Adam Stephen. Washington sent out "advertisements," urging people not to be alarmed by "every false Report they may hear" and to stay at their homes and fields, which would soon be well guarded. But Washington was in Winchester, and backcountry families who lay between him and Shingas's warriors were not so easily convinced.[93] Washington expended energy raising and organizing troops, touring the several stations, and firing off orders that amounted to micromanaging. He imposed brutal discipline, sentencing men to floggings and hanging deserters. He struggled to bring the Virginia Regiment up to even half strength. Building the military forces necessary to withstand the Indian assaults was a slow and painful process. He trained his men in "the Indian Method of fighting," hoping they would be ready for action in the spring,[94] but Washington and his new regiment were no match for Shingas the Terrible.

CHAPTER 6

Frontier Defense and a Cherokee Alliance

THE SEVEN YEARS' WAR pitted Britain and France in a global conflict and dramatic battles on land and sea that ended in 1763 with France defeated on every front. For George Washington, however, it was a frontier war fought against Delawares and Shawnees and in collaboration with Cherokees and Catawbas. Between 1755 and 1758, a total of eight hundred Cherokees and more than two hundred Catawbas, Tuscaroras, Nottaways, and others came to Virginia's aid as allies. While the Virginians remained essentially on the defensive in their frontier forts, their Indian allies carried the war into Shawnee and Delaware country.[1] Washington recognized the vital importance of Indian allies, but, like most British and colonial officers, he experienced and expressed recurrent frustrations in dealing with them. Cherokees and Catawbas experienced their own frustrations in dealing with Washington and the British. The alliance was always precarious and often strained.

After his experiences with Braddock, and acutely aware of the inadequacies of his own forces, Washington knew he needed Indian allies to help defend Virginia's frontier. In September 1755 he invited Andrew Montour to join the regiment, promising that any Indians he brought with him would receive better treatment than they had in the past, and he instructed Adam Stephen to make sure Indians who came to Fort Cumberland were well treated. Three weeks later, hearing that Montour was heading for Venango with three hundred Indians, he wrote asking him to tell his Indian brothers that since Washington now held the chief command he was "invested with power to treat them as Brethren & Allies, which I am sorry to say they have not been of late." He also asked Montour to let Scarouady and other chiefs know that he was on the march against the French and their Indian allies and "how happy it would make Conotocaurious to have an Opportunity of taking them by the Hand at Fort Cumberland, & how glad he would be to treat them as Brothers of our great King beyond the Waters." He sent Christopher Gist to assist Montour in drumming up Indian support—"Never were Indians more wanted than at this time," he wrote. Unfortunately, Montour and Scarouady and the three hundred Indians did not make it to Fort Cumberland.[2]

Unable to recruit Indian allies in the Ohio country, Virginia looked to the South. The Cherokees had ostensibly made a treaty of alliance with Britain a quarter century before when Sir Alexander Cuming, posing as the Crown's emissary, orchestrated a visit to London by a delegation of Cherokee chiefs. One of them was a young man named Ouconecaw, who would later feature in the events of Washington's life as Attakullakulla or Little Carpenter. The 1730 Treaty of Westminster created a chain of friendship between the Cherokees and the king and included a provision that the Cherokees would fight the king's enemies.[3] Getting them to do so, however, required more than simply calling out the warriors. Rather than a commitment to fight someone else's wars, most Cherokees regarded the alliance as a partnership in which the British would uphold their end of the chain by providing trade and protection to Cherokee communities. As the trader James Adair noted, Cherokees regarded themselves as "freemen and equals," not as British subjects.[4]

Cherokees saw their alliance as with the king rather than his colonies, but relations with the British involved dealing with South Carolina and Virginia rather than directly with the king. The two colonies often diverged in their Indian policies, and the issue was complicated by a larger emerging debate about whether and when the empire or its colonies should conduct Indian affairs. When Lieutenant Governor Dinwiddie redoubled his efforts to recruit southern Indian allies for Virginia, he did so as much in competition as in collaboration with Governor Glen of South Carolina, who jealously guarded his colony's role in dealing with the Cherokees, promised to build Fort Prince George at Keowee in Lower Cherokee country, and promised improved trade terms to Cherokee people.[5]

For their part, the Cherokees would not, could not, respond as one to British appeals for help. Connected by a common language (although with several dialects), shared culture, and a kinship system of seven matrilineal clans, Cherokees lived in more than fifty towns scattered across the southern Appalachian Mountains and clustered in several separate regions, known as Overhill, Valley, Middle, and Lower. The Overhill Cherokees inhabited the Little Tennessee and Tellico Rivers in eastern Tennessee; the Valley towns occupied the Little Tennessee and Hiwassee Rivers in northern Georgia and southwestern South Carolina; the Middle towns were in western North Carolina, and the Lower Cherokees in South Carolina. Towns were politically independent, and regional clusters followed their own agendas rather than that of a Cherokee Nation as imagined by the British. Anglo-French conflict exacerbated regional divisions: Lower Cherokees tied to South Carolina by trade generally supported the British; Overhill Cherokees, especially the town of Tellico, more often leaned toward the French. Indian-Indian conflict complicated Cherokee decisions: Overhill Cherokees had connections with the Shawnees; Lower Cherokees who went north to help defend Virginia would have fewer or no qualms fighting against Shawnee enemies, but they would have concerns that their British allies were allied to their Iroquois enemies. Cherokees also worried that sending warriors away to fight would leave their homes vulnerable to assault from the north by Indian raiders or from the south by the Creeks, with whom they had recently ended forty years of intermittent conflict.[6] Many Catawbas and Cherokees saw a campaign with the British as an opportunity to resume age-old fighting against Mingoes and Shawnees rather than to serve the empire.

Dinwiddie held a council with the Cherokees at the governor's house in Williamsburg in September 1755 and sent William Byrd III and Peter Randolph to make a treaty with the Cherokees and Catawbas in February and March and solicit their assistance come spring.[7] The Cherokees sent 130 warriors. When Dinwiddie heard they proposed attacking the Shawnee town on the Scioto River, he ordered Washington in December 1755 to send rangers and other troops to join them. Washington delayed until his regiment was activated in January and remained skeptical, but Dinwiddie continued to pressure him. So Washington ordered Major Andrew Lewis and some 350 men, including a hundred Cherokees led by Ostenaco, to attack the Shawnee towns on the Ohio and Scioto River. Ostenaco, also known as Judd's Friend, was often called by his title Outacite (Mankiller), signifying head warrior (see plate 2). Lewis set out along Sandy Creek, a tributary of the Ohio in what is now West Virginia, in February 1756. The campaign was a debacle. After six weeks of suffering and starvation, their progress halted by flooded rivers, Lewis abandoned the attempt. Washington was not surprised, and reminded Dinwiddie he had often expressed his "uneasy apprehensions on that head." Lewis and his men came home "having done nothing essential," Dinwiddie told Washington. "I believe they did not know the Way to the Shawnesse Towns." Lewis would get another crack at the Shawnee towns on the Kanawha River—but not until eighteen years later.[8]

While Lewis and his men floundered toward the Shawnee villages, Washington left his troops and the Virginia frontier and traveled to Boston. Governor William Shirley of Massachusetts became commander in chief of the British forces in North America on Braddock's death, and Washington went to solicit him in person for a regular officer's commission. He was not successful, but he stopped off in Philadelphia and New York for some shopping, socializing, and card playing.[9]

By the time he was back in the spring, Indians were raiding in greater numbers than ever. They had killed several people not far from Winchester and boldly attacked forts in broad daylight. Despite Washington's efforts to calm the inhabitants, he could not prevent them abandoning their homes and taking flight. His little army could do little to help. "I *see* their situation, *know* their danger, and participate [in] their *Sufferings*; without having it in my power to give them further relief, than uncertain promises," he told Dinwiddie. By the end of April, the Indians had pushed Virginia's frontier back to the Blue Ridge Mountains.[10] In May, Washington started building a fort—called Fort Loudon—on the high ground just north of Winchester. He designed the log-palisaded fort and complained about the slow progress of construction that dragged on for more than two years and was never completely finished. He originally planned for a garrison of one hundred men, but the number fluctuated. The fort served as a deterrent for Indian attacks on the town. It also operated, like Fort Duquesne, as a base for Indian allies raiding the enemy frontier, although the absence of clear Native American archaeological evidence at the fort suggests their presence was temporary.[11]

Washington desperately needed reinforcements and resources, but more than anything he needed Indian allies. "Five hundred Indians have it more in their power to annoy the Inhabitants than ten times their number of Regulars," he wrote. "For, besides the advantageous way they have of fighting in the Woods, their cunning and craft are not to be equaled; neither [are] their activity and indefatigable Sufferings. They prowl about like Wolves and, like them, do their mischief by Stealth. They depend upon their dexterity in

hunting, and upon the Cattle of the Inhabitants for provisions."
Virginia would never be able to defend its frontiers unless it had
Indian allies. "Indians are the only match for Indians; and without
these we shall ever fight upon unequal Terms." In short, "without
Indians to oppose Indians, we may expect but small success."[12]

Dinwiddie was doing his best to provide them, but the Lower,
Middle, and Overhill towns were pursuing their own agendas, not
Virginia's. The Cherokees were allies who had to be courted and cultivated, different chiefs took different positions, and they were adept
at playing European rivals to their own advantage. Lower Cherokees
had long-standing relations with South Carolina. Overhill chiefs negotiated to secure better trading terms and have Virginia build a fort
that would provide protection to their women and children. They also
negotiated with the French on the western edge of their country,
where the governor of Louisiana, Louis Billouart, chevalier de
Kerlerec, planned to build a fort at the mouth of the Tennessee River.
Overhill chiefs sought the same trade and the same assurances of
security from the French that their British allies promised but failed to
deliver with consistency. They made a preliminary treaty of peace and
alliance with Kerlerec in December 1756. Two months later the ubiquitous Silver Heels brought William Johnson news that ten Cherokees
had visited Fort Duquesne and that many more looked likely to join
the French.[13] Cherokees also weighed fears of French retaliation and
the arguments of Shawnee emissaries who came to their towns urging
them to side with the French. Whereas most British officers and officials viewed Cherokee alliance with the French as treachery, Henry
Timberlake, a British officer who served with Washington and later as
a peace emissary to the Cherokees, recognized it as a masterstroke of
policy, equal to those executed by European minsters.[14]

In recognition of Ostenaco's assistance in Lewis's abortive campaign, Dinwiddie invited him to Williamsburg. On his way to and
from the capital the chief stayed with the family of young Thomas
Jefferson. When he arrived he rode down Duke of Gloucester Street
in the governor's coach between lines of militia forming an honor
guard. Dinwiddie promised Ostenaco and Attakullakulla that in
return for sending warriors to come to Virginia's defense he would
provide guns, ammunition, clothing, and supplies and build a fort in
Overhill Cherokee country.[15] He sent Lewis to build the fort—also
called Fort Loudon—across the river from the town of Chota, on the
north side of the Little Tennessee, and recruit warriors.[16]

Ostenaco said he was ready to go to war and eager to see Colonel
Washington. Both Attakullakulla and Hagler, chief of the Catawbas,

said they picked up the war hatchet when they received Dinwiddie's messages but were waiting for the supplies he had promised, which would confirm that Virginia was committed to the alliance. Ostenaco maintained that he needed to be sure his own people were safe before he headed north; Dinwiddie assured him he would send soldiers to garrison the fort and protect his women and children. William Henry Lyttelton, who replaced Glen as governor of South Carolina, reminded Ostenaco of his many promises to take up the hatchet against the king's enemies, and urged him to go to war now with as many warriors as possible.[17] Glen had thought Attakullakulla was a troublemaker in cahoots with the French. Attakullakulla had spent time as a captive of French-allied Indians, and as an Overhill chief he may have had pro-French leanings. But Captain Raymond Demere at Fort Loudon assured Lyttelton that "Little Carpenter is a very sensible Fellow and has a great deal of Influence over the Indians" and was thought to be "a Welwisher to the English."[18] Indeed, having been there in his youth, Attakullakulla made it known that he wanted to visit England again.[19] Colonial officials saw such a trip as expensive, inconvenient, and going over their heads; Attakullakulla likely saw it as a "state visit" to restore the chain of friendship with the king agreed upon in 1730.

Cherokee warriors trickled northward in bands ranging from a dozen to sixty during the spring of 1756, as did some Nottaways and Catawbas. Washington waited anxiously for them to arrive at Winchester and became more anxious once they had arrived.[20] Virginia had no Indian allies except those coming from the south, and he knew how much depended on them. Their assistance was vital, but "One *false* step might not only lose us that, but even turn them against us," he wrote Dinwiddie. He regarded Indians as a dilatory and mercenary lot who expected to be well rewarded "for the least service" and required careful handling.[21] To prevent trouble with the locals he dispatched a sergeant and drummer to beat through the town ordering the soldiers and townspeople "to use the Indians civilly and kindly; to avoid giving them liquor; and to be cautious when they speak before them: as all of them understand English and ought not to be affronted."[22] In the words of his biographer Douglas Southall Freeman, "Washington was almost as uneasy when he had Indian warriors as when he lacked them."[23]

Virginia was short on Indian trade goods and short on competence in Indian diplomacy, as Washington's own recruiting efforts demonstrated. In August 1756 he sent Nottoway messengers to the Tuscaroras to deliver a wampum belt and a speech. Invoking "that chain of Friendship, which has subsisted between us for so many ages past," he asked them to take up the hatchet for their English friends. His ignorance of history could hardly have helped his cause. The "Tusks," as Washington called them, would have remembered what he either forgot or never knew—that most of their nation had migrated north thirty-four years before to join the Iroquois League after the English had driven them out of their North Carolina home-lands. Nevertheless, somewhat surprisingly, thirty-three Tuscaroras "heartily accepted the Invitation." On their way north the following spring, along with thirteen Nottaways, seven Meherrins, and a couple of Saponis, they stopped off at Williamsburg to request arms, ammunition, clothing, and paint. They showed the letter Washington had sent them "and said what the Colonel had writ was very agreeable to them."[24]

Although some Tuscaroras, Nottaways, and Saponis turned out, Cherokees and Catawbas provided most assistance. Washington and Dinwiddie often complained they did not come in the numbers promised and hoped for, and worried that French hands were at work, but many parties made the five-hundred-mile journey to Winchester.[25] Many more Cherokees operated in the Mississippi and Ohio Valleys. When they finally committed to the British, Attakullakulla and many Overhill Cherokees preferred to canoe down the Tennessee and raid French bateaux on the Ohio and Mississippi or the new French fort at Massac, defending their own western frontier rather than trekking north to defend Virginia's frontier.[26] Indian allies intercepted enemy raiding parties, raided French posts, took prisoners for questioning, brought intelligence on enemy movements, acted as mediators with other tribes, and intimidated the French and *their* Indian allies. They inflicted casualties on the Shawnees and Delawares, taking the sting out of their incursions.

Washington and Dinwiddie complained long and loud about the havoc visited on innocent frontier families by Indian scalping parties in the pay of the French, but they sent their own Indian allies out in scalping parties. Virginia offered £10 for Indian scalps, which meant a bounty hunter could earn with one killing what it would take him three months to earn as a laborer. In October 1755, at Dinwiddie's request, the Assembly extended the payment of scalp bounties to "our friendly Indians." Dinwiddie and Washington told their allies they would receive the reward for every scalp or prisoner they brought in. Knowing this "barbarous Method of conducting war" would not sit well with his superiors in London, Dinwiddie blamed the French for introducing it, which left Virginia no choice but to follow suit in self-defense.[27] Washington was not averse to paying scalp bounties. Indeed, he urged Dinwiddie to pay a bonus to Virginian troops who brought in the scalp of a French ensign named Douville; although it was not an Indian's, they deserved a reward because it was "of much more consequence."[28] The House of Burgesses increased the bounty paid on Indian scalps to £15 in 1757, but, fearing that scalp bounties led to indiscriminate killing of any Indians, which only drove more Indians to join enemy war parties, Lieutenant Governor Francis Fauquier repealed the bounty law the following year.[29]

Pennsylvania abandoned its long tradition of pacifism in the spring of 1756. Deputy Governor Hamilton declared war against the Delawares and their allies first in the Indian manner, presenting Scarouady and Andrew Montour with a war belt and hatchet to send to the Susquehanna tribes and the Six Nations, and then with a formal proclamation. Pennsylvania put militia into the field and offered scalp bounties in Spanish dollars or pieces of eight: $130 for the scalp of every adult male over twelve years old, $50 for every adult female scalp, and $700 for Shingas the Terrible's scalp. Pennsylvania offered significantly more ($130) for the capture than the scalp of an Indian woman, but no Indian women were reported captured during the war. Few bounties were paid out, but everyone understood that bringing in a scalp was much less troublesome than bringing in a prisoner.[30]

Washington disagreed with Dinwiddie and the government in Williamsburg about how the war was being run, and he made his feelings known in his letters to them. He denounced "Chimney Corner Politicians" for meddling in military matters that should be left to soldiers. He did not have enough troops, enough supplies and equipment, or enough Indian allies. And the Assembly's strategy of trying to protect the frontier inhabitants by a line of forts was not working. Instead of relying on forts purely for defense, Washington favored using them as bases for dispatching ranger companies and allied Indians against the enemy. He repeatedly argued that Fort Cumberland was unsuitable for defense and unfit for a fortification. The precipitous flight of colonial settlers left the fort exposed as the tide receded, and it was more of a liability to the English than an obstacle to Indian raiding parties, who slipped past it with ease. It should be used for launching offensive operations, or it should be abandoned. Washington advocated building a strong fort at Winchester, which he was doing. Dinwiddie, in failing health, took umbrage at Washington's constant complaints and his whining and petulant tone. Their correspondence became increasingly testy.[31]

Despite the failure of the Sandy Creek campaign against the Shawnees, taking the war to the Indians as Washington recommended did have some impact. In a surprise attack in September 1756, Colonel John Armstrong and three hundred Pennsylvania troops destroyed part of the Delaware town at Upper Kittanning on the Allegheny River. It was hardly a victory: they killed the Delaware war chief Tewea, known to the English as Captain Jacobs, along with his wife and son, but suffered more casualties than they inflicted and rescued only seven of the more than one hundred captives held there.[32] Nevertheless, it demonstrated that Indian settlements west of the Allegheny Mountains, like white settlements east of the mountains, were vulnerable. To escape the expanding war zone, Delawares moved up Beaver Creek to Kuskuski and, with the consent of the Wyandots, settled on the headwaters of the Muskingum and Cayuhoga Rivers and other locations in eastern Ohio. Kuskuski became a cluster of four or five Delaware towns, known as the Kuskuskies, and the political center of the Delawares in the West.[33]

Washington insisted the only way to end Indian raids was to stamp them out at their source. He wanted to strike Fort Duquesne, that "Hold of Barbarians," and he wanted to lead the expedition. Dinwiddie answered that it was not in his power to order an evacuation of Fort Cumberland; John Campbell, Earl of Loudon (after whom the forts were named), was coming to replace Shirley as commander in chief and would decide. Instead, the governor and council responded to Washington's barrage of complaints by strengthening Fort Cumberland with men from the garrison at Winchester and ordering Washington to get himself to Fort Cumberland and establish his headquarters on the front line, not in the comparative safety of Winchester.[34] Washington went behind Dinwiddie's back and over his head. He complained to the Speaker of the House of Burgesses, and he sent the Earl of Loudon a lengthy epistle containing "a Concise, Candid, and Submissive Account of Affairs on the Quarter," in other words a list of complaints. Depending on a chain of forts allowed the Indians to range almost at will across Virginia's frontier, "while we, by our Defensive Schemes and Pusillanimous Behaviour exhaust our Treasury; reduce our Strength and become the Contempt and Derision of these Savage Nations, who are enriching themselves in the meantime with the plunder, and Spoil of our People."[35]

In February 1757 he traveled to Philadelphia to see Loudon in person. Loudon kept him waiting for two weeks—Washington passed the time gambling, shopping, and attending dances—and then gave him short shrift and his orders. There would be no campaign against

Fort Duquesne that year, and Fort Cumberland was to be strengthened and reinforced from Maryland.[36] Loudon's snub aggravated Washington's discontent. He chafed at garrison duty on a frontier far from the centers of power and society in Virginia. Posted "for twenty Months past upon our cold and Barren Frontiers," he felt he had been assigned an impossible task with an inadequate force. Worse, he felt like an exile, "Seldom informd of those oppertunitys which I might otherwise embrace of corrisponding with my friends."[37]

He fell out with Dinwiddie over the conduct of Indian affairs. Like other British and colonial officers, Washington thought Indian allies were unreliable, mercenary, and fickle, and did not trust them. Feeding and supplying them placed a constant strain on the alliance. "The Indians are all around, teasing and perplexing me for one thing and another, so that I scarce know what I write," he told Dinwiddie in April 1757.[38] He complained endlessly about the Cherokees' cost and effectiveness. They watched which way the wind was blowing, sold their services to the highest bidder, and switched sides as it suited them. He assumed that if Indians did not rally to the English cause it was because they were being seduced by the French, and he said as much to the Cherokees.[39] His appreciation of their importance as allies was not matched by an appreciation that they served on their terms, not his, in accordance with their own customs, and for their own reasons.

The Indians' objectives and strategy were consistent. They fought to preserve their independence and security, and they selected their allies and enemies accordingly—just as Washington would do when he allied with former French enemies and fought against former British comrades to win his fight for independence. The Indians expected to be paid for their services and had every reason to expect their British allies would give them gifts. Gift-giving was part of an established pattern of cultural exchange in the Southeast, and the British employed it for decades to lubricate the wheels of diplomacy and to encourage or reward military service. Allies who gave gifts unstintingly demonstrated their power, reliability, and friendship; withholding or giving gifts reluctantly signaled wavering commitment and diminishing strength. Both sides recognized the importance of gifts, but they differed over the "rules of the game" and the obligations gifts created. The British expected that Indians who accepted British gifts should do as the British ordered; the Cherokees accepted the gifts but refused to accept that in doing so they put themselves under British command and control. The British expected the Cherokees to be grateful and act as subordinates; instead they found them demanding and independent. The Cherokees expected the British to be generous and to act like brothers; instead they found them miserly and domineering. Cherokees who were serving on the Virginia frontier were not hunting to feed their families. They expected their allies to outfit them while they were on campaign, to supply and support their families while they were away, and to provide goods to take home, and they became disgruntled by recurrent delays in providing gifts. Cherokees at home expected Lewis's fort on the Little Tennessee to bring direct trade with Virginia but waited in disappointment.[40] Washington distrusted the Indians as mercenary and evidently expected them, unlike his militia or himself, to serve without pay. Indians had little compunction about getting all they could from allies whom *they* did not trust.

Dinwiddie had promised to supply the Cherokees with everything they needed, and he bombarded the Virginia Assembly with requests for presents for Indians defending the frontier.[41] But when Wawhatchee, the head warrior of Keowee, and 148 other Lower Town Cherokees arrived at Fort Loudon with Andrew Lewis in April 1757, there were no goods for them. "I am sure King George does not know now how we are treated," Wawhatchee complained to King George's officers. Captain George Mercer's feeble apology and promise to do better when they returned did little to appease Wawhatchee. He refused to accept the wampum belt Mercer offered him at the end of his speech and stormed out of the council. Cherokees put little stock in Mercer's promise, claiming that whereas the French always gave them what they wanted, "they found from every Action, the Great Men of Virginia were Liars." Mercer implored Washington to do everything he could to push the issue with the government, knowing the Indians would abandon them if they were not properly rewarded.[42] The promised gifts had still not arrived a month later when Wawhatchee and a war party brought in four scalps and two prisoners, and the Indians made their feelings clear. Washington made his feelings about them clear to Dinwiddie; they were, he fumed, "the most insolent, most avaricious, and most dissatisfied wretches I have ever had to deal with." Dinwiddie shared his opinion.[43] But Captain Abraham Bosomworth of the 60th (Royal American) Regiment, who had an Indian wife and served as an agent to the Cherokees, cautioned that Wawhatchee was "a very leading Man in the Nation therefor we must take the greatest Care of him."[44]

In invoking French generosity, Wawhatchee employed a well-worn strategy that played on British anxieties. Still, the French, too, were short of supplies and had the same anxieties. They outmatched the English in their appreciation of the role of gifts in sustaining Indian allegiance, but often lagged behind the English in the quality and quantity of goods they produced. They complained just as much about their dependence on Indian allies and the effort and expense the alliance required. "One is a slave to Indians in this country. They are a necessary evil," General Montcalm's aide Louis Antoine de Bougainville lamented in his journal. The French could no more do without Indians in the woods of America than they could "without cavalry in open country." As independent allies, Indians expected to be consulted and rewarded. At the siege of Fort William Henry in 1757, Montcalm explained the surrender terms to his Indian allies before he signed them but *after* he had negotiated them. The Indians did not feel bound by the terms he had agreed upon. Having given up a season's hunting to serve with his army, they did feel entitled to plunder, captives, and scalps, which they acquired by assaulting the British garrison.[45] Frenchmen were no surer of their Indian allies than Englishmen were of theirs.

Washington and Croghan attended the interrogation of a captive French ensign in June 1757 who indicated that the French were now recruiting allies from the Great Lakes tribes to carry out raids on the frontiers because Ohio Indians were leaning toward neutrality. Indians from the Great Lakes region had been in the Ohio country for decades and had contributed the majority of the warriors who defeated Braddock. Nevertheless, Governor Vaudreuil worried that the Indians on "the Beautiful River" were receptive to English peace overtures.[46]

Like Bougainville, Washington simultaneously recognized and resented his dependence on Indian allies. Unable to give them what they had been promised, he feared losing them altogether. Many Indians left for home when Virginia failed to live up to its side of the bargain. Their options increasingly constrained by an encroaching colonial world, the Catawbas viewed the war as an opportunity to obtain food, clothing, ammunition, and other goods in return for their service as allies.[47] Virginia valued their service but was slow to reward it. When the council heard that Hagler and two chiefs had arrived near Williamsburg in March 1757, it dispatched someone to meet them in a coach and escort them to the capitol, where Hagler was introduced to the council chamber, along with twenty-six other Catawbas who had arrived earlier. Hagler said he had left eighty or ninety warriors on the frontier and had come "to learn if you have anything to propose for our mutual Good." What he really wanted was guns "and everything necessary for war," which Virginia promised to deliver as soon as possible.[48] If the Catawbas thought they got too little for their services, Washington thought they got too much. "The Catawbas have been of little use, but a great expense to this Colony; and are now gone home," he wrote General John Stanwix in May. "The Cherokees I apprehend will follow their example."[49]

Things hardly improved after the British government reorganized the conduct of Indian affairs. In 1755 Edmond Atkin, a thirty-eight-year-old South Carolina merchant living in England at the time, submitted to the Board of Trade a lengthy report on the management of Indian affairs, which, he said, "was on a wretched footing throughout all America." "No people in the world understand and pursue their true National Interest, better than the Indians," he explained. With France competing for their allegiance, there could be no doubt that the prosperity of Britain's North American colonies depended on good relations with the tribes. Atkin recommended centralizing the management of Indian affairs by creating two regional superintendencies. The board agreed. Sir William Johnson was appointed superintendent in the North, and in 1756 Atkin himself was appointed superintendent in the South.[50] The new superintendent assumed jurisdiction over the conduct of Virginia's Indian relations. "You are no longer to have concern with, or management of, Indian affairs," Dinwiddie wrote Washington peremptorily in May 1757. Atkin was on his way to Winchester to take over "that extraordinary Service," and if he had to leave before the Indians returned home, he would appoint a deputy to do business in his absence.[51]

Atkin's appointment only increased Washington's frustrations with the mishandling of Indian allies, and perhaps provided a target to divert criticisms of his own handling of the situation. Washington agreed that Indian affairs should be consolidated in the hands of one person—too many people making multiple promises and no one delivering on them caused endless confusion, and Indians viewed it as perfidious and deceitful—but he didn't think Atkin, a merchant rather than a military man and someone known for his arrogance, was the right person. The new superintendent was so slow getting to Fort Loudon that Washington urged Dinwiddie either to have him get a move on or to give orders for distributing the Indians' presents. "An Indian will never forget a promise made to him," Washington lectured his governor; "nothing ought ever to be *promised* but what is *performed*; and one *only* person be empowered to do *either*." In Washington's opinion Christopher Gist, who had shown him the ropes on his first mission to the Ohio country and pulled him out of the freezing Allegheny River, was the man for the job, even if under Atkin's direction. Gist had little grasp of Indian languages, but he was well acquainted with the manners and customs of the southern Indians, and Washington could vouch for his honesty and zeal.[52] Robert Hunter Morris agreed that Gist knew more than anyone else in Pennsylvania about Indians and Indian country.[53] Dinwiddie's response, perhaps understandably, was cool. Too many officers had made promises they were not authorized to make and had given in to the Cherokees' "clamorous, avaritious Demands." He hoped Atkin would calm things down. Atkin duly appointed Gist as his deputy.[54]

Atkin finally arrived in Winchester on June 3. "A person with a readier pen and having more time than myself, might amuse you with the vicissitudes which have happened in Indian affairs since Mr. Atkin came up," Washington informed Speaker Robinson a week later; "the Indians have been pleased and displeased oftener than they ought to have been." Wawhatchee's Cherokees had "gone off."[55]

Other Cherokees, however, stayed, and more arrived. In June 1757 a party of Virginians and Cherokees ambushed a group of French soldiers. A chief named Swallow Warrior was shot in the head. The Cherokees were so incensed at his death that they killed the two Frenchmen they had taken prisoner.[56] Later that month, Ostenaco arrived with twenty-seven warriors, and more were said to be on the way, to act as "a great Scourge to the prowling Enemy." Although Ostenaco fell ill with fever, his warriors scouted toward Fort Duquesne, gathering intelligence of enemy movements.[57]

Keeping the Cherokees with him was vital, but Washington felt hampered in his efforts to do so, and he let Dinwiddie know it. Indian affairs at Winchester, he wrote, had been impeded by "a train of mismanagement," which, if it continued, "must inevitably produce the most melancholy consequences." In the fall, Atkin departed to attend to Indian affairs in South Carolina, taking Gist and the Indian interpreter with him. In their absence, Washington had to deal with the Indians, but he had no interpreter, no right to hold conferences with them, nothing to give them, and no authority to procure goods for them. Such neglect could drive them into the welcoming arms of the French. The Cherokees, whom he had repeatedly lambasted as mercenary and fickle, were now brave allies who had heartily embraced Virginia's cause and deserved better treatment. Had Washington and his officers not *"strained a point"* to get them things they desperately needed and made extra efforts to keep them contented, the Cherokees would have gone home empty-handed and resentful. Whenever a party arrived, they immediately asked Washington for supplies, which he could not provide, and there was no one to explain the situation to them. Washington was reduced "to such a dilemma as I wou'd most gladly be extricated from." The way things were going, he warned Dinwiddie, "Our Interest with those Indians is at the brink of destruction."[58]

Dinwiddie expressed surprise at Washington's complaints. Atkin had assured him he had put Indian affairs in good order and he had left almost £800 in goods for Indians. Dinwiddie would send more, but presents must be handed out with discretion, he told Washington; Gist had submitted a "monstrous" expense account.[59] Dinwiddie also took exception to Washington's absences on private business while he was supposed to be commanding the defense of the frontier. Washington was back in Williamsburg for the winter because of ill health. (Dr. James Craik, the army physician, recommended the change for the dysentery that still plagued him.[60]) When John Blair (who took over as interim lieutenant governor between Dinwiddie and Francis Fauquier) informed him that seven or eight hundred Indians were on their way to Winchester, Washington replied defensively and sulkily. Despite his poor health, he would go there immediately if he thought it would make a difference. However, as he was not entrusted to manage Indian affairs, other than to direct their raids (and even those were "governed by caprice & whim rather than by real design"), and as there were no arms or supplies to give the Indians when they arrived, he did not see how his being there would help the situation. All that would happen if he were on the spot was that the Indians would blame him, as the commanding officer, for all their disappointments.[61]

Washington was on the defensive in more ways than one. Turning the Virginia Regiment from a collection of volunteers into a professional military force was a significant achievement and a milestone in Washington's maturation as a military leader.[62] Nevertheless, his soldiers were still and always outmatched. "No troops in the universe can guard against the cunning and wiles of Indians," Washington told Speaker Robinson. "No one can tell where they will fall, 'till the mischief is done, and then 'tis vain to pursue. The inhabitants see, and are convinced of this; which makes each family afraid of standing in the gap of danger, and by retreating one behind another, they depopulate the country, and leave it to the Enemy, who subsist upon the plunder."[63] The Indians' tactics were working; Virginia's tactics were not. "I am, and have for a long time been, fully convinced, that if we continue to pursue a defensive plan, that the country must be inevitably lost," he lobbied General Stanwix. The only way to stop the

Indian raids was to snuff them out at the source: Fort Duquesne. Otherwise, so long as the French had the Indians at their command, "what have we to expect by leaving it in Our Rear but absolute Destruction[?]"[64]

Unstated but clearly implied was that Washington could lead a successful campaign against Fort Duquesne.

INSTEAD, THE ASSIGNMENT WENT TO fifty-one-year-old John Forbes, a Scottish officer with almost thirty years of military service and campaign experience in both Europe and North America. In the summer of 1757 the brilliant and temperamental William Pitt, 1st Earl of Chatham, formed a new ministry in London. As secretary of state with responsibility for colonial affairs and international diplomacy, Pitt controlled the conduct of the war. He promptly rebooted Britain's global war effort, with a renewed focus on winning it in North America. Parliament would vote huge subsidies to European allies who would keep French armies bogged down on Continental battlefields; the Royal Navy would sweep French fleets from the seas, destroying their supply lines to America; and reinforcements of British regulars (almost twenty thousand of them, including nine new regiments raised in the Scottish Highlands[65]) would join colonial forces in defeating the French in North America. Loudon was recalled. Forbes was appointed brigadier general to command the expedition against Fort Duquesne, while other armies invaded Canada from Lake Champlain and the St. Lawrence. Forbes appointed an experienced Swiss officer, Colonel Henry Bouquet, as his second-in-command. In almost constant discomfort and pain from the illness that would kill him—possibly stomach cancer—Forbes focused his attention on Philadelphia as his headquarters for supplying the expedition. Bouquet functioned as his operational or tactical commander at the head of the column. It proved an effective partnership.[66]

With Pitt devoting more men, money, and resources to the war in America and footing the bill for recruitment, the Virginia Assembly abandoned conscription and relied instead on a generous enlistment bounty of £10—as much cash as many small planters could bring in during a year—to attract volunteers to the ranks. It also voted to raise a second Virginia regiment and made fifty-year-old William Byrd III its commander, serving under Washington. By June 1758 both Virginia regiments stood at full strength with a thousand men. Virginia never returned to conscription.[67] Much to Washington's satisfaction, Pitt also did away with the regulation that gave regular officers of any rank seniority over provincial officers of every rank; now provincial officers would be junior only to regular officers of equal or superior rank.[68]

Hearing a new expedition was about to be mounted against Fort Duquesne, Washington hurried to get in on the action. He left Williamsburg in late March to resume active command of the Virginia Regiment at Fort Loudon. Then he asked General Stanwix to recommend him to Forbes, "not as a person who would depend upon him for further recommendation to military preferment, for I have long conquered all such expectancies . . . but as a person who would gladly be distinguished in some measure from the *common run* of provincial officers."[69] Forbes began planning his campaign in the spring. His regular and provincial troops and Indian allies were to rendezvous at Winchester.

Before William Byrd III was appointed commander of the 2nd Virginia Regiment, the Earl of Loudon had dispatched him to recruit Cherokees for Forbes's campaign. Byrd spent the spring in Cherokee country but struggled to raise more than a handful. Attakullakulla refused to be rushed, held out for assurances of better trade and more goods than he could get from the French at Fort Massac, and promised to bring more warriors later. Frustrated and "haunted by the Indians" at the Lower Cherokee town of Keowee, Byrd complained to Forbes, "The Squaws are the only good things to be met with here." Like his father, he evidently missed few opportunities for female companionship. In the end, he was able to bring no more than sixty men because some decided to go to Virginia with the Overhill Cherokees at the last minute. "This change proceeds from a Dream," Byrd reported to Forbes, with a sigh. In fact, groups of Cherokees had been setting out since early in the year. Some had gone down the Tennessee River, ostensibly to raid French positions, and many had already joined Forbes.[70]

Forbes feared an Indian attack on his army more than anything else. "Wee are like people in the Dark, perhaps going head long to Destruction," he confided to Colonel Bouquet. Indian allies were his best source of intelligence and best protection against surprise attack.[71] He knew that failure to supply them as promised risked losing them. By late April 1758, 652 Indians—604 Cherokees and 48 Catawbas—had arrived at Winchester, and more were on the way. They had come according to their own seasonal schedule for making war but too early for Forbes's purposes. He was still working on the logistics of supply and had yet to assemble his army. "In short," he wrote Loudon in April, "necessity will turn me into a Cherokee, and don't be surprised if I take F: duQuesne at the head of them, and them only." Indians could be extremely useful if properly looked after, he told General Abercromby, but they were "in want of everything." The Cherokees were so important that he did everything in his power to make sure they had what they needed.[72]

That meant distributing gifts when Indians arrived and when they met in council, outfitting scouts and war parties, provisioning warriors who were far from home, and rewarding them for their services when they returned home. His quartermaster, the still-fractious Sir John St. Clair, who was appointed to the expedition because of his experience in that role crossing the Alleghenies with Braddock, proved barely competent but worked to keep the supplies coming.[73] He and Captain Bosomworth purchased goods from Philadelphia merchants and took measures to prevent trouble, keeping the Indian camp separate, off-limits for soldiers, and alcohol-free.[74] Throughout the spring and summer of 1758, Forbes's Cherokee and Catawba allies received prodigious quantities of merchandise: guns, gunpowder, powder horns, lead, thousands of flints, knives, pipes, kettles, hundreds of shirts, match coats, cloth, blankets, hats, ribbon, shoes, deerskins for making moccasins, scissors, razors, awls, wire, garters, thousands and thousands of wampum beads, tomahawks, gorgets, silver broaches, armbands, vermilion, sugar, and tobacco, as well as rations of food and drink.[75] The effort and expense of keeping the Indians supplied was never enough to keep them fully satisfied or keep them all with the army, but it demonstrated the importance Forbes attached to Indian allies in the success of his campaign.

Washington shared Forbes's appreciation of the need "to please the Indians, who are our steady friends, and valuable allies," as he wrote Forbes. That required, the Indians told him and he told Forbes, "an early Campaigne, and plenty of Goods." Indians came to Fort Loudon almost daily, and many went out in war parties. As usual, Washington lacked arms and clothing to give them. In letters to General Stanwix, Forbes, and Quartermaster St. Clair, he returned to a familiar refrain: Indians were mercenary, expected to be paid for everything they did, and were "easily offended, being thoroughly sensible of their own importance." They seemed to be in high spirits about the upcoming campaign against Fort Duquesne, but he had seen Indian support evaporate before and was eager to get the campaign under way soon, "for on the assistance of these people, does the security of our march, very much depend." No matter how well they were treated or what assurances their chiefs gave, many of the warriors would return home if the troops took a long time to assemble, Washington warned; it was just their nature.[76] He might have added that the Indians wanted to be sure of their allies before they risked their lives fighting alongside them and preferred to hunt and protect their families than to sit on their hands far from home.

In late April, Washington joined Bosomworth, Gist, and other officers in a council with the Cherokees and Catawbas at Fort Loudon. Talking up the justness of the war, the power of Forbes's army, and the strength of the Anglo-Indian alliance, Bosomworth called on "that great Warrior (Colo. Washington)" to witness the mutual promises made. The Cherokees in their response repeated the description of Washington as "that great Warrior."[77]

The great warrior was barely holding his own. The same month, a young warrior called Ucahula and two other Cherokees descended the Monongahela by canoe and landed on the north bank, not far from Fort Duquesne. They lay concealed for two days, lifted a couple of French scalps, and brought back information that the fort was strong on the landward side but protected only by a stockade on the river side. It did not appear to be strongly garrisoned. On the return journey Ucahula came across signs of Indian war parties heading against the Virginia frontier. Washington dispatched a detachment of troops and Indians to try to intercept them but was too late to prevent them falling on the back settlements of Augusta County, where they killed nearly fifty people.[78]

Another Indian foray caused considerable consternation. After the Raven Warrior of Hiwassee, a Cherokee war chief, returned from leading an unsuccessful scouting party and produced two white men's scalps, it turned out he had brought them with him when he came from Cherokee country. Detected in his deceit, which offended his own warriors, the Raven promptly took off for home with thirty followers, calling the English "Cowards and Liars" who had promised a large army and not delivered. When Forbes heard of the Raven's defection, he had his brigade major Francis Halkett (who had served with Braddock when his father and brother were killed) write to Washington, stressing in the strongest terms that everybody under his command should pay the utmost attention to keeping the Indians in a good disposition, and that he must do all he could to bring back the Raven, as well as the other Indians who had left. Forbes did not need disgruntled Cherokees jeopardizing peace talks with the Shawnees and Delawares. Washington must keep them busy by sending them out on scouting parties and send any information he got from prisoners directly to Forbes.[79]

The implied reprimand struck a nerve. Washington fired off two letters—to Halkett and to John St. Clair—on the same day, May 11.

Contrary to what Forbes might have heard, the Catawbas had not brought in a single prisoner or scalp this year, he told Halkett. Only Ucahula had brought in scalps this season. Washington had sent Forbes a full account by the last post of the intelligence Ucahula brought, and he would "have kept him duly informed of every interesting occurrence, even had it not been recommended to me." Washington and Gist had done all they could to prevent Cherokees from wandering off toward Maryland and Pennsylvania, "clearly foreseeing the bad consequences such a peregrination would produce," but those two colonies had "very impolitically" given the Indians presents the year before and encouraged them to return this spring. Then back to an ongoing sore point: "I and my officers constantly have and always will pay the strictest regard to every circumstance that may contribute to put, and keep the Indians in a good humour. But, as Governor Dinwiddie ordered me not to meddle or interfere with Indian affairs on any pretence whatever, the sole management of *them* being left to Mr Atkin, and his Deputy, Mr Gist—and those orders having never been countermanded—neither I nor my officers have adventured to do any thing relative to them, but in a secondary manner, thro' Mr Gist." Since Forbes and his subordinates seemed "to be unacquainted with the Villainy of the Raven Warrior and his Party," Washington explained what had happened. Then he shifted from defense to offense. He could do nothing to stop some parties of Cherokees returning home, unless Forbes's troops assembled "sooner than there seems to be a probability of their doing." And that, he added ominously, "might be of the most fatal consequence to this part of the Continent."[80]

In order to operate effectively in the North, the Cherokees and Catawbas had to be reconciled with the Six Nations. The Iroquois told the governor of Pennsylvania that they and the Cherokees had been at war "ever since we were created." Catawbas in 1750 declared they would fight the Six Nations as long as one of them lived, "and that after Death their very bones shall fight."[81] Arranging a détente between the old enemies shifted the balance of power by confronting the French and their Indian allies with a potentially formidable array of Native power aligned with the British, but dealing with multiple Indian nations required some delicate diplomatic footwork.

The Cherokees became suspicious of British intentions when they heard that their allies were trying to make peace with their Delaware and Shawnee enemies. Recognizing that the security of the Susquehanna Delawares required reaching an accommodation with both Pennsylvania and the Iroquois, Chief Teedyuscung employed

Newcastle (the Seneca warrior whom Washington had given the name Fairfax) as a go-between with Deputy Governor William Denny and attended peace talks at Easton in the summer and fall of 1756.[82] (Newcastle's intermediary efforts cost him his life: he died of small-pox in Philadelphia in November and was buried, at his request, in the Quaker burial ground.[83]) Teedyuscung returned in the summer and fall of 1757 (when he demanded that Charles Thomson act as his clerk) and was given a large white wampum belt depicting three figures—King George, the Iroquois, and Teedyuscung—holding hands in peace.[84]

For that peace to succeed, the British would have to stop their Cherokee allies attacking the Ohio Indians. Washington and other officers faced the challenge of how to convey to the Cherokees and Catawbas at Winchester that the British were talking peace with Teedyuscung and the Delawares without "disgusting them and incur-ring their displeasure."[85] The British were talking out of both sides of their mouths: sending Cherokees to raid the Shawnees and Delawares at the same time as they were negotiating peace with the Shawnees and Delawares. Even the Shawnee band of the pro-British chief Paxinosa on the Susquehanna feared the English might turn the Cherokees against them.[86] Before the British could make peace with the Shawnees and Delawares, they had to help smooth over relations between the Cherokees and the Shawnees and Delawares.[87] At the same time, they had to keep the Six Nations from joining the French.

Meanwhile, the British expedition against Fort Duquesne seemed to be going nowhere fast, as logistical problems continued to delay Forbes's army. The Cherokees became skeptical of the red-coats' intentions, and many warriors grew tired of waiting. Neither "promises nor presents," wrote Forbes, could prevent them from heading for home.[88] St. Clair and Washington did everything they could to keep the Cherokees at Winchester, but to no avail.[89] The presence of smallpox among the British troops may have hastened the exodus.[90] Byrd and his 57 Cherokees reached Winchester at the end of May.[91] But by early June only 186 remained with the army, and most of those left during the summer. Bosomworth held council after council trying to talk them out of it and get them to join the campaign, but the Cherokees laughed at his efforts.[92] Forbes now called the Cherokees "fickle" and "a very great plague." He did what he could to get the expedition moving to placate them, but even the arrival of the Scottish Highlanders, whom Forbes called the Cherokees' "Cousins," and the artillery did not stop them from leaving.[93] On their way south, Cherokees exchanged blows with backcountry settlers and plundered goods they no doubt felt were due them for their unpaid services.[94] The Cherokees' presence, their impatience at the army's inactivity, their threats to leave if supplies and gifts were not forthcoming, and finally their absence—all of these exasperated British officers.[95]

Attakullakulla was supposed to be on his way with two hundred warriors, traveling north as other Cherokees headed south, but his progress was slowed by delays and, some suspected, delaying tactics. In July 1758 they postponed their departure because their medicine men saw omens that warned disease would strike the warriors. The British dismissed such talk, but Attakullakulla told them the Cherokees never undertook anything important without consulting their medicine men. Access to spiritual power was essential to success in war, and omens could deter, delay, deflect, or terminate an expedition.[96] As an additional deterrent, Virginians in the Piedmont region who clashed with Cherokees left some of their victims lying in the road so that other Indians coming to join the army would see them.[97]

Anxious that relations with the Cherokees were literally and figuratively going south, Washington again took the liberty of writing directly to Forbes about the importance of Indian allies. Marching more than one hundred miles through rugged and mountainous country contested by the French and *their* Indian allies would be extremely arduous and perhaps impracticable unless the British were accompanied "by a considerable Body of Indians, who I conceive to be the only Troops fit to Cope with Indians in such Ground." Doubtless haunted by the memory of Braddock's march, he added that success in the woods did not depend on numbers: on the contrary, a handful of "the Skulking Enemy we shall have to deal with" could frustrate and harass an unwieldy body of troops on the march. He urged Forbes to dispatch someone to the Cherokee Nation to cultivate the support of the southern Indians who seemed to be wavering. Heaven forbid that those powerful nations should be lost to the French and turn against the English: if that happened the enemy would be able to destroy the southern colonies "and make themselves Masters of this part of the Continent at least."[98] Everything hinged on Forbes's campaign, a theme Washington continued to press on Bouquet.

By July 1758 Forbes had assembled an army of more than 6,000 that included 1,200 British regulars (mainly Highland Scots), 350 men of the Royal American Regiment, 2,700 provincials from Pennsylvania and 1,600 from Virginia, two companies from North Carolina, and a couple of hundred Marylanders.[99] Though he was dying from his ailment and probably knew his time was short, Forbes was not a man to be rushed, especially by a pushy young officer like Washington, who had advised Braddock to divide his command and send a flying column ahead. Forbes planned his campaign with great deliberation and moved men, munitions, and supplies at what Washington thought was a frustratingly slow pace. It was even more frustrating for the Indian allies who remained.

Washington had no illusions about his Indian allies but could not deny their contribution to the defensive war he was fighting. "The Malbehaviour of our Indians gives me great concern," he wrote Bouquet; "if they were hearty in our Interest their Services would be infinitely valuable; as I cannot conceive the best whitemen to be equal to them in the Woods: but I fear they are too sensible of their high Importance to us, to render us any very acceptable Service." From Fort Cumberland that summer, he dispatched Indian scalping parties to harass the enemy by keeping them in a continual state of alarm, but he always sent some white men to accompany the Indians.[100] Cherokees launched at least seventeen raids toward Fort Duquesne between April and August. Even as their numbers declined, their presence with the army contributed to the Ohio Indians' growing sense that the war was slipping away from the French. As Forbes acknowledged, the Cherokees kept the French and Indians "in awe."[101]

One hundred Cherokees and a contingent of Catawbas led by a chief known as Captain James Bullen (whom Bouquet adopted according to Indian custom) remained with the army.[102] Forbes was heartened by the news that Attakullakulla was finally coming with more warriors, but nervous that the slightest incident might give offense and change things in an instant.[103] At the beginning of August, Byrd wrote Forbes from Fort Cumberland with the news that "every one of my cursed Indians has left me," saying they were tired of waiting. He expected they would "shortly revolt from our Interest."[104] Forbes denounced the Cherokees as "a parcel of Scoundrels" who had "left us in a most Scandalous manner" just when they might have been of service. He now pinned his slim hopes for Indian assistance on Captain Bullen.[105] But British officers and officials thought no better of their Catawba allies than of their Cherokee allies.[106] Captain Bullen was killed before the end of the month.[107] A few Cherokees accompanied the army on the march to Fort Duquesne, but the southern Indian alliance was crumbling.

In the years before the war, Senecas, Delawares, and Shawnees had introduced Washington to the protocols and pitfalls involved in securing Indian allies. In the first years of the war, Cherokees and

Catawbas introduced him to the costs and complexities of maintaining Indian allies. He confronted a dilemma that other imperial officials faced and sometimes argued about: Indian allies expected generous gifts and regular supplies, but they refused to behave as subordinates and often seemed to deliver limited results—did one expend vast amounts to keep them as allies or risk having to expend even more to fight them as enemies? It was an issue Washington would face again as commander of the Continental Army and president of the United States.

CHAPTER 7

Frontier Advance and a Cherokee War

AS IS CLEAR FROM THE WAR'S NAME, Indians were major players in the French and Indian War. How they influenced the outcome of the war, however, is less clear. Indians did not line up on one side or the other of the imperial conflict and fight to the end for King George or King Louis; they waged their own parallel wars and made decisions consistent with their own interests as circumstances changed. In the end, the British victory at Fort Duquesne, when it happened, owed less to their Cherokee allies than to the Indians Washington and the Cherokees had fought against. Washington's war ended in 1758 primarily because the Delawares made peace.

Washington's ideas about fighting in Indian country, like those of the British army, reflected a sharp learning curve. When he first arrived in the Ohio backcountry in 1754, he had requested red regimental uniforms for his troops, thinking the Indians would be impressed. But regimentals were styled after fashionable three-piece suits, with skirted coats, waistcoats underneath, and breeches with tight bands just below the knees. They required a lot of expensive fabric, restricted movement, and offered legs and ankles little protection against underbrush, rocks, and snakes.[1] Four years later, in 1758, he ordered one thousand pairs of tanned deerskin Indian leggings to better equip his men for service in the woods and urged Forbes and Bouquet to permit Virginia militiamen to dress Indian style in buckskins. If it were up to him, he wrote Bouquet, "I woud not only cause the Men to adopt the Indian dress, but Officers also, and set the example myself." If he knew that General Forbes would approve, Washington would not "hesitate a moment at leaving my Regimentals at this place, and proceeding as light as any Indian in the Woods. T'is an unbecoming dress, I confess, for an officer; but convenience rather than shew I think shoud be consulted."[2] Adam Stephen requested and Washington ordered loincloths for his men.[3] Washington, of course, was not "going Indian"; like Daniel Boone, Sir William Johnson, and others who made their way in Indian country, he adopted some Indian ways to achieve his goals—which entailed defeating and dispossessing Indian people. Meanwhile, of course, Indians were adopting elements of European clothing; many of the warriors fighting alongside or against Washington's troops would have worn imported linen shirts, leggings fashioned from woolen cloth, and perhaps a red coat taken at Braddock's field.

Nor did Washington introduce a new way of fighting to Englishmen who were hopelessly entrenched in conventional ways of war. English colonists had been adapting to Native ways of fighting since the seventeenth century, as Indians had adapted to new ways of fighting necessitated by firearms. The British army was already building units of rangers and light infantry, and adapting tactics, clothing, and equipment to the demands of forest fighting. In fact, two weeks before Washington wrote to Bouquet on the subject, Bouquet had suggested that Forbes "make Indians of part of our provincial soldiers," by removing their coats and breeches, "which will delight them," giving them moccasins, blankets, and face paint, cutting their hair, and mixing them with "the real Indians" to give the enemy an inflated impression of the number of Indian allies. Forbes was convinced of the need to adopt new tactics of forest fighting in small companies and had long shared Bouquet's opinion about equipping some of the soldiers like Indians; "in this country, wee must comply and learn the Art of Warr, from Ennemy Indians," he said.[4] As his army advanced, Forbes screened his regulars with American riflemen in the woods. According to the captive James Smith, Indians acknowledged that "Forbes's men were beginning to learn the art of war."[5]

Forbes began moving his troops forward in the spring of 1758, from Philadelphia to Carlisle and Rays Town. Anticipating that a body of light troops might be sent ahead from Fort Cumberland, Washington in July asked Bouquet to use his influence to get him and his regiment included; "I hope without vanity I may be allowed to say, that from long Intimacy, and scouting in these Woods my Men are as well acquainted with all the Passes and difficulties as any Troops that will be employ'd, and therefore may answer any purpose intended by them, as well as any other Body."[6] Bouquet assured Washington that Forbes depended on him and his regiment and would avail himself of his zeal, experience, and knowledge of the country, and he solicited Washington's advice about "making an Irruption into the Enemy's Country with a strong Party." (Washington advised against it until the army was further advanced.)[7]

Nevertheless, Bouquet was not ready to defer to Washington's supposed expertise in dealing with Indians and fighting in Indian country. "It is with the utmost displeasure that I am to inform you, of the unaccountable behavior of *your* Indians," he wrote (emphasis added). Clearly, he implied, the Indians had become accustomed to liberal handouts while at Fort Cumberland. They demanded the same treatment when they joined the army at Rays Town, and when Bouquet was unable to give them what they wanted, they caused trouble among the Indians already there and threatened to leave. Washington must do more to ensure that the king's presents were distributed judicially and equitably among the Indians to prevent such jealousies occurring.[8] As Washington began to cut a wagon road between Fort Cumberland and Rays Town, Bouquet dispatched a contingent of Indians to cover his advance and reminded him to send out flanking parties, "as you are perfectly acquainted w[i]th the dangers of a Sudden attac[k]."[9] Bouquet knew as well as Washington what had happened to Braddock.

Bouquet and Forbes also declined Washington's advice—forcefully and repeatedly offered—on the best route for the expedition. In Washington's opinion, Forbes took the wrong one. Instead of following the road Braddock had blazed from the upper Potomac on the Virginia-Maryland border (which passed close by Washington's land at Bullskin Creek), Forbes elected to build a road from Rays Town, where Bouquet established his main advance depot, Fort Bedford, and strike due west. That route was shorter by about forty miles but meant the army had to hack its way through one hundred miles of forest and across the Allegheny Mountains.[10] Roads had the power to shape the economic and political landscape in eighteenth-century America. Reopening and improving Braddock's road to the Ohio country would secure opportunities for commerce and settlement for Virginia and the Ohio Company. The alternative route would give Pennsylvania traders a direct path and strengthen Pennsylvania's claim to the region. Washington consistently opposed and complained about taking the Pennsylvania route. He lobbied Bouquet, harping on the issue; he wrote Lieutenant Governor Francis Fauquier of Virginia, and, in a letter to John Robinson, Speaker of the House of Burgesses, he attacked

Forbes and Bouquet as being in cahoots with Pennsylvania. Their conduct he said, was "tempered with something—I don't care to give a name to—indeed I will go further and say they are d[upe]s or something worse to P-s-v-n [Pennsylvanian] Artifice—to whose selfish views I attribute the miscarriage of this Expedition, for nothing now but a miracle can bring this Campaigne to a happy Issue."[11]

Both routes presented challenges. After "an interview with Colonel Washington to find out how he imagines these difficulties can be overcome," Bouquet told Forbes, "I learned nothing satisfactory. Most of these gentlemen do not know the difference between a party and an army, and find every thing easy which agrees with their ideas, jumping over all the difficulties."[12]

Washington continued carping as the army hacked its way ponderously along what he thought was the wrong route. In this campaign he spent more time and energy fighting his commanding officer than he did fighting Indians. Forbes, with good reason, believed his preference for Braddock's route from the upper Potomac had less to do with sound military strategy than with giving Virginian land speculators, traders, and settlers first access to the Ohio Valley. He got to the bottom of the Virginian's opposition to the new road when "a very unguarded letter of Col. Washington" fell into his hands. It was, he wrote Bouquet, "a scheme that I think was a shame for any officer to be concerned in." Washington's behavior on the issue, he said with some restraint, "was no ways like a Soldier."[13]

Unlike Braddock, who pushed ahead to keep on schedule, Forbes constructed storehouses and defensive posts along his line of march and built a road that would supply the British garrison once Fort Duquesne fell.[14] The agonizingly slow progress frustrated Washington to no end. "So miserably has this Expedition been managed," he vented in a letter to Sally Fairfax in late September, that he expected that after another month's ordeal and the loss of many more men, it would be abandoned for the season.[15] But Forbes's slow and deliberate advance allowed him time to establish supply depots and intermediate forts along the route and advance with strength. It also allowed time for Lieutenant Colonel John Bradstreet to capture Fort Frontenac on Lake Ontario, thereby severing French supply lines to the interior and cutting off support for Fort Duquesne and its Indian allies. And it allowed Forbes to recover lost ground with the Indians.

Forbes shared many of Braddock's attitudes and antipathy toward colonials and Indians. He was disappointed in the forces from Virginia and Pennsylvania, he told William Pitt: with very few exceptions the officers were a bunch of "broken Innkeepers, Horse Jockeys, & Indian traders"; the men were just as bad, "a gathering from the scum of the worst of people, in every Country, who have wrought themselves up, into a panick at the very name of Indians who at the same time are more infamous cowards than any other race of mankind."[16] But Forbes grasped the importance of Indian diplomacy to his campaign. He understood that in the escalating competition for the Ohio country the Indians' goal was to maintain their independence and keep their homelands intact, and that, as Robert Hunter Morris argued, the French had won over the Delawares and Shawnees under the pretense of restoring their country to them.[17] Forbes knew that if they were to be won back and their power neutralized, the British would have to assure them their lands would be protected when the war was over, something that Braddock had refused to do.

The French-Indian alliance was vulnerable. Pitt was injecting money and men into winning the war in America; the Royal Navy's domination of the Atlantic jeopardized France's ability to supply Indians, and goods manufactured in the mills and factories of industrializing Britain outmatched French goods in quantity, quality, and price. There were signs early in 1758 that raids on the frontier were abating and the western Indians were shifting in favor of the British.[18] And now came Forbes's army, bigger and better prepared than Braddock's had been. Although General Abercromby's frontal assault on Montcalm's forces at Fort Ticonderoga in July 1758 was repulsed with catastrophic losses, the tide of the war was turning, and the Indians could see it. Their scouts watched as Forbes's army clawed its way west over the mountains.[19] Forbes was on the march, Montcalm wrote in September, and he worried he would have many Indian allies. The Iroquois were receiving presents from the English, he said. "Their hearts are with the latter, and their fears with us."[20]

A crucial component of Forbes's strategy was to win over the Delawares and thereby induce other Indians to abandon the fight for the Ohio.[21] Forbes could not, of course, simply go and meet Shingas; he had to proceed with due attention to Native politics and protocol, securing assistance from various quarters to get the peace process in motion. Scarouady, the consistent ally to whom Washington had given his name and who might have helped facilitate the peace process, had died of smallpox in 1757. As a first step, Forbes enlisted the help of Israel Pemberton, head of the Quakers' Friendly Association, to initiate measures to convene a treaty at Easton in Pennsylvania. It was a complicated business that involved dealing with the governors of Pennsylvania and New Jersey and their colonial assemblies as well as the various Indian nations, and that, notably, did not involve Virginia, whose landed interests would not have been likely to countenance any territorial concessions. And, as Sir William Johnson observed, "if they push Peace with one hand and War with another they will have a ticklish & hazardous Part to act."[22]

Indian-Indian diplomacy cleared the way for peace. The Six Nations and Susquehanna Delawares mediated with the Ohio nations. The Cherokees, though by now few in number in Forbes's army, made peace overtures to the Six Nations. Sir William Johnson, who had become accustomed to running British-Indian relations and whom Forbes risked offending by reaching out to the Delawares directly, was crucial in brokering the peace between the Six Nations and Cherokees. Once the Cherokee-Iroquois peace was achieved, messages went to the Ohio nations warning them of dire consequences if they continued to support the French. The prospect of Cherokee and Iroquois power aligned against them was a powerful incentive for Ohio Indians to reconsider their position.[23]

Forbes believed the Delawares were weary of the war and would be glad to have peace.[24] Hearing that the western Delawares might be open to negotiations, the eastern Delaware Teedyuscung acted as go-between. He traveled to Philadelphia and conveyed peace belts between Deputy Governor Denny and the Ohio nations. He met with the Delaware chiefs Shingas and Tamaqua, and in July 1758 escorted their brother Pisquetomen and another headman named Keekyuscung or Ketiuscund to Philadelphia to explore possibilities for peace.[25] As usual, intertribal relations complicated the peace process. At one point a party of Cherokees arrived in Philadelphia while Teedyuscung was negotiating with Denny. Their arrival sent Teedyuscung into "a terrible pannick," and Forbes confessed he was at a loss what to do.[26] Fortunately, the Cherokees sent Denny a peace message and wampum belts to assure the friendly Delawares they had no hostile intentions.[27]

Forbes sent a Moravian missionary named Christian Frederick Post as an envoy to the Indians. Post had lived almost ten years among the Delawares, spoke their language, and had twice married Native wives. (Both converts, they had died in 1747 and 1751.) He undertook three major journeys in 1758, one, accompanied by Charles Thomson, to Wyoming, where he gained information from Teedyuscung about the disposition of Ohio Indians, and two to the Ohio country. In July, escorted by Pisquetomen and carrying a message from the government at Philadelphia, he headed west to the Delawares, Shawnees, and Mingoes. As the historian James Merrell has noted, the Delaware war chief and the German missionary made an unlikely team, and they conducted their mission at great personal danger.[28]

In August, Post reached the four Delaware towns at Kuskuski on the headwaters of the Beaver River. He noted in his diary that the towns held two hundred warriors, which meant a population of roughly a thousand people. Pisquetomen went ahead with four strings of wampum to announce their arrival, and Tamaqua gave Post a warm welcome. But Post thought the messengers who came to invite him to the Indian towns around Fort Duquesne were "very surly." He traveled to Fort Duquesne and, with French officers looking on, delivered his message of peace to three hundred Shawnees, Delawares, Mingoes, and Ottawas. Fearing for his life, his companions hurried Post away, but even they were deeply suspicious. Speaking "in a very soft and easy manner," Shingas asked if the English would hang him, as they had put a price on his head. Post assured him he would be well received, but a Delaware named Shamokin Daniel interrupted him, called him a liar, and accused him of coming only to cheat the Indians out of their land. Back at Kuskuski, Shingas, Tamaqua, Pisquetomen, Delaware George, and other western Delaware chiefs held several conferences with Post. It was, they said, "a matter of great consequence" and required much thought. They were glad to hear the English message of peace, but feared "you intend to drive us away, and settle the country; or else, why do you come and fight in the land that God has given us?" Post assured them that the English intended only to drive away the French, not take the Indians' land. If that was true, the chiefs said, they would send the French home. But they were skeptical, and they refused to consider returning captives before peace was made; "such an unreasonable demand makes us appear as if we wanted brains," they said.

> It is you that have begun the war, and it is necessary that you hold fast, and be not discouraged in the work of peace. We love you more than you love us; for when we take any prisoners from you, we treat them as our own children. We are poor, and yet we clothe them as well as we can, though you see our children are as naked as at the first. By this you may see that our hearts are better than yours. It is plain that you white people are the cause of this war; why do not you and the *French* fight in the old country, and on the sea? Why do you come to fight on our land? This makes every body believe, you want to take the land from us by force, and settle it.[29]

Pisquetomen and Tamaqua belonged to a prominent lineage of Delaware culture brokers. The brothers drew on their influence, their political skills, and the Delawares' traditional role as intertribal peacemakers to mediate a peace that would end the war in the Ohio country and at the same time preserve Indian autonomy. The Quaker trader James Kenny described Tamaqua by this time as "a steady, quiet middle aged man of a cheerful disposition," although the Delaware chief was surely grief-stricken by the death of a daughter while the talks were taking place. Acutely aware of the stakes—and risks—of a British victory, Tamaqua told Post that if the British were prepared to recognize that "the land is ours not yours," the Delawares would ensure that "all Indians from the sunrise to the sunset should join the peace." Again escorted by Pisquetomen, Post hurried back across the mountains with the news and a Delaware peace belt of eight rows of wampum.[30]

The peace process gathered momentum, and Sir William Johnson threw his weight behind it. After many intrigues with the Quakers and the governors and governments of Pennsylvania and New Jersey, and with Johnson exerting his considerable influence, Forbes by mid-August had arrangements in place for a treaty to be held at Easton in Pennsylvania. The chiefs of the Six Nations and all the Indians living east of the Lakes and as far down the Ohio as the Wabash and Illinois Rivers had accepted the belts of invitation and friendship. "I think nothing can prevent a solid peace being established with most of those Indian tribes," Forbes told Bouquet, "as the Indian Claims appear to me both Just and Moderate, and what no man in their senses or in our situation with regard to the Indians would hesitate half an hour in granting them."[31]

By September the treaty was imminent. The Delawares and their neighbors had been driven into the arms of the French and removed to the Ohio, Forbes explained to Pitt, but now Britain could win them back. Their demands were "few, and to me seemingly not unreasonable," and the western tribes would be ready to declare for the British, or at least remain neutral, if they could be given assurances of protection. The chiefs were expected to arrive in Easton at any hour. Forbes regretted the peace talks had not been held earlier and given the Indians time to relocate, because he now had to put his offensive operations into effect immediately, and it would be difficult to distinguish between friendly and enemy Indians.[32]

Even so, there were hurdles to clear. In September, as the army approached its objective, Bouquet gave Major James Grant of the 77th Highland Regiment permission to make an advance on Fort Duquesne. Grant reached the fort undetected, but then blew his advantage by announcing his arrival with drums and bagpipes at daybreak. A sortie by French and Indians routed the British; more than 270 officers and men were killed or missing. Grant, Thomas Gist, and Andrew Lewis, who led the Virginians in the attack force and whom Washington feared dead, were captured. One old Indian told the captive James Smith he could only account for Grant's behavior "by supposing he had made too free with spirituous liquors during the night, and become intoxicated about day-light."[33] Guyasuta, who had guided Washington in 1753 and then gone over to the French after Braddock's defeat, participated in the attack.[34] Yet the French triumph was short-lived. Having scored a victory, many Indians quit Fort Duquesne and returned to their villages. "It was found impossible to retain them," said Bougainville. Forbes's army was on the way, and "its success [was] more than probable."[35]

Time, however, was running out for Forbes. It was now fall. Heavy rains and lack of wagons impeded the army's progress, morale was slipping, and people were questioning the apparent lack of activity.[36] Attakullakulla and about sixty Cherokees joined the army in October and served as scouts, but Forbes was feeling increasingly put upon and out of patience. The Cherokees, he told Bouquet in the middle of the month, were "bullying us," threatening to return home if their demands were not met. Attakullakulla, he told another correspondent, was "as consummate a Dog as any of them."[37] Nevertheless, the Cherokees performed useful service, and Forbes needed Attakullakulla. Hearing that the chief's services as a peacemaker had been requested in Virginia, where returning Cherokees had clashed with colonists, Forbes worried how to manage without him: if Attakullakulla left, no Indians would stay with the army, and there was no word from Easton of how the peace talks were going.[38]

In fact, the Easton conference was winding down as Forbes fumed. More than five hundred Indians, men, women, and children, representing thirteen nations—the Six Nations, Delawares, Conoys, Nanticokes, Tutelos, and others—had turned up in early October, "but what they will now do, God knows," Forbes confided to Bouquet. Croghan and Montour both attended the great council, as did Charles Thomson. Croghan found the assembled Indians "Much Divided and Jelious of Each other," many of them alienated by Teedyuscung. Teedyuscung buckled under Six Nations pressure and accepted their authority over the tribes of Ohio and Pennsylvania, but Pisquetomen and the western Delawares wanted territorial security and independence. Knowing the Indians would never agree to peace as long as they feared that Britain intended to take the Ohio country from them, the negotiators gave the Indians the assurances they needed: the British did not want to settle the land, only to open it to British traders and defend it against the French. Indeed, Pennsylvania actually promised to return the lands west of the Alleghenies that the Iroquois had ceded four years before at Albany.[39] The Ohio Indians wanted to keep settlers out of their country, but they needed to let in traders and their merchandise. The Treaty of Easton seemed to secure them both objectives. Had they been junior partners or pawns in the "French and Indian War," their acceptance of the Easton Treaty might be construed as abandoning their allies. Instead, they were fighting their own war with their own goals, and having achieved those goals, they likely regarded the treaty as the end of the war for them. Pennsylvania published the treaty and sent Post back to the Ohio country with the news to reassure the Indians that the English had no intentions of settling there.[40]

Hurrying along the rough road Forbes had blazed, Post and Pisquetomen caught up with the army, bringing news of the treaty. Forbes immediately sent them with wampum belts and a speech to Shingas, Tamaqua, and other Ohio chiefs, calling on them to return to the villages, sit quietly by their fires with their wives and children, and smoke their pipes in safety while the British took care of the French. They should keep their young men at home so the British did not mistake them for enemies.[41] Washington made provision for ensuring that his Indian allies would not be so mistaken. His orderly book for November 3 recorded: "A number of the Indians who have come over to our Alliance by the late Treaty at Easton are now upon their March to join us to go to War. The troops are therefore to receive them as Friends, & they will be known by Carry[in]g red Handkerchief with white Spots at the end of a Pole."[42] After another round of diplomacy in the Indian towns along Beaver Creek, Shingas and Tamaqua agreed not to interfere as Forbes advanced against Fort Duquesne, and Tamaqua worked to promote the peace among neighboring tribes.

Like building a physical road to Fort Duquesne, opening a diplomatic path from Philadelphia to the Ohio took time and energy.[43] Washington had little patience for the pace of either. Busy griping about the Pennsylvania Road and going behind his commanding officer's back, he paid the Treaty of Easton little attention.[44] As it turned out, the painstaking diplomacy it took to convene the tribes at Easton and the promises made there had an immediate impact on the course of the conflict and were crucial to Forbes's ultimate victory. Fred Anderson in his authoritative study of the Seven Years' War in America calls the Treaty of Easton "the most important diplomatic breakthrough of the war."[45] The French Empire beyond the St.

Lawrence rested on a network of alliances with Native nations. French forts in the west depended for their defense less on palisades and firepower than on allegiance with the Indian people who lived outside the forts. Once those allegiances were removed, even a substantial edifice like Fort Duquesne became essentially indefensible. The Treaty of Easton removed the resistance of the Ohio nations. The French could still call on the Ottawas, Ojibwas, and other Great Lakes Indians, who were their main allies and not party to the Easton Treaty, but their presence near Fort Duquesne was only temporary, and most returned home to go hunting. They had families to support, and French supply lines had dried up after the capture of Fort Frontenac. Smallpox, likely brought by warriors returning from the war, was raging in their villages. Few Great Lakes warriors joined the French in the campaigns of 1758.[46]

In November, Forbes held a council of war that advised against a final advance on Fort Duquesne that season.[47] The next day, Washington and Lieutenant Colonel George Mercer were involved in a tragic incident when the detachments they were leading in the woods at dusk mistook each other for the enemy and exchanged gunfire. By the time the shooting stopped, fourteen men lay dead, another twenty-six wounded. Virginia's Captain Thomas Bullitt, who Washington acknowledged had shown great courage at Grant's defeat, blamed Washington for the calamity and said he did nothing to stop it. Washington conspicuously said nothing about the event in his correspondence at the time, but in the version of events he prepared for David Humphreys thirty years later he figured heroically: he was leading his men to Mercer's assistance, and it was Mercer's troops that initiated the friendly fire; Washington stopped the bloodshed at great personal risk, standing between the two sides and knocking down his men's muskets with his sword.[48]

In any case, Fort Duquesne's fate was already sealed. On November 20 its commander, Captain François-Marie Le Marchand de Lignery, sent a messenger to Kuskuski to rally the Indians to the fort's defense. Christian Frederick Post, who was already in the village and had conveyed his news of peace, witnessed what happened. The messenger spoke and then presented a wampum belt to the assembled chiefs, but the call for warriors fell on deaf ears. One chief announced, according to Post, "I have just heard something of our brethren the *English*, which pleaseth me much better. I will not go. Give it to the others, may be they will go." He threw the wampum belt on the ground. Others kicked it away from them, "as if it was a snake." Finally, one hurled it the length of the room. "Give it to the *French* captain, and let him go with his young men," he said; "he boasted much of his fighting; now let us see his fighting. We have often ventured our lives for him; and now he thinks we should jump to serve him." The French officer stationed at the village "looked pale as death." At midnight he sent messengers to Fort Duquesne bearing the bad news.[49]

Just as Forbes was thinking he would have to defer the assault until the spring, French captives revealed Fort Duquesne was seriously undermanned. Then an Indian scout reported huge smoke clouds rising from the Forks. In spite of Washington's insubordination and scheming over the issue of the Pennsylvania road, his persistent naysaying, and a friendly fire debacle that must have raised doubts about his competence as a commander, Forbes appointed him brevet brigadier general to lead one of the columns that advanced to take the fort.[50] On the morning of November 25, in what must have been a mixture of elation and anticlimactic disappointment, Washington arrived to find Fort Duquesne reduced to a pile of smoldering ruins. The French had blown it up and abandoned the Forks.[51]

Forbes promptly renamed the site Pittsburgh and called for the construction of a fort. He had understood all along that victory depended on the Indians abandoning, or at least not actively supporting, the French, and he acknowledged their importance in his reports the day after the capture of the fort. Anxious to make an alliance with "our real Friends" the Indians, he invited their leading men to meet him and "in a few Words and few Days to make everything easy."[52] He had worked hard at peace for six months, and there had been so many obstacles to overcome and so many different interests to reconcile that he had almost despaired of success, but in the end, he said, it "turned out as I foresaw it would." Now Forbes wanted to complete his work and wrap things up. He intended to leave "as soon as I am able to stand, but God knows when, or if I ever reach Philadelphia."[53] Incapacitated by inflammation in his stomach, midriff, and liver, he departed on December 3, leaving Bouquet to meet with Tamaqua and the other chiefs the next day.[54] Forbes made it to Philadelphia in great pain, but when Indian delegates came to see him, he was too ill to meet with them.[55] He did not live long after his triumph. He died in March 1759. The campaign that Washington had consistently warned could never succeed had succeeded, led by a dying general, making slow and methodical progress, and assisted by intricate Indian diplomacy.

Henry Bouquet made it implicitly clear that Forbes captured Fort Duquesne in spite of, not because of, George Washington. "After God the success of this Expedition is intirely due to the General," he wrote in his report, "who by bringing about the Treaty of Easton, has struck the blow which has knocked the French in the head, in temporizing wisely to expect the Effects of that Treaty, in securing all his posts, and giving nothing to chance; and not yielding to the urging instances for taking Braddock's Road, which would have been our destruction."[56] Instead, Forbes had removed the staging post for French and Indian raids on the Virginia frontier.

With Colonel Hugh Mercer in command, the new British post at Fort Pitt became the center of British diplomatic efforts. The Delawares were relieved to be at peace. Many of the residents of Sawcunk, also known as Beaver's Town or Shingas's Town, had moved farther north to Kuskuski to be out of harm's way. Tired of fighting, they had seen too much of both the English and the French to want to live near either of them.[57] Other tribes took more convincing. Tamaqua and Delaware George continued working to bring neighboring tribes to make peace with the British, and Bouquet and Croghan sent Indian messengers to the tribes, and spies to ascertain Indian inclinations and French activities.[58] As the focus of diplomacy shifted westward, the British held a series of conferences at Fort Pitt. Thousands of Indians came for negotiations between 1759 and 1761, not only Delawares, Shawnees, and Senecas in the Ohio country but also, increasingly, Miamis, Ojibwas, Ottawas, Potawatomis, and Wyandots, nations that were not inclined to adhere to a peace made by the Six Nations and Delawares.[59] The British had learned what the French knew: that in Indian country imperial policies often depended on negotiation and agreement.

They also feared what the French feared: that they risked losing everything if they could not supply the Indians with gifts to lubricate diplomacy and goods to cement the alliance. Washington told Lieutenant Governor Fauquier that the capture of the fort came as a "great surprise to the whole army—and we can not attribute it to more probable causes than those of weakness, want of Provisions, and desertion of their Indians." He expected it to be "attended with happy effects." The tribes on the Ohio were suing for peace, but the best way to secure their friendship was to provide free trade on fair terms and send goods immediately to the Forks. The trade would have to be regulated to ensure that it was carried on by men of principle, and not by "a set of rascally Fellows divested of all faith and honor," and protected in its infancy from "the sinister views of designing, selfish men." Presumably, he did not include the members of the Ohio Company in that characterization. He feared the Forks would be lost and the frontiers exposed again if the garrison was not reinforced in the spring; "lose our footing on the Ohio," warned Washington, and we "lose the interest of the Indians."[60] The French were rumored to be mounting a counteroffensive against Fort Pitt, but Bouquet was more worried about losing the Indians since they had the power to cut off supplies to the fort. Without adequate supplies, the peace with the western Indians—and the fort itself—would remain precarious. Britain would lose all the advantages it had gained at so much effort and expense.[61] Supply problems continued to plague Fort Pitt.

In fact, the threat of a French counterattack and losing Fort Pitt ended in July when the British captured Fort Niagara. The French commander, Pierre Pouchot, said Indians from all parts of North America traveled to Niagara to trade, and Sir William Johnson predicted that if the British could destroy the fort they could shake the French and Indian alliance to its core and undermine France's entire system of Indian trade and power on the continent.[62] Again, Indian-Indian politics and diplomacy played a key role in the British victory. Most of the Six Nations remained neutral for most of the war, but in 1759 they joined the British war effort, partly to reassert their crumbling authority among the nations of the Ohio Country. Johnson and almost one thousand Iroquois warriors accompanied the expedition against Niagara. The local Senecas had given permission for their French allies to build Fort Niagara, but what use were a fort and allies that that could not deliver trade goods? When the British-allied Iroquois arrived, the Senecas met with them in council and decided to sit out the fight rather than fight against their relatives. They stood aside and let the British take care of expelling the French from their land.[63] At Fort Niagara as at Fort Duquesne, Indian inactivity affected the outcome of the war.

DESPITE RECOMMENDING TRADE AS THE way to win over the Indians, Washington had other plans for the Indians' lands that would require their absence, not their presence as trading partners.

Just weeks after he stood amid the smoking ruins of Fort Duquesne, Washington was back at Belvoir, and then Mount Vernon. After five years of military service, the time seemed right to return to civilian life. The war was not over, but the French had been driven from Fort Duquesne, and most of the remaining fighting was in the North. In 1757 he had made plans for rebuilding Mount Vernon.

His participation in Forbes's campaign meant he was absent while construction was under way, and he was anxious to get back.[64] Also, in July 1758, while he was on campaign, his political backers and prodigious amounts of alcohol had won him election from Frederick County to a seat in the House of Burgesses. He was no nearer attaining a royal commission, and there seemed little likelihood that he would. "Nose out of joint," as the historian Francis Jennings suggested, he resigned his command.[65] On January 6, 1759, he married Martha Custis, a wealthy widow who brought two children and some two hundred slaves from her previous marriage to Daniel Parke Custis.[66] In February he took his seat in the House of Burgesses. His position in Virginia society and politics seemed assured.

His attention now turned to settling the Custis estate, running his plantation, and ordering merchandise from England. Still, the fallout from the Indian war followed him into the House of Burgesses, where the members considered petitions from soldiers and civilians seeking compensation for losses and injuries they had suffered. Washington chaired a committee to review the memorial of his cousin and comrade Major Andrew Lewis, who, following his capture at Grant's defeat, spent sixteen months in a Quebec jail, which "greatly impoverished his private Fortune." On Washington's recommendation, the House voted Lewis £350 as reward for his services, compensation for his hardships, and the expenses he incurred "to support and maintain the Dignity of his Character as an Officer."[67]

Washington also followed the news from Indian country. "All is well and quiet on the Ohio," Lieutenant Colonel George Mercer wrote from Winchester in September 1759. Indians were coming in great numbers to mend fences with Bouquet; the French had burned their forts at Venango, Presque Isle, and LeBoeuf and retreated to Detroit, and the British were going to build a strong brick fort at Pittsburgh.[68] Washington's friend Robert Stewart reported from Pittsburgh the same month that the Indians were ready to make a permanent peace. They had brought in nearly fifty captives and promised to deliver more. The Delawares and Shawnees had both suffered heavy losses in the war and, said Stewart, were "greatly incens'd against you, who they call the Great Knife & look on you to be author of their greatest misfortunes." Now there was peace, the Pennsylvanians were busy making money trading with the Indians. Stewart could not understand why Virginians were not active in the fur trade as well—surely some public-spirited gentlemen "must have an Inclination to advance the Interest of their Country by encreasing their private Fortunes."[69]

He may have hoped to push Washington in that direction, but Washington had other ideas. He had turned from building a military reputation to building the landholdings and wealth that would secure his place and his status as a planter. His travels into the Ohio country and the rich lands he saw there convinced him that the West was the land of opportunity—where he would grow rich by renting or selling to other people who settled there. He urged others to move west and start a new life though he showed no interest in doing so himself; for Washington, western lands offered the means to further his ambitions as a Tidewater planter and secure his position as member of the Virginia gentry—in other words, to build an old life.[70]

By 1760 the war against France was winding down with the conquest of Canada. The almost routine capture of French possessions was "becoming a Story too stale to relate in these days we are often at a loss for something to supply our Letters with," joked Washington. Unaware of a storm brewing in the Ohio country, he thought the Cherokees were now "the only People that disturbs the repose of this great Continent."[71]

The military cooperation between Cherokee warriors and British soldiers that contributed to Forbes's victory also brought cultural conflicts and misunderstandings. Disillusioned with the campaign's slow progress, or perhaps assuming his scouting was done, Attakullakulla had headed for home even before Fort Duquesne fell, taking the guns the British had given him. To Forbes such behavior was desertion. Like most British officers, he believed Indian allies should use British guns to fight British enemies. He sent orders to British posts to have the Cherokees arrested and disarmed. Like most other Cherokees, Attakullakulla refused to see accepting British guns as subjecting himself to British control. He regarded Forbes's actions as an assault on Cherokee autonomy and "a stinging personal affront." Attakullakulla was released, but the damage was done.[72]

Cherokees who had gone north to fight with Forbes had been poorly supplied, frustrated by the ponderous progress of the army, and subjected to suspicion and insult, said the trader James Adair; "their hearts told them therefore to return home, as freemen and injured allies." En route, some Cherokees took what they regarded as just payment for their services. Passing through southwestern Virginia, they stole horses and clashed with settlers. Lieutenant Governor Fauquier's revocation of Virginia's scalp bounty had not yet gone into effect, and Cherokee allies made tempting targets. Colonists in the spring and summer of 1758 murdered at least thirty Cherokees on their way home from fighting for the British. Cherokees appealed to

Virginia and to North and South Carolina for satisfaction but received none, and, Adair explained, "when the Indians find no redress of grievances, they never fail to redress themselves." Cherokee warriors took vengeance on backcountry settlers. Attakullakulla went to Williamsburg and met with the governor and council to try to heal the wounds, and some chiefs traveled to South Carolina to apologize, but Governor Lyttelton seized and executed twenty-three Cherokee hostages.[73]

Meanwhile, smallpox raged throughout the Southeast, killing Christopher Gist in the summer of 1759.[74] Catawbas continued to come to Winchester in the summer of 1759, but warriors returning home in the fall took the disease with them. Catawba population dropped by about 60 percent in six months; by 1760, fewer than sixty warriors remained. The Catawba population had dwindled to just 4 percent of what it had been a century before, and the survivors requested a reservation with a stockade fort to protect their women and children when their men were gone. Catawba raiders spread the disease to Cherokee villages in October 1759.[75]

Escalating tensions exploded in full-blown war. Adair blamed provocations and misconduct on the part of Virginia and South Carolina: "We forced the Cheerake to become our bitter enemies, by a long train of wrong measures."[76] Warriors who had fought alongside British soldiers now fought against them. Ostenaco, who had joined Washington as an ally in 1756, now took up arms against the colonists. If the Cherokees united with the Creeks, Stewart wrote Washington, "I tremble for our Southern Colonies!" The Ohio Indians had been enemy enough; imagine how formidable a combination of these nations would be.[77] The dire prospects of a powerful southern Indian alliance would haunt Washington well into his presidency.

The war raged across the South Carolina backcountry. Had Washington remained in the army he would have led the Virginian war effort. Instead, as Fauquier wrote William Byrd III, "Washington has resigned his command of the Virginia forces (and is married to his agreeable widow)." Byrd, who had been second-in-command under Washington, was now appointed commander of the Virginia Regiment and inherited many of the problems that had frustrated Washington—reluctant and ill-trained recruits, inadequate supplies, and uncertainties over pay.[78] Washington could only watch from the wings as his colony went to war against his former allies. He was confident that Britain's generals would have little trouble conquering Canada that summer, but was less sure about the fate awaiting Colonel Archibald Montgomery as he advanced into the heart of Cherokee country: "Let him be wary—he has a crafty Subtil Enemy to deal with that may give him most trouble when he least expects it."[79]

Neither Montgomery's Highland troops nor Byrd's Virginians arrived in time to save Fort Loudon. In August 1760, after a siege of six months, Ostenaco's warriors captured the fort they had wanted the British to erect in their country. Accusing the British of violating the terms of surrender, they killed twenty-three of the garrison, avenging the twenty-three Cherokees executed by Lyttelton, and tortured to death Captain Paul Demere (who had succeeded his brother Raymond as commander). Attakullakulla saved his friend John Stuart's life.[80] Montgomery's army burned the Lower Cherokee towns but, true to Washington's predictions, met stiff resistance in mountainous terrain when he pushed on to the Middle towns and was forced to turn back. The following year, 1761, Lieutenant Colonel James Grant, who had fought alongside Cherokees in the Forbes campaign and who had been ransomed after his capture in the ill-advised raid on Fort Duquesne, invaded Cherokee country with an army of 2,600 men. With Lieutenant Quentin Kennedy's corps of rangers and Indian allies screening his advance, Grant burned fifteen towns, destroyed more than 14,000 acres of cornfields, and drove hundreds of people into the woods and mountains.[81]

Some of Washington's former comrades-in-arms took part in the war. The ubiquitous Silver Heels, who had fought with Washington at Fort Necessity and in Braddock's campaign, served with Grant's Indian allies. According to one British officer, Silver Heels in a drunken fit tomahawked three Indians—a man and two women—who lived near the camp. Only Grant's intercession prevented his execution, which his own clan relatives offered to carry out.[82] Adam Stephen took over command of the Virginia Regiment when Byrd resigned, but the Virginia provincials saw no action, and Stephen dealt with Cherokee peace initiatives rather than Cherokee war parties.[83]

Washington was more concerned with affairs at Mount Vernon and his accounts with the London merchant house Robert Cary and Company, but he kept half an eye on developments in Cherokee country. "We catch the reports of Peace with gaping Mouths, and every Person seems anxious for a confirmation of that desirable Event provided it comes as no doubt it will, upon honourable terms," he wrote to the London merchant Richard Washington (no relation). He believed the Cherokees would make peace on almost any terms, not because they feared British military power but because they were dependent on the supplies that only the British could provide. The Cherokees had been asking for peace for some time. "I wish the Powers of Europe were as well disposd to an accommodation as these poor Wretches are," he wrote to the Cary firm; "a stop would soon be put to the Effusion of Human Blood."[84]

Washington's assessment was accurate. Already ravaged by small-pox, the Cherokees now faced starvation. Attakullakulla, Ostenaco, and Oconostota sued for peace. Attakullakulla, who had been a voice for peace throughout the crisis, impressed one of Grant's officers as an amiable individual and "a Man of great Sense." The Cherokees made peace with South Carolina at Charleston in December 1761.[85] Oconostota, the chief warrior and Attakullakulla's chief rival, made peace with Virginia and traveled to Williamsburg to confirm it. Fauquier thought him a man of integrity, "not talking, as they express themselves with a double tongue."[86] Ostenaco, who had worked to build relations with Virginia before the war, now worked to rebuild them.[87]

Ostenaco urged sending a delegation to England to confer with the king. A royal visit would increase his prestige at the expense of Attakullakulla, and would reduce South Carolina's dominance in Cherokee relations. Fauquier and his council agreed to the visit, reasoning it would impress the Cherokees with the grandeur of the king and the power of his military.[88] Ostenaco and two other Cherokees, Cunne Shote (Stalking Turkey) and Woyi (Pigeon or Pouting Pigeon), accompanied by Lieutenant Henry Timberlake, made the hazardous voyage. They met George III at St. James's Palace, saw the sights, attended the opera, attracted the attentions of English ladies, and had their portraits painted by Sir Joshua Reynolds. Ostenaco came home determined to maintain the alliance.[89] The Cherokees needed peace: "Our women are breeding children night and day to increase our people," he said, "and I will order those who are growing up to avoid making war with the English."[90] In December 1762 the Virginia Regiment that Washington had led for four years was disbanded.[91]

WASHINGTON'S MILITARY SERVICE DURING the French and Indian War had primarily involved fighting Indians. It was hardly an unqualified success. He had embarked on it as a means of personal advancement, and he frequently behaved like a young man on the make. As Edward Lengel acknowledges, "some unattractive facets of Washington's personality arose during the French and Indian War, and they would continue to mark his conduct twenty years later." He made lots of mistakes and did not admit them, and he suffered several defeats. Oversensitive and easily hurt, he sometimes reacted to his own failures by blaming others or falling into despondency. He complained constantly, carped to his superiors, and tried to undermine them. His frustrations in dealing with the British army were matched by British officers' frustrations in dealing with uncooperative colonial assemblies and unreliable provincial troops, and the experience of fighting together generated attitudes that hardened into stereotypes as relations between British armed forces and colonial Americans deteriorated in the troubled times to come.[92] His frustrations in dealing with Indian allies were matched by Indian frustrations in dealing with British and colonial allies. His only victory was questionable—achieved over a party of French soldiers caught off their guard, and marred by the assassination of Jumonville. The image of Tanaghrisson washing his hands in Jumonville's brains surely had an enduring influence on Washington's attitudes toward Indians, and perhaps on his later Indian policies as well.

After witnessing and surviving debacles and disasters—some brought about by his own rash actions in pursuit of victory—Washington had watched a dying general who ignored his advice secure a huge victory without even fighting a battle. Washington had urged an assault on Fort Duquesne, but credit for its capture belonged to Forbes, who succeeded despite Washington's bickering, and to Indian diplomats, who conducted their business off Washington's radar. There were those who questioned Washington's fitness for command. He hardly deserved the military reputation he had acquired by the end of the war, and the Revolutionary War would demonstrate, time and again, that he still had plenty to learn. He experienced and grudgingly acknowledged the effectiveness of the Indians' war of attrition, but, contrary to popular myth, he did not learn how to defeat the British in the Revolution by fighting in the "Indian style" he learned in the French and Indian War.

Nevertheless, he had displayed personal courage in the face of disaster, he had racked up valuable experience, and he had built up a well-trained and effective provincial regiment. As Fred Anderson notes, "the war had been a kind of education, in many aspects of life, for a man who had undergone very little formal education." It took Washington some time to grow into that education, but lessons he learned about leading men; organizing campaigns, supplies, and defense; and the value of patience, planning, and perseverance would serve him well in years to come. He may also, as he found himself powerless to stop Indian warriors filtering past his forces to kill people he was supposed to be protecting, have learned humility.[93]

He had been lucky—to escape with his life and without blame for the debacles in which he was involved—and he knew it. Writing to Adam Stephen in July 1776, when both men were fighting the British, not the French and Indians, Washington noted that he did not let the anniversaries of July 3 and 9 pass "without a grateful remembrance of the escape we had at the Meadows and on the Monongahela." Providence had protected them at Fort Necessity and during Braddock's defeat, and he hoped it would do so again.[94]

PART TWO

The Other Revolution

CHAPTER 8

Confronting the Indian Boundary

WHEN GEORGE WASHINGTON REBUILT Mount Vernon, he placed his elegant new parlor and dining room on the west side of the house.[1] On the other side, in Washington's mind, the Potomac River that flowed past his home always pointed west, to the Blue Ridge Mountains, the Ohio, and beyond. In his house perched on the eastern edge of the continent, with English-style architecture and furnishings, Washington spent a lot of time and energy, as the historian Joseph Ellis says, "dreaming and scheming about virgin land over the western horizon."[2] However, the land was not virgin, and the end of the Anglo-French war did not end the Indians' war to defend it. In fact, just when "we thought ourselves fixed in the utmost tranquility," wrote Washington to his friend Captain Robert Stewart, "another tempest…arose upon our Frontiers, and the alarm spread wider than ever."[3] In response, Britain erected a new barrier that thwarted Washington's dreams and schemes in the West.

The French and Indian War had disrupted the land business, and the Ohio Company lay dormant from 1754 to 1759. Now, with the French driven from the Ohio and his military service over, Washington was eager to jump back into the business. He used his position in the Assembly to push for western land, and he wanted to secure title to lands in the Ohio country. He was determined to get a share—actually far more than his share—of the 200,000 acres of bounty lands on both sides of the Forks of the Ohio that Lieutenant Governor Dinwiddie had promised Virginian soldiers in 1754. As was common with such incentives to enlist, Dinwiddie's bounties were almost certainly intended for rank-and-file soldiers; officers had their own rewards and compensation. Washington insisted that the bounties applied to officers as well, and he argued that they applied only to the men who served in 1754, that is, his command on the Fort Necessity campaign. He made every effort to acquire the best land for himself and buy up the shares of his fellow officers and men. Even before he left the army, in collusion with Captain George Mercer, his former aide-de-camp, and Robert Stewart, Washington sent Christopher Gist's son Nathaniel into the Ohio country to scout out the best land and establish their claims to it before others did. As Mercer told Washington, they would "leave no Stone unturned to secure to ourselves this Land." Others were not far behind. Thomas Bullitt, who had been caught in the exchange of friendly fire with Washington, and Adam Stephen, who took over as commander of Virginia's army after Washington left, both filed surveys of Ohio country lands in Williamsburg in 1760 and lobbied the Assembly to validate their claims, much to Washington's alarm.[4]

Stephen not only competed with Washington for land, he also ran against him for the Assembly seat from Frederick County in 1761. It was the end of their friendship. In the Revolution, Stephen rose to the rank of major general, but after the Battle of Germantown in 1777, amid allegations of drunkenness, he was court-martialed for "unofficerlike behaviour," inattention to duty, and lack of judgment. "From Fort Necessity onward," reckons the historian John Ferling, "every defeat suffered by Washington required a scapegoat."[5]

By the time Washington turned his attention to developing his estate in the 1750s, Virginia planters knew they had to diversify to protect themselves from the boom-and-bust cycles that plagued the tobacco economy. Still heavily dependent on British credit and committed to their plantation system of agriculture, Washington and his contemporaries sought to achieve greater economic independence by developing new crops, new markets, new commercial networks, and new territory. Lands beyond the Appalachian Mountains that had long attracted the attention of eastern speculators now attracted settlers and promised to sustain an expanding plantation economy and support the growth of eastern towns.[6] British population in North America was increasing by leaps and bounds: a quarter of a million in 1700, nearly 1.2 million in 1750, 1.6 million in 1760—and immigrants kept coming. Between 1760 and 1775, 222,000 people arrived in the British colonies from England, Scotland, Northern Ireland, and Germany, and as slaves from Africa, more than the total Native American population east of the Mississippi.[7]

Planter speculators who could obtain a large swath of land from the Indians and then rent or sell it in parcels stood to make huge profits.[8] Unless the British government stood in their way.

Ohio Indians had made peace on condition that the British would leave their country after the French were defeated, an assurance given by Christian Frederick Post and reaffirmed at various times subsequently by British officers and officials.[9] Just a couple of weeks after Fort Duquesne fell, Colonel Henry Bouquet had assured the Delawares: "We are not come here to take Possession of yr hunting Country in a hostile Manner, as the French did when they came amongst you."[10] Nonetheless, Indians were skeptical, and the atmosphere around Fort Pitt—formerly Fort Duquesne—remained tense. Tamaqua warned the British "to go back over the mountain and stay there." If they did not, said Keekyuscung, "all the nations would be against them; and he was afraid it would be a great war, and never come to peace again." Post said that when Tamaqua told Colonel Bouquet to take his soldiers back over the mountains, George Croghan and Andrew Montour, who were acting as interpreters, refused to translate the speech.[11] Croghan, of course, had land claims of his own west of the Appalachians. Pisquetomen asked what the English meant by bringing a great army to the Ohio country, and many Shawnees "believed ye English only wanted to deceive them to their destruction."[12] There was still work to be done if the peace hashed out at Easton was to hold.

Tamaqua continued to do that work. When he arrived at Fort Pitt for a council, the garrison greeted him with a cannon salute. Like most Indian councils, this one was conducted through a tortuous chain of communication: Croghan spoke to Montour, who spoke to the Mingoes and then interpreted the substance of what was said to Shingas, "who sat by him & he spoke it very boldly to ye Delawares." The trader James Kenny, who attended, had difficulty hearing everything that was said in English, but Tamaqua talked about how the king would protect the Indians and confirm their rights. As a mark of his commitment to peace, Tamaqua returned two English women he had taken captive and adopted; one he called his "mother" and the other his "sister."[13]

The British army tried to enforce the Easton Treaty and ejected settlers who illegally squatted on Indian land, but the army's presence encouraged settlement more than it restrained it. Migrants streamed along the roads built by Braddock and Forbes and settled near the military posts. Fort Pitt was a military community that required and attracted traders and tavern keepers, sutlers and settlers, artisans and laborers, camp followers and laundresses.[14] Bouquet—whose own speculative schemes were in Maryland rather than the Ohio Valley—refused bribes from members of the revived Ohio Company who offered him a share of company stock in return for letting them sell titles to squatters already occupying "company land" in Indian country. In the fall of 1761 Bouquet issued a military proclamation requiring squatters who had settled west of the Appalachians to leave. The following spring he sent soldiers to burn down their cabins. Bouquet's proclamation caused alarm in Virginia, and Washington and other Northern Neck planters who owned or claimed grants of land immediately protested to Governor Fauquier.[15]

Confronted with attempts to block settlement in America, speculators turned to London. The Ohio Company began pressuring the government in preparation for the end of the war. In September 1761, in expectation of peace the following winter and assuming that His Majesty's subjects would then be free to settle in the Ohio country, the company submitted a petition stating its case for a grant of lands, or failing that to have its time for settling the lands prolonged.[16] Washington, Adam Stephen, and Andrew Lewis submitted a memorial to the king on behalf of the officers and soldiers who had enlisted to defend Virginia against the French and Indians, asking that they not be blocked from taking up the lands promised by Dinwiddie.[17]

British appreciation of the pivotal power of Native allies during the war diminished once the war was won. The dying General Forbes told his friend General Jeffery Amherst that he had done everything he could to win over the Indians but that it would take a just settlement "to fix them our friends." Forbes had grown to detest (his word) Indians, but he begged Amherst to "not think triflingly of the Indians or their friendship;...twenty Indians are capable of laying half this province waste, of which I have been an eye witness."[18] It was advice Amherst chose to ignore.

At the Treaty of Paris in 1763, France gave up its North American empire, ceding everything east of the Mississippi to Britain. (Its territory west of the Mississippi went to Spain, to keep it out of British hands.) The West, it seemed, was finally open to British settlement. Indians thought differently. In their view the French had no right to give their country to the English. Never having been conquered by the English or the French, nor subject to their laws, they considered themselves "a free people."[19] The Delaware chief Neetotehelemy or Newcomer said he "was Struck dumb" when he first heard of the Treaty of Paris; the English had grown so powerful it seemed "they would be too Strong for God himself."[20]

British garrisons now occupied posts formerly held by the French. Fort Pitt was ten times the size of Fort Duquesne. When the Indians asked why they were building forts, the English, according to French reports, replied that the Ohio now belonged to them, an answer that caused great uneasiness among the Indians, "who, at heart, have no greater love for the English than for the French."[21] They reminded the British of their promises to bring good trade at good prices once the French were defeated; instead, "penned up like Hogs" with forts all around them, the Indians feared destruction.[22] Adding insult to injury, the British terminated gift-giving to Indians— it seemed a logical and necessary way to cut costs after a global war had left the nation bankrupt. Amherst added his own spin. Now the war was over, he saw no reason to supply Indians who would not bother to support their families by hunting if they could do it by begging provisions from the British. Indian Superintendent Sir William Johnson knew it was a mistake but was unable to convince Amherst.[23]

In Indian eyes such actions and attitudes constituted a declaration of hostile intentions and a breach of British assurances that they wanted to trade with Indians, not steal their land. Friends and allies gave and received gifts as testimony of their mutual need, generosity, and commitment, and to maintain and refresh good relations. Withholding gifts as colonists were clearing land and redcoats were occupying posts sent a very different message. Indians who came to Fort Pitt voiced their concerns. "All the Indian nations are very Jealous of the English," a Shawnee chief warned; "they see you have a great many Forts in this Country, and you are not so kind to them as they expected." The French had been generous; the English were not. Building more forts even though the French were defeated and charging high prices for goods "makes us apt to believe every bad report we hear of your intentions towards Us," others said.[24] Their suspicions were further galvanized by the teachings of a Delaware prophet named Neolin, who attributed the evil ways he saw among Indian people to European goods and religions that corrupted them while alcohol and diseases were destroying them. Neolin preached a message of spiritual and cultural revitalization, telling his followers to separate from the British and return to their own ways.[25] When more than 150 people died of an epidemic at Lower Shawnee Town, some said the disease was sent by God.[26] War belts circulated through Indian country.

Washington's old acquaintance Silver Heels was busy again, carrying messages and gathering information for the English, to whom, said the trader Kenny, he was a firm friend.[27] Shingas, who five years before had terrorized the frontier, now had a reputation for treating white people with kindness and generosity, and he and Tamaqua tried to keep the peace they had made. When they were offered a war belt they refused to accept it and "threw it against ye Wall." But the aged Pisquetomen died a year or so later; Delaware George also died, and Tamaqua returned from a mission to Philadelphia "unwell & not so Cheerful as befor[e]."²⁸ Tamaqua and Shingas could not stop the drift to war.

The conflict became known as Pontiac's War, after the Ottawa war chief, but multiple Indian leaders and multiple Indian nations took up arms against the king's men. Washington's former guide Guyasuta played a major part, organizing resistance to the imposition of British imperial authority in Indian country.²⁹ In 1761 he carried a red wampum belt to Detroit, where, "under the nose of the British commandant," he exhorted the Delawares, Shawnees, Ottawas, Hurons, Ojibwas, and Potawatomis to attack British posts.³⁰ Major Henry Gladwin, who took command at Detroit in the summer of 1762, warned Amherst that the Indians were planning to take action to recover their freedom now, rather than wait until the English were more firmly entrenched and made slaves of them.³¹

In a series of devastating attacks, the Indians took nine of the fourteen British posts west of the Appalachians and laid siege to Detroit, Niagara, and Fort Pitt; they sent settlers scrambling back east in panic, and they almost destroyed Britain's hold on the interior of North America. The "sudden Irruption" hit the frontier inhabitants with "as rude a shock" as any they had received during the last war and generated "terrible consternation" all along the frontier, Washington wrote Richard Washington that summer; "confusion and despair prevails in every Quarter."³² Ohio Indians raided settlements along the Potomac and Greenbrier Rivers while, in a reprise of Virginian strategy after Braddock's defeat, Adam Stephen and Andrew Lewis commanded the small forts that attempted to protect the frontier.³³

At Fort Pitt, smallpox broke out among the garrison in June. Amherst in July infamously urged Bouquet "to try to Inoculate the *Indians,* by means of Blankets, as well as to Try Every other Method, that can Serve to Extirpate this Execrable Race," but the deed was already done. Three weeks earlier, on June 24, two Delaware chiefs, Turtle Heart and Maumaltee, came to the walls of Fort Pitt and tried to talk the British into surrendering. The trader William Trent, back at the place where he had tried to build a fort in 1754, confided sarcastically to his diary, "Out of our regard to them we gave them two Blankets and a Handkerchief out of the Small Pox Hospital. I hope it will have the desired effect." His company then submitted an invoice for "Sundries got to Replace in kind those which were taken from people in the Hospital to Convey the Smallpox to the Indians." Turtle Heart and Maumaltee evidently were not infected—they showed up at Fort Pitt again a month later, along with Shingas and other chiefs—but an escaped captive the following year reported that smallpox had been raging among the Indians since the previous spring.³⁴ In August, Bouquet, leading a bedraggled force of Highland soldiers who had survived deadly and disease-ridden campaigns in Cuba and Martinique, fought off an Indian attack at Bushy Run in western Pennsylvania and made it through to relieve Fort Pitt. Like Forbes, Bouquet had learned how to conduct a march through Indian country.³⁵ Pennsylvania resumed paying bounties on the scalps of Indians over ten years of age.³⁶

The war petered out in a series of agreements rather than a resounding British victory. The Indians returned forts and captives, and the British returned to gift-giving and diplomacy in dealing with the tribes. Guyasuta, Tamaqua, and other chiefs met with Bouquet in peace talks. The Delawares and Shawnees reluctantly agreed to return the white captives they had taken during the recent wars. Many of the captives were even more reluctant to return. Some never did.³⁷

Washington took no part in Pontiac's War, but men he knew were in the thick of it, and its repercussions affected his life profoundly. The Indians had waged a war of independence against the British Empire. Their actions at Fort Pitt, Detroit, Michilimackinac, and Niagara sent reverberations across the Atlantic and back again, setting in motion a chain of events that would thrust the colonies into another war of independence twelve years later.

POSTWAR DEPRESSION AGGRAVATED YEARS OF falling prices in Virginia's sole cash crop, plunging Washington and other tobacco planters into debt. Explaining to friend-in-need Robert Stewart in April 1763 why he could not loan him £400, Washington said he had found his estate in terrible shape when he returned from the war. He had had to buy provisions and stock, build buildings, and purchase additional land and slaves, all of which "swallowed up before I knew where I was, all the money I got by the Marriage, nay more, brought me in Debt."³⁸ Nevertheless, Washington continued to live the extravagant lifestyle of a Tidewater planter. Sustaining that lifestyle meant selling his tobacco harvest on consignment to merchants in Britain who in turn sold it on the market, provided credit, and purchased the furnishings, clothing, foods, and wine Washington ordered from England, as well as the clothes and tools used by his slaves and other necessities for running a plantation. The London mercantile firm of Robert Cary and Company bought Washington's goods against the expected profits from sales of his tobacco. But Washington was not the tobacco planter Daniel Parke Custis had been, the depleted soils of Mount Vernon produced poor-quality tobacco, and he was routinely disappointed in the prices his harvest brought. He constantly complained to Cary that his tobacco sold too low, and his goods cost too much, as he struggled to make ends meet as a gentleman planter. The precariousness of Virginia's tobacco economy intensified planters' resentment of their dependence on British merchant firms.[39] In debt to his London creditors to the tune of almost £2,000, Washington hoped the Peace of Paris would bring a change of fortune and a way out of debt. The West was open, the growing population of the colonies needed land, and settlers were poised to flood across the Appalachian Mountains and into the Ohio Valley. Washington eagerly anticipated "the profits to be made from buying good land cheap."[40]

On June 3, 1763, he joined eighteen other Virginian planters in forming the Mississippi Land Company. They included four Lee brothers, two Fitzhughs, Adam Stephen, Thomas Bullitt, and John Augustine Washington, and many of them were already members of the Ohio Company. Three months later they petitioned the Crown for 2.5 million acres of territory ceded by France at the Treaty of Paris four months earlier. The tract lay between the Ohio and Allegheny, included the junction of the Ohio and Mississippi, and embraced land in the present states of Ohio, Indiana, Kentucky, and Illinois. They asked the Crown to build a fort there to protect the settlement from Indian "insults" and requested twelve years in which to settle the lands "if not interrupted by the savages." Washington's timing was unfortunate. The same day he formed the Mississippi Company, Ojibwa warriors seized the British fort at Michilimackinac, setting events in motion that would halt the land sales on which he staked his future.[41]

Washington and his associates were not fazed, however. Instead, they invoked the Indian war to promote, rather than postpone, their scheme. The Indians had broken the Treaty of Easton and were murdering His Majesty's subjects and laying waste to the country. By breaking the treaty that protected their lands west of the Alleghenies, the Indians themselves had "put it in the power of the Crown consistently with Justice, to pursue the political plan of getting that country seated as quickly as possible." Just a few years earlier Washington had warned Robert Stewart in ominous tones of the terrible consequences should the Cherokees and their neighbors unite against the colonies; now, apparently, "the mild and friendly disposition of the Southern Indians" meant that the Mississippi Company's proposed settlement could be made sooner and more safely than one farther north, where the warlike Six Nations were certain to obstruct, and perhaps totally prevent, such a settlement for many years to come.[42]

The Mississippi Company members adopted a line of argument to which Washington would adhere throughout his life: western expansion was best carried out as an orderly process by placing western land in the hands of men of property. The alternative was to leave things as they were, "when people in numbers that have no property and of bad reputation generally are bursting daily thro' the bounds of the settled Colonies, and fixing on the Waters of the Ohio, both lawless and useless to their Country."[43] Nothing came of the Mississippi Company, however, but its claims conflicted with the claims of the Ohio Company, to which Washington and the Lees also belonged.[44]

Washington had other irons in the fire. In 1763 he joined a group of ten investors, mostly members of the Virginia Assembly, who purchased 40,000 acres of swampland on the border of Virginia and North Carolina. The company proposed to drain and develop the land, and each member provided five slaves to do the work. Nothing came of this scheme either, but Washington held on to his 4,000 acres of swampland until 1795.[45] He also shared and promoted "Potomac fever" and began joining organizations for improving navigation on the upper river. In addition, Washington in 1763 expected to acquire a substantial share of the 200,000 acres Dinwiddie had promised to the army that fought in the 1754 campaign, he hoped to benefit from awards of land to British veterans, and he bought into the grant of lands awarded to traders to compensate their losses in Pontiac's War.[46] His portfolio was diverse, and he had a stake in multiple ventures, but Indian actions and imperial reactions jeopardized them all.

Before the French and Indian War, across large stretches of the frontier, Indians and colonists had rubbed elbows in their daily lives—trading, exchanging news, smoking, eating, and sometimes sleeping together. The war shattered patterns of peaceful coexistence. Now, it seemed, peace required keeping Indians and colonists apart. At a time when American colonists and land speculators like Washington were poised to reap the fruits of victory beyond the Appalachian Mountains, the British government decided to halt colonial expansion at the mountains.[47] At a time when Parliament was hoping to reduce troop numbers after the French and Indian War, Pontiac's War convinced the government that it needed to keep a standing army in America, ten thousand soldiers, almost half of them stationed on the frontier to protect colonists and Indians from each other. Some colonial merchants took advantage of the economic opportunities offered by the presence of the army, but most colonists suspected its purpose was to control rather than defend them. Britain had not maintained a standing army in America when the French threatened the colonies; why do so now when there was no French threat? Redcoats who had been less than impressive in wartime remained to threaten colonists' property, liberty, and daughters in peacetime. Worse still, the government asked the colonists to help shoulder the hefty financial burden of maintaining the military establishment in North America. British taxpayers were staggering under the costs of a long global war, and British ministers thought it only reasonable that the American colonies should pay their share. In 1765 Parliament passed the Stamp Act, a measure that is often considered the first step in the imperial crisis that led to the American Revolution.[48]

Pontiac's War did not create the policy of restricting settlement on Indian land, but it made it urgent. Even before the Treaty of Easton, Sir William Johnson had recommended establishing "clear and fixed Boundaries between our Settlements and their Hunting Grounds."[49] In November 1761 the Board of Trade had urged George III to do something to stop colonists settling on land the Indians had not yet sold. The board called it a "most dangerous Tendency" and pointed out that drawing a western boundary and prohibiting settlement beyond it would also keep American settlers within the British commercial orbit and dependent on British manufactures. The farther west settlers migrated, the more difficult it would be for them to import British goods, and the more tenuous their ties to Britain. Better that they be diverted north to Nova Scotia or south to Florida to help develop those colonies than settle in the interior of the continent beyond the reach of the government.[50] Officials in London were already studying proposals to impose a boundary when Pontiac's War pushed the government into action. On September 16 Lord Halifax, incorporating suggestions from two proposals drafted earlier in the summer, presented his plan to the cabinet. The Earl of Hillsborough, the new president of the Board of Trade, made a few revisions, ran the document by the attorney general, and had it back to Halifax by October 4. The Privy Council gave its pro forma approval, and on October 7 the king officially promulgated it.[51] By the standards of eighteenth-century government, the Royal Proclamation was issued at breakneck speed.

The Royal Proclamation of 1763 was Britain's first attempt to administer the new American empire it had won. Its guiding principle was to restore and maintain order on the frontier. Indian relations must be directed from London by a government with an imperial vision of American affairs, not by individual colonies pursuing local agendas. It organized the newly acquired territories into four new colonies—Quebec, East and West Florida, and Grenada—and it established the Appalachian Mountains as the boundary between Indian and colonial lands, reserving for Native peoples a vast territory stretching from the Appalachians to the Mississippi. (In its haste to issue the proclamation, the government had no time to survey the actual patterns of Indian-white settlement, which left enclaves of Indian peoples and lands east of the line and Europeans, including French settlements in the Illinois country, west of the line.) It prohibited any "private Person" from buying "any Lands reserved to the said Indians within those parts of our Colonies where We have thought proper to allow Settlement," and it prohibited purchase or settlement west of the Appalachians. Squatters were to leave immediately. Only the Crown's representatives acting in formal council with Indian nations could negotiate land transfers. Although the Indian trade was declared open to all British subjects, traders needed a pass from the governor or commander in chief of their colony to do business beyond the mountains. The governors of Quebec and the Floridas were authorized to grant land to help populate their new colonies and divert settler pressure to the North and South, but colonial governors could not make land grants west of the Appalachians, a restriction that nullified, or at least put on hold, Dinwiddie's land bounties to soldiers. Intended to remove "all just Cause of Discontent, and Uneasiness" among the Indians, the measures were to remain in effect "until our future pleasure be known." At that time, veterans of the war would be entitled to free land on a graduated scale according to rank, from 5,000 acres for field officers to 50 acres for privates.[52]

In the past, individuals had bought land from Indian people in all kinds of circumstances. Now only the Crown and its official representatives could purchase Indian land; only tribes could sell land, and they must do it in open treaty council. The Crown claimed a right of preemption to those lands—an exclusive right to purchase if and when the Indians chose to sell. In other words, the government effectively said that Indians could sell their lands only to the government. East of the Appalachians, governors and commanders in chief were authorized to purchase Indian lands on the Crown's behalf, but west of the mountains the right belonged to the Crown alone. Colonial governors and individual colonists had no right to claim title to Indian lands there. In short, London, not the colonies, controlled western expansion.[53]

By restricting and regulating access to Indian country, the proclamation intended to avoid further frontier wars and to keep colonists within the British orbit as the empire grew. Ministers latched on to the Appalachians as a clear demarcation line that could be adjusted when time and circumstances allowed; the goal was to control westward expansion, not to stop it in its tracks. The proclamation boundary never existed except as a line drawn on a map; it was an abstract idea that had to be negotiated and implemented in subsequent meetings and treaties with the Indians.[54] With France removed from the scene, the proclamation outlined the foundations for building a new relationship between Britain and the Indian nations. John Stuart and the governors of the southern colonies met with nearly a thousand Cherokees, Creeks, Catawbas, Chickasaws, and Choctaws at Augusta, Georgia, in November, and in the winter Sir William Johnson dispatched runners carrying copies of the document and strings of wampum across Indian country, summoning the tribes to a council. Two thousand Indians, representing twenty-four nations from Nova Scotia to the Mississippi and as far north as Hudson Bay, assembled at Niagara in the summer of 1764. Johnson read the provisions of the proclamation, and the Indians pledged themselves to peace. Gifts and wampum belts were exchanged to seal the agreement and usher in a new era of alliance between equals based on mutual respect and interdependence.[55]

Getting American colonists to accept the proclamation was another matter. Many frontier settlers simply ignored it. Those who had crossed the Appalachians were now squatting illegally on Indian land and might be removed by British troops. Squatters were used to that, however, and the proclamation had limited effect on them, especially as there were no courts beyond the line and the British army lacked the resources to patrol and maintain the line. Scotch-Irish pioneers who had resented English laws at home were unlikely to obey them now they were three thousand miles away. In effect, as the historian Patrick Griffin points out, the proclamation created an area beyond the line that was beyond the law, a no-man's-land "of possibilities for the desperate."[56] Lieutenant Governor Fauquier issued proclamations and tried to enforce the boundary, but he was no more able to keep frontier Virginians off Indian lands than to stop them murdering Indian people.[57] Four years after the proclamation, Indians complained that settlers were making more encroachments on their country than they had before. And colonists not only encroached on Indian lands; they also encroached on the deer and other game Indians claimed as their own, following their prey across boundary lines and claiming that game-rich country like Kentucky constituted common hunting territory, not an Indian reserve.[58]

Land speculators were furious. Unlike squatters, they could not ignore the proclamation. They had pinned their hopes on being able to turn speculations into fortunes when the war was won, the French were expelled, and Indian lands were opened to settlement. Instead, the empire seemed to be favoring the Indians at the expense of men like Washington who had fought in its service. The members of the Ohio Company were shocked to find that the very backcountry lands the Indians had laid waste were now "reserved for these cruel butchers," while His Majesty's subjects were ordered off them. George Mason declared the proclamation "an express destruction of our grant."[59] They could not rent or sell the land they owned or claimed unless they had clear title to it, and now title to the land derived from the Crown, not from the Indians. They could not, now, buy and sell western lands legally. The proclamation not only threatened the Virginia gentry's opportunity to make money speculating in western land; it also threatened their ability to make money selling or renting that land to the farming classes. Settlers, even if they did so illegally, could now acquire Indian land without paying any money to speculators and brokers, who, without legal title to the land, could neither extract payment from them nor evict them. Britain's interference with what they regarded as their right to make enormous profits in the West generated sentiments of rebellious resentment among Virginia gentry.[60]

British policy and the Indian boundary threatened to stifle attempts by Washington and other planters at achieving greater economic independence and to frustrate their vision for the expansion and development of Virginia. Already feeling the effects of imperial restrictions on Virginia's economy, they would not watch their investments in Indian country slip away.[61] Colonial elites who saw themselves transforming wilderness into civil society on the edge of the empire had developed a "settler political theory" that included the right to acquire property by dispossessing and supplanting Native peoples without restriction or interference from the imperial center; for many, the restrictive new policies threatened their rights as settlers and constituted the first step in their alienation from the empire.

The fruits of the victory over France for which they had fought and bled were being denied them; in fact, the old French and Indian barrier seemed to have been replaced by a British-Indian barrier. Washington, Jefferson, Arthur Lee, Patrick Henry, and others denounced British interference as tyranny and demanded freedom. It included the freedom to acquire and sell Indian land at will.[62]

THE PROCLAMATION SLAMMED THE DOOR shut on Washington's land speculations, or almost. Rather than continue struggling to grow quality tobacco on Mount Vernon's light soil, he began to replace tobacco, which had to be exported, with wheat, which could be sold locally, and in 1767 he turned all of his fields over to wheat.[63] But he did not give up on land speculations—nor did anyone else. He needed other sources of revenue, and he knew where to look.

As the historian Joseph Ellis puts it, Washington's various schemes to acquire land in the Ohio Valley "crisscrossed in dizzying patterns of speculation" that were further complicated by border disputes between Virginia and Pennsylvania, overlapping tribal claims, shifting imperial policies, and squatters who claimed land by virtue of occupying it. But, in Ellis's apt summation, "at bottom lurked a basic conflict about the future of the Ohio Country: Washington believed it was open to settlement; the British government believed it was closed; and the Indians believed it was theirs."[64] Washington was not about to abandon his views, his claims, or his schemes. He did not risk being punished by the government if he continued to buy land west of the mountains; the problem was that such purchases were unenforceable in court, and the titles derived from them could be superseded by later title. He might lose his purchase price if the government later granted the land to someone else. It was a risk he was prepared to take. He looked for ways around the new law.[65]

Frustrated by British policy on the ground in America, speculators turned their efforts to changing British policy at the highest levels in London, even lobbying Parliament to approve new colonies west of the Appalachians. Since now only the government could grant title to Indian land, instead of trying to buy land themselves, speculators lobbied the government to buy it for them; once it was purchased, the government could grant it to the speculators, who would in turn divide it up and sell it to settlers. These gentry had connections in high places. The Ohio Company had shareholders in Britain as well as America; some members of the government were also stakeholders in the Ohio Company or other land syndicates.

After 1763 it was common practice to offer shares in land companies to people in positions of power who could decide, or influence those who decided, whether and which land could be purchased. Land speculators and their agents and associates were soon lobbying to have the boundary abandoned or at least moved.[66] George Croghan, after an abortive trip to London to promote his and his associates' claims, announced in 1766: "One half of England is Now Land Mad & Every body there has thire Eys fixt on this Cuntry."[67] Not surprisingly, there were plans to renegotiate the boundary almost as soon as the Royal Proclamation announced it. Those negotiations now had to be carried out by the Crown's official representatives—John Stuart, British superintendent for Indian affairs south of the Ohio, and Sir William Johnson in the North—but it was only a matter of time before the West was reopened.

Washington believed so. Once that happened, he and other men of ambition and mettle could get back to building fortunes and futures on Indian lands. As he advised his neighbor Captain John Posey in June 1767, there was "an opening prospect in the back Country for Adventurers...where an enterprising Man with very little m[o]ney may lay the foundation for a Noble Estate in the New Settlem'ts upon Monongahela for himself and posterity." This was, after all, "how the greatest Estates we have in this Colony were made...by taking up and purchasing at very low rates the rich back Lands which were thought nothing of in those days, but are now the most valuable Lands we possess." Posey had served with Washington during the French and Indian War but was now a deadbeat neighbor perpetually in debt—and in debt to Washington, who had a mortgage on his land. He chose not to follow Washington's advice, preferring instead to follow his example and marry a widow with property, even though she was, according to local gossip, "as thick as she is high, and gets drunk at least three or four times a week."[68]

Washington learned of Johnson's plans for a new Indian boundary in Pennsylvania as early as 1767, and he took steps to purchase lands in the area that would fall to Pennsylvania when the line was redrawn. He turned to William Crawford, whom he had known since their school days. Crawford was born in Westmoreland County, Virginia, and at an early age moved with his family across the Blue Ridge Mountains to Frederick County. Commissioned as an ensign in 1755, he served with Christopher Gist's company of scouts and marched with Washington on Braddock's campaign; as a lieutenant in the Virginia Regiment he marched again with Washington on Forbes's campaign, and he served in Pontiac's War.[69] During his campaigns he

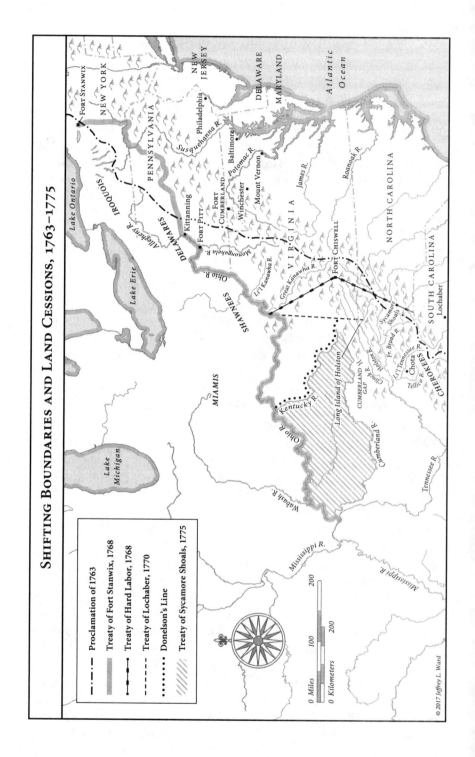

SHIFTING BOUNDARIES AND LAND CESSIONS, 1763–1775

Legend:
- Proclamation of 1763
- Treaty of Fort Stanwix, 1768
- Treaty of Hard Labor, 1768
- Treaty of Lochaber, 1770
- Donelson's Line
- Treaty of Sycamore Shoals, 1775

FORT STANWIX

NEW YORK

NEW JERSEY

DELAWARE

MARYLAND

Atlantic Ocean

Lake Ontario

IROQUOIS

PENNSYLVANIA

Philadelphia

Susquehanna R.

Baltimore

Potomac R.

Mount Vernon

Winchester

Roanoke R.

James R.

NORTH CAROLINA

Allegheny R.

DELAWARES

Kittanning

Fort Pitt

Fort Cumberland

Lake Erie

Monongahela R.

Ohio R.

Li'l Kanawha R.

Great Kanawha R.

VIRGINIA

FORT CHISWELL

SOUTH CAROLINA

Lochaber

SHAWNEES

Sycamore Shoals

Fr. Broad R.

Li'l Tennessee R.

Tellico R.

Chota

CHEROKEES

MIAMIS

Kentucky R.

Long Island of Holston

CUMBERLAND GAP

Clinch R.

Holston R.

Tennessee R.

Ohio R.

Cumberland R.

Lake Michigan

Wabash R.

Mississippi R.

Mississippi R.

0 Miles   100   200
0 Kilometers   200

© 2017 Jeffrey L. Ward

got to know the rich country of the Monongahela Valley, and in 1765 he secured land grants and moved with his wife and three children to the Youghiogheny River, settling at a place called Stewart's Crossing or Crossings in western Pennsylvania. As a man on the spot and an old friend in whom Washington felt he could confide, Crawford was well positioned to act as his agent in the region.[70]

In September 1767 Washington wrote to Crawford proposing a partnership. The letter stands as a bald statement of Washington's tactics for acquiring Indian land ahead of the curve. He asked Crawford to "look me out a Tract of about 1500, 2000, or more Acres" close to his own settlement. Washington was not interested in just any land. "No; a Tract to please me must be rich (of which no Person can be a better judge than yourself)," and, if possible, level and close to river navigation. He wanted Crawford to find the land soon and find a way of "securing it immediately from the attempts of others, as nothing is more certain than that the Lands cannot remain long ungranted." He could circumvent Pennsylvania's practice of making grants in tracts of no more than 300 acres each by making several contiguous entries. He also wanted to collaborate with Crawford to secure some of the most valuable lands in the territory placed off-limits by the Royal Proclamation, and to start the ball rolling now, "for I can never look upon that Proclamation in any other light (but this I say between ourselves) than as a temporary expedient to quiet the Minds of the Indians." The prohibition was bound to be removed in a few years, in which case anyone "who neglects the present opportunity of hunting ou[t] good Lands & in some measure Marking & distinguishing them for their own (in order to keep others from settling them) will never regain it." So if Crawford would do the legwork of seeking out the lands, Washington would take care of the paper work and secure title to them as soon as it was possible, and he would assume all the costs of surveying and patenting. Once the business was concluded, Crawford would get "such a reasonable proportion of the whole as we may fix upon at our first meeting." Washington also intended "to let some few of my friends be concerned in the Scheme & who must also partake of the advantages" to help move the project along. "By this time," he added redundantly, "it may be easy for you discover, that my Plan is to secure a good deal of Land." To avoid censure for his opinion on the proclamation and to avoid giving alarm—or giving the same idea to others—Washington urged Crawford to "keep this whole matter a secret." Do everything "by a silent management" and "under the guise of hunting game," he advised. Once Crawford identified the lands, Washington would have them "immediately surveyed, to keep others off, and leave the rest to time and my own assiduity to accomplish."[71]

Crawford did as he was asked. In fact, he had already been thinking of searching out land beyond the proclamation line under pretense of hunting. He and Washington were on the same wavelength. Washington could depend on him to lose no time and to keep the whole thing "a profound secret," he said. Trading with the Indians was a good way to locate the best land, and for that he would need licenses, which he asked Washington to obtain for him.[72] Crawford identified some suitable tracts of land near Fort Pitt. The next year Washington secured title to a tract on the Youghiogheny River about thirty-five miles southeast of Fort Pitt, his first land west of the Alleghenies. It was the beginning of a lucrative partnership that would last fifteen years.[73] Confident the boundary line would be extended, Washington had Crawford survey a tract of land for him in southwestern Pennsylvania as if acting for himself, "taking all the good lands and leaving out the sorry."[74]

Negotiating a new boundary required preparatory diplomacy and preliminary talks. Since a new boundary would engulf the area through which the Warriors' Path ran, the Iroquois and Cherokees had first to settle their differences. Attakullakulla and several other Cherokee chiefs sailed for New York in November 1767 (where Attakullakulla, who had gone to the theater in London thirty-seven years before, attended a performance of *Richard III*) and then traveled on to Johnson Hall, where Sir William orchestrated a peace in March.[75] Many Iroquois worried more about land-hungry Virginians than they did about Cherokees. "We and our dependants have been for some time like Giddy People not knowing what to do, wherever we turned about we saw our Blood," the Oneida chief Conoghquieson told Johnson. When they went hunting they found the country covered with fences, the trees cut down, and the animals driven away. They wanted a new boundary, too, Conoghquieson said, but it would only work if the governor of Virginia could "keep his people in better order... otherwise the Path will Close up and not be safe to travel."[76]

In April and May 1768, Croghan met at Fort Pitt with 1,100 Indians, including Guyasuta and Tamaqua, to settle differences. A Shawnee chief named Nimwha told the British the Indians were "uneasy to see that you think yourselves Masters of this Country, because you have taken it from the French, who you know had no Right to it, as it is the Property of us Indians." Guyasuta played a more conciliatory role; the Six Nations and their allies had agreed to allow the British to build forts and trading posts, and "to Travel the

Road of Peace," he said. The commissioners thanked him "for his friendly Behavior on this occasion."[77]

While Washington was participating in the gala events welcoming the new governor, Baron Botetourt, to Williamsburg in October 1768, two treaties were being negotiated that hugely affected Washington's prospects of making a fortune in the West. John Stuart followed his instructions and negotiated what became known as the Treaty of Hard Labor with the Cherokees. It moved the boundary west to the Kanawha River but left Kentucky and southwestern Virginia to the Cherokees, contrary to the interests of Washington and other Virginia land speculators.[78] Meanwhile, at Fort Stanwix in New York, Johnson met with some two thousand Iroquois over a period of several weeks to negotiate a new boundary line in the North. Pennsylvania, Virginia, traders seeking compensation in land for losses they had suffered in the war, and various other interested parties sent representatives. Croghan and Montour were present. The home government had authorized Johnson to secure an extension of the boundary down the Ohio River as far as the Kanawha River, where it would meet up with the new boundary Stuart had negotiated with the Cherokees. Instead, in exchange for £10,000 in merchandise, Johnson obtained a cession of territory that stretched another four hundred miles down the Ohio to the mouth of the Cherokee or Tennessee River. The home government rapped Johnson's knuckles for exceeding his instructions, but the treaty suited just about everyone who was present. Britain got a new Indian boundary line; Johnson and Croghan got chunks of land for themselves; Pennsylvania and its traders secured confirmation of their claims. For their part, the Iroquois obtained British confirmation of their claims to lands in the Ohio Valley, effectively diverted the oncoming rush of settlement away from Iroquois country and down the Ohio, and received a huge haul of goods in the process.[79]

The treaty was good news, too, for Virginian land speculators. Virginia's representative at the treaty was Dr. Thomas Walker, the veteran explorer, surveyor, and head of the Loyal Land Company. Walker claimed he was there only as an observer, but he had important agendas to push. His great-grandson later said he was "as great a land-monger as Genl. Washington."[80] Andrew Lewis also made the journey to Fort Stanwix but left before the treaty got under way, hurrying home for the treaty with the Cherokees. If Johnson had obeyed his instructions, the boundary would have stopped at the Kanawha; instead, no doubt prompted by Walker behind the scenes, he pushed the boundary down to the Tennessee River. It seemed that by the

Treaty of Fort Stanwix, Johnson and Walker had opened Kentucky for Virginia to claim.[81]

In 1763 the Royal Proclamation had set the Indian boundary line at the Appalachian Mountains. Five years later the Treaty of Fort Stanwix effectively moved it hundreds of miles to the west. George Washington was back in business.

CHAPTER 9

"A good deal of Land"

THE TREATY OF FORT STANWIX set off a land rush. Arthur Lee resubmitted the Mississippi Land Company's 1763 petition to the king.[1] Thomas Walker revived the dormant Loyal Land Company. Thomas Jefferson, for whom Walker had acted as guardian after his father died, got in on the act, joined two separate land companies, and set about securing 7,000 acres of land west of the Appalachians, although he had no interest in moving west himself.[2] And George Washington redoubled his efforts to get as much good land as he could. In the eight years between the Treaty of Fort Stanwix and the outbreak of the Revolution, as Americans moved from trying to preserve their independence within the British Empire to seeking independence *from* the British Empire,[3] Washington's main concern was acquiring land he thought was due to him—and some he knew was not. Unfortunately, the lands Washington, Walker, and Jefferson coveted were bitterly contested. The Shawnees and Cherokees both claimed the territory ceded at Fort Stanwix as hunting grounds and denied the Iroquois had any right to sell it. Shawnees tried to build a multitribal coalition to resist the British-Iroquois land deal.[4] Rival colonies and companies competed for the same lands.

The Stanwix Treaty seemed to reopen the opportunity for realizing Lieutenant Governor Dinwiddie's promise of 200,000 acres to the Virginia regiment and the Royal Proclamation's promise of 5,000 acres to "reduced" officers who had served in the war. Dinwiddie's proclamation had offered land bounties to encourage men to enlist; it did not, as noted, apply to commissioned officers, and Washington was not a "reduced" officer—he resigned his commission long before his regiment was disbanded after the Cherokee War. Undaunted, he renewed his demands that Dinwiddie's promise be met for officers and soldiers alike, and he pressed his claim to be included in the proclamation's provision.

He petitioned Governor Botetourt and the Executive Council to implement the land bounties Dinwiddie had promised. He argued that only the three hundred officers and men who had joined the Virginia Regiment between February and July 1754—in other words, Washington and the men who served under him in the Fort Necessity campaign—were entitled to the land bounties, thereby excluding "the multitude which afterwards engaged in the course of a Ten years War." His petition also included "some self-serving suggestions under the guise of helpful hints." He urged that some of the bounty lands be set aside along the Monongahela River, and the rest along the Kanawha—in the area William Crawford had already surveyed for him. Since the Ohio territory in question was nominally part of Augusta County in 1769, and the county surveyor (who was Andrew Lewis's brother, Thomas) would no doubt be busy with other duties, Washington recommended that another surveyor be appointed. Clearly, he had Crawford in mind for the position. The country was "settling very fast," Washington pointed out, and poor people "swarming with large Families" would soon occupy all the fertile areas, "whilst none but barren Hills, & rugged Mountains, will be left to those, who have toild, and bled for the Country, & whose right to a part of it is fixed by the strongest Assurances which Government coud give them so long ago as 1754."[5]

Botetourt and the council bought it. With a watchful eye on Pennsylvanian traders and settlers who were claiming lands west of the Alleghenies, the day after Washington petitioned, the council granted permission for Washington and the officers and soldiers who had joined the Virginia Regiment prior to July 4, 1754 (the day Washington surrendered Fort Necessity), to locate 200,000 acres of land on the Great Kanawha and other rivers. Washington was to apply to the president and masters of the College of William and Mary, who licensed county agents, to appoint a surveyor to determine the exact location of the lands. Washington took out an advertisement in the *Virginia Gazette* requesting the officers and soldiers to submit their claims to him so that he could lay them all before the governor and council. He then moved quickly to exert his influence and secure Crawford's appointment as surveyor.

Other Virginians also wanted to increase their share of ceded lands. They objected to the Treaty of Hard Labor with the Cherokees.

Walker of the Loyal Land Company, Andrew Lewis of the smaller Greenbrier Company, and others wanted to redraw the northern boundary of Cherokee country to legitimize their claims to lands in Kentucky.[6] The House of Burgesses petitioned the British government, complaining that if the line stood, lands already granted by regular patent "would be entirely dismembered from this Colony, allotted to the Indians, and entirely lost to the Proprietors," who, after all, had been authorized by law and encouraged by Governor Dunmore "to explore and settle this new Country, at the Risque of their Lives, and at a great Expence." Virginians wanted to extend their boundary with North Carolina westward and effectively annex Kentucky and all land northward to the mouth of the Kanawha River that had been ceded at the Treaty of Fort Stanwix.[7]

Confronted with an invasion of white people into their hunting territories who killed their deer, Cherokees opposed the new boundary proposed by Virginia. Superintendent John Stuart warned that continued actions by "adventurers from your colony" and a further cession of Cherokee land could cause "a general rupture with and coalition of all the tribes on the continent."[8] Nevertheless, with Virginian land speculators exercising their influence and Virginian agents at work, Stuart met with Attakullakulla, Ostenaco, Oconostota, and other Cherokees at Lochaber, South Carolina, in 1770 and negotiated a new treaty that revised the Treaty of Hard Labor and moved the boundary line west.[9] Then a Virginian surveyor and speculator, Colonel John Donelson, got Cherokee delegates to agree to move *that* line west to the Kentucky River.[10]

The new boundary lines formed by the Fort Stanwix and Cherokee treaties pointed like an arrow into the heart of Indian country, but the lines did not hold, and neither did the peace. Escalating rents and hard times drove thousands of people from the Celtic borderlands of Britain to America. In a society where nineteen out of twenty people lived by farming, the influx put pressure on agricultural lands in the East and sent migrants west onto lands the Shawnees and Cherokees still regarded as theirs. Alexander Cameron, British agent among the Cherokees, described to Superintendent John Stuart the pattern of encroachment that remained a feature of American expansion through Washington's presidency and beyond: "The white people upon the frontier are all inveterate against the Indians because they have any land left them. They drive their cows and horses over the line and when any of them are stolen they exclaim against the Indians and would have them all cut off, although upon every little alarm they are ready to desert their interest and all that is dear to them."[11]

Washington denounced such violence against Indians, not least because it sparked hostilities that threatened his land business. In the summer of 1769, three Mingoes returning from a raid against southern tribes were killed on the South Branch of the Potomac. "It seems this Murder (for it deserves no other name) was committed on slight provocation," Washington wrote John Armstrong. He was not optimistic about the chances of bringing the perpetrators to justice, but fortunately, since none of the Indians survived to tell the tale, "we, in consequence, may represent it in as favorable a light, as the thing will admit of, having the knowledge of it confined to ourselves."[12]

With considerable understatement Indians told the governors of Virginia, Pennsylvania, and Maryland in 1771: "We find your people are very fond of our rich land." Settlers had crossed the mountains, then the Fort Stanwix treaty line, and would soon be crossing the Ohio; if the governors could not restrain their people, the chiefs would be unable to control their young men, "for we assure you the black clouds begin to gather fast in this country." Indians who had watched as nation after nation was destroyed saw that "it must be soon their turn also to be exterminated."[13] In 1768 few white people lived in the region that became Kentucky; by the early 1780s there would be more than twenty thousand.[14]

The Treaty of Fort Stanwix left Pennsylvania's western boundary undetermined and the area still contested between Virginia and Pennsylvania. The claims of the Ohio Company became entangled with the claims of a group of Philadelphia merchants who described themselves as the "Suffering Traders" in an area known as the Indiana Grant. The original group of traders expanded to include British politicians and speculators, and their claim for reparations for losses sustained during the Indian war became absorbed into a much larger project that reached the highest levels of government. George Mercer, in London to push the Ohio Company's claim, was "bought off," and the Suffering Traders joined forces with Benjamin Franklin, Sir William Johnson, George Croghan, and influential individuals in England to form a new consortium, known as the Grand Ohio Company or Walpole Company. It planned to develop a new western colony called Vandalia in the ceded lands south of Ohio and petitioned for a grant of 20 million acres within the Stanwix cession that would have swallowed up the Indiana Grant and embraced what is now West Virginia and northeastern Kentucky.[15] Washington and the Ohio Company complained, but they had been beaten at their own game. Meanwhile, settlers who claimed Indian land by occupying, clearing, and defending it felt little obligation to respect the mammoth paper claims of wealthy elites far from the scene.

Washington was still impatient to secure the land while he could. Having obtained permission to survey lands he had already effectively surveyed, he summoned meetings of veterans, induced them to select Crawford as surveyor of the bounty lands, and collected money from them to cover their share of the surveying costs. He also set about buying up the claims of fellow officers when he could get them on the cheap and without making the purchases in his own name.[16] Anticipating that the government would soon make a decision on whether officers and soldiers who were promised land by the Royal Proclamation would be permitted to acquire it west of the Allegheny Mountains, Washington enlisted the help of his brother Charles to discover if any of the officers would sell their rights and at what price. He doubted any of them would sell "upon such terms as I woud buy," because with so many competing grants, "I woud hardly give any Officer a button for his Right," but surely some who needed "a little ready money, would gladly sell." He asked Charles to approach them "in a joking way" and find out what they would take for their grants. If he could buy them for as little as £7 or less per 1,000 acres, he was to do so under his own name and not let it be known that George had "any concern therein." By one argument or another, Washington purchased from his former comrades lots totaling more than 5,100 acres "for a pittance." Through grant and purchase combined, he would acquire over 20,000 acres.[17]

In October 1770 Washington, in company with Dr. James Craik, William Crawford, several others, and their servants, set out on another trip across the Alleghenies and down the Ohio to the mouth of the Great Kanawha, to explore and mark possible sites for future surveys of bounty lands.[18] Traveling by way of Fort Necessity and Braddock's Field, they viewed 1,600 acres of land Crawford had selected for Washington on the Youghiogheny and spent a day at Crawford's home. Subsequent visitors to Crawford's home noted their host was not a model of virtue. In January 1773 Rev. David McClure preached a sermon at Stewart's Crossings and after the meeting rode home with Crawford. "The Captain was very hospitable," McClure recorded in his diary. "He is from Virginia." And then, in Latin: "Holy things are not much observed in his house. He has a virtuous wife, but, alas, he at this time lives in fornication; and the scandalous woman, according to what they say, he keeps not far from his house." Two years later Nicholas Cresswell, a young Englishman traveling in the Ohio country with hopes (vain, it turned out) of securing enough land to establish himself as a gentleman farmer, met Crawford at his mistress's house. No prude when it came to relations with the opposite sex, Cresswell noted in his diary that "this woman is common to him, his brother, half brother, and his own Son, and is his wife's sister's daughter at the same time." Cresswell pronounced them "a vile set of brutes."[19] If Crawford's creative domestic arrangements were in place in 1770, Washington made no mention in his journal; one wonders what Martha would have thought of it all.

At Fort Pitt—described by Cresswell five years later as "small, about 30 houses, the people chiefly in Indian trade"[20]—Washington dined with George Croghan. The two had quarreled back in 1754, but now Washington was mending fences with a view to advancing his land schemes in the region, and Croghan had land claims he wanted to sell, despite—or because of—the fact that the British government rejected them. Working through Crawford, Washington discussed buying 15,000 acres of Croghan's land, as well as the possibility of purchasing his interest in the Walpole Company. But Crawford could not find land of the quality and quantity Washington wanted, and Croghan's claims were all too shaky. Finally, Washington decided against it.[21]

At Fort Pitt, a Seneca chief named White Mingo and a group of Six Nations chiefs came "to bid me welcome to this Country." White Mingo said they remembered Washington from when he went as an ambassador to the French, and they hoped that past differences were now resolved and forgotten. He gave him a string of wampum so "the People of Virginia wou'd consider them as friends & Brothers linked together in one chain."[22]

Washington took on Joseph Nicholson as interpreter and two Indians, an older man called the Pheasant and a young warrior.[23] Departing Fort Pitt, they canoed down the Ohio and made their surveys of land between the Little and Great Kanawha Rivers (lands also claimed by the Walpole Company, which agreed to allow the regimental claims[24]). Croghan and Alexander McKee, the British Indian agent at Fort Pitt, accompanied them for the first day, as far as Logstown.[25] There, they heard rumors (unfounded, it turned out) that Indians had killed two traders downriver. They saw a war party of sixty Iroquois heading south to raid the Catawbas.[26] Washington filled his journal with detailed descriptions of the rich lands he saw, including those "which Captn. Crawford had taken up for me."[27]

Passing the mouth of the Kanawha into what is now West Virginia at the end of October, the group came across the camp of an Indian hunting party. Washington recognized their leader as "an old acquaintance, he being one of the Indians that went with me to the French in 1753." Then Guyasuta was "the young hunter"; now he was "one of the Six Nations Chiefs, and the head of them upon this River," a seasoned warrior and diplomat to whom it was necessary to pay "our Compliments." In the intervening years, Guyasuta had fought in the French and Indian War and Pontiac's War and led attacks on English forts and settlements. David McClure, who saw him a couple of years later, said he looked every inch a warrior, with "a very sensible countenance & dignity of manners." For his part, Washington was now himself a seasoned Indian fighter and land speculator; he had twice invaded the Ohio country with British armies, had defended the Virginia backcountry against Indian raids, and relentlessly coveted Indian lands. Nevertheless, Guyasuta was pleased to see him and treated his party "with great kindness," sharing buffalo meat and insisting they spend the night. The next morning, he expressed the Indians' desire for trade with Virginia and asked Washington to inform the governor of their friendly disposition toward white people. Washington complained that "the tedious ceremony which the Indians observe in their Councellings & speeches" delayed their departure until 9:00 a.m. Eight days later, Washington's party came upon Guyasuta's hunting camp again, now located on Big Sandy Creek. Again Washington was detained the rest of the day by "the Kindness and Idle ceremony of the Indians," but he put the time to good use, "having a good deal of conversation with him on the Subject of Land." Washington wanted to know the distances from the Great Kanawha to the Falls, where the bottom lands were located, and where the soil was rich.[28] (George Washington Parke Custis later narrated an account, "received from the lips of Dr. Craik," of a meeting with "an old Indian" who, recognizing his adoptive father as the soldier who had been invulnerable to Indian bullets at Braddock's defeat, prophesied his future destiny in conventional "Indian speak."[29] Washington's journal makes no mention of such an encounter.)

Washington knew what he was looking for, and so did his Indian guides. At one point, the Pheasant told him about a fine piece of land with a beautiful location for a house and, "in order to give me a more lively Idea of it," sketched it out in chalk on a deerskin. The house would sit on top of a hill overlooking a large stretch of level land, watered by a creek that ran parallel to the Ohio and attracted herds of buffalo that had worn tracks coming to drink.[30] Like other Indians who guided explorers, surveyors, and speculators through their country, the old man seems to have willingly or unwittingly assisted in staking out the best lands for colonizers, but Washington had no way of knowing, and nor do we, if and when the guides diverted his attention from other lands or hurried him past sites that held cultural significance for Native people.

Washington's travels to the Great Kanawha and its tributaries took him past extensive ancient earthworks; the area known as Washington's Bottom is particularly dense with prehistoric mounds. Washington could hardly have missed these mounds, noted a former director of the National Park Service, Roger Kennedy; "these earthen buildings were by far the largest architecture he had ever seen or ever would see." But if he wrote about them in his journals, his words were lost when the pages of his diary for that part of his journey were mutilated, "so chewed by rodents as to be intelligible only in patches."[31]

Reaching the village of Mingo Town on November 17, Washington and his party were compelled to remain there for three days until horses for baggage and riding arrived. The delay gave Washington an opportunity to pen some rare but brief observations on Indian life in his journal. He noted the Indians had hunting camps and cabins all along the river conveniently located for transporting their skins to market by water, and they were all "(even there women)" dexterous in handling canoes. He recorded a cursory description of their subsistence cycle. They would set out in family hunting bands in the fall and move their camps from place to place, traveling two or three hundred miles from their towns by the spring. In May the women were busy planting, "the Men at Market, & in Idleness, till the Fall again; when they pursue the same course again. During the Summer Months they live a poor & perishing life." The Shawnees, Delawares, and Mingoes living on the upper Ohio viewed white settlers on the river "with an uneasy & jealous Eye, and do not scruple to say that they must be compensated for their Right if the People settle thereon, notwithstanding the Cession of the Six Nation's thereto" at the Treaty of Fort Stanwix.[32]

Washington viewed frontier settlers with an equally uneasy eye. They viewed him and his kind much the same way. Washington and other elites had to establish their claims to large tracts of land by going through the proper channels—or at least give the appearance of doing so—and have the lands surveyed and registered. Settlers employed less formal and more violent methods of establishing ownership on the basis of physical occupation. They cleared fields and built fences and cabins with the axe, defended their new property with the gun, and often defied and disputed the legal claims and surveys of their "betters."[33] Washington noted with some alarm that people from Virginia and other colonies were already exploring and marking out all the valuable lands on Redstone Creek and the waters of the Monongahela and as far down the Ohio as the Little Kanawha. He expected they would reach or even pass the Great Kanawha the following summer and be difficult to deal with. They threatened his plans: "A few Settlements in the midst of some of the large Bottoms, woud render it impractable to get any large qty. of Land Together," he noted in his diary.[34]

Toward the end of his journey, Washington met Dr. John Connolly, George Croghan's nephew. Connolly lived in Pittsburgh and shared Croghan's and Washington's lust for western lands. Washington described him as a sensible and intelligent man who had traveled widely over the western country by land and water. By his own account, Connolly had fought in Pontiac's War and then, after peace was established, explored the newly acquired territory, visiting the various tribes and studying their different manners and customs. He told Washington there were excellent lands for settlement on the Shawnee River, as well as in the Illinois country, and he was eager to attract families to live there.[35] Washington reached Mount Vernon on December 1, 1770, after an absence of nine weeks and one day.[36] He had traveled hundreds of miles, and he had seen a lot of land.

Back home, he continued to enlarge his holdings and buy up grants. On December 6 Crawford wrote to inform Washington that he had bought for him Great Meadows, the site of his defeat and ignominious surrender at Fort Necessity in 1754.[37] Washington made overtures to enlisted men about selling their bounty land, warning them that that there was a good "chance of our never getting the Land at all." John Posey, who had served as a captain in the Virginia Regiment, was entitled to 3,000 acres, but the land "being inconvenient for him to seek after," he decided to sell his rights to it "for a certain Sum agreed upon with the said George Washington."[38] Others did the same. Washington even tried without success to get Captain Robert Stobo and Jacob Van Braam, who had both been taken as hostages by the French after the surrender at Fort Necessity, to sell him their grants, but only, he wrote George Mercer, if "they will take a trifle for it, and more than a trifle circumstanced as things are, I will not give."[39] By such tactics, Washington purchased hundreds of bounties from needy veterans who exchanged the uncertain prospect of obtaining land in the future for a small amount of cash in hand, and he bought up valuable riverfront properties.

In March 1771 Washington held a meeting with the officers of the first Virginia Regiment in Winchester, where he had commanded them during the French and Indian War. After he debriefed them on his trip and Crawford's initial surveys, the officers authorized Washington to instruct Crawford to carry out the surveys he had begun on the Kanawha as soon as possible and to give him orders from time to time to give as needed to complete the work.[40] In his surveys for Washington, Crawford included only rich bottom lands, thereby infringing a Virginia law that grants of Crown land be no more than three times as long as they were deep. Then, back at Mount Vernon, he and Washington prepared finished drafts, or "redrew the surveys in accord with the notes that Washington had carefully made the year before." With Washington alone knowing which bottom lands were the best in the tracts, they presented the surveys to the governor's council for approval and showed them to the officers of the Virginia Regiment.[41] As Ron Chernow writes, "Washington proved a natural manager of this enterprise and undertook the necessary surveying work, but his situation was fraught with conflicts of interest, and the entire episode would be shadowed by accusations of sharp dealing from his former men."[42]

Virginian expansion received a boost in September 1771, when John Murray, the Earl of Dunmore, arrived to succeed Governor Botetourt, who had died the year before. A former Jacobite who had made his peace with and made a place for himself in the Hanoverian regime, Dunmore had been building a fortune in real estate as governor of New York, and he accepted transfer to Virginia's governorship reluctantly.[43] Instead of enforcing the Crown's restrictions on western settlement, he befriended men like Walker and Washington, who claimed and coveted tens of thousands of acres beyond the Appalachians and were willing to share part of their claims in appreciation of his support. Dunmore shared their concern that the Walpole Company associates might secure a grant for their colony of Vandalia, and he encouraged settlers near the Forks of the Ohio to assert Virginia's claim to the area against Pennsylvania.[44]

Washington never joined the Vandalia scheme, and he feared the organization threatened his own land schemes. But he could hardly resist the lure of land wherever the opportunity beckoned, as a letter written to George Mercer on November 22, 1771, betrayed: "Colo. Cresap who I have seen since his return from England gave it to me as his opinion, that, some of the Shares in the New (Charter) Government on the Ohio might be bought very Cheap from some of the present Members—are you of this Opinion? Who are they that would sell? And at what price do you think a share could be bought?"[45]

The Royal Proclamation of 1763 had authorized colonial governors to award land grants to veterans as a way of settling the colonies in Florida and Nova Scotia, but Dunmore interpreted it to include lands purchased at Fort Stanwix.[46] Washington, individually and in petitions from the officers of the Virginia Regiment, lobbied Dunmore to permit the surveys for veterans' claims, and appeared in person in the council chamber to present his case. In November 1771 the governor and council ordered the 200,000 acres of bounty land distributed and awarded the tracts, which ranged from 400 acres for each of fifty-two private soldiers who had made claims to 15,000 acres for each of three field commanders, including Washington. Crawford returned to the region to carry out the surveys and by fall 1772 had surveyed thirteen tracts totaling about 128,000 acres.[47]

Washington feared—and complained to Dunmore in June 1772—that squatters were taking advantage of the ban on westward expansion to establish homesteads in territory that was now officially off-limits, "daily & hourly settling on the choice spots." When and if the proclamation was repealed, the squatters would then solicit legal title directly from the British government on the basis of prior occupancy at the expense of officers and soldiers who had suffered in the cause of their country. Of course, such a development would also cut out middlemen and land speculators like Washington.[48]

These were worrying times for Virginian planter-speculators. By the early 1770s, tightening credit and falling prices aggravated a system that seemed to keep them permanently in debt and threaten their way of life, status, and personal independence. It was a system of dependence Washington had railed against. A financial crash in England in 1772 hit tobacco farmers hard: after borrowing heavily from British merchants to expand their acreage, they suddenly faced demands for repayment of loans. As debts mounted and British restrictions increased, Virginia planters began to see economic independence as a prerequisite to liberty.[49] Chief Justice Lord Mansfield's ruling in *Somerset v. Stewart* in 1772, that an African slave from the colonies who set foot in England became free and could not be returned to slavery, fueled paranoia about impending imperial threats to Virginian planters' property rights.[50] Many began to think radical thoughts and to organize.

They also continued to look west for land. Tobacco agriculture always demanded more land, not least in hard times: if prices were low, planters responded by growing more tobacco on more land with more slaves. New land also offered opportunities to generate additional income by renting or selling it to farmers. In 1772 the British government pulled its troops from outposts like Fort Pitt and Fort Chartres to deal with growing tensions in the cities on the seaboard, leaving a power vacuum in the trans-Appalachian West. In the ensuing anarchy, Virginians and Pennsylvanians almost went to war over the Forks of the Ohio. Colonists invaded Indian lands without restraint. Rival land companies and speculators, land jobbers who acted as agents scouting out lands for companies and speculators, and frontier settlers scrambled to grab what they could, taking possession by force if necessary. In a world that was becoming increasingly disorderly, formal claims looked increasingly vulnerable.[51]

On Wednesday, November 4, 1772, in Williamsburg, Washington submitted a petition to Dunmore and the council on behalf of himself and the officers and soldiers of the Virginia Regiment, claiming land under Dinwiddie's proclamation in 1754. He dined that day with Dunmore; on Thursday he dined with Speaker Peyton Randolph, and on Friday with members of the council. He wanted them to allow him more surveys and in the remaining surveys to substitute better tracts of land for the hilly and rocky parts of the originally designated areas. He had not risked his life in war for poor land: "It is the cream of the Land…which stimulates men to such kind of Enterprise," he argued. The councilors rejected his request, but on Saturday they approved patents for land Crawford had surveyed. Washington secured four tracts totaling 20,147 acres—15,000 on account of his own claim and the rest in claims he had purchased from others in his regiment—more than 10 percent of Dinwiddie's total grant.[52] And he was not finished. The next month Dunmore approved a grant to Washington of 10,990 acres on the left bank of the Kanawha River near its confluence with the Ohio.[53]

Washington's share and the shares he acquired from others amounted to more than 23,000 acres along a forty-mile stretch of the Great Kanawha River and almost 10,000 acres on the banks of the Ohio.[54] He planned to establish a permanent settlement on his lands nearer the mouth of the Great Kanawha. His title to all this was cloudy, but he was, in the historian Charles Ambler's words, "to all intents and purposes a modern real estate promoter, promising everything to everybody."[55] And his land was prime real estate. No other claimant received land that was "so good as your Land,"

Crawford told him; the lots Washington acquired were "much the best on the hole River." By manipulating the system Washington secured "the cream of the Country" for himself.[56]

Some veterans protested. When some of the officers went to the Kanawha to see the bounty tract for themselves, they were "a good deel shagreened" that Washington's land was almost all prize bottomland, as was Dr. Craik's land. Never one to take criticism well, Washington was incensed. He responded to an "impertinent letter" from Major George Muse, who had been a lieutenant colonel in the Virginia Regiment, saying he must have been drunk when he wrote it and that he was an "ungrateful & dirty" fellow. In fairness to Washington, he had a history with Muse. Accused of cowardice for withdrawing his company without orders at the Fort Necessity fight, Muse had resigned his commission. He was then appointed colonel of militia defending the Virginia frontier in 1756. After the war, excluded from the land bounty promised by Dinwiddie, he had asked Washington to help him get his share, offering him one-third of the land if Washington would bear the costs of obtaining it. Washington used his influence to get Muse a share, but it was not as much as Muse hoped for, and he blamed Washington.[57]

Having secured more than his own share under Dinwiddie's proclamation, Washington acquired more under the Royal Proclamation. Dunmore in March 1773 issued him a certificate for the amount allowable to reduced colonels—an additional 5,000 acres.[58] According to the historian Bernhard Knollenberg, Washington secured lands to which he was not entitled by either Dinwiddie's proclamation or the Proclamation of 1763, had them surveyed illicitly by someone who was not qualified by law and who laid them out in violation of legal stipulations as to size and location, and enriched himself at the expense of his Virginia comrades-in-arms: "The more he got of the allotted 200,000 acres, the less was available for the enlisted men to whom it was promised."[59] Douglas Southall Freeman, author of a seven-volume biography of Washington, observed that difficulties in developing land did not deter Washington from acquiring more—"and more and more."[60]

Washington's land hunger extended as far west as the lower Mississippi and as far south as Florida.[61] Looking to Florida for the lands to which he felt entitled under the Royal Proclamation of 1763, he engaged James Wood, a Virginian who was traveling to Florida, to act as his agent and have 10,000 acres surveyed for him if he should see "such Lands as he thinks will answer my purpose." Needless to say, he told Wood, "I should choose good Land, or none at all." The proclamation entitled Washington to 5,000 acres; he would purchase the rest himself. In fact, if Wood found good land, easy to acquire, and not difficult to keep under the government's rules, he should increase the amount to 15,000, 20,000, or 25,000 acres: "In short I could wish to have as much good Land located in a Body or contiguous together...as I could save without much difficulty or expence."[62] Nothing came of his Florida speculation because the British government declared Washington ineligible for land grants under the proclamation.

In April 1773 Washington offered to accompany Dunmore on a trip through the western country in the summer. He and Crawford would be only too willing to assist in "facilitating any Schemes your Lordship might have of procuring Lands to the Westward for us, for yourself."[63] But in June, his stepdaughter Martha "Patsy" Custis, who had a history of epileptic seizures, died suddenly. Distraught, Washington remained at home, and Dunmore made the journey without him, visiting Crawford en route.[64] In September, in anticipation that Dunmore would grant land for petitions below the Scioto, Washington instructed Thomas Bullitt, who was surveying lands down the Ohio, to survey 10,000 acres for him: 5,000 to which he was entitled in his own right, and another 5,000 that he had purchased from a captain and a lieutenant. "No time should be lost," urged Washington. He asked Bullitt to get him all the land in one tract if there was enough "of the first quality," but if not, to get it in two or three. He also asked him "to get it as near to the mouth of the Scioto, that is, to the western bounds of the new Colony, as may be, but for the sake of better Land, I would go quite down to the Falls, or even below it; meaning thereby to get richer & wider bottoms, as it is my desire to have my Land run out upon the Banks of the ohio." He also joined the land rush into Kentucky, acquiring a tract that included a salt spring on the Kentucky River, which, he told Crawford, he planned to turn "to an extensive public benefit, as well as private advantage." Bullitt had no authority to do the surveys, and when Dunmore recalled him Washington immediately asked Crawford to obtain a license and survey his 10,000 acres quickly, because once it became known the governor was going to grant patents for those lands, officers from Pennsylvania, Maryland, and the Carolinas would "flock there in shoals," taking every valuable tract of riverfront land.[65]

That the mouth of the Scioto was the site of Lower Shawnee Town and a center of Shawnee culture and economy seems not to have troubled Washington; nor did he hesitate to join the rush into Shawnee hunting grounds. John Connolly, Virginia's agent in the

Ohio Valley, continued to send Washington reports. In June 1773 he wrote describing "a very curious piece of antiquity," earthwork mounds he had seen on the east side of the Scioto River when he was returning from the Shawnee towns. "The Ruins of Fort Pitt twenty years hence, will not exhibit half the labour discoverable at this place," he said. The mounds, and the artifacts he found, induced him to believe that "a Politic, & numerous People" formerly inhabited the country and that these were religious sites rather than fortifications. Connolly was closer to the truth than he knew; scholars are still trying to unravel the ritual significance and the solar alignments of the complex of mounds in the Ohio country. As many Americans would do in the nineteenth century, Connolly assumed that Indian people lacked the labor resources, political organization, and sophistication to create such mounds, and he speculated that the civilization that had built them must have been destroyed by warlike invaders.[66] Like Connolly, Washington subscribed to the belief that Indians did not create civilizations; they destroyed them. He would not have been deterred by, or interested in, the spiritual significance of such sites. Nevertheless, he knew that lands he coveted had an ancient human past.

Inscribed on the flyleaf of his diary for 1773 was a doctored copy of a legal opinion issued sixteen years before, pertaining to a different continent. In 1757 England's attorney general, Charles Pratt, and solicitor general, Charles Yorke, in response to a petition from the East India Company, had issued an official opinion that a grant from the Crown was not required to obtain valid title to land in India: it could be purchased directly from "any of the Indian Princes, or Governments." Someone transcribed and edited a version of the opinion to make it read as if it referred to Indian princes and governments in North America rather than in India. Although, or more likely because, the doctored version was clearly at variance with the 1763 Royal Proclamation, American speculators seized on it to justify their illegal activities.[67]

Washington jealously guarded every tract of land, meticulously planned ways to make them turn a profit, monitored how his agents carried out their duties, and kept a tight grip on the purse strings. One student of his land businesses describes him as "a practical, calculating schemer with an expansive dream."[68] He needed tenants to occupy his lands against rival claimants and to turn his thousands of acres of western lands into a lucrative investment. In July 1773 he advertised his lands on the banks of the Ohio and Kanawha for lease to settlers. The lands were among the first surveyed in that part of the country, the printed broadsheet declared, and were unequaled in "luxuriancy of soil, or convenience of situation." All were riverfront lots, abounding in fish and wildfowl, and with excellent meadows "almost fit for the scythe." River transportation offered easy communication with Fort Pitt and access to market, and settlers could expect to "cultivate and enjoy the land in peace and safety."[69] He also contemplated attracting Palatinate German emigrants as well as Scots and Irish settlers to his western lands, but those schemes did not pan out. He remained on the verge of making his fortune in the West.

EVENTS UNFOLDING IN LONDON, NEW ENGLAND, and Shawnee country in 1774 determined whether Washington's schemes succeeded or failed. After colonists dumped British tea into Boston Harbor in December 1773, Britain responded with a series of punitive measures that included placing Massachusetts under military government, closing the port of Boston until reparations were paid for the destroyed tea, and asserting the right to quarter British troops in unoccupied buildings. Outraged colonists denounced the measures as the "Intolerable Acts."

The government also took steps that infuriated Washington. Dunmore told him that if Crawford was found to be unqualified as a surveyor, the patents granted for land under the proclamation would be declared null and void. Lord Hillsborough, as secretary of state for the American colonies, had declared that American veterans had no rights to bounty land—the land grants promised in the proclamation were restricted to British regular officers. The new colonial secretary, Lord Dartmouth, agreed with Hillsborough and in 1774 informed Dunmore that Virginia veterans were not entitled to bounty lands. The ruling rendered illegal Washington's claims to thousands of acres. Washington was apoplectic. He accused Hillsborough of a "malignant disposition" toward Americans. All officers, Americans and British, provincial as well as regular, should share equally in the land bounties, he argued; there was no reason why Americans who had served the king as faithfully and as well as his British troops should be discriminated against. The decision was based on "Malice, absurdity, & error." As Woody Holton notes, "Hillsborough's declaration fueled Washington's patriotism."[70] "As far as the American west was concerned," comments Joseph Ellis, "Washington was already declaring his independence."[71] By September 1774 he was in Philadelphia as a delegate to the First Continental Congress.

Meanwhile Dunmore and Virginia's land-dealing gentry stepped up their efforts to obtain the Ohio Valley. In the wake of the Fort Stanwix Treaty, tensions and killings increased as immigrants invaded Shawnee lands. Then the British army abandoned Fort Pitt in 1772, withdrawing what little protection it had offered Indians. Settlers, speculators, and Dunmore himself seized the opportunity that opened when governmental authority in the area crumbled. Only the Indians stood in their way.[72]

Often portrayed as nomads with no fixed attachment to the land, Indian people faced a flood of true nomads. Explaining his conduct to the home government, Dunmore said no policy could curb "the emigrating Spirit of the Americans" on the frontiers. Mainly Scotch-Irish and Germans, they "remove as their avidity and restlessness incite them. They acquire no attachment to Place: But wandering about Seems engrafted in their Nature," ever imagining that "Lands further off, are Still better than those upon which they are already Settled." Americans, Dunmore explained, could not conceive that government had any right to stop them taking possession of territory that was uninhabited or occupied only by a few scattered tribes of Indians, or that they needed to respect treaty pledges made to people they considered "little removed from the brute Creation."[73]

Washington's old acquaintance Guyasuta helped contain the escalating conflict. The Seneca chief kept the British Indian Department informed of developments in Indian country and regularly operated as a messenger. In the fall of 1772 he arrived at Johnson Hall, having traveled from the Ohio country via Philadelphia. Sir William Johnson regarded him as "a great Chief of much Capacity and vast Influence amongst all the Nations."[74] He told Johnson in January 1774 that the Shawnees were sure the white people were about to try to take all their country from them. Many Shawnees, especially from the Kispoko and Piqua divisions, harvested their corn, packed up, and moved west from the Scioto Valley rather than "be Hemmed in on all Sides by the White People, and then be at their Mercy."[75] Shawnee chiefs did their best to keep their young men in line, but they could not prevent conflict.

In the spring, Michael Cresap, the son of Thomas Cresap and a frontier trader, land developer, and Indian fighter in his own right, together with a posse of frontier militia, murdered some Indians. Then, at the mouth of Yellow Creek, Daniel Greathouse and another group of thugs murdered thirteen women and children, the family of a Mingo chief, Tachnechdorus, also known as John Logan. The victims included Logan's Shawnee wife and his pregnant sister,

Koonay, the wife of Pittsburgh trader John Gibson. The killers strung Koonay up by the wrists and sliced her open, impaling the unborn baby on a stake, but spared her two-month-old daughter.[76] Crawford took the child "from a woman that it had bin given to" and she was now at his house, he informed Washington. She was eventually returned to Gibson. Logan's grief became immortalized in various versions of a speech attributed to him, especially the one recorded by Thomas Jefferson in his book *Notes on the State of Virginia*. Recruiting Shawnee and Mingo warriors, Logan vowed to exact vengeance. Crawford kept Washington apprised of events that could torpedo his land schemes on the south bank of the Ohio. Hundreds of settlers fled back across the mountains, "and the hole Country Avackquated as far as monogahelia," Crawford wrote as he hurried off to a council with the Indians at Fort Pitt; "a war is every momint Expected." The Shawnees were aggrieved that they still had not been paid anything for the lands the Iroquois had sold. Crawford feared war was unavoidable.[77]

The trader Richard Butler declared in an affidavit that, whatever their intentions for the future, the Shawnees did not want war at the time, but the cold-blooded murders were "sufficient to bring on a war with a Christian instead of a Savage People." He feared the actions and prejudices of the common people would cause a general Indian war because there was little effort to restrain them.[78] When the British Indian agent Alexander McKee heard of the murders, he immediately called a meeting with Guyasuta and other Six Nations chiefs to assure them that rash people were responsible and the governor of Virginia would be sure to give the Indians satisfaction.[79] Guyasuta said the Six Nations would not make common cause with the Shawnees, and neither would other tribes, and "the Shawanese by themselves can't do much Mischief."[80] He worked with the British Indian Department to prevent the war from spreading, went as an emissary to several tribes to isolate the Shawnees, and continued his diplomatic travels through the end of the conflict. On October 15, while a delegate to the Continental Congress, Washington recorded in his diary that he gave Guyasuta £1 14s, although he did not record what for. The chief was passing through Philadelphia on a mission from the tribes in the Illinois and Ohio country to Guy Johnson, who had taken over as superintendent of Indian affairs on the death of his uncle and father-in-law, Sir William, in July.[81]

Dunmore, meanwhile, had no intention of giving the Indians satisfaction. The murders served his interests in sparking a war that opened Shawnee lands for the taking. Pennsylvanians accused "the scheming party in Virginia" of instigating the war as a way to assert Virginia's claims on the Ohio against both Pennsylvania and the Vandalia scheme. An Indian war not only provided justification for grabbing Indian land but would also send squatters scurrying east to safety, leaving the field open for wealthy speculators to amass large holdings, which they could rent to settlers once the war was over. Whether or not Dunmore and Virginia land speculators manufactured the war, as argued by Pennsylvanians then and many historians since, they seized the opportunity to punish and dispossess the Shawnees.[82]

Logan took his revenge by killing settlers, then declared his vengeance satisfied. But many Virginians had been waiting for a chance like this. Connolly told Washington the Shawnees were "a haughty, violent & unthinking tribe" who "constantly shook the Tomahawk over our Heads" and threatened anyone who ventured beyond the Kanawha River. It was time to teach them a lesson and no time for half measures.[83] In a circular letter calling for volunteers, Colonel William Preston urged men to rally to the defense of their lives and properties. Virginians might never again have such a good opportunity to drive their "old Inveterate Enemies" from their country, plunder and burn their towns, destroy their cornfields, and "prevent them from giving us any future Trouble." There were other incentives as well; there would be valuable plunder, and "it is said the Shawnese have a great Stock of Horses." Preston was also a surveyor and land speculator.[84]

The impending war disrupted Washington's operations. Fearful of squatters, Washington tried to beat them at their own game and strengthen his claim to land on the basis of occupancy.[85] In the spring of 1774 he engaged Valentine Crawford, William's brother, to head down the Ohio with carpenters, slaves, and supplies and construct buildings on his land. Then news of the killings broke, and the "Alarming Surcomstances" made it impossible for Valentine to carry out Washington's plans.[86] As settlers streamed back across the mountains in fear of Indian attack, he and others in the area built blockhouses, and Crawford enrolled Washington's men as militia. By summer work was progressing on building a mill, but, Crawford warned, their ability to hold their ground would depend on getting assistance or the Virginian army defeating the Indians. Washington had wanted Crawford to sell his slaves, but that was impossible: "Out here, we have one day peace, and the next day war. It is hard to know how to act, even if you were here yourself." Washington was impatient and critical. "You Seeme to Scencer Me hard in My Condoct of your bisness," Crawford wrote, "but times has been in great Confusion here with us and som of the people I had to deale with was vere grate vilons and tuck great advantages of the times."[87]

In June, Dunmore called out the Virginia militia.[88] By then, Washington wrote to George William Fairfax, the British government had closed the port of Boston and was "endeavouring by every piece of Art & despotism to fix the Shackles of Slavry upon us;" a confederacy of western and southern tribes seemed to be forming against Virginia, and a general Indian war looked inevitable. On top of that, crops were poor after severe frosts in the winter followed by a cruel drought. Never since the first settlement of the colony had the minds of the inhabitants been "more disturbed or our situation so critical," Washington thought. "God only knows what is to become of us."[89]

The war against the Shawnees was soon under way. William Crawford was commissioned a major by Dunmore and led five hundred men in the regiment now commanded by Colonel Adam Stephen. He accompanied Dunmore's army when it moved down the Ohio to attack the Shawnee towns in the Scioto Valley, an area Crawford knew well.[90] Colonel Andrew Lewis with another force descended the Kanawha. Chief Cornstalk and some six hundred Shawnees set out to do battle. The Delawares and Wyandots sent runners to try to deter them, but the Shawnees would not be stopped. "They talked big and said they did not care"; better to be wiped off the face of the earth than have the Virginians live so close to them.[91] They made their stand against Lewis's army at the junction of the Great Kanawha and Ohio Rivers, the area where Washington intended to plant his settlements. At the Battle of Point Pleasant on October 10, the Shawnees inflicted more casualties than they sustained but, outnumbered and outgunned, were forced from the field after a hard-fought, daylong struggle.[92] Cornstalk and his chiefs grudgingly accepted Dunmore's peace terms at Camp Charlotte nine days later, giving up their lands south of the Ohio and sending four hostages to Williamsburg as a guarantee of future good conduct. Crawford was not at the battle, but afterward he led 240 men up the Scioto River and destroyed a Mingo village called Salt Lick Town, near present-day Columbus, where they killed five people and took fourteen prisoners, "chiefly Women & Children." As soon as Crawford got home to Stewart's Crossing he wrote to tell Washington that the expedition against the Shawnees was a great success, resulting in what he hoped would be a lasting peace. Even while on campaign, he added, he had not forgotten Washington's lands and plans: he had taken the opportunity to press his claims with the governor and had a house built on Washington's land opposite the mouth of the Hockhocking.[93]

Washington too thought Dunmore's peace with the Shawnees would last.[94] However, the Shawnee cession really only confirmed what the Treaty of Fort Stanwix had already done, and it was little use to Virginia's land-dealing gentry unless the Privy Council repealed the 1763 proclamation. Instead, in June 1774, in a further move to restrict settlement from the seaboard colonies, Parliament had passed the Quebec Act, transferring jurisdiction over the territory between the Ohio and the Mississippi to Quebec, in effect making it part of Canada. The British government did what it had fought to prevent France from doing. Washington and other Virginia gentry had viewed the Ohio as their river of fortune; the British had turned it into a barrier instead.[95]

As tension escalated between the imperial government and the Virginia elites, Dunmore had to choose where his true allegiance, or his best interests, lay. He chose the empire. In the early spring of 1775, claiming that Crawford was improperly qualified to survey the lands granted under Dinwiddie's proclamation (which he was; he had failed to take the oath of office required of official surveyors of Crown lands), Dunmore planned to annul the land patents Washington had received, a decision that would strip Washington of 23,000 acres. Washington was livid, pointing out the time and expense involved in the surveys, and told Dunmore he found his decision "incredible."[96] Before the end of the year, Dunmore was calling on slaves to help suppress the Revolution, and Washington was calling him "that Arch Traitor to the Rights of Humanity."[97]

Washington emerged from the tangle of intercolonial, interpersonal, and intercompany rivalries as the owner of several potential estates, with thousands of acres scattered across southwestern Pennsylvania and along the Ohio and Great Kanawha Rivers.[98] And he wanted more. But there would be no unrestricted access to Indian land under the British Empire. Washington had hoped the proclamation would be a temporary expedient, soon repealed. He had hoped his Mississippi Company would acquire 2.5 million acres of Indian land but wrote off his investment when he realized the futility of competing with the conflicting claims of powerful investors in London. He had bought up veterans' claims to thousands of acres of bounty lands, but Lord Dartmouth denied the claims. Finally, the Quebec Act killed prospects beyond the Ohio. By 1775, in Woody Holton's words, the total yield of the land rush set off by the Fort Stanwix Treaty amounted to "a pile of rejected land petitions and worthless surveys."[99]

Virginians declared independence from Britain in 1776 and immediately adopted a state constitution that nullified both the proclamation and the Quebec Act. Confronted with the extensive claims of the great land companies, settlers pressured the Virginia Convention to pass a resolution in May 1776 promising preemption rights to actual settlers when lands came on the market. Four hundred acres was fixed as the maximum amount such settlers could claim; speculators, of course, had legal rights to much larger claims. The Virginia legislature in December 1776 created the "County of Kentucky," securing the region speculators had coveted for decades. In 1778 it passed an act providing that the officers and soldiers who claimed land under Dinwiddie's proclamation and had submitted surveys would be entitled to the grants; the questionable patents issued to Washington on the basis of Crawford's surveys would be validated if Virginia won its independence. The next year, the Virginia Land Law opened Kentucky to settlement. Freed from the tyranny of imperial restraints, Virginian gentry could get back to the business of leasing and selling Indian land to yeoman farmers.[100]

IN HIS STUDY OF WESTERN LANDS in the coming of the American Revolution, written more than sixty years ago, Thomas Perkins Abernethy concluded that it did not really matter exactly how many acres various individuals and companies acquired or tried to acquire; what mattered was "that usually the most successful speculators and traders were those who betrayed public trust and used official position to bilk the people." Britain's shifting policies and the unwise legislation of the new states resulted in most lands falling into the hands of speculators and absentee proprietors who made their money exploiting the ordinary people who actually settled and sometimes defended their lands. The scramble for land generated layer upon layer of competing and overlapping claims—spurious grants, dubious titles, military warrants, settlers' "tomahawk rights" and squatters' rights—that covered the West "like shingles on a roof."[101]

In an age and society where seizing Indian land and killing Indian people was taken for granted, Virginians developed a particular reputation for greed and violence in Indian country. Indians feared Virginians more "than all the Rest of the Colonies," said one of Washington's correspondents.[102] "The Virginians are haughty Violent and bloody," wrote the British governor of Detroit, Henry Hamilton; the Indians respected them as warriors but resented their encroachments and distrusted their word in treaties.[103] Indians came to apply "Virginian" to any Indian-hating, land-hungry white people. Washington had killed no Indians and, unlike his grandfather, seized no chiefs, but his actions helped drive Virginians' expansion and contributed to their reputation in Indian country.

The Cherokees bore the brunt of the land grabbing. The treaty lines negotiated by William Johnson and John Stuart did not hold. Instead, wrote Stuart, "amazing great settlements" had been made beyond the boundaries on tracts that individuals had acquired by taking advantage of Cherokee needs and poverty or by forgeries and frauds that the Cherokee Nation never agreed to, "for they are tenants in common and allow no person, however so great, to cede their lands without the consent of the nation obtained in general council."[104] In the spring of 1775, Washington started getting reports of one such transaction. At the so-called Treaty of Sycamore Shoals in March, Attakullakulla, Oconostota, and the Raven of Chota sold Richard Henderson and a group of North Carolina speculators known as the Transylvania Company 20 million acres of land between the Cumberland and Kentucky Rivers for a cabin full of trade goods. Attakullakulla's son Tsí-yu-gûnsí-ni or Dragging Canoe stormed out of the treaty in anger, warning Henderson that the land "was the bloody Ground, and would be dark, and difficult to settle." Undeterred, Henderson intended to divide the land and sell it at twenty shillings sterling per hundred acres. "It is suspected some of our Virga Gentlemen are privately concern'd in it," George Mason confided to Washington. Indian lands that had been kept out of Washington's grasp by British imperial authority seemed to be toppling in a scramble as that authority crumbled; "there is something in that Affair which I neither understand, nor like," he wrote to William Preston, "& wish I may not have cause to dislike it worse as the mistery unfolds."[105] Dunmore issued a proclamation prohibiting Henderson and his associates from taking possession of any of the king's Virginia lands "merely under any Purchase, or pretended Purchase made from Indians."[106]

The actions of men like Henderson—and Washington—undermined the British government's attempts to slow the assault on Indian land. "I know of nothing so likely to interrupt and disturb our tranquility with the Indians as the incessant attempts to defraud them of their land by clandestine purchases," wrote John Stuart in March 1775.[107] In 1776 a delegation of fourteen Indians from the North traveled to Chota in Tennessee and called on the Cherokees to take up arms with them. The Shawnee delegate held up a nine-foot-long wampum belt painted with vermilion as a sign of war and told how the Virginians had taken all their lands, provoked an unjust war, and reduced the Shawnees from a great nation to a handful. It was clear that the Virginians intended "to extirpate them," said the speaker; it would be better to "die like men than to diminish away by inches." Many Cherokee warriors agreed.[108]

CHAPTER 10

The Question of Indian Allies

I N THE SKIRMISHING AROUND Concord in April 1775 that opened the American Revolution, British officers complained that "the rebels followed the Indian manner of fighting, concealing themselves behind hedges [and] trees and skulking in woods and houses, whereby they galled the soldiers exceedingly." A month later, Ethan Allen, leader of Vermont's Green Mountain Boys, asked Kahnawake Indians to help him fight the redcoats. "You know they stand all along close together, rank and file, and my men fight as Indians do, and I want your warriors to join with me and my warriors like brothers and ambush the regulars."[1] It has become a commonplace in American history and popular culture that embattled farmers succeeded in defeating the British military machine by employing Indian ways of fighting. In fact, like British officers, Washington employed irregular operations as an adjunct to the regular campaigns of the main army. He tried to create an army that was modeled on the British army, employed conventional British tactics, and emulated British military culture in which gentlemen officers commanded. In other words, there was nothing revolutionary about the Revolutionary army.[2] Far from abandoning orthodox tactics and fighting Indian style, Washington as commander in chief sometimes advocated tactics, such as full-frontal assaults and marching in line formation while under fire, that were totally alien to Indian concepts of waging war.

However, both sides used scouts, light infantry, ranger companies, Indian allies, and more flexible formations when necessary.

After his experiences in the French and Indian War Washington knew Indians would figure prominently in this one, and Indian allies were essential to an army's capacity to compete in forest fighting. During the French and Indian War, he had urged adopting Indian clothing and tactics; during the Revolution, he ordered snowshoes and moccasins for American troops, specifically asking that they be made in Indian country, preferably by Oneidas, who were allies.[3] In the spring of 1777 James Smith went to Washington and proposed raising a battalion of riflemen "acquainted with the Indian method of fighting, to be dressed intirely in their fashion, for the purpose of annoying and harassing the Enemy." Washington offered him command of an existing battalion of riflemen but did not pursue his "scheme of white-men turning Indians."[4] That summer, when General Horatio Gates's soldiers were reported to be panic-stricken by the Indians and the Tories who dressed and fought like Indians accompanying General John Burgoyne's army, Washington dispatched to their aid Colonel Daniel Morgan and five hundred handpicked riflemen "well acquainted...with that mode of Fighting which is necessary to make them a good Counterpoise to the Indians."[5] Washington wanted a regular army to combat British regulars, but Indian-fighting tactics were best for fighting Indians. He knew that the best people to fight "Indian style" were Indians. But whether, where, and when to employ Indian allies troubled him.

Against the British he developed a strategy that was essentially defensive. Military historians call the strategy Fabian, after the Roman general Quintus Fabius, who defeated Hannibal by a war of attrition. General Arthur St. Clair, for one, saw a clear analogy between the Carthaginian invasion of Italy and the British invasion of America. Writing to Washington in January 1778, he predicted that just as the Romans had adopted a defensive system that saved their country from the brink of ruin, so Washington's strategy "will ultimately crown you with Glory and the Blessings of a free and happy People." Washington agreed, at least in principle, to always "avoid a general Action" and never "put anything to the risque" unless compelled by necessity.[6] As long as the army remained intact, the Revolution could continue, General Nathanael Greene told him; it was "the Stamina of American liberty; and our position and measures should be taken upon this principle."[7]

These were not the strategies Washington favored when fighting Indians. Committed or compelled to wage a defensive war against the British, he consistently advocated offensive war against Indians. His primary goal in the Revolution was to win independence by fighting the British army in the East, but he was also intent on winning lands in the West. Washington was the hero of the Revolution, the man who held the struggling Patriot army together through its darkest hours and secured the victory that gave birth to the new nation. His role as commander in chief of the Continental Army has a different cast viewed from Indian country.

DURING THE FRENCH AND INDIAN WAR, Washington had put himself forward for military office and seethed with resentment when it was denied or deferred. In the Revolution, he had it thrust upon him. His appointment as commander of the Continental Army by unanimous vote of the Continental Congress was "an honour I wished to avoid, as well from an unwillingness to quit the peaceful enjoyment of my Family as from a thorough conviction of my own Incapacity & want of experience in the conduct of so momentous a concern."[8] His reputation stemmed from his service in the French and Indian War, where, despite displaying impressive courage, he had won no battles and, as we've seen, experienced several debacles. His record early in the Revolution would be not much better. The historian Edward Lengel rates his performance on the battlefield in the first year of the war as "practically incompetent," an assessment that many of Washington's fellow officers shared.[9] Washington's appointment had much to do with the fact that as a Virginian he represented one of the largest colonies and a broader colonial unity than if he'd been from New England. In the French and Indian War, he had taken a narrow view of campaigns and pushed Virginia's interests over those of other colonies; now people, as Lengel put it, "identified him not with his colony, but with the frontier, and ultimately with America."[10]

Washington knew a British-Indian alliance would threaten the northern frontier much as the French-Indian alliance had done twenty years earlier. His first instructions to Major General Philip Schuyler, commander of the Northern Department and Congress's chief negotiator with the Iroquois, included watching the movements of Colonel Guy Johnson, the new British superintendent of Indian affairs, doing everything he could to counter his intrigues among the Indians, and gathering information on the disposition of the Indians.[11] Schuyler hardly needed to be told. Like Washington, he was a wealthy land speculator who had served in the French and Indian War, and he was well aware of the influence of the Johnson family among the Iroquois.[12]

Most Indian people wanted to stay out of the struggle as relations between Britain and its colonies escalated into violence. "What have they to do with your Quarrels?" asked the Mohegan preacher Samson Occom, who hoped the whites would not drag the Indians into the fighting.[13] Nevertheless, both sides expected the Indians to take part, as they had in the French and Indian War; they had "been long taught by contending Nations to be bought & sold."[14] John Adams said the French had "disgraced themselves" by employing Indian allies in the last war. "To let loose those blood Hounds to scalp Men, and butcher Women & Children is horrid." Patriot leaders and newspapers played on fears that the British were preparing to do the same in this one.[15] In fact, both sides courted Indian allies, and both sides hesitated to employ them. Messengers and scouting parties crisscrossed the northern borderlands, and reports and rumors of enemy agents in Indian country created a tense environment. Indian communities tried to figure out what was going on and what it would mean for them.

Washington and the Continental Congress were initially reluctant to employ Indian allies, as they were reluctant to use black soldiers. However, recognizing that Britain had the edge—not just in its Indian Department personnel, experience, and connections, but also in having tried to restrain the invasion of Indian lands—the Americans watched developments nervously, worked to keep Indians neutral, and looked for opportunities to win them to the Patriot cause. Many British officers and officials shared Washington's concerns: Indian allies were unpredictable; they fought for their own reasons and in their own way; they were expensive to supply and maintain; they might commit atrocities. Like the Americans, the British worried that if they did not employ Indian allies, the enemy would.[16]

The competition for their allegiance imposed huge strains on Indian communities. Some Indian people in southern and central New England volunteered to join American companies in the first months of the war, fought alongside their colonial neighbors at Bunker Hill, and served the Patriot cause throughout the war, often at great cost. William Apess, a Pequot writing in the next century, said that the Indian town of Mashpee on Cape Cod sent twenty-six men to the war, and all but one "fell martyrs to liberty in the struggle for Independence." The Pequots of Connecticut lost about half of the men who went to fight. Their Mohegan neighbors suffered heavily as well: Rebecca Tanner lost five sons serving in the American army during the war.[17]

The Declaration of Independence asserted that the king had unleashed savage warriors against innocent families on the American frontier. In reality, the first Indians to fight in the war appear to have joined *Washington's* army. Indian men from Stockbridge in western Massachusetts, a mission community of some two or three hundred people from the Mahican, Housatonic, and Wappinger tribes, volunteered as minutemen even before the outbreak of the Revolution. Stockbridges had served alongside the British in the French and Indian War, but the Revolution and its rhetoric offered them hope for reversing their history of indebtedness and land loss. "If we are conquered our Lands go with yours," Captain Solomon Uhhaunauwaunmut told American commissioners, "but if we are victorious we hope you will help us recover our just Rights." Seventeen Stockbridge warriors joined Washington's army, besieging Boston and the British forces under General Thomas Gage, his former friend and comrade-in-arms from the Braddock campaign.[18]

The Stockbridges' arrival caused "much Speculation," said one of Washington's soldiers.[19] Their presence in Washington's army gave the British justification for employing Indian allies of their own. "The rebels have themselves opened the door," announced Gage; "they have brought down all the savages they could against us here, who with their riflemen are continually firing on our advanced sentries."[20] With Stockbridges already engaged in the fighting, the Continental Congress had to decide its policy on employing Indians. (It also had to decide on its policy of employing free blacks, which was, it informed Washington in February, that the black volunteers in his camp could be retained but he should enlist no more. Slaves, of course, were not considered.[21] As the war dragged on and few white men volunteered for service, Washington and Congress revised their reservations: by the end of the war, black soldiers comprised 10 percent of the Continental Army.[22]) In December 1775 Congress decided to call on Indians "in case of real necessity."[23] Six months later it approved employing up to two thousand Indians.[24] Although it did not offer scalp bounties, it also authorized offering the Indians a bounty for capturing British soldiers—a hundred dollars for officers and thirty for privates—which Washington thought would prove "a powerful Inducement to engage the Indians in our Service."[25] If insufficient numbers enlisted, Schuyler wrote Washington, the companies would be made up with white men who lived near the Indians and were at home in the woods, provided they did not exceed one-third of the company strength.[26]

But then Congress clarified its position: the authorization was intended only "*to employ in Canada* a Number of Indians not exceeding two Thousand." John Hancock, president of the Continental

Congress, instructed Washington to stop raising companies of Mahican and Stockbridge Indians.[27] The Stockbridges were troubled at not being used and came to ask Washington why. Considering the Indians' expectations, the problems of raising men, and the danger that some of the Stockbridges might take "an unfavourable part," Washington thought they should be employed.[28]

Congress reconsidered and gave him approval to employ the Stockbridge Indians, if he thought "proper."[29] Hancock informed Washington at the beginning of August, and Washington immediately sent a copy of the congressional resolution to Indian Commissioner Timothy Edwards and to Schuyler, explaining the reasons for the change in policy. He asked Edwards to recruit as many as he could and give them the choice of joining his army or Schuyler's army in the North.[30] Edwards duly conveyed the news to the Stockbridges, and by the third week of August 1776 they had a company ready to march to join Schuyler.[31] They were issued with red and blue caps to distinguish them from enemy Indians.[32] Formerly reluctant to employ them, Washington was now eager, optimistic, and perhaps even a little desperate to have them. His own forces were inadequate. The militia, he said, "come in, you cannot tell how—go, you cannot tell when—and act, you cannot tell where—consume your provisions—exhaust your Stores, and leave you at a last critical moment."[33] His complaints sounded like those he made about Cherokee allies twenty years before.

"Wherever you go, we will be by your sides," Solomon Uhhaunauwaunmut declared. "Our bones shall lie with yours. We are determined never to be at peace with the red coats, while they are at variance with you."[34] Stockbridge men served in New York, New Jersey, and Canada. They served with General Gates in the fighting around Saratoga in 1777, although most of the warriors returned home to help with the harvest before Burgoyne's army surrendered. In October that year Congress ordered payment of two hundred dollars to the Stockbridge chief Abraham Nimham and his men "for their zeal in the cause of the United States."[35] Nimham was killed the next year near New York City when the Stockbridges were cut to pieces by the British cavalry and infantry in a battle that became known as Indian Field.[36] In Washington's words, they "suffered severely."[37] A contingent of Stockbridges under Captain Solomon Hendricks volunteered to take part in General John Sullivan's expedition against the Iroquois in 1779. Hendricks and about twenty Stockbridge volunteers served with Washington's army in the summer of 1780, attached to the light infantry, and Washington said they "conducted themselves with great propriety and fidelity." However, he remained ambivalent about employing them, and as the war shifted south toward Yorktown he paid less attention to his Indian allies. In September 1781 he refused an offer of support; he told the Stockbridge chiefs their help was not required at that time, but he told Major General William Heath "their services never compensated the expense."[38]

The Stockbridges probably felt that the expense never compensated their sacrifices. They suffered heavy casualties in battle—perhaps half their number—and more died after returning home sick. They complained that Captain Hendricks's contingent served "immediately under the direction of his Excellency Genl. Washington and at the close of the campaign received nothing but a little clothing and money to bring them home."[39] Back at Stockbridge, widows struggled to pay off their dead husbands' debts, and the community petitioned the Massachusetts government for assistance with food and clothing. At the end of the war, Washington furnished the Stockbridges with a certificate attesting that they "have remained firmly attached to us and have fought and bled by our side; That we consider them as friends and Brothers."[40] Unfortunately, Stockbridge veterans returned home to find that their white brothers had taken over the town government and much of their land while they were away fighting for liberty. When Stockbridge chiefs petitioned Congress for assistance, the secretary of Congress recommended that the petition be referred to the state of Massachusetts where they lived and that they be dismissed with some presents, "covering according to the indian custom, the bones of those who have been killed in the war with shrouds, blankets or clothing to be delivered to the widows or families of the deceased; the amount not to exceed 100 dollars."[41]

IN THE EARLY STAGES OF THE WAR, Washington was more concerned with Indian activities in the North than with Indian soldiers in his army. He knew the Indians could have a critical impact on the war there, and he found Indian responses to the Revolution in northern New England, Quebec, and Nova Scotia more ambiguous and more worrying than in southern New England. He received reports and emissaries from the northern tribes, but he was touching the edges of an Indian world beyond his reach and perhaps even his understanding. He had dealt with Cherokees, Catawbas, and Ohio tribes during the French and Indian War, but he had no experience with the Indian peoples of Canada and northern New England. He attributed generic Indian traits to them but acknowledged to Schuyler "the little Knowledge I have of these people's policy and real Intentions."[42] The immediate worry was that the British in Canada would unleash Indian raids as the French had done. Schuyler kept tabs on the movements of the Indians and Canadians, supplied Washington with intelligence, and sent him evidence that the British were trying to enlist Indians to fight. Washington found the evidence "incontrovertable."[43]

In September 1775, encouraged by what he heard about the disposition of the inhabitants and the Indians there, Washington dispatched Colonel Benedict Arnold and one thousand men to invade Canada via the Kennebeck River in Maine. Arnold would either provide a diversion for Schuyler's planned advance on Montreal or capture Quebec, which, Washington predicted, "in its present defenceless State must fall into his Hands an easy Prey."[44] He was wrong, but invading Canada as a way to stop Indian raids and win over Indian allies remained a compelling strategy.

The Indian communities on the St. Lawrence River known collectively as the Seven Nations of Canada had grown up in the previous century when refugees from New England and New York had settled around French mission villages. Many of the inhabitants were nominally Catholic, and the British, and sometimes other Indians, often called them French Indians. Now they were exposed to diplomatic pressure and military threat from both sides. British and American agents focused most of their efforts on the Abenaki village at Odanak, then known as St. Francis, and the Mohawk village of Caughnawaga or Kahnawake, which was also the site of the Seven Nations' council fire. Both communities had kinship ties to New England, where, during earlier conflicts, their warriors had taken captives who were adopted by Mohawk or Abenaki families. Both also understood they could be caught in a crossfire. They had little love for the British—after all, they had fought against them for eighty years—but they had to live with the reality of British power in Canada and weigh that against the prospect that Americans might launch a successful invasion. Kahnawakes told the Americans that the British threatened them and that they assisted the redcoats only as an act of self-preservation. Abenakis wanted to avoid a recurrence of what had happened in 1759, when Robert Rogers's Rangers had burned Odanak. Kahnawake and Odanak received overtures from both sides, and they made overtures of their own. The Revolution generated disagreement, division, and shifting allegiances in these communities as it did in many others. Individuals and groups promised and rendered service, generally as scouts, but Kahnawake and Odanak avoided making a full commitment to either side—and thereby avoided making themselves targets.[45]

In August 1775 a chief named Swashan and four other Abenakis from Odanak arrived at Washington's encampment at Cambridge, offered their services, and remained throughout the siege of Boston.[46] The same month, Colonel Jacob Bayley from Cohoss or Cowass in the upper Connecticut Valley brought to the camp a Kahnawake chief named Atiatoharongwen or Louis Cook (see plates 3 and 4). Of Abenaki and African American parentage, as a young man he had fought against Washington at Braddock's defeat. Now Atiatoharongwen was said to be "a Man of Weight, & Consequence" at Kahnawake. He said the British were pressuring the Kahnawakes to fight for them, but his nation was "totally averse," and the Indians would support the Americans if they invaded Canada. Washington did all he could "to cherish these favorable Dispositions."[47]

Atiatoharongwen returned with a group of thirteen people from Kahnawake in January, first visiting Schuyler in Albany and then Washington at Cambridge. John Adams, who saw them at Cambridge, said Atiatoharongwen spoke English and French "as well as Indian."[48] Washington said the chief, "whom I understand is now the first Man in the Nation," intended to apply to him for an officer's commission and promised to raise four or five hundred men when he returned. Washington treated the Kahnawakes with respect and made a point of impressing them with his army's strength.[49]

The "Sundry Sachems & Warriors of the Cognaawaga Nation" told Washington they had been sent by five tribes in Canada "to Inquire into the cause of the Quarrel between the people of England & Our Brothers in this Country." But when they offered military assistance, Washington was "a little embarrassed to know in what Manner to conduct myself." A chief named Jean Baptiste or Ogaghsagighte declared, "I am now in my own Country where I was born (being a New Englander & taken prisoner in his Infancy) and want Liberty to raise men to fight for Its defence." He asked Washington to give them a letter informing Schuyler that if he needed men he had only to call on them and they would join him. Having the Indians abandon neutrality and take an active part seemed to go beyond what Congress had authorized, and then there was the expense. Yet Washington assumed they would join one side or the other and did not want to reject their services when offered. Not knowing the Indians' real intentions or how much Schuyler needed their assistance, he admitted, "how far...I ought to go is a

Question that puzzles me." He decided "to please them by yielding in Appearance to their Demands" and buy time while he consulted with Schuyler and Congress. He ordered Colonel Timothy Bedel to conduct the Kahanawakes safely back to Canada and advanced him £100 to cover expenses. Then he wrote to Schuyler. The Kahnawakes' offer had "put the Matter upon the Footing I wished," he said. "I heartily wish that this Union may be lasting and that Nothing may cast up to interrupt it. The Expediency of calling upon them I shall leave to you—Circumstances and policy will suggest the Occasion."[50]

Schuyler was less than enthusiastic. "If we can get decently rid of their Offer, I would prefer it to employing them," he countered. The expenses in the Indian Department were already "amazing," and Kahnawake allies would only increase them. Besides, their intervention would not have much effect unless the other northern nations joined as well.[51] He need not have worried about an influx of Kahnawake recruits. Jean Baptiste promised more than he could deliver and did not speak for all the Kahnawakes. In May the American agent James Dean returned from Montreal with a more realistic appraisal: the Kahnawakes were friendly but refused to take up arms for the Americans.[52]

Atiatoharongwen, however, would prove a valuable ally to Washington. Congress gave him a commission as lieutenant colonel in 1779, and he became commonly known as "Colonel Louis." He served with the American army, including at the pivotal battle at Saratoga; was at Valley Forge in the winter of 1778; brought intelligence from Indian country; and may have served in General Sullivan's expedition. Relieved to hear that Colonel Louis had returned safely from a mission July 1779, Washington referred to him as "our friend."[53] The next summer, Colonel Louis led a delegation of nineteen French-speaking Indian allies to visit the French general Rochambeau at Newport, Rhode Island. One of Rochambeau's officers noted that the Indian colonel "seemed intelligent" and spoke French "fairly well, and even without an accent."[54] He was likely the "Indian colonel from Canada" who three years later sat down to dinner with Washington and a visiting Italian count at Schuyler's Hudson Valley mansion; the count said he "spoke French and English fluently in addition to five Indian languages."[55]

After weighing the pros and cons, Washington and Schuyler both overcame their initial reluctance to employ Indians. Washington urged Congress to engage Indians as allies because it was impossible to keep them neutral, the king's emissaries were poisoning their minds, and if they turned against the Americans it "would be a Most fatal stroke under our present Circumstances." Schuyler agreed, although he feared it would be virtually impossible to enlist the Indians as allies unless the American forces took Canada.[56]

Eleazar Wheelock, president of Dartmouth College, suggested another line of defense. Wheelock had founded the college in 1769, ostensibly for the education of Indians. Located on the east bank of the upper Connecticut River—a direct route between Canada and Massachusetts, and a warpath traveled by French and Indian raiders—Dartmouth lay vulnerable to attack from the north. Wheelock argued to Washington that sending missionaries to Canada to recruit more Indian students for his college and charity school was a good strategy for preventing Indian attacks.[57] Wheelock had targeted Kahnawake and Odanak in his recruiting efforts and had the sons of chiefs of "the most Respectible Tribes in Canada" at his school. Ten children from Kahnawake and Odanak were there when the Revolution broke out, eight of them descendants of English captives. Wheelock considered the children "as Hostages" and was confident their parents would not go to war while they were at the school. In repeated memorials to Congress, he stressed the vital strategic importance of keeping the Canadian Indian students at Dartmouth and keeping his school on its feet. Congress agreed and appropriated money for that purpose, reasoning that "it may be a means of reconciling the friendship of the Canadian Indians, or at least of preventing hostilities from them in some measure." After Wheelock's death in 1779, his son took over as president and continued to request congressional assistance to retain the loyalty of key Odanak and Kahnawake families. Washington agreed it was good policy.[58]

He had good reason to do so. He expected "a very bloody Summer" in New York and Canada in 1776. The enemy was sure to launch campaigns, and "we are not, either in Men, or Arms, prepared for it." He hoped "that if our cause is just, as I do most religiously believe it to be, the same Providence which has in many Instances appeared for us, will still go on to afford its aid."[59]

Rather than rely on Providence or Dartmouth College to defend the upper Connecticut Valley, Schuyler and the New Hampshire Committee of Safety turned to Colonel Timothy Bedel of the New Hampshire militia. Bedel had attended Wheelock's charity school and had connections at Kahnawake and Odanak. His orders were to assemble a force of rangers and Abenakis as the first line of defense and do his utmost to win and keep the Indians' friendship. With minimal financial resources, he tried to attract Indians to Cowass, the site of an old Abenaki village near present-day Newbury, Vermont, and he sent out word that he was ready to trade, operating on the strategy that "if the Indians Trade with us, we need no Soldiers." The Americans believed that the Abenakis who came to Cowass were from Odanak, but most probably lived in the vast borderland between the two places. There was talk of building a fort at Cowass, but nothing came of it, and Bedel had to rely on local militia and Abenaki scouts to defend the upper Connecticut. By the end of 1778 about thirty warriors and their families had assembled at Cowass, with more arriving daily. Bedel said they were "all Naked" but would make "a very good Guard to this Quarter" if supplied with blankets and leggings. Washington, however, was unwilling to run up Congress's debts clothing the Indians, and, as an invasion of Canada seemed unlikely by this time, he told Bedel to hold off engaging any of the Indians for the present.[60]

Bedel's Indian rangers continued to serve with minimal supplies. Captain John Vincent of Kahnawake, who had fought against Washington at Braddock's defeat, led one company.[61] Swashan, who had joined Washington at the siege of Boston, served as his sergeant. Lewis Vincent, a Huron from Lorette and the third Indian student to graduate from Dartmouth, also served. Responding to one of John Wheelock's requests for support, Washington wrote: "Pleased with the Specimen you have given in Mr. Vincent, of the improvement and cultivation which are derived from an education in your Seminary of Literature, I cannot but hope the institution will become more flourishing and extensively successful." Vincent apparently requested in person that Washington enter him on the payroll as a lieutenant of the corps of Indians. Washington could not grant that request but was willing to make Lewis "a present of the Horse which he rides here" if General Jacob Bayley thought he deserved such a reward.[62]

At the same time that Bedel was dispatching Abenakis northward to scout the woods for signs of enemies, the British were dispatching Abenakis from Odanak to scout the region to the south. The rival scouting parties failed to come into contact—at least that's what the American and British records indicate—and they certainly avoided coming into conflict. By ranging the woods for signs of enemy activity, Abenakis from both communities gave the appearance of participating in the war and managed to keep that war away from their homes and families.[63]

Abenaki ambivalence, or strategy, was reflected in the person of Joseph Louis Gill. The son of white parents who had been captured in separate raids on New England, adopted as Abenakis, and married, Gill grew up Abenaki and was known as "the White Chief of the

Abenakis." Both the British and the Americans courted his support. Gill's son and nephews attended Dartmouth. In the summer of 1778 Gill came to Cowass and asked what the Americans intended to do for their many friends among the Abenakis. In November he said the Abenakis at Odanak were "all willing to Join the United States." In 1779 Washington supported a recommendation that Gill be granted a commission in the American army and endorsed "the fidelity and good services of this Chief, and those of his Tribe." Congress awarded Gill a commission as major.[64] But as the likelihood of an American invasion of Canada diminished, Gill understood that he needed to mend fences with the British and at least make a show of supporting the Crown. He now assured the British that they could rely on Abenaki support. The British did not entirely trust him, but his strategy was consistent with that of Odanak and Kahnawake in these perilous times.[65]

The British-Indian threat from the north was real. Small parties of Indian and Tory raiders evaded a string of blockhouses erected between Lake Champlain and the Connecticut Valley—as French and Indian raiders had evaded Virginian frontier posts in the 1750s—and settlers retreated to safer locations farther south.[66] In 1777 warriors from the Seven Nations of Canada made up the bulk of Burgoyne's Indian allies when he thrust south down the Champlain and Hudson Valley corridor, eventually to meet defeat at Saratoga. Some of the warriors killed a young woman named Jane McCrea. The event served as a powerful propaganda weapon, rallying the New Hampshire militia to assist in defeating Burgoyne. After the war, Americans invoked the murder, made infamous by John Vanderlyn's painting in 1804, to justify treating Indians as savages, although if the killers came from the mission villages they likely were Christians. The attack on Dartmouth that Wheelock feared never came, although raiders came close: in 1780 a war party of 265 Mohawks and Abenakis under British command attacked and burned the nearby town of Royalton in Vermont, carrying off thirty-two prisoners.[67] In the closing years of the war, Governor Frederick Haldimand of Quebec purposely avoided sending Indian raids into Vermont at a time when the independent republic was contemplating reunion with his province.[68]

INDIANS IN MAINE AND NOVA SCOTIA faced a situation similar to that of Kahnawake and Odanak. Agents from the rebel government in Massachusetts (of which Maine was part at the time) and the loyal government of Nova Scotia competed for the allegiance of the

Penobscot, Passamaquoddy, Maliseet (St. Johns) and Mi'kmaq tribes as the keys to controlling the region. In the fall of 1775 two Maliseet chiefs, Ambroise Saint-Aubin and Pierre Tomah, appeared at the Penobscot trading house at present-day Bangor, Maine, and sent a letter to the government of Massachusetts, offering their support and asking that a Catholic priest and goods be sent to them. Massachusetts agreed.[69] Also that fall, five Penobscots joined Benedict Arnold's expedition as guides.[70]

Some Maliseets, Penobscots, and Abenakis visited Washington at Cambridge in the fall of 1775, but at that time he was still unsure whether he was authorized to enlist Indian allies and dismissed them with some presents. In February he sent the Maliseets a letter declining their offers of assistance and asked them to pray for him. According to Colonel John Allan, Washington's letter gave "universal satisfaction." Mi'kmaq and Maliseet people "adored him as a saint for the reason that though he was harassed with war himself, still he tells us (say they) 'to be at peace and if they want help he will grant it and defend us.' That for this their incessant prayers were for his success." They even told Allan "they had turned out one of their chiefs because he had spoken disrespectfully of General *Washington*."[71]

When the American army retreated from Canada and left the northern frontiers exposed, Washington saw that employing Indian allies was absolutely necessary.[72] On July 4, 1776, when John Hancock signed his name in bold letters on the Declaration of Independence, Washington wrote the president of the Congress a letter pressing his case. The British were doing everything they could to incite the Indians, and American efforts to employ the western Indians showed little prospect of success. Congress should make a treaty of alliance with tribes in Maine and Nova Scotia to keep them out of the British camp and also secure their assistance if the enemy attempted an invasion. The General Court of Massachusetts was the body best situated to negotiate it. Four days later, Congress gave Washington permission to "call forth and engage in the service of the United States, so many Indians of the St. John's, Nova Scotia and Penobscot tribes, as he shall judge necessary" and authorized him to request the assistance of the General Court of Massachusetts.[73]

Washington promptly wrote urging the General Court to recruit five or six hundred men from the tribes and have them join his army with all possible speed. He was no longer ambivalent. "At a crisis like the present, when our Enemies are prosecuting a War with unexampled severity—When they have called upon foreign mercenaries, and have excited Slaves and Savages to arms against us, a regard to our own security & happiness calls upon us to adopt every possible expedient to avert the blow & prevent the meditated ruin." Since the eastern Indians had already shown their willingness to join the Americans, he hoped they might serve for less pay and on better terms than the Continental troops, but if not, they would have to be paid the same. He recommended that they enlist for a term of two or three years, or failing that, "such time as they will agree to, provided It is not too short," and, if possible, bring their own firelocks. And the sooner they arrived, the better: "It is unnecessary to suggest to you the necessity of the utmost dispatch in the matter."[74]

Even as Washington was writing his letter, the Massachusetts Council and its president, John Bowdoin, had begun talks with Ambroise Saint-Aubin and ten Mi'kmaq and Maliseet delegates at Watertown in Massachusetts. A couple of Penobscot chiefs arrived soon after. The Indians said they had come because of the letter Washington had sent them, which they brought with them. Then, Washington had declined their help and asked them to pray for him. Now, Ambroise said, "We shall have nothing to do with *Old England,* and all that we shall worship or obey will be *Jesus Christ* and General *Washington.*" After the conference where they were "strongly urged" to join the Americans in their war, the chiefs on July 17 signed "a Treaty for that purpose." It was the first treaty of the newly independent United States. In fact, the Declaration of Independence, signed just two weeks before, was translated for the assembled chiefs, with the interpretation that "you and we...have nothing to do with Great Britain; we are wholly separated from her." The chiefs said that the six villages they represented could furnish about 120 men, but that—as those villages were scattered across great distances and their men dispersed in hunting—they would not be able to come until the next spring. The Maliseets who lived closest promised to return early in the fall with about thirty warriors. Bowdoin said another six villages of Mi'kmaqs, who had not been informed of Washington's letter and therefore had not sent delegates, could probably provide about as many men as the other villages. The Penobscots too seemed well disposed, although, despite promises of payment, they had received no support for the families of their five men who had accompanied Benedict Arnold, two of whom had been wounded, and three taken prisoner. Bowdoin assured them the matter "would be represented to Genl Washington, & that what is right & just he would order to be done." The Indians declared they were "one people with us" and had no doubt their tribes "would be willing to join Genl Washington" once the chiefs got home and called them together to discuss the matter. Bowdoin sent Washington a copy of the proceedings and the treaty.[75]

Taking no chances, the Massachusetts Council sent agents to accompany the Indians to their homes and recruit warriors. Thomas Fletcher, who had come with the Penobscots, was appointed to work with that tribe; Major Francis Shaw, who had brought the Mi'kmaqs and Maliseets, was to work with the Maliseets and Passamaquoddies; Lieutenant Andrew Gilman, who served as an interpreter for the Penobscots for much of the war, was to go to the Abenakis at Odanak. Back in the villages, however, older chiefs were concerned that younger men had exceeded their authority and committed the tribes to involvement in a war they did not want. The American recruiters had limited success. Gilman brought seven Penobscots to Watertown, who enlisted for a one-year term in the fall of 1776; Shaw brought only a few Indians from Nova Scotia, who enlisted but "were fond of Returning back again to their Families." The Massachusetts Council informed Washington that the Indians "must Attend Upon your Excellency," but Washington had no use for them where he was and passed them on to General Heath with instructions to employ them as he thought best.[76]

On Christmas Eve 1776, in his encampment on the west bank of the Delaware River, Washington was surely preoccupied with preparations for the next day's historic crossing. Yet he took time to send letters to the chiefs of the Maliseets and Passamaquoddies. He was glad to hear from Shaw that they had accepted the chain of friendship he had sent them from Cambridge in February, and that they were determined to keep it bright and unbroken. When he first heard that the Passamaquoddies had refused to send warriors to his assistance, he wrote, "I did not know what to think; I was Afraid that some Enemy had turned your Hearts Against Me," but he had since learned they were out hunting, which "Made my Mind easy." He hoped he would always be able to call on them in future. He then updated them on developments elsewhere in Indian country. Despite British efforts to stir up all the tribes from Canada to South Carolina, the Six Nations, Shawnees, and Delawares "kept fast hold of our Ancient Covenant Chain." The Cherokees, on the other hand, were foolish enough to listen and had taken up the hatchet. In response, American armies had invaded their country, burned their houses, destroyed their corn, and forced them to sue for peace and give hostages for their future good behavior. Let that serve as a warning, Washington implied. "Now Brothers never lett the Kings Wicked Councellors turn your Hearts Against Me and your Bretheren of this

Country, but bear in Mind what I told you last February and what I tell you now."[77]

In January 1777 Congress appointed Colonel John Allan as superintendent of the eastern Indians. That summer, the British drove the Americans from the St. Johns River in Maine and Nova Scotia. The Maliseets informed the local British commander that after giving the matter due consideration, they were "unanimous that America is right and Old England wrong" and he should remove his troops, but most of the tribe fled south with Saint-Aubin to Machias on the Maine coast.[78] Pierre Tomah tried to operate between the British and the Americans, offering his services to one or the other as occasion and opportunity demanded.[79] One hundred leading men from the Mi'kmaq, Maliseet, and Passamaquoddy tribes signed an oath of loyalty to the king between September 1778 and January 1779, and other Indian nations in Canada warned the three tribes to stay out of the way as they waged war against the "Boston people."[80] Chief Orono and a company of Penobscots served with the United States and fought in the action at Penobscot Bay in 1779, but, by and large, Indian people in Maine and Nova Scotia were reluctant to get dragged into a war that could catch them between two fires.[81]

WASHINGTON CONTINUED TO SEEK INDIAN allies—and permission to recruit them—as need demanded during the war. In January 1778, in winter quarters at Valley Forge, he wrote a long letter to Congress, describing the sacrifices of his men, outlining the defects in the military and supply system, and recommending improvements. At the end, he also raised again the issue of Indian allies. With the enemy calling on Indians "and even our own slaves" to assist them, "would it not be well to employ two or three hundred Indians" in the coming campaign? Washington remembered from firsthand experience the psychological impact of Indian warriors and Indian ways of fighting, and he argued that a body of Indians combined with American woodsmen would strike fear into the British and foreign troops, especially the new recruits. Once Indians gave up "the Savage Customs" they exercised in their intertribal wars, they would make excellent scouts and light troops.[82] Congress gave him permission to raise as many as four hundred Indians, if they could be recruited on suitable terms.[83]

Washington planned to recruit about half from the North and half from the South. Not forgetting his experience with Cherokee allies during the French and Indian War—and the problems of keeping them adequately supplied—he turned to them again in this war, but with different arrangements for compensation in mind.

As Washington told the Passamaquoddies, the outbreak of the Revolution brought disaster for the Cherokees. Older chiefs like Attakullakulla, who had lived through the war of 1760–61 and subsequently pursued a policy of buying time by ceding space, advocated remaining neutral. Younger warriors led by Dragging Canoe, angered by recurrent land cessions and frustrated by their elders' policies, accepted the war belt when emissaries from the North called on them to fight. Cherokee attacks brought swift retaliation. Expeditions from Virginia, Georgia, and the Carolinas stormed through Cherokee country, burning towns and cornfields, and reducing the people to famine. The older chiefs reasserted their voices and asked for peace.[84] Despite his complaints about Cherokee allies in the last war, Washington wanted Cherokees to join the Indians he recruited in this one.

Nathaniel Gist seemed the obvious person to do the recruiting. He had served under Washington in the Virginia Regiment as a lieutenant in the company of scouts commanded by his father, Christopher Gist; he lived among the Cherokees, and his wife was a sister of the Cherokee chief Corn Tassel or Old Tassel. In January 1777 Washington ordered Gist to raise four companies of rangers and then go directly to the Cherokees, or any other nation where he had influence, and "procure a number of Warriors (Not exceeding in the whole 500) to join the Army under my immediate Command." The Indians were to bring their own weapons and blankets but would be supplied with ammunition and provisions and, instead of presents, which had proved the bane of their service in the French and Indian War, would receive the same pay as soldiers in the Continental Army. If they had their own officers, Gist was to advance them more pay, but not more than American officers received. If raised, this body of Indians was to consider Gist as their leader and obey all orders he received from Washington. Recruiting a company or two of Cherokees, Washington explained to Hancock, would serve two valuable purposes: first, they made excellent scouts, and second, they would function as hostages to help ensure "the good behavior of their Nation."[85]

The Cherokees were in the process of making peace and giving up lands to secure it. In March, Gist traveled to Chota to invite the Overhill Cherokees to meet Virginia's peace commissioners at Long Island, located on the Holston River in northeastern Tennessee, an ancient treaty ground considered sacred in Cherokee tradition. In April, Attakullakulla, Oconostota, and a delegation of thirty chiefs went to Williamsburg to talk peace. It was one of Attakullakulla's last acts. A month later, the Lower Cherokees ceded virtually all their remaining lands in South Carolina at a treaty with Georgia and South Carolina.[86] In July the Cherokees made another treaty with Virginia and North Carolina at Fort Patrick Henry on the Holston, where Gist's ranger company was stationed. Corn Tassel stressed the Cherokees' desire for peace but balked at the amount of land the commissioners demanded. He suggested the Americans demanded so much knowing the Cherokees would refuse and give them an excuse to renew the war. Hoping for justice from a former ally, Corn Tassel asked the commissioners to write a letter to General Washington and have Gist deliver it: "I will leave the difference between us to the great Warrior of all America," he said. It was a mystery to him why the Americans asked for so much land so close to the Cherokees, he said, and he knew the lands were worth far more than what the Americans paid for them. "It spoils our hunting ground; but always remains good to you to raise families and stocks on, when the goods we receive of you are rotten and gone to nothing." The North Carolina delegation insisted this was a matter between the Cherokees and North Carolina alone. At the Treaty of Long Island of Holston, the Cherokees were forced to give up their land in western North Carolina and upper eastern Tennessee.[87] Many Cherokees followed Dragging Canoe west to the Chickamauga River and continued their fight for independence from there.[88]

During the course of the negotiations at Long Island, Colonel William Christian reminded the Cherokees that "our Great Warrior General Washington" had sent them a letter by Gist inviting them to send some warriors to his camp, where they would be warmly welcomed, treated as friends, and free to return safely home whenever they wanted. They would be under Gist's care and be paid and well clothed. The Americans did not want them to fight their battles, just "to see the riches and grandeur of our Army and Country," Christian assured them.[89]

Little or nothing came of it. Talk of forming a mixed corps of Indians and light infantry continued, but by May 1778 Washington was backing away from the idea of having Indians join the army. It was unlikely to succeed because the British had the advantage when it came to buying Indian support with gifts. Besides, he explained at length to Henry Laurens of South Carolina, who had succeeded Hancock as president of the Continental Congress, he had proposed the measure "by way of experiment" at a time when prospects were very different. France had now entered the war, and the British, instead of launching an early offensive, as anticipated, now seemed likely to remain on the defensive. In that case, there would be "very little of that kind of service in which the Indians are capable of being useful," and little point in bringing them such a distance. Washington knew from his experience in the French and Indian War that that would create needless expense and frustrate the Indians. Since the Indians seemed apprehensive about leaving their homes unprotected, they might be just as pleased to learn their services were no longer required. Better, after all, Washington concluded, to tell them to remain peacefully at home and be ready to cooperate with us if called on in the future. As for those who were already on their way to join his army, "I had much rather dispense with their attendance."[90] Cherokee chiefs seeking relief from the United States for their starving people had to invoke their services in the French and Indian War rather than in the Revolution.[91]

Patriot leaders and newspapers downplayed or ignored the service and sacrifices of Indian allies, and publicized and exaggerated the hostilities and atrocities of Indian enemies. The belief that all Indians allied with the British served to unify Patriots during the war and to justify the tribes' dispossession in its aftermath.[92] In truth, Washington never quite overcame his reluctance to use Indians for much more than scouting operations.[93] The need and opportunities for Indian allies demanded his attention at critical times during the Revolution, but he was always more interested in Indian lands than in Indian allies. Ultimately, in his vision, Indian territory, not Indian assistance, would secure the independence of the United States. Instead of being remembered for employing Indians in his armies during the Revolution, Washington would be remembered for sending his armies against them.

CHAPTER 11

Town Destroyer

A LIFE-SIZED BRONZE SCULPTURE in the National Museum of the American Indian in Washington, DC, depicts Washington flanked by an Oneida chief, Skenandoah, and an Oneida woman named Polly Cooper. Polly is carrying a basket of corn. The sculpture commemorates what Oneidas remember as a pivotal moment in the Revolution and the nation's struggle for independence. It also reminds us that Washington's relations with the Six Nations during the Revolution often revolved around corn. For most Iroquois people, however, the relationship involved burning cornfields. Recalling in later years the villages laid waste by Washington's troops, they called him Town Destroyer, the name he claimed from his great-grandfather.

Although as a Virginia planter Washington mainly grew tobacco and then wheat, corn was the dominant food crop throughout most of North America. Corn cultivation had spread north from Mexico before Europeans came to America. Indian peoples grew corn across large areas of the continent, from the Rio Grande to the St. Lawrence. After men cleared the fields, women hoed the soil and planted the corn, dropping several kernels in holes three or four feet apart in small hillocks formed by hand. Planting beans and pumpkin seeds together with corn added nitrogen to the soil. The growing cornstalks served as beanpoles and also afforded shade to the pumpkin vines. The Iroquois referred to corn, beans, and squash as the "sacred three sisters." European colonists grew imported crops like wheat, oats, and barley, but they also adopted the indigenous corn agriculture. Corn was higher in nutrition than most other grain crops, and it gave higher yields. In New England and Virginia, Native knowledge and food surpluses helped the earliest colonists survive their first hard years. Indian people taught English settlers how and when to plant, cultivate, and harvest corn, and how to grind it into meal, preserve it through the year, and cook it with beans to make succotash.

Corn soon became the proverbial staff of life for many European colonists, as it had been for many Native peoples for centuries. Indian crops, combined with Euro-Indian farming techniques, produced prolific yields. Thomas Jefferson grew Indian corn, and he also employed indigenous planting techniques such as hilling in his "revolutionary garden." Washington planted his cornfields in straight rows for ease of weeding. Although a wheat farmer, he thought corn was more nourishing than wheat bread "as food for the negroes."[1] Corn not only fed colonists and their slaves; it also sustained colonial armies that often relied on Indian fields and storehouses to feed the troops and keep the campaign alive. Washington understood the centrality of the "three sisters" to Indian life, and he knew the military importance and vulnerability of Indian cornfields. Iroquois crops and stores of corn were an important source of provisions for the British army and Loyalists, as well as for Washington's soldiers at Valley Forge.[2] They also offered easy targets for invading armies.

In 1757–58, following his participation in the French and Indian War, Washington had been quick—too quick, some said—to leave his men to defend the frontier while he went to Boston, Philadelphia, or Williamsburg. In the winter of 1777–78, he stayed with his army, what was left of it, as it shivered and starved at Valley Forge, and he held it together. This, more than any battle he fought, says the historian John Ferling, "was the time of his transfiguration." As never before, he came to be seen as a heroic figure, the savior of his country, dedicated to the army and the cause.[3] There were Indians with him at Valley Forge. In early January, Albigence Waldo, a surgeon from Connecticut, was called to administer to an Indian soldier, "an obedient good natur'd fellow," who died before Waldo reached his hut. The Indian had no doubt signed up for money like many others, Waldo noted in his diary, but he had served his country faithfully, fighting "for those very people who disinherited his forefathers."[4]

More Indians joined Washington's bedraggled little army in the spring when a group of Oneidas journeyed more than 250 miles from their homes in upstate New York, bringing stores of dried corn. Polly Cooper is said to have cooked for the troops, showed them how to prepare hulled corn soup, and refused any payment. The army—and the Revolution—survived. Later, so the story goes, a grateful Martha Washington took Polly shopping in Philadelphia and bought her a hat and shawl.[5] It is difficult to imagine that a group of people traveling such a distance could have carried enough corn to feed an army, but the story endures and is commemorated in the statue as a symbol of the Oneidas' contribution to the birth of the nation.

Why would the Patriot army, in winter camp in the midst of one of the most populated and fertile areas in the American colonies, be starving, and why would Oneidas care? The answer to the first question is relatively simple. The Revolution in 1778 was hardly an outpouring of patriotic unity. Rather than a band of farmers turned freedom fighters united in sacrifice for the cause, Washington's army was a motley collection of indentured servants, recent Scotch-Irish immigrants, unemployed laborers, emancipated slaves, misfits, and no-hopers—the poorest of the poor, many of whose services were paid for by more prosperous Americans who had bought out their own service. Most farmers in southeastern Pennsylvania went about the business of growing and selling food—and many of them sold it in Philadelphia to the British army, which paid hard cash in pounds sterling, not to the Continental Army, which paid in worthless paper currency. Washington worked incessantly to win the hearts and minds of local farmers, merchants, and officials and keep his men supplied despite what he called "the Horrid Intercource" between the country and the city.[6] Why Oneida Indians stepped up to save the Revolution when Pennsylvania farmers failed to do so requires more explanation.

The chain of friendship between the Iroquois and the British had endured through tumultuous times before the colonists split with the Crown. Six Nations chiefs had steered their people through perilous currents of imperial conflict, and sometimes had cooperated with imperial and colonial officials in transferring huge amounts of land from other Indian peoples. Whereas Indian-white relations in Pennsylvania unraveled into bloodshed in the 1750s and '60s, the economic, social, kinship, and religious ties that Iroquois people built with colonial neighbors generally survived, strained but intact. Mohawks and Oneidas had adapted European agricultural techniques and raised livestock. They participated in the cash economy of the Mohawk Valley, with the result that the Indian and colonial communities in the area became economically interdependent and their material cultures merged. Such ties made conflict all the more bitter when it came.[7] Neutrality had served the Iroquois well in past conflicts between Britain and France, and it seemed for a time as if it might work again in what looked like an English civil war. "It was a family quarrel," the Iroquois told Major General Philip Schuyler; "they would not Interfere, but remain neuter and hoped we would not desire more of them."[8] Washington's position regarding the Six Nations as of February 1776 was that "we don't want them to take up the hatchet for us, except they chuse it, we only desire that they will not fight against us."[9]

That meant paying special attention to Iroquois emissaries and conveying an impression of American strength and generosity to counteract British propaganda. In the spring of 1776, some Mohawks from Canajoharie on the Mohawk River traveled to Boston and requested a commission to raise men and to fight against the British. As they did not appear to Washington "to be Persons of any Sort of Consequence," he sent them on their way with a few presents and suggested they go and see General Schuyler. But he knew Indians were watching events in New England as intently as he and Schuyler were watching events in Indian country, and he recognized the propaganda potential in the Mohawks' visit: they had seen the king's troops abandon Boston, and it would "be Good Policy to hasten them home as fast as possible, that they may Communicate the Intelligence, their Tale will Carry more Conviction than the Report of twenty white men."[10] Schuyler agreed. During a conference with the Iroquois in Albany in May, he had the Indians attend his review of Major General John Sullivan's troops and had his soldiers "Continually walking the Streets in Order to induce the Belief of a greater Number than there really was," to contradict Tory agents who told the Indians that the American forces were weak.[11]

Schuyler and the other commissioners suggested that the Iroquois send a delegation to New York to visit the great warrior George Washington, and then proceed to Boston and Philadelphia to meet American leaders. When a delegation of twenty-one Iroquois complied, a nervous Schuyler suggested that Washington detain them or send them on to Philadelphia or other places, "that they might serve as a Kind of Hostages" to keep other Iroquois peaceful. Washington agreed and kept the Indian delegates in Philadelphia in June for that purpose. He heard that they returned home the next month "with very favourable Ideas of our strength and resources."[12] Nevertheless, things hung in the balance in Iroquois country, and Washington knew it. "Our Situation," he wrote Schuyler, "is rather delicate & Embarrassing." The Mohawks and many other Iroquois were attached to John Johnson, Sir William's son, who was exerting his influence against the Patriots, and although it made sense to try to capture Johnson and other Tories, to do so risked incurring the Indians' resentment.[13]

Once John Hancock sent Congress's approval for employing Indian allies, Washington hastened to get the word to the Six Nations. He urged Schuyler and his fellow commissioners to make an alliance with them on whatever terms seemed most likely to secure their friendship, without waiting for further directions from Congress. "The Situation of our Affairs will not suffer the Delay."[14] Schuyler met with the Six Nations at German Flatts on the Mohawk River in August 1776, although he feared that asking them to actively support the American cause might prove counterproductive.[15] In October, when two Cayuga (or possibly Kahnawake) sachems expressed an inclination to visit Washington, Schuyler "greedily embraced" the opportunity and sent them on. They spent three or four days with Washington, who, as Schuyler had suggested, "shewed them every Civility in My Power & presented them with such Necessaries as our Barren stores afforded and they were pleased to take." He also gave them a tour of the military installation to dispel notions spread by Tory agents that the army was weak. The chiefs "seemed to think we were amazingly strong" and departed, Washington hoped, "with No Unfavorable Impressions."[16]

Conscious of their vulnerable position on the edge of colonial settlement, the Oneidas had to weigh multiple factors and respond to many forces as the Revolution divided their neighbors and divided the longhouse. The Oneida sachem Conoghquieson had worked closely with Sir William Johnson in fashioning the Treaty of Fort Stanwix that diverted the tide of colonial settlement away from Iroquois country.[17] But the Oneidas derived far less from their relationship with Johnson than did his Mohawk neighbors and relatives. The treaty placed the boundary line west of the Oneida Carrying Place, the portage linking the Mohawk River–Hudson waterway to Wood Creek and Lake Erie, which Oneidas regarded as an essential source of future income. Relations with the British became increasingly strained. As Oneidas came to depend more heavily on farming, animal husbandry, and trade with colonial settlers, their relations with the other Iroquois tribes, already tested by their exposure to missionaries, also became more tenuous.[18]

When the Revolution broke out, the Oneidas were initially determined to stay out of the war. In June 1775 their chiefs issued a declaration of neutrality. They were "altogether for Peace," they said, and did not want to meddle in the disputes "in these times of great confusion." In fact, they actively tried to maintain a broader Iroquois neutrality.[19] But the neutral ground they tried to cultivate was shrinking rapidly, and cracks appeared in the ancient unity of the Iroquois League. As happened throughout Indian country, militant younger voices challenged the cautious authority of older chiefs. "Times are altered with us Indians," said one Onondaga chief. "Formerly the Warriors were governed by the wisdom of their uncles the Sachems but now they take their own way & dispose of themselves without consulting their uncles the Sachems—while we wish for peace and they are for war."[20] Oneidas and Cayugas disagreed over what course to take, and some Indians said the league had never witnessed such fierce debate in all its history.[21] Ultimately, Oneidas saw supporting their Patriot neighbors as their most viable option.

Historians have long recognized the influence of the New Light Presbyterian missionary Samuel Kirkland in winning over the Oneidas, and so did Washington. Congress in July 1775 recommended employing Kirkland to win the friendship and neutrality of the Six Nations.[22] "All Accounts agree that much of the favourable Disposition shewn by the Indians may be ascribed to his Labour & Influence," Washington told Hancock in September.[23] Kirkland and the Mohawk war chief Joseph Brant (see plate 5) had been friends at Eleazar Wheelock's school in Lebanon, Connecticut, where they first met in the summer of 1761, when Brant was eighteen, Kirkland nineteen. Brant taught Kirkland Mohawk; Kirkland helped Brant with his English. Brant returned to Mohawk country after he left school; Kirkland went as a missionary to Kanonwalohale, the largest of the four main Oneida villages. As tensions escalated between Britain and its colonies, Brant reaffirmed his ties to the Church of England, the Johnson family, and the Crown; Kirkland edged the Oneidas away from the Church of England, the Johnsons, and the Crown. With the outbreak of the Revolution, Brant and Kirkland became bitter enemies, each exerting his influence in the tug-of-war for Indian allegiance.[24]

Washington said Kirkland had an "uncommon Ascendency" over the Oneidas.[25] Many trusted him because of his commitment to the community, demonstrated by his efforts to create schools, convert people to Christianity, and curb alcoholism.[26] He also, so far, had kept his pledge not to use his mission to speculate in Indian land. Kirkland influenced the flow of information into Oneida country, talked up the benefits of an American alliance, and acted as a conduit between the Oneidas and Congress. He asserted that by interpreting the actions of Congress to a number of sachems, he did "real service to the Cause of the Country, or the Cause of Truth & Justice." Conoghquieson was not so sure; he said Kirkland caused a lot of trouble "by always collecting news and telling us strange matters of the white people."[27]

In the summer of 1775 Kirkland accompanied his friend Skenandoah to Boston. Skenandoah had embraced Kirkland's New Light Presbyterianism and was inclined to embrace the Patriot cause as well. Washington went out of his way to make sure Skenandoah was well treated, gave him a tour of the army, and wrote him a letter of introduction to the Massachusetts Provincial Congress. Skenandoah, he said, was a chief "of Considerable Rank in his own Country"; the Oneidas were "very friendly to the Cause of the United Colonies," and Skenandoah's report when he returned home would "have important Consequences to the publick Interest."[28] The following spring "our Staunch Friends the Oneidas" brought Schuyler word that some of the Six Nations had gone to Niagara to join the British, and some Oneidas set out to prevent tribes in Canada from defecting.[29] The Americans planned to build a fort on the site where Fort Stanwix had stood, and Schuyler was confident the Oneidas, who lived only twenty-four miles away, would provide early warnings of enemy movements in the area.[30] In July 1776 Skenandoah and one hundred Oneidas attended Schuyler's conference with the Iroquois at German Flatts, where Kirkland preached a service in the Oneida language. (Joseph Bloomfield, a captain in the Continental Army, said the Oneida congregation listened with such reverence and sang so beautifully that "their devout Behaviour struck me with Astonishment & made me blush with shame for myself and my own People.")[31] Another delegation of six Oneidas visited the American forces early in 1777, asking for accurate information about the state of affairs so they could relate it to the Grand Council, and Kirkland brought them to see Washington at his headquarters. Again Washington did all he could to treat them well and to impress them with the strength of his army. He also told them France was about to join the war, knowing the news would have a considerable impact on several nations and help secure their neutrality, if not an outright commitment to the American cause.[32]

Other students of Wheelock worked for the Patriot cause in Oneida country. James Dean was born in Connecticut in 1748, and as a boy accompanied his missionary step-uncle to the village of Oquaga or Onoquaga on the Susquehanna River. The Oneidas adopted him, and by the time he was thirteen he was "a perfect Indian boy, in language, manners and dress." Wheelock admitted him to Dartmouth free of charge in return for his services as an interpreter. Two years after his graduation, Wheelock sent Dean in the spring of 1775 to strengthen his school's ties with the Indian communities on the St. Lawrence, and he recommended him to the Continental Congress as "the fittest man I know on Earth" for employment among the western and northern tribes. Congress sent Dean to Kanonwalohale, where he worked with Kirkland to win over the Oneidas.[33] Wheelock also recommended Joseph Johnson, a Mohegan preacher and schoolteacher, to Washington as someone who was acquainted with the intrigues of British agents among the Iroquois and had been successful in his efforts to counteract them.[34]

Meanwhile Joseph Brant traveled to London in 1776. On his return, according to the British Indian agent Daniel Claus, he proved the most loyal friend to His Majesty's cause and urged his warriors to defend their lands and liberty against the Americans, "who in great measure began this Rebellion to be sole Masters of the Continent." What was more, Brant was proficient in Christianity, his English was flawless, and he had translated part of the New Testament into Mohawk.[35] The Mohawk was clearly a formidable presence in war or peace. Washington would confront him as an enemy and then court him as an ally.

The widening divisions in the Iroquois League came to a head in 1777. After smallpox struck Onondaga in the winter of 1776–77, the central council fire—the symbol of the league's unity—was ritually extinguished for the first time, leaving the tribes free to follow their own paths.[36] The Oneidas split with most of the others and sided with the Patriots. In the summer Iroquois warriors fought with both the British and American armies. Britain launched a campaign to cut off New England from the other colonies. General John Burgoyne advanced from Montreal down the Champlain-Hudson Valley, and Brigadier General Barry St. Leger drove into Iroquois country and laid siege to Fort Stanwix. Oneida warriors rallied to assist their neighbors and resist the invasion of their homeland. About sixty joined General Nicholas Herkimer and the Tryon County militia in an effort to relieve the fort. Ambushed by the British and their Mohawk and Seneca allies at the Battle of Oriskany, the Americans suffered heavy casualties. As many as thirty Oneidas died. The Senecas suffered similarly heavy casualties in a fight that pitted Iroquois against Iroquois. Mohawks and Oneidas subsequently destroyed each other's villages, and although Iroquois warriors generally avoided fighting other Iroquois during the remainder of the war, the Revolution had become an Iroquois civil war.[37]

The Oneidas sent warriors to join General Horatio Gates and the American army opposing Burgoyne, and they participated in the victory at Saratoga that helped propel France into the war. In the spring of 1778, when Washington proposed enlisting Indians to join his army at Valley Forge, he had the Oneidas and Tuscaroras specifically in mind. He asked Schuyler and the northern commissioners to recruit two hundred warriors, primarily from the Oneidas, who "have manifested the strongest Attachment to us throughout this Dispute."[38] Schuyler told Washington that in the presence of the other Iroquois nations, the Oneidas and Tuscaroras "announced their Determination to Sink or swim with us." Nevertheless, they feared retribution and requested assistance in building a fort to protect them against other Iroquois; they were reluctant to send their young men away to fight and leave their homes defenseless against Seneca attacks.[39]

After a three-week journey, forty-seven Oneidas arrived at Valley Forge in mid-May. Washington assigned them to reconnaissance missions under the command of the marquis de Lafayette. The Oneidas performed well and suffered several casualties at the Battle of Barren Hill on May 20. Washington was impressed, but news of French intervention had reached Valley Forge a couple of weeks before the Oneidas did, and, anticipating that the British would be increasingly on the defensive, he now saw less need for Indian allies. In mid-June the Oneidas began to return home.[40] Both Lafayette and Washington were grateful for their assistance.[41]

Washington's supply problems were not over, and Valley Forge was not the last time he had to resort to Indian corn. Writing from Morristown on Christmas Eve that year, he told Congress that, lacking flour, he had ordered Indian corn from the forage department; "thus we are obliged to attempt to save the men at the expense of the Horses."[42] Nevertheless, news of the French alliance boosted his optimism, and, even before the Oneidas arrived at Valley Forge, he was planning ahead for the eventual victory that now seemed more certain. He dashed off a letter telling his stepson not to sell land to meet expenses. With paper currency depreciating, the money he got would "melt like Snow before a hot Sun." Instead of selling, Washington intended to keep buying land, and he advised his stepson to do likewise. "Lands are permanent—rising fast in value—and will be very dear when our Independency is established, and the Importance of America better known."[43] Washington was occasionally

interested in Indian allies; he was always—even amid the hardships
of Valley Forge—interested in Indian land.

WHILE WASHINGTON CULTIVATED THE ONEIDAS and Tuscaroras
as allies, he planned to "extirpate" the Iroquois nations that sided
with the British. Their warriors carried out devastating attacks on the
frontiers of New York and Pennsylvania, burning large stretches of
the country between the Ohio and the Susquehanna, and in 1778
Joseph Brant's warriors and John and Walter Butler's Tory Rangers
inflicted heavy losses on American soldiers and civilians at Wyoming
and Cherry Valley.[44] There was little Washington could do: "To
defend an extensive frontier against the incursions of Indians and
the Banditti under Butler and Brant is next to impossible," he wrote
in response to New York governor George Clinton's pleas for help.[45]
He hoped their losses might cause the Iroquois to desist but could
not predict how they would act. British intrigues, combined with the
Indians' inherent "disposition to ravage," drove them to commit outrages.[46] Washington and his officers justified expeditions into
Iroquois country as necessary retaliations. Iroquois people suspected
that the driving force behind Washington's campaigns was not retaliation but land. Some historians agree.[47]

In late February 1778 the Continental Congress formally authorized Washington to plan and execute an expedition for the "chastisement of the savages."[48] In June Congress voted almost $1 million for
campaigns against Detroit and the Six Nations. Washington argued
against them. The time was not right; the season was too far advanced
to organize an effective campaign, and diverting limited resources
against the Indians would leave other areas vulnerable to British attack.
Washington had seen firsthand the horrors perpetrated by Indian
raids, but in the broader scheme of the war, defending frontier inhabitants was secondary "to matters of higher moment" and military operations elsewhere. The frontier settlers would have to wait. Congress
deferred the campaign against Detroit. The campaign against the Six
Nations was postponed until the next year.[49]

Meanwhile, in June a delegation from the Senecas, the primary
target for an expedition against the Six Nations, came to Washington's
encampment on the New Jersey side of the Delaware River. Accompanied by a few Oneidas and Tuscaroras as peacemakers, they hoped to
exchange a white captive for a chief named Astiarix, who had been
captured on the Virginia frontier. Washington's aide James McHenry
recorded an account of the meeting in his diary. The Seneca speaker

gave a bold and impassioned speech. He acknowledged his people were at war with the Americans, but, as he came on a peaceful errand, "he was sure that the great American Warrior woud not with-hold his Freind whom he sought. They were both great Warriors, & must know each other, & must both be inspired by the same generous Sentiments." Washington treated the Senecas civilly but took a hard line. He knew nothing about the whereabouts of Astiarix, he said, and threatened that if they did not cease their hostilities, as soon as the British army was gone, he "would turn our whole force against them & the other Indian Nations who have taken a like blody part against us and cut them to pieces." He hoped that when they returned home the accounts they gave about the strength of the Continental Army and the British evacuation of Philadelphia would have the desired effect on the disposition of their people.[50]

Washington and his senior officers were all of the opinion that, as General John Stark put it, "we never Shall be safe, in this Country, till an Expedition is Carried into the Indians Country, & Effectually, Root out these nefarious Wretches, from the face of the Earth."[51] The Senecas received a stay of execution. Iroquois communities that lay within closer striking distance were not so fortunate. Located on the upper Susquehanna River near present-day Windsor, New York, Oquaga was an Oneida town, but by the eve of the Revolution it was a mixed community with many Mohawk, Tuscarora, and Mahican residents. Although it had impressed visitors as a model Christian Indian community, it was riven between Christians and non-Christians and between an Anglican faction and a Presbyterian faction. Joseph Brant used Oquaga as his headquarters for launching raids in the Susquehanna Valley, and Governor Clinton urged Washington to destroy the place. In October 1778, Washington ordered an expedition against Oquaga and Unadilla, "places of Rendezvous for the Savages & Tories who infested them—and where they deposited their plunder." As Lieutenant Colonel William Butler and the 4th Pennsylvania Regiment advanced, the inhabitants abandoned Oquaga. Butler said, "It was the finest Indian town I ever saw." Nestled on both sides of the river, Oquaga consisted of about forty log cabins, many with shingled roofs, stone chimneys, wooden floors, and glass windows, as well as communal longhouses. Butler's soldiers burned the town and destroyed two thousand bushels of corn. Years later a veteran of the expedition boasted they found several small children hiding in the cornfields and impaled them on bayonets.[52]

As Washington said of himself, no man knew better than he the need to wage offensive war against Indians. He recognized, as he had on the Virginia frontier twenty years earlier, that defensive tactics played into the Indians' hands: "Supported on the one hand by the British, and enriching themselves with the spoils of our people, they have everything to gain and nothing to lose." His ideas about fighting Indians had not changed; the only effective strategy was to invade Indian country.[53] Unlike the young man in a hurry who had lobbied for an attack on Fort Duquesne, however, Washington was now commander in chief, with a broader perspective, and he preferred to wait than to risk all. Throughout the late fall of 1778 and the winter of 1779 there was much talk of launching expeditions—against Canada, against Detroit, against the Iroquois. His friend and protégé Lafayette favored a Canadian invasion with French officers. Washington opposed it. He may have done so because Gates, who had won a major victory at Saratoga while Washington had none, championed it and would have likely been its commander; he may have been fixated on New York, but at least on paper he took a longer view. Suppose the expedition succeeded, and then France retook Canada and rebuilt its Indian alliances, he posited. With Spain in possession of the lands west of the Mississippi, the young American nation would be hemmed in, a prospect, he informed Henry Laurens in November, that "alarms all my feelings for the true and permanent interests of my Country." Like Washington in 1758, Washington in 1778 remained "convinced that the only certain way of preventing Indian ravages is to carry the war vigorously into their own country," and fretted that an invasion of Indian country was not under way, but he had learned, perhaps from General Forbes twenty years earlier, that patience and preparation were preferable to haste: "I fear we must content ourselves with defensive precautions, for the present." His arguments prevailed with Congress.[54]

Diverting a substantial part of the Continental Army to a western Indian campaign far from the main theater of war and from its logistical base represented a considerable risk. Washington had formerly thought the best way to end Indian raids was to invade Canada, not Iroquoia.[55] Escalating Iroquois raids and consultations with Generals Greene and Schuyler convinced him that striking deep into Seneca country would stifle the raids at their source. It was a common strategy, executed in other assaults on Indian country in 1779. In April, Colonel Evan Shelby led an expedition against the Chickamauga Cherokees on the lower Tennessee River, burning, Thomas Jefferson informed Washington, eleven towns and twenty thousand bushels of corn.[56] In May, Colonel John Bowman and three hundred Kentucky militia crossed the Ohio and burned the Shawnee town at Chillicothe.[57]

The expedition against the Iroquois that summer is commonly called Sullivan's campaign, after the general who led the main thrust. In fact, the expedition was Washington's from start to finish. He conceived it, gathered information about the country and communities it targeted, planned it, secured congressional support and funding for it, oversaw and orchestrated its multiple components, and eagerly awaited reports coming in from the front. It was one of the most carefully planned campaigns of the war. With meticulous attention to detail and stressing the need for "the profoundest secrecy" in making inquiries and plans, Washington consulted with Greene, Schuyler, and Brigadier General James Clinton; he corresponded with officers and civilians; he interviewed frontiersmen and former captives; he sent out spies, and he circulated questionnaires as he compiled the information he considered vital to success. What was the topography in Iroquois country? Which water routes provided access, and how navigable were they? Where were the various Indian towns, what were their populations, and how many miles separated them? Which towns should bear the brunt of the attack? How many men would be needed, and what proportion of the army should be frontiersmen and rangers accustomed to Indian fighting? Would artillery be necessary? What supplies would be necessary, in what quantities, and at what locations? Should support posts be established as the army advanced? Would the British interfere? He compiled in his own handwriting a table with answers to his questions and appended relevant extracts from other sources. He sketched his own map of the New York/Pennsylvania frontier.[58] His efforts demonstrated the seriousness of the Iroquois threat, but they also reflected the value of the prize. It has been suggested that his preoccupation with preparations for the Iroquois campaign diverted his attention from the growing dispute between Benedict Arnold and Joseph Reed, president of the Pennsylvania Supreme Executive Council, a feud that fueled Arnold's alienation from the Patriot cause.[59]

Washington wanted the intended invasion to "distract and terrify the Indians" and hoped that in the confusion some old men, women, and children would be taken prisoner. If the army did not manage to defeat the Iroquois warriors, it would at least destroy their villages and the year's crop.[60] Greene advised that to "scourge the Indians properly" American forces should invade their country by multiple routes "and at a season when their Corn is about half grown." The goal was simple: drive the Indians away, destroy their grain, and return home. Washington would have to use Continental troops "or else the Work wont be half done."[61] In other words, the expedition was to do what French and British armies had done when fighting Indians—burn their homes and food and leave them to starve.

At first, Washington wanted to strike Niagara, the hub of the British-Iroquois war effort.[62] He hoped the Oneidas might be induced to persuade their relatives to betray the fort but acknowledged this was a long shot. An American campaign against Niagara had to find its way across Iroquois country, knowledge best obtained via Kirkland and Dean from the Oneidas. But Washington knew the Oneidas would be reluctant to wage war on fellow Iroquois and cautioned that information about the geography of Iroquoia be obtained "in such a manner as not to give them any suspicion of the real design."[63]

Schuyler initially recommended the Mohawk Valley as the main invasion route, but Greene argued strongly for the Susquehanna; Washington accepted his advice, and Schuyler concurred.[64] Washington originally envisioned sending an expedition from Fort Pitt as a third prong of the invasion and ordered Brigadier General Lachlan McIntosh to explore the possibility of transporting troops up the Allegheny River in large canoes and then heading overland to Lake Erie. But, concerned about supplies, accurate information, and timing, he reduced the expedition to a feint.[65] When Colonel Daniel Brodhead took over as commander at Fort Pitt, Washington encouraged him to fuel rivalry between the Wyandots and Mingoes; inducing the former to attack the latter would create a "useful diversion."[66]

Although the Iroquois harassing the frontiers were predominantly Mohawks and Senecas, Washington's first strike targeted the Onondagas. Most Onondagas were still neutral, many had close ties to Washington's Oneida allies, and some were actually allied to the United States by early 1779. Nevertheless, when Schuyler suggested it, Washington approved a surprise attack on "the Onondaga capital village." He said it offered good prospects for success at little risk and an opportunity "to pay them in their Coin."[67] Joseph Brant's first biographer, William Stone, noted in 1838 that the attack on Onondaga might look like "a harsh if not unnecessary measure," but at the time Washington thought a blow against the political and military nerve center of the Iroquois League would reverberate through the confederacy.[68] In April, over Oneida protests, Colonel Goose Van Schaick and 550 troops invaded Onondaga country. They burned fifty longhouses, destroyed cattle and stores of corn and beans, killed a dozen people, and took thirty-four prisoners.

Brigadier General Clinton had warned Van Schaick to make sure his soldiers did not abuse the Indian women. "Bad as the savages are," he said, "they never violate the chastity of any women, their prisoners." As one might expect, official reports of the expedition said nothing about mistreatment of infants and sexual abuse of female prisoners, but Iroquois traditions assert, and other sources seem to confirm, that American soldiers killed babies and raped women. Three years later, an Onondaga chief told the British that when the Americans attacked his town "they put to death all the Women and Children, excepting some of the Young Women, whom they carried away for the use of their Soldiers & were afterwards put to death in a more shameful manner." Van Schaick's campaign drove hungry Onondagas west to the Senecas and the British at Niagara, although some sought refuge with their Oneida neighbors to the east.[69] Washington congratulated Van Schaick on the successful outcome of a campaign that, he declared in general orders, brought "the highest honor" to the commander and his officers and men.[70]

Back in 1776 Schuyler had told Washington that if the Cayugas declared against the United States he would cut them off immediately; they were within striking distance of Fort Stanwix. The Senecas, on the other hand, were out of reach.[71] In May 1779 the Cayugas sent out peace feelers. Washington's first inclination was to have none of it, suspecting they intended only to evade the immediate threat and would resume their hostility as soon as they could do so with safety and success. However, the advantages to be gained from dividing the Iroquois persuaded him that it might "be politic enough to make a partial peace with some of the tribes."[72]

Washington first offered the command of the Iroquois campaign to Gates, with instructions that if did he not feel up to the task, he should pass it on to Major General John Sullivan, which, as expected, he did.[73] Sullivan, a hard-drinking New Hampshire lawyer and an ambitious officer with a volatile temper and a mixed record in the war so far, was not enthusiastic either and took a week to accept. He knew that he was up against a formidable enemy and that American troops faced a challenge in Indian country, but said his New Hampshire soldiers were "all marksmen, and accustomed to the Indian mode of fighting."[74]

Washington corresponded with Sullivan throughout the spring and summer as the general organized the campaign and got it under way. Mindful of what had happened to Braddock, Washington gave detailed advice: guard against surprise; establish intermediate posts to safeguard communications and convoys; leave enough men to garrison the posts but not so many as to seriously deplete the attacking force. And while Washington deplored and denounced British and Indian terror tactics and raids on American settlements, he had no qualms about ordering Sullivan to employ terror tactics and wage total war against Iroquois settlements: "The immediate objects are the total destruction and devastation of their settlements and the capture of as many prisoners of every age and sex as possible. It will be essential to ruin their crops now in the ground and prevent their planting more." As the army cut its swath, Sullivan was to dispatch detachments to lay waste all the neighboring settlements so that the country would "not be merely overrun but destroyed." The best defense was attack, Washington explained to Sullivan: peace "would be fallacious and temporary" unless the Iroquois were driven far from the frontiers and terrorized by "the severity of the chastisement they receive." He forbade Sullivan to listen to any peace overtures until he had totally destroyed their settlements, and then only if they gave hostages as security.[75] Writing to Lafayette on July 4, Washington said he expected the invasion would "extirpate them from the Country which more than probable will be effected by their flight as it is not a difficult matter for them to take up their Beds and Walk."[76] As several thousand American soldiers, including roughly one-quarter of the Continental Army, prepared to descend upon the Iroquois in a coordinated, three-pronged assault, Sullivan's officers drank a toast (one of many toasts) promising "civilization or death to all American savages."[77]

Washington told Sullivan that the success of his campaign depended on the speed of his movements and urged him to "proceed as light as possible."[78] Instead, Sullivan dilly-dallied, citing one supply problem after another, and even complaining to Congress about deficient support from Washington. Washington lost patience—and his cool—and ordered him to get a move on. Sullivan finally marched against the Iroquois on August 9, two months later than Washington had hoped.[79]

Once Sullivan got going, he did as he was ordered, taking precautions against ambush and devastating the country as he advanced. He led three brigades of Continental troops north up the Susquehanna; James Clinton and a fourth brigade advanced west from the Mohawk Valley, destroying five Indian villages. Their combined force numbered roughly 4,500 men. Meanwhile, Daniel Brodhead left Fort Pitt on August 11 with 600 men and eight Delaware guides and marched against the Seneca and Munsee towns on the upper Allegheny River, a region never far from Washington's mind and crucial to his Ohio country plans. Guyasuta sent word to the British at Fort Niagara asking for help, but the British could spare no troops, wrongly expecting that any American assault would head for Niagara or Detroit.[80]

The Oneidas evidently wanted little part in it. Samuel Kirkland served as chaplain and James Dean served as an interpreter and guide in the early stages of the campaign, but only four Oneidas accompanied the expedition, including Hanyerry or Hanyost Thaosagwat, who had fought at Oriskany. Sullivan complained they seemed to be "totally unacquainted with every part of the country" through which he marched, which assumes, of course, that the Oneidas were actually trying to lead the army to Iroquois villages.[81] A party of Stockbridge Indians acted as advance scouts for the army.[82]

Sullivan and Clinton rendezvoused at Tioga in late August. At the end of the month they fended off a force of six hundred Tories and Iroquois led by John Butler and Joseph Brant at Newtown on the bank of the Chemung River east of present-day Elmira, New York. The Indians left a dozen dead, including a woman, whom the soldiers "scalped immediately." They also skinned the legs of two dead Indians and "Drest them for Leggins." One officer preferred to record the incident in abbreviations: "Sm. Skn. By our S. fr Bts" (Some skinned by our soldiers for boots). As they would repeatedly during the expedition, the Americans found that Iroquois towns were not unlike those of frontier settlers. Many houses were built of hewn logs framed together, with doors, glass windows, and wooden floors; some were painted. Sullivan told Washington that Chemung "was most beautifully situated, contained a chapel with between thirty and forty other houses, many of them large and tolerably well finished. There were fields of corn, the most extensive that I ever saw with great quantities of potatoes, pumpkins, squashes, and in short every other thing which any farmer could produce—the whole of which was destroyed root and branch." One soldier said the fields were so large he could hardly believe it. The troops put the town to the torch and spent two days destroying whatever they could not eat.[83]

When Washington heard of the victory at Newtown, he immediately wrote urging Sullivan to press on and achieve the two goals of the expedition. One was to push the Indians as far as possible from the American frontiers and create a refugee crisis for the British. "The other is the making the destruction of their settlements so final and complete as to put it out of their power to derive the smallest succor from them in case they should attempt to return this season."[84]

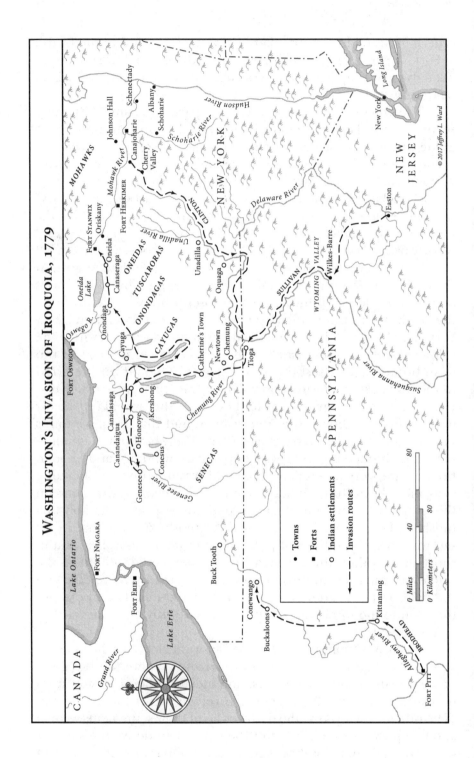

WASHINGTON'S INVASION OF IROQUOIA, 1779

CANADA

Lake Ontario

Grand River

Lake Erie

FORT NIAGARA

FORT ERIE

MOHAWKS

Johnson Hall

Schenectady

Albany

Schoharie

Schoharie River

Mohawk River

Canajoharie

Cherry Valley

FORT HERKIMER

NEW YORK

Hudson River

Long Island

New York

NEW JERSEY

© 2017 Jeffrey L. Ward

FORT STANWIX

Oriskany

Oneida

Oneida Lake

Canaseraga

ONEIDAS

TUSCARORAS

ONONDAGAS

Onondaga

Cayuga

CAYUGAS

Unadilla River

Unadilla

Oquaga

CLINTON

Delaware River

FORT OSWEGO

Oswego R.

Canadasaga

Canandaigua

Honeoye

Kershong

Catherine's Town

Newtown

Chemung

Tioga

SULLIVAN

WYOMING VALLEY

Wilkes-Barre

Easton

Genesee

Conesus

Genesee River

Chemung River

SENECAS

PENNSYLVANIA

Susquehanna River

Buck Tooth

Towns
Forts
Indian settlements
Invasion routes

Conewango

Buckaloons

Kittanning

Allegheny River

BRODHEAD

FORT PITT

0 Miles 40 80
0 Kilometers 80

With the army's provisions growing sparse but surrounded by an Iroquoian cornucopia, Sullivan put his troops on half rations, which they gladly put up with, wrote one of the soldiers, "being anxious to extirpate those Hell-Hounds from off the face of the Earth."[85] Then Sullivan resumed his march, burning towns and crops as the people fled before his advance.

Despite Washington's instructions to net prisoners, Sullivan's troops took very few. Outnumbered and outgunned, the Iroquois usually managed to keep their women and children beyond the army's reach.[86] The soldiers also murdered noncombatants whom they could have taken captive. At French Catherine's Town, a settlement of about thirty houses, they found an old Indian woman. Some of them wanted to kill her, but Sullivan spared her, fed her, and learned from her that the warriors and the women in her village had debated whether to fight or flee from the American army. Sullivan left the old woman with food and shelter, an act of humanity that attracted comment from many of his officers. It was an isolated incident in a campaign of terror and destruction. A young woman who had apparently stayed behind to help the old woman was shot. When the army returned several weeks later, they found her naked body lying in a mud hole. The murder, and presumably rape, of the young woman, wrote one officer, was "supposed to be done by some of our soldiers."[87]

The army lived off the land—or rather it lived off Iroquois fields, orchards, and stores—as it marched through some of the most fertile territory in the country. Time and again, officers described in their journals well-built towns, vast fields of corn, beans, squash, pumpkins, potatoes, and watermelons, and orchards of apple, peach, plum, and cherry trees. Dr. Jabez Campfield, a surgeon in the 5th New Jersey Regiment, said the amount of corn in the towns was far beyond what anybody had imagined and feared that the methods the army employed would be "ineffectual for its destruction."[88] The soldiers ate well on Iroquois food, and veterans of the campaign would remember the fertility of these lands when the war was over. Some officers felt qualms about what they were doing. Campfield hoped the Indians ("these rusticks," he called them) would be made to see reason just by the advance of the army, without suffering the extremes of war; "there is something so cruel, in destroying the habitations of any people, (however mean they may be, being their all) that I might say the prospect hurt my feelings."[89]

Most soldiers went about their work either with grim determination or in good spirits.[90] In town after town, they burned the

houses, some of which were single-family dwellings and others sub-
stantially built longhouses between sixty and eighty feet in length
that lodged several families.[91] They destroyed corn in the fields and
corn in the storehouses, and cut down orchards or girdled the bark
of fruit trees so that they would perish from the frost in the coming
winter. Corn could be replanted and cornfields regrown, but the
orchards represented a long-term investment of time and attention.
Destroying them sent a clear message that there would be nothing
for Iroquois people to return to.[92] At one town the soldiers found an
old woman and a man too infirm to walk. Sullivan would not allow
them to be hurt and ordered that a house be left standing for them,
but as the army was marching away some soldiers secured the door
and set it on fire, burning both the house and the old couple within.[93]

In mid-September the army reached Chenussio or Genesee
Castle, the largest of the Seneca towns and, prisoners told Sullivan,
"the grand Capital of the Indian Country." About 128 well-built
houses nestled in the bow of the river on rich bottom lands where
there were too many cornfields to count, one officer thought, "there
being not less than 700 acres in the place." The Senecas had
ambushed and killed an American advance party, including Hanyost
Thaosagwat, whose body they hacked to pieces, and when the army
entered Genesee they found and buried the bodies of an officer,
Lieutenant Thomas Boyd, and a soldier who had been tortured,
scalped, and "mangled in a Most Horrid Manner." They put the town
to the torch. The troops spent from six in the morning until two in
the afternoon destroying two hundred acres of gardens and cornfields. They threw some of the crops into the river; most they pulled
up, piled in large heaps mixed with dry wood taken from the houses,
and set on fire.[94] As the army headed for home, detachments broke
off to destroy outlying villages en route. Four Oneidas came with a
message from their nation asking that the Cayugas' villages be spared,
but Sullivan was intent on carrying out Washington's orders to the
full when it came to burning towns.[95]

Washington monitored the campaign's progress. He wrote to
Lafayette on September 12 that he hoped his "plan of chastisement"
would convince the Indians of two things: first, that their cruelties
would not go unpunished; second, that the nation that had insti-
gated them to take up arms and commit acts of barbarism was unable
to protect them. In other words, the Iroquois had brought this tempest down on their own heads. Unlike the British and Indian attacks
on American settlements that Washington denounced, Sullivan's
campaign was just retribution. By the end of September, Washington

PLATE 1. George Washington, by Charles Willson Peale, 1772. The forty-year-old Washington posed for his first portrait wearing his old French and Indian War uniform. Gift of George Washington Curtis Lee, Washington and Lee University, Lexington, Virginia.

PLATE 2. Sir Joshua Reynolds painted this portrait of the Cherokee chief Ostenaco, also known as Judd's Friend and Outacite, during his visit to London in 1762. Gilcrease Museum, Tulsa, Oklahoma.

PLATE 3. In 1790 Washington subscribed and made partial payment for copies of John Trumbull's painting of *The Death of General Montgomery*. In March 1798 Trumbull sent him proofs of his first engraving and then four copies. *PGW, Ret.* 3:14, 361. Yale University Art Gallery.

PLATE 4. Trumbull sketched Louis Cook (Atiatoharongwen), whom he identified
as an Oneida, and used him as the model for the Indian warrior in *The Death of
General Montgomery*. Yale University Art Gallery.

PLATE 5. Joseph Brant (Thayenda-negea), by Gilbert Stuart, 1786. The famous Mohawk had his portrait painted several times and twice by Stuart. This one was formerly owned by the Duke of Northumberland.

PLATE 6. *Portrait of Ki-on-twog-ky* (Cornplanter), by F. Bartoli, 1796. The Seneca chief was a central figure in Washington's dealings with the Six Nations. Collection of the New-York Historical Society.

PLATE 7. Henry Knox, by Charles Willson Peale, c. 1784. Knox was Washington's secretary of war and the chief architect of the first president's Indian policy. Courtesy of Independence National Historical Park, Philadelphia.

PLATE 8. John Trumbull painted the seventy-five-year-old Oneida chief Good Peter (Agwerondongwas) in 1792, the year before his death. Yale University Art Gallery.

PLATE 9. Arthur St. Clair, first governor of the Northwest Territory and the general defeated by the Northwestern Indian Confederacy in 1791. Portrait by Charles Willson Peale, 1782. Courtesy of Independence National Historical Park, Philadelphia.

PLATE 10. Timothy Pickering, by Charles Willson Peale, c. 1792. Pickering served as U.S. treaty commissioner, secretary of war (briefly), and secretary of state under Washington. Courtesy of Independence National Historical Park, Philadelphia.

PLATE 11. Indians were a common sight on the streets of the nation's capital during Washington's administration, as illustrated in this view by English engraver William Birch, who came to Philadelphia in 1794. *The City of Philadelphia in the State of Pennsylvania, North America, as it appeared in the Year 1800, consisting of twenty eight plates drawn and engraved by W. Birch & Son.* Published by W. Birch, 1800. Dartmouth College Library.

PLATE 12. Washington enlisted the Seneca chief Sagoyewatha or Red Jacket as an intermediary in his negotiations with the Northwestern Confederacy. Red Jacket wears the peace medal Washington gave him. Thomas L. McKenney and James Hall, *History of the Indian Tribes of North America,* vol. 1 (Philadelphia: E. C. Biddle, 1836).

PLATE 13. *Apotheosis of Washington* or *Commemoration of Washington*, by John James Barralet, 1802. Lady Liberty and an Indian figure mourn as Father Time and an angel carry Washington to heaven, where, apparently, Handsome Lake encountered him in his vision. Collection of Fraunces Tavern Museum, New York City.

expected Sullivan to "have completed the entire destruction of the whole settlements of the Six Nations, excepting those of the Oneidas and such other friendly towns as have merited a different treatment." He pictured men, women, and children fleeing in distress and confusion to Niagara more than one hundred miles away, with Brant and the Butlers at their head.[96]

By the end of the campaign, according to Sullivan's estimate, his army had destroyed forty towns, 160,000 bushels of corn, and vast quantities of fruit trees and vegetables. "Every creek and river has been traced, and the whole country explored in search of Indian settlements, and I am well persuaded that, except one town situated near the Allegana, about 50 miles from Chinesee there is not a single town left in the country of the Five nations."[97] Sullivan was a braggart, and it was a bit of an exaggeration; he appears to have been rather expansive and inclusive in his definition of what constituted a "town." Congress passed a resolution thanking Washington and Sullivan and set aside the second Thursday in December as a national day of thanksgiving. Washington, perhaps because of Sullivan's early dilatoriness, was sparing in his praise for his general. Sullivan resigned soon after, claiming ill health.[98]

There was devastation enough. The Seneca scholar Arthur C. Parker said that "ruin was spread like a blanket over the Iroquois country." Sullivan's count of forty towns did not include the towns destroyed by Van Schaick and Brodhead. Like Sullivan, Brodhead found large towns with as many as 130 houses, some of them large enough to accommodate three or four families, surrounded by large cornfields. His soldiers burned ten towns and spent three whole days destroying the towns and cornfields. Brodhead estimated they destroyed more than 500 acres and took $30,000 in plunder.[99] Washington received news of Brodhead's success on the heels of Sullivan's return: "This in a great measure completes the destruction, not only of the Country of the Six Nations, but of their Allies on the head of the Allegheny River," he wrote to Gates.[100]

The plunder taken by Sullivan and Brodhead's men was not insignificant. Indian communities were tied into Atlantic networks of commerce, and Indian participation in the fur and deerskin trades meant that the products of British mills and workshops sometimes flowed into the lodges of Indian hunters more readily than into the cabins of frontier framers. American soldiers who plundered Indian villages in the Revolution, like archaeologists who excavated the sites in modern times, often found Sheffield steel knives, china, glassware, and other valuable items. When Sullivan dispatched Colonel Peter

Gansevoort to destroy the small Mohawk settlement at Tionondaroga, often called the Lower Mohawk Castle, at Fort Hunter in New York, Gansevoort surprised the village and took the inhabitants prisoner. Rather than put the houses to the torch, he allowed several frontier families who had been driven from their homes by Indian attacks to occupy the Mohawks' houses, which "were very well furnished with all necessary Household utensils, great plenty of Grain, several Horses, Cows, & wagons." Gansevoort saw what would have been obvious to many of the soldiers: "These Indians live much better than most of the Mohawk River farmers." The chapel at Fort Hunter contained a set of communion silver that Queen Anne had donated after the visit of Mohawk "kings" to London in 1711, but when rebel troops plundered the town, they turned the chapel into a tavern. Alarmed that Sullivan had ordered an attack on a community that had been consistently peaceful and resided there under assurances of peace from the commissioners of Indian affairs, Schuyler wanted the prisoners freed. Washington agreed and ordered their release.[101]

Sullivan's estimate of food destroyed did not include that consumed by his thousands of troops over the course of the six-week campaign.[102] Relating her life story in old age, Mary Jemison, who was living with the Senecas, said that when Sullivan's troops reached the Genesee River, they destroyed every article of food they could lay their hands on. They burned the corn or tossed it into the river, killed the few cattle and horses they found, destroyed the fruit trees, "and left nothing but the bare soil and timber." Jemison and her people had "not a mouthful of any kind of sustenance left, not even enough to keep a child one day from perishing with hunger."[103]

At Niagara, as Washington planned, the British faced a refugee crisis as Indian families who had lost everything flooded in.[104] By late September more than five thousand homeless and hungry people huddled around the fort, seeking food, shelter, and clothing. Some dispersed to relieve the pressure, but, as one of the coldest winters on record gripped northern New York, refugees in makeshift camps suffered exposure, disease, and—with supply routes from Montreal impassable—starvation.[105] Others settled at Buffalo Creek, where they built a new community and attempted to rebuild their league after the war. The scorched-earth campaign and terror tactics that Washington ordered and Sullivan executed caused untold human misery. A decade later Seneca chiefs meeting Washington in Philadelphia told him, "When your army entered the country of the Six Nations, we called you Town Destroyer; and to this day when that name is heard, our women look behind them and turn pale and our children cling to the necks of their mothers."[106]

Washington believed the Sullivan and Brodhead campaigns had had been so successful in laying waste Iroquois country and the headwaters of the Allegheny that they would bring peace to the northern frontier.[107] In addition to destroying enormous quantities of food, the Sullivan campaign demonstrated that in terms of intelligence gathering, operational planning, tactics, and leadership, Washington had made significant progress by 1779 in building an army that could confront the British in a protracted war.[108]

The expeditions stunned the Iroquois but did not break their war effort. If anything, they stiffened their resolve and strengthened their allegiance to the British. Sullivan's campaign confirmed what the British had been telling them all along (and what Washington had told Lafayette): that the Americans were intent on destroying them. Driven to Niagara with his fellow Senecas, Sayengeraghta, a chief also known as Old Smoke, declared that the Americans wanted nothing less than to wipe the Indians from the face of the earth and take their land; that was the cause of the war "between the King and his disobedient Children."[109] Even as they were taking refuge at Niagara, Iroquois warriors vowed to take revenge on the Americans as soon as they had placed their women and children in safety. James Madison told Jefferson that Sullivan's campaign seemed "rather to have exasperated than to have terrified or disabled them." One of Sullivan's officers summed up the effects of his campaign: "The nests are destroyed but the birds are still on the wing."[110]

The Iroquois had no choice but to fight on. Come spring, they resumed their raids on the American frontier, looking for food and vengeance. According to John Butler fifty-nine parties totaling almost 2,300 men went out from Niagara between February and September 1780. They killed 142 Americans and took 161 captives, destroyed 2 churches, 157 houses, and 150 granaries, and drove off 247 horses and 922 cattle. In New York, the raids led by Brant, Butler, and the Seneca war chief Cornplanter (see plate 6) that spring destroyed 1,000 homes, 1,000 barns, and 600,000 bushels of grain. Pennsylvania fared little better. The Susquehanna Valley, through which Sullivan's army had marched before following the Chemung River into Seneca country, suffered at least thirty-five separate raids from 1780 to 1782.[111] Washington's war on Iroquois homes and food generated more, not fewer, raids on American settlers. Despite the devastation of American scorched-earth campaigns, according to the British Indian agent Daniel Claus, the Six Nations maintained they still held the balance of power on the continent.[112] Indians and colonists who had once coexisted now burned each other's homes with equal vigor and violence.

The Oneidas fared little better than those who fought against the Americans. Their allegiance to the United States made them a target for retaliation by the British and other Iroquois nations. In the winter of 1779 they still had not received help building their picket fort and faced the threat of starvation. Other Iroquois pressured them to renounce their American alliance. The Senecas threatened to strike them hard, and the Oneidas braced for an attack.[113] Governor Haldimand of Quebec advocated threatening to execute more than thirty Oneida prisoners to guarantee the good conduct of the rest of the nation, and the fear of assault drove the Oneidas to evacuate their towns. In August 1780 Joseph Brant put Kanonwalohale and Kirkland's church to the torch.[114] The Oneidas fled east to Schenectady, where, like those Iroquois driven west to Niagara, they lived the rest of the war in squalid refugee camps. James Dean accompanied them. Convinced that it was both good policy and justice to support a tribe "who have manifested so strong an attachment to us as the Oneidas have done," Washington did what he could to help, but it was not much. In the winter of 1781 he sent Schuyler articles of clothing for the Oneidas that he had selected from the army's depleted stores; the quality was not good enough for his troops, but it was enough to make the Indians comfortable at least. He could promise nothing in terms of provisions. The troops at Albany and Schenectady had been short of food all winter, he told the Board of War: "When our magazines are full, the Indians will participate, when scanty, they must share accordingly."[115] In the spring Congress approved Schuyler's measures for relieving the Oneidas and Tuscaroras from the suffering they had incurred as a result of their fidelity to the United States, and provided him $1,000 to purchase blankets for them.[116]

Despite their losses and suffering, Oneidas continued to assist the Patriots. A handful witnessed the surrender of the British army under General Charles Cornwallis at Yorktown in October 1781.[117] When Washington went to Schenectady in the summer of 1783, two hundred Oneidas and Tuscaroras turned out to honor him, although emissaries presented him with a memorial reciting their losses and requesting rum, and powder and ammunition for hunting.[118] The Oneidas later petitioned Congress to compensate them for the frame houses, wagons, farm equipment, livestock, kitchen utensils, clothing, teacups and saucers, punch bowls, looking glasses, jewelry, and many other items they lost during the war.[119] Like the Mohawks at

Tiononderoga, the Oneidas apparently had enjoyed a material standard of living at least equal to that of their white neighbors.

Washington and most historians have explained the Sullivan-
Clinton campaign as a war measure, to avenge and terminate Iroquois
attacks on the frontier. But it was also a measure to prepare for peace.
Washington understood that when terms were drawn up ending the
war, it would be a hollow victory if his new nation got only a strip of
territory along the Atlantic and no lands to the west into which it
could expand. The officers and men who destroyed so many crops
and orchards in Iroquois country came home with reports of rich
lands for the taking in upstate New York and Pennsylvania. Being
able to claim the fertile lands of Iroquoia on the basis of conquest
during the war would be essential to American success at the peace
talks. "Not many leaders of 1779 saw the great prize, but Washington,
the seer, did," wrote the historian A. C. Flick in 1929.[120] Of course, the
seer's vision also embraced the Ohio country.

CHAPTER 12

Killing Crawford

THE REVOLUTION WAS A MESSY AFFAIR in the West. In western Pennsylvania, Kentucky, and the Ohio Valley, the collapse of the imperial order left a power vacuum and a kaleidoscope of contests. Frontier populations not only rebelled against the king, they also fought to build new societies on their own terms amid the upheaval and violence of a revolution that was also, increasingly, a race war. Indian communities fought to fend off embryonic republics that demanded their land and, increasingly, their destruction. British and American agents, operating out of Detroit and Fort Pitt, competed for the allegiance of the tribes in the Ohio country. Local struggles for power and authority—between Virginia and Pennsylvania, between the Continental Congress and frontier settlers, between poor western settlers and wealthy eastern land speculators, between Indians and settlers, between the Delawares and the Six Nations—often took precedence over the bigger struggle between colonists and Crown.[1] The Revolution here sometimes turned neighbors into killers, when frontier militia attacking Indian villages and Indian warriors raiding frontier settlements knew the people they were fighting.[2] It was also a continuation of the war for the lands of the Ohio country that Washington had helped instigate in 1754.[3] It was an opportunity to get lands Washington had coveted for a quarter of a century. Congress and the individual states needed land there to pay the warrants they issued in lieu of pay during the war. Western settlers found in the war opportunities to rid contested lands of Indian inhabitants.

Washington had ambivalent attitudes toward frontier settlers. These were the same people who squatted on his lands, disputed his title, and defied his authority. Like many other members of the eastern elite, he often blamed frontier whites as much as Indians for bloodshed in the region. At the same time, like other land speculators, he relied on settler families to brave the dangers of frontier warfare and to help secure lands he intended to develop.⁴ As commander, he outsourced much of the war in the West to frontier whites, who furnished militia for expeditions against Indian villages and collected bounties on Indian scalps.

The war in the West continued long after, indeed heated up after, Lord Cornwallis surrendered at Yorktown, in part because Washington and his fellow Americans wanted to lay claim to as much of the Ohio country as they could before the peace terms ending the Revolution were decided. The presence of settlers or militia on the ground added weight and legitimacy to the claim. Washington and William Crawford had worked long and hard to get their hands on the best Ohio lands before the Revolution, but their lands stood idle and unsold while the war continued. Winning the Revolution in the West would remove the last obstacle. But victory in the West proved elusive, and the cost was high—although much higher for Crawford than for Washington.

THE REVOLUTION IN THE WEST began as a contest of words and wampum belts, as Indian leaders negotiated with British and American agents and with other Indians. In one of its last acts, the Virginia House of Burgesses in June 1775 elected Washington, Thomas Walker and his son John, Adam Stephen, Andrew Lewis, and Captain James Wood, "or any three or more of them," as commissioners to meet with the chiefs of the Ohio Indians as soon as possible "at such place as they shall find most proper."⁵ Their job was to confirm the Treaty of Camp Charlotte, where the Shawnees had ceded their lands south of the Ohio River to Dunmore, and allay the tribes' concerns. Washington had other business to attend to, of course, and Thomas Walker became the chairman of the commission. (Walker was subsequently appointed commissioner for the middle of the three Indian departments that Congress created; his son John was appointed a commissioner for the Southern Department.)

The "most proper" place for dealing with the Ohio tribes was Fort Pitt (which John Connolly and the Virginia militia had occupied and renamed Fort Dunmore after the British left), the place Washington

had helped capture seventeen years earlier. Congress established a
military department at Pittsburgh but diverted few troops or resources
from the main theater of war in the East, leaving the burden for their
own defense on the shoulders of the inhabitants.[6] Nevertheless,
Pittsburgh's strategic location rendered it important to the broader
revolutionary struggle and a center for military and diplomatic campaigns into Indian country.

Delegates from the Ohio Iroquois, Delawares, and Shawnees
met at Fort Pitt in June and July 1775 to arrange for a fuller meeting
in the fall with the commissioners from Congress and Virginia and
restore their "antient friendship."[7] In a council that dragged on for
five weeks in September and October, the commissioners asked the
Indians to stay home, take care of their women and children, and go
about their usual occupations.[8] Most Indians would have been happy
to do just that, and avoid getting embroiled in a conflict they regarded
as a British civil war that would likely catch them in its crossfire.
Guyasuta attended the council, as did two of Washington's other
acquaintances from the Ohio country, Silver Heels and White Mingo.
Guyasuta had been a key player in Pontiac's War, but he worked tire-
lessly to keep his people out of this one. He had inherited
Tanaghrisson's role as half king, "appointed by the Six Nations to take
care of this Country, that is of the Indians on the West side of the
River Ohio," and was a strong voice for peace in the council talks.
He assured the Virginians that the Six Nations held fast to the chain
of friendship and presented wampum belts to the Wyandots,
Delawares, Shawnees, and Ottawas to bind them in friendship as well.
He even urged Virginia and Pennsylvania to settle *their* differences.[9]

Virginian actions undermined Virginian overtures and assurances. Shawnee chiefs said Virginians were building forts and settling in Kentucky, hunting north of the Ohio, and driving away the
game. They repeated a familiar refrain; the Indians had been pushed
steadily west as American population increased, and now they feared
the Virginians were determined to go to war with them and take
what was left of their country.[10] The Virginian case was not helped
when two men in hunting shirts took a shot at White Mingo not far
from the treaty grounds.[11]

During the talks, Guyasuta declared that "the Six Nations are
the head of all the other Tribes here present."[12] However, the
Delaware war captain Quequedegatha or Koquethagechton, commonly known as White Eyes, demonstrated that the thirteen states
were not the only ones asserting independence. Addressing his
"Brethren the White People and Uncles the Six Nations," and with

Guyasuta present, White Eyes announced the Delawares now lived on land given to them in Wyandot country and told the Six Nations to "not permit any of your foolish People to sit down upon it." According to some accounts, he metaphorically cast off the petticoat the Iroquois had formerly placed on the Delawares, exchanged the corn hoe and pounder for guns, and with a dramatic sweep of his arm claimed all the land beyond the Allegheny River![13] Like the colonists who had thrown off their alliance with the Crown, the Delawares would need allies elsewhere. After the conference White Eyes traveled to Philadelphia, where he spent the next six months negotiating with Congress. He asked for a minister, a schoolteacher, and assistance in adopting agriculture. Congress promised to send an agent to instruct the Delawares in American-style farming.[14]

White Eyes advocated gradual acculturation as the path to the future, and peace with the Americans as the best strategy for Delaware security.[15] Nonetheless he did not speak for all Delawares. Religion and revolution divided Delawares as well as colonists. Some embraced the Moravian faith and followed a Christian life in the mission villages. White Eyes, war captain of the Turtle clan, and Gelemend or John Killbuck, chief of the Turtle clan, supported the work of Moravian missionaries and favored a neutral and then pro-American stance, as did many of the Turkey clan. Hopocan or Captain Pipe of the Wolf clan and his followers distanced themselves from the missions and later moved to Sandusky, settling closer to the Wyandots and the British at Detroit. The Delaware chief Pachgantschihilas or Buckongahelas was openly hostile to the missionaries and their teachings and wanted them expelled from Indian country.[16]

George Morgan, the American Indian agent at Fort Pitt, recognized that, as "grandfathers" of the Algonquian family of Indian nations, the Delawares occupied a key position in intertribal diplomacy. He worked with White Eyes, dispatching runners with speeches and wampum belts to bring multiple nations to Fort Pitt for a council in the spring of 1776.[17] The Indians, he found, were "much confused & unsettled in their Resolutions."[18]

Guyasuta, however, remained constant: he said he had "but one heart" and would continue to work for peace.[19] At a meeting with the Americans and the western tribes at Fort Pitt in July, he presented a wampum belt sent by the Six Nations to the Shawnees, Delawares, Wyandots, and other western Indians, informing them that the Iroquois were determined to take no part in the war and urging them to do the same. The British at Niagara had tried to enlist Seneca support, but "we must be fools indeed to imagine that they regard us

or our Interest who want to bring us into an unnecessary War,"
Guyasuta said. Then, turning to the Virginians and Pennsylvanians
present, he warned: "We will not suffer either the English or
Americans to march an army through our country."[20] At the end of
the month, Congress instructed the commissioners of Indian affairs
to thank Guyasuta for his conduct at Niagara and invite him to visit
the great council fire at Philadelphia.[21] In the fall, more than six
hundred Indians showed up at Fort Pitt and made a treaty that confirmed the Ohio River as the boundary of their lands. Guyasuta again
assured the Americans that the Indians would mind their own business and not join either side, no matter how much pressure the
British at Niagara and Detroit applied, "for if any of our young
Warriors should be cut off it would occasion us great Grief." He
asked the Americans to restrict their campaigns against the British to
the coast, and not come into Indian country to fight, which would
risk alienating the tribes.[22] In private meetings, Guyasuta and White
Mingo warned the commissioners that the hearts of the Ojibwas
"were black and ill affected towards us."[23]

Cornstalk and other Shawnee chiefs also told Morgan they
intended to remain neutral and preserve their friendship with the
white people. As the Fort Pitt conference drew to a close, Cornstalk
asked Morgan to record his words and send them to Congress.
Congress had asked the chiefs several times to explain the causes of
their complaints against the Americans; Cornstalk was surprised they
had to ask:

> All our lands are covered by the white people, and we are jealous that you still
> intend to make larger strides. We never sold you our Lands which you now
> possess on the Ohio between the Great Kanawha and the Cherokee River, and
> which you are settling without ever asking our leave, or obtaining our con-
> sent. Foolish people have desired you to do so, and you have taken their
> advice. We live by Hunting and cannot subsist in any other way. That was our
> hunting Country and you have taken it from us. This is what sits heavy upon
> our Hearts and on the Hearts of all Nations, and it is impossible for us to think
> as we ought to whilst we are thus oppressed.[24]

He was talking about lands Washington and other Virginians coveted. Although Cornstalk continued to assert the Shawnees' desire
for peace, he did so with diminishing confidence. The war party was
gaining strength, and he could not restrain his warriors.[25] Three
Shawnees and two Cherokees, including a chief named Hanging
Maw, kidnapped Daniel Boone's daughter Jemima and two of her
friends in July. (Fearing they might be raped or killed, Boone and his

neighbors gave chase and recovered the girls, although Jemima said the Indians treated them kindly.) Shawnee delegates carried the war belt to the Cherokees in August.[26] Meanwhile, Congress had shifted from trying to secure Indian neutrality to actively soliciting Indian allies.

In early October 1777 Cornstalk and two other Shawnees visited the American garrison at Fort Randolph on the Kanawha River, at the site where he had fought the Virginians exactly three years earlier. The post commander took them hostage to prevent other Shawnees from joining the British. A month later, American militia murdered and mutilated the prisoners. The governors of Virginia and Pennsylvania sent urgent apologies to the Shawnees; George Morgan conveyed Congress's regret, and Patrick Henry denounced the murders, but it was too little and too late.[27] Outraged Shawnees retaliated against frontier settlers, and the Ohio River became a war zone, crossed and recrossed by Shawnee raiding parties and Kentucky militia who burned villages, plundered homes, and lifted scalps with equal ferocity.

American actions made it impossible for Indians to ignore British warnings that the rebels intended to steal their country and destroy them. Many saw their best chance in siding with the redcoats, who had offered at least token protection for Indian lands, rather than with the Americans, who were clearly hell-bent on taking them. Guyasuta abandoned his neutral stance: he, White Mingo, and other Seneca chiefs went to war in late 1777.[28] "The western Indians are United against us," Brigadier General Edward Hand informed Washington in September. He had called out the militia but could not get them to do duty at Fort Pitt nor assemble in sufficient force to mount a campaign into Indian country.[29] In November, Washington sent William Crawford to join Hand's command.[30]

William Crawford entered the Revolutionary service as a lieutenant colonel of the 5th Virginia Regiment, then took command of the 7th Virginia Regiment, and then raised a new regiment, the 13th, west of the Alleghenies. "If a War With the Westerly Endians happen I am to go there," Crawford wrote Washington in September 1776, though he doubted such a war would happen. By February he had changed his tune and warned Washington that an Indian war was likely, and for the reasons the Indians had given during the summer.[31] Despite the looming threat of war, and despite the deaths of his brother, Valentine, and half brother, Hugh Stephenson, to illness, Crawford continued to look out for Washington's business interests west of the Alleghenies, where squatters occupied Miller's

Run, his largest tract in Pennsylvania, on a branch of Chartier Creek.[32] Washington's time and attention was "so constantly taken up & ingrossed by public Matters," he wrote Crawford in February, "that I scarce bestow a thought on my private Affairs beyond my family at Mount Vernon."[33] Nevertheless, he kept an eye on his own future as well as that of his country, and on the lands that were key to both.

After his transfer, Crawford participated in the first American invasion of Indian country from Pittsburgh. In February 1778 General Hand led a force of five hundred men to capture British stores reported to be at an Indian town on the Cuyahoga River. The campaign petered out in bad weather, and the troops managed only to kill one old man, four Indian women, and a boy. Captain Pipe's brother was among the dead. "In performing these great exploits," wrote Hand, one soldier was wounded and another drowned. The expedition became known as the "squaw campaign." Washington learned of it in March.[34]

In May he appointed Brigadier General Lachlan McIntosh to succeed Hand. He had "great expectations" of McIntosh, who possessed good sense and lengthy experience dealing with Indians in Georgia and South Carolina.[35] Two regiments were stationed at Fort Pitt, the 8th Pennsylvania under Colonel Brodhead and the 13th Virginia under Colonel William Russell. Since Indian affairs in the West demanded officers who were familiar with the country and with Native languages and customs, Washington sent Colonel John Gibson to take temporary command of the 13th, with Russell returning east to command Gibson's old regiment. Russell and Crawford had been rivals for command of the 13th, and Washington did not want Gibson's temporary appointment to prejudice Crawford's claim in future. If there were in be two regiments on the frontier, Washington wanted Crawford in command of one of them.[36] Under McIntosh, Crawford commanded the militia of the western counties of Virginia, constructed Fort McIntosh at what is now Beaver, Pennsylvania, and participated in an expedition against Detroit.[37]

McIntosh found things in a bad way at Fort Pitt. Distressing accounts of Indian attacks and atrocities came in from the frontier settlements, the militia was dispirited and deserting, and with a garrison of only about one hundred men, Hand had done nothing to help the settlers. Washington was disappointed to hear of the state of affairs and that more vigorous measures had not been taken.[38]

There was still hope the Delawares might cling to their neutrality, but their hold was precarious. Other Indians warned that if they persisted in their attachment to the Virginians, they would treat them as Virginians. The Wyandots, whose lands the Delawares were living on, pressured them to join the emerging anti-American coalition. War parties passed through the Moravian mission villages with scalps and captives, sometimes threatening, sometimes cajoling the pacifist converts. At Lichtenau on the Muskingum River, Rev. David Zeisberger on June 15, 1777, heard reports that the Indian nations on both sides of the lakes and as far west as the Mississippi had united to wage war against the colonies. "If this were true, then the entire *Delaware Nation* and we would be in danger of being attacked by other *Nations* and we would certainly all be destroyed," he wrote in his diary. "Our heavenly father will have to look at this situation and do what is best."[39] A year later White Eyes sounded desperate, telling George Morgan: "If you do not assist me now as soon as possible then I shall be ruin'd & destroy'd."[40]

The United States made its first treaty with a foreign nation in February 1778, when Benjamin Franklin negotiated a defensive alliance with France in Paris; the United States made its first formal treaty with an Indian nation in September 1778, when commissioners Andrew Lewis and Thomas Lewis negotiated a defensive alliance with the Delawares at Fort Pitt. Washington was pleased Lewis was conducting the treaty, but he doubted it would achieve its goals.[41] White Eyes, John Killbuck, and Captain Pipe represented their respective divisions. The commissioners began by reviewing the many treaties the Indians had broken. "You alone of all the Western Indians seem inclined to hold fast the Chain of friendship," they told the Delawares, "and even in this instance it has Contracted some Rust, of a very Dangerous Nature." They offered a large wampum belt, on which the thirteen states and the Delaware Nation were depicted in black (purple) beads against a white background of peace; if the Delawares accepted it, the United States would consider them "as their own people" and require nothing of them "but what will be for mutual Good and Happiness." The Delawares accepted and, on September 19, signed a treaty of confederation, perpetual peace, and friendship. In the third article they agreed to let American troops pass through their country, to provide them with corn and provisions, and to assist them with warriors; the United States agreed to build a fort to protect Delaware women and children while their warriors were away. In the sixth and final article the United States guaranteed to the Delawares and their heirs "all their territorial rights in the fullest and most ample manner." The article also contained the remarkable stipulation that any tribes friendly to the

United States might in future be invited to join the confederation and "form a state whereof the Delaware nation shall be the head, and have a representation in Congress." Whether the provision was an instance of wartime expediency or a rare moment when Indians and colonists imagined a shared future is debatable. The two commissioners and the three chiefs signed the treaty in the presence of, among others, McIntosh, Brodhead, and Crawford.[42]

The treaty seemed to offer the Delawares the security and independence that White Eyes had worked hard to achieve.[43] However, the prospect of an Indian state with guaranteed boundaries must have been an alarming one to land speculators like Washington and his colleagues in Congress, and the likelihood of such a thing becoming reality was slim. The treaty did little to stop American settlers who were mounting their own invasion. "The emigration down the Ohio from this quarter I fear will depopulate it altogether, unless I have orders to put a timely stop to it immediately," McIntosh wrote Washington the following March. He expected almost half the people who remained at Pittsburgh to follow suit later in the spring, heading for Kentucky and the Illinois country. "Their design of securing land is so great, notwithstanding the danger of this country, they will go."[44] Like Hand, McIntosh struggled to reconcile the goals of Congress with the demands of the people inhabiting the western frontier.[45]

By permitting American passage across their territory, the Delawares reversed the policy spelled out by Guyasuta at Fort Pitt two years before and opened the way for McIntosh to march against the British supply base and center of Indian operations at Detroit. McIntosh's expedition, however, invaded and exited Indian country with much bombast and little effect. His bedraggled and hungry army never came close to Detroit. Instead, when he called a council with Delawares at Fort Laurens and warned the tribes to make peace or face the wrath of the United States, the Indians "Set up a General Laugh."[46] McIntosh's soldiers did manage to kill one Indian, possibly their best Native friend in the Ohio country. White Eyes set out as a guide for the expedition but never returned. Americans claimed he died of smallpox, but Morgan said he was murdered by some of the militia.[47]

Captain Pipe and his warriors moved closer to the British-Indian alliance. Still, many Delawares endeavored to remain at peace. John Killbuck told Morgan that the written treaty contained things "to which I never agreed." He had looked over the articles and found they were "wrote down false." The Delaware council made a formal complaint to Morgan that their intent in making the treaty was to remain at peace, not go to war. They agreed to guide American armies through their country, not to take up arms for the United States. Morgan, who had his own agenda to pursue and axes to grind, declared, "There never was a Conference with the Indians so improperly or villainously conducted."[48] Meanwhile, he reported, Americans continued to invade Indian lands and had purchased about 70 million acres west of the Ohio.[49]

In the spring of 1779 Morgan arranged for Killbuck and a Delaware delegation to meet with representatives of Congress and tell their side of the story. At Morgan's house in Princeton, New Jersey, the chiefs drew up a message reasserting their neutral stance and asking Washington and Congress to prevent any further breaches of the alliance. They wanted to meet with Washington in person, but Morgan assured him the meeting would not take much time because the chiefs had "thrown aside the use of wampum" and wanted Washington's answer in writing. The Delawares denied they ever agreed to take up the tomahawk and war belt as written into the Treaty of Fort Pitt, and they had returned them to Morgan. They pointed out they had accepted the invitation from Congress to bring three of their children to school. (White Eyes's eight-year-old son, George, and John Killbuck's sixteen- and eighteen-year-old sons, John Jr. and Thomas, enrolled in the College of New Jersey, the future Princeton, where they lived in Morgan's home.) If these children lived, said the Delawares (and it was a big if, given the high mortality rate among Indian students at colonial schools), they would have great influence in Delaware councils. The chiefs were willing to send more students so "that our Nation may the sooner and more effectually be brought to embrace civilized Life, and become one People with our Brethren of the United States." Nothing could give clearer testimony, they thought, "of their firm Resolution to continue an inviolate Friendship with the United States to the end of time." Moreover, Delawares had established a mission town where they lived as Christians under the guidance of the Moravian David Zeisberger. All this demonstrated their peaceful intentions. "As a free & independent People (which the Delaware Nation have ever declared themselves to be)," the chiefs outlined the boundaries of their lands. They prayed God would give Washington and Congress wisdom and virtue to establish a permanent union between their respective nations, and reminded Congress it had failed to provide the trade it had promised, leaving the Delawares short of food and clothing.[50] McIntosh accused Morgan of framing the speech himself and putting it "into the Mouths of a few Delaware Chiefs" while most of the nation was at war.[51]

The Board of War had assured the chiefs that General Washington would receive them with his characteristic "tenderness and friendship."[52] In fact, Washington was less interested in hearing the Delawares' grievances than in neutralizing them as allies of the British. After leaving Morgan's home, the six chiefs met Washington in May 1779 at his headquarters at Middlebrook. He was "a little at a loss what answer to give," he told Congress. "But as an answer could not be avoided, I thought it safest to couch it in general but friendly terms" and refer them to Congress in Philadelphia for more specifics. "Brothers," he told the Delawares, "I am a warrior. My words are few and plain, but I will make good what I say. 'Tis my business to destroy all the enemies of these states and to protect their friends." If the Delawares had any inclination to join the British, a "boasting people," they should forget it. The king of France "has taken up the hatchet with us and we have sworn never to bury it till we have punished the English." Instead, he advised them "to learn our arts and ways of life and, above all, the religion of Jesus Christ. These will make you a greater and happier people than you are."[53] It was a harbinger of policies to come. Although his own religious beliefs remain ambiguous (according to his biographer Ron Chernow, this was his most explicit reference to Jesus[54]), Washington as president would continue to promote Christianity as the path to happiness for Indians.

He staged a military review for the chiefs. Martha, who watched from a carriage, accompanied by the wives of Nathanael Greene and Henry Knox, wrote to her daughter-in-law: "Some of the Indians were fine looking, but most of them appeared worse than Falstaff's gang. And such horses and trappings! The General says it was all done to keep the Indians friendly towards us. They appeared like cutthroats all."[55] Her husband harbored similar sentiments. The same day he delivered his address to the Delawares, he confided in a letter to his brother John Augustine that "all the Indians from the extremest North to the South, are bribed to cut our throats."[56] Nevertheless, he recognized the importance of keeping the Delawares' friendship. When a soldier murdered a young Delaware man at Fort Pitt in May 1779, Washington ordered him court-martialed. "Exemplary punishment" was absolutely necessary, he told Brodhead, and should be carried out in the presence of Delaware chiefs.[57]

The Delaware delegates made it safely to Philadelphia in May, despite several plots by colonists to murder them en route.[58] There the chiefs met the French envoy.[59] They repeated their desire to remain neutral to the congressional Committee for Indian Affairs. Pipe and other warriors were joining the British-Indian war effort, however, and, despite the chiefs' insistence that these warriors had been expelled from the nation, Congress regarded all Delawares with increasing suspicion.[60] As escalating violence became a racial war, in which killings and atrocities begat more killings and atrocities, the Ohio country was no place for neutrals. The Delawares were in a perilous position. So were Washington's western lands and the prospects for settlement and profit. "Your houses Down the river is all burnt by the Endians," Crawford informed him in August.[61]

Meanwhile, Washington changed commanders at Fort Pitt. Daniel Brodhead, McIntosh's lieutenant and senior officer of the 8th Pennsylvania Regiment, told Washington McIntosh was "almost universally Hated by every Man in this department;" all the officers were disgusted with him, and Brodhead doubted any would serve under McIntosh in another campaign. Congress put the Western Department under Washington's direct command, and Washington urged Brodhead to reach an understanding with McIntosh. Brodhead promised to try but could not promise success.[62] McIntosh also had strained relations with Morgan, the Indian agent and deputy commissary at Fort Pitt, who criticized the Fort Pitt treaty, competed with McIntosh for influence among the Delawares, and quarreled with him over supply measures. Morgan's friend Gouverneur Morris described McIntosh to Washington as an indolent dullard. In March 1779, when McIntosh asked to be relieved from a command that had "become exceedingly disagreeable," Washington appointed Brodhead in his place.[63]

Brodhead was anxious for action. With one thousand men and the necessary resources, he told Washington, he could defeat the Munsees and Mingoes on the Allegheny, strike the Shawnee towns on the Scioto, and push on to Detroit.[64] Once again Washington faced the challenge of limited resources and competing objectives. In the spring of 1779 he ordered Brodhead to make preparations to support Sullivan's campaign against the Iroquois but at the same time cultivate peace with the western tribes. Once the campaign was under way, Brodhead could warn the western Indians that if they interfered, the Americans would turn their whole force against them and "never rest till we have cut them off from the face of the Earth."[65] Washington wanted "to chastise the Western savages" as soon as he could, but an expedition into their country would have to wait until the Iroquois campaign was successfully completed. In the meantime, Brodhead should conserve his dwindling resources, concentrate on defense, and hold the American frontier at the Ohio.[66] Forced to choose between contesting British occupation of major cities in the East or supporting a rebellious population in the West, writes the historian Daniel Barr, "Washington essentially gave up on the western Pennsylvania frontier."[67] Brodhead's defensive measures involved forming three companies of rangers, frontiersmen who fought, dressed, and painted their faces like Indians.[68] Having advocated such measures himself many years before, Washington no doubt approved. Brodhead also sent the Shawnees a speech telling them to listen to peace and ignore the intrigues of British agents, but Shawnee warriors burned it in defiance.[69]

Like Washington, Brodhead bristled at being confined to defensive duties. He told Washington he wanted to launch a major strike against the Mingoes, "who will not and ought not to be treated with but at the point of the Bayonet," and Washington thought it could act as a diversion for Sullivan's expedition.[70] In the fall of 1779 Brodhead got his chance to go on the offensive, leading the western thrust of the American campaign into Seneca country in conjunction with Sullivan and Clinton's invasion from the east and attacking Seneca and Munsee towns on the upper reaches of the Allegheny River.[71] But Indian attacks only intensified. In the spring of 1780 the Pennsylvania Council authorized payment of $1,500 for every male prisoner and $1,000 for every Indian scalp. Brodhead feared bounty hunters would scalp friendly Delawares and spark a general Indian war.[72]

Brodhead, a Pennsylvanian, competed for resources and reputation as an Indian fighter with George Rogers Clark, a Virginian who, like Washington, had set himself up as a surveyor and begun his career in the upper Ohio country. Clark had experience fighting Indians in Kentucky and made a name for himself in 1778–79, invading the Illinois country, capturing Vincennes by a forced winter match, and taking prisoner the notorious "hair-buying general" Henry Hamilton, the British governor of Detroit. Convinced that negotiating with Indians was wrong-headed, Clark offered them a simple choice between a white wampum belt signifying peace and a "bloody belt" threatening destruction. He backed up his words by tomahawking Indian captives and tossing their bodies into the river in plain view of the garrison at Vincennes.[73] He declared that "to excel them in barbarity was and is the only way to make war upon Indians" and looked for an excuse to exterminate the Delawares who had settled on the forks of the White River. When Delawares plundered and killed a party of traders, Clark seized the opportunity to make an example of them and demonstrate "the horrible fate of those who dared to make war on the Big Knives." He attacked the Indian camps. Clark's men killed many Delawares on the spot, took others to Vincennes and put them to death, and took women and children captive.[74]

Clark's campaign earned him fame as "the Washington of the West" who won the region for the United States, but it was a pretty hollow conquest. The British remained in control at Detroit, and Clark's power and presence soon evaporated.[75] Even so, Clark saw in the Illinois country an opportunity to seize territory from the British Empire and extend Virginia's territorial claims north and west of Kentucky, even if some of his militia suspected the objective was to execute a land grab.[76] His alleged conquest strengthened the United States' bargaining position at the peace negotiations in Paris.

Clark also invaded Shawnee country. Spearheading the defense of the Ohio country, the Shawnees raided settlements; forced the Americans to abandon Fort Randolph, where Cornstalk had been murdered; and effectively closed the Ohio River to American traffic. Henry Hamilton described them as "inveterate against the Virginians," and Shawnee and Delaware war parties brought scalps and captives to Detroit every day in May 1780.[77] Governor of Virginia Thomas Jefferson wanted the Shawnees driven from their country and advocated turning other tribes against them.[78] Clark led one thousand men against the Shawnee villages. When the Shawnees made a stand at Piqua on the Mad River, he turned his six-pound cannon on the village council house, where many of the people had taken refuge. His men killed some old people they found hiding in the cornfields and spent three days burning the crops. Some plundered graves for burial goods and scalps. Shawnee losses were slight, but the destruction of their corn hit them hard that winter, and many took refuge with the British at Detroit.[79] The war of attrition was taking a toll. As one Shawnee said, they had been fighting the Virginians for almost twenty years.[80] Washington remained convinced that capturing or destroying Detroit was the only way to secure peace and security on the western frontier, and he continued to correspond with Brodhead about plans for a campaign, but nothing came of it.[81]

Recognizing that the United States lacked the means to retain the affections of Indians who were well disposed or win over those who were not, Washington ordered Brodhead to foment divisions among the nations of the Ohio country.[82] Although Delawares who visited Fort Pitt appeared friendly, and Delawares from the Moravian villages provided the garrison with food, Brodhead believed the majority favored the British. He heard, feared, or simply claimed that Delaware war parties were planning to attack Pittsburgh and warned Washington to expect a general Indian war. In April 1781 Brodhead, to whom the Delawares had given the honorary name Maghinga Keesoch (Great Moon) two years before, assembled a force of three hundred Continental soldiers and Pennsylvania militia and marched against the Delaware capital at Coshocton. John Killbuck, who had been commissioned as a colonel, accompanied him with a party of Delawares. Coshocton was "completely surprised." Finding only fifteen warriors there, probably youths who were not away with the rest of the men, the militia took them prisoner, tried them, found them guilty of raiding and killing, and sentenced them to death. They then bound, tomahawked, and scalped them. They took another twenty or so noncombatants prisoner, and burned and plundered the town. Brodhead said the plunder sold for £80,000, an enormous sum. Indians denounced the attack as an unprovoked massacre; Brodhead tried to pass it off as a battle (in which, strangely, "I had not a man killed or wounded") and to pin blame for atrocities on the militia, whom he could not control.[83]

It didn't save him. In early May, Washington ordered Brodhead to answer charges in a court-martial. Hearings dragged on into August. Brodhead was acquitted, but Washington removed him from command, replacing him with Colonel Gibson.

Worse was to follow.

EVEN INDIANS WHO CONVERTED TO CHRISTIANITY and refused to fight were not safe from racial violence. As the Delawares had told Washington, some of them had embraced Christianity. Moravian missionaries began converting Delawares and Mahicans in the 1740s, and by the time of the Revolution they had founded several villages in the upper Muskingum (now the Tuscarawas) Valley. The Delawares who lived there were pacifists, but in the vicious warfare of the Ohio country, their neutrality rendered them suspect in the eyes of militants on both sides. In the fall of 1781 the Wyandots compelled them to relocate to Sandusky, where the Wyandots and British could keep a closer watch on them. They allowed them to return to their villages in the winter to gather corn, but reports that the Christian Delawares were aiding and abetting the Wyandots made them a target for retaliation by Americans, who, as they had shown in murdering Cornstalk and White Eyes, rarely distinguished between Indian friends and Indian foes. In March 1782 Colonel David Williamson and two hundred militiamen from Washington County in Pennsylvania marched to the village of Gnadenhütten, which means "huts of grace" in German. They rounded up the inhabitants, separated the men and the women and children into two houses, and debated how to put them to death. A proposal to set fire to the houses and burn them alive was rejected: some thought this "too Barbarous"; others "did not think it tormenting enough." Instead, the next day, the militia bound the Indians together in pairs, systematically bludgeoned them to death with wooden mallets, and then scalped and burned them. Ninety-six men, women, and children perished. Having "no further Opportunity of murdering innocent People, and no Stomach to engage with warriors," the militia headed back to Pittsburgh with "a great haul" of furs, horses, and other plunder, killing several more peaceful Indians on the way.[84]

When the killers arrived with scalps and plunder, the post commander, William Irvine, did nothing. In reality, he knew he could do nothing. He communicated news of the massacre to Washington and to his wife. In his letter to his wife, he said the perpetrators spared neither age or sex. "What was more extraordinary, they did it in cold blood, having deliberated three days, . . . fell on them while they were singing hymns and killed the whole. Many children were killed in their wretched mothers' arms. Whether this was right or wrong, I do not pretend to determine." Irvine understood that people who had had "fathers, mothers, brothers or children, butchered, tortured, scalped by the savages" felt very differently about killing Indians than did people who lived farther east in "perfect safety." He implored his wife, whatever her own opinions might be, to keep them to herself, lest any sentiments she expressed be attributed to him. "No man knows whether I approve or disapprove of killing the Moravians," he said.[85] Irvine asked Washington for assistance to alleviate the suffering of some friendly Indians who took refuge at Fort Pitt, and Washington took steps to provide it.[86] But when George Croghan's son, William, arrived at Fort Pitt in April, he found "the Country taulks of Nothing but killing Indians, & taking possession of their lands."[87] Irvine gave in to demands for another expedition against Sandusky.

News of Gnadenhütten spread like wildfire through Indian country and to the British at Detroit.[88] Delawares who had moved repeatedly to find a safe place to live saw once again, in the words of David Zeisberger, that "the world is on all sides too narrow for us." Many moved again, across the Mississippi to Spanish-held territory or north to Canada.[89] Others stiffened their resistance. Citing

American attacks that killed women and children in Shawnee and Onondaga towns and the slaughter of Delawares at Gnadenhütten, Indian speakers told the British at Niagara they would not sit back and wait for the same fate to befall them. They would redouble their attacks on the Americans, treat them as they were treated, and show them no mercy.[90]

When Washington heard what had happened at Gnadenhütten, he warned soldiers in the western theater not to let themselves to be taken alive. The expedition against Sandusky was already under way: 480 mounted volunteers commanded by Colonel William Crawford, with David Williamson, the perpetrator of the Gnadenhütten massacre, as second-in-command. Many of the militia had been with Williamson at the slaughter. Irvine's instructions were "to destroy by fire and sword (if practicable) the Indian town and settlements at Sandusky, by which we hope to give ease and safety to the inhabitants of this country."[91] In other words, Crawford was to do in northern Ohio what Washington had sent Sullivan to do in Iroquois country. The Moravian missionary John Heckewelder said it was "strongly suspected that the object of the expedition was to complete the work begun at Gnadenhütten" and finish off the Moravian Indians living on the Sandusky River. The men took coils of rope with them to pack plunder and secure horses.[92] After a two-hundred-mile march, Crawford's army reached the Sandusky in early June.

This time, instead of finding a village of Moravian pacifists, they ran into Wyandot, Delaware, and other warriors, supported by British rangers. The Americans lost more than fifty men, and retreat turned into rout. Williamson and most of the soldiers escaped. Crawford was not so fortunate. He and nine or ten others—including his son-in-law William Harrison, his nephew William (Valentine's only son), Dr. John Knight, a Scottish surgeon with the expedition, and a guide named John Slover—were captured and taken back to Sandusky. Indian women and boys tomahawked five of the captives. They stripped the others and painted their faces painted black, marking them for death by torture.

Even in murder and torture, this was a world where killers and victims often knew each other. According to Heckewelder, Crawford called for a Delaware chief named Wingenund who lived in a nearby village and who in more peaceful times had been his friend and visited him in Pittsburgh. Wingenund was "a great and good man" known for his humanity, but he replied that by associating with the murderer Williamson, Crawford had made it impossible for him to interfere.[93] Captain Pipe, whom Brigadier General Josiah Harmar described as "much more of a gentleman than the generality of these frontier people,"[94] and who had pledged perpetual peace with Crawford four years earlier at the Treaty of Fort Pitt, now presided over his execution. He made a speech, and then the Delawares exacted grim retribution for the slaughter of their relatives at Gnadenhütten. They shot Crawford with burning powder, scorched his body with firebrands, scalped him, and poured hot coals on his raw head before burning him at the stake. A baptized Moravian named Joseph did the scalping. Crawford's son-in-law and nephew were tortured to death as well. "So it was that Colonel Crawford...made atonement for Williamson's crime," said Heckewelder. Major John Hardin, who reported Crawford's death to the Virginia authorities, agreed: "How can you expect any other[?]" he asked; the Moravian killings were "Every day Retaliated for."[95] Indians told the British Crawford was "the principal Agent in the Murder of the Moravians, and he was burned with Justice and according to our Custom."[96]

When Irvine first wrote, on June 16, 1782, to tell Washington of the disaster, he had not learned the details of Crawford's fate, only that he was missing. Washington was saddened by "the loss of Colonel Crawford, for whom I had a very great regard." (He later offered to loan money to Crawford's widow so she would not have to sell her slaves to meet her dead husband's debts.)[97] But then Dr. John Knight made it back to Pittsburgh, emaciated and barely able to speak. Knight had witnessed Crawford's torture and execution and fully expected to receive the same treatment himself, but managed to escape. The guide John Slover also escaped and staggered in a week later. Both told a harrowing tale and gave grisly details of Crawford's execution. Knight said Simon Girty, the former Indian captive and Seneca adoptee who went over to the British in 1777, was present, and Crawford had begged him to shoot him, but Girty ignored the request. There was little he could have done. William Harrison, Crawford's son-in-law, was quartered and burned. The reason the Indians gave for "this uncommon barbarity" was "retaliation for the Moravian affair."[98]

Washington was shocked. But even in his sorrow, he recognized the Indians were incensed by "the treatment given their Moravian friends." Any Americans who fell into their hands could expect "the extremest tortures that could be inflicted by savages." No one, he warned Irvine again, should let himself be taken alive.[99] He did not acknowledge, and perhaps did not allow himself to think, that he and Crawford had helped create the violence and hatred to which Crawford fell victim.

Contemporaries understood, and historians have acknowledged, that Crawford's torture and execution was an act of revenge, but they often implied that since Crawford was not at Gnadenhütten, he was simply the wrong man in the wrong place. The culturally mandated vengeance to which Crawford fell victim did not require that the perpetrator of past deeds be the one to suffer for them. On another level, however, the retribution was personal. Pipe and the Delawares knew Crawford, and they knew what he stood for. The spirits of the slain Moravians cried for vengeance, but the Delawares also vented their outrage on a surveyor, land speculator, and soldier who had threatened their lands and lives for years.

BY THE CLOSING YEARS OF THE REVOLUTION, Washington's efforts to keep the western tribes neutral or even win their alliance by diplomacy were in shambles. In the early years of the war, Guyasuta, Cornstalk, White Eyes, and George Morgan had worked hard to preserve peace; Delaware leaders had visited Washington and Congress, stayed at Morgan's home, pledged peace and friendship with the United States at the Treaty of Fort Pitt, and reaffirmed their alliance by sending their sons to school. Now Cornstalk and White Eyes lay dead at American hands, Gnadenhütten lay in ruins, and American actions drove more and more Indians over to the British. The cycle of savagery and revenge that played out at Gnadenhütten and Sandusky continued. Atrocity begat atrocity, and unrestrained violence became a way of life on the frontier.[100] Ohio Indians ramped up their attacks after Gnadenhütten. Guyasuta, who had worked so hard to stay out of the war, attacked Hannastown in western Pennsylvania in July 1782 and burned it to the ground.[101] Shawnee war parties ranged the frontier. In August they attacked Bryan's Station at present-day Lexington, Kentucky, and then ambushed a Kentuckian force that included Daniel Boone at Blue Licks on the Licking River, killing more than seventy of them, including Boone's son Israel.[102] George Rogers Clark invaded Shawnee country again in the fall. He burned five villages, destroyed their corn, and spread desolation. The Shawnees refused to be drawn into open battle and suffered few casualties, although they said "the white Savages Virginians" committed atrocities.[103] With each American invasion, Shawnees moved their villages farther north, away from the Ohio River. On the other side of the Ohio, outrage at Crawford's torture produced volunteers "who pant[ed] after revenge" and threatened to "continue for years a scene of mutual bloodshed."[104]

Washington and the British both denounced and distanced themselves from the atrocities.[105] Writing to Irvine, Washington blamed the frontier inhabitants. Writing to Congress, he suggested the violent actions were "conducted with the approbation at least, if not the Authority of individual States." None of the atrocities were "committed under my Direction, or by any parties of Continental Troops; nor have they been sanctified by any Orders from me," he said. Indeed, "my Mind revolts at the Idea of those wanton Barbarities which both sides have in too many Instances, been the unhappy Witnesses to." Writing to Sir Guy Carleton, the British commander, he blamed the Indians, who had in some measure brought things on themselves by their own barbarous conduct. As for the Indians' claims that Crawford's death was justified, Crawford "was not in the least concerned in the unhappy Massacre of the Moravian people." Washington repeated that none of the atrocities were carried out by his orders. "The Cruelties exercised on both Sides are intirely repugnant to my Ideas," he assured Carleton.[106]

The vicious border warfare of the Revolution produced atrocities on both sides, but Americans placed the blame squarely on the shoulders of the Indians and their British backers. As in the Seven Years' War and Pontiac's War, the violence and terror they experienced in fighting Indians united whites in fearing and hating Indians. Crawford's torture and execution joined a host of reports of Indian atrocities, real or imagined, that appeared in American newspapers, fueled American propaganda, and made killing Indians a patriotic act.[107] Indians saw what was happening. The Americans charged them with many acts of cruelty that they never committed and publicized them in "their false Papers" as "a pretence to hurt & murder us," they told the British; "if we had the means of publishing to the World the many Acts of Treachery & Cruelty committed by them on our Women & Children, it would appear that the title of Savages would with much greater justice be applied to them than to us."[108]

Thomas Jefferson had depicted Indians in the Declaration of Independence as merciless savages doing the bloody work of a tyrannical king without regard to age or sex. The story of the capture and torture of William Crawford, Washington's friend, helped imprint Jefferson's image in the national memory of the war in years to come. The slaughter at Gnadenhütten was downplayed, and the desperate diplomacy of White Eyes, Cornstalk, and Guyasuta as they tried to keep the peace was all but forgotten. Indians had fought like savages to kill the nation at its birth; now the nation was alive and growing, they must atone for their crimes by forfeiting their lands.[109]

While Washington's efforts to achieve peace and order in the West disintegrated into a nightmare of violence, his efforts to acquire Indian lands continued unabated long after Yorktown secured victory in the East. Washington had no way of knowing what victory would mean in territorial terms when peace was signed. After all, the British government had drawn boundary lines over enormous swaths of territory before and had included the Ohio country within the borders of Quebec in 1774. Quebec did not rebel and fight for independence from the empire. What if Britain insisted on keeping the Ohio country as part of Quebec? During peace talks in Europe, mediating neutral powers suggested an armistice on the basis of *uti possidetis*, letting each side keep the territory it controlled at the time peace was made.[110] Indians, most of whom were now allied with the British, controlled the Ohio country, and Britain might, as it did in later years, propose establishing the trans-Appalachian West as an Indian buffer against American expansion, something France and Spain also favored.[111]

The United States was unable to establish its authority over the Ohio country and struggled to keep pace with the violence perpetrated against Indians.[112] But while Washington decried the violence, he knew that military strikes against the Indians—whether conducted by federal forces or local militias—were necessary to establish a demonstrable claim to the western lands he had long coveted for himself and now coveted for the new nation. This was the basis of Clark's "conquest" of the Northwest for the United States. In the contest for Indian lands between eastern elites and western settlers, building homes and planting fields established and reinforced claims to possession; destroying Indian homes and cornfields likewise weakened their claims to possession.[113] Washington certainly authorized expeditions into the Ohio country to preempt or retaliate for Indian attacks, but driving Indian people from their homes and fields was more important than killing them. In 1779 Washington had adamantly opposed a joint Franco-American invasion of Canada; in 1782, with Yorktown won and peace talks in Paris well under way, he now proposed such an invasion to General Rochambeau, depicting the annexation of several Canadian provinces as "matters of great moment" that would help sever the British-Indian connection. He left little doubt, writes the historian John Ferling, "that he saw the acquisition of this vast region as important for those who wished to speculate in, or settle on, the frontier lands of New England, New York, and the trans-Appalachian West."[114] Nothing came of his suggestion, but Washington knew what the Indians knew: the war in the West was a war for Indian land.

Never expecting to be betrayed by their British allies in the peace terms, Indians repelled American invasions with increasing unity of purpose.[115] Then, suddenly it seemed to them, the war was over. When Washington received news of the preliminary terms of peace, he sent three Oneidas in the spring of 1783 with a message to Brigadier General Allan Maclean, the British commander at Fort Niagara, asking him to prevent the Indians from committing acts of cruelty "disagreeable to them and to inhabitants of the United States." Maclean wrote back in anger asking Washington why, if he really wanted to prevent "disagreeable consequences," he had condoned attacks on Indians from Fort Pitt, and why did he allow newspapers to print lies that were a disgrace to any nation and served only to inflame tempers? Maclean would observe the cease-fire, but he awaited official confirmation.[116] When the definitive Peace of Paris was signed in September 1783, Britain not only recognized American independence but also ceded to the United States all territory east of the Mississippi, south of the Great Lakes and north of Florida. The peace did not mention Indians. British diplomats in Paris had handed Washington and his new nation the rich Ohio country they had been unable to win during the war.

MEANWHILE, FAR BEYOND THE WEST that Washington knew, the trans-Mississippi West was also experiencing revolutionary upheaval, albeit brought about by germs, not men. At the siege of Boston, with smallpox in the city, Washington had worried that the British would use the disease as "a weapon of Defence," and there were rumors of plots to unleash germ warfare. Smallpox hit the American army retreating from Canada in 1776. John Adams told Abigail it was "ten times more terrible than Britons, Canadians and Indians together."[117] Washington had thousands of his soldiers inoculated in 1777, but smallpox continued to flare up, and it plagued Philadelphia, Charleston, and other cities as well as Boston. It struck Onondaga in the winter of 1776–77; the Creeks and Cherokees in the fall of 1779; Chickamaugas in the spring of 1780; Oneidas in December 1780; Senecas in the winter of 1781–82. Yet the death tolls in the East were nothing compared to the horrors unfolding in the West. Smallpox broke out in Mexico City in September 1779; by December it had killed eighteen thousand people. From there it spread in all directions, reaching the silver-mining districts of northern Mexico and mission villages in California and New Mexico. Indians who visited San Antonio and Santa Fe to trade for horses became infected and spread the disease along well-traveled trade routes across the Great

Plains. The great trading villages of Mandans, Hidatsas, and Arikaras on the Great Bend of the upper Missouri became death traps. The Arikaras, who numbered around twenty-four thousand in the mid-eighteenth century, lost 75 to 80 percent of their population. People who came to the Missouri River villages to trade passed the disease to neighbors. Sioux winter counts—calendars of significant events drawn on hides—recorded the epidemic in 1779–80. On the southern plains, Comanches said two-thirds of their people died. Shoshonis likely carried the disease home from Spanish settlements in New Mexico. They infected the Blackfeet. It spread to the Crees, Assiniboines, and Ojibwas. An estimated thirty thousand Indian people died on the Canadian plains. On the shores of Hudson's Bay, traders reported Indians dying every day in the winter of 1783–84. Smallpox reached the Columbia River and spread among the dense populations along the Northwest Coast. In 1793 the English explorer George Vancouver saw Indians with pockmarked faces, abandoned villages littered with bones, and skeletons scattered along the beach.[118]

Washington knew nothing of this, but the slaughter going on offstage, as it were, during the Revolution had significant consequences for the nation he was building. Images of Washington crossing the Delaware or presiding over the British surrender at Yorktown depict the United States winning independence from an empire in the East; images of Plains Indian villages laid waste by smallpox help explain how the United States subsequently built its own empire in the West.

CHAPTER 13

Building a Nation on Indian Land

THERE WERE NO INDIANS at the Peace of Paris in 1783 when Britain handed over their lands to the United States and the new republic acquired an empire. The lands that Washington and others had explored and surveyed, as well as lobbied, connived, and fought for, were now there for the taking. The Continental Congress had kept the war effort afloat on the expectation of such an outcome, issuing land bounties to recruit soldiers and borrowing money from France and the Netherlands in anticipation of future land sales. Now the new nation stood poised at the brink of one of the greatest land rushes in history. It also faced enormous challenges in securing those lands.

With an estimated population of 150,000,[1] Indians remained the dominant power in the trans-Appalachian West, and Washington knew they would not let their country be wrested from them without another fight.[2] When they got wind of the peace treaty in Paris, Indians at Fort Niagara told Brigadier General Maclean they "could never believe that our king could pretend to cede to America what was not his own to give, or that the Americans would accept from Him what he had no right to grant." They were not going to take it lying down.[3]

The thirteen states had achieved independence but did not yet constitute a nation, let alone an imperial republic with a manifest destiny to occupy the continent. A more likely prospect in 1783 was that North America would continue to be divided among several empires, Indian confederacies, and multiple sovereignties that might include more than one American republic if individual states and settlements of Americans "who imagined futures outside the United States" went their separate ways.[4] The Appalachian Mountains loomed as a barrier that threatened to keep East and West apart. American frontier settlers with few feelings of national loyalty often looked southward down waterways that connected them to New Orleans rather than eastward over mountains that separated them from Philadelphia or New York. Could the infant nation resist these powerful centrifugal tendencies? Could it survive as a line of states along the Atlantic coast hemmed in by the Appalachians, or could it, as Washington envisioned, build a democratic federal republic spanning half a continent? To achieve the latter, the government had to secure the loyalties of western settlers, manage the land rush, and acquire the land from the Indians. It had to measure, divide, and use the land to pay the nation's debts, reward veterans, satisfy land companies, and create new states. How it did so not only shaped the American landscape, it also established the territorial foundation and the territorial system of the United States and in large measure determined the relationship of the central government to the states.[5]

The last paragraph of the Declaration of Independence asserted "that as Free and Independent States, they have full Power to levy War, conclude Peace, contract Alliances, establish Commerce, and to do all other Acts and Things which Independent States may of right do." When it came to levying war, concluding peace, contracting alliances, and establishing commerce with Indians, it was not entirely clear who "they" were—only the confederation of states, or could individual states do so as well? The Articles of Confederation, drafted in 1777 but not in effect until 1781, gave Congress "the sole and exclusive right and power" of regulating the Indian trade and managing Indian affairs, "provided that the legislative right of any state within its own limits be not infringed or violated."[6] This rather ambiguous statement of central authority over Indian affairs contributed to confusion in national and state relations with the tribes.

Following British precedent, the Confederation Congress planned initially to establish an Indian boundary line that could be renegotiated as the tide of settlement pushed westward. But the US government was no better able than the imperial government to maintain such a boundary and was not the only player in the game. Individual states made their own treaties with Indians, often in defiance of federal wishes, and sometimes challenged the authority of the federal government to conduct Indian affairs. Between 1783 and 1786 twenty-one major treaties were signed, but Congress negotiated only six of them; Spain made four, Britain one, individual states seven, and private interest groups three.[7] The northern states and Virginia ceded their claims to land north of the Ohio to the federal government, but south of the Ohio, Virginia retained its claims to Kentucky; North Carolina did not cede Tennessee until 1789; and Georgia claimed Alabama and Mississippi until 1802. The founding generation had to create a national government from the top down at a time when the idea of a national government was unpopular. They had to create a cohesive national identity that would bind together diverse citizens in disparate regions at a time when, as Joseph Ellis put it, "the vast majority of American citizens had no interest in American nationhood."[8] They had to defy predictions that, having thrown off the political stability provided by Crown and empire, the new republic would degenerate into tyranny or anarchy.

Indian land played a crucial role in constructing the American nation-state, providing a source of revenue and room for growth. It also contributed to the formation of a shared national identity. Before the Revolution, the fears and realities of Indian warfare contributed to the development of a white racial consciousness, in which disparate groups of European colonists shared pervasive anti-Indian sentiments.[9] During the Revolution, the fears and realities of Indian warfare contributed to the development of an American racial consciousness.[10] After the Revolution, westward expansion contributed to the development of a white American consciousness.[11] Various individuals and groups had different ideas about who should acquire Indian lands and how those lands should be allocated. Political leaders were not unanimous in their support for territorial expansion; some feared that contests for Indian land might increase divisions and exacerbate centrifugal tendencies, and some antifederalists warned that expansion would dismember the fragile union.[12] Settler colonists, states, and the federal government competed for rights and authority in western lands. Nevertheless, Washington's America built a nation on Indian lands and built an identity in the collective process of acquiring those lands.

Having won independence from the British Empire, the United States created a different kind of empire and governed its own colonial territories. A postcolonial republic became simultaneously a settler empire, but imperialism and republicanism could be deemed compatible if the lands into which the nation expanded were "vacant" and "domestic space." The federal government might disparage the treaty-breaking assaults of settler colonists on Indian lives and lands—and Washington decried their lawless occupation of lands to which he claimed title—but nation-building and settler colonialism went hand in hand. As the late Patrick Wolfe explained, settler colonialism operated on the "logic of elimination," removing or destroying indigenous people to make their land available. The US government absorbed frontier settlers' takeovers of Indian land; sanctioned, turned a blind eye to, or lamented their killing of Indian people; and invoked on-the-ground "settler sovereignty" to exert jurisdiction and control over Indian country.[13]

American territorial expansion also contributed to an emerging *Indian* identity. Colonial policies fomented and fueled recurrent divisions among and within tribes, and Indian leaders were not unanimous in opposition, but multiple tribes united to resist the assault on their homelands. When Washington and his peers talked about Indian land, they called it "hunting territory," which implied a more transient occupancy and a lesser value than farming land; with no deep attachment to the land, Indian hunters could, as Benjamin Franklin said, be easily persuaded to give it up as game diminished.[14] In fact, Indians clung tenaciously to their land even as the game diminished. Washington viewed land as a commodity to be surveyed and measured, bought and sold, and accumulated. Tied to their homelands by cycles of life and death, kinship, ceremony, and subsistence, Indian peoples viewed them as sites of tribal creation and sources of tribal identity. As American demographic and military assaults intensified, diverse Indian peoples found common cause in defending all Indian lands. As American agents pressured them to adopt new ways of living and believing, many Indian people who fought for their lands also fought to be Indian.[15]

In doing so, some said, Indians were not only resisting American expansion and settlement but were also defying God's will. In May 1783, as Americans waited for news of the peace being negotiated in Paris, Ezra Stiles, a Congregationalist minister and president of Yale, delivered a sermon to the Connecticut Assembly entitled "The United States Elevated to Glory and Honor." Stiles predicted that the states would "prosper and flourish into a great American Republic; and ascend into high and distinguished honor among the nations of the earth." If population continued to grow at present rates, he predicted, Americans in two to three centuries would number two or three hundred million people. Indian populations, on the other hand, were plummeting. A numerous population was necessary to give value to the land. The Indians must give way to the rising nation. Stiles likened them to the "*Caananites* of the expulsion of Joshua" and called Washington the "American Joshua ... raised up by God."

When Joshua and the Israelites attacked Canaan and took Jericho, according to the Bible, "they utterly destroyed all that was in the city, both man and woman, both young and old, and ox, and sheep, and ass, with the edge of the sword." In some instances, Stiles argued, war was "authorized by heaven," and "the extirpation of the *Cannanites* by *Joshua*" was one such instance. In building the new American Israel, the extirpation of Indians by the American Joshua was clearly another.[16]

Washington invoked no Old Testament God to justify genocide. He shared Franklin's belief that as a matter of both justice and policy Indians should have the opportunity to give up their lands by consent in treaties, and he hoped the process could be carried out with a minimum of bloodletting.[17] He was also deeply concerned with how the international community and posterity would judge his nation's treatment of its Native people. But he shared Stiles's vision of a rising nation. Indian land was the best resource and hope for the future and the basis of the new empire he had helped to create.[18]

In the words of one biographer, Washington in the run-up to the Revolution "had become an American nationalist before there was an American nation." With the Revolution won, before he resigned his command, from his headquarters in Newburgh on June 8, Washington sent circular letters to the state governments, calling for national unity and laying out his vision for a great continental republic.

> The Citizens of America, placed in the most enviable condition, as the Lords and Proprietors of a vast Tract of Continent, comprehending all the various soils and climates of the World, and abounding with all the necessaries and conveniences of life, are now, by the late satisfactory pacification, acknowledged to be possessed of absolute freedom and Independency; They are, from this period, to be considered as Actors on a most conspicuous Theatre, which seems to be particularly designated by Providence for the display of human greatness and felicity.

The Republic was at a critical juncture; the states must decide between a strong and a weak national government. "This is the time of their political probation, this is the moment when the eyes of the whole World are turned upon them, this is the moment to establish or ruin their national Character forever." They could give the federal government the authority it needed to govern effectively and secure the fruits of the Revolution, or they could relax the powers of the Union, leaving the separate states "to become the sport of European politics." The United States must present a united face to the world if its treaties and foreign policies were to be taken seriously. The choice, in Washington's view, was whether the new nation would be "respectable and prosperous, or contemptible and miserable."[19]

Ordinary citizens beset by heavy taxes at the end of a long war faced real hardships and had legitimate grievances, but when Daniel Shay and disgruntled farmers in western Massachusetts rebelled against taxation in 1786, Washington saw it as "melancholy proof... that mankind left to themselves are unfit for their own government."[20] The rebellion also aggravated fears that the Republic would not survive its infancy. Washington fully expected the British to interfere: they were already stirring up trouble among the Indian tribes on the frontier and were sure to make the most of any opportunity "to foment the spirit of turbulence within the bowels of the United States."[21] The British were equally apprehensive of American intrigues among *their* Indians. "I do not believe the World ever produced a more deceitful, or dangerous set of Men, than the Americans," wrote Allan Maclean; "they are become such Arch-Politicians by eight years of practice, that were old Matchiavell [*sic*] alive, he might go to School to learn Politics more crooked than his own; we therefore cannot be too cautious."[22]

Washington thought the precarious republic's security, prosperity, and future depended upon creating a strong government, creating a national market in Indian lands, and turning hunting territories over to commercial agriculture and economic development. Converting Indian homelands into American real estate would provide homes for citizens, fill the empty treasury, and ensure the nation's survival and growth. He realized that his vision for the United States meant prying the continent away from the peoples who inhabited it, but he hoped it could be done with a minimum of bloodshed. He would only "extirpate" them if they refused to give up their land and left him no choice.[23]

In the French and Indian War, Washington had tried to build his reputation by grasping after power; at the end of the Revolution, he secured his legacy by declining power.[24] Two days before Christmas 1783, he formally and famously resigned his commission as commander in chief, handed back his authority to Congress, and retired to Mount Vernon. Washington's act demonstrated the insight, in Abigail Adams's assessment, "that if he was not really one of the best intentioned men in the world he might be a very dangerous one." It marked Washington for greatness. "The moderation and virtue of a single character probably prevented this revolution from being closed, as most others have been, by a subversion of that liberty it was intended to establish," said Thomas Jefferson.[25] Contemporaries and historians likened him to Cincinnatus, who defeated Rome's enemies and then gave up his power and returned to his plow. They could have found parallels closer to home in Indian war chiefs, who, before escalating conflict and the intrusion of colonial rivals undermined traditional patterns of balance and behavior, were accustomed to relinquishing their temporary leadership upon returning home to villages where the guidance of older civil chiefs prevailed. Eighteenth-century Indian people would have seen little remarkable in Washington's action.

Washington turned his attention to his personal affairs that had been neglected during nine years of military service.[26] Having won a war for American freedom, he returned to running a plantation based on African slave labor.[27] He even let himself relax: a visitor to Mount Vernon in 1785 said the general passed the bottle around "pretty freely" at dinner and "got quite merry" drinking champagne.[28] He focused much of his energy on completing reconstruction of Mount Vernon. He bought additional adjacent or neighboring property, and he looked again to his western lands. At the close of the Revolution, Washington owned approximately 58,000 acres west of the Alleghenies: 4,695 acres in southwestern Pennsylvania, 9,744 along the Ohio River, and 43,466 along the Great Kanawha.[29] Now independence was won, there was nothing to dispute his right to the lands he had accumulated. He had yet to realize any profit from them, but settlers moving west as the nation grew would surely change all that.[30] As he watched over the nation's growth, he managed to weave together national agenda and private interests. "Few public figures in American history could match Washington's record of virtuous and selfless service, but even he stumbled when the vast potential of the frontier West was at stake," notes his biographer John Ferling. "As always, he convinced himself that the nation was the chief beneficiary of his actions."[31]

Washington did not, and could not, retire from charting the direction of the new nation. He had fought and resigned to save the Republic, and he remained deeply invested in ensuring its survival and its expansion. "Retired as I am from the world, I frankly acknowledge I cannot feel myself an unconcerned spectator," he told John Jay in 1786.[32] As the Confederation government stumbled along, Washington led efforts to reform and strengthen the central government and to forge the thirteen states into a united and expanding nation. Doing so required linking the East to the emerging regions of the West by creating a national navigable water route, developing a national land policy, and building a national army to defeat Indian resistance.[33]

Two letters, both written on October 12, 1783, and both to Frenchmen, conveyed the westward orientation of his vision for the new nation. Following a three-week tour of the Hudson and Mohawk River corridor, Washington pored over maps and reports to get an overview of the vast inland navigation of the country and was "struck with the immense diffusion and importance of it," he told the comte de Chastellux, a friend of Lafayette traveling in the United States; he said he would not rest until he had "explored the western country, and traversed those lines...which have given bounds to a new empire."[34] Responding the same day to a suggestion from Lafayette that he make a grand tour of European capitals as a kind of victory parade, Washington countered with a journey of the imagination—a tour of America's "New Empire," starting in Detroit, going down the Mississippi River, then heading back through Florida and the Carolinas.[35]

As a young man, Washington had seen the Virginia backcountry as terrain for attaining personal wealth and status. By the end of the Revolution, his vision of the West embraced all the land between the Appalachians and the Mississippi as a national asset best developed by a strong central government.[36] During the French and Indian War, he had fought to open the West to Virginia, while keeping it closed to rival Pennsylvania. But before the end of the Revolution, when Maryland would not ratify the Articles of Confederation as long as Virginia held on to so much western land, he urged his home state to relinquish its claims to the western empire he had fought to build.[37] Always intent on promoting the Potomac as a way to bring trade from the West to his own part of Virginia, he now extended his interests to New York and tried, with Governor George Clinton, to buy the land around Fort Schuyler (formerly Fort Stanwix) that dominated the portage between the Mohawk River and Wood Creek, and ultimately the link between the Hudson and Great Lakes water systems. When that failed, he bought a tract of 6,000 acres near present-day Utica in partnership with Clinton. (In 1793 he sold two-thirds of his half for £3,400).[38] He supplemented his personal knowledge of the West, acquired on military expeditions and tours in the Ohio Valley and western Pennsylvania, by building an extensive network of correspondents who furnished him with news, information, and observations on land, rivers, and Indians. He was absolutely convinced of the importance of the West to the nation.[39]

In early May 1783, even before the Peace of Paris formally transferred the lands west of the Appalachians to the United States, Washington wrote Alexander Hamilton, as chairman of the congressional committee on establishing peace, justifying the need for a military force to secure the ceded territory. The US Army after the Revolution comprised a mere six hundred men, stationed at West Point, Fort Pitt, and the federal arsenal at Springfield, Massachusetts, and Congress was reluctant to take measures to strengthen it. Suspicion of large standing armies as a threat to the liberties of a country went back to colonial times and to England. But Washington knew the United States needed a regular force to garrison its posts, protect its trade, and defend its frontiers. Better to create an army that would "appear respectable in the Eyes of the Indians," and then reduce it, than to have to increase it in the wake of some disaster, he said with some prescience.[40] In June, Washington wrote urging Congress to settle disbanded soldiers on the frontiers. The veterans, "a brave, a hardy and respectable Race of People," not only would provide protection for frontier families but also, in their proximity to Indian towns, "would be the most likely means to enable us to purchase upon equitable terms of the Aborigines their right of preoccupancy; and to induce them to relinquish our Territories, and to remove into the illimitable regions of the West."[41]

By September, when the Peace of Paris was finally signed, Washington had modified his views somewhat. He was influenced by General Philip Schuyler's recommendations to Congress in the summer that, rather than pushing the Indians farther west (and potentially into the arms of the British), the United States should permit them to remain on portions of their homeland, which they would gradually cede as American settlement advanced.[42] Writing to James Duane, chairman of a congressional committee charged with formulating Indian policy for the new nation, Washington laid out at considerable length his ideas on "the line of Conduct proper to be observed not only towards the Indians, but for the government of the Citizens of America, in their Settlement of the Western Country." As a statement of his thinking on nation-building and Indian policy, it merits considerable quotation.

Formerly an accomplished land grabber himself, Washington saw the dangers of unrestrained land grabbing now that he was in a position of authority. Letting land jobbers, speculators, and monopolists, or even settlers, overrun western land was "inconsistent with that wisdom and policy which our true interest dictates, or that an enlightened People ought to adopt," and was likely to generate disputes both with the Indians and among Americans. And for what? It would make a few avaricious men wealthy at the expense of the many, for the people who engaged in this business contributed nothing to the government and did not even abide by its laws and, unless restrained, would cause a lot of trouble and probably a lot of bloodshed. After eight years of war in which the Indians had fought alongside the British, "a less generous People than Americans" might have driven the Indians beyond the Great Lakes.

> But as we prefer Peace to a state of Warfare, as we consider them as a deluded People; as we perswade ourselves that they are convinced, from experience, of their error in taking up the Hatchet against us, and that their true Interest and safety must now depend upon *our* friendship. As the Country, is large enough to contain us all; and as we are disposed to be kind to them and to partake of their Trade, we will from these considerations and from motives of Comp[assio]n, draw a veil over what is past and establish a boundary line between them and us beyond which we will *endeavor* to restrain our People from Hunting or Settling, and within which they shall not come, but for the purposes of Trading, Treating, or other business unexceptionable in its nature.

In other words, reinstate the kind of boundary line he had opposed and ignored when the British imposed one in the 1763 proclamation.

The government must be careful "neither to yield nor to grasp at too much" in establishing this boundary, but the line would not be permanent. The Indians "will ever retreat as our Settlements advance upon them, and they will be as ready to sell, as we are to buy," Washington reasoned, optimistically. Anyone who had experienced an Indian war, or even estimated the expense of waging one, knew that a policy of purchasing land was the wisest and cheapest way of dealing with the Indians. Unless the government adopted such measures and soon, Washington predicted, "a parcel of Banditti" would take over the western country, "bid defiance to all Authority while they are skimming and disposing of the Cream of the Country" (a phrase Washington had applied to lands he himself had skimmed), and deprive veterans of the land bounties Congress had promised them, or spark renewed hostilities with the Indians.

He unrealistically imagined that extending American settlement gradually would dispossess Indian people of their land without recourse to war. In fact, he regarded the settlement of the West and making peace with the Indians as "so analogous that there can be no definition of the one without involving considerations of the other."

> I am clear in my opinion, that policy and œconomy point very strongly to the expediency of being upon good terms with the Indians, and the propriety of purchasing their Lands in preference to attempting to drive them by force of arms out of their Country; which as we have already experienced is like driving the Wild Beasts of the Forest which will return us soon as the pursuit is at an end and fall perhaps on those that are left there; when the gradual extension

of our Settlements will as certainly cause the Savage as the Wolf to retire; both being beasts of prey tho' they differ in shape. In a word there is nothing to be obtained by an Indian War but the Soil they live on and this can be had by purchase at less expence, and without that bloodshed, and those distresses which helpless Women and Children are made partakers of in all kinds of disputes with them.[43]

Washington's letter to Duane also formulated a plan for forming new states in the West, envisioning two states in what became Ohio and Michigan, which later became the basis for the organization of what was then called the Northwest Territory. The committee, which also included Richard Peters of Pennsylvania, Arthur Lee of Virginia, Benjamin Hawkins of North Carolina, and Daniel Carroll of Maryland, echoed many of Washington's recommendations. Congress adopted the general plan and incorporated some of his actual words in its report of October 15, 1783, which guided American Indian policy until the last years of the Confederation government. The Indians wanted peace, said the report, but would not give up their land without a fight. Nevertheless, they were the aggressors in the war and had to make atonement, "and they possess no other means to do this act of justice than by compliance with the proposed boundaries"; in other words, by giving up their land.[44] Unfortunately, the process of acquiring Indian lands would not be nearly as orderly as Washington and the committee imagined.

The United States in 1783 faced a situation not unlike the one Britain faced in 1763. It had a huge new empire on its hands yet was virtually bankrupt. The government had debts amounting to an estimated $40 million, but under the Articles of Confederation it lacked the power to impose taxes. Its only source of revenue was the land ceded by Britain. Now the states had thrown off the authority of the Crown, they were no longer bound by the Royal Proclamation and its restrictions. Nevertheless, many states continued to prohibit private purchases, and the federal government asserted its authority over Indian affairs and Indian lands for the same reasons the British government had. Concentrating land purchases in the hands of government persisted as best practice and wise policy.[45]

The new republic struggled with the same problem that had confounded the old empire—how to control the frontier and hold back a land rush: "Sundry persons are preparing to settle upon lands within the U.S which have not been purchased from the Indian natives," a congressional committee reported in 1783.[46] Unlike imperial officials, republican leaders were supposed to represent and respond to the will of the people, but simply opening new territory in a chaotic scramble for lands could threaten the social order of the young republic before it was properly established. Congress in 1783 prohibited people from settling or purchasing Indian lands outside states' borders without its express authority.[47] But Washington himself had set a precedent for defying a distant government and speculating in Indian lands, and Americans had few qualms about continuing the tradition.

THE CONFUSION OF COMPETITIVE LAND grabbing before the Revolution had produced a patchwork of overlapping claims. Washington's finances were in what he called a "deranged situation" after the Revolution, and he looked to his western properties as his chief source of revenue. Expecting "something very handsome from that quarter," he was anxious to secure his titles and have his lands start generating income, but with his papers in disarray, he worried that others might be surveying or settling lands he had claimed under Dinwiddie's proclamation and the Royal Proclamation.[48] He said he had patents signed by Dunmore for 30,000 acres, and survey rights to an additional 10,000 acres, patents for which were suspended because of the disputes with Britain. He believed his title was "indisputable." Of the 30,000 acres, 10,000 lay on the Ohio, the rest on the Great Kanawha, all, as he repeatedly described it, "rich bottom land, beautifully situated on these rivers, & abounding plenteously in Fish, wild fowl, and Game of all kinds." Because his lands were located on the south side of the Ohio where the Indians had no claims, settlers would be free from the disturbances that settlers north of the river were likely to experience.[49] He circulated an advertisement for leasing the 30,000 acres on the Ohio and Great Kanawha in March 1784 but was unsuccessful.[50] A week later he wrote to the Virginia lawyer Edmund Randolph explaining the losses he had sustained on his lands acquired under Dinwiddie's grant because of Indian hostilities and asked him to do what he could on his behalf.[51]

In September 1784, accompanied by Dr. Craik and his son, his nephew Bushrod Washington, and their slaves, Washington set out to tour his western land and visit the Kanawha if it was safe to do so. He was not going to explore the country or search out new lands "but to secure what I have," he told Craik, who had lands close to his.[52] In other words, he was going to inspect his bounty lands on the Ohio and Kanawha to keep them out of the hands of speculators and retrieve lost rents. Tenants had fallen behind on payments during the war, and squatters had occupied some of his lands; as Ron

Chernow put it, "the American Cincinnatus, badly strapped for cash, was reduced to a bill collector."[53] Eager to obtain information about the best routes connecting eastern and western rivers and to facilitate the inland navigation of the Potomac, he also discussed the prospects with Daniel Morgan and "many other Gentlemen" during his tour.[54]

It was a difficult trip. His route took him via Fort Cumberland, Braddock's Road, and Great Meadows, the site of Fort Necessity, although he made no comment about his past experiences at these places. Worse, a land rush was under way: Indians that summer told the Spanish governor of St. Louis that Americans were spreading "like a plague of locusts in the territories of the Ohio River."[55] The great land speculator was feeling the heat of the competition. The "rage for speculating" in the lands beyond the Ohio left hardly a valuable spot without a claimant, he complained. "Men in these times, talk with as much facility of fifty, a hundred, or even 500,000 Acres as a Gentleman formerly would do of 1,000 acres." Defying Congress's proclamation, "they roam over the Country on the Indian side of the Ohio, mark out Lands, Survey, and even Settle them." Unless timely measures were taken, Washington predicted, it would "inevitably produce a war with the western Tribes."[56]

Washington also checked up on Gilbert Simpson, with whom he had contracted before the Revolution to improve his land and manage his mill on a branch of the Youghiogheny River (called Washington's Bottom; now, more decorously, Washington's Run). Ill health and other issues had hampered Simpson, and Washington had demanded a full accounting of his operations. Finding his mill in disrepair and unrented, he terminated the partnership. He appointed Major Thomas Freeman of Redstone, Pennsylvania, to oversee his western affairs, settle tenants on his lands, collect rents, and "in all cases by fair and lawful means to promote my interest in this country." He would not lease to people who did not intend to reside there; he wanted, he told another of his agents, to rent to "an industrious class of reputable people" who would improve his lands.[57] He was willing to sell some lands if the terms were right, but knowing his carefully selected tracts would increase in value, he preferred to lease them and was not inclined to compromise on his terms.[58]

In western Pennsylvania, in the area the state had named Washington County, he found several families squatting on his 2,813-acre tract at Miller's Run. They were Scotch-Irish Calvinists, and they were angry and defiant. They felt they had earned the right to settle there and challenged the legality of Washington's title. Washington called them "willful and obstinate Sinners" and hired a lawyer to sue

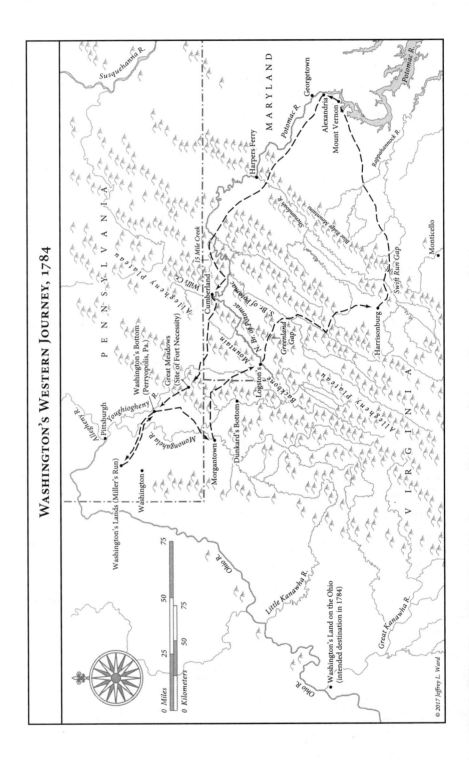

WASHINGTON'S WESTERN JOURNEY, 1784

them for trespass and have them evicted unless they paid him rent. He was determined to obtain "full justice." The case dragged on for two years, as Joseph Ellis says, "pitting the most powerful figure in the nation against a feisty delegation of impoverished farmers." Washington won his case, but the squatters moved away rather than pay him rent.[59] Learning that some of his lands were being offered for sale in Philadelphia and Europe, Washington intended, with no sense of irony, to rescue them "from the hands of Land Jobbers & Speculators."[60]

In 1787 he appointed Colonel Thomas Lewis, surveyor for Augusta County, to manage his lands on the Ohio and Great Kanawha. Promoting his lands to prospective settlers—this time farmers from Scotland—Washington emphasized again their fertility and safety from Indian attack (though he was eager for a treaty that would provide an additional buffer by opening the other side of the river to settlement).[61] Whereas Jefferson envisioned an "empire of liberty" in the West, where independent yeoman farmers would work their own property in a land-owning democracy, on Washington's western lands tenant farmers would pay rent to an absentee landlord.[62] Washington was not alone. In Kentucky the practices of wealthy investors and the land policies that favored them ensured that most frontier settlers remained landless tenant farmers instead of becoming independent property owners, who were supposed to provide the backbone of the Republic. When Kentucky became a state in 1792, two-thirds of adult white male residents owned no land; they lived as tenants on enormous landholdings belonging to distant landlords, or they squatted on lands, "not knowing or caring who claimed to own them."[63]

Despite Washington's confidence that his lands were safe, rumors of Indian hostilities kept him from visiting his lands on the Great Kanahwa. The Indians were angry that settlers were invading their lands and the government had not yet held a treaty, which they interpreted as evidence of hostile intentions on the part of the United States.[64] As a result, his western tour "was less extensive" than he intended.[65] In Joel Achenbach's words, Washington's "Grand Tour of America had been downsized into a mere business trip to his western properties, and now even that was turning into a bust."[66] Washington returned to Mount Vernon by a more southerly route and reached home before sunset on October 4. The 680-mile trip was his last visit to the Ohio country.[67]

Washington's plans for a comfortable retirement rested on income from his lands at Washington's Bottom, Miller's Run, and the Great Kanawha. But his trip showed him these were precarious assets at best: the first was producing no revenue; squatters occupied the second; Indian hostility restricted access to the third. Removing such obstacles to turning a profit on frontier investments, Washington decided, would require government action. In a sense, Edward Larson explains, "his long journey back from retirement to the Constitutional Convention and the presidency began with his trip to the frontier in 1784."[68]

The journey also renewed his commitment to making the Potomac River the gateway to the West. In the weeks after his return, he wrote letter after letter to influential individuals in Virginia and Maryland promoting the project. The more he thought about it, the greater the advantages appeared, he said. As the Indians were dispossessed, the West would be linked to the East by commerce, which required clearing rivers and building canals to connect the Potomac and the Ohio. It was time to open the way for western produce to flow to American markets before it got diverted "into another channel," namely to New Orleans. Developing the Potomac water route served Washington's personal interests as well as the nation's agenda. It would alleviate western settlers' dependence on the Spanish-controlled Mississippi, strengthen ties between the eastern and western states, and link his Tidewater properties with his holdings in the West, enhancing their value. The Potomac canal never came to fruition, but its potential for opening the West and uniting the nation figured continuously in Washington's thinking, conversation, and correspondence.[69]

James Madison shared Washington's enthusiasm for the project.[70] So did Jefferson, who had the canal "much at heart" and lobbied for it with his friends in the Virginia Assembly. "All the world is becoming commercial," Jefferson said, and the citizens of "our new empire" must have as large a share as possible of the West's resources. Connecting the Potomac to the Ohio would bind the nation together and enhance the economy of Virginia in particular.[71] Whereas Jefferson felt western settlers were bound to the United States by their republican sentiments and needed minimal control from the federal government, Washington placed far less faith in them to do the right thing and thought commercial connections were necessary to bind them to the nation.[72]

A week after he returned from his trip, Washington lobbied Virginia governor Benjamin Harrison to revive the enterprise and form a company to undertake making the Potomac navigable to the Ohio. Recycling reflections he had penned in his journal, he reminded Harrison that the state of affairs in the West was anything but orderly. Frontier settlers regarded the government with suspicion and eastern elites with resentment; individual states competed for territory, and foreign powers loomed in the North and South. It was vital to bind all parts of the union together by bonds of self-interest, especially in the region immediately west of the middle states.

> For what ties, let me ask, shou'd we have upon these people? How entirely unconnected with them shall we be, and what troubles may we not apprehend, if the Spaniards on their right, & Gt Britain on their left, instead of throwing stumbling blocks in their way, as they do now, should hold out lures for their trade and alliance? What, when they get strength, which will be sooner than most people conceive (from the emigration of foreigners, who will have no particular predilection toward us, as well as from the removal of our own Citizens), will be the consequence of their having formed close connections with both or either of those powers, in a commercial way? It needs not, in my opinion, the gift of prophecy to foretell.

From his own observation, Washington added, the western settlers stood, "as it were, upon a pivot. The touch of a feather would turn them either way."[73]

Westerners had little reason to commit to a union that seemed on the verge of falling apart. Separatist tendencies surfaced in Kentucky and Vermont, where residents were courted by Spain and Britain, respectively. By 1783 Kentucky had twelve thousand white inhabitants; two years later, thirty thousand, half of them from Virginia. Deprived of property and prosperity by Eastern elites and their land policies, and attracted by the possibilities of better trade down the Mississippi, many Kentuckians "turned their eyes to New Orleans, and may become riotous and ungovernable," said Washington. Resentful Kentuckians were soon demanding self-government and separation from Virginia.[74] In western North Carolina settlers formed their own state, Franklin, and looked to their own leaders rather than the state government for access to Indian lands and protection from Indian attacks. Adam Stephen, who had learned to respect the Cherokees after serving against them and making peace with them in 1761, feared that "the Wild men" of Franklin intended to drive the Cherokees out of their country and would force them into war. Leaders like Governor John Sevier, who burned Cherokee towns during the Revolution, built and maintained their reputation on speculation and Indian fighting. The movement for secession in Franklin raised the specter that any settlement with any grievance might, as Governor Alexander Martin of North Carolina feared, claim the right to separate and declare its independence and expose the frailty of "a pusillanimous Government, that either is unstable, or dares not restrain the lawless designs of its Citizens."[75]

Virginia must take the lead in linking the West to the East. The Potomac, Washington told Jefferson in 1788, "will become the great avenue into the Western Country; a country which is now sett[lin]g in an extraordinary rapid manner, under uncommonly favorable circumstances, and which promises to afford a capacious asylum for the poor and persecuted of the Earth."[76] The illusion that the river flowing past Mount Vernon provided the most direct access to the West stayed with him all his life and played a significant role in the decision to locate the national capital on the Potomac in 1790.[77] Meanwhile, if the nation was to be built on western lands, it must secure them quickly lest it fly apart before it had chance to fully form.

THE NEED TO STRENGTHEN the national government and make expansion a national project was urgent, but the federal government was not the only player active in the field. Jurisdictional disputes with the states over Indian lands and Indian affairs were central issues in debates about federalism and the union.[78] Regional divisions and federal-state tensions complicated and jeopardized Indian policy.

As had Britain, the United States preferred to achieve its goals by treaty rather than by war, and obtain Indian lands by purchase rather than by risky and expensive military campaigns. But whereas the Six Nations declared their intention to live in peace and friendship with Congress "provided their intentions be agreeable and leave our possessions undisturbed,"[79] Congress insisted that it had acquired all territory east of the Mississippi by right of conquest and that the defeated Indians must relinquish lands as atonement for the atrocities they had committed and the expenses the United States had incurred fighting them. They could have no complaints about the boundaries that were imposed.[80] Treaty commissioners representing "the Thirteen Fires" of the United States employed the rhetoric and symbols of council-fire diplomacy, but they dictated more than they negotiated. "We are now Masters of this Island, and can dispose of the Lands as we think proper or most convenient to ourselves," General Schuyler lectured the Iroquois.[81] Joseph Brant told the British that Schuyler was as "Saucy" as the devil and the Indians who met with him behaved shamefully. Dismayed that "after our friends the English left us in the lurch, still our own chiefs should make the matter worse," Brant began "to prepare my death song for vexation will lead one to rashness."[82]

The federal government had to assert its authority over the state of New York in dealing with the Six Nations, and New York was in a mess. Still recovering from the devastation of the war, the state confronted the intrusion of congressional authority within its borders, lingering land claims by the state of Massachusetts, and separatist Vermonters trying to establish an independent republic on its eastern border. Agents from New York, Massachusetts, and Congress held councils with Indians, while private operations like the Genesee Company of Adventurers, organized by members of the Hudson Valley elite in 1787, also negotiated leases.[83] Schuyler called on New York to let federal commissioners conduct its Indian diplomacy, but Governor Clinton and other state leaders insisted that under article 9 of the Articles of Confederation—which gave the United States the power to deal "with the Indians, not members of any of the states, provided that the legislative right of any state within its own limits be not infringed or violated"—any attempt by the federal government to deal with the Six Nations constituted a violation of the state's rights.[84] New York intended to make its own treaty.

As chair of the Committee on Indian Affairs, James Duane supported the exclusive right of Congress to make treaties; as the first mayor of New York City, he sided with Clinton in opposing that policy as a threat to his own state. In the summer of 1784 Duane advised Clinton that since Congress had clear authority to make treaties with Indian nations that were independent of the states, New York must treat the Six Nations not as nations but "as ancient Dependants on this State, placed under its protection...with the Management of whom Congress have no concern." The state should play hardball in negotiating with the Iroquois and strip them of any attributes of nationhood. "If we adopt the disgraceful system of pensioning, courting and flattering them as great and mighty nations, we shall once more, like the Albanians be their Fools and Slaves, and this Revolution in my Eyes will have lost more than half it's Value." New York should dictate terms, dispense with wampum belts, and stop calling the tribes nations "or any other Form which would revive or seem to confirm their former Ideas of Independence."[85]

New York sent commissioners to deal with the Seneca chief Cornplanter and about twenty delegates from the Six Nations at the Treaty of Fort Stanwix that fall, as did Pennsylvania.[86] Commissioners from the United States—Oliver Wolcott of Connecticut, Richard Butler of Pennsylvania, and Arthur Lee of Virginia, accompanied by 150 troops and the marquis de Lafayette—joined those from New York and Pennsylvania. The competing federal and state claims confused the negotiations. "Here lies some Difficulty in our Minds," said Brant, "that there should be two separate Bodies to manage these Affairs, for this does not agree with our ancient Customs."[87]

Declaring that they, not New York, had full authority to make peace with the Indians, the federal commissioners demanded huge cessions of Iroquois country as the price of that peace. "You are a subdued people," they told them. Divided by the war and abandoned by the British, the Iroquois delegates ceded much of Seneca land in western New York and Pennsylvania as well as all their territory west of Pennsylvania, essentially giving up all claims to the Ohio country, and gave hostages to guarantee their compliance.[88] When Washington saw the terms of the treaty, he thought the Six Nations had given "all that the United States could reasonably have asked of them." He hoped that their example would influence the Ohio tribes—"the Western gentry," as he called them—and smooth the way for the commissioners who were on their way to Fort Pitt.[89] But when the Iroquois delegates returned home they were met with scorn. The Six Nations in council refused to ratify the treaty on the grounds that King George had never given up their lands and that delegates were not authorized to cede the territory. When Cornplanter, along with Guyasuta and other chiefs, met Brigadier General Josiah Harmar, now commander of the American army, at Pittsburgh in July 1785, he brought the original articles of the Fort Stanwix Treaty with him and "said they were burdensome, and wished to deliver them up."[90] The United States proceeded as if the treaty were valid.

The Fort Stanwix Treaty exposed divisions within the United States as well as within the Six Nations. New York not only negotiated its own treaty but attempted to derail the federal negotiations. "What think You of the State of New York undertaking a Treaty of its own Authority?" one congressional delegate, Jacob Read, asked Washington. "If this Conduct is to be pursued," Read warned, "our Commissioners are Rendered useless."[91] James Monroe, then also a congressional delegate traveling through the area, witnessed the negotiations and expressed alarm to James Madison that New York making its own treaty raised the question of the political status of tribes and whether states had primary authority over Indian peoples living within their boundaries. Madison, who was touring New York State with Lafayette and also attended the treaty, insisted the federal government had priority over the states in Indian affairs. He feared that states' intrusions on the treaty-making power of the national government could destroy the authority of Congress and that states' treatment of Indians threatened the reputation of the United States.[92]

That said, on a visit to Mount Vernon the next year, Madison asked Washington's advice about buying land in the Mohawk Valley. Washington, who had just purchased a tract there, replied it was "the very spot his fancy had selected of all the U.S." Madison and Monroe together bought 900 acres of land on the edge of Oneida territory in 1786. Sounding a lot like Washington had twenty years earlier, Madison regretted they were not able to purchase more, for "my private opinion is that the vacant land in that part of America opens up the surest field of speculation of any in the U.S." With twelve to fifteen feet of topsoil in the Fingers Lakes region, Oneida land impressed European visitors as some of "the richest and most fertile on our globe."[93]

Washington lamented the interference of individual states in Indian affairs. So long as they set up competing claims to Indian land and pursued their own short-term interests, the federal government was "a name without substance," he told Secretary of War Henry Knox (see plate 7). The states' insistence on conducting their own dealings with Indians highlighted the larger issue of states' rights. "We are either a United people under one head, & for Fœderal purposes," he explained to James McHenry, "or we are thirteen independent Sovereignties, eternally counteracting each other." Knox agreed: "We are entirely destitute of those traits which should Stamp us *one Nation*." He feared that some of the states' views "sooner or later must involve the Country in all the horrors of civil War."[94]

The Confederation Congress thanked the Oneidas for their support and services during the Revolutionary War, and while the Treaty of Fort Stanwix imposed punitive terms on the other Iroquois, article 2 secured the Oneidas and Tuscaroras "in the possession of the Lands on which they are settled."[95] The state of New York and most of its citizens had other ideas. They coveted the fertile lands closest to them, which belonged to their wartime allies the Oneidas, rather than lands farther west that belonged to their wartime enemies. In a series of treaties marked by fraud, deception, and intimidation, the Oneidas rapidly lost most of their homeland. At the Treaty of Herkimer in June 1785, over the protests of their chief Good Peter (see plate 8), they ceded about 200,000 acres to Governor Clinton for $11,500. Although Samuel Kirkland had lost some influence as a result of participating in Sullivan's expedition, the Oneidas evidently requested that lands be set aside for both him and James Dean; the state granted 2,650 acres to Dean and 320 acres to Kirkland, with another 320 acres held in trust for his successor as a missionary. In January 1788, in an attempt to circumvent a state law that prohibited private purchases of Indian land without legislative approval, the Hudson Valley landowner John Livingston and the Genesee Company got some Oneidas to agree to lease them all Oneida land for 999 years for an annual rent of $1,000. The New York legislature promptly rejected the company's request and authorized Governor Clinton to negotiate with the Oneidas, Onondagas, and Cayugas for their land. At the Treaty of Fort Schuyler in September 1788, the Oneidas ceded most of their remaining lands, about 5 million acres, for $5,000 in cash, clothing, and provisions, money to build a sawmill and gristmill, and an annuity of $600.[96] New York made similar treaties with the Cayugas and Onondagas before the Constitution went into effect giving the federal government the sole authority to make treaties. In each treaty the Indians granted all their lands to the state of New York, and the state then appropriated for the use of each tribe a portion of the lands they had ceded. On these state-owned reservations, they were to take up American-style agriculture and could also sell or lease their lands, under state supervision.[97]

In 1790 Timothy Pickering negotiated an agreement to compensate the Oneidas for their losses in the Revolution. Good Peter told him that his people's loyalty to the United States had reduced them to landless poverty.[98] A treaty made in 1794 provided up to $5,000 for individual losses, promised to rebuild and maintain the sawmill and gristmill, and paid $1,000 to replace the church that was destroyed when Brant burned Kanonwalohale.[99] But New York's assault on the lands of the Oneidas and other tribes within its borders proved relentless. "The York People have got almost all our country; and for a very trifle," said Cayuga and Onondaga chiefs.[100] In 1825 the marquis de Lafayette was touring the United States on the fiftieth anniversary of the Revolution. At Oriskany, Rome (the site of Fort Stanwix), and Utica, he received a rapturous welcome from the citizens of Oneida County. Almost lost in the crowds, three Oneidas came to see him, old comrades in the Revolution. They told him they could no longer support themselves by hunting and were miserable having to subsist by agriculture. Lafayette "entreated them to regard the Americans as their brothers forever."[101]

In the South, at the Treaty of Hopewell on the Keowee River in South Carolina in the winter of 1785–86, Benjamin Hawkins and the other federal commissioners met with delegates from the Cherokees, Choctaws, and Chickasaws to establish relations and confirm boundaries. The treaty stipulated that any squatter who remained on the Indian side of the boundary after six months would forfeit the protection of the United States and the Indians could "punish him

or not as they please," a provision that convinced many frontier settlers the government had no concern for their safety.[102] Georgia and
North Carolina also sent commissioners. Hawkins told Jefferson some
months later that nothing was more important to him than preserving the Indians' rights in the treaties. North Carolina's commissioner, William Blount, on the other hand, went there primarily to
protect his land investments in the great bend of the Tennessee River
and to coerce the Cherokees and Chickasaws to accept the Tennessee
as their northern boundary. (Blount pushed for North Carolina to
cede its western land to the nation because that would put his speculations under federal protection.) He told the commissioners that if
they fixed any other boundaries with the Cherokees, his state would
consider it an infringement of its legislative rights. Governor Richard
Caswell told Congress the same thing.[103] Even Hugh Williamson,
who represented North Carolina at the Constitutional Convention
and advocated a strong federal government, advised his state governor in 1788 that with Britain and Spain tampering with the Indians
and only a handful of national troops in service, "North Carolina must
depend on her own Prudence or her own strength for the Measure
of Peace that she may enjoy with the neighbouring Indians."[104]

Indian nations, like the new American nation, had to deal with
internal divisions and competing policies. During the Revolution,
Chickasaw chiefs had defiantly rejected American threats and overtures and generally supported Britain. But King George did not
stand by them, and the withdrawal of British trade after 1783 compelled them to look elsewhere for supplies and allies. Some turned
to the United States; others turned to Spain. Both powers sought
Chickasaw friendship to bolster their efforts to gain control of the
lower Mississippi Valley, and they competed to secure Chickasaw permission to establish trading posts on the bluffs overlooking the river.
The Chickasaws sought to take advantage of both powers, but the
diplomatic shuffling intensified divisions within the nation.[105]

In July 1782 the principal Chickasaw war chief, Piominko, also
known as Piomingo or Mountain Leader, and other headmen initiated peace talks with Virginia.[106] A year later, they sent their first message to Congress, asking why it had not reached out to them when so
many others had. They had received invitations to trade from Spain,
Georgia, and the Illinois country; the Virginians wanted to make a
treaty with them for part of their land, and they expected the settlers
on the Cumberland River also would demand land soon, "as we are
informed they have been marking Lines through our hunting Ground."
Receiving so many talks from so many sources was confusing, the

Chickasaws said: "We are told that the Americans have Thirteen Councils composed of Chiefs and Warriors. We know not which of them we are to listen to." If the president of Congress was "the head Chief of a grand Council which is above these Thirteen Councils," why had they not heard from him? They hoped Congress would stop the encroachments on their land and provide the trade they needed. They could always trade with the Spaniards, of course, but they preferred not to, "as our hearts are always with the Americans."[107] Piominko and a delegation of chiefs made a treaty with Virginia at French Lick near Nashville in November 1783. One of the chiefs, Red King, blamed their past conflicts with the Americans on bad advice from the English, "Like Two puppies thrown together and provoked to Fight." Piominko declared that peace was settled and claimed that he "was the first that proposed it."[108]

An emerging rival, Ugulayacabe or Wolf's Friend, and other Chickasaw delegates, together with Choctaws and Upper Creeks, made a treaty with Spain at Mobile in June 1784, in which they secured continued access to manufactured goods by granting Spain a monopoly on their trade. At Hopewell two years later, Piominko and his party granted the same trade monopoly to the United States.[109] Piominko and Ugulayacabe were both determined to preserve Chickasaw land and independence; they differed over how to do it.

Indian nations' conflicts with other Indian nations complicated their relations with non-Indian nations. In aligning with the Americans, Piominko alienated the Creek chief Alexander McGillivray and the alliance he was building with Spain. After a Creek war party killed Piominko's brother and nephew as they were returning home from a mission to New York in the summer of 1789, Piominko's Chickasaws engaged in open conflict with the Creeks. Ugulayacabe sometimes collaborated with McGillivray to undermine Piominko and advance the Spanish-Indian alliance he opposed.[110]

The more numerous Choctaws farther down the Mississippi faced a similar situation and the same choices, their predicament heightened by the precipitous decline of the whitetailed deer population as Choctaw hunters harvested thousands of deerskins to purchase manufactured goods and rum.[111] A chief named Franchimastabé led a delegation to the Mobile treaty with Spain; another chief, Taboca, led the delegation that traveled hundreds of miles over two months to Hopewell and made a treaty with the United States. Taboca went on to visit Philadelphia and New York in the summer of 1787. "General Washington treated him with great civility," the Spanish governor of Natchez informed the governor of Louisiana. "The general's house was open to him at all hours and he was made welcome at the most private times." Taboca returned home laden with gifts. When Stephen Minor, a Pennsylvanian working for Spain, sat down to eat at Taboca's home several years later, "a Spanish flag was waving over us," but the chief "also had portraits of General Washington, of his wife, of Governor Penn and various others."[112]

Southern Indians recognized the potential for playing off Spanish and American rivals, as they had once played off French and British rivals. The United States represented one source of trade and protection; Spain offered another. American and Spanish officials trying to follow shifting tribal foreign policies saw only the tips of intratribal politics as one party or another extended feelers and made agreements.[113] The United States had called the treaty conference at Hopewell partly in response to the Spanish treaty at Mobile. But the advantages offered by American allegiance were always tempered by American land hunger, and Indians knew it. With three thousand settlers ensconced in the fork between the French Broad River and the Holston, the question the Cherokee chief Corn Tassel posed to the US commissioners at Hopewell was surely rhetorical: "Are Congress, who conquered the King of Great Britain, unable to remove the people?" Corn Tassel was under no illusions about the purpose and effectiveness of American treaties: "We always find that your people settle much faster shortly after a Treaty than Before. It is well known that you have taken almost all our Country from us without our consent," he noted wryly in 1787. "Truth is, if we had no Land we should have Fewer Enemies."[114]

THE FEDERAL GOVERNMENT FIRST EMBARKED on a program of national expansion in the lands north and west of the Ohio River. The region became the testing ground for a new republic to build a new kind of empire.[115] Various states had claims to these lands, but Maryland had insisted that the landowning states cede their claims to Congress—in effect making the land "public land"—as a condition of its ratifying the Articles of Confederation. The states gradually agreed. Virginia, which claimed almost 177 million acres of western land, more than any other state, ceded all its territory north and west of the Ohio in 1784 "for the common benefit," except for 4 million acres between the Scioto and Little Miami, known as the Virginia Military District, which it reserved to honor the land bounties it had promised its soldiers in the Revolution. Connecticut, which had competing claims with Pennsylvania, relinquished its claims except for 3.25 million acres in northern Ohio that became known as the Western Reserve. The states' cessions created a single public domain under the control of the federal government, which not only shaped western land policy and patterns of settlement but also speculated itself in western lands.[116] Selling the lands northwest of the Ohio to its citizens gave Congress the opportunity to pay off its debts and generate much-needed revenue. The rich lands and rivers of Ohio were the key to settlers' hopes, land speculators' fortunes, and the nation's future.

Instead of unleashing a chaotic land rush, the government envisioned extending the nation westward in an orderly process: lands would be systematically surveyed in townships and then sold and settled by the "right" sort of people. That process involved coordinating national and private interests, a model that Washington himself had perfected. Well-placed and well-heeled speculators used their political connections and financial clout to get a head start. Congress collaborated with them in their pursuit of profits, and the government forged a reciprocal relationship with land companies in developing the Ohio country as it did with railroad companies in developing the trans-Mississippi West in the second half of the nineteenth century.[117] Speculators purchased vast tracts of land on credit, in anticipation they could quickly resell lands to settlers and generate the cash for future payment. They also bought up at a fraction of their face value the unpaid notes of the Continental Congress, veterans' land bounties, and military warrants and used them to buy land. Military warrants—scrip for claims to western land—had been used as war bounties and incentive payments to encourage soldiers to reenlist during the Revolution. Many veterans who lacked the opportunity or the means to move west sold their warrants, often for a pittance, to wealthier men who offered ready cash.

In 1784 the Confederation Congress set up a committee, chaired by Thomas Jefferson, to consider plans for distributing the national domain and formulate a blueprint for the future development of the territory west of the Ohio. Washington did not serve on the committee, but members sought his advice and opinions, and his experience and interests in the West carried weight.[118] The committee recommended that after the land was acquired from the Indians, it be surveyed and divided into territories. Once its population reached twenty thousand, a territory could begin the process of becoming a state on a par with the original thirteen states. The federal government thus laid out a plan for filling the nation's coffers and paying off its crushing war debt as territories were settled, townships grew, and new states joined the union.[119]

Washington wanted to implement a process of "compact and progressive Settling" that would strengthen the Union and "admit law & good government." Sparse settlements scattered across several states or a large territory would have the opposite effects, he explained to both Henry Knox and Hugh Williamson in the spring of 1785, opening the field "to Land jobbers and speculators, who are prouling about like Wolves in every shape"(the same image he had conjured up for Indians in his letter to Congress) and injuring "the real occupiers & useful citizens; and consequently, the public interest." Fearful that a country on the move might fly apart, he wanted an orderly national advance in which the territory designated for a new state would be laid out and a certain amount of the land settled, or at least granted, before the process of surveying and distributing land for the next state began.[120]

Congress incorporated Washington's basic ideas into the Northwest Ordinance of 1785.[121] The ordinance again prohibited illegal intrusions and ordered squatters to depart. It provided for the survey and sale of lands once the United States acquired title from the tribes. Unlike the method of metes-and-bounds surveys in place south of the Ohio, where settlers claimed irregular areas and marked their boundaries by landscape features such as streams and rocks, the country north of the Ohio would be surveyed and divided into squares before it was occupied. Starting at the western boundary of Pennsylvania, running north to Lake Erie, and running west from where the Pennsylvania borderline intersected with the Ohio River, the ordinance stipulated the West would be divided into square townships measuring six miles by six miles; townships would be further divided into thirty-six sections of one square mile, or 640 acres. Townships were arranged in north-south rows called ranges; ranges, townships, and sections were all systematically numbered. The surveyors were to measure the lines by chains, mark them on trees, and describe them exactly on plats. Thomas Hutchins, the US geographer, and surveyors from the various states surveyed the first tracts of land in eastern Ohio, known as the Seven Ranges. The secretary of war was to choose by lot one-seventh of the land to compensate veterans of the Continental Army. The remaining lots were to be sold at auction. The ordinance established a pattern of land settlement and land ownership by which the United States surveyed, measured, and divided the continent into squares as it marched west.[122]

Washington's attitude to the passage of the ordinance was "better late than never."[123] Nevertheless, it gave him occasion to share his vision for the West with Lafayette:

> I wish to see the sons & daughters of the world in Peace & busily employed in the more agreeable amusement, of fulfilling the first and great command-ment—*Increase & Multiply:* as an encouragement to which we have opened the fertile plains of the Ohio to the poor, the needy & the oppressed of the Earth; any one therefore who is heavy laden, or who wants land to cultivate, may repair thither & abound, as in the Land of promise, with milk & honey: the ways are preparing, & the roads will be made easy, thro' the channels of Potomac & James river.[124]

In order for Congress and the land companies to secure control of those fertile plains and set the nation on its orderly path of expansion, the government had to deal with the noncompliance of its own citizens who squatted there and the resistance of the Indians who lived there. Federal troops burned squatters' cabins and crops and ordered squatters back across the river, but too few troops and too many squatters scattered over too much territory rendered the task impossible.[125]

The Indians presented a more formidable obstacle. Having acquired the claims of the Six Nations to the Ohio Valley at the Treaty of Fort Stanwix, the United States turned its attention to the tribes who actually lived there.[126] At the Treaty of Fort McIntosh in January 1785, US commissioners Richard Butler, George Rogers Clark, and Arthur Lee demanded large cessions from most of the Ohio tribes. When the Indians objected that the king of England had no right to transfer their lands to the United States, the commissioners brushed their objections aside and dictated terms to them as a defeated people. The Shawnees did not attend, and there could be no peace without them. Washington rated the Shawnees "among the most warlike of the Ohio Indians," but with other tribes making peace, he predicted "their spirit must yield, or they might easily be extirpated."[127]

The Mekoche division of the Shawnees met with Butler and Clark at Fort Finney at the mouth of the Great Miami River in January 1786. Butler during the Revolution had a reputation as a hothead, given to fistfights and exchanging black eyes with fellow officers.[128] Clark's idea of diplomacy was to let the Indians know he would just as soon tomahawk them as talk with them. The two men were not inclined to negotiate. Instead, they demanded all land east of the Great Miami. Years of conflict had taken a toll on the Shawnees:

"Many of the young fellows which have grown up through the course of the war, and *trained like young hounds to blood,* have a great attachment to the British," Butler noted in his journal of the treaty; the chiefs were averse to war but lacked the influence to restrain their warriors. The Shawnees objected to the Americans' demands and asked that the Ohio River remain the boundary. "God gave us this country, we do not understand measuring out the lands, it is all ours," they said. But when the Shawnee speaker offered the wampum belt on which he spoke, the commissioners refused to accept it. Butler picked up the belt "and dashed it on the table"; Clark pushed it off the table with his cane and ground it into the dirt with the heel of his boot. The Americans then threw down a string of black and white wampum, symbolizing the choice between war and peace. The Americans had defeated the British, and the country now belonged to the United States, they declared. The Shawnees could have peace on American terms or destruction by American arms.[129] Moluntha, Painted Pole, and other chiefs grudgingly ceded the land and gave hostages but complained: "This is not the way to make a good or lasting Peace to take our Chiefs Prisoners and come with Soldiers at your Backs."[130] They were right: before the year was out, Moluntha, holding a copy of the peace treaty, was tomahawked in cold blood when Benjamin Logan and a force of Kentucky militia attacked and burned his village.[131]

Butler was appointed superintendent of Indian affairs for the Northern District in August 1786. His bullying at Fort Finney stood in stark contrast with the conduct recommended that same year to the *British* superintendent of Indian affairs in the list of "Instructions for the good Government of the Indian Department" sent by Guy Carleton, Lord Dorchester: "As these People consider themselves free and independent and are in fact unacquainted with control and subordination they are alone to be governed by address and persuasion and they require the utmost attention to Ceremonies and external appearances with an uncommon share of patience[,] good temper and forbearance."[132] The contrast was not lost on the Indians, who long remembered the insult to the wampum belt.

Washington wrote to Butler conveying his "sincere regard" for him and his pleasure at his appointment as superintendent. He wanted to know more about the situation in the Ohio country, he said: "the real temper & designs of the Western Indians," the politics of the people, and navigation on the waterways. He also asked Butler to assist him in meeting a request from Lafayette on behalf of Catherine the Great of Russia for a vocabulary of the languages of the Ohio Indians. Butler, who had traded among the Shawnees and had a Shawnee wife, complied. In November 1787 he sent Washington a vocabulary of Shawnee words compiled by himself and Delaware words done by John Killbuck, "an Indian of that nation who has been Educated at Princetown College at the Expence of the U.S. & patronage of Congress." Along with the vocabulary, Butler sent Washington what little information he had been able to gather from oral tradition and their old men on the origins and history of the Shawnees.[133] Washington forwarded the vocabulary to Lafayette for Empress Catherine, together with a shorter vocabulary of southern Indian words compiled by Benjamin Hawkins and a copy of a Delaware-English spelling book produced by Rev. David Zeisberger for use in the Moravian mission schools on the Muskingum River.[134] (The following year, George Morgan sent Washington a Shawnee grammar and vocabulary that he had had composed, together with the Lord's Prayer in Shawnee, for the Russian empress, who had "ordered a universal dictionary to be made of all languages."[135]) Washington thanked Butler for his observations on Indian history and traditions, and allowed himself a rare moment of reflection on the indigenous past: "Those works which are found upon the Ohio and other traces of the country's being once inhabited by a race of people more ingenious, at least, if not more civilized than those who at present dwell there, have excited the attention and enquiries of the curious to learn from whence they came, whither they are gone and something of their history." But what excited Washington's attention and curiosity, he made clear, was the land, the distances between rivers, and trade and navigation routes in the Ohio country.[136]

He was not the only one. In March 1786 a group of self-described "reputable, industrious, well-informed men" of "wealth, education, and virtue" met at a tavern in Boston and formed the Ohio Company of Associates. Most of them were New Englanders, and most were veterans of the Revolutionary War who had not been adequately paid for their services. The company planned to sell stock to speculators and then petition the federal government for enormous grants of land. It offered one thousand shares at $1,000 in continental paper currency to raise up to $1 million and then purchase 1.5 million acres of land from Congress, ostensibly with the goal of settling veterans in the territory beyond the Ohio. In effect, the Ohio Company would buy land the United States had won during the war by giving back to Congress the nearly worthless paper it had issued to finance that war.[137]

The associates appointed as company directors General Samuel Parsons, a Harvard graduate who had served in the Revolution and negotiated the Treaty of Fort McIntosh; Rev. Manasseh Cutler, a former lawyer, doctor, merchant, and chaplain in the Revolutionary army and now pastor of the Congregationalist church in Ipswich, Massachusetts; and General Rufus Putnam, a surveyor, land speculator, and engineer who had served in the French and Indian War and with Washington in the Revolution. Winthrop Sargent, a Harvard graduate who had served in Henry Knox's artillery regiment in the Revolution, was secretary.[138] Putnam played on his connection to Washington to promote his own and his company's land schemes and, like Washington, saw his own interests and the national interest as compatible if not identical. "I am *Sir*," he had told Washington a couple of months after the Peace of Paris, "among those who consider the *Cession* of so grate a tract of Territory to the United States in the Western World as a very happy circumstance; and of grate consequence to the American Empire." And he was impatient to get at that territory: the settlement of the Ohio country occupied "many of my thoughts, and much of my time," he told Washington. Thousands would emigrate to that country as soon as Congress made provision for granting lands. Putnam submitted a petition in 1784 and warned that the officers would not "lie long upon their Oars, waiting the decision of Congress." In 1785 Congress made Putnam the surveyor of western lands.[139]

The members of the Ohio Company promoted their scheme as an opportunity for settling the West and paying down the national debt that Congress could not afford to miss.[140] Cutler sold shares to leading government officials, including Arthur St. Clair, who was president of Congress at the time, and the secretary of the Confederation's Treasury Board, William Duer.[141] Duer was a political and business crony of Alexander Hamilton and became his assistant secretary in the Treasury Department after the Constitution was adopted. Duer was also a business partner of Secretary of War Knox, who also owned stock in the Ohio Company.

Washington told Thomas Cresap that he was not a member of the Ohio Company, did not know who its members were, and was not involved in its affairs.[142] Nevertheless, he "took a decided interest" in promoting schemes for settling Ohio. Settlements north of the river would give added security to his lands on the south bank; he was anxious to bind the West to Virginia and the East; he sympathized with the veterans' complaints, and many of the men promoting the project were former comrades-in-arms. Who better to settle the West, Washington asked, than "the disbanded Officers and Soldiers of the Army, to whom the faith of Government hath long since been pledged, that lands should be granted at the expiration of the War?"[143]

A congressional committee in fall 1786 reported that the Indian opposition comprised the Shawnees, Miamis, and Lakes Indians, joined by "a banditti of desperadoes" made up of "outcasts from other nations" who had moved into the Ohio country "for the purpose of war and plunder."[144] It was rather more than that. Two months later, delegates from the Iroquois, Shawnees, Delawares, Hurons, Ojibwas, Potawatomis, Ottawas, Piankashaws, Weas, Miamis, and Cherokees gathered in council at Brownstown, a Wyandot town near Detroit, and sent Congress a message denouncing its divisive policies of making separate treaties. "As landed matters are often the subject of our councils with you, a matter of the greatest importance and of general concern to us," they said, all treaties with the United States should be "with the general voice of the whole confederacy, and carried on in the most open manner, without restraint on either side." The treaties at Fort Stanwix, Fort McIntosh, and Fort Finney were "partial treaties" and therefore "void and of no effect." The chiefs proposed making another treaty and, as a first step toward peace, asked Congress to remove surveyors and settlers from lands on the Indian side of the Ohio River. They were determined their demands should "appear just and reasonable, in the eyes of the world."[145]

In the spring of 1787 Washington traveled to Philadelphia, where he would preside over the Constitutional Convention as it worked to form a more perfect union, but even as he did so, the Indian tribes beyond the Ohio were forming a union of their own to resist the American expansion to which Washington was committed. Indian power stood squarely in the way of the new nation's ability to turn real estate into revenue and alleviate the postwar tax burden on its citizens. The threat of Indian war kept surveyors and settlers out of the lands they coveted. "Had it not been for the hostile appearances in the Indians," Massachusetts congressman Nathan Dane told his state assembly in 1786, "7,000,000 acres of the land belonging to the United States would now have been surveyed, and ready for sale."[146]

In July 1787, in one of its last acts, the Confederation Congress issued another land ordinance, commonly known as the Northwest Ordinance. Cutler went to New York and, at dinners and private meetings, worked on members of the government and key members of Congress to get them to agree to the Ohio Company's purchase of land in the Northwest Territory.[147] He also worked out a deal with Duer that would give another company, the Scioto Company, an option on an additional 3.5 million acres.[148] On July 27 Congress, some of whose members held stock in the Ohio Company, passed the Northwest Ordinance and approved granting the Ohio Company a total of 5 million acres of land. The Ohio Company kept 1.5 million acres for itself and allowed Duer and his cronies in the Scioto Company to acquire the other 3.5 million.[149] (The Scioto Company sold land through agents to European emigrants but never paid the government for the land, and immigrants arrived to find they had been swindled.) The government's price for the land was nominally one dollar an acre, but it deducted one-third for poor-quality lands and surveying expenses, reducing the cost to sixty-six cents per acre.[150] Cutler got Congress to agree to accept payment in depreciated government securities and devalued military warrants, so the real cost to the company was more like eight or nine cents per acre.[151] Cutler pronounced it "the greatest private contract ever made in America."[152] Before long, "almost every army officer owned shares in the Ohio Company."[153]

Written by a congressional committee chaired by James Monroe, the Northwest Ordinance created a blueprint for national expansion and a uniform model of statehood. The Northwest Territory, some 220,000 square miles of it, would be surveyed, divided into districts and lots, sold, and settled. The territory would have its own territorial government, with a governor, a secretary, and judges appointed by Congress. Once the adult male population reached five thousand, they would elect an assembly. The ordinance provided for proportionate representation of the people in a territorial legislature, freedom of religion, trial by jury, habeas corpus, and judicial proceeding according to common law. It encouraged education and schools; it prohibited slavery and involuntary servitude north of the Ohio. It stipulated that "not less than three nor more than five States" should be formed in the territory. Unlike colonial status under the British Empire, territorial status was temporary: once its population reached sixty thousand, a territory could petition to become a state. The ordinance harnessed the potentially divisive forces of western expansion into a national project. Eventually Ohio, Indiana, Illinois, Michigan, and Wisconsin entered the Union as states carved from the Northwest Territory. Ultimately, more than thirty states entered the union through the process it established.

At the same time as the ordinance committed the nation to expansion onto Indian lands, however, it also pledged that the United States would observe the "utmost good faith" in its dealings with the Indians. Their lands would not be taken from them without their consent, and they would not be attacked except "in just and lawful wars authorized by Congress."[154] In keeping with Washington and Knox's views, Congress would try to acquire Indian land by treaty rather than by war. Knox doubted that Indians and whites could ever be good neighbors: the former were determined to defend their lands and the latter determined to have them. But if it appeared "that we preferred War to Peace," Knox wrote in his report to Congress in July, "the United States may have the verdict of mankind against them; for men are ever ready to espouse the cause of those who appear to be oppressed provided their interference may cost them nothing." The result would be "a stain on the national reputation of America." And if national honor was not enough to require such a course of action, the nation's financial situation rendered it "utterly unable to maintain an Indian war with any dignity or prospect of success." A war would cost much blood and much more money, but Indian lands could be bought for a small amount. A congressional committee accepted Knox's recommendations. The government must deal with Indians on an equal footing. Treaty commissioners should stop using "a language of superiority and command" and convince the Indians "of the Justice and humanity as well as the power of the United States and of their disposition to promote the happiness of the Indians." Instead of dictating treaties and demanding Indian lands by right of conquest, the United States would return to the British practice of negotiating treaties and purchasing Indian lands.[155] The new US Congress reaffirmed the Northwest Ordinance in its first session.

Washington and others entertained notions that colonial status could be temporary for Indians as well as western settlers. Territories shed their colonial status when they became states; Indians could shed it when they became "civilized" and incorporated into the Republic. But the fact that the Indians' lands were the basis for territorial expansion, state formation, and nation-building meant that federal colonial control over Indians would be indefinite.[156] The fact that Indians would resist meant that the rhetoric of "just and lawful wars" in the Northwest Ordinance was less an aspiration to high ideals than a justification of the violence inherent in US Indian policy. What Patrick Wolfe labeled "intentional fallacies"—declared good intentions that were never going to come to fruition—became a hallmark of US Indian policy.[157]

The new governor of the Northwest Territory was Arthur St. Clair, former president of the Congress (see plate 9). Born in Scotland in 1734 or 1736, St. Clair had attended the University of Edinburgh, purchased a commission in the British army, and served in the French and Indian War under Jeffery Amherst at the capture of Louisburg in

1758 and James Wolfe at the capture of Quebec in 1759.[158] After the war he married the niece of Governor James Bayard of Massachusetts and settled in western Pennsylvania. During the Revolution, he fought at Trenton, Princeton, Ticonderoga, Brandywine Creek, and Yorktown and developed a close relationship with Washington. His abandonment of Ticonderoga in 1777 brought an inquiry, but he was exonerated and ended the war a major general. He was elected president of the Confederation Congress in 1787. In his fifties, St. Clair was corpulent and suffered from gout, but he brought military and political experience to the position of territorial governor, and he owned Ohio Company land. Like Washington, St. Clair wanted to see the country settled in an orderly manner. Arriving at Marietta, the model town established by the Ohio Company at the mouth of the Muskingum River in the spring of 1788, he made it the seat of his territorial government and named the area Washington County.

This was exactly how Washington thought the nation should grow. "No Colony in America was ever settled under such favorable auspices as that which has just commenced at the Muskingum," he wrote in a letter to one correspondent "If I was a young man, just preparing to begin the world or if advanced in life, and had a family to make a provision for, I know of no country, where I should rather fix my habitation." With an efficient government, America would be the best country in the world for hardworking, frugal people with a little capital; "the lowest class of people" would also benefit because there were "plenty of unoccupied lands," equal distribution of property, and ample means of subsistence. The only obstacles were the Indians and the difficulty of transportation, and both could be dealt with by the proper application of federal power.[159]

As the Constitutional Convention wrapped up its business, Washington wrote his land agent in western Pennsylvania instructing him not to sell his property for two dollars an acre; once the new Constitution was ratified, Washington had "no doubt of obtaining the price I have fixed on the land, and that in a short time." (He eventually sold it for more than seven dollars an acre). It was, notes John Ferling, "a remarkably candid letter" offering "a clue to the private interests that combined with his nationalistic concerns to bring him to Philadelphia."[160]

Washington and his fellow delegates were not the only ones creating a stronger union. As the states debated and then voted to ratify the Constitution, so the Indians, Joseph Brant and several Seneca chiefs told Samuel Kirkland in July 1788, had been debating for a long time what was best for themselves and decided "that the Indian interest must be one; that they must all unite as Indians independently of white people." To that end, some twenty chiefs from the Six Nations had gone as an embassy to the southern and western nations to argue the case for a plan of general union. They had traveled for seventeen months and recently returned, having conferred with twenty-two different tribes from the Great Lakes down to the Mississippi and as far south as the Upper Creeks, and they had received belts from all of those nations signifying their compliance with the proposal. Brant and the Seneca chiefs asked Kirkland if he did not think that every true friend of the Indians would approve of the scheme; wouldn't the Great Spirit approve? Their immediate objective was the peace and good of the Indians, not war with either Britain or the Americans, although they acknowledged it would put them in a better state of defense, in the event a war did break out. And after all, they observed to Kirkland, "Congress could not blame them for such a conduct, neither ought they to be jealous of them; for what had Congress done, but to unite thirteen states as one; all their wisdom and strength to become one."[161] The new United States would have to contend with the uniting Indian nations.

PART THREE

The First President and the First Americans

CHAPTER 14

An Indian Policy for the New Nation

F ROM THE TIME THE UNITED STATES was born, images of Indians, which Europeans had used for centuries to represent the New World, began to appear on American maps, medals, and buildings as emblems of an independent American nation based on freedom.[1] The association of American Indians with American freedom continued. In 1988, just after the bicentennial of the US Constitution, the House of Representatives, with the Senate concurring, issued a declaration that "the original framers of the Constitution, including, most notably, George Washington and Benjamin Franklin, are known to have greatly admired the concepts of the Six Nations of the Iroquois Confederacy" and that the confederacy influenced the formation of the Republic and provided a model for the Constitution.[2]

The evidence is circumstantial, but here is the logic behind the argument: an Onondaga chief named Canasatego recommended to the colonists in 1744 (on July 4, incidentally) that they form a federation of their governments as the Six Nations had done; Franklin took note of this speech and published it; Franklin called the Albany Congress in 1754 where some of the colonies drew up their first plan of union; the colonists were negotiating with the Iroquois while the Continental Congress met in 1775 and 1776. And thus the founding fathers discussed the Iroquois federation when they debated the Constitution. Washington, who presided over the debates in the Constitutional Convention, said nothing to indicate such a debt, though not everything gets written down, and influences may have seeped from the decentered federated governance of the Iroquois into the new federal system of the United States without being documented. While some people took this as an article of faith, most scholars see all this as a stretch. Few accept the role of the Iroquois in shaping the US Constitution. A war of words and essays ensued and continues to this day, with people taking sides in what became a yes-or-no debate.[3]

Whether or not the founding fathers modeled the Constitution on Iroquoian structures and philosophies of governance, they certainly took Indian nations into account as they built their own, if in a less celebratory way than the 1988 declaration. Concerns about the government's weakness in dealing with Indian nations, implementing Indian policies, and defeating Indian enemies featured prominently in correspondence and debates about creating, drafting, and ratifying the Constitution, and in arguments for a stronger federal state and a stronger national army. Many western settlers and people farther east with a financial stake in western lands supported the Constitution because they hoped a stronger federal government and army would defend them, or their investments, against Indian attack. Georgia became the first southern state and the fourth state in the nation to ratify the Constitution in large part because it was embroiled in conflict with the Creek Nation.[4] Debates about the sovereignty of the United States acknowledged the sovereignties of Native nations as well as of the states and federal government. As the legal scholar Gregory Ablavsky puts it, Indian issues were refracted "through the lens of federalism."[5]

The framers of the Constitution managed to resolve or set aside conflicting interests in their effort to create a more perfect union, but the sparely worded principles of the document they crafted provided few specifics about how to develop a functioning federal government or to conduct Indian affairs. "We are in a wilderness without a single step to guide us," James Madison fretted to Thomas Jefferson.[6] When Washington was inaugurated in April 1789, he had yet to work out the forms and functions of the office he had assumed. On his personal copy of the Constitution he bracketed and noted in pencil those sections outlining the responsibilities of the president. But how should the president be addressed? What were the powers and limitations of the office? What, indeed, were the powers and limitations of the new federal government? Article II stated simply, "The executive Power shall be vested in a President of the United States," but how the first president read those words and how he applied that power established important precedents. Washington told the Boston selectmen in 1795 that "the Constitution is the guide which I never can abandon." In fact, what Washington did has often proved more significant than what the Constitution said.[7]

The new president who took office in 1789 looked west, and so did the new nation. "The Western Country is daily growing into greater importance," Washington's old comrade Adam Stephen wrote James Madison that year. "The Strength and Vigour of the United States ly in the Mountains and to the Westward."[8] But Washington knew that if westward expansion was to unite rather than divide the states, it must be a national endeavor, with the federal government controlling Indian affairs and the process of acquiring Indian lands. Between 1789 and 1791 he visited all thirteen states, carrying his vision of an expansive republic and stressing the need for a strong central government to the people.[9]

The Constitution gave the federal government increased powers—to raise taxes, regulate commerce, raise an army, call out state militias, govern federal territories, and make treaties—so many powers, in fact, that alarmed states and citizens responded by demanding protections in what became the Bill of Rights.[10] The Constitution also reaffirmed the federal government's authority over Indian affairs. Under the Articles of Confederation, Congress could only regulate trade and manage affairs with Indians who were "not members of any state" and could not infringe on the legislative rights of any state within its own borders. It had been a source of considerable tension. The Constitution granted the president the power to make treaties with the advice and consent of the Senate, and the commerce clause gave Congress exclusive authority to "regulate Commerce with foreign Nations, and among the several States, and with the Indian tribes," saying nothing about federal authority ceasing at state borders and thereby eliminating the division of authority between the central government and the states that had plagued Indian policy during the Confederation.

The federal government and its chief executive had the opportunity for a new start in Indian affairs and the power to define and implement a national Indian policy. Yet the five words "and with the Indian tribes" were a slim foundation on which to build. What Indian policy should look like, and what the executive branch's broad discretion to conduct Indian affairs meant in concrete terms, generated vigorous debate and extensive deliberation. The new president worked to develop a federal Indian policy with his secretary of war, Henry Knox, and to a lesser extent Thomas Jefferson, who arrived back from Paris, where he had served as ambassador, in November

1789 to find he had been appointed secretary of state. In doing so they produced a substantial archive of correspondence and meetings among the president, his cabinet, and state executives, as well as records of treaty negotiations, letters, reports, and instructions to and from officials and Indian agents in Indian country. Washington's administration based its assertion of federal authority over Indian affairs not solely on the commerce clause but also in the broad array of powers granted by the Constitution to the federal government and denied the states, notably the right to make treaties or to wage war. As commander in chief, the president assumed responsibility for conducting war against Indians. Federal Indian policy developed "bit by bit" as Congress, responding to the executive, enacted laws to regulate trade and intercourse with the tribes.[11]

Different people had different hopes and expectations as the new government took shape. Madison anticipated that the increased security it afforded purchasers of western lands would attract speculation, and accelerate population movement and the formation of new states. George Nicholas, a Kentuckian, warned Madison that the government must defend settlers from Indian attacks to stop them drifting into Spanish territory: "No people will remain long under a Government which does not afford protection."[12] Brigadier General Harmar was more forthright, telling Knox he hoped the new government would begin to operate soon and "sweep these perfidious villains off the face of the earth."[13] Benjamin Hawkins of North Carolina hoped the Senate would "do something effectual" in Indian affairs but recognized the problems in working out a boundary line: Indians hoped Congress would protect their lands, while whites feared Congress would scupper their land speculations, he told Madison.[14] Washington knew that the challenges he faced in Indian country could not be resolved easily. Many of the anomalies that characterized US-Indian relations in the Confederation era—promoting westward expansion while trying to prevent frontier conflict, signing treaties with tribes as sovereign nations while persistently attempting to erode their independence, negotiating with compliant but unauthorized chiefs, dealing with the separate agendas of individual states, and trying to impose unpopular restraints on people who could vote officials out of office—persisted for decades to come.

Though in search of a practical Indian policy, Washington was not immune to larger philosophical, legal, and constitutional considerations about Indian affairs. As the founding fathers sought to secure a place for the new republic among the nations of the world, they also had to determine what was the place of Indians in the new nation. The Indians in a sense were resident "foreign nations." This was their homeland, but they had no desire to become part of the new nation that was being built on it. The United States claimed exclusive sovereignty and territorial control, but how should it deal with the Indian nations?[15] The founders turned to writings on international law to guide them. "The circumstances of a rising state make it necessary to consult the law of nations," Benjamin Franklin wrote to a friend in the Netherlands who had sent him a copy of *The Law of Nations*, the influential treatise on international law written by Swiss philosopher and legal theorist Emer de Vattel. (Washington borrowed a copy of *The Law of Nations* from the New York Society Library in October 1789, evidently on permanent loan.) Sovereign nations made treaties in which they recognized one another's rights and maintained the balance of power. For the infant United States, international diplomacy entailed making treaties and alliances with Indian nations as well as European nations and paying attention to the rituals of the council fire as well as the etiquette of court.[16]

There was widespread agreement that the law of nations should govern relations between the United States and Natives, but European texts said little about indigenous peoples, and Vattel was ambiguous on their status. Washington and his government therefore had to translate international law principles from Europe and apply them to Indian country. The administration asserted its authority to deal with Indian nations as it would with foreign nations, made treaties with them, and recognized aspects of their sovereignty, but it did not consider Indians to be fully independent polities. It drew on Vattel's position that a nation-state possessed a uniform sovereignty over its national territory to establish its right of preemption to land inhabited by Indian people. Since the Indian nations existed within the borders of the United States, and its government possessed ultimate sovereignty over this territory, the sovereignty of the United States limited the sovereignty of the Indian nations. As territorial sovereign, the government insisted that Indians could not sell their lands to anyone but the United States or make alliances with any other nation.[17] The Revolutionary generation also deployed Vattelian precepts to justify the conquest, dispossession, and assimilation of indigenous peoples: so-called civilized nations had the right to take possession of "part of a vast country" from "erratic" and "savage" nations who lived by war and plunder rather than by farming.[18]

The Washington administration recognized Indian nations as possessing much greater sovereignty than the Confederation government had recognized. This stemmed from its deliberations about the laws of nations and the nature of federalism but also reflected the reality that Indian nations were powerful and independent. Recognizing Native sovereignty was the right thing to do, but it was also the expedient thing to do. Indians, of course, as Washington was to discover, were unimpressed. When the government tried to get them to acknowledge they were under the exclusive protection of the United States and no other power, they resisted. Much of their power, as it had in the colonial era, rested on their ability to deal with other nations. They insisted they were free, independent, and equal nations. As George Rogers Clark had noted at the end of the Revolution, Indians were as ready to make war on Britain as on the United States if either offended them.[19] If the infant United States was to succeed, it must impress Indian nations as well as European nations with its national power.[20]

Instead, said Alexander Hamilton, the young republic was hemmed in by Indian power and European powers. The tribes on the western frontier ought to be regarded as natural enemies of the United States and natural allies of Britain and Spain, he wrote in *The Federalist Papers*, "because they have most to fear from us and most to hope from them." Since the territories of Britain, Spain, and the Indian nations stretched the length of the Union from Maine to Georgia, posing a common danger to all the states, security required common measures on the part of all the states.[21] Hamilton was determined to give the United States the military and financial resources to project national power against foreign powers and Indian peoples and to sustain territorial expansion. That meant a standing army supported by loans and taxes. Whatever method the United States employed to secure Indian lands—war or treaty—it needed a strong government to carry it out and the money to pay for it.[22]

The illegitimate son of a Scottish merchant in the West Indies (John Adams called him "the bastard brat of a Scottish pedlar"), Hamilton was brilliant, flamboyant, thirty-something. He was an unlikely ally for Washington, yet they joined their efforts to create a strong government and centralized financial institutions and economic policy.[23] In the developing competition between Jeffersonian and Hamiltonian philosophies and practices of government, Washington believed Hamilton's offered the best approach for western expansion. Jefferson hoped the "free" lands of the West would help stave off industrialization and preserve the young nation's agrarian character. Washington hoped to harness the resources of the West to transform the nation's economy and believed that Hamilton's program would provide the financial muscle to thwart British and

Spanish ambitions, dispossess the Indians, and open new frontiers. Only a strong union with a strong army could win the West.[24]

It was clear the nation would continue to advance across Indian country; it had little choice. The government remained dependent on the acquisition and sale of western land to pay off its Revolutionary War debt, fund its operations, provide property for its citizens, and essentially hold things together. Without territorial expansion, writes the historian Alan Taylor, "American leaders dreaded that some medley of class or civil war and foreign intervention would destroy their risky experiment in American independence, republican government, and federal union. Only the continued consumption of Indian land to make private property could sustain the American social order that combined inequality with opportunity."[25] The citizens of the new republic shared their president's obsession: "It would be a difficult matter to find a man of property in the country, who is not concerned in the buying or selling of land, which may be considered in America as an article of trade," a visiting Englishman observed in the 1790s.[26]

The Confederation Congress in its last months had authorized Governor Arthur St. Clair to make a general treaty with the tribes in the Northwest Territory to confirm their earlier land cessions, instructing him not to depart from the treaties that had already been made unless he could obtain "a change of boundary beneficial to the United States." Purchasing Indian land was not the primary goal, but he should seize "any opportunity that may offer of extinguishing Indian rights to the westward, as far as the river Mississippi."[27] Knox recommended modifying the instructions to authorize paying for the lands acquired in earlier treaties based on the right of conquest. The Indians so resented those treaties that rather than submit to them they would prefer continual war, and in the present political crisis and with an exhausted treasury, Knox warned, that would be "an event pregnant with unlimited evil." Congress appropriated an additional $20,000.[28] If St. Clair failed to secure peace and war was inevitable, Knox told him, he should wage it vigorously and end it quickly, "for a protracted Indian war, would be destruction to the republic, under its present circumstance."[29]

In January 1789 St. Clair made two treaties at Fort Harmar, the main garrison in the Ohio country. One was with Cornplanter, Guyasuta, and other representatives of the Six Nations; the other with Wyandots, Delawares (including Captain Pipe and Wingenund), and some Ottawas, Ojibwas, and Potawatomis. The Indians confirmed earlier land cessions, but St. Clair's tone—he told Washington he found the negotiations "tedious and troublesome"—did little to convince the Indians of "the Justice and humanity as well as the power of the United States."[30] Most Indians stayed away, and many of those who attended the treaty disavowed it later. But a treaty was a treaty, and if the Indians broke this one they could, in the Washington-Knox construction of a just Indian policy, be "extirpated." Like Washington, St. Clair worried that westward migration might depopulate the eastern states. Emigrants were already flooding down the Ohio and pushing on to the rich lands beyond, he informed Washington in August. "The Spirit however has gone forth, and cannot now be restrained."[31] The Indian nations who boycotted the Fort Harmar Treaty announced their determination to fight, sent war pipes to the various tribes, and sent a delegation to Detroit to ask the British for ammunition.[32]

Meanwhile, Indians continued to raid across the Ohio, and Kentuckians continued to retaliate against any and all Indians.[33] Colonel John Hardin and the Kentucky militia launched an attack on Wea villages on the Wabash in the spring of 1789 that killed and scalped a dozen men, women, and children, including, Knox informed Washington, "a number of peaceable Piankeshaws, who prided themselves in their attachment to the United States."[34] Such indiscriminate killings undermined Washington's efforts to avoid conflict with the Wabash Indians and to wage just wars. In his view the United States must adopt more diplomatic means of dealing with the tribes, at least as a first step. Then, "if after manifesting clearly to the Indians the dispositions of the General Government for the preservation of peace, and the extension of a just protection to the said Indians, they should continue their incursions, the United States will be constrained to punish them with severity."[35]

Washington wanted Indian relations in the United States to demonstrate to the world that his nation was the equal of European nations in humanitarianism and waging civilized war.[36] Knox agreed with him on the need to inject greater morality into the conduct of Indian affairs: "Indians possess the natural rights of man" and should be treated with "justice and humanity," he wrote the president.[37] How the United States treated Indians would affect how other nations viewed American democracy.

Washington's thinking, and his conflicting commitments, reflected the dilemmas and ambiguities of the nation's Indian policies. Convinced that both his personal fortune and the nation should be built on Indian lands, Washington had few qualms about separating Native peoples from their homelands and hunting territories.

He envisioned, developed, and implemented policies that would do just that. At the same time, he hoped to make dispossession a peaceful process, deal with Indian tribes as sovereign nations, and treat them with justice and humanity. George Thatcher, representing the Maine district of Massachusetts in Congress, reduced the complexities and challenges of forging Indian policy to a simple option: either exterminate the Indians or abandon settlement of the western country. "There is no other alternative," he said; "Indians & white people cannot live in the same neighborhood of each other."[38] Washington tried to find a third path that would allow the United States to deprive Indians of their land with minimal bloodshed.

As an individual and as president he struggled to reconcile the contradictions of an Indian policy that tried to combine expansion with honor.[39] In practice, that often meant making treaties with Indians to secure peace and land, and waging war against Indians who refused and resisted. For frontier settlers, it usually meant nothing. Men like George Rogers Clark thought that war was the only way to deal with Indians and that treaties were an absurdity without it.[40] Frontier settlers thought that treaties protected Indians and left innocent citizens exposed to the horrors of Indian war.[41] They ignored government restraints, broke treaties, and preferred to expel Indians from their lands by killing them.

Washington attempted to leaven national land grabbing with sprinklings of humanitarianism. Thirty or forty years later, US Indian policy as articulated by Andrew Jackson justified dispossessing and removing Indians on the racist assumption that they were incapable of change and would always be "savages." Washington and other founding fathers tended to subscribe to Scottish Enlightenment teachings that explained human difference as the product of environment and experience. "Savages we call them," wrote Franklin, albeit in an attempt to poke fun at European pretensions, "because their manners differ from ours, which we think the Perfection of Civility; they think the same of theirs."[42] With education and assistance, "savages" could become "civilized." In other words, with proper social engineering on the part of government, Indians could overcome their disadvantages and learn to live, dress, farm, believe, and behave like Americans.[43] Reading the words of Washington, Knox, and Jefferson as they formulated policies to dismantle Indian lands and cultures and justified those policies as serving the Indians' best interests, one cannot help but see hypocrisy, arrogance, and deceit. Certainly, Washington, Knox, and Jefferson never doubted they would take away the Indians' lands. However, they also spent much time, energy, and ink devising policies that would give Indian people something in return. The formula they developed—land for civilization—became a strategy for American expansion and a hallmark of US Indian policy for one hundred years. So did the readiness to wage war on Indians who refused the deal.

The humanitarian challenge was there from the start. Even before the Peace of Paris, the Countess of Huntingdon, a reform-minded religious leader prominent in the Methodist movement in England, tried to enlist Washington's support in helping the Indians. In 1784 she circulated to Washington and the governors of several states a proposal to send from Britain at her own expense pious Methodist men and women who would settle on the American frontier, convert Indians to Christianity, and serve as role models to help them improve their lives. Washington expressed support for the project and agreed with Lady Huntingdon that civilization must come before Christianity. "It has ever been my opinion," he wrote her, "that all attempts to reclaim, & introduce any system of religion or morality among them, would prove fruitless, until they could be first brought into a state of greater civilization; at least that this attempt should accompany the other." He forwarded the countess's proposal to Congress. Congress rejected the plan—it could only dispose of land to secure revenue, and it opposed placing on the frontier "those religious people" who had been such bitter enemies in the Revolutionary War. Nothing came of the scheme, but the humanitarian challenge remained on Washington's mind.[44] He also took the opportunity to send Lady Huntingdon a newspaper advertisement soliciting settlers for his lands on the Ohio and Kanawha Rivers.[45]

Washington and Knox worked together to develop the nation's Indian policy. Indian affairs were conducted through the Department of War rather than the Department of State (or the Department of Foreign Affairs, as it was then called), and Secretary of War Knox pressed Washington throughout the summer of 1789 to make reform of Indian policy a priority.[46] In June and July, Knox issued major statements of Indian policy, in the form of reports or memoranda to Washington. As he had before, he rejected the financial and ethical costs of going to war to acquire Indian land and argued the financial and ethical benefits of making treaties. Military operations were risky and expensive, and the nation could not afford them at present. What was more, using force would be unjust. As prior occupants, the Indians possessed rights to the soil that could only be taken from them "by their free consent, or by the right of Conquest in case of a just War." To dispossess them on any other principle would constitute a violation of natural laws and national justice. "The principle of the Indian right to lands they possess being thus conceded," Knox argued, "the dignity and interest of the nation will be advanced by making it the basis of the future administration of justice towards the Indian tribes." The United States should follow the British model of dealing with the tribes. Indians should be considered as foreign nations, not as subjects of the states; land transactions should be carried out by treaties; and treaties should be conducted, sanctioned, and honored by the federal government. Treaties would enable the United States to expand in an orderly and peaceful manner because Indians who saw their game diminish as American settlement increased would sell their hunting territories cheaply. Expansion was inevitable, but the destruction of Indian people was not, if they could be civilized and incorporated into American society. "How different would be the sensation of the philosophic mind to reflect," Knox asked rhetorically, if "instead of exterminating a part of the human race by our modes of population we had persevered through all difficulties and at last had imparted our Knowledge of cultivation and the arts to the Aboriginals of the Country, by which the source of future life and happiness had been preserved and extended."[47]

Extending the blessings of civilization to Indians would cushion their inevitable dispossession and ensure that the nation acquired their lands by commendable means. Since civilization meant farming, not hunting, Indians, of course, would need much less land. The idea that Indians would give up their lands in exchange for civilization had been suggested during the Confederation period, but under Washington it became both a fundamental component and a central justification of United States Indian policy.[48]

To symbolize these good intentions, Knox recommended following the practice, used by Britain, Spain, and France for decades, of presenting Indian chiefs with silver medals. These peace medals, as they came to be known, served as marks of distinction, badges of allegiance, and symbols of the wearer's willingness to follow the path of progress offered by the government. The first American peace medal was struck in 1789; others, with slight changes in design, were adopted during Washington's presidency (see figure 3). Washington's medals typically were large, oval, silver discs bearing an engraving. On the obverse, the president, wearing a uniform and with a sword by his side, stands at the right gesturing toward an Indian on the left who smokes a peace pipe. The Indian's tomahawk lies at his feet. In the background a man plows a field behind a team of oxen, and a house sits in the distance. The message was that Indians could attain

Figure 3 Drawing of the engraved silver medal like the one Washington presented to Red Jacket, and which Red Jacket wears in his portrait (see plate 12). The medal depicted a peaceful and prosperous future for Indian people who accepted the first president's offer of friendship and his "civilization" program.

peace and progress by giving up their weapons and their way of life. The arms of the United States are displayed on the reverse. Later medals often bore a president's head in profile on the obverse and hands clasped in friendship on the reverse. Almost every American president from Washington in 1789 to Benjamin Harrison in 1889 (the exceptions being John Adams and the short-lived William Henry Harrison) had peace medals made and presented to Indian leaders.[49]

Washington flagged the new Indian policy in a message to Congress on August 7, 1789. The government should, of course, protect its citizens from attack, but "a due regard should be extended to those Indian tribes whose happiness in the course of events so materially depends on the national justice and humanity of the United States."[50] Washington's government-controlled Indian policy—acquire land by purchase, establish and maintain clear boundaries, regulate commerce, introduce agriculture and other aspects of American civilization, and resort to just war only if and when the Indians refused such reasonable offers—would secure the nation's expansionist goals and at the same time reflect honor on the United States in the eyes of the world.

In another message to the Senate the next month, Washington addressed the status of Indian treaties. Like all other treaties and compacts made by the United States, they "should be made with caution and executed with fidelity." Nations generally did not consider any treaty negotiated by ministers or commissioners to be final and conclusive "until ratified by the sovereign or government from whom they derive their powers," he advised the Senate. The United States had adopted this practice in making treaties with European nations, "and I am inclined to think it would be adviseable to observe it in the conduct of our treaties with the Indians."[51] Consistent with the international treaty provisions outlined in the Constitution, treaties with Indian nations came to be ratified by a two-thirds majority vote in the Senate.

In the first annual presidential address to Congress—what is now the State of the Union Address—delivered in person in the Senate Chamber in Federal Hall on January 8, 1790, at the beginning of the second session, Washington assessed the nation's prospects looking forward and the challenges facing the new government. National defense was first on the list. Congress must take steps to establish the necessary armed forces, for "to be prepared for war, is one of the most effectual means of preserving peace." He had hoped that adopting "pacific measures" toward hostile tribes would have relieved the inhabitants on the southern and western frontiers from their attacks, but since that was not the case the government must be prepared to afford protection to those areas and, if necessary, punish aggressors. Wrapping up this first State of the Union Address, the president looked forward to working with Congress in "ensuring to our fellow Citizens the blessings, which they have a right to expect, from a free, efficient and equal Government."[52] High on the list of expectations for many citizens was access to Indian land. "Pacific measures" on the part of the United States depended on Indians giving up their land.

IN ADDITION TO DEALING WITH Indian nations and with foreign powers exerting their influence in Indian country, Washington had to deal with states that resented and resisted the federal government's application of its new authority in dealing with "their" Indians, and settlers who rejected the federal government's efforts to curb their land grabbing. Unbridled expansion could (as Knox fretted) depopulate eastern states, depreciate eastern land values, and sever ties between East and West in the embryonic union; western expansion must be orderly and ordered. Peace between the Indians and the frontiersmen was necessary before western lands could be surveyed, sold, and settled. Bringing order to the West, protecting its citizens against the Indians (and the British), securing access to the Mississippi, and integrating the region into the new nation were major tests of the new government and the new president.

Knox had recommended treating tribes like foreign nations, not as subjects of individual states, and he insisted that under the Constitution the United States had "the sole regulation of Indian affairs, in all matters whatsoever." Washington informed Governor Thomas Mifflin of Pennsylvania that the United States possessed "the only authority" to regulate intercourse with the Indians and redress their grievances. The administration endeavored to prohibit state governments, in Edmund Randolph's words, "from inter-medddling with the Indian tribes, to the utmost limit of the constitution," but it was an uphill battle.[53]

Washington knew that encroachments on Indian lands were the root cause of most conflicts. He placed much of the blame on squatters. Eastern elites looked askance at frontier settlers who seemed almost as savage as the Indians, and many members of government attributed to them the violence and disorder on the frontier. They shared much in common with older Indian chiefs who struggled to restrain their own warriors.[54] Whereas the federal government treated the Indians as neighbors whose rights should be respected, the French diplomat Louis Guillaume Otto explained to his minister for foreign affairs, "It is generally agreed here that the American emigrants established on the frontiers are the scum of mankind and infinitely more ferocious, more perfidious and more intractable than the savages themselves."[55] Ironically, given his own past and even present interests, Washington also blamed land speculators, who, to justify their purchases of Indian land, often denied the government's right of preemption and claimed that Indians possessed absolute title, and the right to sell their land to whomever they wished. "It will be fortunate for the American public if private Speculations in the lands, still claimed by the Aborigines, do not aggrevate those differences, which policy, humanity, and justice concur to deprecate," he wrote Jefferson.[56]

The tension between a central government seeking to impose order and groups of frontier citizens generating disorder became an enduring feature of American expansion.[57] But Washington also knew that destabilizing Indian societies advanced the national project, pushing Indian peoples to a point where they gave up their land.

Frontiersmen did much of the dirty work of expansion. The federal government deplored their actions as contrary to its declared policies but did little to stop them. Even imposing what little control it could on the frontier risked losing westerners' loyalties and votes.

Western expansion could unify the nation, but establishing the institutions necessary to carry it out risked widening existing divisions. The government had to maintain peace and protect prospective settlers from Indian raids if it hoped to generate revenue by selling western lands. That required strong government and a strong military. "The angry passions of the frontier Indians and whites are too easily inflamed by reciprocal injuries, and are too violent to be controuled by the feeble authority of the civil power," Knox warned Washington. There could be no justice or observance of treaties where every man avenged his own supposed wrongs. Only a federal army, "the sword of the Republic," could administer justice and preserve peace. Raising revenue therefore depended on raising and funding an army, and the new nation—a nation born in war—debated what kind of military force a republican government should be able to call upon.[58]

Many Americans deemed a "well-regulated militia," as the Second Amendment to the Constitution termed it, the best defense against both aggression from without and tyranny within, but Washington knew a national government required a national military. Responding to a proposal in the Constitutional Convention to limit a standing army to three thousand men, he reputedly countered with a proposal that no foreign enemy should invade the United States with more than three thousand troops.[59] Knox felt that "a small corps of well-disciplined and well-informed artillerists and engineers, and a legion for the protection of the frontiers and the magazines and arsenals" were all the military forces the United States required for the moment, and he advised Congress to reject a standing army in favor of a "well-constituted militia." However, Knox knew all too well that the nation's armed forces were inadequate if the general Indian war he feared became a reality. In the end, the federal government exercised its authority under the Constitution to raise a national army, and the states retained their own militias. In April 1790 Congress authorized a further increase in the regular army to 1,273 officers and men for a term of three years and added four more companies of infantry. Privates' pay was three dollars per month, minus one dollar for clothing and medical expenses.[60]

The new nation had to finance its military and other institutions. It fell to Alexander Hamilton, the head of the new Treasury

Department, to put the nation's finances in order and map out its future prosperity. He tackled the national debt first. The foreign debt—the amount owed to France, Spain, and Dutch bankers—amounted to $12 million; the domestic debt—the amount owed by the federal and state governments to their own citizens—was about $42 million and $25 million, respectively. Five months after taking office, Hamilton in January 1790 presented Congress with a forty-thousand-word Report on Public Credit, laying out his proposals for paying off the debt. They included the controversial plan for the federal government to fund at their full face value the promissory notes it had issued to soldiers during the Revolution and assume the war debts of the individual states. Consolidating the states' debts into a national debt would relieve states of the need to raise taxes, give investors a stake in the new government, and bind states and citizens to the national government. In May 1790, as part of his plans for centralizing public finances, Hamilton introduced to Congress a proposed tax on whiskey, the first federal tax on an American product (it was passed the following March). In December 1790 he issued a second report, outlining his plans for a national bank, modeled in part on the Bank of England that had proved an effective engine of national growth. For Hamilton and Washington, centralized financial institutions and economic policy were essential to the nation's stability and future.[61] Jefferson feared that such measures threatened the gains of the Revolution and the principles on which the Republic was founded.

Hamilton's plans threatened to divide rather than cement the new union. Many veterans had sold their promissory notes at a fraction of their face value; wealthy investors who had snapped them up at cents on the dollar stood to make a killing if Hamilton's proposal went into effect. Senator William Maclay of Pennsylvania, who saw it as a scheme "to make immense fortunes to the Speculators who have amassed vast quantities of Certificates for little or nothing," was amazed "that mankind could be so easily duped."[62] Three states—Massachusetts, Connecticut, and South Carolina—owed nearly half the total state debts and were eager for the federal government to assume those debts. Virginia, Maryland, and Georgia, on the other hand, had paid off much of their debt and were not anxious to pay federal taxes to help retire the debts of those states that had not. Congress became deadlocked on the issue until, at a dinner arranged by Jefferson, Hamilton and Madison agreed to a compromise: southern states would accept the national assumption of state debts in return for moving the capital to the Potomac after it had been at

Philadelphia for ten years. (The capital moved to Philadelphia in August 1790.)[63] Hamilton's plan to charter a national bank further divided the regions: southern agriculturalists saw no need for it and feared it was an instrument for northern merchants and speculators. After its difficult passage through Congress early the next year, Washington signed the bank bill into law.[64] Congress postponed tackling an even more divisive issue between North and South by resolving that it had no authority to interfere in the emancipation of slaves.[65] In doing so, it left southern Indian country open to invasion by cotton planters and their slaves.

It could not postpone dealing with issues that divided East and West. The national government's inability to defeat the Indians and secure free navigation of the Mississippi disgruntled western settlers; its tax on whiskey infuriated them. Distilling corn and grain into whiskey for easier transportation, sale, and bartering was an important component of western farmers' economy. The whiskey excise aggravated existing divisions that pitched East against West, city against country, mercantile against agricultural interests. Eventually, faced with a tax rebellion on the frontier, the first president would have to quell resistance among his own citizens as well as among the Indians.

The Cherokees felt the effects of the contradictions and limitations in federal Indian policy as they struggled to recover after the Revolution. Hundreds of settlers from North Carolina breached and ignored the boundaries established at the Treaty of Hopewell in 1785. General Joseph Martin warned Knox there was such "a thirst" for Cherokee lands that some people would do everything they could to prevent a treaty.[66] In May 1789 twenty-four Cherokee chiefs and warriors in council at Chota drew up a talk to send to "our elder brother General Washington, and the Great Council of the United States." They had heard that Congress now had the power to carry out its commitments, and they asked it to remember the Treaty of Hopewell, where they had given up all the land they could spare, and stop the invasion of what lands they had left. "We are neither Birds nor Fish," they said; "we can neither fly in the air nor live under the water, therefore we hope pity will be extended towards us: We are made by the same hand and in the same shape with your selves." They wanted to live in peace and friendship with the United States and asked Washington to send them an agent. "Let us have a man that dont speak with two tongues, nor one that will encourage mischief or blood to be split. Let there be a good man appointed, and war will never happen between us. Such a one we will listen to; but such as have been sent among us, we shall not hear, as they have already caused our nation to be ruined and come almost to nothing."[67]

The talk was carried north by a delegation that included their current agent, Bennett Ballew, who was the son of a white father and a Cherokee mother, and an elderly chief named Keehteetah or Keenettehet, also known as Rising Fawn. Rising Fawn found the journey too much for him; after traveling more than a hundred miles he turned back. He sent Washington a letter, signed with his mark. "Greate & Beloved Brother," he wrote, "I have thought the Day Long to See you, Since I heare So much good of you, I think you are the man that can Settle our Land in Peace." He hoped "the greate Spirit above will Put it into your hearte to Do us all the good you can."[68]

The delegation arrived in New York in mid-August, and Ballew presented the Cherokees' grievances to "the beloved President." They had hoped to live quietly on their lands within the boundary lines established at Hopewell, but as many as three thousand families had crossed the treaty lines. A few young warriors had retaliated against repeated injuries and killed one of those families, which brought dreadful vengeance down on the Cherokee people. Their cornfields were laid waste, "some of their wives & children were burnt alive in their town houses," and some of their chiefs had been killed in cold blood under a flag of truce. Tennessee militia in 1788 had murdered Corn Tassel and his son, "who were characterised by their kind offices to the white people, & veneration for the American flag, insomuch that for many years, it was constantly flying at their door."[69]

What Knox called the "disgraceful violation" of the Treaty of Hopewell demanded Washington's attention. It threatened to undermine the government's efforts to chart a just Indian policy and assert its authority over its own citizens. If the United States permitted such a blatant demonstration of contempt for its authority, it would be futile to try to extend the arm of government to the frontiers, Knox advised him. "The Indian tribes can have no faith in such imbecile promises, and the lawless whites will ridicule a Government which shall on paper only, make Indian treaties and regulate Indian boundaries."[70] Washington shared Knox's fear that the powerful tribes of the South, with as many as fourteen thousand warriors, might form a confederation against the United States. Far better to have them form a barrier against the colonies of Spain. "The fate of the southern States," he had informed the Senate in August 1789, "may principally depend on the present measures of the Union towards the southern Indians." He blamed the treaty violations entirely on disorderly white people inhabiting the frontiers of North Carolina, but since North Carolina was not yet a member of the Union (it entered in November), there was little the federal government could do for the moment.[71] Lacking the power to remove the trespassers, it could only negotiate a new boundary. Washington instructed the commissioners sent to do so to explain to the Cherokees the difficulties arising from North Carolina's claims and to assure them the United States had not forgotten the Hopewell Treaty. As soon as those difficulties were removed, the United States would do justice to the Cherokees.[72]

Washington's assurances of future justice and protection of Indian lands likely rang hollow. In May 1790, after North Carolina ceded its Tennessee Valley lands to the federal government, Congress established the Territory South of the Ohio River (the Southwest Territory). The United States became a political presence in the region, and the authority of the federal government came into direct contact with the Cherokees and Chickasaws. Many people living south of the Ohio River welcomed the assertion of federal authority in the area, but the honeymoon period was short-lived. Frontier settlers and land speculators expected the federal government to assist their economic progress and provide protection against Indian attacks. Washington and his administration needed to curtail speculation that cost the government millions of dollars in revenue, curb encroachments on tribal lands that provoked the Indian attacks, and avoid getting involved in an Indian war.[73]

Washington set foxes to guard the chicken coop. In August he appointed North Carolina commissioner William Blount as governor of the new territory; he was also appointed superintendent of Indian affairs.[74] The next month, Blount visited the president at Mount Vernon (and described him in a letter to his brother as "great and amiable," but as awesome "as a God"!)[75] Two months later Blount fretted he had not yet received any instructions on Indian affairs and feared lest the letters had fallen into the hands "of some unfriendly Land Speculator."[76] He knew how such men operated. Blount was himself a notorious land speculator who owned more than a million acres of Tennessee land. Indians called him "the dirt king." True to form, in his new office he was more interested in land than in peace.[77] He appointed fellow land speculators to territorial offices and made John Sevier brigadier general of the militia. Sevier, former governor of Franklin and future governor of Tennessee, was a well-known Indian fighter; Washington later said he "never was celebrated for any thing...except the murder of Indians."[78] Washington repeated his assurances that the federal government would respect the Treaty of Hopewell in a message to the Chickasaws in December 1790, and went so far as to declare: "The United States do not want any of your lands, if any bad people tell you otherwise they deceive you, and are your enemies and the enemies of the United States."[79] The Chickasaws must have found it difficult to put much faith in the declaration.

IN TRYING TO APPLY A COMPREHENSIVE POLICY for the whole frontier and attempting to negotiate and enforce fair treaties, Washington found himself in the same position as the Crown before the Revolution.[80] The Trade and Intercourse Act, first passed by Congress in July 1790 and subsequently strengthened, embodied Washington and Knox's principles. It also bore striking similarities to the Proclamation of 1763 that Washington had railed against, evaded, and undermined. The act stipulated that traders in Indian country must be licensed by Congress and no sales of lands by Indians "shall be valid to any person or persons, or to any state, whether having the right of pre-emption to such lands or not, unless the same shall be made and duly executed at some public treaty, held under the authority of the United States." Like the proclamation, the act sought to minimize frontier conflict by centralizing land transactions and declared invalid any land deals not approved by Congress.[81] It provided the kind of federal regulation of Indian affairs that Washington wanted.

In October 1791 Washington asked Attorney General Edmund Randolph to examine the laws of the federal government relating to Indian affairs, in particular those that provided protections for the Indians' lands, restrained states or individuals from buying them, and prohibited unauthorized trade. Randolph was also to suggest auxiliary laws to deal with any defects in the existing laws, so that the executive could enforce them. Unless the government took such measures and imposed adequate penalties to "check the spirit of speculation in lands," the nation would be constantly embroiled in conflict and "appear faithless in the eyes not only of the Indians but of the neighboring powers also." Agents of the Tennessee Yazoo Company were at that moment advertising land for settlement in the Muscle Shoals region in the great bend of the Tennessee River, despite disapproval of the Creeks and Cherokees, and probably the Choctaws and Chickasaws as well.[82] Blount and Sevier were both part of the Tennessee Yazoo Company.[83]

In his annual message to Congress, delivered on October 25, 1791, Washington laid out six basic principles that should govern United States Indian policy:

1. An "impartial dispensation of justice" toward Indians.
2. A "defined and regulated" method of purchasing Indian lands, since this was "the main source of discontent and war."
3. A regulated and fair trade.
4. "Rational experiments...for imparting to them the blessings of civilization."
5. "That the Executive of the United States should be enabled to employ the means to which the Indians have long been accustomed for uniting their immediate interests with the preservation of peace"; in other words, the president should have authority to give presents to Indians.
6. Adequate penalties should be imposed on those who infringed Indian rights, broke treaties, and thereby endangered the peace of the nation.

These principles reflected Washington's belief that following "the mild principles of religion and philanthropy" in dealing with "an unenlightened race of men, whose happiness materially depends on the conduct of the United States," was both the honorable thing to do and sound policy. The message was referred to a special committee in the House of Representatives, which reported a bill, but the legislation died without further action.[84]

In his next annual message Washington called Congress's attention to the fact that the Trade and Intercourse Act was about to expire. He recommended appointing agents to live among the Indians and urged Congress to devise a plan "for promoting civilization among the friendly tribes, and for carrying on trade with them, upon a scale equal to their wants."[85] Congress responded by passing a revised and more robust Trade and Intercourse Act in 1793 that incorporated much of Washington's six-point program. It authorized the president to appoint Indian agents and included a new clause that provided for an annual appropriation of $20,000 to be used at the president's discretion for promoting agriculture and the "civilized arts" among the tribes.[86]

Indian people differed over whether and at what rate they wanted to accept the new programs. The Moravian missionary John Heckewelder had reported in 1788 that Cornplanter, Half Town, and other Seneca chiefs said they wanted teachers, but an old Seneca got up and said "he did not need a teacher, because he was already too old to learn anything new. Such people had better keep away." An Oneida said: "If you are looking for a preacher, you had better choose a better one than we have because ours preaches what he does not practice."[87]

From colonial times, those who sought to improve Indian lives had put their faith in a Christian education. Unfortunately, young Indians placed in the white man's educational institutions commonly experienced disorientation, hardship, and sometimes tragedy.[88] The three Delaware boys who had enrolled in the College of New Jersey in 1779 were no exceptions. Placed under the care of George Morgan, who secured quarters for them, and supported by congressional funding, they each ran into trouble. The oldest, Thomas Killbuck, was homesick and became addicted, it was said, to "Liquor & to Lying." His half brother, John Killbuck, two years his junior, got one of Morgan's maids pregnant, and she gave birth to his child. Thomas and John both asked to return to their people. A congressional committee in 1785 reported they had not been attentive to their studies for some time, "but either have been wholly Idle, or Employed in some branches of Mechanic Arts, which can avail them little on their return among their Countrymen." Congress gave permission for them to go home, and John's wife and child went with him to Ohio. George Morgan White Eyes, the son of the murdered chief, who was seven or eight years old when he started school, did better. He won a prize at his grammar school commencement and described his time at the college as his "happiest moments." He lived for a time at Morgan's home, but when Morgan had to travel west on business for two or three months, he requested the Board of Treasury to assume responsibility for White Eyes, which it could not do without congressional approval. He sent White Eyes to live in New York, where he evidently neglected his studies. The Board of Treasury dragged its feet and objected to certain expenses. In June 1789, "reduced at last to the disagreeable Necessity of applying for relief," White Eyes wrote directly to Washington. He was dependent on Morgan's charity for food and clothing and complained of "cruel Usage." Better that Congress had left him in the wilds of his Native country, he said, than "to experience the heart breaking Sensations I now feel." He hoped the president might find him some kind of employment to support him. A month later, he asked Washington for assistance in returning home to see his mother and friends "as I have no other person to apply to." In August, White Eyes wrote again: "I am very sorry that the Education you have given & Views that you must have had when you took me into your Possession, & the Friendship which my Father had for the United States (which I suppose is the chief Cause) are not sufficient Inducements, to your further providing for me." Washington's private secretary, Tobias Lear, recorded charges for clothes furnished "for Geo. M. White Eyes by

direction of the President of the U. S." in September, and reimburse-
ment of those funds by the secretary of war in December. Congress
was still providing funds for White Eyes in June 1790, but he subsequently sold what belongings he had, moved to Ohio, and rejoined
the Delawares. In the winter of 1795 White Eyes was employed by
General Anthony Wayne, the commander of the American army, as
an emissary to the western tribes, and a British Indian agent reported
him "working mischief as fast as he can." According to one account
he was killed in a drunken brawl in 1798; another account includes
a George White Eyes among a group of Delawares killed by an Osage
war party in 1826.[89]

Rev. Samuel Kirkland sent Washington his plans for educating
Indians, which combined both Christian and agrarian goals.[90]
Washington gave appropriate vocal support to both, but he put his
faith in agriculture rather than in missionaries and colleges.[91] He
surely had George White Eyes in mind when he wrote that the kind
of education given "to those young Indians who have been sent to
our Colleges" was not "productive of any good to their nations" and
was even, "perhaps, productive of evil." Instead, Washington believed,
"humanity and good policy must make it the wish of every good citizen of the Unites States, that husbandry, and consequently civilization should be introduced among the Indians."[92]

In this, as in other elements of his Indian policy, Washington
appears to have been influenced by Timothy Pickering; at least the
two men agreed on the fundamentals. Pickering was a Continental
Army veteran who had settled in the Susquehanna Valley in northern Pennsylvania and served in Washington's administration as post-
master general, federal Indian commissioner, and secretary of war
after Henry Knox. "In many ways," writes the historian David
McCullough, "Pickering might have served as the model New Englander for those who disliked the type. Tall, lean, and severe-looking,
with a lantern jaw and hard blue eyes, he was a Harvard graduate...proud, opinionated, self-righteous, and utterly humorless"
(see plate 10).[93]

Like Washington, Pickering believed the federal government
needed to restrain lawless settlers and carry out settlement in an
orderly manner; like Washington, he had a personal stake in acquiring land. In line with Enlightenment thinking about human and
societal development, Pickering attributed the Indians' "savage"
state to environment and experience, not to racial characteristics:
like other peoples, Indians could achieve a level of civilization if they
learned and practiced the arts of civil life. "I cannot admit the idea,"

he told Washington, "that their minds are cast in a mould so different from that of the rest of their species as to be incapable of improvement." Vocational education was the key. Many people, perhaps most, thought that civilizing Indians was a utopian dream and pointed to those Indian youths who, after several years in school or college, returned to their own country and "again become mere savages." But it was not the Indian students that were the problem, Pickering explained; it was the kind of education they received. Harvard in the seventeenth century, and Eleazar Wheelock's school in the eighteenth century, taught Greek, Latin, Hebrew, and other classical subjects to Indian students they identified as future leaders or potential missionaries, but this was the wrong track, thought Pickering: "We spare no pains or expence to give them what is called *Learning*: but never teach them a single art by which they may get a subsistence." When they returned to their tribes, they had to eat; not knowing how to farm, they became hunters, and "being hunters, they soon become savages; and all their civil learning is lost upon them." Instead of educating Indians like the sons of men of independent fortunes, what they needed, Pickering thought, was the same education that the sons of common farmers in New England received. Teach them only reading, writing, and arithmetic, "and while they are acquiring these arts, let them *practically* learn the art of husbandry." Give each Indian student a cow, a yoke of oxen, a plow, a cart, and other necessary domestic animals and farming implements, and they would "need no other gifts; they have land in abundance, inviting the hand of Cultivation." Establishing what Pickering called "these schools of humanity" among the tribes would cost less than mounting a single campaign against them, and, as Washington himself argued, once Indians became farmers, "they will find their extensive hunting grounds unnecessary; and will then readily listen to a proposition to sell a part of them, for the purpose of procuring, for every family, domestic animals & instruments of husbandry." Like Washington, Pickering took for granted the superiority of American civilization and assumed that, given the chance, Indians would strive to attain it. Like Washington and generations of American reformers to come, he sympathized with Indians but was impatient with their refusal to see the obvious benefits of civilization and their delay in taking up the new way of life being offered them, which was their only course of survival. Like Washington, Pickering condemned the encroachment of frontier settlers on Indian lands but never questioned that the United States would expand and take those lands.[94] Of course, Washington's plans and Pickering's arguments ignored the fact that tribes like the Cherokees, Creeks, and Iroquois had been farming for centuries.[95]

The Indian policy that Washington envisioned and implemented continued with variations for more than one hundred years. Indian tribes were nations, but they were not fully independent nations like Britain and France; their sovereignty was limited by the sovereignty of the United States, and their autonomy declined as the United States grew. They would give up most of their land—voluntarily by purchase if possible, by coercion or conquest if necessary, and inevitably, as they made the transition from hunting to agriculture. There would ultimately be no room left for Indian tribes, but individual Indians could survive as farmers. They must adjust to their new circumstances by learning to live as white men.

CHAPTER 15

Courting McGillivray

T HE FIRST BIG TEST FOR WASHINGTON and Knox's new federal Indian policy came in the South, where still-powerful Indian nations resisted American expansion and exploited the rivalry between Spain and the United States. In an effort to avoid an all-out Indian war and the possibility of international conflict, the president delved into relations between the Creek confederacy and the state of Georgia, as well as Creek relations with Spain. Doing so involved asserting the authority of the national government over a state that regarded federal interference in its Indian affairs as a dangerous threat to its rights and liberty. Making the first treaty since the adoption of the Constitution forever affected how the president and Senate conducted their business under the Constitution's advice-and-consent provision. It also involved winning the allegiance of the most diplomatically astute Native leader of the age, a Scots Indian named Alexander McGillivray.

Like Washington, McGillivray was trying to build a confederation into a unified nation. The Creeks or Muskogees were a loose confederacy of fifteen to twenty thousand ethnically and linguistically diverse people living in more than fifty autonomous towns (*talwas*) and satellite towns (*talofas*). Creek homelands stretched across northern Florida, western Georgia, northern Alabama, and eastern Mississippi, a block of territory as big as a modern state.[1] By the end of the eighteenth century, the confederacy was divided into the Upper Creek towns on the Tallapoosa, Coosa, and Alabama Rivers in present-day Alabama and the Lower Creeks on the Ocmulgee, Chattahoochee, and Flint Rivers in Georgia.[2] Creeks who had migrated into northern Florida in the course of the eighteenth century developed a new identity as Seminoles and built an increasingly independent nation during the Revolutionary era.[3] Creeks generally sided with Great Britain during the Revolution, but their actual involvement was limited; no armies burned towns in Creek country as they did in Iroquois, Delaware, Shawnee, and Cherokee country, and the Creeks did not suffer significant losses. At a time when the US Army numbered in the hundreds, reports on the military strength of the southern Indian nations estimated that the Creeks could field between four and six thousand well-armed warriors, a figure, said Washington to one of his generals, that "behoves us the more to cultivate their friendship." Geographic and political realities meant that Alexander McGillivray could never, as the historian Joseph Ellis imagines, "deploy over five thousand warriors at a moment's notice," but the Creeks nonetheless represented a formidable force.[4]

McGillivray asserted himself as the "Beloved Man" or principal chief of the Creeks after the Revolution. He was a new kind of Creek, whose life and leadership reflected and promoted far-reaching changes as non-Indian traders who married Creek women, and their bicultural children, exerted increasing influence and inculcated capitalist values and practices in Creek society.[5] The son of the Scottish trader Lachlan McGillivray and Sehoy Marchand, a French-Creek woman of the powerful Wind clan among the Upper Creeks, Alexander attended school in Charleston, South Carolina, and acquired business experience in Savannah by working in the counting house of a merchant named Samuel Elbert. When the Revolution broke out, Lachlan, like many other Highland Scots in the South, remained loyal to the Crown and lost his plantation. He returned to Scotland.[6] Alexander returned to Creek country to live with his mother's people. Physically frail and chronically ill, afflicted with rheumatism, migraine headaches, alcoholism, and syphilis—a visitor to his home in 1791 said he was thirty-two but looked forty-five[7]— McGillivray had no reputation as a warrior, but his mental abilities, political savvy, and connections outweighed his military limitations. He was literate and studied Greek, Latin, English history, and literature. He also lived very differently from most Creeks: he accumulated personal wealth and property, owned slaves, managed a large plantation at Little Tallassee on the banks of the Coosa, and functioned effectively in the Atlantic market economy. The British and the Creeks recognized the value of McGillivray's education and training in colonial society and his influential connections in both societies.

During the Revolution, the British appointed him deputy superintendent of Indian affairs. He presented himself to Spain, Britain, and the United States as the leader of all the Creeks, and acted like it, although his power was more impressive in appearance than in reality.[8] He inspired mixed assessments. Colonel Arthur Campbell, a former Indian captive, Indian agent, and veteran of Virginia's Revolutionary War campaigns against the Cherokees, described him to Washington as an insolent "half-breed" who needed to be checked.[9] But Pensacola governor Arturo O'Neill (an expatriate Irishman in the service of imperial Spain) thought McGillivray had more influence among the Creeks than any other individual.[10] Washington and Knox agreed.

The Creeks had become so accustomed to being courted by rival colonial powers that it had made them "haughty" and "full of their own importance," complained one British agent.[11] They were shocked by the news of the Peace of Paris. One chief dismissed it as "a Virginia Lie." McGillivray denounced it as a shameful act of betrayal: after the Indians had answered calls for help and fought for the king, Britain had made peace for itself and divided their lands between the Spaniards and Americans. The king had no right to give up a country he never owned.[12] Britain returned Florida to Spain, but the boundary line between Spanish Florida and the new United States remained vague. Spain, the United States, Georgia, and North Carolina all claimed territory north of the 31st parallel and east of the Mississippi, as of course did the Indian nations who lived there. "The whole Continent is in Confusion," McGillivray wrote O'Neill. "Before long I expect to hear that the three kings must Settle the matter by dividing America between them."[13] The United States, Spain, and Britain all vied for control of Creek country and influence within the Creek Nation. The United States took the position that most Creeks lived on American soil, and Georgia claimed the Mississippi as its western boundary. But Spain viewed the Tennessee River as the northern limit to its territory and tried to use the tribes who lived there as buffers against its aggressive new republican neighbor.[14] Like the Ohio country in the 1750s, the American Southwest was an area many contested but none controlled.

Following Britain's withdrawal, McGillivray and the Creeks adjusted to the new international situation and charted new foreign policies. "As a free Nation we have an undoubted right to chuse what Protection we think proper," McGillivray told Esteban Miró, the Spanish governor of Louisiana, and he preferred "the protection of a great Monarch...to that of a distracted Republic."[15] Although a

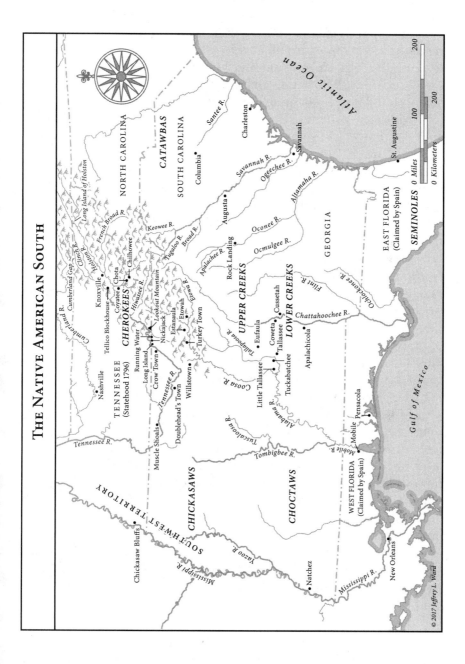

THE NATIVE AMERICAN SOUTH

Spanish alliance was preferable to an American one, McGillivray made the best of the chaotic new situation and played the field. Arthur Campbell described his tactics to Washington in August 1789. Sometimes he threatened the southern states with war; at other times he appeased them with talk of a treaty. At the present time he was working to form a league among the four southern Indian nations, with himself at their head, "that he may, with the aid of Britain, be able to bid defiance to Spain as well as the United States."[16]

Although Britain had relinquished Florida, many Loyalist refugees continued to live among the Indians, and traders and agents still promoted British interests, influence, and intercourse. Since Creek country extended to the sea, it was accessible to British traders from the West Indies.[17] When Spain took over Florida, it allowed the Loyalist Scottish merchants Panton, Leslie & Company, headquartered in the Bahamas, to stay on. Although it did not grant a formal monopoly, Spain permitted the company to sell British guns, gunpowder, goods, and cloth to help keep the Creeks and Seminoles in the Spanish interest. McGillivray issued the licenses traders needed to operate in Creek towns and oversaw the flow of valuable commodities into Creek country. He also served as a secret partner for Panton, Leslie & Company and grew wealthy as the company extended its operations from Florida to the Mississippi. Centering its business empire at Spanish Pensacola, it effectively controlled the whole southeastern trade, with trading posts and packhorse trains operating from Nassau in the Bahamas to western Tennessee.[18]

Meanwhile, Georgian frontiersmen and speculators were grabbing Creek lands in the western region of the state. Southern states needed Indian lands to repay their debts and reward their veterans after the Revolution. Georgia in 1780 passed a headright law granting every adult white male head of household who had not served Britain in the Revolutionary War 200 acres of backcountry land, with an additional 50 acres for each of his dependents. Subsequent acts gave veterans priority in obtaining headrights. The system generated confusion and overlapping land clams as speculators amassed multiple headrights by buying up the land warrants of the poor, and it ensured constant pressure on Creek land.[19] The Assembly offered land grants to veterans in the area between the Ogochee and Oconee Rivers, which it named Washington County, but the Creeks treated the Americans they found there as trespassers.[20] Creeks called Georgians *Ecunnaunuxulgee*, roughly translated as "people greedily grasping after the lands of the red people."[21] Georgia ratified the Constitution—"If a weak state with powerful tribes of Indians in its rear and the Spaniards on its flank did not incline to embrace a strong national government," it must be due to "either wickedness or insanity," Washington commented. But unlike the northern states, Georgia did not cede its western land claims to the federal government until 1802. It relied on disposal of those lands to satisfy its land-hungry citizens and settle its dues.[22]

On a personal level, McGillivray sought to avenge himself upon the United States for the financial losses that he had suffered with the confiscation of his Loyalist father's property. He also realized that the Spaniards posed less of a threat to Creek lands than did the Americans and could offer protection against Georgian frontiersmen. And the United States could not match Spain in providing trade. Congress was burdened by heavy war debts in Europe and at home, he told O'Neill; consequently, the Americans "had no trade for us, they were poor." Claiming to speak for the entire Creek Nation and playing on Spanish fears of an American invasion, McGillivray courted Spanish officials to establish a favorable relationship with the Creeks. He said the southern states were trying to win over the Creeks, which could turn the Indians from Spain's friends to dangerous neighbors, and he warned that the Americans would try to involve the Indians in plans to seize places like Mobile or Pensacola.[23]

Spanish officials responded by calling a meeting with the Creeks at Pensacola in 1784. McGillivray acted as the Creeks' principal spokesman for the negotiations. At the Treaty of Pensacola, signed on June 1, the Creeks acknowledged themselves under Spanish protection and swore to "Maintain an Inviolable Peace and fidelity" with his Catholic Majesty's provinces and subjects and with the neighboring Indian tribes. In return, King Carlos III declared his paternal love for the Creeks, and Spain promised to keep their lands secure and protect their towns that lay within Spanish territory. Spain agreed to provide the Creek Nation with a "permanent and unalterable commerce," unless prevented by war, and the Creeks agreed to exclude all traders except those holding Spanish licenses. The treaty also appointed McGillivray as the Spanish commissary for the Creeks, at a monthly salary of fifty pesos, about $600 per year, the equivalent, points out the historian Claudio Saunt, of "what a Creek hunter might have grossed over a quarter of a century." McGillivray emerged from the treaty as the key intermediary between the Creek and Spanish nations.[24]

However, many Creeks objected to McGillivray's increasing authority and affiliation with Spain. Although McGillivray presented himself as a national leader, various Creek towns and divisions did

Figure 4 John Trumbull
sketched Hoboithle Mico and
several other members of the
Creek delegation "by stealth"
during their visit to New York
in the summer of 1790.

Yale University Art Gallery.

not agree, and other *micos*, meaning "kings" or "chiefs," played different roles.[25] While McGillivray was courting the Spaniards, a dissenting faction under the leadership of Hoboithle (or Hopoithle)
Mico, also known as the Tame King, Tallassee King, or Good Child
King (see figure 4), dealt with the Americans. After Georgian representatives invited the chiefs of the Creek Nation to Augusta to make
peace, Hoboithle Mico, Eneah Mico (also called Cussitah Mico or
the Fat King), and a handful of followers turned up and, on November
1, 1783, conceded to Georgia's demand for the cession of Creek
lands between the upper waters of the Oconee River and the Ogeechee
River.[26] McGillivray called Hoboithle Mico "a roving beggar, going
wherever he thinks he can get presents"; Marinus Willett, a former
officer in the Continental Army and emissary to Creek country,
described him as "a weak man of little influence and easily perswaded
to any thing."[27] But Hoboithle Mico and Eneah Mico were peace
chiefs whose assigned role was to pursue peaceful relations with
Georgia and the Carolinas, and they likely attracted a greater following than McGillivray acknowledged.[28] McGillivray called the Augusta
Treaty unjust and absurd. He was furious that the signers had denied
his leadership and claimed it was they who spoke for the nation. He
called for a council at the Upper Creek town of Tuckabatchee to
make this minority group "give an account of themselves." Georgia
insisted that the agreement was binding on the whole Creek Nation
and proceeded to take over the ceded lands throughout 1783 and
1784.[29] Confident in the protection that he had acquired from Spain

at Pensacola, McGillivray dispatched war parties to remove the Georgians from the disputed lands.[30]

The federal government tried to offset the advantage Spain gained by the Treaty of Pensacola and to prevent the escalating clashes between Creeks and Georgians from embroiling the United States in a war from which it which it stood to gain nothing.[31] In 1785, Congress resolved to hold conventions with the southern Indians to establish boundary lines and extinguish "as far as possible all occasion for future animosity, disquiet and contention."[32] Appointed as peace commissioners were Benjamin Hawkins, a Princeton graduate and member of the Continental Congress, Lachlan McIntosh, Joseph Martin, a Virginian Revolutionary general now serving as Indian agent for North Carolina, and the South Carolina general and politician Andrew Pickens, who had fought against the Cherokees in 1760–61 and in the Revolution. In June they invited the Creek headmen and warriors to meet at Galphinton on the Ogeechee River in late October.[33]

McGillivray responded that he was pleased the United States wanted to settle affairs with the Creeks, but the effort was long overdue. He had expected the country to resolve its differences with the Indians soon after achieving independence. Whereas Georgians had assumed they had the Creeks at their mercy and "their talks to us breathed nothing but vengeance," Spain had promised to protect Creek territory and provide free trade through the Floridas. "We want nothing from you but justice." McGillivray told the commissioners. "We want our hunting grounds preserved from encroachments. They have been ours from the beginning of time, and I trust that, with the assistance of our friends, we shall be able to maintain them against every attempt that may be made to take them from us."[34] Everyone understood who he meant by "our friends." Although he said he would attend the meeting, in the end he stayed away and tried to sabotage it instead. Boycotting the Galphinton conference allowed him to demonstrate his loyalty to the Treaty of Pensacola and follow Governor O'Neill's advice not to negotiate with the Americans.[35] Delaying an agreement between the Creeks and the Americans also bought him time to see what he could get from both the Spanish and the Americans.[36] As they had at Augusta, Hoboithle Mico, Eneah Mico, and a handful of Creeks defied McGillivray's leadership and attended the Galphinton congress. To his satisfaction, however, fewer than twenty Indians traveled to meet the commissioners.[37]

McGillivray was not the only one trying to derail the conference. Georgia feared that the federal commissioners would encroach on its state rights and might negate the cession of Creek lands it had obtained at Augusta.[38] Georgia's government did everything it could to delay, and if possible prevent, the federal commissioners' meeting with the Indians.[39] It refused to provide the required funds for the negotiation, forcing the commissioners to draw on US funds.[40] State delegates circulated a rumor that the commissioners intended only to reconfirm the Augusta Treaty, which aided McGillivray's efforts to discourage Creek attendance.[41] Georgia's commissioners—Edward Telfair, William Few, and James Jackson—protested the proposed treaty as an infringement of Georgia's sovereignty and refused to agree on any terms except those for maintaining friendship. McGillivray said the quarreling between the two sets of commissioners made them look "Completely ridiculous, in the eyes of the Indians."[42] The federal commissioners finally decided that they "could not treat with so few of their nation, there being but two towns properly represented, instead of about one hundred," and departed. Georgia's commissioners remained behind and signed a treaty with the few chiefs present who claimed to speak for the whole Creek Nation. The Treaty of Galphinton confirmed the treaty made at Augusta and included a further cession of lands extending from the forks of the Ocmulgee and Oconee Rivers to the source of the St. Marys River.[43]

The Galphinton Treaty only increased hostilities on the Creek-Georgia frontier. Hoboithle Mico later told Henry Knox that only one town—Tallassee or Great Tallassee on the eastern side of the Tallapoosa River—was properly represented at the treaty; Okfuskee farther up the Tallapoosa was partially represented, and common Indians with no authority attended from three other towns. Hoboithle Mico insisted he and the other chiefs present never consented to the land cession: "I tried to scratch & destroy the paper while the man was writing but it was prevented," he said. He told the commissioners he had no right to cede the lands: they belonged to the whole nation, and the nation as a whole must decide. When the nation discussed the cession in a general meeting in June 1784, the thirty-five towns represented protested against it unanimously.[44]

McGillivray refused any responsibility for what Hoboithle Mico and Eneah Mico had done and opposed the land cessions they made.[45] "Georgians are encroaching on our hunting Lands," he wrote O'Neill in March 1786. "I have repeatedly warned them of the ill consequences of such measures, & the dangers it might bring upon them, but they do not listen to it & Still persist in their encroachments."[46] He appealed to Spanish officials for guns and ammunition to help the Creeks defend their territory.[47] He traveled to New Orleans and secured renewed commitments of support from Governor Estevan Miró. Then he held a meeting at Tuckabatchee, where Creek chiefs "drew up some very spirited resolutions" demanding that Georgians withdraw "within the natural limits of the Ogeechee River" and threatening force they did not comply.[48]

In an attempt to avoid all-out war with the Creeks, Georgia appointed commissioners to negotiate a cession of the disputed lands along the Oconee River.[49] At the Treaty of Shoulderbone Creek in November 1786, Hoboithle Mico, Eneah Mico, and their supporters once again showed up, and McGillivray as usual stayed away. Intimidated by the Georgia commissioners' strong-arm tactics, the chiefs confirmed their previous land cessions at Augusta and Galphinton, promised satisfaction for thefts and killings committed since those treaties, and marked out the cession of an additional block of land by designating the Oconee River as the Creek-Georgia boundary line.[50] In what was becoming a routine pattern, McGillivray and his followers denounced the treaty as illegitimate and condemned Hoboithle Mico and Eneah Mico as American pawns. Confident he had Spain's support, McGillivray continued to resist Georgian encroachment and defy American threats. If resorting to war to get what could not be obtained through peace efforts was the mark of savages, he wrote, then "what savages must the Americans be, and how much undeserved applause have your Cincinnatus, your Fabius obtained." He said that names like "man killer" or "the great destroyer" would be more appropriate.[51] For the Creeks, this was more than a dispute over property: "Our lands are our life and breathe [*sic*]. If we part with them, we part with our blood," declared Hallowing King of Coweta.[52] The conflict with Georgia escalated. In the list of twelve "Vices of the Political System of the United States" Madison drew up in 1787, the second was state encroachments on federal authority, such as "the wars and Treaties of Georgia with the Indians."[53] In this case, the state's actions threatened to embroil the nation in a war it could ill afford.

Spain feared the consequences of a Georgia-Creek war almost as much as Washington did, and urged McGillivray to make peace if he could. McGillivray told Governor Miró in June 1788 he did not trust the Americans, "who are a sett of crafty, cunning, republicans, who will endeavor to avail themselves of every circumstance in which I cannot speak or act with decission."[54] A year later, in June 1789, he sent warriors to Pensacola to get arms and ammunition, "as we are threatened hard by the Americans with the displeasure of their King Washington."[55] McGillivray may have been aware of the heated debate going on about whether, in a world full of monarchs, the president of the Republic should have a regal title.[56]

Washington meanwhile was learning all he could about the situation in Creek country. In July, Knox sent him a comprehensive report, accompanied by extensive correspondence, relating to the southern Indians. He explained the division between the Upper and Lower Creeks and noted that most Creek towns lay within the territory of the United States but that some of the southernmost towns of Lower Creeks or Seminoles were in Spanish territory, stretching toward the southern tip of Florida. He provided background on McGillivray—"his abilities and ambition appear to be great"—and reviewed the treaties at Augusta, Galphinton, and Shoulderbone, concluding that the cause of the war between Georgia and the Creeks was "an utter denial on the part of the Creeks of the validity of the three treaties." Congress had resolved, a year before, to notify the Creeks that if they persisted in refusing to make a treaty on "reasonable terms," the United States would send troops to protect the frontier, but Knox recommended devising other means to end the hostilities.[57] To be sure, "national dignity" demanded punishing the Creeks for their "intransigence," but, Knox informed Washington in January 1790, the armed forces of the United States consisted of one battalion of artillery, comprising 240 men, and one regiment of infantry, comprising 560 men. The army was thus "totally inadequate" for taking on the Creeks, estimated at 4,500 warriors. Knox reckoned to do so would require raising an army of 5,000 men, which would cost $1.5 million each year to maintain. In the circumstances, it seemed expedient to negotiate. Congress should authorize the president to appoint three commissioners to travel to Georgia and make a peace with the Creek Nation.[58] Washington believed that the crisis required immediate action and that the only way to resolve it was to have US commissioners negotiate an agreement with Georgia and the Creeks.[59] By inserting the federal government into the dispute, he hoped to avoid war and sever the Creeks' ties to Spain.

Speculators speculated on what it might mean for them. Writing from New York on August 8, 1789, Hugh Williamson relayed what inside information he could to his friend John Gray Blount, an avid speculator like the other Blount brothers, William and Thomas. Knox had communicated many papers on Indian affairs to Congress, Williamson reported, and the congressmen were busy reading them behind closed doors. He had it on good authority that Congress was likely to adopt Washington's recommendation and appoint treaty commissioners, in which case Blount could be sure that no more lands would be bought from the Indians. The Indians would be assured that if they abided by the terms, no whites would breach the boundary lines, no land sales would be made except to the United States, and troops would be stationed on the frontier to "equally curb the White and Red Savages." The effect would be to drive up the value of lands "fairly purchased from the Indians," and since many members of Congress had substantial landholdings that fell into this category, they would be likely to support the measure. Williamson suggested that Blount exchange the tracts he held in a region the state had not purchased from the Indians for lands nearer Nashville; that "would be a great Speculation." The lands not already purchased from the Indians were not likely to be purchased for years, "and in this private Belief was I in Carolina I would endeavor to make Exchanges accordingly."[60] In Washington's America, those in the know about Indian policy communicated what they knew to those in the Indian land business.

THE RECENTLY RATIFIED CONSTITUTION PROVIDED general guidelines on how to make a treaty. Article II gave the president "Power, by and with the Advice and Consent of the Senate, to make Treaties, provided two thirds of the Senators present concur." Article IV declared all treaties made under the authority of the United States to "be the supreme Law of the Land; and the Judges in every State shall be bound thereby, any Thing in the Constitution or Laws of any State to the Contrary notwithstanding." But the Constitution remained silent on the specifics about how treaties were to be carried out with the Indians. Two principal questions arose: How exactly did the Senate "advise and consent," and were treaty agreements with Indian nations to "follow regular treaty procedures?"[61] The negotiations with the Creeks would provide the answers.

Congress debated the appropriate amount and then voted funding for the treaty commissioners and for carrying out the negotiations with the Creeks. The House Speaker signed the bill; it was sent to the Senate for Vice President John Adams's signature on August 20, 1789, and the president signed it the same day.[62] Washington also took seriously the stipulation that the president should act with the advice and consent of the Senate. He was conscious of the need to establish proper protocol and thought oral communication was essential because discussing the issues in writing "would be tedious without being satisfactory." Consequently, he informed the

Senate on August 21 that he would appear in person in the Senate Chamber the next morning at eleven thirty "to advise with them" on the terms of the treaty to be negotiated with the Creeks.[63]

There was a lot riding on it. Since the southern tribes could raise so many warriors, attaching them to the United States was "highly worthy of the serious attention of Government," Washington explained to the Senate. The goal was not only to secure peace on the frontier but also to create a buffer against the colonies of a European power, "which, in the mutations of policy may one day become the enemy of the United States." The fate of the southern states might well depend on making an alliance with the southern Indians. Unsure about what instructions the treaty commissioners should receive, Washington and Knox prepared a series of questions for the Senate to consider. The first two questions regarded the Cherokees, Choctaws, and Chickasaws and were dealt with quickly. The rest dealt with the Creeks in "a series of either/or proposals for the Senate's judgment." If the commissioners found that the Creek Nation had been fully represented at the three Georgia treaties and the treaties were "just and equitable," should they insist on formal renewal and confirmation of those treaties? If the Creeks refused, should the commissioners tell them military force would be employed to compel them? How should the commissioners attempt to obtain a cession of the lands if they judged that the three treaties had been made without adequate representation or under coercion? Considering the importance of the Oconee lands to Georgia and of a Creek allegiance to the United States, what should the commissioners do if the Creeks refused all offers to cede the lands in question— issue an ultimatum or make a new treaty that included the disputed lands within the boundaries assigned to the Creeks? Finally, Washington inquired if the $20,000 appropriated for treaties could, if necessary, be applied entirely to a treaty with the Creeks.[64] On Saturday, August 22, Washington and Knox walked in person to the Senate Chamber armed with their questions.[65]

It did not go well. Washington may have anticipated a formality; instead he got a fiasco. John Adams was Washington's vice president, but he was also ex officio president of the Senate. No one knew exactly what the proper protocol was, what forms of address should be employed, or how to act when the president of the United States came to the Senate. An awkward scene ensued, recorded in the journal kept by William Maclay. Maclay had served in Forbes's campaign in 1758 and in Bouquet's command at Bushy Run in 1763, and was one of Pennsylvania's representatives at the Treaty of Fort Stanwix in

1784. He was now a senator from Pennsylvania and a caustic critic of Adams, Washington, Hamilton, and the new Constitution. (He described Washington sarcastically as "the greatest Man in the World" and suggested that Hamilton used the president's renown to silence criticisms of his own dirty dealing).[66] When Washington entered the chamber, he took Adams's chair, and Knox sat beside him, facing the Senate. Adams joined the other senators. Knox handed Washington a document, which Washington handed to Adams. Adams proceeded to read it aloud, but his voice was drowned out by carriages passing in the street outside. "Such a noise!" wrote Maclay. "I could tell it was something about Indians, but was not master of one sentence of it." Robert Morris, the other senator from Pennsylvania, said the traffic noise was so great he had not heard the bulk of the paper, and asked for it to be read again. They closed the windows. Adams reread the document and asked the Senate, "Do you advise and consent?" There was a "dead pause," said Maclay. When Maclay asked to see supporting documents, Washington gave a look of "stern displeasure." Maclay and Morris suggested the matter be submitted to a committee to review the materials: "I saw no chance of a fair investigation of subjects while the President of the United States sat there, with his Secretary of War, to support his opinions and overawe the timid and neutral part of the Senate," Maclay wrote. This prompted a debate on the meaning of "advise and consent" and about doing business by committee. Adams tried in vain to move things along and get the Senate to consent, but they were awash in procedural difficulties. *"This defeats every purpose of my coming here!"* exclaimed Washington in exasperation—or what Maclay called a "violent fret." After he had cooled down, he agreed to put things off until Monday, and the discussion was postponed. When Washington returned two days later he was "placid and serene," and the matter was concluded, but, he was overheard to say, he would "be damned if he ever went there again" to request Senate approval on Indian treaty business.[67]

No president since has gone to the Senate Chamber to seek either advice or consent on a treaty. Washington reasoned that the Constitution subjected the final treaty, not treaty-making itself, to the advice and consent of the Senate; it assigned initiating, negotiating, and drawing up the terms of the treaty to the president alone. Appearing in person before the Senate, said Washington, put the president of the United States in the awkward situation of being subordinate to his own vice president as president of the Senate. Maclay thought the president wanted the Senate simply to rubber-stamp his actions. In future, the president initiated treaties and nominated appointments first and then requested the Senate's consent (not advice) on paper, not in person. The president would appear in the Capitol only at joint sessions of Congress and at the president's choice of time and place. Instead of developing a consultative partnership with the Senate, Washington increasingly turned to his department heads, and the cabinet emerged as the president's de facto council and sounding board. By limiting the advise-and-consent provision of the Constitution, Washington helped establish the power of the president to act in foreign affairs *before* seeking input from the legislative body and to set foreign policy. A mishandled meeting over the terms of an Indian treaty, writes Ron Chernow, "may have done more to define the presidency and the conduct of American foreign policy than an entire bookshelf of Supreme Court decisions on the separation of powers."[68]

After the debacle in the Senate, the president turned his attention to the Creeks. Even before Washington actually took the oath of office, American commissioners had sent them an invitation to a conference at Rock Landing on the Oconee River to resolve their land disputes with Georgia. Things would be different now that all Americans were governed by a president, "like the old King over the great water," they promised: "He will have regard to the welfare of all the Indians; and, when peace shall be established, he will be your father and you will be his children, so that none shall dare to do you harm."[69] The commissioners overestimated Washington's authority over his citizens and the Creeks' willingness to be anyone's children.

As treaty commissioners at Rock Landing, Washington appointed Revolutionary general Benjamin Lincoln; Cyrus Griffin of Virginia, who had been the last president of the Continental Congress; and David Humphreys, who had been Washington's aide-de-camp during the Revolution and later aspired to write his biography. It was, he impressed on them, "an object of high national importance" to be at peace with the Indian nations of the South and win them over "by a just and liberal system of policy." The commissioners were to ascertain whether the chiefs who had signed the treaties at Augusta, Galphinton, and Shoulderbone represented all the Creeks; whether coercion or subterfuge had been employed; and, accordingly, whether the cessions of territory between the Ogechee and Ocmulgee Rivers were binding. Given the hostilities that had ensued from those contested treaties, Washington insisted that in this treaty the whole nation "must be fully represented and solemnly acknowledged to be so by the Creeks themselves." The commissioners were to make clear that the United States did not want the Creeks' lands, only to be

their friends and protectors and treat them with justice and humanity. But since the disputed lands had already been opened to settlers,
it would be "highly embarrassing" to return them. To get the Creeks
to accept the cession, he advised offering them a safe port through
which their trade would flow and offering the leaders gifts, bribes,
and military titles. He also urged them to win the allegiance of
McGillivray.[70]

Once they arrived at Savannah, the commissioners sent messages to the Cherokees, Choctaws, and Chickasaws, telling them that
the United States was strong and "our great warrior, General Washington," was now "the head-man of all our councils, and the chief of
all our warriors." Washington wanted the Indians to know "that the
United States regard the red men with the same favorable eye that
they do the white men, and that justice shall always be maintained
equally between them."[71] The commissioners sent notices announcing their mission to McGillivray and to Georgia governor George
Walton. Americans knew that no treaty with the Creeks would hold
without McGillivray.[72]

On September 20 the commissioners arrived at Rock Landing.
Hoboithle Mico, Eneah Mico (Cussetah King), and Hallowing King
came to see them and expressed their hopes for a lasting peace. They
smoked "the pipe of friendship" with the commissioners and brushed
their faces "with the white [eagle's] wing of reconciliation in sign of
their sincere intention to wipe away past grievances."[73] McGillivray
sent the commissioners a note insisting that he meet with them in
private before the treaty opened.[74] When he arrived he had an entou-
rage of nine hundred warriors. It was a demonstration of the power
that McGillivray believed had forced the government to negotiate.
The Americans had "fondly thought that they could Seize with
Impunity every foot of Territory belonging to the Red Natives of
America," he told Miró. Now "these haughty republicans" had sent
commissioners "to bend & Sue for peace from the people whom they
had despised & marked out for destructing."[75]

The next day McGillivray dined with the commissioners. He
impressed Humphreys with his ability to hold his liquor. The commissioners drew up a draft of the proposed treaty and, after participating in the black drink ceremony with the Creeks, presented the
treaty and repeated their assurances that Washington, "who led our
armies to conquest wherever he turned his face," was determined to
see justice done to the Indian nations. "You know him," the commissioners said, "and he never speaks the thing which is not." The chiefs
met in council late into the night. Then McGillivray informed the

commissioners they had some objections, principally regarding the boundary.[76] As he explained to William Panton, the treaty terms assumed the sovereignty of the United States over the Creeks, left the contested lands between the Oconee and Ogeechee in Georgia's possession, and prohibited the Creeks from making treaties with any other nation or state, which would require them to terminate their treaty with Spain. Humphreys tried to ease McGillivray's concerns and argued that the disputed lands had been ceded to Georgia in an earlier treaty, but his "arts of flattery, ambition and intimidation were exhausted in vain." Humphreys was a man with few insights into his own limitations, and McGillivray dismissed him as a "puppy" and "a great boaster." After informing Humphries, "By G—— I would not have such a Treaty cram'd down my throat," McGillivray brought the meeting to an abrupt halt by decamping with his followers and heading for home.[77] William Irvine told Madison that Humphreys personally offended McGillivray, who, after hearing what the commissioners had to say, "observed it was the old story" and "went off in wrath."[78]

"The Parties have separated without forming a Treaty," the commissioners reported to Knox the next day. In their view McGillivray was entirely to blame.[79] The United States could never depend on McGillivray, Humphreys told Washington; ego and financial gain dictated his conduct. The commissioners agreed that the boundary issue was secondary; McGillivray's main objective was to see if he could get better terms from Spain than from the United States.[80] McGillivray had "the good sense of an American, the shrewdness of a Scotchman, & the cunning of an Indian," Humphreys told Washington. Humphreys did not think much of McGillivray: he was "so much addicted to debauchery that he will not live four years," he said; he dressed "altogether in the Indian fashion," and he was "rather slovenly." Nevertheless, he acknowledged that McGillivray's influence was "probably as great as we have understood it was" and that he could be very useful to the United States, "if he can be sincerely attached to our Interests."[81]

Although the negotiations broke up without a formal treaty, the Creeks sent Washington a white eagle-tail fan as a symbol of peace, which Benjamin Lincoln presented to him after he returned to New York on November 10.[82] The commissioners lodged their official report with Knox on the seventeenth, with further observations on the Creek situation on the twentieth, and Washington received it on the afternoon of the twenty-first. He gave it a quick reading, promising (in his diary) to read it again, with more attention, later. The next day, a Sunday, he spent the evening in close conversation with the commissioners about the negotiations and "their opinion with respect to the real views of Mr. McGillivry." He recorded their views in his diary:

> The principles of [his] conduct they think is self-Interest, and a dependence for support on Spain. They think also, that having possessed himself of the outlines of the terms he could Treat with the United States upon, he wished to Postpone the Treaty to see if he could not obtain better from Spain. They think that, though he does not want abilities, he has credit to the full extent of them and that he is but a short sighted politician. He acknowledges however, that an Alliance between the Creek Nation & the United States is the most Natural one, & what they ought to prefer if to be obtained on equal terms. A Free port in the latter seems to be a favourite object with him.[83]

In his "Memoranda on Indian Affairs," Washington noted the reasons McGillivray gave for walking away from the peace talks; from his conversations with Humphreys he had expected full justice and restoration of the contested Oconee hunting grounds, but finding there was no such provision in the treaty, he had resolved to return home and defer making peace until the next spring. The Creeks "sincerely desire a Peace, but cannot sacrafice much to obtain it," he said. Washington also made a note of the "Influential Characters" among the Creeks, placing McGillivray first among the Upper Creeks, followed by the White Lieutenant of Okfuskee and Mad Dog (Efau Hadjo) of Tuckabatchee; among the Lower Creeks, Hallowing King (commanding the war towns) and Cussetah King or Eneah Mico (commanding the peace towns), along with Tallassee King (Hoboithle Mico), Tall King, White Bird King (Fusatchee Mico), the king of the Seminoles, and the king of the Euchees, merited attention. The leader of the American nation needed to know who the leaders of the Creek Nation were.[84]

Clearly intrigued by McGillivray, Washington was not ready to give up. The crisis of affairs with the Creeks required the United States to try "every honorable and probable expedient...to avert a War with that tribe," Knox advised him in February 1790.[85] Three weeks later, Washington wrote Knox, expressing his approval for bringing McGillivray to New York as a way of avoiding that war.[86] "The President, who does not change his principles easily, wants to try the medium of negotiations a second time," Louis Guillaume Otto, secretary of the French legation in the United States, reported to the French minister of foreign affairs; "and if he succeeds in getting some savage plenipotentiaries to come here, he is too adroit to let them leave without having obtained and signed a permanent peace."[87]

Washington sent as his special emissary to McGillivray Colonel Marinus Willett, a very different character from Humphreys. Willett's mission, Washington noted in his diary, "was not to have the appearance of a Governmental act." Willett carried with him a passport Washington had authorized guaranteeing safe conduct to "such of the Chiefs of the Creek Nation as may desire to repair to the seat of the General Government on the business of their Nation," and a letter of introduction from former commissioner and now US senator Benjamin Hawkins of North Carolina. Hawkins introduced Willett as an honorable gentleman with whom McGillivray could talk openly, rebuked the Creek leader for refusing to treat with the United States when he had been solemnly invited to settle the disputes "on terms of mutual advantage," and urged him to consider going to New York to make peace.[88] Willett assured McGillivray that Washington did not desire Creek lands and would respect the tribe's claims. A treaty made at New York would be "as strong as the hills and lasting as the rivers," he said.[89]

McGillivray, like Washington, was not ready to give up on peace. A treaty with the United States might bolster his resistance against Georgia and increase his bargaining power with Spain. Like the federal government, he was concerned by the activities of the Yazoo speculators. Georgia's original charter had located the colony's western border at the Mississippi, and in December 1789 the Georgia legislature, most of whose members were shareholders in the speculation, announced the sale of more than 20 million acres in the region of the Yazoo River, an area in present-day Alabama, Mississippi, and Tennessee disputed by Spain and the United States, to three out-of-state land companies in Virginia, Tennessee, and South Carolina, collectively called the Yazoo Companies, at a cost of roughly four-fifths of a cent per acre. Washington and his government opposed the brazen scheme, maintaining that Georgia should cede its rights and that the national government rather than the state government should dispose of the Yazoo lands. What was more, the lands were still occupied by Indians, and Indian land could only be acquired by war or treaty. The Constitution—which Georgia had ratified—granted both powers to the federal government. McGillivray and Washington shared a common interest in blocking a scheme that threatened Creek territory and federal authority.[90]

McGillivray also had to rethink his position as the controller of Indian trade. In 1788 the Spanish had temporarily curtailed Indian trade goods, rendering McGillivray's connection with Panton, Leslie & Company less lucrative. In 1790 the looming threat of war between

Britain and Spain over Nootka Sound in the Pacific Northwest—where vessels from both nations competed for the sea-otter trade with the coastal Indians before sailing across the Pacific to China and exchanging the pelts for tea, silk, and spices—rendered Creek reliance on Spain, and the trading status of Panton, Leslie & Company, even more precarious. It also presented Washington with a potential foreign policy crisis if the nations went to war in the American hemisphere. Meanwhile, William Augustus Bowles, a former Loyalist from Maryland living in Creek country, presented himself as McGillivray's rival as leader of the Creek Nation and took advantage of the disruption in commerce to insert himself and his merchant backers in the Bahamas as competitors with Panton and Leslie.[91] In the circumstances, turning to the United States offered the Creeks an alternative supply of manufactured goods and offered McGillivray the opportunity to control it. Of course, McGillivray knew that bribery was common in treaty negotiations and that he could expect to return from New York an even wealthier man.[92]

A Creek delegation had traveled to London, the imperial capital, in the 1730s. Now McGillivray decided to lead a delegation to the American capital. He sent runners summoning Creek chiefs to council to hear Willett, who declared that a treaty "ratified with the signature of Washington and McGillivray would be the bond of Long Peace and revered by Americans to a very distant period." McGillivray told William Panton he did not hesitate to accept the invitation.[93] Panton and Miró attempted to stop him, but by the time they heard of it, McGillivray had already left for New York. The United States wanted to reject the Georgia land grants because it wanted those lands itself, Panton said; "their pretension to Justice and humanity is all a bubble and it is obvious to me that McGillivray will find it so before he returns."[94]

McGillivray was no fool. He knew that "all the eagerness which Washington shows to treat with me on such liberal terms is not based...on principles of Justice and humanity."[95] As he departed from Little Tallassee at the beginning of June, McGillivray wrote Miró explaining his reasons for wanting to make "a good Peace," as Spain had encouraged. At the same time, he suggested his journey could serve Spanish interests: "Tho I do not pretend to the ability of a Machiavel in Politics, Yet I can find out from my Slender abilities pretty near the disposition of the American Politics so far as they respect the Spanish Nation, & Your Excellency may depend on receiving a faithful account of every matter whenever I may return."[96]

He set off with Willett, a nephew and two servants, and eight Upper Creek warriors.[97] More chiefs joined them at Stone Mountain, and Hoboithle Mico joined them at General Pickens's plantation in mid-June. Willet had originally planned to sail to New York by ship, but the Creeks claimed a "mortal aversion" to water so the group traveled overland.[98] McGillivray rode on horseback at the head of the procession or with Willett in a carriage, and twenty-six chiefs and warriors followed in three wagons.[99] Washington had Knox ask the governors of Virginia, Maryland, and Pennsylvania to furnish the Creek delegates "with whatever might be deemed a proper respect that they might be kept in good humour."[100] William Blount, hearing of McGillivray's journey north, saw it as evidence of a retreat after having rebuffed the federal treaty commissioners the previous fall: he was now traveling to Congress to supplicate for the same terms they had offered him on his own soil. "He is I suppose like most other great Men," Blount mused; "if so the more he is seen the less he is admired."[101]

The Creeks' progress took on the appearance of a state visit. They attracted large crowds, and McGillivray was welcomed by prominent citizens and civic leaders in the towns they passed through. At Guildford Courthouse in North Carolina, a woman broke from the spectators and approached McGillivray, who recognized her as a former captive he had freed. They embraced in a tearful reunion, which Willett described as "truly affecting." In Virginia, the Creeks dined with dignitaries, including Governor Beverley Randolph, at Richmond and attended a theater performance at Fredericksburg. Willett and McGillivray were shown Washington's birthplace. More public dinners and theatrics followed in Philadelphia. Americans drank toasts to "the Creek Washington."[102] Although he no doubt appreciated all the attention, McGillivray found the trip "tedious & fatiguing," in part owing to a "Violent indisposition" that seized him along the way.[103]

Finally, on July 21, 1790, the delegation ferried across the Hudson River into New York. McGillivray, who reports said looked "like a white man," and his followers, who were "adorned with feathers, beads, earrings, and silver gorgets," disembarked to church bells, cheering crowds, and a salvo of cannon fire.[104] Officers and members of New York City's Tammany Society, wearing what they imagined to be Indian costume and carrying bows, arrows, and tomahawks, escorted the Creeks up Wall Street to Federal Hall, where Congress was in session, then to Washington's house, and finally to the City Tavern on Broadway, where Knox and Governor Clinton hosted them at dinner. The society members were doing more than simply welcoming the visitors; in the early Republic such appropriation and parodying of Native practices constituted a public declaration of an emergent national identity that laid claim to an aboriginal American identity, incorporated "noble" Indian traits such as courage and freedom, and distinguished Americans from Europeans; it could also be seen as a declaration that Americans had replaced, or were replacing, Indians as rulers of the land.[105] It was the biggest celebration since Washington's inauguration. "We hope good from this visit," wrote Jefferson.[106]

Still weak from the pneumonia that had almost killed him in the spring, Washington left most of the negotiations to Knox. McGillivray, who was also unwell, lodged at Knox's home—perhaps so the secretary of war could keep a close eye on him—while the rest of the delegation roomed at the Indian Queen Hotel and outside the city at Richmond Hill in Greenwich Village. Writing to her sister, Abigail Adams said that "my Neighbours the Creek savages" were lodged nearby. "They are very fond of visiting us as we entertain them kindly, and they behave with much civility." They were the first Indians she had seen, and she thought them "very fine looking Men." After dinner one of the chiefs conferred an Indian name on her, the meaning of which she did not understand. Dressed in European clothing and light skinned, McGillivray spoke English "like a Native." He impressed Abigail as "grave and solid, intelligent and much of a Gentleman, but in very bad Health."[107]

The events attracted international attention. Spain and Great Britain watched from the wings. Carlos Howard, one of a number of Irish officers who entered Spanish imperial service and who was now secretary to the governor of East Florida, was dispatched to join José Ignacio de Viar, the Spanish agent in New York. Howard contacted McGillivray as the chief made his way from Philadelphia, offering his own and Viar's services and "to clarify any ambiguities" he might have about Spanish policy.[108] He reminded McGillivray of their joint opposition to the Americans, their trade agreements, and the Pensacola treaty. Howard said US officials did not leave McGillivray alone for a minute and "also appointed people to watch and follow my footsteps."[109] Yet he still managed to communicate with McGillivray throughout the negotiations, reminding him that Spain had always wanted the Indians to be at peace with the Americans—just not at Creek or Spanish expense.[110]

The British, too, kept a careful eye on the negotiations. If the Nootka Crisis erupted into open war, alliance with the Creeks would offer Britain an opportunity to seize Spanish-held territory in Florida and Louisiana. The British government assigned an agent, George

Beckwith, to discover the exact terms of any treaty and gain McGillivray's confidence.[111] Beckwith enjoyed a close relationship with Alexander Hamilton and so had greater access to the treaty talks than did his Spanish counterparts. Beckwith thought McGillivray was "a man of talents and ambition"; he thought Washington's talents were greatly overrated.[112]

The Treaty of New York was the first US-Indian treaty negotiation held outside of Indian country. The Creeks were in the city for more than three weeks. They attended endless meetings, informal conferences, and dinners, and they saw the sights. McGillivray did most of the talking, and his negotiations would have been conducted in English. "He had more conversation with General Washington, and his great men, than we," White Bird King recalled later. One critic suggested that the treaty was "patched up" in Knox's "closet."[113]

On one occasion, Washington took the principal chiefs into the room where the artist John Trumbull had recently completed the president's portrait. According to Trumbull, "when the door was thrown open, they started at seeing another 'Great Father' standing in the room" and approached the portrait with wonder and astonishment. Whether or not the other chiefs were as openmouthed as Trumbull described, McGillivray would not have been overawed. Before they left New York, Trumbull surreptitiously sketched portraits of several of the Creeks.[114]

On August 4, 1790, Washington notified the Senate the treaty negotiations were "far advanced." The Creeks would agree to cede to Georgia the lands east of the Oconee River, hand over all captives, and acknowledge the sovereignty of the United States. In return the United States would give back the lands south of the Altamaha River. Knox "readily concurred" with the Creeks that the three treaties signed with Georgia at Augusta, Galphinton, and Shoulderbone were fraudulent and invalid.[115] Only weeks after Congress passed the Indian Trade and Intercourse Act, regulating commerce with the tribes, Washington asked the Senate to approve a secret article authorizing duty-free passage of Creek trade goods through American ports in the event that the tribe's regular channels of trade became obstructed. "As the trade of the Indians is a main means of their political management," he explained, "the United States cannot possess any security for the performance of treaties with the Creeks, while their trade is liable to be interrupted or withheld, at the caprice of two foreign powers." The Senate immediately gave its consent. With this agreement, McGillivray achieved his main goal in coming to New York. And since it was understood that Washington's government would allow no merchant to do business in Creek country without McGillivray's approval, the arrangement effectively gave McGillivray a monopoly on the trade.[116]

During the negotiations, McGillivray expressed his willingness to see the Creeks become "cultivators and herdsmen instead of Hunters." Knox responded that the government would "cheerfully concur in so laudable design." The government further agreed to educate and clothe up to four Creek youths at any one time.[117]

On August 7 the articles of the treaty were read. The treaty document opened by announcing perpetual peace and friendship between the two peoples, and the Creeks acknowledged themselves to be under the protection of the United States "and of no other sovereign whosoever," meaning Spain in particular. It contained routine provisions, such as prisoner exchange, punishment of crimes under American law, return of property, protection of Indian hunting grounds, and placing American interpreters among the Indians. Article 12 stipulated that the United States would from time to time furnish the Creeks with domestic animals and farm implements in order to elevate them "to a greater degree of civilization."[118] The Creeks had the right to expel white trespassers on their land, but the eastern boundary of Creek country was set at the Oconee River; in other words, McGillivray gave up the lands between the Ogeechee and the Oconee that he had refused to part with at Rock Landing.

Presumably the secret articles helped him change his mind. In addition to the provision for a trade monopoly, the secret articles gave McGillivray a commission as brigadier general with an annual salary of $1,200, more than the stipend he received from Spain. Lesser Creek chiefs would receive smaller amounts. The public treaty was written on three sheets of parchment stitched together and with seals affixed at the bottom. Knox signed for the United States. McGillivray signed first, and twenty-three other chiefs made their marks according to their towns. Eight other people signed as witnesses.[119] Only McGillivray signed the secret articles.[120] A few days later he sent Carlos Howard "an exact compendium" of his negotiations and the terms of the treaty, insisting on the purity of his motives, and claiming he had resisted accepting the honorary commission as brigadier general as long as he decently could.[121]

Washington presented the treaty to the Senate the same day Knox and McGillivray signed it. "While I flatter myself that this treaty will be productive of present peace and prosperity to our southern frontier," he told the senators, "it is to be expected that it will also in its consequences be the means of firmly attaching the Creeks and the neighboring tribes to the interests of the United States." There was cause for concern, however: the Creeks ceded to Georgia the disputed land on the Oconee River but retained hunting rights southwest of the junction of the Ocmulgee and Oconeee, and Georgia claimed a tract of land between the Ocmulgee/Oconee junction and the St. Marys River to the south, which the Creeks said constituted "some of their most valuable hunting ground" and "absolutely refuse[d] to yield."[122]

It was the first treaty made under the Constitution. The Senate ratified it by a vote of 15–4 on August 12. Washington and Jefferson signed it the next day in a formal ceremony held in the House Chamber at Federal Hall. Everyone present, including the Spanish and British representatives in the large audience, were aware of the treaty's public provisions, but it's not clear exactly who knew about the secret clauses.[123]

The ceremony was the federal government's last official function in Federal Hall. It caused quite a stir. The galleries were filled with people curious to see and anxious to be seen. The cabinet members, officers of government, members of Congress, and ambassadors of foreign courts whom Jefferson had invited were seated "according to their rank." After Martha and other members of the president's family took their seats, McGillivray led the Creeks in singing a song of peace. McGillivray wore a brigadier general's uniform; the others wore colonels' uniforms in blue faced with red, headscarves ornamented with feathers and wreaths, face paint, earrings, and nose jewelry. Washington appeared, wearing "Vestments of rich purple satin," and "a reverential silence" descended. With all eyes on him, he ascended to his chair, and his secretary, Tobias Lear, read the articles of the treaty. Then the president rose from his seat and delivered a formal address to the assembled citizens and Creek chiefs. With an interpreter translating and the Creeks voicing their approval at the end of each sentence, Washington declared the treaty just and equal and stated the mutual obligations of the contracting parties. He called on the Creeks to do all they could to conciliate their people and wipe away animosities, "and he supplicated the great spirit, the Master of breath, to forbid an infringement of a Contract, formed under such happy auspices." Then the formal signing took place. Washington presented McGillivray with tokens of peace: a string of beads and a paper of tobacco for the calumet pipe of friendship. McGillivray gave a short speech and wampum in return. The Creeks advanced one by one, clasped the president's right arm, and sang a second song of peace, thereby concluding "this affecting, important, and dignified transaction." The president invited the attendees to take punch at his house, and later there was "a grand dinner" for the Indians, which four Kahnawakes who were in New York seeking compensation for their services during the Revolution also attended. National songs and dances ended the celebrations. One eyewitness, who described the events for her parents the next day, felt she had been a spectator at a scene which "succeeding Centuries may not repeat."[124]

The president proclaimed the treaty the next day, and it was quickly published and circulated in the nation's newspapers.[125] Both sides appeared pleased with the finished product. The United States had avoided an Indian war, established peace with the most powerful Indian nation in the South, secured space for Georgia settlers on Creek land, and enhanced the standing of the national government over the state. Knox claimed the treaty was "new and honorable evidence of the vigilance and wisdom of the executive of the U.S."[126] McGillivray told Representative William Smith of South Carolina at dinner that ever since he took over leadership of his nation, his life had been taken up with war or preparation for war, and he could now "anticipate with pleasure the tranquil enjoyments of peace." Smith thought he could not be in better hands than Washington and Knox, "who vie with each other in acts of friendship."[127] McGillivray said later that he had "been obliged to give up something in order to secure the rest."[128] The "something" was the land between the Oconee and the Ogeechee; the "rest" included American recognition of his "office as head chief of the Creeks," an annual stipend, the promise of a free port, and guaranteed continuance of his monopoly on trade. He also secured American promises to protect Creek territory against further encroachments. When the Creek delegates returned home and told what they had seen and done, one town commemorated the treaty by taking a new name: Nuyakv, pronounced "nu-yaw-kah," which is what the delegates heard when the residents of the city said "New Yorker." According to the author and Indian rights advocate Suzan Shown Harjo, whose ancestors lived in the town, the delegates to the New York Treaty were "the founding fathers of Nuyakv."[129]

Washington wrote to Lafayette with the news of the treaty before the Creek chiefs left town. "This event will leave us in peace from one end of our borders to the other, except where it may be interrupted by a small refugee banditti of Cherokees and Shawnee, who can be easily chastised or even extirpated if it shall become necessary." Such action would only be applied in extreme circumstances "since the *basis* of our proceedings with the Indian Nations has been, and shall be *justice,* during the period in which I may have anything to do in the administration of this government."[130] The letter conveyed the twin elements of Washington's Indian policy: peace and justice if possible, extermination if necessary.

DESPITE THE MUTUAL SATISFACTION of the parties who made it, the treaty failed to become, in Knox's words, "the instrument of our future peace and happiness."[131] Those who were left out of the negotiations protested.[132] The Oconee River boundary was farther west than Creeks wanted and farther east than Georgians wanted.[133] Georgians resented the celebrity status accorded to McGillivray in New York and denounced the treaty as illegitimate, an act of betrayal by the federal government. Exercising powers far beyond what the new constitution allowed and in a clear breach of their state's rights, the government had taken the Creeks' side in the controversy and, by not including the cessions made at Galphinton and Shoulderbone, handed back more than 3 million acres of land that rightfully belonged to Georgia. "The Indians to the South are to be treated with humanity, and those to the North are to be butchered, that the United States may enjoy their property," a Georgia congressman declared, bluntly pointing out the sectional differences in Washington's Indian policy.[134] And the government's promise of agricultural instruction suggested that the Creeks, rather than giving up rich farming lands that Georgians coveted, would, literally, be putting down more roots. Georgians continued to encroach into Creek territory in open defiance of the treaty. Washington described those Georgians dissatisfied with the treaty as "Land Jobbers, who, Maugre [despite] every principle of Justice to the Indians & policy to their Country would, for their own immediate emolument, strip the Indns. of all their territory if they could obtain the least countenance to the measure."[135] Although he did not see it, he could have been describing himself twenty years earlier.

Lacking the military and financial resources to exert the dominance it claimed over the southern Indian nations, the United States had to keep peace with them. Washington recognized that the Creek treaty was only a foundation for peace and that the United States must fulfill its treaties with other tribes in the area—namely, the Treaty of Hopewell with the Cherokees, Choctaws, and Chickasaws, which, he told the Senate, frontier settlers "had openly violated."[136] During the negotiations in New York, McGillivray had "protested strongly against the behavior of the new western companies, in the terms in which Georgia has formed them," and said he had "the word of the government that said companies will be broken up." The Trade and Intercourse Act passed that July prohibited purchases of Indian land without congressional approval, rendering such land sales illegal. Washington maintained that Georgia's land sales to the Yazoo companies also violated federal treaties with the Choctaws and Chickasaws. He issued a proclamation on August 26, announcing the new law and requiring all officers and citizens of the United States to observe the nation's Indian treaties or "answer the contrary at their peril."[137] The Yazoo Companies shelved their plans, and the Georgia legislature nullified their grants in 1791, but the issue of the Yazoo lands was not over.[138]

Knox called McGillivray "the soul of the Creek nation,"[139] but dissenting Creeks criticized McGillivray's actions in New York and disputed his claim to represent the entire nation. He may have represented the Upper Creeks, and most of the delegates were Upper Creeks, but perhaps only four Lower Creeks went to New York, and no Seminoles.[140] There also seems to have been some disagreement among the Creeks in New York. At least twenty-seven, and according to newspaper accounts as many as thirty, chiefs traveled to the city.[141] But only twenty-four signed the treaty.[142] It is uncertain if the others refused to sign—Knox indicated that ill health may have prevented them from doing so.[143] Creek people may have balked at the Oconee cession, of land that belonged mainly to the Lower Creeks, or at article 12, which promised to turn them into farmers and herdsmen.[144] Louis LeClerc de Milford, a Frenchman turned self-described Creek chief, said McGillivray ceded Washington "precisely the same land that the Georgians wanted to take by force from the two micos [Hoboithle Mico and Eneah Mico]...and for which reason we had waged a terrible war with the Anglo-Americans." He said Creek chiefs were greatly displeased with the treaty and refused to ratify it.[145] Six years later, one of the chiefs said McGillivray did not show the treaty to the Creeks when he returned home, and the nation did not hear of the cession of the Oconee lands "till lately."[146]

Spain also sought to nullify the Treaty of New York. It took several months for the Spaniards to obtain a complete copy, and McGillivray disclosed the secret articles to them piecemeal and partially. Miró regarded it as a violation of the Treaty of Pensacola, "inasmuch as they accept the gifts and protection of those states." Carlos Howard saw it as part of a campaign by the US government to sow discord and turn the Indians against Spain. As far as

Spanish colonial officials were concerned, McGillivray would have to be replaced unless he disavowed the Treaty of New York. They did everything they could to foment opposition to the treaty among the Creeks.[147]

Preexisting divisions within Creek society, Spanish intrigues, opposition to McGillivray, Georgia's resentment at the imposition of federal authority in its Indian affairs, and dissatisfaction with specific terms in the treaty all contributed to its failure. Georgia's representatives in Congress had voted against ratification. Instead of recognizing the state's rights, Representative James Jackson railed on the floor of the House some months later, the federal government had given away 3 million acres of Georgia's land. "A savage of the Creek nation had been sent for, brought to the seat of government, entertained and caressed in a most extraordinary manner," and sent home loaded with favors. Jackson wanted Washington to lay the whole treaty—including the rumored secret articles—before the House. "The constitution declares, that treaties shall be the supreme law of the land," he said. "But will Congress permit the laws of the U.S. should, like the laws of Caligula, be hung up on high, out of sight, in order to draw the inhabitants of America into snares?" Georgia's senators and representatives "growl exceedingly," said Hugh Williamson; other people not in the business of land jobbing "seem to think the Treaty well made."[148] The stipulated boundary line was not surveyed because the Creeks would not cooperate with the American surveyors.[149] Violence along the Creek-Georgia frontier continued.

Foreign intrigue swirled. William Augustus Bowles masqueraded as the self-styled director general of the Creek Nation. While McGillivray and his delegation were in New York negotiating with Washington, Bowles and a delegation of eight Creeks and Cherokees were in Quebec meeting with Lord Dorchester. As McGillivray's delegation sailed out of New York, Bowles's delegation sailed for London, where they stayed for five months. Although the Indian delegates dined with the Spanish ambassador in London, Bowles lobbied to gather British support for a scheme to wrest West Florida from Spanish control. By August 1791 he was back in Creek country, denouncing McGillivray's land cession at New York and causing Washington and Knox considerable concern. The Spanish governor of Louisiana, Francisco Luis Hector, baron de Carondelet, who hoped to forge a multitribal confederation to block American expansion, threatened that if McGillivray did not reverse the Treaty of New York, Spain would shift its support to Bowles. But Bowles was a loose cannon—in January 1792 he and his followers sacked one of Panton,

Leslie & Company's stores—and Spain removed him from the scene. Bowles was imprisoned, shipped to Havana, then to Spain, and then to the Philippines. He would be back.[150]

Washington and Knox continued to try to fashion an effective peace. They knew that open war with the Creeks, "in the present crisis of European affairs, would be a complicated evil of great magnitude" and, as Knox put it, "would generate all sorts of Monsters."[151] They could no longer achieve peace by working with McGillivray. When John Pope visited McGillivray at his Little Tallassee plantation in 1791 (he found him supervising the building of a log cabin "embellished with dormer Windows" and said he had about fifty slaves), the Creek chief proudly showed him the gifts Washington had given him—a set of gilt-bound books and a gold epaulette. He considered the latter a great honor and said he prized it "far above Rubies and much fine Gold."[152] But Spain made him a better offer— an annual stipend of $2,000—and in July McGillivray signed a treaty at New Orleans with Carondelet, in which he renounced the Treaty of New York, gave up his American salary, and returned to his Spanish alliance. "It is far from my heart," he told Carondelet, "to wish to have the least dependence on a people I know to be the Natural & determined enemy of all the Indian Nations & whom it is Incumbent on us to resist." It was never his inclination to be on good terms with the Americans, he added six weeks later.[153]

In January 1792 Washington appointed as agent in Creek country James Seagrove, a Revolutionary War veteran, member of the Georgia legislature, and businessman with a mercantile store at Coleraine on the St. Marys River. "To develop Mr. McGillivray, will be a work of considerable delicacy," Knox told Seagrove with some understatement. Despite Bowles's presence, McGillivray was still a major player in Creek country, and until "he shall throw off the mask entirely," the United States should treat him as a friend while at the same time keeping "an eagle's eye" on him.[154]

Seagrove sent Washington alarming accounts of developments, even as he tried to undermine McGillivray. McGillivray had been playing a double game, and so long as he had a say in the Indians' councils, the United States had no chance of success: "He is an Enemy in his heart to our Country & measures & is now so totally under the influence & direction of Spain & Panton, that he cannot or dare not, serve the United States if he was so inclined."[155] Washington, convinced that Spain was behind his Indian troubles in the South as Britain was in the North, wanted Seagrove to counteract Spain's "nefarious schemes." If there was unequivocal evidence of McGillivray's duplicity and treachery, Seagrove was to do everything he could to destroy his standing in the Creek Nation and, if he could, take his place.[156] Seagrove was certain the Spaniards had left no stone unturned to set the Indians against the United States. They had McGillivray on their side, and the agent feared they intended to employ Bowles as well.[157]

Washington may have been somewhat relieved, therefore, to hear "that our friend McGillivray was dead—and that Bowles who was sent to Spain had been *hanged.*"[158] Chronically ill, given to alcoholism, and physically weak, McGillivray fell ill with a fever and died in February 1793 at William Panton's home. The *Gentleman's Magazine* in London, which seven years earlier had not known who McGillivray was, noted the passing (prematurely in one instance) of "the celebrated chief of the Creek nation and an ally of the United States."[159] Bowles had not been hanged. He escaped from the Philippines, made his way via England back to Florida, and resumed his career of intrigue among the tribes, playing on their problems with Spain and the United States and trying to achieve the position he claimed for himself as the head of an Indian state under British protection. Captured again and incarcerated in a Spanish dungeon in Havana, he died in 1805.

In September 1793 Knox urged Seagrove to bring "about a dozen of the real chiefs" of the Upper and Lower Creeks to Philadelphia in the winter and brighten the chain of friendship by meeting the president and Congress. Seagrove should avoid the same chiefs who had come in 1790 and bring instead eminent chiefs like the White Lieutenant and Mad Dog. If they agreed, it would help "to avert the impending storm."[160]

The Creek crisis was the first challenge or opportunity for a national Indian policy as envisioned by Washington and Knox, in which the federal government would attempt to achieve its goals by treaty and resort to arms as a last resort. In arranging and negotiating the Treaty of New York, Washington made his first foray into treaty-making under the Constitution, applied the new treaty-making provisions, established the procedures for sharing his responsibility with the Senate, and succeeded in bringing the leaders of a powerful Indian nation to his seat of government instead of going to theirs. As such, the treaty represented a significant beginning in presidential treaty-making and established the precedent of bringing Indian delegations to the capital.[161] Five years after the Treaty of New York, Washington used the treaty-making power to enforce a policy he could not get through the House. After Georgia opened to settlement 5 million acres of Creek land protected by the Treaty of New York, the president asked Congress for a bill restraining the state. The Senate passed it, but the House voted it down. Fearing that war with the Creeks might spread to involve Britain and Spain, Washington, after Congress had adjourned, appointed a federal commission that overrode Georgia and arbitrated the dispute with the Creeks. Viewing it as a matter of foreign policy, Washington then secured the consent of the Senate after Congress reconvened.[162]

The new president's efforts to deal fairly with southern Indian nations and protect their lands stemmed from concerns of power and policy more than justice and humanity and did not extend far beyond Creek country. The Creeks in 1790 were a force to be reckoned with. The Catawbas by this time were not. In the spring of 1791, when Washington was touring the southern states, a delegation of Catawba chiefs came to see him. They were concerned, he noted in his diary, "that some attempts were making or would be made to deprive them of part of the 40,000 Acres" which had been guaranteed to them by treaty but was being impinged upon by a road on the boundary line between the two Carolinas. During the French and Indian War, the Catawbas had sent scouts and warriors to help Washington defend the Virginia frontier, although he did not like them very much or value their services highly. Now they, or their sons, came to him for help, or at least reassurance. Washington said nothing more about it in his diary. Five years later, a dozen Catawbas turned up at Mount Vernon. Washington complained to Secretary of War James McHenry: "I have already, been incommoded, at this place, by a visit of several days, from a party of a dozen Cuttawbas; & should wish while I am in this retreat, to avoid a repetition of such guests." As historian James Merrell notes, the incident reflects how the Catawbas' world had changed. Previously courted as allies, they were now dismissed as a nuisance. Washington, like most Americans, deemed them "hardly worth a second thought, or even a first."[163]

CHAPTER 16

The Greatest Indian Victory

I N THE SOUTH, WASHINGTON tried to curtail the assault on Indian lands and prevent war; in the Northwest Territory, he moved quickly to acquire the Indian lands he deemed essential to the nation's future, a move that virtually guaranteed war. He ordered Governor St. Clair to avoid war with the Indians "by all means consistently with the security of the frontier inhabitants, the security of the troops, and the national dignity," but "to punish them with severity" if they persisted in their hostility.[1] Washington's instructions were consistent with the national Indian policy he and Knox developed: attempt to acquire Indian lands by treaty, but if the Indians broke the treaty or refused to make a treaty on reasonable terms, the United States "would be exonerated, from all imputations of injustice" and would use force to impose peace on the Indians "or to extirpate them."[2] In reality, the United States lacked the military forces or the finances to sustain a war of extermination. Washington saw his campaigns against the Indians in the Ohio country as "punitive strokes" that would force them to accept American domination. He badly miscalculated.

Washington and Knox also underestimated the extent of Indian resistance north of the Ohio and misattributed its causes. They blamed it on recalcitrant Shawnees, renegade Cherokees, and some of the Wabash tribes; Washington called them "some bad Indians, and the outcast of several tribes who reside at the Miamiee Village." Instead of listening to "humane invitations and overtures" from the United States, "an incorrigible banditti" of no more than two hundred warriors persisted in raiding the frontier, taking lives and captives.[3]

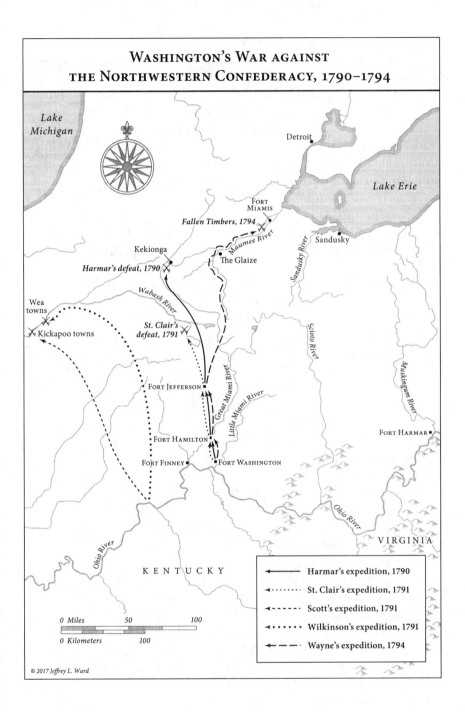

WASHINGTON'S WAR AGAINST
THE NORTHWESTERN CONFEDERACY, 1790–1794

Lake
Michigan

Detroit

Lake Erie

FORT
MIAMIS

Fallen Timbers, 1794

Kekionga

Maumee River

The Glaize

Sandusky

Sandusky River

Harmar's defeat, 1790

Wabash River

Wea
towns

Kickapoo towns

St. Clair's
defeat, 1791

Scioto River

Muskingum River

FORT JEFFERSON

Great Miami River

Little Miami River

FORT HARMAR

FORT HAMILTON

FORT FINNEY

FORT WASHINGTON

Ohio River

VIRGINIA

Ohio River

KENTUCKY

◄———	Harmar's expedition, 1790
◄·········	St. Clair's expedition, 1791
◄- - - - -	Scott's expedition, 1791
◄••••••	Wilkinson's expedition, 1791
◄— — —	Wayne's expedition, 1794

0 Miles   50   100

0 Kilometers   100

© 2017 Jeffrey L. Ward

Washington assumed British agents were at work among the tribes, which they were, but the seeds of Indian discontent lay in American land grabbing rather than foreign intrigue. Indians did not need the British to convince them that the United States was intent on their destruction.[4] The policy of bringing Indian communal lands into the national domain and transforming them into private property generated recurrent and steadfast resistance among the tribes. War was preferable to a peace that depended on Indians giving up their homelands and the way of life those lands sustained.

As was to be expected, the British took a rather different view than did the president of the United States. "The Indians in America seem to be forming a Grand League and Covenant, which promise to disturb the new Constitution of that country," the *Times* of London informed its readers, "and the arguments used by the Indians in support of their taking up arms, is founded on the true national Rights of Man." The Americans had stolen their country from them by force of arms and without provocation, they said. John Graves Simcoe, lieutenant governor of Upper Canada, dismissed American rhetoric about a fair and humane Indian policy. The US government threw off "all appearance of moderation and justice in respect to the Indian Nations" as soon as the Peace of Paris was signed, he said; "the division of the Country into Provinces was among their first public Acts, the extirpation of the Indians was their Philosophical language: and the sale of their lands was held forth as the avowed foundation of their National Wealth." It was not surprising that the Indians united to defend themselves and the result was all-out war. Instead of treating Indians with respect as independent neighboring nations, added a British traveler, frontier people stole their land and "shot them with as much concern as they would either a wolf or a bear." Americans had no one but themselves to blame for their Indian wars.[5]

The British were biased, of course, but there were those in the United States who shared their views. Benjamin Hawkins reminded Washington that during the Revolution, when the United States needed them, "we acknowledged the Indians as brothers" and "as possessors of the soil on which they lived." But after the war, anxious to pay off veterans with land, "we seem to have forgotten altogether the rights of the Indians," treated them as "tenants at will," and seized their lands. This, said Hawkins, was the source of their hostility.[6] Even the land speculator Rufus Putnam acknowledged that, although the British no doubt encouraged them, the real cause of the conflict was the Indians' fear that the Americans intended to steal their lands.[7]

The "Miamiee Village" Washington referred to was actually a cluster of villages, often called the seven "Miami towns" but inhabited by multiple tribes around the principal town of Kekionga on the Maumee River in northwestern Ohio.[8] Lieutenant Ebenezer Denny mapped and described a complex of Miami, Shawnee, and Delaware villages on both branches of the river, with hundreds of wigwams and log cabins surrounded by vast fields of corn.[9] Refugees from the Ohio country and beyond had gathered there, distant from the threat of American assault and near the source of British supplies and support at Detroit. By 1790 these towns were the center of Indian resistance to American expansion and to Washington's vision for America. "All those Scoundrels now Sir profess to hold the Americans in the most Supreme Degree of Contempt," Winthrop Sargent, who was secretary of the Northwest Territory, wrote territorial governor Arthur St. Clair that summer. "They will they say send their Women to fight us & with Sticks instead of Guns."[10] As he had done with the Onondaga and Seneca towns in the Revolution, Washington targeted Kekionga for destruction to stamp out resistance at the source.

The Indian confederacy he confronted was a loose and fragile alliance, built and maintained by collaborative coalition leadership, collective vision, and intertribal consensus. Rather than waging a single "Indian war," the various tribes were fighting a coordinated set of national wars in defense of their homelands.[11] Three broad tribal groupings comprised the bulk of the confederacy: the Iroquois; the Miamis, Shawnees, and Kickapoos; and the Three Fires of the Ojibwas, Ottawas, and Potawatomis. After the Revolution the Mohawk chief Joseph Brant had been a forceful voice in organizing an Indian confederacy and articulating the need for a united Indian stand on land sales, but now he was prepared to negotiate a compromise and accept the Muskingum River as the boundary between Indian and American land rather than insist on the Ohio.[12] The Miami war chief Little Turtle (Mishikinaakwa) (see figure 5) and the Shawnee war chief Blue Jacket (Waweyapiersenwaw) took a more militant stand. Some Wyandots and Delawares favored compromise, but the Shawnees, Miamis, and Kickapoos rejected such talk and stood firm on holding the Ohio as the boundary; Brant called them "unreasonable."[13] Warriors from the Three Fires also joined the fight, although they sometimes wavered in their commitment to fighting for a boundary at the Ohio River, a long way from their own homelands. The Ojibwas, the largest and most populous of the three tribes, were geographically scattered around the Great Lakes, occupying more

Figure 5 The Miami war chief Mishikinaakwa or Little Turtle was a key figure in the Northwestern Confederacy that resisted American expansion beyond the Ohio. In later life, he met Washington and adopted his policies as the best path for his people's future.

Courtesy of the Ohio History Connection, SC 2086.

than fifty villages in what is today Michigan, Wisconsin, Minnesota, and southern Ontario. Most warriors who joined the fight came from the Michigan peninsula.[14]

Following Washington's instructions, St. Clair continued to offer the Indians peace as he simultaneously prepared for war. But he had little hope or expectation that peace could be achieved.[15] He agreed with Knox that it was time to launch an invasion and punish the Indians "for their hostile depredations, for their conniving at the depredations of others, and for their refusing to treat with the United States when invited thereto." Delivering "a sudden stroke" against the Indians' towns and crops would demonstrate the power of the United States. It would also, Knox reminded Washington, "be highly satisfactory" to the people on the frontiers.[16] With Kentuckians seething at the government's apparent neglect of their safety and their economic interests, and Hamilton's proposed tax on whiskey before Congress, Washington was under mounting pressure to strike the Indians or risk losing the West.[17]

Knox dispatched Brigadier General Josiah Harmar of Pennsylvania, a thirty-seven-year-old veteran of the Revolutionary War, with 320 regulars and 1,133 militia from Pennsylvania and Kentucky to destroy the villages at Kekionga. Harmar left Fort Washington, present-day Cincinnati, at the end of September, confident of victory, but his confidence was misplaced, and Washington may not have shared it. Before the campaign got under way, he had Knox write confidentially to Harmar that he had heard reports the general was "too apt to indulge yourself to excess in a convivial glass" and that there must be no hint of such behavior.[18] Moreover, many of the militia were old men and young boys hardly able to bear arms, with an "indifferent" assortment of muskets. Ebenezer Denny said they "were not of that kind which is calculated for Indian Expeditions; they were drafts & substitutes, many of them had never fired a rifle in their lives."[19] In the face of Indian opposition, land sales had fallen short of financing the kind of military establishment needed to win an Indian war.[20]

This ragtag army, led by a general with an undistinguished war record, faced Indian warriors determined to defend their homes and families and led by a formidable trio of war chiefs.[21] Little Turtle had defeated a French expedition against Detroit in 1780. Now in his forties, he was a seasoned warrior with a strong following.[22] Blue Jacket had fought during the Revolution and built a reputation as the premier war chief of the Shawnees. Oliver Spencer, a white captive, said he was "one of the most brave and most accomplished of the Indian chiefs." Although Blue Jacket was nearing fifty years of age, Spencer described him as a muscular six-footer with an open and intelligent countenance, "the most noble in appearance of any Indian I ever saw." On the day Spencer saw him, Blue Jacket was wearing a scarlet frock coat laced with gold and with gold epaulets on the shoulders, a colored sash around his waist, red leggings, and moccasins ornamented with quill- or beadwork. He had silver bands on his arms, and a large silver gorget and medal of King George III hung from his neck.[23] The Delaware war chief Buckongahelas or Pachgantschihilas, whom Moravian missionaries knew as a mild-mannered, friendly, humane, "gallant and generous" man, had few illusions about the Americans. Prior to the massacre at Gnadenhütten, he had warned the inhabitants not to trust "the long knives" who "will in their usual way, speak fine words to you, and at the same time murder you!" "I admit that there are good white men, but they bear no proportion to the bad," the Moravian missionary John Heckewelder heard him say. "They enslave those who are not of their colour, although created by the same Great Spirit who created us. They would make slaves of us if they could, but as they cannot do it, they kill us. There is no faith to be placed in their words." Buckongahelas was committed to the confederacy. Delawares said he was "such a man among them as General Washington was among the white people."[24]

To avoid an unintended international incident, Knox ordered St. Clair to inform the British commander at Detroit that the campaign was directed only against hostile Indians, not the British posts.

Evidently, Alexander Hamilton had already conveyed much the same information to the unofficial British envoy, George Beckwith. Major Patrick Murray, the post commander, replied that Britain was unconcerned, and promptly sent messages to warn British traders in the Miami villages. The British Indian Department observed and encouraged the Indians' preparations.[25]

While Harmar invaded in the East, Major John Francis Hamtramck invaded in the West. Leaving Vincennes on the lower Wabash with three hundred regulars and three hundred Kentucky militia, he burned an abandoned Piankashaw village at the mouth of the Vermilion and then headed for home. Harmar also burned abandoned villages. The Indians were accustomed to burying grain to conceal it from enemies, and as Harmar's forces approached they evacuated their towns, hid as much corn as they could, and moved their women and children out of harm's way.[26] Kekionga was empty when Harmar reached it on October 17. His men burned everything they could. The next day at Chillicothe, a neighboring Shawnee town, they destroyed about eighty cabins and wigwams and "a vast quantity" of corn and vegetables. On the nineteenth, Colonel John Hardin and three hundred men went in pursuit of Indians and fell into an ambush. The militia fled, and the regulars had to cover the retreat back to the main body. On October 21, after Harmar's column had burned Kekionga and five other villages and destroyed twenty thousand bushels of corn, the army began its march back to Fort Washington.[27]

As it did so, Harmar sent Major John Wyllys with 340 militia and 60 regulars to attack the Indians as they returned to Kekionga. The Indians lured the militia into giving chase, and then caught and killed Wyllys and most of regulars at the village. By the time Harmar's army limped into Fort Washington, it had suffered more than two hundred casualties, lost a third of the packhorses, and abandoned much equipment. At first Harmar claimed a victory, but it quickly became clear the campaign was a humiliating defeat.[28]

By November 2 Washington was concerned that there had been no news from Harmar. "I am not a little anxious to know the result of it," he told Knox.[29] As the first reports trickled in, he "prepared for the worst," confiding to Knox "that my forebodings with respect to the Expedition against the Wabash Indians are of disappointment; and a disgraceful termination under the conduct of B. Genl Harmar." Washington had appointed Harmar, but now he fumed, "I expected *little* from the moment I heard he was a *drunkard*. I expected *less* as soon as I heard that on *this account* no confidence was reposed in him by the people of the Western Country. And I gave up *all hope* of Success, as soon as I heard that there were disputes with *him* about command."[30] In the historian John Ferling's assessment, the reports of insobriety were unfounded and Washington was simply looking for a scapegoat. If Harmar was such a drunkard, why leave him in command of the army?[31] A court of inquiry exonerated Harmar, and blame for the defeat fell on the militia.[32] Still, Knox informed the discredited general, with a degree of understatement, "It would be deficiency of candor on my part were I to say your conduct is approved by the President of the United States, or the public."[33]

Senator William Maclay of Pennsylvania took a dim view of the whole thing. "A war has actually been undertaken against the Wabash Indians without any authority of Congress," he wrote, when the first suggestions of a defeat reached the Senate in early December. "Mind what comes of it." Then, when the official information followed: "The ill-fortune of the affair breaks through all the coloring that was given to it." Maclay was convinced that Washington and his government fomented the Indian war as a pretext for raising an army that could be employed to cow its own citizens into submission.[34] Thomas Jefferson shared those suspicions and also condemned the tactics. "The federal council has yet to learn by experience, what experience has long taught us in Virginia, that rank and file fighting will not do against Indians," he wrote in implicit criticism of the Virginian veteran of Braddock's defeat who was now commander in chief. He hoped the next expedition would "be made in a more auspicious form."[35]

Indian raids intensified after Harmar's defeat, and the alarm spread to the frontiers of Washington's home state.[36] In the Ohio country, speculators could not sell land to emigrants who were now afraid to emigrate. They hoped the president would dispatch another invasion in the spring.[37] Marietta and other frontier communities that were supposed to be the vanguard of civilization now faced a full-blown Indian war. Rufus Putnam bombarded Washington that winter with requests to send troops and do it soon, before the settlements were "swallowed up." The only way to prevent an all-out attack on the frontiers come spring, Putnam preached to the choir, was to carry the war into the Indians' own country. If the government defeated the Indians and protected the settlers, it could reasonably expect a rapid sale of its lands that might pay off millions of dollars of the national debt. If it left its citizens at the mercy of the Indians, the consequences were obvious: no more lands would be sold, and they would probably be snatched up by speculators who paid no regard to the laws of the United States or the rights of the Indians—precisely what Washington hoped to avoid.[38]

Knox echoed Putnam's warnings. Things could not remain as they were, he told Washington. Another campaign into Indian country was essential to stop the Indians wreaking havoc on the frontiers in the spring. If the rapidly increasing frontier population did not receive protection from the government, it might look elsewhere and lean toward separation. Knox now estimated the Wabash Indians could muster about 1,100 warriors, with perhaps another 1,000 joining them from more distant tribes; that being so, it would take an army of 3,000 men to convince the Indians of the futility of resistance and "the absolute necessity of submitting to the justice and mercy of the United States." The army would quash resistance, destroy towns and food supplies, capture as many women and children as possible, and build a fort at the site of the Miami village. It was the same strategy Washington had advocated in the French and Indian War and implemented during the Revolution: *"That is, by carrying the war into the enemy's country, prevent in a great degree their invading the frontiers."*[39] Even Jefferson, who usually preferred gift-giving to war as a more cost-effective tactic for dispossessing Indians of their land, told Washington, "I hope we shall give the Indians a thorough drubbing this summer."[40]

Knox duly requested expansion of the regular army to 3,000—1,200 regulars, 1,300 volunteer levies enlisted for four months, and 500 rangers at a cost of $100,000—in preparation for a new offensive in the summer.[41] On March 3, 1791, Congress authorized raising a second regiment of 912 men and authorized the president to raise 2,000 levies and a body of militia for six months. The next day, Washington appointed St. Clair to command the army. "Your knowledge of the country north-west of the Ohio, and of the resources for an army in its vicinity, added to a full confidence in your military character, founded on mature experience, induced my nomination of you to the command of the troops on the frontiers," the president wrote to his general.[42] The levies were to be raised from the various states, assemble at Fort Pitt, and then float downriver to Fort Washington. From there St. Clair would march to Kekionga and build a fort "in the heart of the Miami villages" that would keep the Indians in check. Knox was certain that "disciplined valor will triumph over the undisciplined Indians."[43]

So was Washington. As "the great chief of the thirteen fires," he sent the Indians at the Miami towns a message "unmixed with fear, and dictated by the pure principles of humanity," giving them a last chance: they must see reason, make peace, and take up farming, or suffer the consequences. "The United States are powerful, and able to send forth such numbers of warriors, as would drive you entirely out of the Country," he warned. The campaign "would occasion some trouble to us, but it would be absolute destruction to you, your women and your children."[44] Like Sullivan's officers who had drunk a toast as they set out to invade Iroquois country in 1779, Washington offered the Indians a choice between "civilization or death." It reflected a consistent formula in his Indian policy.

The Indians, too, had been preparing for renewed war in the spring. After the American attacks, they moved their villages down-river to an area known as the Glaize, which now became the center of their resistance. Blue Jacket traveled to Detroit in the fall to request British food and clothing for families whose fields and homes the Americans had destroyed, and a promise of assistance in the fighting to come. The commander at Detroit promised to do what he could but cautioned that he had no authority to commit troops "as I am only a Small Finger on the hand of your Father at Quebec."[45]

Brigadier General Charles Scott, who had served under Washington in Braddock's campaign, kicked off the 1791 campaign. Washington instructed him to assemble "men of reputation," meaning known Indian fighters, and to fight "according to your mode." He directed them to take captive Indian women and children to be held as hostages. In late May, Scott and eight hundred Kentucky mounted militia crossed the Ohio and headed for the Wabash Valley, where they destroyed a group of Wea villages known as Ouiatenon and other towns farther upriver. They met no opposition, and most of the Indians who were killed died trying to escape cross the river in canoes or by swimming. Scott reported killing thirty-two people, but did not specify age or gender, and took fifty-eight captives. Five Americans were wounded. The captive Indian women were taken first to Fort Steuben and then to Fort Washington, where they remained in prison next to the army barracks for almost a year. As the historian Susan Sleeper-Smith points out, Washington had pushed his war against Indian women to another level; in addition to targeting their homes and crops, he now turned to kidnapping them.[46] This was the way to fight Indians, exulted George Nicholas, Kentucky's first attorney general; Scott had not encountered much opposition, "but more real service was effected than by the expedition last fall which cost so much blood and treasure." St. Clair could expect little trouble when he launched his campaign in the summer.[47] News of Scott's success sent Ohio Company shares soaring in value.[48]

In August, St. Clair dispatched Lieutenant Colonel James Wilkinson and five hundred mounted troops on a second raid into the Wabash Valley. Wilkinson burned a cluster of villages along the Eel River and then reburned the Ouiatenon villages that Scott had destroyed and the Indians had since rebuilt. Knox forwarded the news of Wilkinson's success to Washington, and Washington laid the reports before Congress.[49] So far, so good.

ST. CLAIR, HOWEVER, WAS HAVING TROUBLE. He was supposed to advance into Indian country on the heels of Scott's campaign. Instead, he was delayed by illness and did not reach Fort Washington and assume command until mid-May. At that point, he had barely one hundred men present and fit for duty. The start date of July was abandoned. Incompetence and corruption in supplying the army caused further delays. The provisions contract for the campaign was first awarded to a New York merchant named Theodosius Fowler, who transferred the contract to William Duer.[50] Duer, who had played an important role in the Ohio and Scioto Companies' machinations in 1787, had resigned from his position as assistant secretary of the treasury to pursue a career in contracting and speculating. He received more than $75,000 in cash advances from the government to purchase army supplies but used some of it to fend off creditors and invested some of it in land speculations. He loaned his friend Henry Knox $10,000, and they formed a secret partnership speculating in land in Maine.[51] Knox appointed as quartermaster general another friend and business associate, the Philadelphia merchant Samuel Hodgdon. Knox's younger brother, William, was Hodgdon's chief assistant.

The quartermaster general was supposed to deal with contracts and inspection in Philadelphia, buy boats and horses, arrange for the manufacture of artillery shells at Pittsburgh, and have everything shipped downriver, before proceeding himself to Fort Washington. Although Hodgdon had enough funding to get the job done, recurrent deficiencies and problems arose. Clothing was shoddy and was slow reaching Fort Pitt. Knapsacks ripped and leaked. Shoes were too small and split after a few days' wear. Packsaddles were too big, and new ones had to be made. The lightweight tents were suitable only for a summer campaign. Many of the firearms were in poor repair and some unfit for use. Gunpowder was packed in casks that leaked and let in moisture; the cartridge paper was flimsy. The beef supplies were insufficient, and the meat was sometimes barely edible.[52]

St. Clair had to employ local coopers, carpenters, wheelwrights, and gunsmiths in Cincinnati while he waited for the quartermaster and supplies to arrive.[53] "For God's sake, put the matter of provisions on the frontier in perfect train," Knox wrote Duer privately in late June.[54]

Troops trickled into Pittsburgh during the summer, but low water levels on the upper Ohio prevented General Richard Butler, St. Clair's second-in-command, from moving them downriver. As the summer ticked by, Washington began to fret. Knox communicated the president's growing concern to St. Clair and Butler. In July, Washington, "exceedingly anxious" to have the campaign begin as soon as possible, ordered Butler to descend the Ohio immediately with all the troops at his command. In August, Washington was "by no means satisfied by the long detention of the troops on the upper part of the Ohio, which he considers unnecessary and improper" and feared it was "an unhappy omen." The delays were jeopardizing the campaign, and unless all parts of the army made great exertions to make up for lost time, the money invested in the campaign would be wasted, and "the measures from which so much has been expected will issue in disgrace."[55] Butler's troops finally headed downriver. Butler, Quartermaster Hodgdon, and three companies of the 2nd Regiment arrived at Fort Washington on September 10.[56] But the powerful army that Washington had threatened would destroy any Indians who resisted did not materialize. In Kentucky so few men and officers volunteered that one thousand "reluctant citizens" had to be drafted.[57] Most of the soldiers were raw recruits with little or no preparation for a campaign into Indian country, and regular officers complained the militia lacked training and discipline.[58]

St. Clair had serious doubts whether the campaign should go ahead so late in the season. But Washington needed a victory, and he needed it soon. St. Clair said later that Knox wrote repeatedly "in the name of the president, in the most positive terms, to press forward the operations."[59] On September 1 Knox wrote: "The president enjoins you, by every principle that is sacred, to stimulate your exertions in the highest degree, and to move as rapidly as the lateness of the season, and the nature of the case will possibly admit."[60] St. Clair assured Knox a week later that "every possible exertion shall be made to bring the campaign to a speedy and happy issue."[61] On October 1 he asked Knox to assure Washington "that nothing can exceed the anxiety I feel to have the operations of the Campaign begun." He would rather have started the campaign two months earlier but was sparing no effort.[62] Pressured by his commander in chief, St. Clair pushed ahead.

The army headed north from Fort Washington along an Indian path that ran between the Ohio and the Glaize. The problems continued to mount. As Forbes had done in 1758, St. Clair constructed a supply route with a series of garrisoned posts at intervals along the way, sending supplies forward from each post as the troops advanced. Hacking its way through the woods, with oxen pulling the artillery and many of the wagons, the army made slow progress, sometimes advancing only a few miles each day, and even at that pace it frequently stalled as it waited for supply wagons to catch up.[63] Soldiers wearing shoddy clothes and shoes and sheltering in thin and leaky tents suffered misery when the weather turned wet and then freezing. Disease and desertion thinned the ranks, and levies left as their six-month terms expired. St. Clair himself was so sick he sometimes had to be carried on a litter. Courts-martial, floggings, and hangings further reduced morale. At one point, fearful that deserters would plunder the supply train coming up behind, St. Clair sent Major Hamtramck and the 1st Regiment back to protect it.[64]

By the time St. Clair reached the Wabash River on November 3, discharges, desertions, and the absence of the 1st Regiment had reduced his army to about fourteen hundred effective men.[65] Still, he was confident it would resume its march the next day, reach the Miami villages, and build a fort. He anticipated little or no resistance.[66] Indian scouts had been monitoring the army's progress, running off horses and lifting an occasional scalp, but Piominko and a contingent of Chickasaw warriors who had come to scout for St. Clair saw little sign of the enemy. They missed the Indian army.[67]

When the Shawnees and Miamis got word of St. Clair's invasion, they had sent war belts and painted tobacco, calling on other nations to join them.[68] Delawares, Shawnees, Kickapoos, Miamis, Wyandots, Ottawas, Ojibwas, and Potawatomis, together with some Conoys and Nanticokes, Mohawks from Canada, and a few Creeks and Cherokees, gathered at the Glaize. Simon Girty, Alexander McKee (whom Washington had met during his trip to the Ohio country in 1770[69]), and Matthew Elliott of the British Indian Department, together with various French and British traders in the vicinity, supported and supplied the coalition.[70] Indian men prepared for war by fasting, abstaining from sexual intercourse, observing rituals that gave them access to spiritual power, and drinking herbal concoctions to cleanse their bodies before combat. On October 28, 1,040 warriors set out to do battle, singing prayers as they went. Girty, who counted them, said they "were never in greater Heart to meet their Enemy, nor more sure of Success."[71]

They covered fifty miles in four days. When St. Clair made camp on November 3, they were just two or three miles away. During the night, they advanced through the woods to the outskirts of the American positions. According to Joseph Brant and John Norton, a Cherokee-Scot and adopted Mohawk who wrote his account based on talking with Indian people years after the event, the tribes lined up in a crescent or half-moon formation. The Shawnees, Delawares, and Miamis under Blue Jacket, Buckongahelas, and Little Turtle occupied the center; the Ottawas, Ojibwas, and Potawatomis took the left wing; the Wyandots and Iroquois, the right.[72] Spiritually and tactically ready for combat, they waited for dawn.

They attacked just before the sun was up and just after the soldiers had been dismissed from parade. They routed the Kentucky militia, who were camped ahead of the main body of the army across a creek, and sent them reeling into the other battalions as the men scrambled to arms, throwing the army into disorder.[73] The warriors quickly enfiladed the American position—St. Clair recalled his army was surrounded in a matter of minutes. Firing from the trees, they picked off the American officers and the artillery crew, silencing the guns.[74] Some officers managed to mount hastily assembled bayonet charges, but the Indians simply melted away until the charges lost their momentum, and then they resumed their deadly target shooting.[75] Amid the chaos and confusion, noncombatants and camp followers— mostly women and children—huddled in terror in a hollow square within the American lines.[76] The lines contracted and crumbled under the relentless assault, rendering soldiers and noncombatants even more vulnerable. Most of the officers fell, including Richard Butler, whom Shawnee warriors tomahawked and scalped.[77]

By midmorning discipline was unraveling and resistance breaking down. Around 9:30 a.m. St. Clair ordered a desperate retreat. It quickly turned into a rout. Soldiers ran for their lives, throwing aside muskets, cartridge boxes, and anything that impeded their flight; "the whole Army Ran together like a mob at a fair," Lieutenant Colonel William Darke told Washington.[78] Stores, equipment, artillery, wagons, horses, and wounded were abandoned to the Indians.[79] Most of the survivors made it into Fort Jefferson by sunset; more wounded and stragglers stumbled in the next day. The dazed remnants of the US Army staggered back to Fort Washington on the afternoon of November 8. The army lost 630 killed (37 officers, 593 enlisted men) and 32 officers and 252 enlisted men wounded, in addition to noncombatants and captives. "I think the Slaughter far Grater than Braddocks," Darke told Washington, which surely conjured up nightmare memories in the president's mind.[80] Indian losses were relatively light: 20 or 30 killed and perhaps 50 wounded, according to different estimates.[81] It was the biggest victory American Indians ever won and, proportionately, the most severe defeat the United States ever suffered. The nation's only army lay in ruins. "The fortunes of this day have been as the cruellest tempest to the interests of the Country and this Army, and will blacken a full page in the future annals of America," wrote Winthrop Sargent, who served as adjutant general.[82]

Precisely when Washington received news of the disaster is unclear. According to his private secretary, Tobias Lear, a mud-spattered officer arrived at the president's home in Philadelphia during a dinner party. Leaving the room to receive the dispatch, Washington composed himself and returned to his guests. Only after they had left did he fly into a rage against St. Clair, striking his forehead in fury. Here in this very room, he had warned him: "Beware of surprise! You know how the Indians fight us. He went off with that, as my last solemn warning, thrown into his ears." And still St. Clair had allowed the army to be surprised and cut to pieces. He was "worse than a murderer," and the blood of the dead was on his hands. But then the storm passed. "This must not go beyond this room," Washington told Lear; "General St. Clair shall have justice."[83]

News of the disaster reached Philadelphia through various routes, appearing in western newspapers and transmitted east before St. Clair's official report—he sent three copies—arrived. Unofficial reports arrived on December 8; partial reports appeared in Philadelphia newspapers the next day.[84] "The late calamity to the Westward has produced great sensation here," wrote Jefferson, who hoped the defeat would prevent enlarging the regular army and increase reliance on militia.[85] Ebenezer Denny, carrying one of St. Clair's reports, made it to the capital on December 19 after an eight-hundred-mile odyssey. The next morning Henry Knox called at his quarters and took him to the president's house, "where we breakfasted with the family, and afterward had much talk on the subject of the campaign and defeat."[86] By then, it was old news. Washington had informed Congress of "the misfortune" in a brief message a week before, on December 12. The loss to the nation was considerable, he acknowledged, "yet maybe repaired without great difficulty, excepting as to the brave men who have fallen." He provided copies of St. Clair's reports and a list of the officers who had been killed and wounded.[87] The Senate and the House ordered the message and enclosures to be read and tabled.[88]

As news of the disaster and the magnitude of the losses sank in, correspondents, the press, and Congress debated how it could have happened and who was responsible.[89] The commander in chief did not escape criticism for a military expedition badly conceived and badly executed, and he received plenty of advice on what to do next. William Darke wrote him a long and detailed account of the defeat the same day that St. Clair wrote his report. He offered to meet with Washington during the winter and answer any questions he might have about the campaign.[90] But Darke's son died of wounds sustained in the defeat, and in February 1792 Darke published in the press an anonymous diatribe against Washington for having sent an infirm and bedridden general into battle.[91] George Nicholas agreed that St. Clair's infirmities rendered him "totally unfit" for a command that would have taxed a strong and healthy man.[92]

Frontier settlers renewed their alarmed calls for protection. A "Citizen of Georgia" asked Washington why the government was waging an "inhuman and unprofitable War" against the Indians in the Northwest whose only crime was defending their own territory, while on Georgia's frontiers innocent families were being butchered by Indians in violation of the treaty Washington had made with McGillivray.[93] Newspapers printed rumors of escalating Indian war, accounts of the western settlers' peril, and letters, often written under pseudonyms, denouncing the war as unjust and the government's Indian policy as driven by the interests of land speculators.[94] Tobias Lear told Washington the war was extremely unpopular in New England, where everyone he spoke with thought it stemmed "from a wish on the part of the United States to obtain lands to which they have no just claim."[95] William Stoy, a German minister, physician, and member of the Pennsylvania legislature, blamed wrongheaded and hypocritical policies predicated on taking Indian lands by right of conquest from Britain: "What would your Excellency think if I or Some body else was powerful enough to rob you of your Estate?" he asked Washington.[96]

Many of Washington's correspondents criticized aggressive land policies that did not give peace a chance. Quakers, appalled by the bloodshed, urged him to return to pacific measures.[97] Benjamin Hawkins declined to comment on the battle itself—"You are a military Judge," he told Washington—but he made his position quite clear: "I am for peace." He attributed the defeat to the government's policies in Indian country and its "feeble efforts" to make peace. Indian policy was being dictated by those "at the head of affairs to the Westward" who were all for war, he said; "this is their harvest." The Indians were "wholly unacquainted with the real disposition of our government."[98] Aaron Burr agreed. Widespread opinion held that peace was possible, he told Washington. The Indians were fighting because they believed the government intended to take their lands, and they would cease once those misapprehensions were removed; unfortunately, since hostilities broke out, the government had not conveyed to them any direct assurances to the contrary.[99] Other correspondents argued that victory over the Indians was a prerequisite to real peace, and that without it St. Clair's soldiers had died in vain. The question was how best to achieve that victory.[100]

As the debate was fought out in the press, Knox came in for scathing criticism. He and his supporters were quick to defend his policies. But the opposition increasingly coalesced around the secretary of the treasury: Hamilton wanted the war in order to maintain the national debt and promote his financial policies, and he had authorized his crony William Duer to supply the army.[101] The delays in carrying out the campaign rendered it incapable of success, said George Nicholas, and those delays were the fault of the quartermaster and contractor: "As long as men who are strangers to the country in which they are to act are appointed from motives of friendship &c. the business will have a similar end," he told Madison.[102] In Congress, critics of the government questioned Washington and Knox's plans to overhaul the militia system and expand and fund the regular army. "We are preparing to squander away money by millions," railed one congressman, "and no one, except those who are in the secrets of the Cabinet, knows for what reason the war has been carried on for three years."[103] An emerging Republican faction squared off against Hamilton and the Federalists.

Congress conducted an official investigation into the disaster. St. Clair, who wanted to clear his name and then resign his command, requested an inquiry into his conduct. Washington replied that there were not enough officers of sufficient rank left in service to form a court of inquiry. He asked St. Clair to resign immediately, so a successor could be appointed and dispatched to the frontier, and assured him the congressional inquiry would afford the opportunity to explain his conduct "in a manner satisfactory to the public and yourself." Newspapers reprinted the exchanges between the president and his disgraced general.[104] In discussion with his cabinet Washington said he disapproved of St. Clair "not keeping his army in such a position always to be able to display them in a line behind trees in the Indian manner at any moment."[105]

Congress established a special committee. It was the first congressional investigation under the new Constitution.[106] The committee's sessions were held in public, and its investigations went far beyond St. Clair to uncover the causes of the disaster. It raised questions

about the authority of the new federal government and the account-
ability of elected officials, and traced the failures and mismanagement to the secretary of war and secretary of the treasury. Knox, who
had initially told St. Clair he was not to blame for the defeat, now
tried to pin the blame squarely on the general's shoulders.[107] When
Congress requested relevant documents, Washington, conscious of
establishing precedents, consulted his cabinet—Jefferson, Hamilton,
Knox, and Attorney General Edmund Randolph. They concluded
that Congress had every right to request documents from the president but recommended that Washington release those papers which
"the public good would permit" and "refuse those the disclosure of
which would harm the public good." The notion that the president
had the right to withhold documents that might be deemed detrimental to the public good was thus established, and with it the foundation for what became known in the twentieth century as executive
privilege. Washington eventually decided that disclosing the papers
would not harm the national interest and was necessary to give
St. Clair a fair hearing. He ordered Knox to provide the House with
the relevant documents and had copies made for the committee.[108]

The committee reached unanimous agreement and communicated its report to the House of Representatives in May 1792. It
absolved St. Clair of any responsibility for the defeat. Instead, it
blamed congressional delay in apportioning funds for the campaign,
the troops' lack of discipline and experience, the lateness of the
season, and, most of all, "the delays consequent upon the gross and
various mismanagements and neglects in the quarter master's and
the contractor's departments." Although Washington and Knox were
not identified by name, the committee made it clear that St. Clair
was under orders from the top to forge ahead despite serious delays
and deficiencies; those orders were so "express and unequivocal" as
to "preclude the commander in chief from exercising any discretion
relatively to that object."[109] The committee did not recommend
taking action against any government official. Knox, Hodgdon, Duer
(from debtor's prison, where he had been since March 1792), and
St. Clair all subsequently submitted memorials, but the committee
did not change its conclusions.[110] Although the committee blamed
contractor fraud rather than leadership, St. Clair spent the rest of his
life trying to clear his name. In 1812, by which time he was an old
man, he published by subscription his own 275-page *Narrative of the
Manner in which the Campaign against the Indians, in the Year One Thousand
Seven Hundred and Ninety-one, was Conducted, under the Command of
Major General Arthur St. Clair.*[111]

The Indian victory put the United States in a precarious position. Frontier inhabitants were alarmed at the prospect of being left defenseless in the face of renewed Indian raids. The destruction of St. Clair's army reaffirmed their concerns that the federal government lacked the resolve to bring order in the West.[112] Land speculators fretted over their investments. Encouraged that the experiment in republicanism was faltering, the British stepped up the pressure to reach an accommodation. Elated by "the astonishing success of a few Indians... who have opposed and destroyed, the whole American force," Alexander McKee hoped the United States, "now convinced of the difficulty of Subduing a Brave & warlike race of People, may listen to the Voice of Equity and Reason and Establish a firm and lasting Peace on the Principles of natural Justice & Humanity."[113] The British government advocated turning the Northwest Territory into a neutral Indian barrier state. Such a state would be independent of both Britain and the United States, closed to further settlement but open to trade; it would protect Indian lands from American expansion, protect Canada from American aggression, and help maintain British influence among the Indian nations.[114] But Washington consistently maintained that the only irreparable loss of St. Clair's defeat was the men who died there. Everything else could be recovered if the government stayed the course in its policies toward the Indians and its efforts to take control of the West and its lands.[115] He was proved right, but building a new army took time and money. Buying the time to do it and ensuring that the Indian war did not spread required him to balance a strategy of preparing for war even as he negotiated for peace.

CHAPTER 17

Philadelphia Indian Diplomacy

WASHINGTON HAD LEARNED the rudiments of Indian diplomacy as a young man in Indian country, but in the early 1790s he conducted his Indian diplomacy in and from Philadelphia. These were critical years. The Indian war was going from bad to worse; British and Spanish agents encouraged the tribes, and conflict between Britain and Revolutionary France created a foreign policy crisis that threated American neutrality. Washington dealt with Indian diplomacy at a frenetic pace. He met prominent Indian leaders who came to Philadelphia to establish relationships with the new president, get a clear reading of the government's intentions, and chart their own courses in light of US policies. He talked, smoked, and dined with Indian chiefs. He dispatched peace emissaries into Indian country, even as he dispatched armies into Indian country. He asked individual Indians to negotiate on his behalf, embracing indigenous diplomatic practices and traditions that the United States had spurned in its initial dealings with Indian nations.[1] It was, wrote Anthony Wallace some fifty years ago, "the climax of a political generation during which 'Indian Affairs' was the major public business of an entire nation" (see plate 11).[2]

Washington's Indian diplomacy was always about land, but in his first administration, isolating, dividing, and defeating the Northwestern Confederacy took priority. Doing so required talking and making peace as well as threatening and waging war. The two approaches went hand in hand: if he could achieve the nation's goals without recourse to war, he would; if his peace efforts failed, they would justify the war he then had to wage.

IMPLEMENTING THIS DOUBLED-EDGED POLICY required some delicate diplomatic footwork, and Washington turned for help to the Iroquois, whose country he had invaded a dozen years before. Fearful that the conflict with the Northwestern Confederacy might spread into a general Indian war all along the frontier, he had to keep the Six Nations out of the fight. Alexander Hamilton spelled out the situation for him: "You are sensible that almost every person here is interested in our Western lands; their value depends upon the settlement of the frontiers, these settlements depend on Peace with the Indians, and indeed the bare possibility of a war with the six Nations, would break up our whole frontier."[3] The government asked Iroquois chiefs to act as intermediaries with the western Indian nations as it negotiated a peace settlement, or at least bought time for its army by appearing to negotiate a peace settlement. It also hoped, rather optimistically, that the Six Nations might assist the United States in its war against the western tribes. Washington wanted the Iroquois to be pliant instruments of his policy, and many western Indians castigated them as American tools, but the Iroquois were practicing a peace-making tradition that stretched back hundreds of years. They were past masters of the art of diplomacy.[4]

Cultivating the support of the Six Nations required sending American emissaries into Iroquois country. Washington appointed Timothy Pickering as federal commissioner to head the Iroquois initiative. The New Englander faced a steep learning curve. He held his first council, with more than two hundred Senecas and a few Onondagas, at Tioga Point on the Susquehanna (near present-day Athens, Pennsylvania) in November 1790. Following the murder of two influential Turtle clan Senecas at Pine Creek in Pennsylvania, Washington wanted Pickering to assure the Six Nations that the offenders would be punished and to head off a potential cycle of revenge by giving gifts to "cover the dead," according to Iroquois custom and at the request of peace-minded Seneca chiefs.[5] Prior to the meeting, Pickering sent the Senecas word that in future all their business with the citizens of the states would "be conducted by the authority of the United States, through their President, or Great Chief: that I was appointed by him to wash off the blood of their murdered brothers, & wipe away the tears from the eyes of their friends."[6] At the conference, Pickering reported to Washington, "I

studied to please them in every thing within the limits of your instructions: the sole object of my mission being to soothe their minds."
The Indians wanted peace; they appreciated the gifts Washington
sent, and the conference went well. Only the acquittal by a Pennsylvania jury of the one suspect who had been apprehended marred
Pickering's satisfaction. He found it mortifying that most frontier
inhabitants considered it no crime to kill Indians in peacetime.
Unless some examples were made, he would have to hold many
more meetings like the one at Tioga Point.[7]

A novice in the art of doing business in Indian country, Pickering fumbled his way through the protocols and rituals of diplomacy.
"I was an utter stranger to the manner of Indians," he confessed to
Washington after the council. But Pickering was a different kind of
American treaty commissioner, with a different attitude toward
Indians and different goals—he was not there to ask for land. After
listening to the Indians recite the wrongs they had suffered at the
hands of the whites, he told Washington, "a man must be destitute of
humanity, of honesty, or of common sense" who did not sympathize
with them.[8] The contrast with previous federal and state treaty commissioners who had dictated terms and demanded land was not lost
on the Iroquois, who made allowances for his inexperience.

Pickering found a good teacher. The Seneca chief Sagoyewatha,
known to the Americans as Red Jacket (see plate 12), was not known
for his prowess in war; his enemies called him Cowkiller, referencing
a story that he had fled a battle and daubed himself with the blood
of slaughtered cattle to give the impression he had been in combat.
But he was an accomplished orator and a master of council-fire
diplomacy and stood as a spokesman for those of the Six Nations
who remained in New York. A Quaker observer who saw Red Jacket
in conference with Pickering recorded in his diary: "His appearance
& manner would cut no inconsiderable figure on the floor of a
British Parliament, or an American Congress. I do not remember to
have seen any statesman make a more majestic appearance."[9]

Red Jacket and Farmer's Brother (Honanyawas) instructed
Pickering in the ritual of condolence that was a foundational element of the Iroquois League and the Great Law of Peace; it eased
the grief of bereaved kin, ensured that negotiators were "of good
mind," and "cleared the path" so that talks could begin.[10] Red Jacket
alternately lectured and tutored Pickering on how to conduct himself. He listened as Pickering explained the Constitution and the
terms of the Trade and Intercourse Act, but when the commissioner
urged Iroquois men to give up hunting and become farmers like the

Americans, Red Jacket pointed out that the Great Spirit intended Indians and whites to walk different paths. The Six Nations wanted to brighten the chain of friendship with General Washington, as they put it, but they must be allowed "to follow our ancient rules" as the white people followed theirs. "We can then as well agree as if we followed one rule." It was an argument Red Jacket would reprise many times in the years to come. He impressed Pickering as "a man of great ambition." The Iroquois in turn honored Pickering by giving him the name Connesauty. Washington expressed his "entire Approbation" of Pickering's conduct and offered to appoint him superintendent of Indian affairs in the North, an offer Pickering declined as conflicting with his appointments by the state of Pennsylvania.[11]

Meanwhile, Washington was meeting a chief who did not attend Tioga and who was on the outs with many Six Nations leaders. The Allegheny Seneca chief Cornplanter or Kayenthwahkeh could not be ignored. Sometimes called Obeal or Captain Abeel after his father, an Albany trader named John Abeel, Cornplanter was a member of the Wolf clan through his mother, who seems to have been related, possibly a sister, to Guyasuta.[12] Along with Sayenqueraghta of the Turtle clan, he was one of the two war chiefs of the confederacy that the Senecas were entitled to name.[13] A rival of both Joseph Brant and Red Jacket, both like him members of the Wolf clan, Cornplanter had earned a reputation fighting against the Americans during the Revolutionary War. But at the Treaty of Fort Stanwix in 1784, he had grudgingly accepted the American terms, an act for which he was vilified by Brant as well as many Senecas at Buffalo Creek. The next year he moved his band away and resettled on the Allegheny River, closer to American settlements. In 1786 he had traveled to Philadelphia and then to New York City, the capital at the time, where he addressed Congress. The Ohio Company in 1788 granted him one square mile of land in recognition of his service to the United States and "the Friendship he has manifested to the Proprietors of Land purchased by the Ohio Company."[14] In 1789, along with Guyasuta and several other Seneca chiefs, Cornplanter signed the Treaty of Fort Harmar, confirming the cession made at Fort Stanwix. The historian Alan Taylor portrays him as "an ambitious and eloquent man with a powerful mind, an often overbearing will, and flexible scruples," who coveted private property and "would make many compromises with the Americans rather than eat crow served by Red Jacket or Joseph Brant." Rather than attend Tioga as one of a number of Seneca chiefs, he preferred to go to Philadelphia, speak with the president in person, and position himself as the key player in

Iroquois-US relations.[15] But Cornplanter was motivated by more than ego and self-interest. He had plenty to say to Washington.

Accompanied by Half Town, Big Tree, New Arrow, and Guyasuta, Cornplanter arrived in Philadelphia in October 1790. The delegation first met with the Pennsylvania Executive Council. "When I was young and strong our country was full of game," Guyasuta told the council, but white people had driven away the game, and now "we are old and feeble and hungry and naked, and...have no other friends than you." Cornplanter acknowledged that the shifting power dynamics demanded a redefinition of the relationship. "In former days when you were young and weak I used to call you brother, but now I call you father," he told them.[16]

Rev. Samuel Kirkland brought his influence and interpretive skills to bear. Traveling from Oneida country at the government's request and expense to meet with the Seneca delegates, he arrived in December. Kirkland had known Cornplanter for five or six years and counted him a good friend. Cornplanter told him the purpose of their visit was to represent "the abuses which the Seneka Nation had suffered from the white people," obtain an adjustment to the boundary line established in 1784, ask Congress for assistance to promote agriculture "& gradually introduce the arts of civilized life among the Senekas," and, last, discuss the western Indians. Kirkland spent three weeks with the Seneca delegation and admired Cornplanter's sobriety, sagacity, and Christianity. "He seems raised up by Providence for the good of his nation," he wrote in his journal. When they had first met, Cornplanter "was so strongly attached to the traditions of the fathers that the truths of Christianity could not have a fair hearing from him," Kirkland said; "but now, by an over-ruling Providence, he has become very attentive."[17]

Between December 1, 1790, and February 1791, the chiefs addressed a series of speeches to the man they called Town Destroyer. (The British obtained copies of the proceedings.[18]) Reviewing their treatment since the end of the Revolution, Cornplanter said the Iroquois had accepted Washington's invitation to attend the peace talks at the Treaty of Fort Stanwix. "You then told us we were in your hand, and that, by closing it, you could crush us to nothing, and you demanded from us a great country, as the price of that peace which you had offered us;...our chiefs had felt your power, and were unable to contend against you, and they therefore gave up that country." Then the Americans had acted "as if our want of strength had destroyed our rights," but "your anger against us must, by this time, be cooled," he said; "we ask you to consider calmly, Were the terms dictated to us by your commissioners reasonable and just?" No sooner had the chiefs signed their treaty with the United States than commissioners from Pennsylvania had pressured them into ceding a large chunk of what is now northwestern Pennsylvania, for a sum of $5,000. The Livingston leasing scheme and a contentious land sale to speculators Oliver Phelps and Nathaniel Gorham further eroded the Seneca homeland, and Phelps had reneged on his promised payments. "You have compelled us to do that which has made us ashamed," Cornplanter said. Signing the Fort Stanwix Treaty had put Cornplanter's life in danger, and one of the signatories had even contemplated suicide. All the treaties and land deals rested on the assumption that the king had ceded the Indians' land to the United States, but that was not the case. The king could not have ceded what the Indians had not ceded to him; "the land we live on, our fathers received from God, and they transmitted it to us, for our children and we cannot part with it."[19] They were custodians of the land and could not sell it even if they wanted.

It took Washington almost a month to reply. He waited for Pickering's full report on the Tioga negotiations and to be briefed by Knox, to whom he had forwarded the Senecas' speeches. Knox in turn forwarded their complaints to Governor Clinton, asking for information about the Livingston and Phelps purchases, about which Knox and Washington knew little or nothing, so the president could answer Cornplanter "with precision and effect."[20] Knox then reviewed and contextualized their complaints and gave his assessments of the chiefs. Though not a sachem, Cornplanter was an accomplished war captain and "a very active partizan against our frontiers" in the Revolution "but by no means cruel or blood thirsty." Since then his attachment to the United States and his role at the treaties at Fort Stanwix and Fort Harmar had earned him the hatred of many of his people and the enmity of Joseph Brant. Now in his early forties, Cornplanter was "a man of truth" and had "never been known to be drunk, certainly not habitualy so." Knox thought him "the fittest person to make use of to manage the six nations." Brant was too close to the British; Farmer's Brother, the principal sachem, was "a great drunkard" and had lost standing; Red Jacket and Big Tree lacked Cornplanter's talents or influence. To bind Cornplanter to the United States with ties of self-interest, Knox recommended paying him an annual pension of $250 in his choice of money, goods, livestock, or farming utensils, with a similar amount distributed among other chiefs who appeared friendly to the United States. Preaching to the choir, Knox repeated his conviction that civilizing

the tribes "instead of extirpating them" would enhance the government's reputation. Most important for the moment, however, was to
make sure Cornplanter and the Senecas kept their young men from
joining the western Indian alliance.[21]

Two days after he got Knox's briefing, Washington replied to
the Senecas. He assured them he would protect their lands as defined
by the Treaty of Fort Stanwix. The evils Cornplanter described had
happened because the central government had been weak and the
individual states had acted on their own to acquire Indian lands, but
things were very different now. Their remaining lands were safe
because the Constitution gave the federal government exclusive
authority to deal with the Indian nations, and the Trade and
Intercourse Act contained additional protections. In words that must
have sounded reminiscent of British assurances after the Proclamation
of 1763, Washington explained that Indian lands could only be purchased at public treaties held under the auspices of the United
States. "The general Government will never consent to your being
defrauded, but it will protect you in all your just rights," including
the right to sell their lands to whomever they wished and not to sell
if they so chose, he said. He also claimed that the preparations for
war were a last resort, necessitated by the western Indians' continued
hostilities and refusal of peace offers.[22]

The Senecas were appeased but not assured. "Father," said
Cornplanter, "your speech, written on the great paper, is to us like
the first light of the morning to a sick man, whose pulse beats so
strongly in his temples and prevents him from sleep. He sees it, and
rejoices, but he is not cured." In other words, "Yeah, right." The
Senecas wanted restoration of lands lost at Fort Stanwix, not confirmation of the loss. Washington replied that they themselves had
already confirmed it: the boundaries they established at Fort Stanwix
and reaffirmed at Fort Harmar must stand. Even so, Cornplanter
assured Washington of his people's pacific intentions and the government made arrangements for him to go to the Miami and Wabash
villages on a peace mission that, Washington said, would "render
those mistaken people a great service, and probably prevent their
being swept from the face of the earth."[23]

Cornplanter had all he could do to prevent his own people
from being swept from the face of the earth. Survival meant adapting
to new situations and adopting new ways of living. In what must have
been music to Washington and Knox's ears, he asked them "to teach
us to plow and to grind corn; to assist us in building saw mills, and
supply us with broad axes, saws, augers, and other tools, so as that we

may make our houses more comfortable and more durable; that you will send smiths among us, and above all that you will teach our children to read and write, and our women to spin and weave." Like Washington and Pickering, Knox believed that teaching agricultural skills was more useful than sending Indian children to eastern schools, and he promised to send a schoolteacher and one or two farming instructors.[24] Before the Senecas left, the Pennsylvania legislature granted Cornplanter three tracts of land totaling 1,500 acres.

Governor St. Clair had hoped some of Cornplanter's Senecas would accompany his expedition; the government was more concerned with keeping them out of the Northwestern Confederacy and employing Cornplanter as an emissary.[25] He was supposed to go with Colonel Thomas Proctor, who had been an artillery officer during Sullivan's campaign, to deliver Washington's final peace offer and ultimatum, which Knox described as "inviting the hostile Indians to peace, previously to striking them." Cornplanter had Proctor present his case in council at Buffalo Creek, but the Iroquois were not impressed, and when the British commander at Fort Niagara refused to furnish a boat, Proctor abandoned his mission.[26]

Few Iroquois were convinced by Washington's assurances that their lands were now safe. Not everyone in the settler republic approved of a federally controlled and just Indian policy. Speculators continued to operate in Iroquois country, and the state of New York continued to conduct its own negotiations. Washington was furious. What did it say to the Indians if the left hand seemed not to know what the right hand was doing? he asked Hamilton in exasperation. "That we pursue no system, and that our declarations are not to be regard[ed]." State interferences and individual speculations "will be the bane of all our public measures."[27] Worse, Iroquois delegates had been assaulted and robbed on their way home, and some Senecas trading in Pennsylvania had been murdered. "We hope you will not suffer all the good people to be kill'd," Cornplanter and his fellow delegates told Washington, "but your People are killing them as fast as they can." Washington knew there was little prospect of peace "so long as a spirit of land jobbing prevails, and our frontier Settlers entertain the opinion that there is not the same crime (or indeed no crime at all) in killing an Indian as in killing a white man."[28]

As St. Clair gathered his forces in the summer of 1791, the government dispatched Pickering to keep the Six Nations neutral, at the least, during the impending conflict. Pickering met with about a thousand Iroquois at Newtown Point (Elmira, New York) in July. Things did not go well. Red Jacket had asked that Congress "speak to us of nothing but peace." Pickering, however, following Knox's instructions, tried to get the Iroquois to send warriors to assist St. Clair and boasted of American power. Red Jacket was quick to exploit the misstep. Grandstanding before the assemblage, he took Pickering to task for talking war when he should have been talking peace, mocked his mistakes in council protocol, and ridiculed his assertions of American superiority. Plain-speaking Pickering was no match for the Seneca orator. He dropped his request for warriors and salvaged the council by reaffirming American friendship and Washington's promises of protection for their land and rights. Pickering said he and Red Jacket "parted as friends."[29]

Pickering and Washington promised more than they could deliver. When Governor Clinton of New York protested that his state claimed a right of preemption to Indian lands within its borders—in other words, New York Indians could sell their lands only to the state of New York—Washington backed down.[30]

At Newtown, Pickering invited a Six Nations delegation to visit the president after the corn harvest and discuss plans for introducing agriculture. Offering the chiefs bribes and pensions would serve little purpose because if the British offered them more they'd take the highest bid, he explained to Knox; with few exceptions, they were "as corrupt as the ministers of any court in Europe." But bringing them to see the nation's capital would counter British claims that the United States was "poor, mean, & contemptible." With more than forty thousand inhabitants, large streets laid out on a grid plan, bookstores and printers, and a bustling wharf, Philadelphia impressed the French traveler Jacques-Pierre Brissot de Warville two years earlier as "the metropolis of the United States. It is certainly the finest town, and the best built; it is the most wealthy, though not the most luxurious." Pickering intended it to similarly impress Iroquois visitors: "The dignity of the President & the splendor of his house—the number of attendants, the magnificence of entertainments...cannot fail to strike them with surprise and to excite their reverence," he thought. "The public buildings in Philadelphia—the extent & populousness of the city, the vast quantities of goods in every street, and the shipping at the wharves will so much exceed any thing they have seen before, and so far surpass their present ideas that they cannot fail to wonder and admire."[31] Such thinking would bring Indian delegations to the nation's capital for the next hundred years.[32]

St. Clair's defeat delayed the visit but made it all the more pressing. The United States set to work to exploit divisions in the Indian confederacy. The loose and fragile coalition of many nations had less unity and unanimity of purpose now it had repulsed the invasion. The Shawnees, Miamis, and Delawares remained resolute to halt American expansion at the Ohio River, but Joseph Brant and the Six Nations, as well as the Ojibwas, Ottawas, and Potawatomis, were willing to consider a compromise boundary.[33] The government sent messages warning the Six Nations and southern Indians to remain "fast friends" as it redoubled its efforts to crush the hostile tribes and again tried to enlist the Six Nations as mediators with the western tribes.[34]

It commissioned Rev. Samuel Kirkland to bring a delegation to the capital. Kirkland, accompanied by the Oneidas Skenandoah, Good Peter, and Peter Otsequette, and Hendrick Aupaumut, a Stockbridge Mahican, traveled to the western reaches of Iroquois country to invite chiefs from the Onondagas, Cayugas, and Senecas. Brant warned that "the real design of the invitation was not on the paper—but behind it," and he and Cornplanter stayed away.[35] But so many wanted "to see the Great Council of the 13 fires," and get a glimpse of the famous General Washington, that Kirkland brought about fifty people. Red Jacket, Farmer's Brother, Good Peter, and many other chiefs accompanied the missionary down the Susquehanna Valley, arriving in Philadelphia on Tuesday March 13, where they were welcomed with a cannon salute. Washington invited a group of the delegates to dinner the following Monday.[36]

The marquis de Lafayette had adopted Peter Otsiquette or Ojekheta when he was a teenager. After several years in France, where he received an education, learned French and English, and became accustomed to moving in polite society, Otsiquette had returned home in the summer of 1788. Three years later he impressed the businessman and land investor Ekanah Watson as "probably the most polished and educated Indian in North America," well versed in "music and many branches of polite and elegant literature," who in his manners resembled "a well-bred French man." After less than a week in Philadelphia, Otsiquette died suddenly. He was buried in the cemetery of the Second Presbyterian Church. Ten thousand people attended the funeral, no doubt impressing the visiting chiefs with the "populousness of the city." Big Tree also died while in Philadelphia and was buried in the Friends burial ground.[37]

Before Washington met the delegates, Pickering gave him some blunt advice. He must negotiate in good faith and deal only with the introduction of agriculture and other civilized pursuits, not the acquisition of land:

Indians have been so often deceived by White people, that *White Man* is among many of them, but another name for *Liar*. Really, Sir I am unwilling to be subjected to this infamy. I confess I am not indifferent to a good name, even among Indians[.] Besides, they recieved, and expressly considered *me*, as *"your Representative*["]; and my promises, as the promises of ["] *The Town Destroyer.*" Sir, for your honour & the honour & interest of the United States, I wish them to *know* that *there are some white men who are incapable of deceiving.*[38]

In his opening speech, Washington stressed his wish to keep the alliance with the Six Nations strong and presented a belt of white wampum, symbolizing his desire for peace. With the consent of the Senate, he proposed establishing a fund to provide $1,500 each year to provide the Iroquois with clothing, livestock, and farming tools; farmers and teachers would instruct their men to farm, their women to spin and weave, and their children to read and write. Knox and Pickering then turned to the real business at hand: getting the Iroquois to use their influence with the western tribes to make peace.[39]

The Iroquois delegates were not bought so easily. Good Peter had experienced the devastation of Oneida country in the Revolution and the assault on Oneida lands in the 1780s, and he was known for his intelligence and integrity. Kirkland, who once attended a council where Good Peter "spoke for an hour like an Apollo & with the energy of a son of Thunder," said "his equal is no where to be found among all the Indian nations."[40] Responding to Washington's speech via Pickering a week later, Red Jacket returned to the tricky question of New York State's right of preemption over Iroquois lands, a right Washington had implicitly denied in his negotiations with Cornplanter in December 1790, and then rather tamely accepted in the face of Governor Clinton's protests the following year. "The President," Red Jacket announced, "has in effect told us that we were freemen; the sole proprietors of the soil on which we live. This is the source of the joy; which we feel—How can two brothers speak freely together, unless they feel that they are on equal ground." The Seneca politician was putting words into Washington's mouth, but with a disastrous Indian war on his hands and Iroquois neutrality an absolute necessity, Washington said nothing to contradict him. Although there was peace among the Iroquois, there was still "some Shaking among the original Americans at the setting sun," Red Jacket said. Washington had said *he* was not the cause of the hostilities in the West, so Red Jacket pointedly asked him, *"What do you thin[k] is the real cause?"* (emphasis in the original). As far as the Iroquois could see, murdering Indians and stealing their land in fraudulent treaties were the principal problems, and the president and Congress must resolve them if they truly wanted peace. "You have manifested a desire to put the burthen of bringing you and the Western Indians together, upon our shoulders: but it is too heavy for us to bear without your assistance."[41]

Washington presented Red Jacket with a peace medal, which the Seneca wore in later portraits, evidently proud of it and his association with the first president.[42] As he had when McGillivray and the Creeks came to New York, the artist John Trumbull painted portraits of several of the visiting chiefs, including Good Peter (see plate 8).[43] On April 22 Washington dined with twenty-two Iroquois, their interpreter, and Kirkland. A few days later, after a month in the capital, the chiefs left Philadelphia laden with gifts from the government.[44]

Pickering was relieved to see them go. He had issued the original invitation, but knew nothing about the delegation coming until Knox crossed the street one day and told him the Indians were on their way. "I believe I must get you to negotiate with them," said Knox. "Do think of it." Pickering bore the brunt of the negotiations and found the business "very burthensome": the written proceedings would fill a hefty volume, and besides the formal speeches there was "a multitude of *conversations*." He had scribbled down the Indians' speeches as the interpreters translated them, and then he transcribed and corrected them, often working at night and on Sundays. Was he entitled to any compensation? he asked the secretary of the treasury.[45]

JOSEPH BRANT DID NOT PARTICIPATE in the Newtown Point council or the Philadelphia delegation. His was an absence the US government dared not accept. Allan Maclean, commander at Fort Niagara, said Brant was "better educated & Much More intelligent than any other Indian." The British made him a captain in the Indian Department, provided a pension for his sister, Mary or Molly, the widow of Sir William Johnson and an influential clan mother, and set aside lands (purchased from the Mississaugua Ojibwas) on the Grand River in Upper Canada (present-day Ontario) for Brant and his people.[46] Brant's ties to Johnson and visits to England gave him connections in important circles. Governor Clinton described him to Washington as "a Man of very considerable information, influence and enterprise" and reckoned his friendship "worthy of cultivation at some Expense."[47] Many regarded Brant as the most important Indian of his day, and Brant seems to have agreed. He was also the Six Nations leader most closely aligned with the Northwestern Confederacy. He had defiantly articulated the stance against piecemeal land sales, and he remained a powerful voice for Indian unity.

However, Brant wanted unity to strengthen the Indians' bargaining position in reaching a peaceful settlement, not to sustain an endless war against American expansion. He regretted that the breach between the Indians and the United States was wider than ever, he told Clinton in early 1791; Harmar's expedition had "spread the Sore where it was not felt before,... [and] all that will be gained in the end, will not be adequate to the Expense in Blood and Treasure."[48]

If the United States could win over Brant, it would reinforce Iroquois neutrality and at the same time weaken the Northwestern Confederacy and the British-Indian alliance. During the Revolution, Washington had hoped that some Iroquois might be induced to kidnap Brant.[49] Now he tried to get him to Philadelphia and secure his help. Pickering sent the first invitation by letter, but, fearing that would not be sufficient inducement, Knox turned to Kirkland, Brant's former classmate. Brant and Kirkland had parted ways during the Revolution; living at Grand River, Brant seemed firmly in the British orbit, but his relationship with the British colonial government was often testy. He had returned frustrated from a second visit to London in 1786 and was disappointed by Britain's reluctance to give full support to the Indian resistance movement. Shawnees and other hard-liners for whom the stakes were higher suspected Brant because of his willingness to compromise on the Ohio boundary, especially after his absence from the victory over St. Clair. Uncertain circumstances plus his own ego and ambition made Brant receptive to the flattering invitations Pickering, Knox, and Kirkland all sent, promising a grand reception as befitted a man of his importance. "The President of the United States will be highly gratified by receiving and conversing with a chief of such eminence as you are, on a subject so interesting and important to the human race," Knox wrote him in February 1792. Kirkland even pledged his honor and his life for Brant's safety.[50] Brant accepted the invitation, telling the British that since his requests for assistance from them had produced only evasive answers, he was going to Philadelphia to assess American intentions and the prospects for peace.[51]

In undertaking such a journey Brant surely anticipated getting more than just answers. It took him almost a month to reach Philadelphia. He set out from the Grand River in May, made his way through the country Washington's armies had razed in the Revolution, and traveled down the Hudson to New York, then on to the capital. He received the reception he had been promised. Washington met with him the day after his arrival. "I have brought the celebrated Captn. Joseph Brant to this City, with a view to impress him with the equitable intentions of this government towards *all* the Nations of his colour," Washington wrote privately to his friend Gouverneur Morris just before the meeting.[52] The president and his cabinet wined and dined Brant. Jefferson noted on June 21, a Thursday: "He dined with the P. yesterday, will dine with Knox to-day, [George] Hammond on Sunday, the Presdt. On Monday &c."[53] But Brant was not overly impressed by Philadelphia or dinners with Washington: he had been twice to London and dined with royalty and aristocracy, and, as at Mount Vernon, dinners at his Grand River mansion were served by black servants dressed in livery.[54] Knox met with him several times to try to convince him of Washington's "humane disposition" toward Indians and talk him into getting the western chiefs to come to Philadelphia, where "the President would have the satisfaction of forming an acquaintance with the Chiefs," and making a treaty would be more efficient than sending commissioners into Indian country, as points of dispute could be settled as they arose and "adjusted exactly according to his wishes."[55]

The government offered Brant a secret pension of $1,500 (six times what it paid Cornplanter), land for himself, and a reservation for the Mohawks on the American side of the border. He left Philadelphia on June 28, "apparently in the best dispositions," according to Jefferson. Although Brant said he refused the offers, preferring "the interests of his Majesty, and the credit of my nation, to my own private welfare," he likely departed a wealthier man. He also left Knox and Washington believing he would be instrumental in reaching a settlement with the Northwestern Confederacy. It is also not beyond the realm of possibility that Washington and Brant, both Freemasons, reached some private understanding. Before he left, Brant went to see George Hammond, Britain's first minister to the United States, and told him of the American offer. Knowing Hammond would convey the information up the line, Brant used the visit to bolster his own position and put pressure on the British.[56] He continued to work for a settlement, but, as the British well knew, he had his own agenda. He was not about to do the Americans' bidding. Back in Upper Canada, Brant dined with Lieutenant Governor and Lady Simcoe in November 1792. "He has a countenance expressive of art or cunning," the lady noted in her diary, evidently imbibing her husband's views.[57]

As Washington pursued his diplomatic initiatives with the Indians in Philadelphia, so the British pursued theirs. When Hammond arrived in town in October 1791, Jefferson gave him a frosty reception and made clear his rancor toward Britain; Washington treated him with politeness and respect.[58] In addition to negotiating a commercial accord with the United States, the twenty-seven-year-old Yorkshireman had instructions to try to mediate a peace between the Indians and the Americans, and secure a new boundary between Canada and the United States that would include an Indian reserve as a barrier to American expansion. Preoccupied with events in Revolutionary France, Britain was not likely to support the Indians in open war against the United States, but if it could mediate a new border with an Indian buffer zone, the Indians would be appeased and Canada safeguarded. The Indian victory over St. Clair in November seemed to open the door for such a proposal, and Hammond engaged in multiple discussions with Jefferson and Hamilton, though the scheme made little headway.[59]

Washington adamantly opposed calling in the British to act as mediators. In cabinet discussion in March 1792, he, Knox, Jefferson, and Hamilton agreed never to accept British mediation. (The others were unaware that Hamilton had privately appealed to Lord Dorchester via the agent George Beckwith to use his good offices in bringing the Indian war to a close.)[60] Washington laid out his own position in a letter to Gouverneur Morris. British interference was the root of all difficulties with the Indians, and Britain's mediation would never be requested and would be rejected if offered. The United States would conduct its own Indian diplomacy, offering the tribes the usual choice between war and peace, and "will never have occasion, I hope, to ask for the interposition of that Power or any other to establish peace within their own territory." The administration was doing all it could to convince the Indians "that we neither seek their extirpation, nor the occupancy of their lands (as they are taught to believe)" except those purchased in fair treaties, but if they still refused to "listen to the voice of peace, the sword must decide the dispute; and we are, though very reluctantly, vigorously preparing to meet the event."[61] Hammond continued to explore the possibilities of British mediation and Indian boundaries with Hamilton and, more testily, with Jefferson but gained no traction.[62]

The British were equally suspicious of Washington's attempts to secure Iroquois mediation. "I cannot but regret the Six Nations having sent deputies to Philadelphia," Lieutenant Governor Simcoe wrote; "it is certain no Method will be left undone to cajole them into a War against the Western Indians."[63] Fearing that the Republic's aggression against the Indians would spill over into his own colony, and pinning his hopes on the Indian confederacy to contain American expansion at the Ohio, Simcoe saw Brant's moderation as a threat to unity and viewed Brant himself with suspicion after he had been to Philadelphia to talk with Washington. "There is no person, perhaps, who thinks less of the talents or integrity of Mr. Washington than I do," he wrote.[64]

AMERICAN EFFORTS TO REACH OUT to the western tribes came up empty. In January 1792 Knox dispatched two agents, Captain Peter Pond and William Steedman, on a mission impossible: to persuade the victorious Indians to ask the United States for peace. "We cannot ask the Indians to make peace with us, considering them as the aggressors," Knox explained; "they must ask peace of us." Traveling in the guise of traders, Pond and Steedman were also to gather what information they could about the confederacy; in other words, they were spies.[65] In April, Knox sent Colonel John Hardin and Major Alexander Trueman, who had survived the campaigns in 1790 and 1791, respectively, to tell the western tribes that the United States did *not* want to take their lands and drive them out of the country. Quite the contrary, the United States wanted to impart to them the blessings of civilized life, teaching them to cultivate the earth, raise domesticated animals, live in comfortable homes, and educate their children. The Indians should not be fooled by their recent victory into thinking they could escape ruin if the war continued. They should send chiefs to Philadelphia, where chiefs of the Six Nations were currently having talks, and make peace.[66] George Nicholas thought it shameful that a handful of savages should have destroyed two armies and reduced the United States to asking for peace.[67] But Trueman and Hardin did not get far: Indians killed and scalped them both as they traveled from Fort Washington to the Miami villages.[68] Cornplanter said the emissaries should have taken the appropriate road for making peace via the Six Nations, not the road via the Ohio that had been made bloody and where they were taken for enemies.[69]

Washington viewed their deaths as "lamentable proof of Indian barbarity" that should "stimulate every nerve to prepare for the worst."[70] When the Six Nations delegation was on its way, Washington and his cabinet agreed they should be well treated but not trusted too much.[71] Now Knox felt that the last hope for reaching out to the western tribes rested on the "Indians who were in this City for that purpose."[72] Washington agreed. If those attempts also failed, he told Jefferson, there was no alternative left "but the Sword."[73]

The potential emissaries hardly constituted a united team. The Senecas, Hendrick Aupaumut, Colonel Louis Cook, and Brant each had their own agendas. Cornplanter and Red Jacket did not speak for all the Senecas, and the Senecas did not speak for the rest of the Six Nations. Brant called Aupaumut a "Yanky Indian," but Aupaumut was not just Washington's mouthpiece. Drawing on the Mahicans' historic role as diplomats and mediators and their long-standing ties with the Delawares, Shawnees, and Miamis, Aupaumut stated, "We look upon ourselves as the front door, by and through which you can go through all the different Tribes." At Washington's request he traveled west four times in the early 1790s in an effort to broker peace, but he undertook the missions to reassert Mahican influence and prestige rather than simply advance American interests.[74] The western tribes would more likely listen to a message delivered by an Indian whom they regarded as friend and who had never deceived or hurt them, he said, and he took with him "ancient wampum" that recorded past agreements.[75] He urged the Indians to make peace, argued the benefits of aligning with the United States rather than the British, and likened the American republic to traditional indigenous governance where leaders derived their power from the consent of the governed. In his journal, though, he confided he was careful "to say nothing with regard of the conduct of the [New] Yorkers, how they cheat my fathers, how they taken our lands Unjustly, and how my fathers were groaning as it were to their graves, in loseing their lands for nothing, although they were faithful friends to the Whites; and how the white people artfully got their Deeds confirm in their Laws, &c."[76] In speaking to the western Indians about the Americans, he distinguished between Big Knives, frontier whites who lied, stole, and killed, and President Washington, who was honest, wise, and just.[77]

Louis Cook also lent his support to the peace initiatives. After his services with Washington during the Revolution, Cook had settled on a farm in Oneida country and played a prominent leadership role, primarily facilitating land sales. He was a bitter rival of Brant and complained that in courting the Mohawk, Washington undermined the peace efforts of the Kahnawakes, Stockbridges, and Senecas. "My father has struck me," he said, "by raising Brant so high and employing him to make peace who is the enemy of peace."[78] Cook thought he was entitled to reward for his services, and Knox recommended that Washington approve paying him $100.[79] Other Oneidas who had served with Washington and received officers' commissions wanted to know why Cook received preferential treatment; he was the only one to be placed on half pay (Knox had declined their requests two years before). They asked the president to see justice done to them as well as to Cook.[80] Washington was knee-deep in intertribal, intratribal, and interpersonal politics.

With the exception of Aupaumut's mission, Knox reported to Washington, all the peace overtures miscarried, "whether conducted by Whites or Indians." The British did everything they could to derail any peace talks. Brant and some of the Six Nations chiefs got sick, although whether Brant's illness was medical or political is unclear. Good Peter died.[81] "The whole Confederacy will feel the loss of *Good Peter*," wrote Kirkland.[82]

In May 1792, Washington appointed Rufus Putnam a brigadier general and sent him in company with Aupaumut with a message for the tribes who were going to meet in council at the Miami River. Putnam was to make it clear "that we want not a foot of their land."[83] Such duplicity required delicate handling. "No idea of purchasing land from them ought to be admitted," Washington told Knox; "for no treaty, or other communications with the Indians have *ever* been satisfactory to them when this has been the subject." Instead, negotiators like Putnam should be informed of the principles and general outlines of the treaties, "notwithstanding the right of disannulling is reserved to the Government—Illiterate people are not easily made sensible of the propriety, or policy, of giving a power, & rejecting what is done under it."[84]

Seeing little prospect of making peace with the northwestern Indians, Putnam headed instead to Vincennes to try and detach the lower Wabash tribes from the confederacy. The Moravian missionary John Heckewelder accompanied him, and Putnam enlisted William Wells, a former Miami captive and son-in-law of Little Turtle, as an interpreter.[85] But the chiefs who signed the treaty were not committed members of the Indian confederacy, and maybe, as Washington noted in his journal, "not Chiefs."[86]

Nevertheless, at the end of the negotiations Putnam invited them to send a delegation to visit Washington in Philadelphia. Fifteen or sixteen men and three women from the Kaskaskias, Piankashaws, Peorias, Potawatomis, Mascoutens, and other tribes accompanied Heckewelder on the journey, carrying a wampum belt of peace to present to the president. The Kaskaskia chief Jean Baptiste DuCoigne also carried a letter of introduction from Washington's land agent on the Kanawha, together with certificates from western citizens like George Rogers Clark attesting to their regard for the chief. DuCoigne had visited Jefferson at Monticello in 1781—Jefferson gave him a bronze medal and smoked the pipe with him; DuCoigne gave Jefferson several painted buffalo skins and named his son after him—and renewed his acquaintance with the secretary of state soon after the delegation arrived in late December 1792.[87] Washington was anxious to know if anyone had spoken with the Indians about land since they arrived in the city, and he had Knox give the interpreters strict instructions "not to communicate to the Indians a single sentence relative to purchasing their Lands."[88]

Eight of the Indian men and the three women met with Washington at his house on February 1, 1793, from noon until midafternoon. Six chiefs and two women dined with him again on February 4. DuCoigne presented Washington with a black pipe to smoke in remembrance of "our chiefs who have come here and died in your bed." (Two men had died of smallpox in the first month of the visit, five more died from being inoculated, and at least one person died of pleurisy.[89]) A white pipe was then passed and smoked to clear the air for peace talks to proceed. "Father, your people of Kentuckey are like Musketoes, and try to destroy the red men," DuCoigne said, "but I look to you as to a good being. Order your people to be just. They are always trying to get our lands. They come on our lands. They hunt on them; kill our game & kill us. Keep them then on one side of the line and us on the other." Other members of the delegation— war chiefs, civil chiefs, and women—reiterated the same sentiments, punctuating their talks with strings of white wampum and smoking the calumet pipe. "Father, you are rich," concluded DuCoigne; "you have all things at command, you want for nothing. You promised to wipe away our tears. I commend our women & children to your care."[90]

The delegation remained in Philadelphia until May. Washington reminded them as they left to consider the power they had seen and "what the bad Indians may expect in the end if they do not hearken to the voice of peace!" He gave each chief a medal to wear as a symbol of loyalty to the United States and provided a letter of protection to help ensure a safe journey home. The white wampum belts and peace pipes the Indians had given him were deposited, ironically, in the War Office.[91]

Washington submitted the Treaty of Vincennes to the Senate in February while the chiefs were still in the city. The fourth article of the treaty guaranteed the Indians "all the lands to which they have a just claim" and recognized their right to sell or not as they wished. Concerned that it did not grant the United States the exclusive right to purchase the Indians' lands in the future, the Senate postponed discussion of the treaty until the next session of Congress. The Indian delegates apparently were not informed. Since most of the chiefs who came to Philadelphia had died of smallpox, Knox told Washington it would have been improper and futile "to have attempted with the remainder any explanation of the fourth article of the treaty."[92] The Senate refused to ratify the treaty in January 1794. The delegates from the Wabash had died for nothing.

KNOX EXPECTED THE PEACE OVERTURES to the Northwestern Confederacy would also amount to nothing. Since the Indians would demand "more than we can grant consistently with any sort of dignity," he confided to General Anthony Wayne in early September 1792, the United States should prepare for war.[93] Unsuccessful in their attempts to reach out to the western tribes or enlist Brant's help, Washington and Knox had to rely on Red Jacket. That same month, Red Jacket, Farmer's Brother, and Cornplanter carried an American peace offer to the Glaize in northwestern Ohio, where so many nations were assembled "that we can not tell the names of them."[94] In addition to Shawnees, Miamis, Delawares, Wyandots, Ottawas, Ojibwas, and Potawatomis, there were Sauks and Foxes from the upper Mississippi; some Creeks and Cherokees from the South; Conoys, Nanticokes, and Mahicans from the East; and deputies from the Six Nations in New York and the Seven Nations in Canada.[95] According to Aupaumut, Brant, still ill, sent his nephew Tawalooth with a message warning the tribes not to be deceived. "I have myself seen Washington, and see his heart and bowels; and he declared that he claims from the mouth of Miamie to the head of it—thence to the land of the Wabash river, and down the same to the mouth of it; and that he did take up dust and did declare that he would not restore so much dust to the Indians, but he is willing to have peace with the Indians."[96]

Red Jacket said the Americans were extending the hand of peace and might accept the Muskingum River as a compromise boundary. "Don't be too proud Spirited and reject it, [lest] the great Spirit should be angry with you," he warned. The Shawnees accused the Senecas who had been to Philadelphia of doing Washington's dirty work and trying to split the confederacy. "We know what you are about," sneered the Shawnee chief Messquakenoe or Painted Pole. "Speak from your heart and not from your mouth." Picking up the wampum on which Red Jacket had spoken, he threw it at the Senecas' feet. "The Farmer's Brother then put the String which had been thrown down, over his head & hanging down his back they then moved away & remained an hour."

When they returned, Red Jacket said it was true they had been to Philadelphia. "Washington asked us what was the cause of the uneasiness of the Western Nations, we told him it was in regard to their Lands." Washington did not say he would give up the lands, but he did promise to "satisfy the owners of the land, if it had been sold by people who were not the real owners thereof." In their talks with Washington, Farmer's Brother said, they "heard nothing false from him, but what breathed the strongest desire of cultivating peace and Friendship with all Nations of our Colour on this Island on the ground of justice and humanity." The western Indians, however, understood that Washington's idea of justice still entailed taking their land. "You say Washington will make us a compensation if our land was not purchased of the right owner," said Painted Pole; "we do not want compensation, we want restitution of our Country which they hold under false pretences." They could accept no peace unless the Americans agreed to the Ohio River boundary. The Americans intended to build forts and drive all the Indians out of the country, but the allied tribes had twice defeated their armies while the Iroquois sat by doing nothing. They saw no need to compromise now. Still, Washington said he wanted peace so they would talk peace. Since "General Washington did not let us know the terms on which he would make peace," they agreed to meet his representatives the following spring and listen to his offer.[97]

The western Indians also viewed Brant with suspicion after his visit to Philadelphia and called on him to join them when they met with the Americans. Brant agreed to attend, but made it clear *he* had not been bought by American dollars or fooled by Washington's words when he visited Philadelphia. Stand united, he warned the Shawnees and Delawares. "General Washington is very cunning, he will try to fool us if he can. He speaks very smooth, will tell you fair stories, and at the same time want to ruin us. Perhaps in a few days, he may send out a flag—that will only be to blindfold us. It will not do for one man to turn about and listen to that flag. We must be all at it, as we are all united as one man."[98]

Back on home ground at Buffalo Creek in November, Red Jacket urged delegates from the western nations to meet the Americans at Sandusky. The western Indians had no objection to a meeting, "provided it is for our Interests" and provided American armies were not on the move. "The Americans came into our Country, we defeated them, we consider ourselves sole proprietors of this Land," they declared; "and tho' Washington is *lately* become a great man, we are resolved to receive no messages from him by the Bloody road."[99] Washington had violated diplomatic protocol by sending a peace message via a warpath, but the Indian confederacy was not closing the white path of peace. Once again, Red Jacket denied Shawnee accusations that he was an American pawn.

In preparation for the conference at Sandusky, Knox compiled a list of possible commissioners. To assure the public that the government was acting in good faith, Washington insisted they be men known for their talents and integrity, "clear of every Suspicion of a wish to prolong the War," and intent on making peace. "Characters uniting these desiderata," he noted, "do not abound." He asked Senator Charles Carroll of Maryland and Charles Thomson, who both declined, and then nominated Benjamin Lincoln, Timothy Pickering, and Beverley Randolph, governor of Virginia from 1789 to 1791.[100]

Half a dozen chiefs of the Six Nations arrived in Philadelphia on January 20, 1793. Again Washington gave clear instructions that no one speak to them about buying land.[101] On February 11 Washington, Knox, St. Clair, Pickering, and Rufus Putnam dined with Hendrick Aupaumut, Louis Cook, and the other Iroquois, who promised their chiefs would attend the Sandusky conference.[102] Washington briefed his cabinet on the importance of the upcoming negotiations, and for the first time in American history the cabinet submitted to the president its written corporate opinions. He instructed Jefferson as secretary of state to review the treaties, asked his cabinet to consider the appropriate role for Quakers who wished to attend the treaty as observers, and furnished the commissioners with detailed instructions prepared by Knox. They were to wind up the talks by August so that General Wayne would have time to carry out his expedition before the end of the campaign season in the event of an unsuccessful outcome.[103] An unsuccessful outcome was more than likely: Knox's instructions stated "explicitly" that the United States could not return any lands the Indians had already ceded.[104] According to Jefferson's notes on the cabinet discussion in February, Washington "declared he was so much in the opinion that the treaty would end in nothing that he then in the presence of us all gave orders to Genl. Knox not to slacken the preparations for the campaign in the least but to exert every nerve in preparing for it."[105]

The peace commissioners set out in April. En route, they received "a written speech, and four strings of white wampum, sent by the Western Indians to the President" and designating Sandusky as the meeting place.[106] Delegates from sixteen tribes assembled at the foot of the Maumee rapids, where the British agent Alexander McKee had a trading post, and held their own discussions before meeting the commissioners.

Lieutenant Governor Simcoe had limited expectations. He hoped for a just and secure safe peace, he wrote McKee, "but I own I dread the selfish & ambitious Projects of Mr. Washington & his

Colleagues in Office will frustrate what must be the wish of every honest Man in America."[107] He was not impressed with the commissioners: "Lincoln was very civil, Randolph able and of the rakish or Virginian cast of character, and Pickering a violent, low, philosophic, cunning New Englander."[108] Narrowly interpreting the meeting as an effort to settle specific tribal land claims, one of the commissioners, according to Simcoe, had "expressed his Surprize that so many Nations should be assembled who had no business with the Lands in dispute, & with whom no treaty would be held." This gentleman seemed to forget, wrote Simcoe, "that the Indian Confederacy is of an Older Day than the Union of the states, and that the Creeks are as much concerned as the People of Massachusetts, Rhode Island, &c, &c."[109] The prospects for peace were slim: neither the commissioners nor General Wayne expected it, and the United States had sent the commission "as necessary to adjust the ceremonial of the destruction and pre-determined extirpation of the Indian Americans." From Simcoe's perspective, the main goal of Washington's Indian diplomacy was to secure an alliance with the Six Nations and to turn them against the western Indians and ultimately Britain as well.[110]

Brant on the other hand believed "this is the best time to obtain a good Peace, and if lost, may not be easily regained," and again suggested ceding land east of the Muskingum River.[111] But his compromise gained no traction with the Indians or with Simcoe, who expected little from him after he had been hobnobbing with Washington. "This Cunning and self interested Savage *chooses* not to understand the difference between a fair Peace, and one upon any terms," he told George Hammond.[112]

The Indians suspected the Americans of duplicity, talking peace while their army readied for war. The commissioners assured them that "our Great Chief, General Washington, has strictly forbidden all hostilities against you" until the peace talks were finished. Unable to strictly forbid anyone from doing anything, Brant recommended restraining the Indian warriors until the treaty took place. Ignoring Brant's suggested compromise, the Indians sent the commissioners a message that there could be no peace as long as white settlers were living on their lands. Were the commissioners authorized to fix the Ohio River as the boundary? That was out of the question, the commissioners replied: the Indians had ceded the lands north of the Ohio by treaty, and American settlers were already living there. The best the government could do was reconsider its claim to possess the Indians' lands by right of conquest and to "concede this great point, by express authority of the President, & acknowledge the right of soil to the country to be in the Indian nations so long as they desire to occupy." The United States claimed only those lands already ceded and the exclusive right of purchase when the time came for the Indians to sell their lands. A Wyandot chief, with Simon Girty interpreting, put the issue simply: "We regard this side of the Ohio as our property. You say you cannot remove your people; & we cannot give up our lands. We are sorry we cannot come to an agreement." Girty then said the Wyandot chief said the commissioners might as well go home; when his interpretation was questioned, he amended it to say they should wait for the Indians' answer.[113] In a multinational summit conducted via convoluted translation chains, there was ample opportunity for misinterpretation, willful or not: James Dean had translated the commissioners' opening speech into Oneida; Brant's nephew then translated it from Oneida into Shawnee, and another interpreter translated it from Shawnee into Ojibwa.[114]

After two weeks of fruitless negotiations, the Indians made a counterproposal: instead of spending vast amounts of money waging war on Indians or buying their lands, why didn't the government pay its citizens to relocate back on the other side of the Ohio? The Indians demanded only "the peaceable possession of a small part of our once great Country." They could retreat no further and were resolved "to leave our bones in this small space, to which we are now confined." Delegates from all the tribes except Brant and the Iroquois affixed their marks to the message. John Heckewelder characterized the speech as "Impertinent & Insolent, & intended to put an end to Treaty Bussiness."[115] It did. Lincoln, Randolph, and Pickering packed their bags. "The Indians have refused to make peace," they reported to Knox.[116]

Brant left the negotiations "much disappointed." The Shawnees, Delawares, and Miamis had "carried everything their own way." He predicted, with some accuracy, that if those three nations were not able to withstand the Americans, they would lose their country and be driven to the Mississippi, unless assisted by the British, which was unlikely; "the consequences then must be fatal to those Indians as time must ere long convince us." He blamed McKee and other British agents for exerting undue influence.[117] Mckee denied it, although he protested too much.[118] Whether or not Brant had made a deal with Washington, his visit to Philadelphia and his willingness to compromise rendered him suspect in the eyes of the hardliners and their British backers. Simcoe said the western Indians regarded him "as a Traitor to their Interests, and totally in the Service of the United States."[119] Simcoe himself did not go that far. Although Brant was "artful" and out for himself, he informed his superiors, he could also be "a Man of Principle." In the precarious situation the Iroquois occupied between the western nations and the United States, Brant always put the Indians' interests first and then, despite his trip to Philadelphia, had a slight preference for the British over the Americans.[120]

All peace efforts having failed, war was inevitable, Knox immediately informed Wayne; "judge whether your force will be adequate to make those audacious savages feel our superiority in arms."[121] Jefferson said much the same but admitted: "We expected nothing else, and had gone into the negociations only to prove to all our citizens that peace was unattainable on terms which any one of them would admit."[122] Washington assured Congress in his annual message on December 3, 1793, that his government had made every reasonable effort to negotiate peace consistent with "the essential interests and dignity of the United States."[123] Indian intransigence, not American aggression, was to blame for the impending bloodshed.

Having satisfied himself and his citizens that he had made good-faith efforts to secure peace, Washington turned to winning the war for the Old Northwest.

CHAPTER 18

Achieving Empire

WASHINGTON'S VISION FOR THE WEST entailed not only acquiring Indian land but also imposing federal authority and order in a region of international, intertribal, and interstate competition, and conflicting loyalties, violence, and disorder. In the North, he dispatched federal forces to defeat Indian resistance and regional rebellion. In the South, he refrained. For all the challenges his administration faced fighting an Indian war north of the Ohio, it feared an Indian war south of the Ohio even more. Washington and Knox knew Spain was trying to build a multitribal coalition, and if the southern nations united with the northern nations in a general Indian war, they would set the entire frontier ablaze. Keeping the Republic safe required preventing that nightmare from becoming a reality, and that, Washington knew, meant keeping on good terms with the powerful tribes bordering the southwestern frontiers. Friendship with the tribes required halting rampant assaults on their lands. Doing that threatened the fragile loyalty of people who thought the federal government should promote expansion, protect its citizens, and wage war against Indians and who resented the difference in how federal power was applied in the Northwest Territory and the Southwest Territory.[1]

As the new nation endeavored to strengthen ties between the North and the South, so did the old nations. Emissaries from the Northwestern Confederacy tried to enlist the support of the Creeks and Cherokees. Most Cherokees wanted peace and kept their distance from the Northwestern Confederacy, and Washington was anxious that they continue to do so. However, the Chickamauga Cherokees who had migrated to western Tennessee during the Revolution and established new towns—often referred to as the Five Lower Towns—continued their fight and made common cause with the Northwestern Confederacy. Some historians have drawn parallels between the Chickamauga and American struggles for independence and even between the Chickamauga leader Dragging Canoe and Washington himself.[2] If there were parallels, Washington did not see them. "The Chiccamogas, aided by some Banditti of another tribe, in their vicinity, have recently perpetrated wanton, and unprovoked hostilities upon the citizens of the United States in that quarter," he told Congress in 1792. In other words, they were terrorists, not freedom fighters.[3] After Dragging Canoe died in March 1792, Chickamauga leadership passed to Kunoskeskie, also known as John Watts, whom Knox described as "a bold, sensible, and friendly half breed," but Chickamauga resistance continued to complicate US-Cherokee relations.[4]

Recognizing that American settlers had shattered the boundaries established by the Treaty of Hopewell, Knox in early 1791 instructed North Carolina governor William Blount to negotiate a new treaty with the Cherokees, as a sequel to the treaty just made with the Creeks in New York. Blount met 1,200 Cherokee people in a conference on the Holston River in June. His idea of negotiating a new treaty was to tell them the Treaty of Hopewell was defunct and they must sell the land between the Clinch and French Broad Rivers as well as a twenty-five-mile tract south of the French Broad. John Watts, Bloody Fellow, Doublehead, and the other chiefs balked at giving up such amounts of land, but by threat, coercion, or other means, Blount secured their reluctant acquiescence. Forty-one chiefs and warriors signed the Treaty of Holston on July 2, relinquishing 2.6 million acres of land and agreeing to return captives and forgo retaliation for crimes. Blount told Governor Charles Pinckney of South Carolina he wanted more land but it was the best he could do. He said the chiefs left "well pleased." In fact, the chiefs sent a delegation to Philadelphia to protest the treaty. "I was desirous of going to General Washington and Congress to see whether I could obtain better satisfaction," Bloody Fellow said. Bloody Fellow (as principal spokesman), Nontuaka, Chutloh or Kingfisher, Teesteke, Kithagusta or the Prince, and two interpreters set out before the end of the year.[5]

Washington proclaimed the Treaty of Holston on November 11, before he learned of St. Clair's defeat the week before.[6] By the time the five chiefs arrived in Philadelphia on December 28 on board a vessel from Charleston, South Carolina, news of the disaster

on the Wabash had sunk in. On January 4 the Cherokees met with
Washington, who asked them to meet with Knox. Over the course of
several days, in talks with Knox at his home, they voiced their complaints about the Holston Treaty. Nontuaka had met Washington
before, in New York in 1789, and when he returned had "sent good
talks to all the nations, of the kindness with which he was treated,
and of the good intentions of General Washington to do justice to
the red people about their lands. We hope General Washington has
not forgotten his good talks to Nontuaka," Bloody Fellow said; "we
desire nothing more." Bloody Fellow assured Knox they would keep
the peace but asked the government to increase their annuity to
$1,500, expel squatters from Cherokee land south of the ridge sepa-
rating the waters of the Tennessee and the Little River, and stop the
projected settlement at Muscle Shoals, an area North Carolina speculators had eyed for some time. Blount had tried to acquire the
Muscle Shoals lands at the Holston Treaty, but the Cherokees insisted
they could not sell as them, "as they were clearly not our property"
but "common hunting grounds" belonging to the four nations.
Bloody Fellow also asked Washington to send them an agent "who
shall protect us in our lands, and be our friend; and who will explain
all things, and at all times. He shall reside with us, and we will take
care of him."[7]

Washington appointed Leonard Shaw, a recent Princeton graduate, to accompany the chiefs on their journey home and serve as
their temporary agent, and took the opportunity to reaffirm relations with the Cherokees. Their requests, Washington told Charles
Pinckney, who had secured the Cherokees' passage from Charleston,
"were of a nature to be readily complied with," and he submitted
their request to the Senate along with Knox's report recommending
approval. The Senate approved the increase in annuity payments just
two days later: $500 was a small price to pay to appease the Cherokees
in the midst of an Indian war. The formal document revising the
Treaty of Holston was completed and signed on February 17. The
Cherokees, who had been delayed by severe winter weather that
closed New York harbor, sailed for home the next day, with an additional $500 in goods and gifts from the federal government and the
Quakers of Philadelphia.[8]

Bloody Fellow returned home "fully satisfied and pleased," and
Washington followed up by giving him "the more honorable name of
General Eskaqua" or Iskagua, meaning "Clear Sky."[9] Nontuaka told
the Cherokee National Council: "When we left our father, the
President, and General Knox, my heart was easy."[10] It did not remain

easy for long. Settlers and speculators like Blount would not stop encroaching on Cherokee land, and Washington's government could not stop them from doing so. After waiting six months for the redress the Cherokees had been promised, Bloody Fellow declared, "Congress are Liars general Washington is a Liar & governour Blount is a Liar."[11] The Scottish traders William Panton and John McDonald worked as Spanish agents to break down Bloody Fellow's relations with the United States. McDonald, who married a Cherokee woman, fought alongside the Cherokees during the Revolution, and lived the rest of his life with the tribe, escorted Bloody Fellow and other chiefs to Pensacola. From there they traveled to New Orleans in November 1792 to negotiate with Baron Carondelet, along with representatives from the Chickasaws and Choctaws, and ask for assistance against American thefts of their lands.[12] Blount put a price of five hundred pesos on McDonald's head.[13]

Like Carondelet, Chickasaws and Choctaws watched with concern as American power expanded in the East. But Indian power in the West posed a more immediate threat. The Osages dominated the prairies between the Missouri and Arkansas and controlled the intertribal gun trade. Well-mounted and well-armed Osage warriors battled Indians who crossed the Mississippi to hunt and escape growing American pressure; they pushed other prairie tribes south and west, and they pillaged traders. According to one Chickasaw chief in 1793, the Osages were "at war with all men, white and red, steal the horses, and kill all the white men they find." Unable to match Osage power, Spain tried to deal with them on their terms. Carondelet granted a monopoly on trading with the Osages to Auguste Chouteau and his younger half brother Pierre, members of the French family that had founded St. Louis in 1764, built its commercial empire trading with the Osages, and spent much time living with the tribe. At the same time, Carondelet tried to build a multitribal buffer against the Osages as well as against the United States. Faced with the Osage threat, Choctaws and Chickasaws set aside their differences and looked for trade and alliance with Spain or the United States or both.[14]

When the Cherokee delegation left for Philadelphia, the Choctaws and Chickasaws gave Bloody Fellow a white wampum belt and asked him to convey a message to the president. "Tell General Washington, that the Carolina people ought not to be appointed to hold talks with Indians, as they always ask for lands." He should appoint someone who wanted justice, not land, they said.[15] Piominko had signed the Treaty of Hopewell, befriended General James Robertson, the founder of Nashville, and led the Chickasaw scouts in

St. Clair's campaign. Knox recommended that he be "rewarded liberally" for his services and cultivated as someone who might be able to unite the Chickasaws and Choctaws as allies of the United States.[16] He sent messages to the Choctaws and Chickasaws, telling them the president had received their talk and inviting them to send warriors to serve in the next campaign. He also sent Piominko and several other chiefs silver medals and "rich uniforms" and "a great white belt" from Washington "as a perpetual evidence of the pure intentions and strong affections of the United States to the Chickasaw nation." The president invited Piominko and other chiefs to Philadelphia so he could convince them in person "how desirous he is to promote your happiness." The peace medal and a uniform were subsequently delivered to Piominko and to the Chickasaw chiefs William and George Colbert.[17] Washington hoped the favorable impression Bloody Fellow's delegation had received during their visit would have a good effect on the Creeks, Choctaws, and Chickasaws.[18]

In April 1792 Blount turned back three Chickasaws on their way to Philadelphia carrying a letter from Piominko to Washington. But in August he held a conference at Nashville, which most of the Chickasaw chiefs attended, including Piominko and his rival Wolf's Friend or Ugulayacabe. Piominko traced the Chickasaw lands on a map and said his only wish was to have the boundaries confirmed and secured. Blount lied: "The United States do not want to take land from any red people; they have land enough." Ugulayacabe, a big man wearing a scarlet coat trimmed with silver lace and sheltering under "a large silk umbrella" in the heat of the day, handed Blount a string of white beads as a token of peace and friendship, but when he said he got all the supplies he needed from the Spaniards, Blount "looked at him with evil eyes." Ugulayacabe told him that in the event of a war between Spain and the United States he would take no part, but he would never allow the Americans to advance any farther into Chickasaw country.[19] General Robertson's pronouncement "Never was a people more attached to a nation, than the Chickasaws are to the United States" was an exaggeration.[20]

Chickasaw foreign policy was a challenge for Washington's administration. In need of allies and ammunition as they confronted the threat of war with the Creeks and raids by the Osages, the Chickasaws explored an alliance with the United States as one of their options, but Spain was an active suitor. Carondelet was willing to pay "any price" to win the friendship of Ugulayacabe and Piominko as a check on American expansion and on Osage power.[21] He redoubled his diplomatic efforts with the Choctaws and Chickasaws, and in

October 1793 Ugulayacabe and one group joined delegates from the Cherokees, Creeks, Choctaws, and other nations in making a treaty of alliance with Spain at Nogales.[22] Piominko and another group set out for Philadelphia to remind Washington of promises that had been made to supply them with arms and ammunition. They turned back because of yellow fever in the city.[23]

A year later, in July 1794, five chiefs (including Piominko and George Colbert), seven warriors, four boys, and an interpreter, completed the thousand-mile journey to Philadelphia. John Quincy Adams, who attended the reception "and assisted in smoking the pipe with them," noted in his diary that some of the Chickasaws wore US Army uniforms. After the ceremonial smoking of the pipe, Washington gave a short speech, stopping at the end of each sentence for the interpreter to translate his words. He thanked them for their assistance against the misguided tribes northwest of the Ohio. "I love the Chickasaws," he said, "and it will always afford me sincere satisfaction, to be instrumental to their happiness in any way or manner." As a means of introducing them to "the blessings of civilized life," he offered to support at public expense any Chickasaw boys who wished to learn to read, write, and manage a farm, and return them whenever the Chickasaws wanted. He also offered to have Knox make travel arrangements if the chiefs wanted to see New York City. Knox had furnished Washington with commissions for some of the chiefs, which "delivered by your hands will have greater value." Piominko, who was unwell, declined to speak but said he would do so in a few days. The Chickasaws did ask questions—with "a mixture of curiosity and animosity," Adams said—about the Cherokees who had recently been there. Then, after cake, wine, and punch were served, they shook hands and departed. More meetings were held during the next ten days. Piominko asked for a document that explicitly stated the eastern boundaries of Chickasaw territory. Washington provided the document and declared Chickasaw country under the protection of the United States.[24] Ugulayacabe, meanwhile, was talking to the Spaniards.[25]

As so often happened, land-hungry and Indian-hating frontiersmen undermined Washington's policies and peace initiatives. "The difficulty of deciding between lawless Settlers & greedy (land) Speculators on one side, and the jealousies of the Indian Nations & their banditti on the other, becomes more & more obvious every day," Washington lamented to Knox.[26] In December 1792 he issued a proclamation, offering a reward for the apprehension of "certain lawless and wicked persons" who had burned a Cherokee town and killed several people.[27] He invited John Watts, Little Turkey, and other chiefs to come to Philadelphia, but they were hesitant to travel while there were hostilities between the Creeks and other Indians and between Indians and settlers.[28]

Then, in June 1793, only a few days after the Cherokees had received Washington's invitation, said the Cherokee chief Hanging Maw, Captain John Beard, or Baird, and a group of Tennessee mounted infantry attacked Cherokee leaders who, at Blount's request, had assembled for peace talks at Hanging Maw's house. They killed and wounded a dozen people, including Hanging Maw's wife.[29] The Cherokees would not be coming to Philadelphia, Hanging Maw explained in a letter to Washington, whom he recalled meeting "when we were both young men and warriors." They liked his talk of restoring peace and making their lands safe, but the white people had spoiled it. "The heads of our land thought well of going to Philadelphia, but some of them now lie dead, and some of them wounded. You need not look for us to go there at this time." This was the third time whites had killed Cherokees when they were talking in peace. The dead had to be avenged. The territorial secretary, Daniel Smith, begged them to wait for the government to punish the perpetrators, because the president was "a great and good man, and will keep his word."[30] The Cherokees did not buy it. A large war party set out to destroy Knoxville; instead they attacked a fortified farmstead known as Cavett's Station, where they killed thirteen men, women, and children.[31]

The violence played into Spanish hands. Manuel Luis Gayoso de Lemos, governor of the Natchez District, told Indian delegates that some Americans on the frontiers were "like mad dogs doing evil to whomever they meet," and neither Washington nor Congress could do anything to stop them.[32] After yet another spate of killings, Washington reassured the Cherokees that summer that he was determined to treat "his red children . . . with the same humanity and justice as his white children." He directed Blount to bring the perpetrators to justice and again invited Hanging Maw and the chiefs to Philadelphia in the fall of 1793. They would be well treated if they came; "by being face to face, the remembrance of all former injuries will be done away," and "we may establish a firm and lasting peace and friendship."[33] It would take a lot more than that.

American officials on the ground pretty much agreed with Gayoso. "To speak of peace with the Creeks, is a crime not to be forgiven, by a very great proportion of the people in this country," Seagrove told Knox, while Daniel Smith feared that the "Spirit for war against Indians pervades people of all Ranks so far that no order of Government can stop them."[34] Georgians continued to encroach on Creek lands, frontier killings escalated, and war with the Creeks looked increasingly inevitable. In 1793 ten delegates from the North-western Confederacy traveled through the South, calling on the Creeks to take up arms and join them.[35] Blount argued that the only way to make "our perfidious Yellow Brethren to the South" behave was to wage "vigorous national war" against them.[36] Creek chiefs sent "our friend and father General Washington" a message asking if Blount and the settlers on the Cumberland were under his government or not. If the president wanted peace with the Indians, he must restrain his own people.[37]

In fact, pressured by Georgia and South Carolina, Washington was considering a military solution. He read reports from the Creek agent James Seagrove and alarmed Georgia citizens. He consulted with Knox, and with General Andrew Pickens of South Carolina and Blount, who were both in Philadelphia at the time.[38] Pickens, like Washington (and unlike Blount), was concerned with his own and his country's reputation in dealing with the Indians but also, like Washington, committed to national expansion on Indian lands.[39] Blount and Pickens urged assisting the Chickasaws in their war against the Creeks and also embroiling the Choctaws in the conflict: "It certainly would be good Policy to use Savages against Savages," they told Knox.[40] Marinus Willett, however, warned the president that "the leading men of Georgia" would stop at nothing to get hold of Creek lands and cautioned him to investigate matters thoroughly before launching an offensive.[41] Washington did just that. He gave the question a lot of thought and discussed it with his cabinet, which split over whether to secretly engage the Choctaws to support the Chickasaws. Jefferson and Knox were in favor; Hamilton and Randolph opposed. Washington, like Randolph, approved "of the general policy of employing Indians against Indians" but feared it might entangle the United States in conflict with Spain, and it was neither ethically defensible nor good policy to involve the Choctaws in war without a clear exit strategy, as we might term it today.[42] In the end, the president and his cabinet decided against military action: the ongoing war with the Northwestern Confederacy and the tumultuous state of affairs in Europe would make a war with the Creeks "extremely disagreeable."[43] Spanish efforts to prevent a Creek-Chickasaw war proved effective, and both nations joined the Spanish-backed alliance at the Treaty of Nogales in October 1793.[44]

In the spring of 1794 Knox invited another Cherokee delegation to Philadelphia. About twenty chiefs, including Nontuaka,

Tekakiska, Doublehead, and Keenaguna (Lying Fawn), arrived by boat from Charleston in early June. Washington met with them in his house on Market Street on June 14, along with Knox, Jefferson, Hamilton, and Pickering. He told them they must stop their young men stealing horses and murdering settlers and promised his government would try to keep its young men from doing Cherokees harm. As for the Cherokees' concerns about lands on the Cumberland, the cessions had been confirmed by the Hopewell and Holston Treaties, and more than ten thousand people were now settled there. The treaties that had been made could not be altered. However, he did promise to increase their annuity from $1,500 to $5,000. "The great pipe was smoked by all," Washington recorded in his journal. "Delivered a speech to them in writing. Several of them spoke & after having eaten & drank plentifully of Cake & wine, they departed seemingly well pleased." Twelve days later thirteen chiefs reaffirmed the Treaty of Holston in return for increased annuities and supplemental articles that clarified misunderstandings arising from the treaty.[45]

Blount would have preferred the president to make the Cherokees "feel the Horrors of War." While Doublehead "and his sanguinary Brothers are received and caressed at Philadelphia," Blount's frontier constituents were "daily Suffering at the Hands of their Associates in Iniquity." Only the restraining hand of government would stop them from killing and stealing, said Blount, sounding like Creek and Cherokee chiefs in their talks to Washington.[46] But Washington's policies withheld that restraining hand and restricted Blount to defensive measures. Instead, Blount looked the other way as territorial militia took the offensive. In September 1794 Major James Ore and a force of five hundred Kentucky and Tennessee militia attacked the Chickamauga towns on the Tennessee River. They burned the towns at Nickajack and Running Water and killed "upwards of fifty."[47] (Ore could not be sure because many were shot in the river.) Blount's report of the victory reached Washington at the end of October.[48] Blount followed up on the blow by warning the Cherokees that war with the United States would destroy them as a people.[49] In November he met with Hanging Maw, John Watts, Bloody Fellow, and other Cherokee leaders at Tellico Blockhouse on the Little Tennessee River, where they, too, agreed to accept the land cession made at the Treaty of Holston.[50]

The land-grabbing Blount was not the man to bring peace and harmony to Indian relations. His meddling in intertribal affairs and readiness to resort to war worried Washington. "Upon the whole, Sir," the new secretary of war, Timothy Pickering (Knox had retired in December), wrote Blount in March 1795, "I cannot refrain from saying that the complexion of some of the Transactions in the South western territory appears unfavourable to the public interests." The president had promised peace and protection to the Cherokee chiefs in Philadelphia the previous summer and was determined to avoid a war with the Creeks if possible. Peace on the frontiers could not be expected so long as state and territorial officials allowed American citizens to steal Indian land and turned a blind eye to unauthorized campaigns. Since Congress alone had authority to decide upon an offensive war, and Congress had not seen fit to do so, the secretary reminded the governor, Blount should forget any plans for offensive operations and cultivate peace with the tribes.[51]

Chickasaw-Creek relations remained volatile, and Chickasaw delegates returned to Philadelphia in 1795 seeking support. Washington had planned to head home to Mount Vernon before the middle of July, but hearing a delegation of Chickasaw and Choctaw chiefs was on the way to see him on official business, he delayed his departure. Three Chickasaw and five Choctaw chiefs and their interpreters arrived in Philadelphia on July 3 and returned home after an audience with the president. Washington and his family left the city on July 15, but he was back in late August when a second group of Chickasaws arrived: William Colbert (Cooshemataha), William McGillivray (Coahama or Red Cat), and John Brown. Washington referred them to the talk he had given to the previous delegation and again declined their requests for assistance against the Creeks. "It was never the design of the United States to interfere in the disputes of the Indian Nations among one another unless as friends to both parties, to reconcile them," he explained, which was not true but expressed his position in this case. Assisting the Chickasaws would involve the United States in open war with the Creeks, and only Congress, "the Great Council of the United States," had the power to declare war. "I have no authority to begin such a war without their consent." However, he would send provisions to alleviate the Chickasaws' suffering after a drought in their country, and he promised to work through diplomatic channels to induce Spain to remove the post they had built at Chickasaw Bluff, "an unwarrantable aggression as well against the United States, as the Chickasaws, to whom the land there belongs."[52] The Spaniards, with the support of Ugulayacabe and his faction, had built the post of San Fernando de las Barrancas on bluffs along the east bank of the Mississippi in the spring.

Washington was actually trying to arrange peace between the Creeks and Chickasaws as soon as possible; he wanted to be able to tell Congress in his address that the government was at peace with all the Indian nations and had also settled differences between the two tribes.[53] The Creeks and Chickasaws made peace in late 1795. (The Spaniards urged them to do so in order to present a united front to American aggression.)[54]

Peace between the Creeks and Georgia remained elusive, however. The aggressions of Georgia settlers, grants of millions of acres by Georgia's legislature to land companies, the state's insistence on its right to deal with Indians and buy Indian lands, Spanish intrigue and influence, the ambitions and activities of individual adventurers, divisions in the Creek confederacy, and the inabilities of leaders, whether Indian or white, to control their warriors all kept the region in continual turmoil.[55] In 1794 the former militia commander Elijah Clarke and a group of Georgians who planned to set up an independent republic in Creek country built a string of forts between the Oconee and Ocmulgee Rivers in flagrant violation of the Treaty of New York; Knox had to order the governor of Georgia to call the state militia into federal service and remove them.[56] In December 1794 the Georgia legislature appropriated lands to pay state troops from territory guaranteed to the Creeks by the Treaty of New York. Speculators in the Tennessee, South Carolina, Virginia, and Georgia Yazoo Companies greased the palms of members of the Georgia legislature, which sold them 35 million acres of fertile land stretching from Muscle Shoals on the Tennessee River to the mouth of the Yazoo River near present-day Vicksburg for $500,000 and passed laws promising to extinguish Indian claims. This second Yazoo land fraud was so egregious that even the citizens of Georgia revolted against it. The Assembly repealed the act, and the new state constitution in 1798 prohibited land sales to monopolies. However, Georgia's insistence that citizens, not monopolies, should reap the benefits of acquiring Indian lands brought little relief for the Creeks.[57]

The best Washington could do was to try to keep the toxic mixture from exploding into an all-out war. He withheld approval of the Georgia legislature's sale of the state's territorial claims to private land companies. In an effort to settle the question of a boundary line, he inserted the federal government in a treaty negotiation between Georgia and the Creeks over land that both claimed. He nominated Benjamin Hawkins, George Clymer of Pennsylvania, and Andrew Pickens as commissioners.[58] At Coleraine on the St Marys River on the southern border of Georgia, the federal commissioners, three Georgia commissioners, and more than four hundred Creeks spent a month trying to settle their differences. The Creeks looked to the federal government. "As soon as I saw the establishment of the forts made by Clarke, broken up by Washington's warriors, it was a satisfactory demonstration that General Washington meant nothing but [our] good: and consequently, we have all determined to confide in him," said Fusatchee Mico (White Bird King). They would listen to the talks of his agent as if "they were the words of Washington himself." The Georgia commissioners protested against the conduct of the treaty and the assertion of federal authority, but the resulting agreement, at the end of June 1796, confirmed the cession of lands between the Ogeechee and Oconee Rivers made in the Treaty of New York six years earlier, made provision for running a temporary boundary with Georgia, increased the annual Creek subsidy to $6,000, and provided for the establishment of a second government trading post in Creek country. It marked the beginning of a brief period of relative peace, although Hawkins was kept busy trying to run a workable boundary line with the southern nations until 1798.[59] Peace sent land prices soaring and surveyors scrambling.[60] Demand for Creek lands would only escalate.

WASHINGTON SUCCEEDED IN AVOIDING ALL-OUT WAR in the South. That was not the case in the North, and perhaps it was never really the intention. While peace initiatives with the Northwestern Confederacy were getting nowhere, the United States rebuilt its forces; indeed, it built the kind of national army Washington had wanted all along. Following Knox's plan, Congress in March 1792 passed legislation that made "more effectual Provision for the Protection of the Frontiers" and overhauled the US Army. The two infantry regiments and the artillery battalion then in existence were to be completed to full strength. Three additional regiments of 960 men each were authorized, to be enlisted for a term not exceeding three years and to be discharged as soon as the United States secured peace with the Indian tribes. Instead of a regimental structure with the infantry, cavalry, and artillery in distinct units, Washington and Knox divided the 5,120 men into four sublegions, each of 1,280 men, commanded by brigadier generals. Each sublegion was organized into two battalions (eight companies) of infantry, one battalion (four companies) of riflemen, one company of artillery, and one troop of dragoons. Washington was not willing to abandon combined regular-militia operations, and the act also authorized the president to call militia cavalry into service and employ Indian scouts as he saw fit. Nevertheless, the burden of fighting the war shifted from irregular soldiers

to a new and more professional military. The government appropriated $1 million to fund the new army, which received more supplies
and better training than either Harmar or St. Clair's armies.[61]

In the spring of 1792, despite misgivings about the value of
militia, Congress had responded to St. Clair's defeat and the threat
of Indian attacks on the frontiers by passing two militia acts. The first
authorized the president to draft state militias into a federal force
"whenever the United States shall be invaded, or be in imminent
danger of invasion from any foreign nation or Indian tribe," and when
necessary to ensure that the laws of the United States were "faithfully
executed," as prescribed in the Constitution. The second provided
for the organization of state militias, requiring every able-bodied free
white male citizen of the states between ages eighteen and forty-five
to enroll and arm himself with a musket or firelock, bayonet and
belt, spare flints, knapsack, pouch, and cartridge box with no fewer
than twenty-four cartridges. Although the Militia Act initially required
consent of a federal judge, Congress later removed that restriction,
giving the president "all-but-unfettered powers" to raise troops and
send them into combat without a declaration of war by Congress.[62]

Washington's two previous appointments of commanders to
lead expeditions into the Ohio country had proved disastrous. He
had to get this one right. He drew up a memorandum describing the
strengths and weaknesses of the available options to head the new
army and then discussed them with his department heads. Benjamin
Lincoln, Lachlan McIntosh, Edward Hand, Daniel Morgan, Rufus
Putnam, Charles Pinckney, Charles Scott, James Wilkinson (who,
unknown to the president, was on Spain's payroll as a spy and exploring the possibility of adding Kentucky to Spanish territory!), and
Anthony Wayne were all on the list. Washington chose Wayne, whom
he described as "more active & enterprising than judicious & cautious…Open to flattery—vain—easily imposed upon—and liable to
be drawn into scrapes.…Whether sober—or a little addicted to the
bottle, I know not." Jefferson's notes of the meeting were more suc-
cinct: "Wayne. Brave and nothing else." He deserved credit for the
battle at Stony Point during the Revolution, "but on another occasion run his head against a wall where success was both impossible
and useless."[63] George Hammond, the British minister in Philadelphia, told Lieutenant Governor Simcoe that Wayne was the most
active, vigilant, and enterprising officer the Americans had and
would make every exertion "to efface the Stain, which the late defeat
has cast upon the American Arms." He added that Wayne's talents
were "*purely* Military," and should he defeat the Indians, he was rash

enough to try and seize the British posts.[64] Wayne had made it known several years before that there could be no lasting peace with the Creeks until they experienced the military superiority of the United States and that, given the proper authority and means, he could "organize & discipline A Legionary Corps" and get the job done in short order.[65] Now he was to get his chance against the northern tribes. Nevertheless, he made it clear he would accept the appointment only if the army was his to command as he saw fit, subject to supervision only by the secretary of war and the president.[66]

Washington also offered an appointment as brigadier general to Marinus Willett, his intermediary with Alexander McGillivray. Willett declined on principle. He had always believed that the best policy was to avoid an Indian war, and he had never been convinced by the reasons given for this one, he wrote Washington. He knew from experience it was not difficult to preserve peace with Indians, and although he believed he knew how to defeat them, fighting them "would be the last choice of my mind." The kind treatment they had shown him made him their advocate rather than their enemy. He expressed his hope to the president "that the Gentleman who is going out against the Indians" would have "as pasific a disposition" as was possible in the circumstances and be "the happy instrument" of achieving peace.[67]

The fact that the gentleman in question had earned the nickname "Mad Anthony" during the Revolution suggested that a pacific disposition was unlikely. Wayne operated on the conviction that there could never be lasting peace until the Indians were defeated in battle. Despite his nickname, he set about the task of molding his army with methodical determination. Knox warned him to avoid at all costs pitting raw recruits against Indians, and the new general was determined not to repeat the mistakes of his predecessors. Having seen what had happened to St. Clair, he refused to march until his army was fully prepared. He trained his soldiers to be an effective fighting force in Indian country, a process that involved, among other things, staging war games and sham Indian attacks.[68] He intended to screen his march with Indian guides, scouts, spies, and cavalry, and to attack, not be attacked.[69] He was confident the military improvements he implemented and the force he put into the field would demonstrate "not only to the savages, but to the World, that the U S of America are not to be insulted with impunity." Bombast aside, Wayne was out to teach the Indians a lesson.[70]

While Wayne was at Pittsburgh and vicinity from the fall of 1792 to early 1793, Guyasuta—"old Quiashuta, Chief of the Allegheny"—

visited him several times to talk and once, in company with Cornplanter and others, to dine. Delaware, Shawnee, and Miami chiefs
also came with tentative peace offers, which Wayne suspected were
designed to gain time to gather in winter provisions and withdraw
their women and children "from pending destruction" as well as
reconnoiter his positions and numbers.[71] At that point, Washington,
too, wanted to delay things. The army was not nearly ready, officers
were still enlisting boys and riffraff, and he feared that if the United
States did not convince the Indians of its just intentions toward them,
it would face "a powerful opposition from their Combined force."
Put another way, negotiating in good faith could help divide that
opposition. He recommended that Wayne keep six or eight Chickasaws and Choctaws with him and treat them well as an inducement
to attracting more if needed.[72] Knox (Pickering had not yet taken
over as secretary of war) suggested to Alexander McGillivray that one
or two hundred Creek warriors might be employed to good advantage with the army, but McGillivray did not bite.[73] Piominko, on the
other hand, sent Chickasaw warriors and tried to get the Choctaws to
fight the Kickapoos "for the benefit of the Americans."[74]

Wayne moved his army from Fort Washington up the Miami
River to Fort Jefferson, where he awaited the outcome of the peace
talks at Sandusky. When the express message arrived from the commissioners in early September that the talks had failed, Knox (writing Washington from the outskirts of Philadelphia, as there was still
yellow fever in the city) hoped Wayne would advance his whole force
from Fort Jefferson by October 1. Wayne now had a trained and
disciplined force of 2,200 regular infantry augmented by 1,500
mounted Kentucky militia under General Scott. It was a force equal
to what all the tribes between the Great Lakes and the Ohio could
muster, said Knox; "God grant him success."[75] Washington's annual
message to Congress in December, however, cautioned that the lateness of the season would delay the expedition until the next year.[76]

Wayne spent the time constructing Fort Greenville as his new
headquarters, about six miles from Fort Jefferson. From there, he
could protect convoys and frontier settlements from Indian attacks
and strike against the Miami villages.[77] He sent a detachment of men
forward to St. Clair's battlefield, where they buried the remains of
the dead and built a fort named Recovery. A company of artillery
and a company of riflemen occupied it for the winter.[78]

Meanwhile there was much saber rattling. Washington's old
comrade Louis Cook participated in a delegation from the Seven

Nations of Canada to Guy Carleton, Lord Dorchester, the governor of Quebec, that winter. Dorchester told them he would not be surprised if Britain and the United States were at war within the year, in which case the boundary line "ought then to be drawn by the Warriors." In March 1794 Washington received from George Clinton a copy of a speech made to him by Cook and a copy of Dorchester's speech. Anticipating war, Cook contemplated removing his wife and children from St. Regis, the Mohawk community of Akwesasne on the border of New York and Canada. Some people who refused to believe that Britain had any hostile intentions toward the United States thought the speech spurious, but Washington had no doubts about its authenticity or the British government's efforts to keep the Indian nations stirred up in an effort to alter the border between Canada and the United States.[79]

Wayne shared Washington's sentiments and anticipated conflict with Britain, although Knox warned him to avoid any action that could be construed as American aggression against a foreign nation.[80] That spring British troops began building Fort Miamis at the rapids on the Maumee River. This was more than holding a fort on the basis that the United States had not met its Peace of Paris commitments; it constituted armed occupation of a site within the Republic's territorial borders. It seemed to the Indians that the redcoats were ready at last to provide open assistance against the Americans. As Wayne advanced, Indians made repeated requests to the British to honor their promises and lend support because time was running out.[81]

The Indian confederacy was no longer the force that had defeated St. Clair. American diplomacy and divergent tribal agendas had divided its councils. Putnam's treaty with the Wabash tribes at Vincennes had effectively detached the western flank of the confederacy.[82] At the end of June, Blue Jacket ambushed a party of dragoons from Fort Recovery, but when the Ottawas led an assault on the fort itself, the American artillery drove them off. The Ottawas had had enough, and most headed for home. Many Ojibwas and Potawatomis followed. The confederacy lost about half its warriors. Little Turtle saw the writing on the wall. In July he visited Detroit to find out what assistance to expect from the British. The Indians could not keep fighting as they had; if the British did not assist them, they would not be able to stop the American army. The British commander thought Little Turtle "the most decent, modest, sensible Indian I have ever conversed with," but his hands were tied.[83] Little Turtle began to advocate making the best peace the Indians could get.

As Wayne's army marched along the Auglaize River, Indian families abandoned the villages that had served as the core of the resistance movement. People loaded canoes and ponies and hurried away with small children; old women burdened with heavy packs struggled after them.[84] In August, Wayne built Fort Defiance at the junction of the Maumee and Auglaize Rivers. The fortunes of war were uncertain, Wayne wrote, but "that great & good man Our Virtuous President" would have no reason to regret the trust he had shown him.[85]

The Indian force diminished further on the eve of its showdown with Wayne. Taking advantage of an area strewn with uprooted trees after a tornado at a place called Fallen Timbers, Blue Jacket drew up his warriors to fight on August 19. When Wayne's army halted and the expected battle did not take place that day, warriors who had fasted in ritual purification prior to combat began to disperse in search of food. Wayne's army appeared the next morning.

The Indians fought in the crescent formation that had proved so effective in engulfing St. Clair's army, with the Shawnees on the left wing. As at St. Clair's defeat, their initial assault put to flight a unit of mounted volunteers advancing in front of the main army. This time, however, the ranks behind steadied and held. The American cavalry turned the Indians' flanks, and the infantry's bayonet charge drove the warriors from the battlefield. They fled to Fort Miamis, where they expected to receive sanctuary if not outright assistance from the British garrison. But the gates of the fort remained barred. That dispirited the Indians more than the outcome of the battle, said John Norton. They had fought with inferior numbers, in a disadvantageous position, and had not suffered great casualties. They could have fought another day and reversed the defeat, but the British betrayal "they did not know how to remedy."[86]

Wayne and the British commander exchanged heated words but no gunfire. London was far more concerned about events in Revolutionary France than about its Indian allies, and the commander was not about to start a war with the United States. Wayne's army was in no position to start assaulting British posts. Nevertheless, although a British garrison remained on their soil, Americans anxious to establish themselves as an international power interpreted the showdown at the fort as a significant assertion of sovereignty: for the first time, the young nation had demonstrated the ability to enforce its will by force of arms.[87]

As in Sullivan's campaign during the Revolution, the American victory lay in crops destroyed more than warriors killed. Wayne's soldiers burned the vast Indian cornfields that stretched along the banks of the Auglaize and Maumee Rivers. In his report of the battle, Wayne said he had never "beheld such immense fields of corn in any part of America from Canada to Florida." Putting them to the torch destroyed "the grand emporium of the hostile Indians of the West." With the Indians' towns and crops laid waste and American troops on their hunting grounds, Wayne estimated there were seven or eight thousand hungry mouths to feed, far beyond the capacity of the British to provision them.[88] According to William Clark, later of Lewis and Clark fame but then a lieutenant in Wayne's army, the destruction of the Indians' homes and cornfields while the redcoats watched in silence convinced them the British had neither the power nor inclination to protect them.[89] According to Alexander McKee, Wayne's soldiers "left Evident marks of their boasted Humanity"; they not only scalped and mutilated the Indians who were killed in the battle but also dug up Indian graves and drove stakes through the decomposing corpses.[90]

In September, Wayne built a fort—Fort Wayne—on the site of Kekionga. The news of his victory reached Washington on September 30.[91] Nothing changed popular sentiment like success, Edmund Randolph wrote Washington three days later. People who had formerly spoken about Wayne in derogatory terms now said they knew all along "that the President would never appoint an incompetent man to the command of the army."[92] Wayne's victory did not silence criticism of Washington, but after Harmar and St. Clair's disasters, it saved his reputation. The federal government and its new army had finally answered westerners' calls and defeated the Indians.

On the heels of the victory, the government asserted its authority in ways westerners had not bargained for. In his annual message to Congress in November 1794, two dozen paragraphs, Washington devoted more than a paragraph to only two domestic issues. He covered Indian affairs in two paragraphs.[93] Before that, he spent two-thirds of the entire address on the Whiskey Rebellion, when settlers in western Pennsylvania refused to pay the tax the federal government levied on whiskey, invoking similar arguments to those they voiced on the eve of the Revolution. For a time it looked as if a settler revolt like that which had occurred in 1776 might occur again.[94] The Whiskey Rebellion threatened to spread across the Ohio Valley, and it surpassed the Indian war in the concerns and correspondence of Washington and his ministers that summer. The morning after he received the news of Fallen Timbers, Washington set off for the Pennsylvania frontier to help organize an army to quash the rebellion and enforce compliance with the whiskey tax.[95] He and Hamilton personally led the army of thirteen thousand men for a time.[96] As

George Nicholas noted to Madison, the armed force the government dispatched against the Indians paled in comparison with that it dispatched against its own citizens; it was, he said, "a spectacle which I never expected to have lived to see."[97] The display of military power was all that was needed—in fact, more than was needed—for the rebellion to crumble. The assertions of federal military power in western Pennsylvania and northern Ohio both demonstrated the determination of the Washington administration to secure control of the West. "Lawless banditti," whether Indian or white, must respect the authority of the United States.[98]

EVEN AS WAYNE WAGED WAR, Washington tried, as he said, "to tranquilize the Indians by pacific measures."[99] Keeping the Six Nations from joining the western tribes fighting Wayne was essential; with British agents at work and Iroquois lands under assault, it took some effort. General Israel Chapin, the agent to the Iroquois, was instructed to employ every means to keep the Six Nations favorably disposed toward the United States "and to buy Captn B[ran]t off at almost any price."[100] To assuage Iroquois resentment about American encroachments, Washington asked Pennsylvania governor Thomas Mifflin to suspend his state's plans for a settlement at Presque Isle on Lake Erie, which Mifflin reluctantly agreed to do.[101]

Six Nations chiefs understood they had leverage and played their cards well. In council with Chapin at Buffalo Creek in July 1794, Cornplanter voiced concern about Pennsylvania's encroachments and Presque Isle. His stance perhaps hardened by the rebuke he had received from the western tribes the previous year, he called on the president to give them justice and protect their land, warning, "Brother, If you do not comply with our request, we shall determine on something else, as we are a free people." Knowing Washington's tendency to blame Indian difficulties on British intrigues, he cautioned the president not to think their minds were corrupted by a foreign power: "You know, General Washington, that we, the Six Nations have always been able to defend ourselves, and we are still determined to maintain our freedom.... The only thing that can corrupt our minds is not to grant our request." Chapin assured the Iroquois that Washington was their "firm friend" and promised to forward their speech to him as soon as possible.[102] Timothy Pickering described Cornplanter's speech as "rude & threatening" and said the principal chiefs were displeased by it, although they allowed it to be sent to the president. "It is not a new thing, I presume," Pickering could not help adding, "for the majority of an Assembly silently to acquiesce in a measure repugnant to their sentiments."[103]

In September, not yet aware of Wayne's victory and with Knox still secretary of war, Washington had dispatched Pickering to negotiate with the Six Nations. While American soldiers were building Fort Wayne, more than 1,500 Iroquois, including Red Jacket, Cornplanter, Handsome Lake, and other prominent leaders, gathered to meet with Pickering at Canandaigua, a Seneca village burned by Sullivan in 1779 and now an American town of forty houses.[104] Brant stayed away. He gave as his reason a previous commitment to meet with the Great Lakes tribes, but in a letter to Chapin he complained "the President of the United States does not seem to come to the main point in question (the line that was proposed) however attentive he may be in other matters." If Washington would agree to the proposed line and to a meeting at Buffalo Creek, Brant would do all he could "to complete the good work of peace."[105] Brant and Cornplanter pursued different paths, but they had few illusions about their situation. "You know my friend," Cornplanter wrote Brant during the negotiations at Canandaigua, "that we are despised by the whites on both sides, that we are a poor, tho' independent people[;] the reason we are despised by both parties is because they both want to be the greatest people." Many Iroquois suspected Cornplanter was Washington's man and were uneasy at his frequent meetings with Pickering during the negotiations, telling him that as a war chief he should leave the business of treaty-making to the sachems. But they identified Pickering as the president's representative and, as Red Jacket said, "took General Washington by the hand" and addressed their speeches as if they were speaking to him.[106]

Pickering told the Iroquois he had come "to heal the wounds which have been given by disposing of your lands, and to point out the way in which you can avoid future strife." The Oneidas felt especially wounded. After assisting Washington in the Revolution they had seen their homeland shrink from 5 or 6 million acres to one-quarter of a million acres. They "had much to say about the many deceptions which had been practiced upon them by the white people." Pickering acknowledged that some white people imposed on the Indians, exploiting their ignorance in computing the value of their lands, plying them with alcohol, and getting them to sign papers that had not been properly interpreted. The best way to avoid trouble in the future, he suggested, was for the Iroquois to adopt white ways and become literate; then they would be able to match white men and avoid being cheated.[107]

Pickering's immediate goal was to keep the Iroquois out of the war that was winding down in the West. News of Fallen Timbers reached Canandaigua in September before negotiations had started.[108] When the Treaty of Canandaigua was finally signed on November 11, the United States confirmed Oneida, Cayuga, and Onondaga lands in New York and even restored some lands to the Senecas.[109] Three weeks later, Pickering signed a second treaty with the Oneidas, awarding them, and their Stockbridge and Tuscarora allies, compensation for their services during the Revolution.[110]

Washington asked Congress to authorize making a large wampum belt to symbolize his new friendship with the Six Nations. Six feet long, five inches wide, and containing ten thousand beads, the George Washington Covenant Chain Belt, as it became known, depicted two figures at the center standing on either side of a house, representing the Mohawks and Senecas as keepers of the eastern and western door, respectively, of the Longhouse, their arms linked to those of thirteen other figures in an alliance of peace with the original states.[111]

The treaty had rather different meanings for Washington and for the Iroquois. Washington saw it as resolving problems the United States faced in its dealings with the Northwestern Confederacy and with the Six Nations. For Iroquois people it was, and remains, a clear recognition of Haudenosaunee sovereignty and the seminal document in their relationship with the United States. An annual commemoration and celebration of the treaty occurs each November 11 in Canandaigua with both US and Iroquois dignitaries present; the covenant belt is displayed, and the treaty goods promised in the treaty, including treaty cloth, are delivered. "In light of the history of other roads taken, some of which are among the most tragic and dishonorable in American history," wrote the late Seneca scholar John Mohawk, "the Canandaigua Treaty stands as a symbol of what might have been almost as much as it is a symbol of what came to be."[112] Washington recognized Pickering's services by promoting him to replace Knox as secretary of war. Unfortunately, Philip Schuyler and other powerful New Yorkers continued to erode the Iroquois homeland in defiance of federal law and treaties.[113]

The Indian war was over, but the causes of conflict remained. Unscrupulous traders and land speculators continued to operate in Indian country. Only "the strong arm of the Union" and robust laws could prevent their abuses, Washington said. Peace with the Indians required fair trade and fair treaties, and by "fair treaties" he meant "that they shall *perfectly* understand every article and clause...that these treaties shall be held sacred, and the infractors on either side punished exemplarily."[114]

In Ohio, Indian delegations trickled in over the course of the winter and sounded out the possibilities for such a treaty. Secretary of War Pickering conveyed to Wayne the president's ideas about this impending treaty, along with his detailed instructions about the conduct of the negotiations, the amount of gifts and how they should be distributed, the general boundary line, and what Wayne could yield on and what he could not.[115]

Finally, the western Indians assembled at Greenville. Few Shawnees showed up, but Little Turtle, Black Hoof, Blue Jacket, Buckongahelas, Painted (Red) Pole, Egushawa, and dozens of other men who had fought to defend the Ohio boundary since before the Revolution did. Guyasuta was not there. In January 1794 Cornplanter had reported: "He is alive & that is all." He likely died in the year between Fallen Timbers and Greenville.[116] One of the first Indians Washington had met in the contested Ohio country, Guyasuta did not live to see its final cession.

Wayne presented the Indians with a prepared treaty for signing. In return for $20,000 in goods, they ceded most of Ohio to the United States. The new boundary ran from present-day Cleveland sixty miles south, then due west to Fort Recovery, and then southwest until it hit the Ohio River just west of Fort Washington. The Indians also ceded sites of forts beyond the line, including Fort Defiance, Fort Wayne, and the future site of Chicago.[117] Washington was there in spirit, as both sides invoked his name. Although there is no record of a meeting with the president before 1796, Little Turtle presented Wayne with "papers which have been given to me by General Washington, the great chief of the United States. He told me they should protect us in the possession of our lands, and that no white person should interrupt us in the enjoyment of our hunting grounds, or be permitted to purchase any of our towns or lands from us; that he would place traders among us, who would deal fairly." Tarhe, the Crane, though severely wounded in the arm, was the sole survivor of four principal chiefs of the Sandusky Wyandots, the others having been killed at Fallen Timbers. He now accepted a new relationship with the United States. "Now this day the good work is completed. I inform you all, brother Indians, that we do now, and will henceforth, acknowledge the fifteen United States of America to be our father,...you must call them brothers no more." New Corn, a Potawatomi, asked Wayne to take their old, British, medals "and supply us with General Washington's." Wayne handed out peace medals, which the Indians should consider "as presented by the hands of your father, the Fifteen Fires of America"; they in turn should hand the medals "down to your children's children in commemoration of this day" when the United States received them "under the protecting wings of the eagle." Then Wayne announced: "The great business of peace, so long and ardently wished for, by your great and good father, General Washington," was now accomplished.[118] The Indians were to find Washington a different kind of father than they were accustomed to. Fathers in Algonquian or Iroquoian society were indulgent relatives who provided protection and gave gifts; this new father would exercise his paternal authority to control and change their lives.[119]

Washington waited anxiously for the official report of the treaty and asked Pickering to relay the gist of it as soon as it arrived in the War Office. Was the Indian representation complete? Did Wayne meet, exceed, or fall short of his instructions, and in what instances? What were the boundaries? Did the negotiations proceed harmoniously, or were they interrupted with difficulties, and if so by whom? Finally, on September 28, Pickering sent him a copy of the treaty with the news that Wayne had "obtained more land than was expected."[120] Even so, Washington cautioned Pickering ten days later, until the final results of treaty negotiations with Britain were known, "and from the intimations of Captain Brant," Wayne should not withdraw his garrisons, and "we ought not...build too much in the present moment, on the treaty of peace with the Western Indians."[121]

AGREEMENTS REACHED ON THE OTHER side of the Atlantic helped to reinforce Wayne's gains on the ground. Writing to John Jay in London, ten days after Fallen Timbers but still a month before he received the news of Wayne's victory, Washington rehearsed his standard complaints that the old enemy was behind all the difficulties with the Indians and the murders of innocent women on the frontiers. The British government might disavow their actions, "but no well-informed person had any doubt" that its agents seduced Indians who were at peace and armed Indians who were hostile to the United States. There could never be peace until Britain surrendered the posts.[122]

In the Jay Treaty, signed in November 1794, Britain and the United States reached a conciliatory settlement. Among other provisions, the British finally gave up the posts on the northern frontier that they had held since the Peace of Paris and that Washington regarded as a source of intrigue among the Indians. But the treaty also allowed Indians continued access to British trade north of the border. It created a firestorm. Critics maligned it for doing too little, too late, making too many concessions, leaving British connections with the Indians intact, and jeopardizing American neutrality by aligning with Britain against Revolutionary France. Crowds burned copies of the treaty and effigies of Jay. Jefferson, Madison, and their Republican followers attacked the administration, and Washington received a flood of petitions denouncing the terms as surrendering to Britain. He expressed his own misgivings to Hamilton in private.[123]

Jay said the treaty was the best that could be achieved, and in some ways it represented a diplomatic triumph. It isolated the Ohio Valley Indians from Britain, and by defusing a crisis with Britain, it strengthened the United States' negotiating position with Spain over its southwestern border. The Senate ratified the treaty 20–10, exactly the two-thirds majority needed, and Washington signed it. The president's prestige helped carry the vote, but it was a costly victory. The debate over ratification—carried out in newspapers, pamphlets, broadsides, and town meetings as well as in government circles—reflected a shifting political landscape. Federalists and Republicans disputed the nature and meaning of the American Revolution, the French Revolution, the presidency, the Constitution, and the empire they were building in the West. The one-party, deferential political culture that Washington knew was giving way to a combative two-party system and a rowdy culture of popular politics and public opinion.[124]

The British had to employ some nimble diplomatic footwork to assure the Indians that by giving up the posts they had not abandoned their allies again and that trade with the tribes would continue uninterrupted.[125] In May 1796 a proposed visit to Philadelphia by chiefs from the Sioux, Puans (Ho-Chunk or Winnebago), and other tribes west of the Great Lakes was postponed for at least a year. Pickering advised Washington that it would be better to hold off trying to win the western tribes' allegiance until the United States had secured possession of the western posts. He feared the British might redouble their efforts to retain the Indians' allegiance and use it as a pretext for procrastinating on delivery of the posts.[126]

Ratification of Jay's Treaty was helped by news of Thomas Pinckney's treaty. Pinckney, who had sailed to Madrid in the spring of 1795, concluded the Treaty of San Lorenzo in the fall. Spain granted the United States free navigation of the Mississippi, right of deposit at New Orleans for three years, and a border with Spanish Florida at the 31st parallel. Spain also agreed to hand over its posts at Nogales, Natchez, and San Fernando de las Barrancas, although the transfer did not occur until 1797. As Washington observed in his notes on the treaty, each nation agreed to restrain its Indian allies from attacking the other, and trade with the Indians was "to be open, & mutually beneficial to each."[127] After the Spanish evacuation of San Fernando, the Americans established a post at Chickasaw Bluff (the future Memphis, Tennessee).

The news of the treaties with the Indians, Britain, and Spain, as well as with the Barbary powers of North Africa that had been the source of raids on American shipping, came in quick succession and generated an enthusiastic response. When Anthony Wayne returned to Philadelphia in February 1796, thousands turned out to see him, cannons were fired and bells rung in his honor, and there was a fireworks display. In January 1794, when the United States was at odds with Britain, Spain, the Indians, and the Barbary powers, John Adams had almost despaired of the situation, but May 4, 1796, as he was about to sign the bills for the various treaties to go into effect, "seemed a Day of Universal and perpetual Peace, foreign & domestic."[128]

Indian people were less optimistic. The retraction of British and Spanish support struck Indians as ominous. Although Piominko's friendship and his opposition to a Spanish-Indian alliance had helped the United States secure access to the lower Mississippi Valley, many Choctaws and Chickasaws felt betrayed by Spain's withdrawal across the Mississippi. Why had the Spaniards abandoned the Chickasaws to the Americans "like smaller animals to the jaws of the Tiger and the bear"? Ugulayacabe demanded. "We perceive in them the cunning of the Rattle snake who caresses the Squirrel he intends to devour."[129]

IT HAD TAKEN WASHINGTON AND his government more than three years to recover from the Indian victory over St. Clair's army. Washington said the United Sates expended "a million, or more dollars annually" on what he called "self defence against Indian tribes."[130] Between 1790 and 1796 the United States spent $5 million, almost five-sixths of the total federal expenditures for the period, fighting the war against the Northwestern Confederacy. Virginia and Pennsylvania also contributed men, money, and materiel to the war effort. But now the threats of separatist plots diminished and western land values soared. The federal government could finally generate income from sales of western land to pay down its debt.[131]

The United States was still a long way from consolidating its control of the trans-Appalachian West. American assertions of sovereignty in the area remained somewhat tentative. Indian nations continued to demand Washington's attention, and threats of foreign involvement with the tribes lingered. Nevertheless, the United States began pushing into the interior of continent with what the historical geographer D. W. Meinig describes as a unique and powerful "fusion of capitalism, individualism, and nationalism." "Never had so many people acting in their own private interest under conditions of great political freedom had access to such a large area of fertile lands, parceled by a simple efficient system into readily marketable units...and never had such a wide array of private interests been further motivated by a deeply emotional corporate interest to act as a unified body of people with a mission to expand relentlessly, subordinating any other people that stood in its way."[132] The nation was on the rise and on the move, Washington declared in his message to Congress in December 1795: "Our population advances with a celerity, which, exceeding the most sanguine calculations, proportionately augments our strength and resources, and guarantees our future security."[133]

Anthony Wayne died in December 1796, mission accomplished. But the boundary he secured at Greenville was no more effective in checking American expansion than the Proclamation Line of 1763 or the Fort Stanwix boundary in 1768 had been. Washington admitted Indians had legitimate complaints against Americans who encroached on their lands and were "not to be restrained by any law now in being, or likely to be enacted." He was not unsympathetic to the Indians' plight, though he had done much to produce it. "They, poor wretches, have no Press thro' which their grievances are related; and it is well known, that when one side only of a Story is heard, and often repeated, the human mind becomes impressed with it, insensibly."[134]

The defeat of the Northwestern Confederacy and the Treaty of Greenville opened Kentucky to a flood of migration—its population almost tripled between 1790 and 1800, reaching 220,955—and drove up land prices. Washington called the rate of increase "almost incredible." It also brought an increased federal presence, which few Kentuckians relished, but the proximity of the federal army in the Northwest contributed to the economic boom and helped fasten the young state to the Union.[135] At the same time, southerners took note that the federal government had deployed its power and resources regionally, to protect settlers, secure lands, and stimulate national growth in the Northwest Territory rather than the Southwest Territory.[136] Securing the lands beyond the Ohio that were vital to the nation risked dividing the nation.

So did slavery, which was on the march in the South. In 1793 Eli Whitney invented a new kind of cotton gin that made possible efficient harvesting of the short-staple upland cotton that grew away from the coast, where long-staple Sea Island cotton grew. The new technology gave a boost to cotton production, a boost to westward expansion, and a boost to slavery. Washington predicted that the increase in cotton growing "must be of almost infinite consequence to the prosperity of the United States," and he was right. Tobacco gave way to cotton as the primary crop of southern agriculture. In 1790 the United States produced 1.5 million pounds of cotton; in 1800 it produced 36.5 million pounds, and the numbers kept growing by leaps and bounds. Soon the South produced most of the raw cotton that fed the hungry mils of industrial Britain. Locked into a system of single-crop agriculture that depleted and eroded the soil, the southern plantation economy depended on limitless sources of cheap land and cheap labor. As cotton spread across the South, Indians were expelled from their lands to make way for African slaves. A nation built on Indian land was also built on African labor. In Sven Beckert's words, "The peculiar combination of expropriated lands, slave labor, and the domination of a state that gave enormous latitude to slave owners over their labor was fabulously profitable for those positioned to embrace it."[137]

Washington did not participate personally in the cotton boom, but he had done his share in setting Virginia, the South, and the nation on a path that was environmentally destructive and, ultimately, politically disastrous, and he avoided doing anything about slavery that might jeopardize the nation's unity.[138] He had envisioned expelling Indians from their land to make way for free white farmers, preferably tenants renting from men like himself. Instead, as the nation expanded across the South, Indians were expelled to make way for unfree black field hands and an industry that depended on the cotton mills of Lancashire and the children who labored in them. Western expansion coupled with the expansion of slavery would force the nation to confront the issue the founding generation had avoided and would tear apart the Union that Washington worked so hard to construct.

Washington's faith in western land as key to the future of individuals as well as the nation remained strong. When Alexander Spotswood asked his advice about selling up and moving west with his family, Washington resorted to his own lifelong philosophy and practice: "It has always been my opinion that new countries (by this I mean the interior of our own) are the best to lay the foundation of wealth, in as much as lands which, comparatively speaking, are to be had there cheap, rise in a fourfold ratio to what they do in the Atlantic Sea." Until communication between East and West improved, "the principal demand for the product of the land is to be found in the emigrants who resort to it. To this cause also is to be ascribed the rapidly increasing prices of those Lands." Better to invest in land than in slaves, he told Spotswood.[139]

However, Washington struggled to sell, rent, or derive profit from his own holdings in the West. Strapped for cash, he started selling his lands. In 1791 he had sold his Ohio and Kanawha lands to a French speculator, John Joseph de Barth, but de Barth's fortunes took a hit in the French Revolution, and Washington agreed to void the contract.[140] As Wayne was advancing to his showdown with the western tribes, Washington decided to liquidate his western real estate assets.[141] He made arrangements for selling the "de Barth lands" and his other western landholdings. (He even asked his secretary, Tobias Lear, then in Scotland, to talk up his lands during his travels.) His "Memorandum on Land" listed a total of 57,332 acres, with tracts in Kentucky, on the Little Miami, on the Great Kanawha, on the east side of the Ohio River, and in western Pennsylvania, as well as in the Great Dismal Swamp. His lands, as always, were "the cream of the country," but he said repeatedly that years of experience had shown that holding property in distant land was "more productive of plague than profit."[142]

Finding buyers and renters for his lands at the rates he wanted continued to occupy his attention and frustrate his expectations. In 1795 he sold most of his Pennsylvania lands to two buyers. After renting his Miller's Run property, he finally sold it in 1796 to Colonel Matthew Ritchie for $12,000; Ritchie paid $3,000 as a down payment but was often delinquent on subsequent payments, and after he died in 1798 his heirs were even less reliable, with the result that the property would revert to Washington's heirs on his death. He sold his lands near the remains of Fort Necessity for $7.20 an acre. Colonel Israel Shreve offered to purchase Washington's Bottom on the Youghiogheny River, but after making a down payment of $2,693 he proved delinquent also, prompting a series of heated letters and threats of legal action from Washington. Washington expected to receive about $22,000 from his two Pennsylvania tracts, but by the time of his death he had received little more than half that amount.[143] In 1795 and 1796 he was still trying to sell his lands on the Ohio, the Kanahwa and the Little Miami and in Kentucky.[144] In February 1796 he placed advertisements in newspapers in Alexandria and Phila-delphia offering to lease four of his Mount Vernon farms and to sell four tracts of land along the Ohio (9,744 acres), four tracts on either bank of the Great Kanawha (23,266 acres), and three tracts on the Little Miami River (3,051 acres)—a total of 36,000 acres dating from the days when he had received bounty lands for his service in the French and Indian War.[145] He asked Rufus Putnam to post notices in Marietta and elsewhere. He was, as he explained, "disposed to sell all the lands I hold on the Western Waters."[146] But he was unable to get the rates he wanted, and his lands on the Ohio and Great Kanawha remained "undisposed of" a year later.[147] He refused $8 an acre for his prime meadow lands on the banks of the Ohio and Great Kanawha, and held out for $10.[148]

Washington had set the nation firmly on the path of westward expansion and laid the foundations of the nation's empire in Indian country, but he was giving up on his own quest for a private empire in the West.[149]

CHAPTER 19

Transforming Indian Lives

"IT IS A STRIKING FACT," wrote the Moravian missionary John Heckewelder, "that the Indians, in their uncivilized state, should so behave towards each other as though they were a civilized people." Others who knew them well made similar observations. Indians, for their part, pointed out that their supposedly civilized white neighbors often displayed decidedly uncivilized and un-Christian behavior.[1] For Washington, however, civilization had less to do with present conduct and living Christian lives than with future progress— for both Indians and the United States. A society based on private property could not accommodate tribal societies based on communal landholding, and Christian or not, Indians could have no place within the United States if they continued to hunt, hold their lands in common, and live separate from American jurisdiction.[2] Getting Indian people to reorient their economies, societies, and values around American concepts of agriculture, family, and property would prepare them to assume their place in the new nation as individuals rather than as members of sovereign tribes; it would also free unused hunting territory to fuel the nation's growth. Remaking Indian lives was necessary to bring Indian people and Indian lands into American society. Their "father" George Washington would oversee this benevolent policy of amalgamation.[3]

With Indian military resistance—for the time—quelled and new boundaries secured, Washington and his administration looked to deliver on the other promise of his Indian policy and step up the tempo of injecting civilization into Indian communities. Just as the

United States could not expand without depriving Indian people of their lands, neither, so it believed, could it extend the blessings of American civilization without ridding Indian people of their "savage" ways, which also entailed depriving them of their lands. Treaties that furnished domestic animals, plows, and spinning wheels were designed not only to make hunters into farmers but also to transform gender roles, alter labor patterns, and change people's relationships with both the land and the animals with which they shared the land.

On December 29, 1794, Knox submitted his final report on Indian affairs to Washington. Washington forwarded it to Congress the next day. Knox said nothing about Wayne's victory four months earlier or the disastrous campaigns of 1790–91. Instead, he emphasized the humanitarian aspects of US Indian policy since the adoption of the Constitution: making treaties of peace with the Indians "upon principles of Justice" and extending to them "all the blessings of civilized life" that their condition would allow. Continuing such policies would reflect "permanent honor upon the national character." There were problems, of course. Rapacious frontier settlers continually encroached on Indian land, and if the powerful Indian nations south of the Ohio united in war against the United States, it would dwarf the conflict the nation had just fought north of the Ohio. It would be necessary to establish military posts and police the frontiers. But the secretary of war was no warmonger. "The United States can get nothing by an Indian war, but they risque men money and reputation," he said, repeating a by now familiar refrain. And peace required more than simply preventing war. Since the United States was more powerful and "more enlightened" than the Indians, the nation had a responsibility to treat them well. Instead, Knox lamented, "it is a melancholy reflection that our modes of population have been more destructive to the Indian natives than the conduct of the conquerors of Mexico and Peru. The evidence of this is the utter extirpation of nearly all the Indians in most populous parts of the Union. A future historian may mark the causes of this destruction of the human race in sable Colours."[4]

For Knox and Washington, saving Indian people from destruction meant transforming Indian lives. Washington recommended what he termed "rational experiments" for imparting the blessings of civilization and believed, or at least hoped, that the United States would not need to fight Indians if it traded with them.[5] The best way to secure their attachment was "to convince them that we are just and to show them that a proper and friendly intercourse with us would be for our mutual advantage."[6]

The twin instruments for carrying out this policy were Indian agents and government trading posts. Agents placed in the principal Indian towns would act as liaisons between the tribes and the federal government, protect the Indians' boundaries against encroachment, and assist Indian people in building a new way of life. In his annual messages in 1793 and 1794, Washington called on Congress to establish a system of government factories or trading posts in Indian country to better regulate trade. "Next to a rigorous execution of justice on the violators of peace, the establishment of commerce with the Indians in behalf of the United States is most likely to conciliate their attachment," he said. "But it ought to be conducted without fraud, without extortion, with constant and plentiful supplies, with a ready market for the commodities of the Indians and a stated price for what they give in payment and receive in exchange." He returned to the theme in his seventh annual address, delivered in the Senate Chamber on December 8, 1795. There could be no peace on the frontiers—and Washington had Georgia specifically in mind—unless Indians were afforded legal protection from murderous whites and provided with fair trade, and the work of civilizing the Indians would "reflect undecayed luster on our national character."[7] The government's Indian diplomacy also incorporated a civilizing component. Like Knox, Pickering favored giving gifts to lubricate the wheels of diplomacy, but he thought the gifts should be more transformative than martial: farm tools and cattle rather than medals and uniform coats. Washington endorsed a mix of both kinds of presents.[8]

With limited funding, the War Department set up the first two government trading posts in Creek country at Coleraine on the St. Marys River (moved in 1797 to Fort Wilkinson on the Oconee) and in Cherokee country at Tellico on the Little Tennessee, already the site of an army blockhouse. The trading posts were to provide Indians with goods at cost and required substantial subsidies to undercut private traders and oust foreign competitors. Ironically, because American merchants in New York, Philadelphia, and Baltimore had exhausted their supplies, the posts could not begin operating until shipments of Indian goods arrived from London in the fall of 1795. In 1796 Congress passed legislation authorizing the president to establish factories at his discretion and allocated $150,000 for the purpose. It also increased restrictions on private traders in Indian country and provided annual funding for the purchase of livestock and agricultural implements for Washington's "civilization" program. The trading posts fulfilled a diplomatic role and became sites of political and cultural negotiation as well as economic exchange between Indians and the US government. Other posts followed early in the nineteenth century.[9]

In the Scottish Enlightenment thinking that informed Washington's views, human societies developed in stages from hunters to herders to farmers. To survive on the small amount of land that remained to them, Washington believed, Indian men must give up the gun and the bow and take up the plow. If they could not do it directly, they should adopt livestock and become herders as a transitional phase. They must learn to inhabit and treat their tribal land as individual plots of property. They must clear fields and plant corn, wheat, and hay; erect fences to protect their crops; pen their livestock; mark their boundaries; and build cabins for their families. They might continue to hunt during the winter months to procure pelts for trading, but that phase would pass as they became self-sufficient farmers capable of feeding and clothing themselves and participated in the market economy by exchanging agricultural surpluses for the manufactured goods they formerly purchased with pelts. As they spent less time hunting, they would need less land and sell "surplus" acreage to the United States.

Washington's program of social engineering involved imposing a social revolution in Indian communities, reorganizing life around intensive agriculture. Most eastern woodland peoples had farmed for centuries. Indian women using hoes and digging sticks produced the vast "emporium" that Wayne described and destroyed after his victory at Fallen Timbers. But now men, not women, were to do the farming, and they were to do it with horse- and oxen-drawn plows. Plowing bit into the soil more deeply than hoeing; it destroyed native plant species, created new habitats dominated by domesticated species, and transformed the landscape.[10] Villages surrounded by communal fields would give way to dispersed family farms with individual plots of land demarcated by fences; tribal ethics of sharing and reciprocity would be replaced by Anglo-American principles of property and inheritance.

Western, male-centered gender roles would be imposed. As men spent more time at home, the nuclear family, with the male at its head, would supplant the clans, which in many tribes were matrilineal. Instead of planting and harvesting in the fields, women would raise children, prepare meals, and sew clothes in their homes, modeling their domestic lives on those of white American women. Children would go to school to study reading, writing, and arithmetic rather than learn the old stories from their grandparents; they must prepare for their new lives as farmers and housewives instead of accompanying their fathers and mothers into the forests and fields.[11] Although the government wanted Indian women to take up spinning, Native American Indian women, like Anglo-American women, were already buying increasing quantities of factory-made cloth.

In implementing its programs, the federal government turned for assistance to the Quakers and other religious groups committed to what they saw as the salvation of Indian people. Quakers enjoyed a reputation for honesty and integrity among Indians and furnished a model of white American society at its best. In addition to working as missionaries, they tried to instill in their Indian neighbors an economy based on plow agriculture and animal husbandry, a Protestant work ethic, and what they regarded as morally upright personal conduct. The Indian Affairs Committee of the Baltimore Yearly Meeting first met in 1795; it directed its efforts to the tribes of the Old Northwest, and in time would work closely with Little Turtle's Miamis. The Philadelphia Friends formed a similar committee dedicated to promoting the civilization and welfare of Indian people and focused on the Iroquois in New York State. Pickering, who became secretary of state in December 1795, endorsed and supported the Quakers in their efforts.[12]

Cornplanter also supported the Quakers. He met them during his visits to Philadelphia and viewed them as allies in his people's efforts to survive by accommodating with the United States and adopting American ways of life. The first Quaker missionaries arrived among the Allegheny Senecas in 1798 and set up a demonstration farm as a model for the transition to an agricultural way of life.[13] Cornplanter himself set an example of adjustment and accommodation. He built a sawmill in 1795 to provide income for his family. In 1797 he traveled to Philadelphia again. In his "last address to you as the great Chief of the fifteen fires," on February 28, a fragment of which survives, he asked Washington, "If we should dispose of part of our County and put our money with yours in that strong place, will it be safe? Will it yield to our children the same advantages after our heads are laid down as it…at present produces to us?"[14] By the time Washington died, Cornplanter was building himself a new house.

Joseph Brant already had an elegant house and enjoyed many of the trappings of "civilized life," but he was not so solicitous of the president. Now fifty-four, he accompanied Cornplanter on the arduous winter journey to Philadelphia in 1797. He met Robert Liston, George Hammond's replacement as British minister to the United States, attended a dinner hosted by Aaron Burr, and sat for another portrait, this time by Charles Willson Peale. But he did not keep the appointment the new secretary of war, James McHenry, made for him with Washington.[15]

Nor were all Senecas as amenable as Cornplanter to Washington's civilization plans. Just as some white captives resisted the acculturative pressures and attractions of Indian life more strongly than others, so Indian responses varied from willing acceptance to outright rejection. Cornplanter sent his son, Henry Abeel, to a Quaker school in Philadelphia, and the young man utilized his education, serving as interpreter at the Treaty of Canandaigua. But by the fall of 1795 it had become "evident that he could derive no advantage by continuing here." On Saturday, November 14, Knox dropped Washington a note telling him to expect the young man to stop by before he left for home.[16] Mary Jemison, an adopted white captive who lived her adult life as a Seneca woman, said she had seen many instances where young Indians were taken from their families, placed in school before they had had an opportunity to contract many Indian habits, and kept there until adulthood, but she had "never seen one of those but what was an Indian in every respect after he returned. Indians must and will be Indians," she concluded, "in spite of all the means that can be used for their cultivation in the sciences and arts."[17] What Knox and Washington saw as failure and disappointment, others saw as cultural resilience. Red Jacket asked for a sawmill when he was in Philadelphia in 1792, but he was scrupulously selective in his adoption of American ways and skeptical of civilization and Christianity as practiced by Americans. Half a dozen years after Washington's death, he remained a forceful spokesman for Iroquois cultural and religious independence.[18]

He was not alone. David Zeisberger, a Moravian missionary who lived and worked among the Delawares, said they thought that God had created Europeans and Indians to lead different ways of life, just as different species of animals did. For one species to adopt another's way of life was contrary to God's will, and the same principle applied to Indians and Europeans. They recognized that Europeans were "industrious and clever" and that trading with them gave Indians many things they would otherwise lack, and they acknowledged that whites were "very ingenious, because of their ability to manufacture a great variety of things," but they regarded their way of life "as wearisome and slavish as compared with their own." With good reason, Zeisberger added, they suspected that whites were just after their land.[19]

Many Indians refused the future Washington offered them. Observers lamented that Indians clung stubbornly to their old ways. Indian people responded that their dealings with white men who stole, lied, and cheated them out of their lands offered little incentive to become "civilized." Some found a haven in a world turned upside down by joining or building Christian communities; others continued to find stability, order, and decency in Indian ways. So did some non-Indians. Before the Revolution, Benjamin Franklin, Hector St. John de Crèvecoeur, and others had noted that while few Indians chose to become "civilized," many people went willingly to live with Indians. Indian society, said Crèvecoeur, exerted a "singular charm" on Europeans; Franklin said that people who had lived with Indians and then returned home soon "become disgusted with our way of life." Washington's policies of civilization evidently did little to change the fact that some people preferred to live with the Indians. Francis Baily, an Englishman traveling the backcountry in 1797, observed that people like this were to be found throughout Indian country, "yet you seldom hear of an Indian renouncing his mode of living or his country, and imposing upon himself the bonds and shackles of civilized society."[20]

Nevertheless, Indians had been adopting aspects of American society, economy, and religion for generations, and they continued to do so. Many raised livestock, made cloth, participated in the cash and market economy as merchants, consumers, and laborers, and lived in dispersed single-family homesteads rather than communal villages or longhouses. The government's policies institutionalized processes that were already under way. Even by the criteria Washington applied, some of his "savage" enemies were quite "civilized" before he offered them a systematic program of change.

Delawares had long since adopted many elements of so-called civilized life. They acquired pigs, cows, and chickens from Europeans, and fences in Delaware villages protected their cornfields from their cattle. Although most preferred to live in traditional wigwams, some Delawares built houses, sometimes with two stories and a chimney. As the historian Gregory Dowd notes, the inventory of White Eyes's personal effects at the time of his death gives insight into the changing material culture of Ohio Indians as well as White Eyes's role as an intermediary: buckskin leggings, breechcloths, a pipe tomahawk, and a wampum belt, along with scarlet breeches, four jackets (one of them made of scarlet silk and laced with gold trimming), three green coats, a fur cap, a beaver hat, three pairs of shoes, a rifle, a silver medal bearing a portrait of King George III, and a pair of spectacles.[21] White Eyes married a white captive, ran a tavern, operated as a trader, and encouraged conversion and gradual acculturation as part of a strategy for survival and security in a changing world.[22]

Indian people had also for years been converting to Christianity, accepting elements of Christian teachings, and building new Christian communities. Delaware converts to the Moravian faith lived in mission villages such as the well-ordered Christian community Nicholas Cresswell visited, where the church service was conducted with more decorum than "I ever saw in any place of Worship in my life."[23] Good Peter served as a deacon in his Oneida church. The Mohegan minister Samson Occom led a movement of New England Indian people after the Revolution to Oneida country, where they established a new, Christian Indian community. Christian Mahicans from Stockbridge joined them. Educated at the Stockbridge mission school, the Mahican sachem Hendrick Aupaumut imagined that incorporating Christian beliefs and other aspects of "civilization" would revive the Indians' cultures, strengthen their communities, and secure them a place in a republic where Christian Indians and Christian Americans could coexist. He advocated adopting American-style agriculture as the best path forward for Indian people and credited "the great men of the United States" with trying "to lift us up the Indians from the ground, that we may stand up and walk ourselves."[24]

Aupaumut's Stockbridges, like Good Peter's Oneidas, were not only Christians; they had also served, suffered, and sacrificed alongside their American neighbors during the Revolution. Surely, Aupaumut had good reason for his optimistic vision of the future. Unfortunately, Christianity and loyalty were not enough to satisfy policies that associated civilization with property. Civil and Christian Indian communities that practiced communal values and preserved communal lands must embrace programs that would break up those values and open up those lands.

Like most other Americans, Washington was less interested in the Indians' religion than in their land. His benevolent policies might prove as lethal as his military assaults, and they generated mixed responses. Leaders like Aupaumut hoped for inclusion. Others, recognizing that a way of life built on buying and selling individual property threatened their communities and their existence as a people, saw separation as the key to survival, and rejection of white ways as the recipe for cultural revitalization. Others were more flexible and selective. Although he steadfastly resisted the invasion of Shawnee lands, Blue Jacket sent his son to Detroit to be educated. Two American women who had been taken captive during the Revolution recalled that Blue Jacket and his French-Shawnee wife slept in a four-poster curtained bed and ate with silver cutlery. Both women said he was kind to them: one considered herself fortunate to have been taken into Blue Jacket's family; the other liked to visit Blue Jacket's home, where they always offered her tea.[25]

During the negotiations with General Wayne at the Treaty of Greenville, Blue Jacket, speaking on a string of blue wampum, asked if two chiefs from each nation could pay Washington a visit "and take him by the hands: for our younger brothers have a strong desire to see that great man, and to enjoy the pleasure of conversing with him." Blue Jacket's language suggests naïve Indian "children" calling on the Great White Father, but as his biographer John Sugden points out, Blue Jacket was a shrewd operator. The Shawnees had been engaged in almost continuous war against the Americans since 1774, and no Shawnee chief had yet visited the seat of government of the new nation. As a war chief and member of the Pekowi division, Blue Jacket now deferred to Painted Pole, a civil chief of the Mekoche division, as premier chief, but he understood that meeting Washington in Philadelphia could help maintain his own leadership status as the Shawnees entered a new era of peaceful dealings with the United States. Colonel John Francis Hamtramck observed in April 1796: "Blue Jacket is used to good company and is always treated with more attention than other Indians."[26]

In the fall of 1796, "agreeably to the Unanimous request of all the Chiefs who signed the Treaty of Greene Ville," a delegation duly embarked from Detroit for Philadelphia to talk with their great father. In addition to the Shawnees, the delegates represented the Wyandots, Delawares, Ottawas, Ojibwas, Miamis, Potawatomis, Eel River, Weas, Piankashaws, Kickapoos, and Kaskaskias. Wayne forwarded the names of the chiefs to Secretary of War James McHenry. They included "the famous Shawanoe Chief Blue Jacket, who, it is said had the Chief Command of the Indian Army" against St. Clair, and Little Turtle, "who also claims that honor, & who is his rival for fame & power." In fact, Little Turtle refused to travel in Blue Jacket's company.[27]

When the chiefs met with Washington in late November, Blue Jacket acknowledged that he had long been attached to the British and fought against the Americans, but now those days were over. Painted Pole presented the Wabash Indians' complaint that the Greenville treaty line had been taken too far to the west and asked that it be modified to run down the Great Miami to the Ohio, but Washington replied that no changes could be made, as the treaty had been ratified.[28] Instead, the president repeated his message of survival through cultural change and was free with his advice to his "children." (He used the term deliberately, scoring out the word "brothers" in one draft of a speech.) The Treaty of Greenville had established peace and friendship, but it was not enough for the Indians to live in friendship with the Americans; they must learn to live like Americans.

> More than all this is required to render your Condition comfortable. Your lands are good. Upon these you may raise horses and large Flocks of Cattle, by the sale of which you may procure the conveniences and necessaries of life in greater abundance, and with less trouble than you do at present. You may also, by a little more industry raise more Corn and other Grain, as well for your families, as for the Support of your Stock in winter. I hope the Nations will maturely reflect upon this subject, and adopt what cannot fail to make them happier. When the Government shall be informed that they have taken this wise course, and are sincerely desirous to be aided in it, they may rely upon receiving all necessary assistance.

He referred them for any further business to the secretary of war, "who will furnish such of you as have acquired the title of Chiefs or Warriors with a Testimonial of the same import as that delivered up by Blue Jacket as a proof of my Esteem and Friendship."[29]

After meeting the president, the chiefs toured Philadelphia. They were not the only Indian delegates in town. At Charles Willson Peale's museum at Fifth and Chestnut Streets, they found themselves face-to-face with a delegation of southern Indians who were also getting the tour—not only Creeks and old allies like the Chickamauga Cherokee John Watts but also Choctaws and Chickasaws, including Piominko and George Colbert, who had assisted the Americans in the late war. After what must have been an awkward initial encounter, the delegates arranged a second meeting at the museum, and then Blue Jacket and Red Jacket asked Secretary McHenry to convene a formal peace conference on December 2.[30] The multiple delegations filled the president's calendar. He had dined with "four Setts of Indians on four several Days" the week before, John Adams told Abigail, and Adams joined him for dinner with John Watts and a large number of Cherokee chiefs and their wives on December 3.[31] The visit was the last time Washington saw Piominko, who died in 1798.

The northern delegates left with good words and commissions from Washington but no alterations in the Greenville boundary. On the way home Painted Pole grew ill at Pittsburgh and, despite the best efforts of three American doctors, died on January 28. He was buried in Trinity Church graveyard. Blue Jacket survived as the principal leader of the Shawnees as they embarked on a difficult new path, but he was almost sixty, and he was being eclipsed in American eyes by Little Turtle.[32] Many Shawnees left Ohio and moved to

Missouri. Most of those who stayed followed the lead of their principal chief, Black Hoof, in adapting to a changing world.[33]

Anthony Wayne said Little Turtle possessed "the spirit of litigation to a high degree" and may have been "tampered with" by land speculators.[34] James Wilkinson gave St. Clair's nemesis a much more positive recommendation in the letter of introduction to Washington with which he furnished Little Turtle at Pittsburgh: "I think Sir, you will find Ideas more correct, and a mind more capacious in this Chief, than any of his race."[35] In one of his last public functions as president, Washington invited Little Turtle to his home and presented him with a ceremonial sword, a gun, and a medal displaying the likenesses of both men.[36] The physician Benjamin Rush inoculated Turtle against smallpox by variolation—a process that involved infecting the patient with live smallpox matter. He was the first American Indian to receive federal inoculation, and he stayed at Rush's home for several weeks while he recovered.[37] He was also treated for gout and rheumatism at the government's expense.[38]

Little Turtle became something of a regular visitor to the nation's capital, first at Philadelphia and then at Washington, and he met three presidents. On his visit to Philadelphia in 1798, John Adams acknowledged Little Turtle was "certainly a remarkable man."[39] Hamtramck described him to Hamilton as "the Oracle of the Indians."[40] Gilbert Stuart painted his portrait, although the original was destroyed when the British burned the White House in the War of 1812. On visits to the capital Little Turtle wore a blue suit "in the American fashion," but he put his Native clothes back on when he returned home. He returned east in 1801–2 and requested an agency and government trading post for the Miamis, in part to restrict and regulate the lethal liquor trade. Evidently Washington's earlier promise to send fair traders had not yet been implemented. At Jefferson's urging, Little Turtle agreed to be vaccinated and took home live vaccine with instructions on how to administer it to his people.[41] Aided by his son-in-law William Wells, who became a US Indian agent, Little Turtle urged the Miamis to make the transition to a new way of life. When he died, in July 1812, the sword, gun, and medal Washington had given him were interred with him as burial goods.[42]

AS HIS PRESIDENCY PROGRESSED, WASHINGTON looked increasingly to the larger southern nations, particularly the Cherokees and Creeks, as test cases for the civilization programs he had developed. In February 1795 he was able to inform Congress that hostilities with the Cherokees had ceased and there was "a pleasing prospect of permanent peace with that nation."[43] The best recipe for that peace, Washington believed, was to transform Cherokee warriors into self-supporting yeoman farmers who could be integrated into American society. Even as the Treaty of Holston in 1791 affirmed boundaries separating Cherokee and American territory, it promised to lead Cherokees "to a greater degree of civilization" and furnished farming implements to make them "herdsmen and cultivators, instead of remaining in a state of hunters."[44]

He feared time was running out for the Cherokees. They were a people in crisis. The warfare from 1776 to 1794 had brought defeat, division, and burned villages. In that period they had surrendered more than twenty thousand square miles of prime hunting territory, with profound impact on their economy, which depended on the deerskin trade. Game, which was once plentiful, was growing scarce in the lands they retained, and, Washington said, "you know that when you cannot find a deer or game to kill, you must remain hungry." Cherokee society placed the highest value on harmony, yet disorder was everywhere—generations divided, towns competed, and people struggled to maintain proper relationships with other people, with the environment, and with the spirit world. According to the historian William McLoughlin, Cherokees "were no longer sure of their place in the universe" and "had lost control of their destiny as a people." Washington offered them a path forward with the promise of equal citizenship in the United States if they would change and become herdsmen and farmers. Instead of succumbing to despair, tribal leaders looked to his civilization program "to prepare them and their children for a new Cherokee world," and the Cherokees began a remarkable comeback.[45]

In August 1796, near the end of his second term, the president published an address to the Cherokee Nation, laying out a road map for them to follow in order to coexist with Americans. Ever since white people first came to America, he said, many good men had given much thought to how the condition of the Natives of the country could be improved, and many attempts had been made to do so; all these attempts had been "nearly fruitless." The growth of American settlement was destroying the Indians' hunting way of life. They should learn to live like American farmers. Some Cherokees already kept cattle and hogs; they should add sheep to give them clothing as well as food. They could raise livestock not only for their own needs but to sell to white people. They should grow cotton, wheat, and flax. The government would provide an agent to advise and instruct them, and the agent would furnish plows and other agricultural implements, and award medals to the best farmers. Their wives and daughters should learn to spin and weave, and the government would hire a woman to teach them how. Washington held himself up as a role model. "What I have recommended to you, I am myself going to do. After a few moons are passed, I shall leave the great town and retire to my farm." There he would work on increasing his livestock and growing his crops, and employ women (meaning slave women) in spinning and weaving, "all of which I have recommended to you, that you may be as comfortable and happy as plenty of food, clothing and other good things can make you."

The Cherokees would serve as a role model and a test case, as "the experiment made with you may determine the lot of many nations." If the civilization program succeeded with the Cherokees, the government would give the same assistance to all the tribes; if it failed, "they may think it vain to make any further attempts to better the condition of any Indian tribe." He encouraged the Cherokees to emulate the United States in convening a council once or twice a year, made up of the wisest councilors from each town, to discuss the affairs of the nation. (Although Cherokees held occasional national councils, such as occurred at Chota in 1776, their government operated through town council meetings, custom, clan, and kinship.) So his talk would be known and remembered, Washington had it printed and distributed throughout the Cherokee Nation, with one, "signed by my own hand, to be lodged in each of your towns." Having heard that some chiefs wished to see him in Philadelphia, Washington sent word that he would be happy "to receive a few of the most esteemed," but not before November.[46]

As the historian Theda Perdue points out, his address to the Cherokee Nation really only addressed Cherokee men. Although women exercised considerable influence in Cherokee and other southern Indian societies, in Washington's vision of the Indian future, men would exercise their proper power and control, women would be subordinate, and patriarchal families would replace matrilineal clans. The new economic order that transformed hunters into farmers threatened the traditional gendered division of labor. Cherokee women took up spinning and weaving more readily than Cherokee men took up farming and generally adjusted with less difficulty to new roles and expectations.[47]

Washington's agents of change were already at work in Cherokee country. When Leonard Shaw was appointed agent in 1792, his instructions were to convince all the Indians of "the uprightness of the views of the President of the United States" and his desire to improve their situation in every way he could. Shaw was to collect materials for a history of all the southern tribes, endeavor to learn their languages, and compile vocabularies. Knox had spelled out the philosophy behind the plan: the idea that the difference between civilized and savage ways of life was based on different "races of men possessing distinct primary qualities" was fallacious; the differences arose from "education and habits." Consequently, Shaw's job was to teach them agriculture and "useful arts." Shaw married a Cherokee woman but struggled in vain to curb warfare on the frontier, protect Cherokee lands against encroachment, and secure the Cherokees fair treatment in their dealings with William Blount.[48]

In 1794 Washington appointed Silas Dinsmoor as his "beloved agent" to the Cherokees (see figure 6). A first lieutenant in the Army Corps of Engineers, Dinsmoor had graduated three years earlier from Dartmouth College, where he would have encountered some Indian students. At Knox's request, Dinsmoor took charge of the Cherokee deputation visiting Philadelphia at the time, sailed with them back to Charleston, and accompanied them home. He remained with the Cherokees for five years. His duties were to visit every town to oversee their progress in achieving Washington's vision and instruct the Cherokees "in the raising of stock, the cultivation of land, and the arts." He ordered spinning wheels for the women.[49]

Dinsmoor was the first agent to make significant efforts to transform Cherokee men from hunters to farmers.[50] According to Dinsmoor's son, an old Cherokee chief named Bloody Knife at first opposed the new agent and his program but was eventually won over and became his father's friend.[51] Reviewing his services years later, Dinsmoor wrote that when he first went to Cherokee country, the men did the hunting and the women were the farmers, millers,

Figure 6 Silas Dinsmoor, Hawkins's deputy and Washington's principal agent among the Cherokees in the mid-1790s.

Dartmouth College Library.

cooks, woodcutters, and water carriers. He introduced plowing and cotton growing by the men and cotton manufacture by the women. "In this I received personally, the express approbation of the two first Presidents of the United States."[52]

Dinsmoor was not the only person offering the Cherokees a program of culture change. About the same time, Governor Gayoso persuaded Bloody Fellow to hand over his eleven-year-old son for schooling. Gayoso believed it was important that the young men who would one day govern the Indian nations should "have a Spanish education and heart"; he also thought having Bloody Fellow's son in a Spanish school would help ensure the chief's good conduct. Bloody Fellow agreed to let the boy take a Christian name, Charles, along with that of his family, Bloody Fellow Swan, and evidently was willing to have Charles go to Spain. Gayoso, however, feared the risks of accident and disease, and the boy went to the public school in New Orleans.[53]

Dinsmoor's instructions required him to end hostilities between the Indians and their white neighbors, a difficult task in a borderland region where Cherokees and Scotch-Irish settlers shared similar codes of revenge and killings were commonplace. With the cooperation of "good & virtuous" people, he made headway in removing prejudices, restricting retaliatory revenge, and restoring trust and tranquility.[54] Peace was "the general talk of this country," Dinsmoor said in March 1795, but progress was not uniform. He believed the Cherokees really wanted to bury the hatchet and shed no more blood; "would to God the frontier people were of the same mind."[55]

Dinsmoor urged the government to establish a clear boundary. The Treaty of Holston had stipulated that three persons appointed by the United States and three on behalf of the Cherokee Nation should mark the boundary, but the line still had not been run and was out of date. Washington agreed and understood the magnitude of the challenge. In February 1796, transmitting a report on the "daring designs of certain persons" to take possession of lands the United States had solemnly guaranteed to the Cherokees by treaty, the president recited his familiar refrain on the need to prevent such intrusions "and the mischievous consequences, which must necessarily result therefrom."[56] In July he instructed his cabinet to consider how to start running a clearly marked boundary line between the United States and the Cherokees as soon as possible. "The Indians urge this; the law requires it, and it ought to be done," he said, "but I believe Scarcely any thing Short of a Chinese Wall, or a line of troops, will restrain Land Jobbers, & the encroachment of settlers upon the Indian territory."[57]

He was right. He appointed Dinsmoor, Benjamin Hawkins, and Andrew Pickens as commissioners to survey and mark the line, but congressional delays in funding meant the measure had to be postponed until 1797. The commissioners met with Cherokee chiefs and warriors in April to ascertain and mark the line in accordance with the Holston Treaty.[58] Francis Baily, the Englishman traveling through Cherokee country that summer, said the Indians disputed "every inch of ground with the Americans" and generally sent a party to watch the surveyors appointed to run a treaty line "in order to see that they do not go wrong." Baily also encountered a group of squatter families waiting in the wings for the business to be completed. They had encroached on Indian country before, and the government had ordered them to remove; in fact, "the President actually sent a detachment of the army into the country to enforce his commands." "This," said Baily, "was the bone of contention, which was the subject of conversation in every place I went into." People living within the limits of US territory shared the squatters' outrage, "as they all hate the Indians, and think a little deviation from justice is a thing to be overlooked where their two interests clash with each other."[59] It was a problem neither the first president nor any of his successors would resolve.

In 1798, with John Adams now president, Dinsmoor convened the Cherokees to meet at short notice with American treaty commissioners and obtained provisions for a treaty held at Tellico. The goal of the treaty, as Secretary of War McHenry gently phrased it, was "to dispose the minds of the Cherokees to make a sale of such part of their land as will give a more convenient form to the State of Tennessee." The Cherokees balked at selling any more land, but finally thirty-nine chiefs, including Bloody Fellow, Rising Fawn, and Little Turkey, agreed to cede three more tracts of land on the northeastern border of Cherokee country, between half a million and a million acres in North Carolina and Tennessee. The United States promised to guarantee the rest of their country "forever, as contained in former treaties." Dinsmoor attended as a witness. "You must," Adams wrote to the Cherokees, "be convinced, that the United States can have your good only in view in keeping Mr. Dinsmoor in your Nation."[60]

Dinsmoor insisted on protecting the Cherokees' land, but as a treaty commissioner he also helped separate them from their lands. His son believed Dinsmoor considered himself honor-bound to look after the interests of the tribe as well as the interests of the United States.[61] Doing both simultaneously was possible under Washington's construction of Indian policy that equated depriving Indians of hunting territory with moving them toward a more settled state as farmers. Dinsmoor became an instrument of the twin aspects of the policy: dispossession and civilization.

On Christmas Eve 1798, en route to see the secretary of war in Philadelphia, Dinsmoor stopped off at Mount Vernon to pay his respects to the retired president. He handed over a letter of introduction from Benjamin Hawkins. Dinsmoor, Hawkins reminded Washington, was "one of those chosen to carry into effect the benevolent plan devised by you, for bettering the condition of the Indians in the southern parts of the United States," and he had faithfully and ably carried out the task. In spite of violent resistance from "the mischief makers in this quarter," the plan had succeeded; the Cherokees "are no longer to be called Savages, they are a decent orderly set of people, who possess unbounded confidence in the Justice of our government, and are worthy of its continued attention," Hawkins assured the president. Dinsmoor spent Christmas at Mount Vernon. Washington is said to have given him a sword he had worn during the Revolution.[62]

When John Adams dismissed Dinsmoor in 1799, Hawkins told the Indians that it was the work of their enemies who made misrepresentations to the new president.[63] In 1800–1 Dinsmoor served as purser on the frigate USS *George Washington,* delivering tribute to Algiers to protect American shipping from the Barbary pirates. When Thomas Jefferson entered the White House, he recalled Dinsmoor to the Indian service. In 1802 he was appointed temporary agent to the Choctaws in southern Mississippi, a post he held for twelve years, implementing the same government programs he had initiated among the Cherokees.[64]

The Cherokees made some fairly radical changes in governance and how they dealt with the United States. They placed limits on clan vengeance and established a police force.[65] Cherokee towns for most of the eighteenth century functioned as autonomous bodies and made collective decisions based on tradition, kinship, and consensus; now, Cherokees began to create mechanisms for speaking with a single national voice in dealing with the United States, its treaty commissioners, and agents, and a class of leaders, often mixed-blood and wealthy, began to emerge as mediators with the nation-state.[66]

In the face of growing pressures from the outside, some Cherokees succumbed to alcoholism. Some began to migrate west to Arkansas. Others withdrew deep into the Great Smoky Mountains, where they could live their old ways with little interference. Most continued to follow traditional ways and practice traditional ceremonies as a way of maintaining or restoring order in the midst of change and upheaval, but they adopted those parts of Washington's civilization program they thought might bring greater economic and political security.[67] In the next generation, the Cherokees built a modern Indian nation, adopting American-style agriculture, a written language, and a written constitution modeled on that of the United States. Principal Chief John Ross, who led the tribe for five decades, credited Washington and his wise and humane policies with setting the Cherokees on the path to becoming "a civilized Christian people." Ross named one of his sons George Washington; he named another Silas Dinsmoor.[68]

IN CHEROKEE COUNTRY, WASHINGTON'S CIVILIZATION program in the 1790s offered a lifeline for people struggling to rebuild their nation in the wake of catastrophic defeat. Creek country had witnessed no such defeat. Creek power, and the prospect of Creek alliances with European or other tribal nations, continued to pose a formidable potential challenge to the expanding United States. Washington saw civilization as the path to peace, and he wanted his prescription to work in Creek country more than anywhere else.

The Creeks accepted parts of the new programs. James Seagrove had been out of his depth in Creek country, kept in a constant state of alarm by foreign agents, rival chiefs, and intertribal factions. Washington replaced him in 1796 and appointed Benjamin Hawkins as principal temporary agent to the four southern nations, and to oversee the "civilization program" among the Creeks (see figure 7). The Indians already knew and respected Hawkins, Washington said. "I have chosen him for this office because he is esteemed for a good man; has a knowledge of Indian customs, and a particular love and friendship for all the Southern tribes." Hawkins threw himself into the work. He left the US Senate, took up residence in Creek country, and remained there until his death in 1816. He spoke Muskogean, the language of most Creek people. They gave him, or he assumed, the honorary title of *isti atcagagi*, "beloved man," and to some extent he stepped into the power vacuum left by Alexander McGillivray's death a few years earlier.[69] He toured Creek country, communicating "the benevolent views of the government" to the inhabitants and gathering information to help him in his work.[70]

As Washington had done when traveling in Indian country, Hawkins kept note of fertile lands that would be suitable for agriculture. Both looked at Indian land with a calculating eye, assessing its

Figure 7 Benjamin Hawkins, treaty commissioner and chief architect of Washington's "civilization policy" among the southern Indians.

potential for improvement, weighing its commercial possibilities, and figuring how to increase its capital value. As with Washington, the religious studies scholar Joel Martin points out, there was much Hawkins did not see: he "never saw Muskogees' fields and streams in the ways that Muskogees saw them, animated with a thousand non-human spirits."[71] In the view of Washington and Hawkins, Indian lands, however extensively cultivated, had yet to realize their potential. Properly managed and farmed, Creek lands would be more productive. Creek farmers who adopted modern techniques would become more efficient, and they would need less land.

In article 12 of the Treaty of New York the government had pledged, as we've seen, to supply the Creek Nation with domestic animals and implements of husbandry. That was the toehold of a comprehensive plan to transform warrior hunters into yeoman farmers and women farmers into farmers' wives. Hawkins intended to implement that plan by introducing new technologies, scientific agriculture employing improved strains of seeds and plants and the latest

methods of fertilization, a new economic system that would free the
Creeks from dependence on hunting, free them of much of their
hunting territory, and give them better food, more things, and a
better life. Creek people would have access to manufactured goods
and other commodities at the new government trading posts where
they would purchase with cash, not on credit, and develop values of
labor and property.[72]

In fact, of course, Hawkins found Creek society already adjust-
ing to change. The deerskin trade had been a mainstay of southeastern Indian economy throughout most of the eighteenth century,
and Creek men had shifted from subsistence hunting to commercial
hunting, participating in an emerging frontier exchange economy
that involved Indians, colonists, and slaves and reshaped the cultures
of each group. But overhunting had produced a dramatic decline in
the deerskin trade and, as noted, Eli Whitney's invention of the
cotton gin in 1793 created a boom in the cotton industry, and escalating demand for Indian land to be worked by African slaves.[73]
Traders had entered Creek country along old paths in the eighteenth
century, but new roads were opening the land to growing numbers
of settlers and slaves. A network of trails and paths connected Creek
towns to other Indian towns and to American towns and ports.[74]
Hawkins regularly heard people speaking Scotch, French, Spanish,
English, and African languages, as well as Muskogean and Yuchi, and
he could have added Cherokee, Choctaw, Chickasaw, Shawnee, and
Mobilian, the lingua franca trade language of the Southeast.[75]
Boundary lines did not keep settlers off Indian land, and they were
porous. Creeks and Americans passed back and forth in the give-and-
take of daily economic exchange; to drink, socialize, and form liaisons; to graze and recover livestock; to steal horses.[76]

Many Creeks raised hogs and cattle and grew cash crops for sale
to whites. Ranching offered an alternative to the declining deerskin
trade, and the Creeks were well on their way to becoming ranchers by
the time Hawkins arrived in 1796. He listed almost every town as having
herds of livestock and said Creeks liked raising stock better than any
other aspect of the civilization plan. Contrary to Washington's expectations, however, ranching required the Creeks to use more, not less, of
their lands, even as it involved them in the larger frontier economy as
practiced by Americans. Panton, Leslie & Company still retained more
than one-third of the Creek trade, and almost all the Chickasaw and
Choctaw trade, at the time of Washington's death, but the old trading
relationships were changing. Whereas the British had traded manufactured goods for deerskins, Americans, increasingly, traded for land.[77]

In place of communal fields cultivated by time-honored practices, Washington and Hawkins wanted to see individual plots of land fenced in and rendered productive by modern techniques. Some Indian people fenced common areas for herding livestock, but for Hawkins, fences were a key marker of progress, indicating adoption of the new way of life that Washington envisioned and that he himself was trying to implement. Communities without fences had an appearance of indolence and poverty; those with fences displayed order, industry, prosperity, and good living. Fences not only kept cattle and hogs out of planted fields; they also represented adoption of new concepts of individual land ownership.[78]

Creek women were more open to change than most Creek men, for whom hunting, along with war, was a traditional marker of masculinity and status. When he first arrived, Hawkins said, women welcomed him to their towns, prepared meals and lodging for him, gave him tours of their towns and fields, and talked with him at length about the civilization plan and what it would mean for them. They hoped it would prove true and said they would follow the advice of the president and the instructions of his agent.[79] They started growing cotton and making homespun cloth, and some of them became supporters of his program. Spinning and weaving gave them greater economic independence and greater access to manufactured goods via the market economy. But Indian people were always selective in accepting what white men had to offer, and Creek women resisted the complete revolution in gender relations Hawkins proposed. When one woman suggested that he marry her widowed daughter, Hawkins "lectured her on the merits of patriarchy" and said he would only take a wife if she obeyed him and if her children and property belonged to him. The woman refused: "She would not consent that the women and children should be under the direction of the father, and the negotiation ended there."[80]

In his "Sketch of the Creek Country" written in the last years of Washington's life, Hawkins listed thirty-seven Creek towns (*talwas*), twelve on the Chatahoochee and twenty-five on the Coosa and Tallapoosa, some of which had smaller satellite towns. He also listed the Seminole towns, "as they are Creeks." In fact, the Creeks at this time had a total of perhaps seventy-three towns—forty-eight Upper Creek towns clustered in the valleys of the Coosa, Tallapoosa, and Alabama Rivers, and twenty-five Lower Creek towns on the Flint and Chatahoochee Rivers—and a total population between fifteen and twenty thousand.[81] That population had multiple lines of potential fracture based on age, gender, language, clans, and towns; there were growing rifts between those who favored adopting American changes and those who opposed them, and gaps were widening between poor Creeks and wealthy métis who came to think of land as property and property as private wealth. Scottish traders who had married into southern Indian communities and their influential sons were reorienting Creek society toward a market economy, and some were more concerned with acquiring wealth and property than maintaining traditional ties of sharing and reciprocity.[82] Robert Grierson, a Scottish trader, had married a Creek wife and had five children with her. He owned a plantation, three hundred cattle, and thirty horses, Hawkins recorded, and he grew and manufactured cotton. He employed Indian women to gather cotton in the fields, eleven "red, white and black" hands in spinning and weaving, and part of his family in preparing the cotton for them. His wife and daughter both spun, and he expected more of the Indian women to take it up.[83]

At a time when what he called "the spirit of party" was tearing at the political fabric of his own society, Hawkins lamented its existence in Creek society. Factionalism prevailed "more or less in every town in the nation," he said. Hoboithle Mico, "the first man that gave the land away to the white people," according to one Creek, was now at the forefront of resistance to the new programs, and Hawkins singled him out as a troublemaker. The agent developed a working relationship with Hoboithle Mico's rival, Efau Hadjo or Mad Dog, whom he described as "one of the best informed men of the land and faithful to his national engagements." Efau Hadjo owned five black slaves and livestock. He was used to receiving gifts from British and French agents and expected them from the United States.[84] Generational tension added to the unrest. Old chiefs struggled to govern young men "who are rude and disorderly in proportion to the intercourse they have with white people." Older people complained that contact with whites had a detrimental effect on the morals and behavior of the young.[85]

Washington, too, feared that this was the case. During the negotiations at Coleraine, Hawkins and the other commissioners pushed the advantages of establishing schools in Creek country. When the chiefs' sons who attended grew up, they would be able to conduct the affairs of their nation like the white people did, keeping their own records without being cheated. But Cussetah Mico, also known as Eneah Mico, countered that educated Indians invariably turned out worthless and caused trouble. The commissioners assured them Washington knew that young Indian men educated in American towns turned out badly and attributed it to associating "too much with our bad people." Creek youths, however, would be educated in Creek towns, under the supervision and direction of their elders. Cussetah Mico was not persuaded. "This subject was further enlarged upon, but received with such dislike by the Indians, that it was postponed."[86]

In keeping with Washington's recommendations that Indians form national legislatures modeled on that of the United States, Hawkins claimed he persuaded Creek town chiefs to establish a national council and to replace the system of clan vengeance with recourse to laws. The national council, in which representatives from all the towns met annually, seems to have predated his arrival, but now it exercised greater authority over domestic affairs and attempted to suppress blood revenge and retaliatory killings. The United States could now deal with a centralized body representing the Creeks as a whole; Hawkins thought it "indispensable, to enable the nation to fulfill its engagements with us." But it also prompted shifts in clan and town loyalties and generated further divisions within Creek society.[87]

As did Indian peoples in the North, many Cherokees, Creeks, Chickasaws, and Choctaws accommodated to American ways as the best way to survive in the new nation. Some attempted to increase their status with both the United States and their own people by selectively adopting attributes of "civilization." Those attributes included European styles of clothing, furniture, and household goods; Christianity; literacy in English; plowed fields; fenced property; and cotton cultivation.[88] And African slaves. Many Indians and Africans had shared lives of enslavement in the colonial South, and they built relationships, shared aspects of their cultures, and sometimes made families. But later in the eighteenth century, as they were enveloped by a society in which slave labor was the foundation of tobacco and cotton production and was a symbol of status, southern Indians began to hold increasing numbers of African slaves. As the United States moved toward a rigidly biracial society, Indian slaveholders adopted increasingly racial attitudes that conflicted with traditional notions of kinship. By the time Washington died, many Creeks and Cherokees held and regarded African slaves much as their white neighbors did.[89]

Despite his own increasingly ambivalent attitudes about slavery, Washington was optimistic that his plan for peace and progress in Indian country was working. First on the agenda in his eighth and final message to Congress, delivered on December 7, 1796, was a review of his Indian policy and its achievements: measures adopted to maintain the friendship of the tribes and preserve peace on the frontiers, protecting settlements from unruly individuals who could not be restrained by their tribes, on the one hand, and protecting the Indians' treaty rights, on the other, and always "to draw them nearer to the civilized state; and inspire them with correct conceptions of the Power, as well as justice of the Government."[90]

Hawkins believed his hard work among the southern tribes had given them so much confidence in justice "that the malice or wickedness of the enemies of our government cannot destroy it."[91] In May 1798, at a meeting of Upper and Lower Creeks and Seminoles assembled in the town square at Tuckabatchee, Efau Hadjo handed the agent a wampum belt as a "token of friendship to General Washington and his children." The belt comprised six strands: two white ends, two rows of blue beads on each edge, and two rows of white through the middle to represent the path of perpetual peace linking "the hands of the people of the United States and the people of my land." Efau Hadjo offered the belt in the hope "that they may never again be separated or at enmity."[92]

One likely disturber of perpetual peace exited the scene in 1797. William Blount's schemes finally caught up with him. On July 3 Washington received a letter enclosing correspondence from Senator Blount to an Indian interpreter, James Carey, who had served as Indian agent while Blount was governor and Indian superintendent. Blount's correspondence had been intercepted and sent to Philadelphia, with a copy to Mount Vernon. Despite being an avid speculator in western lands, Blount was in poor financial shape and in 1796 began plotting to involve the Creeks and Cherokees in conspiracy with the British and attack Spanish Florida and Louisiana.[93] He urged Carey to foment Indian suspicion and hostility against Hawkins, who was now governor of the Southwest Territory, and anyone else in the Spanish or American interest. He also directed Carey to spread the word among the southern Indians that it was Washington, not Blount, who was responsible for any discontent they might have in regard to their boundary line. Washington was outraged at this attempt "to poison the minds of the Indians, and destroy the utility and influence of the agents employed by the government for the express purpose of preserving peace and harmony with the Indians," and expressed his "sovereign contempt" for Blount. The evidence of conspiracy was laid before Congress, and on July 8 Blount was expelled from the Senate.[94] Hawkins hoped Blount's downfall would check "a base system for the destruction of the four nations, by the Ecunnaunuxulgee (people greedily grasping after all their lands)."[95]

The optimism proved unfounded. It would take more than Blount's fall to protect Indian land. As Washington had noted, it would take a Chinese Wall. For an elected government to use troops to keep its own citizens off Indian land was politically inadvisable even if it had the will and resources to do so, and their assault undermined the policies of civilization and orderly transfer of land devised by Washington and applied by Hawkins.

For a time things seemed to be going well. In the last year of Washington's life, Hawkins reported, Creek people were "ploughing, spinning and weaving, and begin to be attentive to the raising of stock," three hundred women and children were clothed in homespun, "and we had for market, 1000 beef cattle and 300 hogs."[96] Washington and Hawkins imposed changes with what they saw as the best of intentions. In fact, their policies produced uneven results, mixed reactions, and a troubled legacy. Washington did not live to see his efforts among the Creeks unravel in tragedy and bloodshed; Hawkins did. Divisions within Creek society hardened—over the civilization plan, land sales, and whether to negotiate with or defy Americans and their incessant demand for land. Many Creeks sought to redefine their place in a world of changes imported and orchestrated from outside and to remake themselves as Creeks. The yearning grew into a movement of spiritual and cultural rejuvenation that ultimately led to civil war within the Creek Nation and war with the United States. The aged Hoboithle Mico, who had shaken hands with Washington in New York in a pledge of perpetual friendship, condemned the recurrent land cessions and the civilization program, opposed Hawkins and the chiefs on the national council, and took a leading role in the Creek resistance. In 1811 he dictated a letter to King George III, requesting British assistance; in 1813 he died fighting the Georgians. After a series of devastating, some would say genocidal, campaigns, Andrew Jackson killed eight hundred Creeks at the Battle of Tohopeka or Horseshoe Bend in 1814. He then dictated the Treaty of Fort Jackson, confiscating 23 million acres of Creek land. Many Creeks from Nuyukv, the town named in honor of the 1790 treaty with Washington, died fighting the Americans.[97]

In the end, Washington's hopes, intentions, and policies to do something for Indian people could not compete with the human and economic forces arrayed against them. After visiting the United States in the mid-1790s to survey agricultural lands and labor practices, the English aristocrat farmer William Strickland lamented that the operations of unscrupulous speculators threatened "to extirpate the much injured owners of the soil" and that their annihilation was too often pursued with relentless determination and "spoken of with atrocious pleasure." As long as such things were allowed, and Strickland acknowledged they could not be prevented, "it is in vain for the government of the country to attempt the civilization of the Indian, or the amelioration of their condition by the introduction of the arts and comforts of civilized life."[98]

Washington and Strickland corresponded regularly, and the president wrote letters of introduction to Jefferson and others when the Englishman traveled south from Philadelphia. Washington would have read Strickland's book when it was published, but Strickland's account of Indian dispossession would have told him nothing he did not already know.

CHAPTER 20

A Death and a Non-Death

WASHINGTON SPENT A LIFETIME turning Indian homelands into real estate for himself and his nation. He rarely, if ever, acknowledged that the thousands of acres he acquired and owned in the West were Indian lands, but he spent the last years of his life, as he had spent the previous forty, planning, corresponding, and fretting about properties carved out of Indian country.[1] As he neared the end of his presidency and retired, as he was fond of saying, "to the shades of my own Vine and Fig tree," Indians faded from his correspondence.[2] But Indian land occupied his pen and mind as much as ever as he looked toward life's end.

The retired president was land rich and cash poor. When friends and family asked for financial help he often pleaded poverty. "You are under the same mistake that many others are, in supposing that I have money always at Command," he told his nephew Samuel Washington in July 1797. The situation was "so much the reverse of it" that before he retired from the presidency he had had to sell almost 5,000 acres of his lands in Pennsylvania and his shares in the Dismal Swamp Company just to make ends meet.[3] Washington no doubt had a cash flow problem, but he was one of the richest men in America, with his wealth tied up in land he had spent more than forty years accumulating.[4]

Nevertheless, the western lands he had worked so hard to acquire continued to give him, as he frequently said, more plague than profit. Speculators like Washington operated on the assumption that lands acquired for a song would sell for a fortune when settlers flooded the country, but things did not always work out that way. As James Ross advised him in February 1798, the country beyond the Ohio was opening up; adventurers with money would snap up high-quality lands at moderate prices, and that would "greatly retard the sale of high priced lands upon the Kenhawa and on this side of the Ohio," where Washington's holdings lay.[5] Washington in 1797 had considered exchanging some of his Great Kanawha lands for some of Daniel McCarty's Sugar Land holdings in Loudon County, at a ratio of three acres to one.[6] Nothing came of it. Instead, in December 1797 Washington leased his lands on the Great Kanawha to James Welch, a speculator from Greenbrier County, who agreed to make annual payments until he had paid $200,000, when the land would become his. But Welch failed to pay his rent and never bought any land. Frustrated and angered by Welch's promises and excuses and his failed schemes to raise the money, Washington warned him he was not someone to be trifled with. "I am in extreme want of the money which you gave me a solemn promise I should receive the first of January last," he wrote in April 1799. However Welch might have succeeded deceiving others, "you shall not practice the like game with me, with impunity. To contract new Debts, is not the way to pay old ones."[7] When Washington did sell or lease lands, he had trouble getting payments and threatened legal action, which involved him in acrimonious correspondence, with Israel Shreve, for example.[8]

Other schemes were slow to generate income or just did not work out. Washington negotiated with Archibald McClean, a Scottish printer who had relocated to Alexandria, to lease, exchange, or purchase his 587-acre Round Bottom tract in the Ohio country, near present-day Moundsville, West Virginia. He conveyed the property to McClean in August 1798, and the next year McClean settled tenants on it. But final payment had not been made at the time Washington drew up his will, and discrepancies regarding the actual acreage and terms of the deed meant the subsequent history of the property was "filled with legal difficulties." He also concluded a complicated bargain for his additional Ohio lands between modern Marietta, Ohio, and Point Pleasant, West Virginia, and his Kanawha tracts. According to this deal the purchaser signed a thirty-year lease, paid $5,000 down, and pledged to pay off the balance in three annual payments of $5,000 each, beginning in 1806.[9] When John Gill fell behind in the rent for his tract at Difficult Run, Washington agreed to accept articles suitable only "for cloathing my Negros" in partial payment. Gill finally asked to be released from the agreement, leaving Washington in possession of the tract at the time of his death.[10] In addition to the time and trouble involved in trying to attract emigrants, leasing, and renting, the retired president received notice that he was behind with taxes that had accrued on his Kanawha lands in Greenbrier and Kanawha Counties between 1789 and 1797.[11] And he continued to have to explain his right to some of the lands he had acquired all those years ago by military claim.[12]

In January 1799, less than a year before his death, he wrote his nephew Samuel again, explaining why he could not give him money. He had expected to receive several thousand dollars from selling land west of the Alleghenies, but he had "received not one" and had little expectation of receiving payment.[13] The month before he died, he was making inquiries into the "supposed value" of his tracts on the Ohio, Kanahwa, and Little Miami. His many efforts to peddle the three tracts had proved futile.[14]

On December 10, 1799, Washington wrote out instructions for the coming year for his estate manager, James Anderson, a Scottish farmer he had hired in 1796. Among many other carefully laid out tasks, Anderson was "To visit my Lands in the Western Country (at my expence), so soon as the weather becomes temperate and settled in the Spring, Reporting the circumstances under which they are— and what they are cap[able of]—will be expected, It being of importance for me to receive a just, & faithful acct respecting [them]." They were the last lines he wrote about his western lands.[15] In his final days, after a lifetime's endeavor, he was still trying to get accurate information about his western lands and still agonizing over how to get a profit from them.

He remained adamant that internal commerce was essential to national unity and progress and continued to have faith that the Potomac canal project would secure the nation's future and his family's fortunes: "I have every day additional reason for supporting my former opinion, and new proof of its advantages," he wrote in January 1798. But even as he continued to work on behalf of the Potomac Company, the company's fortunes and prospects continued to decline.[16] His western canal project was no more successful than his western land ventures in turning a profit. He had to seek bank loans during the last two years of his life. If his goal in his land dealings was financial independence, he had made little progress.[17]

In preparing his last will, Washington made a list of landholdings and estimated their total value at $488,137. But, he acknowledged with a sigh, "My estate, though it might sell on credit for a tolerable sum, has been and probably will continue to be an unproductive one."[18] He left instructions to sell it all and divide the proceeds among twenty-three heirs.[19] The will ran on for twenty-nine pages, many of them devoted to the schedule of landholdings he prepared. In addition to 8,000 acres divided over five farms at Mount Vernon, it listed twelve separate tracts in Virginia, four in Ohio, five on the Great Kanawha, two in Maryland, the tract at Great Meadows in Pennsylvania, three in the Northwest Territory, two in Kentucky, and one in New York. He explained how he had acquired each tract and estimated what it was worth.[20] On the Ohio River, including those on the Little Kanawha, he had a total of 9,744 acres of land "of the first quality" that he valued at $97,440. He had 23,341 acres on the Great Kanawha, and there was "no richer, or more valuable land in all that Region." Conditionally sold to James Welch for $200,000, they would command considerably more if the terms of the sale were not met. His 3,051 acres on the Little Miami he valued at $15,251, and 5,000 acres in Kentucky at $10,000. Whatever nostalgic value they may have had for him, his 234 acres at Great Meadows, where he fought the French in 1754, were worth $1,404.[21] He had sold nearly all his land in Pennsylvania (although final payment on the Miller's Run tract had not been made), most of his land in New York, and his share in the Dismal Swamp reclamation project. His landed property was, as Edward Lengel says, "immense."[22] Including his Shenandoah lands, Washington still had 45,000 acres in the West when he died.

Washington insisted that Native American farmers must adopt new agricultural practices. Increasingly, he came to believe that white American farmers must do the same. While his western lands failed to bring him the profits he'd hoped for, he invested time, money, and energy in making his Mount Vernon lands more productive. He continued to increase his holdings, negotiating with William Harrison to acquire control of his adjoining property.[23]

He corresponded with the leading scientific agriculturalists in Britain—Arthur Young, Sir John Sinclair, and William Strickland—and regarded Britain's National Board of Agriculture as "one of the most valuable Institutions of Modern Times," which "must be productive of great advantages to the nation and to mankind in General."[24] He was impressed by Scottish agriculturalists and favored attracting immigrants from the Scottish Highlands because they were "a hardy industrious people, well calculated to form new settlements."[25] However, when Richard Parkinson, an English farmer and agricultural author, visited Mount Vernon in 1798 with a view to renting 1,200 acres, he saw little sign of improvement and was not impressed. He deemed Washington's sheep and cattle of poor quality, and pronounced the land so barren that he would not have taken it even if

Washington had given him it. Parkinson's own farm near Baltimore failed, and in his book he recommended that prospective English emigrants stay at home rather than compete with poor lands and slavery in America. He included narratives of William Crawford's capture and execution to show "how dangerous it is for the migrant to venture far into the country."[26]

Washington, too, worried about the related problems of poor lands and slavery. Through a lifetime of acquiring land, he had acted like the rest of the Virginia planter class, who dominated the government and made sure that the best property went to "the best people" rather than to family farmers. Instead of yeoman farmers working the land with care for a precious commodity and planting a variety of crops, planters acquired vast amounts of land cheaply and exhausted it with single-crop agriculture and slave labor, keeping it "under constant cultivation," as Washington said, "until it will yield scarcely anything at all."[27] He acknowledged Strickland's criticisms of American agriculture as wasteful, making little effort to improve land, with the result "that we ruin the lands that are already cleared and either cut down more wood if we have it, or emigrate into the western Country."[28] He adopted a seven-field, seven-year crop rotation system on his Mount Vernon estates.

How to get rid of the other problem occupied his thoughts increasingly. Had he not been opposed to "selling negros, as you would do cattle at a market," he wrote in 1794, "I would not, in twelve months from this date, be possessed of one as a slave. I shall be happily mistaken, if they are not found to be a very troublesome species of property ere many years pass over our heads."[29] According to Ron Chernow, Washington's "secret agenda" in selling his western lands was to use the proceeds to emancipate his slaves.[30] But his desire to free slaves ran counter to the effects of his constant desire to promote westward expansion. Whites moving west in great numbers helped entrench slave labor in eastern Virginia, where a greater proportion of those who stayed were, or became, slaveholders.[31]

Despite his growing personal aversion, Washington remained publicly silent on the question of slavery.[32] A French traveler, Jacques-Pierre Brissot de Warville, who visited Mount Vernon, observed that the biggest obstacle to freeing slaves lay "in the character, the manners and habits of the Virginians. They seem to enjoy the sweat of slaves." He believed beginning the revolution in Virginia and preparing the way for emancipation was a task worthy of such a great man as Washington. But Washington was slow to move against slavery, thinking it "dangerous to strike too vigorously at a prejudice which had begun to diminish; that time, patience, and information, would not fail to vanquish it."[33]

Although Washington may have been relatively humane in his treatment of his slaves, he nonetheless subjected them to an inhumane system, and they reacted accordingly. Between 1760 and his death in 1799, at least forty-seven of his and his wife's slaves—perhaps 7 percent of the slaves he owned and managed during his lifetime, ran away.[34] Writing to Lawrence Lewis in the summer of 1797, Washington confided: "I wish from my Soul that the Legislature of this State could see the policy of a gradual abolition of Slavery; It might prev[en]t much future mischief."[35] He knew posterity would judge him and his generation, but he never spoke out or advocated any measures against the institution. As Joseph Ellis points out, slavery and Indian policy are conspicuously absent from Washington's Farewell Address, crafted in five months of collaborative correspondence with Alexander Hamilton, who put the president's ideas into prose. Both slavery and Indian policy were controversial and divisive issues, and the president wanted to leave on a unifying note. To do anything about slavery at the present time, Washington feared, would jeopardize the unity of the nation. That debate was best left to a future generation.[36]

There were more than three hundred slaves at Mount Vernon in 1799. Some Washington owned outright, some he controlled as part of Martha's dowry, some he rented by contract, and some he hired for a time because of their artisanal skills.[37] He had too many "working Negroes" by half for effective employment, he told Robert Lewis, "and I shall never turn Planter thereon." He was caught in a labor system that was both inhumane and inefficient:

> To sell the overplus I cannot, because I am principled against this kind off traffic in the human species. To hire them out is almost as bad, because they could not be disposed of in families to any advantage, and to disperse the families I have an aversion. What then is to be done? Something must, or I shall be ruined; for all the money (in addition to what I raise by Crops and rents) that have been *received* for Lands sold within the last four years, to the amount of Fifty thousand dollars, has scarcely been able to keep me a float.[38]

He had come to regard slavery as immoral and impractical and wanted to free his slaves, but only after his death did he publicly express his will, in his will.[39] By then it was clear that setting the nation on a path of expansion had also opened the way for slavery to move west.

On December 12, 1799, Washington was caught outdoors in snow, sleet, and rain; he woke with a sore throat the next morning, and by the morning of the fourteenth he was desperately ill. His old friend Dr. Craik was sent for, but doctors could do little to ease his pain and suffering—he had a streptococcus infection that produced such severe swelling around the glottis that he was scarcely able to breathe. He died about ten thirty that night. He was sixty-seven.

His death prompted an outpouring of grief and veneration for the man who had led and saved the Revolution. But, as his Farewell Address had testified, he had not yet secured the political stability and future of the nation he had helped to create, and now the repercussions of new revolutions, in France and Haiti, were shaking the Atlantic world. As François Furstenberg shows, much of the response "had more to do with the state of the nation than it did with Washington."[40]

IN THE COURSE OF ALMOST fifty years, Washington grew from a young man out of his depth in the cultural practices, foreign policies, and geopolitical strategies of Indian country to the most powerful man on the continent, whose policies and precedents affected the lives and futures of thousands of Indian people. He had spent his life grasping for Indian land, although he never called it that. He had fought alongside Indian allies, and he had waged war against Indian people, Indian towns, and Indian crops. He had learned and practiced the essentials of Indian diplomacy, employed treaties as the primary means of obtaining Indian land, and insisted that the government accord those treaties the same respect as it did treaties with other nations. When he entered Indian country as a young man, he addressed Indians as brothers and negotiated the terms of his relationship with them; as president, he addressed them as children and mandated policies for them. The settler colonial society he represented grew from one held back by Indian power and anxious for Indian allies to an imperial republic that was on the move, dismantling Indian country to create American property, and dismantling Indian ways of life to make way for American civilization. His insistence that the federal government exercise exclusive responsibility for Indian affairs asserted national authority over Indian tribes and over individual states and prepared the way for the role of "big government" in western expansion and Indian affairs in the nineteenth century. The Indian wars and diplomacy that secured the West for the nation also increased the power of the federal government and its army as the instrument of western expansion. He had set in motion campaigns and policies that brought the federal government and its agents into almost every aspect of Indian life, from waging war and negotiating land sales to planting crops and reordering gender relations.[41]

The expansionist forces Washington unleashed and directed were part of an explosion of English-speaking settler societies that produced new and more enduring forms of empire in large areas of the world. Indigenous peoples elsewhere and later fared little better at the hands of the British Empire than did Native Americans in Washington's settler republic.[42] Nevertheless, the first president initiated policies that committed the United States to an imperial path and a colonial relationship that plagued Indian people for generations to come, and he set precedents that established the framework for determining what place Indian tribes would occupy in the new nation. Washington never questioned that Indians must and would relinquish their lands to the growing republic, but the power and presence of Indian nations and the foreign policies pursued by Indian leaders pressured his administration to turn from claiming Indian lands by right of conquest and instead base its Indian relations on law and restraint. Washington and Knox endeavored to establish a place for Indians within the constitutional framework and to establish treaty-based relationships with the tribes within the framework of the law of nations. As Knox recommended, the Washington administration drew on the international law concept of sovereignty to determine Native status and recognized Indian tribes as separate nations, and in doing so helped to establish sovereignty as a central issue in Indian law. At the same time, it asserted ultimate sovereignty over the territory of the United States and insisted that this sovereignty limited Indians' freedom to make alliances with foreign nations or sell land to anyone except the United States. It did not claim or exercise the unbridled power of later years; nevertheless, it laid the groundwork for more aggressive assertions of federal authority after Indian autonomy waned significantly in the late eighteenth century and then declined rapidly in the nineteenth century. From not recognizing Native nations as nations like the United States or France, it was a short step to treating Indians as "domestic dependent nations"; from extending US sovereignty over Indians and denying Indian nations equal sovereignty, it was a short step to asserting plenary power over them and denying their sovereignty.[43] From the Washington-Pickering model of educating Indians in the useful arts and agriculture rather than as scholars, it was just a step to educating Indian students to become members of the underclass, as occurred in nineteenth-century boarding schools.

By some definitions of the term, Washington's civilization program constituted genocide by another name. But Washington saw his policies as setting Indians on the road to survival, not destruction, giving them the opportunity to remake themselves as American citizens. Inclusion in American society, as understood by Washington and subsequent makers of Indian policy, required Indian people to cease being Indian; in effect, their survival, paradoxically, required their "disappearance." When Thomas Jefferson became president he continued Indian policies that, as a member of Washington's cabinet, he had help to develop: dealing with tribes as sovereign nations, acquiring land by treaty rather than by war, and promoting a program of civilization. Jefferson pushed things further. Washington's policy of assimilating Indians as their best chance of survival became in Jefferson's mind a simple choice between assimilation and extinction, either of which would free their land; "by mourning the passing of the Indians into oblivion or civilized invisibility," wrote the historian Anthony Wallace, Jefferson "gave moral justification to the seizure of lands he said they no longer needed."[44] As envisioned by Washington, the government factories or trading posts would not extend credit to Indians: the goal was to make them economically independent producers who purchased goods with cash, not to sink them in debt. But even before Washington died, the factories were beginning to lure Indians into debt, and Jefferson made it a central, albeit covert, component of his policy of Indian dispossession.[45]

Jefferson's acquisition of the Louisiana Territory in 1803 gave the United States another outlet for dispossession, a third option between assimilation and extinction.[46] But the process of dispossession continued along paths well worn during Washington's presidency. Washington had tried to establish federal control over the conduct of Indian affairs, but tensions with the states continued to complicate US Indian policy to the detriment of Indian people. Appalled by what he saw during his visit to America in the 1830s as policies of Indian removal were being implemented east of the Mississippi, Alexis de Tocqueville recalled Washington's declaration to Congress that the United States as "more enlightened and more powerful than the Indian nations" was honor-bound to treat them with kindness and even generosity. But this "virtuous and high-minded policy" had not been followed. The Union treated the Indians with less cupidity and violence than the several states, but in Tocqueville's view the two governments were equally lacking in good faith. "The states' tyranny forces the savages to flee, and the Union's promises make flight easy. Both are means to the same end."[47]

Indians had given Washington hard lessons in war and diplomacy. Their lands had fueled but never satisfied his hunger for a personal fortune in the West and provided the foundation for building an imperial republic. Indian power had frustrated the ambitions of the empire he served, stalled the expansion of the nation he led, and compelled him to do business with tribal leaders. Their victories had prompted him to rethink how Americans raised, trained, and funded their armies and how they fought their wars. Their presence on the land, and his insistence that they be expelled from their lands, presented him with philosophical and political dilemmas as he wrestled to combine expansion with honor, dispossession with justice. He expended prodigious amounts of attention, energy, money, and ink formulating and implementing his Indian policies. He achieved his goal of acquiring Indian land and achieved his vision of an expansive republic, but he failed to balance expansion onto Indian lands with justice to Indian people.

The rapid migration of a vibrant population that Washington celebrated in his message to Congress in December 1795 ensured that the Washington-Knox vision of expansion with honor remained a chimera. As the president acknowledged in that same message, there could never be peace as long as frontier settlers murdered Indians with impunity. Neither Washington nor any of his successors resolved the problem he articulated: "To enforce upon the Indians the observance of justice, it is indispensable that there shall be competent means of rendering Justice to them." Although Washington did not mention Indians in his Farewell Address, he urged Americans to "observe good faith and justice towards all nations" and "give mankind the magnanimous and too novel example of a people always guided by an exalted justice and benevolence."[48] Indians, unmentioned, surely inhabited the retiring president's vision of a just and harmonious future, but he also surely realized that including them in that vision was a vain hope. He had seen too much evidence to the contrary to believe that the better angels of Americans' nature could prevail when Indian land was at stake.

History seemed to show that an expansive territory was lethal to republics. Washington believed that an expansive, indeed expanding, territory, properly managed by a strong and enlightened central government, was the salvation and future hope of his republic. He recognized and worried that this meant the dispossession and possible destruction of Indian peoples, and their "plight" as his American empire advanced elicited his sympathy and his concern for the nation's honor. But he did not let his concerns divert him from his primary purpose of building a nation. Instead, to do Indians justice and offer them a future, he implemented programs to transform their lives and save them from themselves.

The year after his death, Washington achieved his vision of a capital on the Potomac. Indian delegates continued for generations to visit the seat of government named after the first "Great Father," and many recalled his promises as they asked for justice. But as the historical geographer D. W. Meinig observed, they too often found that "the new city of Washington was what St. Petersburg was for the Finns, Peking for the Miao, or Constantinople for the Serbs: the seat of a capricious, tyrannical power."[49]

Despite the assaults that Town Destroyer launched on Indian country and Indian cultures, however, some Native Americans joined other Americans in mourning Washington's passing (see plate 13). On the national day of mourning, February 22, 1800, in Knoxville, Tennessee, nine Cherokee chiefs and many "common Indians" marched in a military funeral procession along with Governor John Sevier (whom Washington had dubbed an Indian killer) and other prominent citizens to mark "the loss of their great father Washington."[50] Indian speakers invoked his memories, words, and promises, like Efau Hadjo, who spoke of "our old friend, General Washington, who gave us the good talks for our land," and held up the first president's policies and practices as the standard for assessing subsequent relations.[51] Although Cornplanter complained about the loss of Seneca lands, toward the end of his life he "praised George Washington" and showed visitors three documents signed by the first president, "which he kept wrapped in a linen cloth in a valise." Writing early in the twentieth century, the Seneca scholar Arthur C. Parker said Iroquois people remembered with gratitude Washington's magnanimity and his attempts to do them justice and mentioned him "with reverence in their native feasts."[52]

Much of this, of course, was the rhetoric and strategy of diplomacy: Indian leaders knew they could leverage Washington's image and reputation among Americans to help secure Indian goals. Chief John Ross regularly invoked his memory as his Cherokee people resisted efforts in the 1820s and '30s to relocate them west of the Mississippi. Another Cherokee chief, Bloody Fellow, had called Washington a liar in 1792, but now that the government was riding roughshod over treaties that guaranteed the Cherokees possession of their remaining lands, Ross honored the first president for acting with justice and upholding the treaties he made. Time and again, he referred to him as "the Great Washington," "the illustrious Washington," "the venerated Washington." From where Ross stood, Washington's presidency looked like a golden age.[53] Washington's efforts to reconcile the competing aspects of his Indian policies seem hypocritical, knowing what we know now, but he devoted more time, thought, and ink to the problem than did most of his contemporaries, and most other presidents. Some, perhaps many, Native Americans revered his memory as they looked back from a time when US Indian policy veered from assimilation in the name of "civilization" to ethnic cleansing under the name of removal.

SIX MONTHS BEFORE WASHINGTON DIED, a Seneca named Handsome Lake fell into a dead sleep. A brother of Cornplanter, Handsome Lake had fought against the British at Devil's Hole in 1763 and against the Americans during the Revolution. He had also participated in the post-Revolutionary treaty councils that had dismantled Iroquois land and unity. Like his people, he felt the loss of military and political power, endured poverty and cultural assault, and faced a bleak future dictated by former enemies. At first it seemed that Handsome Lake was just another hard-drinking Indian who had lost his life to alcohol, another individual who had followed the tragic path prescribed for his people. Unlike those of Washington's death, however, reports of Handsome Lake's demise proved to be premature. He awakened and reported having had a vision in which he journeyed to heaven and also saw the torments of hell. Other visions followed. In Handsome Lake's near-death experience, the Creator had given him a new gospel and a message of rebirth for his people.[54]

Handsome Lake offered Haudenosaunee people a way to live a good life based on traditional values even as American society threatened to engulf them. By 1799 the Iroquois who had once dominated the northeastern United States were confined to reservations in small areas of their traditional homelands or lived in exile in Canada. The Senecas who remained in western New York had once held some 4 million acres; now they lived on fewer than 200,000 acres divided into eleven separate tracts.[55] They rebuilt their communities but were under pressure from missionaries, land speculators, settlers, and the state and federal governments. Renouncing his former life of drunkenness, Handsome Lake embarked on a mission to bring the *Gaiwiio*, "the Good Message," to his people. His teachings combined traditional beliefs and elements of the Great Law of Peace with some Christian additions adopted from Quaker missionaries. He preached that people should live in peace with the United States and with one another. He denounced alcohol, factionalism, and the breakdown of family life, and he emphasized the importance of education and farming. In place of a society based on matrilineal, extended families that traditionally inhabited the clan mothers' longhouses, and in which women were allowed to divorce their husbands simply by excluding them from their houses, Handsome Lake espoused a new social gospel in which men now did the farming, and husbands headed the nuclear family. He urged people to adopt plows, spinning wheels, frame houses, reading and writing English, and schooling. At the same time, his teachings incorporated thanksgiving festivals and other ceremonies from the old religion and denounced the sale of lands. The Longhouse Religion that developed based on his teachings met opposition from both traditionalists and Christians, but by reviving and reshaping traditional morality and values, Handsome Lake offered hope in a time of spiritual crisis and staggering transformations, and a way for Senecas to preserve their identity, autonomy, and lands through resilience and adaptation rather than outright resistance. The Longhouse Religion and the code of values Handsome Lake preached became a source of endurance, and it had enduring appeal.

According to the anthropologist Lewis Henry Morgan, who published his famous work *The League of the Iroquois* in 1851, one of "the modern beliefs engrafted upon the ancient faith" merited particular notice. It related to Washington. In Iroquois belief, there was no place for white men in the Indian heaven, "but an exception was made in favor of Washington." Despite unleashing devastation on Seneca towns during the Revolution, as president he was kind to Indians when he could have killed them all, protected their rights, and advocated policies "of the most enlightened justice and humanity." Evidently they did not blame Washington personally for the losses they had suffered during his lifetime and during his administration. When he died, he was not permitted to go into the presence of the Great Spirit but, "dressed in his uniform, and in a state of perfect felicity," resided just outside the Iroquois heaven, "destined to remain through eternity in the solitary enjoyment of the celestial residence prepared for him by the Great Spirit."[56]

Whether the Great Spirit, Handsome Lake, or Morgan put the revered first president on his celestial pedestal is difficult to say. Nevertheless, some Senecas clearly held Washington and his memory in reverence. The same the year Morgan published his *League of the Iroquois*, Ely S. Parker was installed "as leading Sachem of the Iroquois Confederacy." As part of the ritual, the peace medal that was "given by the great Washington to my tribal relative, Red Jacket," was hung around his neck "to be retained and worn as evidence of the bond of perpetual peace and friendship established and entered into between the people of the United States and the Six Nations of Indians at the time of its presentation."[57] Parker would later serve as Ulysses S. Grant's secretary when Robert E. Lee surrendered at Appomattox and as the first Native commissioner of Indian affairs.

Washington had offered the Senecas *his* vision for their future. His message preached complete cultural transformation as the path to survival in a world where people of Indian descent lived among Americans by becoming Americans. Handsome Lake's people chose a rather different course. They borrowed from Quaker teachings and made a new Iroquois religion; they borrowed from American society to build a new, Iroquois way of life. They adopted American technology, farmed like their American neighbors, lived in log homes, worked in the market economy, and sent their children to school. But they did not stop being Haudenosaunee. They preserved beliefs and values, kinship ties, and customs, maintaining an unchanging core beneath the surface of change. Washington believed that Indians who adopted the new ways he offered them would, eventually, cease to be Indians. Instead, they took some of what he offered, kept what they could of their old ways, and created new ways to be who they were. Indian societies shuddered under the shock of assault, and then held.[58]

George Washington, the campaigns he launched, and the policies he initiated had huge impacts on Native America. Washington's vision of a nation built on Indian land was realized. But his vision of the future for Indian people was not. Instead of adopting Washington's recipe for their survival, Indian people adapted it. Instead of changing and *ceasing* to be Indians, they changed and *continued* to be Indians. Instead of abandoning their traditions, cultures, and values, they built on their Native American past to give themselves an American future.

ATIATOHARONGWEN, COLONEL LOUIS COOK, outlived Washington by fifteen years. He may not have lived to regret his relationship with Washington, but he lived to see the shortcomings of Washington's promises and policies for Indian people. Even Indians who had fought for the United States and befriended the president could not receive the fair and honorable treatment Washington spoke so much about. In the spring of 1796 Cook and a delegation of chiefs from St. Regis (Akwesasne) and Kahnawake, representing the Seven Nations of Canada, traveled to New York City to negotiate with the state government for compensation for the loss of lands and signed a treaty extinguishing their claims to the lands. During the negotiations they repeated the position consistently taken by Indian people that non-Indian nations could not transfer to one another Indian lands that Indians had never given up. Invoking the law of nations in their own way, they "bid defiance to the world to produce any deed, or sale, or gift, or lease, of any of the lands in question, or any part of them, from us, to either the King of France or Britain, or to either [any] of the United States." They had lived in peace, and their rights had been ignored: "It seems that, before a nation can get justice of another, they must first go to war, and spill one another's blood," but as a Christian people they hoped never to have to resort to such measures.

> Brothers: We intreat you only to look back, and consider the privileges your brother Indians formerly enjoyed, before we were interrupted by other nations of white people, who feign themselves to us as brothers, and let justice take place betwixt you and us, in place of arbitrary power; for that, brothers, you very well know, is a thing that never gave contentment to any people or nation whatsoever.

> Brothers: Formerly we enjoyed the privilege we expect is now called freedom and liberty; but, since the acquaintance with our brother white people, that which we call freedom and liberty, becomes an entire stranger to us; and in place of that, comes in flattery and deceit, to deprive poor ignorant people of their properties, and bring them to poverty, and, at last, to become beggars and laughing stocks to the world.

Rather than dwell on the past, they hoped for a better future, in which the white people "would do by us as you would wish to be done by."

> Brothers, this is what we wish for: that every brother might have their rights, throughout this continent, and all be of one mind, and to live together in peace and love as becometh brothers; and to have a chain of friendship made between you and us, too strong ever to be broke, and polished and brightened so pure as never to rust.[59]

The chiefs' words echoed some of the rhetoric of Washington's speeches, but their vision for America as a place of universal rights far exceeded his. For Louis Cook, a man of Native American and African American heritage who had served with Washington in the Revolution and worked with him in dealing with the western tribes, it was a vision that remained elusive. The expanding republic that Washington helped launch depended on Indians giving up their land and Africans giving up their labor; only white men enjoyed the rights Cook wished for.

In a letter to the president, Oliver Wolcott Jr., who had replaced Hamilton as secretary of the treasury in 1795, emphasized something that Washington fully understood: "The power of making Treaties, is the same thing as the power of *pledging the faith of one nation to another.*"[60] Yet despite his well-intentioned efforts to establish nation-to-nation relationships, Washington's Indian policies eroded the Indian rights he claimed to protect and undermined the Indian sovereignty he claimed to respect. In the dark years to come, Indian sovereignty was submerged further still. But instead of disappearing into American society, Indian tribes remained within the American nation. Their sovereignty was never extinguished, and resurfaced with a more robust assertion of Native rights in the second half of the twentieth century.[61] The nation-to-nations relationship between the federal government and Indian tribes today in some ways resembles that which Washington, in many of his writings and some of his policies, aspired to establish. But assaults on the rights and resources of Native peoples continue. It remains to be seen if the relationship can ever measure up to Louis Cook's vision of a chain of friendship "too strong ever to be broke, and polished and brightened so pure as never to rust."

ABBREVIATIONS

American Archives	*American Archives.* Peter Force, comp. 4th ser., 6 vols., Washington, DC, 1837–46; 5th ser., 3 vols., Washington, DC, 1848–53.
ASPIA	*American State Papers: Documents, Legislative and Executive, of the Congress of the United States, Class II: Indian Affairs.* Walter Lowrie and Matthew St. Clair Clarke, eds. 2 vols. Washington, DC: Gales & Seaton, 1832–34.
Bouquet Papers	*The Papers of Henry Bouquet.* S. K. Stevens, Donald H. Kent, and Autumn L. Leonard, eds. 6 vols. Harrisburg: Pennsylvania Historical and Museum Commission, 1951–54.
CVSP	*Calendar of Virginia State Papers.* William P. Palmer, ed. 11 vols. Richmond: Virginia State Library, 1875–93.
CO 5	Colonial Office Records, ser. 5, National Archives (formerly Public Record Office), Kew, England.
CO 42	Colonial Office Records, ser. 42, National Archives, Kew, England.
CRP	*Colonial Records of Pennsylvania.* Samuel Hazard, ed. 16 vols. Harrisburg and Philadelphia: T. Fenn, 1838–53. Vols. 1–10: *Minutes of the Provincial Council of Pennsylvania;* vols. 11–16: *Minutes of the Supreme Executive Council of Pennsylvania.*
DAR	*Documents of the American Revolution, 1770–1783 (Colonial Office Series).* K. G. Davies, ed. 21 vols. Shannon: Irish University Press, 1972–81.
DHFFC	*Documentary History of the First Federal Congress, 1789–1791.* Linda Grant De Pauw et al., eds. 22 vols. to date. Baltimore, MD: Johns Hopkins University Press, 1972–.
Diaries of GW	*The Diaries of George Washington.* Donald Jackson and Dorothy Twohig, eds. 6 vols. Charlottesville: University Press of Virginia, 1976–79.

Dinwiddie Papers	*The Official Records of Robert Dinwiddie, Lieutenant-Governor of the Colony of Virginia, 1751–1758.* R. A. Brock, ed. 2 vols. Richmond: Virginia Historical Society, 1883–84.
Draper Mss.	Lyman Draper Manuscripts, Wisconsin State Historical Society. Microfilm copy at Baker Library, Dartmouth College.
EAID	*Early American Indian Documents: Treaties and Laws, 1607–1789.* Alden T. Vaughan, gen. ed. 20 vols. Bethesda, MD: University Publications of America, 1979–2004.
	Vol. 2: *Pennsylvania Treaties, 1737–1756.* Donald H. Kent, ed.
	Vol. 3: *Pennsylvania Treaties, 1756-1775.* Alison Duncan Hirsch, ed.
	Vol. 4: *Virginia Treaties, 1607–1722.* W. Stitt Robinson, ed.
	Vol. 5: *Virginia Treaties, 1723–1775.* W. Stitt Robinson, ed.
	Vol. 9: *New York and New Jersey Treaties, 1714–1754.* Barbara Graymont, ed.
	Vol. 13: *North and South Carolina Treaties, 1654–1756.* W. Stitt Robinson, ed.
	Vol. 15: *Virginia and Maryland Laws.* Alden T. Vaughan and Deborah A. Rosen, eds.
	Vol. 18: *Revolution and Confederation.* Colin G. Calloway, ed.
Executive Journals	*Executive Journals of the Council of Colonial Virginia.* R. McIlwaine et al., eds. 6 vols. Richmond: Virginia State Library, 1926–66.
FO	Foreign Office Records, National Archives, Kew, England.
Forbes HQ Papers	The Headquarters Papers of Brigadier-General John Forbes relating to the Expedition against Fort Duquesne in 1758. University of Virginia Library. Microfilm copy at the David Library of the American Revolution, Washington's Crossing, Pennsylvania.
GWPLC	George Washington Papers at the Library of Congress, 1741–99. Manuscript Division, Library of Congress and online at memory.loc.gov
Haldimand Papers	Correspondence and Papers of Governor General Sir Frederick Haldimand, 1758–91. British Museum, London, Additional Manuscripts 21661–892.
IALT	*Indian Affairs: Laws and Treaties*, vol. 2, *Treaties*. Charles J. Kappler, comp. Washington, DC: Government Printing Office, 1904.

JCC	*Journals of the Continental Congress.* Washington C. Ford et al., eds. 34 vols. Washington, DC: Government Printing Office, 1904–37.
JHBV	*Journals of the House of Burgesses of Virginia.* H. R. McIlwaine et al., eds. 12 vols. Richmond: Colonial Press, 1906–15.
JPP	*The Journal of the Proceedings of the President, 1793–1797.* Dorothy Twohig, ed. Charlottesville: University of Virginia Press, 1981.
Knox Papers	Henry Knox Papers owned by the New England Historic Genealogical Society and deposited in the Massachusetts Historical Society. Microfilm copy at Baker Library, Dartmouth College. 55 reels.
MPHC	*The Collections of the Michigan Pioneer and Historical Society.* 40 vols. Lansing: Michigan State Historical Society, 1874–1929.
NYCD	*Documents relating to the Colonial History of the State of New York.* Edmund B. O'Callaghan et al., eds. 15 vols. Albany, NY: Weed, Parsons, 1853–57.
NYPL	New York Public Library.
NYPL, GW	New York Public Library, George Washington Papers.
PCC	Papers of the Continental Congress, 1774–89. National Archives, Washington, DC. Microfilm 247.
PGW, Col.	*The Papers of George Washington: Colonial Series.* W. W. Abbot, Dorothy Twohig, et al., eds. 10 vols. Charlottesville: University Press of Virginia, 1983–95.
PGW, Confed.	*The Papers of George Washington: Confederation Series.* W. W. Abbot et al., eds. 6 vols. Charlottesville: University Press of Virginia, 1992–97.
PGW, Pres.	*The Papers of George Washington: Presidential Series.* Dorothy Twohig et al., eds. 18 vols. to date. Charlottesville: University of Virginia Press, 1987–.
PGW, Ret.	*The Papers of George Washington: Retirement Series.* W. W. Abbot et al., eds. 4 vols. Charlottesville: University Press of Virginia, 1998–99.
PGW, Rev.	*The Papers of George Washington: Revolutionary War Series.* W. W. Abbot et al., eds. 23 vols. to date. Charlottesville: University of Virginia Press, 1985–.
PTJ	*The Papers of Thomas Jefferson.* Julian P. Boyd et al., eds. 42 vols. to date. Princeton, NJ: Princeton University Press, 1950–.
Pickering Papers	Timothy Pickering Papers. Massachusetts Historical Society, Boston. Microfilm copy at Baker Library, Dartmouth College. 69 reels.

Schuyler Papers   Philip Schuyler Papers, Indian Papers, 1710–96,
                           boxes 13–15, reel 7. New York Public Library.
Simcoe Correspondence   *The Correspondence of Lieut. Governor John Graves
                           Simcoe, with Allied Documents relating to His
                           Administration of the Government of Upper Canada.*
                           Earnest A. Cruikshank, ed. 5 vols. Toronto:
                           Ontario Historical Society, 1923–31.
St. Clair Papers   *The St. Clair Papers: The Life and Public Services of
                           Arthur St. Clair . . . with his Correspondence and Other
                           Papers.* William Henry Smith, ed. 2 vols.
                           Cincinnati: Robert Clarke, 1881.
Territorial Papers   *The Territorial Papers of the United States.* Clarence
                           Edwin Carter, ed. 28 vols. Washington, DC:
                           Government Printing Office, 1934–75.
WJP   *The Papers of Sir William Johnson.* James Sullivan
                           et al., eds. 14 vols. Albany: University of the State
                           of New York, 1921–65.
Writings of Washington   *The Writings of George Washington from the Original
                           Manuscript Sources, 1745–1799.* John C. Fitzpatrick,
                           ed. 39 vols. Washington, DC: Government Printing
                           Office, 1931–44.

NOTES

INTRODUCTION

1. *JPP*, 42–43; *PTJ* 25:112–18, 133.
2. *JPP*, 49–50.
3. *Territorial Papers* 4:307.
4. *JPP*, 309–10.
5. *Territorial Papers* 4:349–50; *Writings of Washington* 33:412, 418, 424; James Thomas Flexner, *George Washington: Anguish and Farewell, 1793–1799* (Boston: Little, Brown, 1969), 157.
6. *ASPIA* 1:54.
7. Quote from Franklin B. Hough, ed., *Proceedings of the Commissioners of Indian Affairs Appointed by Law for the Extinguishment of Indian Titles in the State of New York*, 2 vols. (Albany, NY: Joel Munsell, 1861), 2:370.
8. Kirkland quoted in Alan Taylor, *The Divided Ground: Indians, Settlers, and the Northern Borderland of the American Revolution* (New York: Knopf, 2006), 271.
9. M. A. LaCombe, *Political Gastronomy: Food and Authority in the English Atlantic World* (Philadelphia: University of Pennsylvania Press, 2012).
10. *Writings of Washington* 35:146, 302n; John to Abigail Adams, Dec. 4, 1796, in C. James Taylor et al., eds., *The Adams Papers: Adams Family Correspondence* 11:430, http://rotunda.upress.virginia.edu/
11. *JPP*, 11, 31.
12. *PGW, Pres.* 13:72 ("momentous").
13. For example, Carol Berkin, *A Sovereign People: The Crises of the 1790s and the Birth of American Nationalism* (New York: Basic Books, 2017) explains the role of four crises—the Whiskey Rebellion, the Genet Affair, the XYZ Affair, and the Alien and Sedition Acts—in emerging American nationalism but does not mention the crisis generated by the Indian destruction of the American army in 1791.
14. Rev. John Heckewelder, *History, Manners, and Customs of the Indian Nations Who Once Inhabited Pennsylvania and the Neighboring States* (Philadelphia, 1876; New York: Arno Press, 1971), 150.
15. Daniel H. Usner, "'A Savage Feast They Made of It': John Adams and the Paradoxical Origins of Federal Indian Policy," *Journal of the Early Republic* 33 (2013): 607–42; David Andrew Nichols, *Red Gentlemen and White Savages: Indians, Federalists, and the Search for Order on the American Frontier* (Charlottesville: University of Virginia Press, 2008); Gregory Ablavsky, "The Savage Constitution," *Duke Law Journal* 63 (2014): 999–1089; Gregory Ablavsky, "Beyond the Indian Commerce Clause," *Yale Law Journal* 124 (2014–15): 1012–90; Leonard J. Sadosky, *Revolutionary Negotiations: Indians, Empires, and Diplomats in the Founding of America* (Charlottesville: University Press of Virginia, 2009); Paul Frymer, *Building an American Empire: The Era of Territorial and Political Expansion* (Princeton, NJ: Princeton University Press, 2017), ch. 2.
16. John Ferling, *The Ascent of George Washington: The Hidden Political Genius of an American Icon* (New York: Bloomsbury, 2009), 6.
17. Lois Mulkearn, ed., *George Mercer Papers: Relating to the Ohio Company of Virginia* (Pittsburgh, PA: University of Pittsburgh Press, 1954), 9.

18. Quoted in Thomas Perkins Abernethy, *Western Lands and the American Revolution* (New York: Russell & Russell, 1959), 21.

19. *The Journal of Major George Washington: An Account of his First Official Mission, Made as Emissary from the Governor of Virginia to the Commandant of the French Forces on the Ohio, October 1753– January 1754*, facsimile ed. (Williamsburg, VA: Colonial Williamsburg Foundation, 1959), v.

20. Charles H. Ambler, *George Washington and the West* (Chapel Hill: University of North Carolina Press, 1936), 86.

21. Colin G. Calloway, *The American Revolution in Indian Country: Crisis and Diversity in Native American Communities* (Cambridge: Cambridge University Press, 1995); Robert G. Parkinson, *The Common Cause: Creating Race and Nation in the American Revolution* (Chapel Hill: University of North Carolina Press, 2016).

22. Warren R. Hofstra, ed., *George Washington and the Virginia Backcountry* (Madison, WI: Madison House, 1998), 81, 87.

23. Dorothy Twohig, "The Making of George Washington," in Hofstra, ed., *George Washington and the Virginia Backcountry*, 32, n. 41.

24. Edward Redmond, "George Washington: Surveyor and Mapmaker," https://www.loc.gov /collections/george-washington-papers/articles-and-essays/george-washington-survey -and-mapmaker/; W. W. Abbot, "George Washington, the West, and the Union," in *George Washington Reconsidered*, ed. Don Higginbotham (Charlottesville: University Press of Virginia, 2001), 198–211.

25. Abbot, "George Washington, the West, and the Union," quotes at 211; "more than anything else" quoted in Don Higginbotham, *George Washington: Uniting a Nation* (Lanham, MD: Rowman & Littlefield, 2002), 63.

26. Thomas P. Slaughter, *The Whiskey Rebellion* (New York: Oxford University Press, 1986), 194; Woody Holton, *Unruly Americans and the Origins of the Constitution* (New York: Hill & Wang, 2007), 268; Douglas Southall Freeman, *Washington*, 1-vol. abridgement by Richard Harwell of the 7-vol. *George Washington* (New York: Simon & Schuster, 1992), 601. See, for example, Hamilton's estimate of expenses for 1790 and 1791; Harold C. Syrett et al., eds., *The Papers of Alexander Hamilton*, 27 vols. (Charlottesville: University of Virginia Press, 1961–87), 9:471–74.

27. *St. Clair Papers* 2:50.

28. Jeff W. Dennis, *Patriots and Indians: Shaping Identity in Eighteenth-Century South Carolina* (Columbia: University of South Carolina Press, 2017).

29. Boyd Stanley Schlenther, *Charles Thomson: A Patriot's Pursuit* (Newark: University of Delaware Press, 1990), ch. 2 (immersed at 35; adopted at 42); Boyd Stanley Schlenther, "Training for Resistance: Charles Thomson and Indian Affairs in Pennsylvania," *Pennsylvania History* 50 (1983): 185–217; *EAID* 3:194, 256–57; [Charles Thomson], *An Enquiry into the Causes of the Alienation of the Delaware and Shawanese Indians from the British Interest, and into the Measures taken for recovering their Friendship* (London: Printed for J. Wilkie, 1759), esp. 80–81; *Bouquet Papers* 2:195n (adopted).

30. Lee claimed to have married Bright Lightning, daughter of a Seneca named Kaghswaghtaniunut, a.k.a. Belt of Wampum, who accompanied Washington on his mission in the Ohio country in 1753 and served as one of Braddock's scouts at Fort Cumberland. David L. Preston, *Braddock's Defeat: The Battle of the Monongahela and the Road to Revolution* (New York: Oxford University Press, 2015), 109, 381n; John E. Ferling, *The First of Men: A Life of George Washington* (New York: Oxford University Press, 2010), 108.

31. Pekka Hämäläinen, "The Shapes of Power: Indians, Europeans, and North American Worlds from the Seventeenth to the Nineteenth Century," in *Contested Spaces of Early America*, ed. Juliana Barr and Edward Countryman (Philadelphia: University of Pennsylvania Press, 2014), 32–68.

32. Ablavsky, "Beyond the Indian Commerce Clause."

33. *PTJ* 29:64, 172, 295, 525.

34. Janet Catherine Berlo, "Men of the Middle Ground: The Visual Culture of Native-White Diplomacy in Eighteenth-Century North America," in *American Adversaries: West and Copley*

in a Transatlantic World, ed. Emily Ballew Neff and Kailyn H. Weber (Houston: Museum of Fine Arts, 2013), 104–15; James F. O'Neill, *Their Bearing Is Noble and Proud: A Collection of Narratives regarding the Appearance of Native Americans from 1740–1815* (Dayton, OH: J.T.G.S. Publishing, 1995); Timothy Shannon, "Dressing for Success on the Mohawk Frontier: Hendrick, William Johnson, and the Indian Fashion," *William and Mary Quarterly* 53 (1996): 13–42.

35. Terry G. Jordan and Matti Kaups, *The American Backwoods Frontier: An Ethnic and Ecological Interpretation* (Baltimore, MD: Johns Hopkins University Press, 1989), 122; Colin G. Calloway, *New Worlds for All: Indians, Europeans, and the Remaking of Early America*, 2nd ed. (Baltimore, MD: Johns Hopkins University Press, 2013), 179.

36. Carolyn Raine, *A Woodland Feast: Native American Foodways of the 17th and 18th Centuries* (Huber Heights, OH: Penobscot Press, 1997).

37. *The Journal of Nicholas Cresswell, 1774–1777* (New York: Dial Press, 1924), 121.

38. *Journal of Captain Thomas Morris* from *Miscellanies in Prose and Verse* (London, 1791; n.p.: Readex Microprint, 1966), 11, 17.

39. Alfred W. Crosby, *Ecological Imperialism: The Biological Expansion of Europe, 900–1900* (Cambridge: Cambridge University Press, 1986), 157–58.

40. Calloway, *New Worlds for All*, 29; John C. Fitzpatrick, *George Washington, Colonial Traveller, 1732–1775* (Indianapolis: Bobbs-Merrill, 1927). Manasseh Cutler, a Massachusetts clergyman, fellow land speculator, and practicing physician whom Washington knew, compiled a list of more than 350 indigenous medicinal plants and credited Indians for many of them.

41. Celia Barnes, *Native American Power in the United States, 1783–1795* (Teaneck, NJ: Fairleigh Dickinson University Press, 2003).

42. Eric Hinderaker, *Elusive Empires: Constructing Colonialism in the Ohio Valley, 1673–1800* (Cambridge: Cambridge University Press, 1997), 260–70; Richard White, *The Middle Ground: Indians, Empires, and Republics in the Great Lakes Region, 1650–1815* (Cambridge: Cambridge University Press, 1991), 413. For earlier manifestations of anti-Indian identity, see Jill Lepore, *The Name of War: King Philip's War and the Origins of American Identity* ((New York: Knopf, 1998); Peter Silver, *Our Savage Neighbors: How Indian War Transformed Early America* (New York: Norton, 2008); David J. Silverman, "Racial Walls: Race and the Emergence of American White Nationalism," in *Anglicizing America: Empire, Revolution, Republic*, ed. Ignacio Gallup-Diaz, Andrew Shankman, and David J. Silverman (Philadelphia: University of Pennsylvania Press, 2015), 181–204; Parkinson, *Common Cause*.

43. James H. Merrell, *The Indians' New World: Catawbas and Their Neighbors from European Contact through the Era of Removal* (Chapel Hill: University of North Carolina Press, 1989), 280.

44. *PGW, Col.* 1:236–40.

45. As will become clear in the pages that follow, I find little to admire in the young Washington except his courage, plenty to admire in the older man. Douglas Southall Freeman, who wrote a seven-volume, Pulitzer Prize–winning biography, acknowledged that Washington was "not a likeable young man," too much of a careerist. "Those who liked him did not know him fully," he wrote to the historian Allan Nevins in 1948, but "the great fact is that Washington grew." Michael Kammen, introduction to Freeman, *Washington*, xviii.

46. Kammen, introduction, xx.

47. David Hackett Fischer, *Washington's Crossing* (New York: Oxford University Press, 2004).

CHAPTER 1: VIRGINIA'S INDIAN COUNTRY

1. Stephen R. Potter, *Commoners, Tribute, and Chiefs: The Development of Algonquian Culture in the Potomac Valley* (Charlottesville: University of Virginia Press, 1993), 20–24; James D. Rice, *Nature and History in the Potomac Country: From Hunter-Gatherers to the Age of Jefferson* (Baltimore, MD: Johns Hopkins University Press, 2009), 130–34; *EAID* 4:xxii.

2. David Waldstreicher, ed., *Notes on the State of Virginia by Thomas Jefferson, with Related Documents* (Boston: Bedford/St. Martin's, 2002), 142–52; Anthony F. C. Wallace, *Jefferson and the Indians: The Tragic Fate of the First Americans* (Cambridge, MA: Harvard University Press, 1999).

3. *EAID* 4:xxii, 5:xix ("umbrage"), 1; 15: ch. 1 (laws).

4. *EAID* 4:268, 5:1.

5. Stuart Banner, *How the Indians Lost Their Land: Law and Power on the Frontier* (Cambridge, MA: Harvard University Press, 2005).

6. *EAID* 15:1.

7. Robert Beverley, *The History and Present State of Virginia*, ed. Susan Scott Parrish (Chapel Hill: University of North Carolina Press, 2013), 107–10, 119, 140–43.

8. April Lee Hatfield, *Atlantic Virginia: Intercolonial Relations in the Seventeenth Century* (Philadelphia: University of Pennsylvania Press, 2004), ch. 1; Audrey Horning, *Ireland in the Virginian Sea: Colonialism in the British Atlantic* (Chapel Hill: University of North Carolina Press, 2013), ch. 4.

9. Kristalyn Marie Shefveland, *Anglo-Native Virginia: Trade, Conversion, and Indian Slavery in the Old Dominion, 1646–1722* (Athens: University of Georgia Press, 2016), 10; *EAID* 4:1, 3.

10. Frederic W. Gleach, *Powhatan's World and Colonial Virginia: A Conflict of Cultures* (Lincoln: University of Nebraska Press, 1997), 3.

11. Philip L. Barbour, ed., *The Complete Works of Captain John Smith*, 3 vols. (Chapel Hill: University of North Carolina Press, 1986), 1:247, 2:175.

12. Rice, *Nature and History in the Potomac Country*, 53–56, 113–21; William Cronon, *Changes in the Land: Indians, Colonists, and the Ecology of New England* (New York: Hill & Wang, 1983), ch. 7.

13. Helen C. Rountree, *Pocahontas's People: The Powhatan Indians of Virginia through Four Centuries* (Norman: University of Oklahoma Press, 1990), population figures at 68–70; Lorena S. Walsh, *Motives of Honor, Pleasure, and Profit: Plantation Management in the Colonial Chesapeake, 1607–1763* (Chapel Hill: University of North Carolina Press, 2010), 73 (planting tobacco, not corn).

14. Camilla Townsend, *Pocahontas and the Powhatan Dilemma* (New York: Hill & Wang, 2004); Gleach, *Powhatan's World and Colonial Virginia*; Alfred A. Cave, *Lethal Encounters: Englishmen and Indians in Colonial Virginia* (Santa Barbara, CA: Praeger, 2011); Michael Leroy Oberg, *Dominion and Civility: English Imperialism and Native America, 1585–1685* (Ithaca, NY: Cornell University Press, 1999).

15. Rountree, *Pocanhontas's People*, 78–79.

16. J. Frederick Fausz, "'Engaged in Enterprises Pregnant with Terror': George Washington's Formative Years among the Indians," in *George Washington and the Virginia Backcountry*, ed. Warren R. Hofstra (Madison, WI: Madison House, 1998), 116–17.

17. William Waller Hening, *The Statutes at Large: Being a Collection of All the Laws of Virginia* (Richmond, VA: Samuel Pleasants, 1810–23), 1:322–26; David Hackett Fischer and James C. Kelly, *Bound Away: Virginia and the Westward Movement* (Charlottesville: University Press of Virginia, 2000), 71, 78; *EAID* 4:65–70 ("Geese" at 68); Shefveland, *Anglo-Native Virginia*, 18.

18. Shefveland, *Anglo-Native Virginia*.

19. Fausz, "'Engaged in Enterprises Pregnant with Terror,'" 118; Mary Thompson memo, June 18, 2001, Iroquois Indians, vertical file, Fred W. Smith National Library for the Study of George Washington ("across from Mount Vernon").

20. Matthew L. Rhoades, *Long Knives and the Longhouse: Anglo-Iroquois Politics and the Expansion of Colonial Virginia* (Teaneck, NJ: Fairleigh Dickinson University Press, 2011), 25.

21. Beverley, *History and Present State of Virginia*, 59.

22. James D. Rice, *Tales from a Revolution: Bacon's Rebellion and the Transformation of Early America* (New York: Oxford University Press, 2012); James D. Rice, "Bacon's Rebellion in Indian Country," *Journal of American History* 101 (2014): 726–50; Cave, *Lethal Encounters*, ch. 8.

23. Ron Chernow, *Washington: A Life* (New York: Penguin, 2010), 3–6.

24. Fausz, "'Engaged in Enterprises Pregnant with Terror,'" 120; Rice, *Nature and History in the Potomac Country*, 137.

25. *EAID* 15:88–89, 93, 104–26; Krystalyn Marie Shefveland, "The Many Faces of Native Bonded Labor in Colonial Virginia," *Native South* 7 (2014): 68–91; C. S. Everett, "'They shalbe slaves for their lives': Indian Slavery in Colonial Virginia," in *Indian Slavery in Colonial America*, ed. Alan Gallay (Lincoln: University of Nebraska Press, 2009), ch. 2.

26. Alan Gallay, *The Indian Slave Trade: The Rise of the English Empire in the American South, 1670–1717* (New Haven, CT: Yale University Press, 2002); Eric E. Bowne, *The Westo Indians: Slave Traders of the Early Colonial South* (Tuscaloosa: University of Alabama Press, 2005); Paul Kelton, *Epidemics and Enslavement: Biological Catastrophe in the Native Southeast, 1492–1715* (Lincoln: University of Nebraska Press, 2007); Robbie Ethridge and Sheri M. Shuck-Hall, eds., *Mapping the Mississippian Shatter Zone: The Colonial Indian Slave Trade and Regional Instability in the American South* (Lincoln: University of Nebraska Press, 2009); Robin Beck, *Chiefdoms, Collapse, and Coalescence in the Early American South* (Cambridge: Cambridge University Press, 2013), ch. 3; David J. Silverman, *Thundersticks: Firearms and the Violent Transformation of Native America* (Cambridge, MA: Harvard University Press, 2016), 56–72.

27. Peter H. Wood, "The Changing Population of the Colonial South: An Overview by Race and Region, 1685-1790," in *Powhatan's Mantle: Indians in the Colonial Southeast,* ed. Peter H. Wood, Gregory A. Waselkov, and M. Thomas Hatley (Lincoln: University of Nebraska Press, 1989), 39.

28. Rountree, *Pocahontas's People,* chs. 6–7. James H. Merrell, *The Indians' New World: Catawbas and Their Neighbors from European Contact through the Era of Removal* (Chapel Hill: University of North Carolina Press, 1989, 2009) is the classic study of change and continuity among the Native peoples of the southern Piedmont.

29. Quoted in L. Scott Philyaw, *Virginia's Western Visions: Political and Cultural Expansion on an Early American Frontier* (Knoxville: University of Tennessee Press, 2004), 87.

30. Margaret Connell Szasz, *Indian Education in the American Colonies, 1607–1783* (Albuquerque: University of New Mexico Press, 1988), 67–77.

31. Everett, "'They shalbe slaves for their lives,'" 69; Shefveland, "Many Faces of Native Bonded Labor," 81; Patrick Wolfe, "Land, Labor, and Difference: Elementary Structures of Race," *American Historical Review* 106 (2001): 871, 874.

32. *Executive Journals* 3:286.

33. Cave, *Lethal Encounters,* 171–72; Wood, "Changing Population of the Colonial South," 38, 40–43 (fewer than 1,000).

34. Beverley, *History and Present State of Virginia,* 182, 214.

35. Rufus Rockwell Wilson, ed., *Burnaby's Travels through North America* (New York: A. Wessels, 1904), 62.

36. Warren R. Hofstra, "'A Parcel of Barbarian's and an Uncouth Set of People': Settlers and Settlements of the Shenandoah Valley," in Hofstra, *George Washington and the Virginia Backcountry,* 93; Rice, *Nature and History in the Potomac Country,* 210–15.

37. David Hackett Fischer, *Albion's Seed: Four British Folkways in America* (New York: Oxford University Press, 1989); Patrick Griffin, *The People with No Name: Ireland's Ulster Scots, America's Scots Irish, and the Creation of a British Atlantic World, 1689–1764* (Princeton, NJ: Princeton University Press, 2001); Warren R. Hofstra, "'The Extention of His Majesties Dominions': The Virginia Backcountry and the Reconfiguration of Imperial Frontiers," *Journal of American History* 84 (1998): 1281–312; James G. Leyburn, *The Scotch-Irish: A Social History* (Chapel Hill: University of North Carolina Press, 1962), 192 ("hard neighbors").

38. Marion Tinling, ed., *The Correspondence of the Three William Byrds of Westover, 1684–1776* (Charlottesville: University of Virginia Press, 1977), 2:493.

39. Philyaw, *Virginia's Western Visions,* xix, 22–23.

40. *EAID* 4:268–69; *NYCD* 5:670; Rhoades, *Long Knives and the Longhouse,* ch. 1, esp. 41, 46.

41. Daniel K. Richter, "War and Culture: The Iroquois Experience," *William and Mary Quarterly* 40 (1983), 557–59; Daniel K. Richter, *The Ordeal of the Longhouse: The Peoples of the Iroquois League in the Era of European Colonization* (Chapel Hill: University of North Carolina Press, 1992), chs. 8–10; James H. Merrell, "'Their Very Bones Shall Fight': The Catawba-Iroquois Wars," in *Beyond the Covenant Chain: The Iroquois and Their Neighbors in Indian North America, 1600–1800,* ed. Daniel K. Richter and James H. Merrell (Syracuse, NY: Syracuse University Press, 1987), ch. 7.

42. *Executive Journals* 4:13, 15, 22–25, 225; Sarah S. Hughes, *Surveyors and Statesmen: Land Measuring in Colonial Virginia* (Richmond: Virginia Surveyors Foundation and Virginia

Association of Surveyors, 1979), 74; *EAID* 4:346–62; Rhoades, *Long Knives and the Longhouse*, ch. 2; Rice, *Nature and History in the Potomac Country*, 188–205; Annette Gordon-Reed and Peter S. Onuf, *"Most Blessed of the Patriarchs": Thomas Jefferson and the Empire of the Imagination* (New York: Liveright/Norton, 2016), 27 (Jefferson's birthplace).

43. Rice, *Nature and History in the Potomac Country*, 198–99; Hofstra, "'A Parcel of Barbarian's and an Uncouth Set of People,'" 93.

44. Timothy Silver, *A New Face on the Countryside: Indians, Colonists, and Slaves in South Atlantic Forests, 1500–1800* (Cambridge: Cambridge University Press, 1990), 164.

45. Silver, *New Face on the Countryside*, 171–85; Virginia DeJohn Anderson, *Creatures of Empire: How Domestic Animals Transformed Early America* (New York: Oxford University Press, 2004).

46. Walsh, *Motives of Honor, Pleasure, and Profit*, chs. 5–8, figures at 405.

47. Bruce A. Ragsdale, "Young Washington's Virginia: Opportunity in the 'Golden Age' of a Planter Society," in Hofstra, *George Washington and the Virginia Backcountry*, 39, 41–42.

48. Walsh, *Motives of Honor, Pleasure, and Profit*, 3.

49. T. M. Devine, *The Tobacco Lords: A Study of the Tobacco Merchants of Glasgow and Their Trading Activities* (Edinburgh: John Donald, 1975), ch. 4; Bruce A. Ragsdale, *A Planters' Republic: The Search for Economic Independence in Revolutionary Virginia* (Madison, WI: Madison House, 1990), 13–41.

50. Devine, *Tobacco Lords*, 3, 18–30, 178.

51. *EAID* 5:25.

52. Rhoades, *Long Knives and the Longhouse*, 100–101.

53. James H. Merrell, *The Lancaster Treaty of 1744 with Related Documents* (Boston: Bedford/St. Martin's, 2008), 30, 59 (Tachanoontia); Warren R. Hofstra, *The Planting of New Virginia: Settlement and Landscape in the Shenandoah Valley* (Baltimore, MD: Johns Hopkins University Press, 2004), 41–43, 172–77; Daniel P. Barr, *A Colony Sprung from Hell: Pittsburgh and the Struggle for Authority on the Western Pennsylvania Frontier, 1744–1794* (Kent, OH: Kent State University Press, 2014).

54. Philyaw, *Virginia's Western Visions*, ix–x.

55. Rice, *Nature and History in the Potomac Country*, 2–3.

56. Ragsdale, "Young Washington's Virginia," 53–55; Walsh, *Motives of Honor, Pleasure, and Profit*, 256–67, 519–20 (Carter).

57. Hughes, *Surveyors and Statesmen*, 1, 72, 84.

58. Hughes, *Surveyors and Statesmen*, 32 (Gunther's chain); Andro Linklater, *Measuring America: How the United States Was Shaped by the Greatest Land Sale in History* (New York: Penguin/Plume, 2002), 40 ("frontier math" figures); Gunther's chain exhibited at the Lunder Center, the Clark, Williamstown, MA, Aug. 2016.

59. David A. Clary, *George Washington's First War* (New York: Simon & Schuster, 2011), 16–17; Hughes, *Surveyors and Statesmen*; Hofstra, *Planting of New Virginia*, 21 ("land stealer"), 110–13.

60. Hughes, *Surveyors and Statesmen*; Philyaw, *Virginia's Western Visions*, 29, 34.

61. On Washington's early training and subsequent career as a surveyor, see Philander D. Chase, "A Stake in the West: George Washington as Backcountry Surveyor and Landholder," in Hofstra, *George Washington and the Virginia Backcountry*, 159–94.

62. Robert D. Mitchell, "'Over the Hills and Far Away': George Washington and the Changing Virginia Backcountry," in Hofstra, *George Washington and the Virginia Backcountry*, 68 (ten thousand settlers); Stephen Brumwell, *George Washington: Gentleman Warrior* (London: Quercus, 2010), 28–29.

63. *Diaries of GW* 1:13, 15, 18.

64. Hofstra, "'A Parcel of Barbarian's and an Uncouth Set of People,'" 87–114.

65. Hofstra, "'A Parcel of Barbarian's and an Uncouth Set of People,'" 88.

66. *PGW, Col.* 1:8–9; Chernow, *Washington*, 22–23; John Ferling, *The Ascent of George Washington: The Hidden Political Genius of an American Icon* (New York: Bloomsbury, 2009), 12–13.

67. Chernow, *Washington*, 23; Willard Sterne Randall, *George Washington: A Life* (New York: Henry Holt, 1997), 55; Edward Redmond, "George Washington: Surveyor and Mapmaker," https://www.loc.gov/collections/george-washington-papers/articles-and-essays/george-washington-survey-and-mapmaker/ (Bullskin Creek purchase).

68. Mitchell, "'Over the Hills and Far Away,'" 68. *PGW, Col.* 1:8–37 provides a comprehensive overview and complete listing of Washington's surveys in this period.

69. *PGW, Col.* 1:16; Edward G. Lengel, *First Entrepreneur: How George Washington Built His—and the Nation's—Prosperity* (Boston: Da Capo, 2016), 21–22.

70. *PGW, Ret.* 4:512–19; Linklater, *Measuring America*, 45; Redmond, "George Washington: Surveyor and Mapmaker."

71. On Ferry Farm, and Washington's childhood there, see Philip Levy, *Where the Cherry Tree Grew: The Story of Ferry Farm, George Washington's Boyhood Home* (New York: St. Martin's Press, 2013); Philip Levy, *George Washington Written upon the Land: Nature, Memory, Myth, and Landscape* (Morgantown: West Virginia University Press, 2015).

72. Edward G. Lengel, *General George Washington: A Military Life* (New York: Random House, 2005), 17–18.

73. See, for example, William G. McLoughlin, *Cherokee Renascence in the New Republic* (Princeton, NJ: Princeton University Press, 1986), 10–16; Rennard Strickland, *Fire and the Spirits: Cherokee Law from Clan to Court* (Norman: University of Oklahoma Press, 1975), ch. 2; John Phillip Reid. *A Law of Blood: The Primitive Law of the Cherokee Nation* (New York: New York University Press, 1970).

74. Peter Charles Hoffer, *Sensory Worlds in Early America* (Baltimore, MD: Johns Hopkins University Press, 2003), 76.

75. Russell Thornton, *The Cherokees: A Population History* (Lincoln: University of Nebraska Press, 1990), 28–31; Samuel Cole Williams, ed., *Adair's History of the American Indians* (1930; New York: Promontory Press, n.d.), 244; Paul Kelton, *Cherokee Medicine, Colonial Germs: An Indigenous Nation's Fight against Smallpox, 1518–1824* (Norman: University of Oklahoma Press, 2015), 10–11, 87–91, 97–101.

76. Kathryn Holland Braund, *Deerskins and Duffels: The Creek Indian Trade with Anglo-America, 1685–1815* (Lincoln: University of Nebraska Press, 1993, 2008), 87–88, 97–98 (export figures); William L. McDowell Jr., ed., *Colonial Records of South Carolina: Documents relating to Indian Affairs, 1750–1754* (Columbia: South Carolina Archives Department, 1958), 1:453.

77. McDowell, *Colonial Records of South Carolina*, 52–53; Tom Hatley, *The Dividing Paths: Cherokees and South Carolinians through the Era of Revolution* (New York: Oxford University Press, 1993), 69–70.

78. W. Stitt Robinson, "Virginia and the Cherokees: Indian Policy from Spotswood to Dinwiddie," in *The Old Dominion: Essays for Thomas Perkins Abernethy*, ed. Darrett Bruce Rutman (Charlottesville: University Press of Virginia, 1964), 21–40, Byrd quoted at 26; *EAID* 5:2, 17–18, 113–24, 155–56.

79. Stephen Warren, *The Worlds the Shawnees Made: Migration and Violence in Early America* (Chapel Hill: University of North Carolina Press, 2014), 140–41, 166–68 (Warriors' Path); 162–64, 176–77 (Lower Susquehanna).

80. Gregory Evans Dowd, *A Spirited Resistance: The North American Indian Struggle for Unity, 1745–1815* (Baltimore, MD: Johns Hopkins University Press, 1992).

CHAPTER 2: THE OHIO COMPANY AND THE OHIO COUNTRY

1. Kenneth P. Bailey, *Thomas Cresap, Maryland Frontiersman* (Boston: Christopher Publishing House, 1944), 86.

2. Matthew L. Rhoades, *Long Knives and the Longhouse: Anglo-Iroquois Politics and the Expansion of Colonial Virginia* (Teaneck, NJ: Fairleigh Dickinson University Press, 2011), 107–8; Woody Holton, "The Ohio Indians and the Coming of the American Revolution in Virginia," *Journal of Southern History* 60 (1994): 456; *Executive Journals* 5:172–73; James Titus, *The Old Dominion at War: Society, Politics, and Warfare in Late Colonial Virginia* (Columbia: University of South Carolina Press, 1991), 10–11 (thirty-six grants).

3. Kenneth P. Bailey, *The Ohio Company of Virginia and the Westward Movement, 1748–1792* (Glendale, CA: Arthur H. Clark, 1939), 35–36.

4. Lois Mulkearn, ed., *George Mercer Papers relating to the Ohio Company of Virginia* (Pittsburgh, PA: University of Pittsburgh Press, 1954), viii, xi, 233–36.

5. Mulkearn, *George Mercer Papers*, 246–47; Bailey, *Ohio Company of Virginia*, 298–301; CO 5/1327:7–8, 26–28, 53–57.

6. CO 5/1338:45–47; *Executive Journals* 5:295–96; Bailey, *Ohio Company of Virginia*, 25–31.

7. Bailey, *Ohio Company of Virginia*, 70; *Writings of Washington* 1:18.

8. Mulkearn, *George Mercer Papers*, 147.

9. *Executive Journals* 5:296–97; David Hackett Fischer and James C. Kelly, *Bound Away: Virginia and the Westward Movement* (Charlottesville: University Press of Virginia, 2000), 152–53; Craig Thompson Friend, *Kentucke's Frontiers* (Bloomington: Indiana University Press, 2010), 24.

10. Bailey, *Thomas Cresap*, 89–90; Bailey, *Ohio Company of Virginia*, 103–22, quotes at 112–13.

11. Andrew Gallup, ed., *The Céloron Expedition to the Ohio Country, 1749: The Reports of Pierre-Joseph Céloron and Father Bonnecamps* (Bowie, MD: Heritage Books, 1997). The translated inscription on the plates is in *CRP* 5:510–11.

12. *NYCD* 10:293–94.

13. Daniel P. Barr, *A Colony Sprung from Hell: Pittsburgh and the Struggle for Authority on the Western Pennsylvania Frontier, 1744–1794* (Kent, OH: Kent State University Press, 2014), 36–37.

14. Thomas Wildcat Alford, *Civilization and the Story of the Absentee Shawnees* (Norman: University of Oklahoma Press, 1936), 44; Vernon Kinietz and Erminie W. Voegelin, eds., *Shawnese Traditions: C. C. Trowbridge's Account* (Ann Arbor: University of Michigan, 1939), 16–17.

15. Michael N. McConnell, *A Country Between: The Upper Ohio Valley and Its Peoples, 1724–1774* (Lincoln: University of Nebraska Press, 1992), chs. 1–5; Michael N. McConnell, "Kuskusky Towns and Early Western Pennsylvania Indian History, 1748–1778," *Pennsylvania Magazine of History and Biography* 116 (Jan. 1992): 33–37; Richard White, *The Middle Ground: Indians, Empires, and Republics in the Great Lakes Region, 1650–1815* (Cambridge: Cambridge University Press, 1991), ch. 5; Helen Hornbeck Tanner, ed., *Atlas of Great Lakes Indian History* (Norman: University of Oklahoma Press, 1987), 44 (Cuyahoga); Cayuga quote in *NYCD* 10:206.

16. Charles A. Hanna, *The Wilderness Trail*, 2 vols. (New York: G. P. Putnam's Sons, 1911), 1:352 (Thomas quote); White, *Middle Ground*, 223–27 (proxies at 223).

17. *CRP* 5:146–47, 151. The council reported that the warriors belonged to "a Tribe of Indians, being a mixture of the Six Nations" (156). Hanna, *Wilderness Trail* 1:329; McConnell, *A Country Between*, 71; Eric Hinderaker, "Declaring Independence: The Ohio Indians and the Seven Years' War," in *Cultures in Conflict: The Seven Years' War in North America*, ed. Warren R. Hofstra (Lanham, MD: Rowman & Littlefield, 2007), 105–6.

18. *NYCD* 6:593–94; McConnell, *A Country Between*, 79.

19. White, *Middle Ground*, 225.

20. *EAID* 2:193; *CRP* 5:358; Reuben G. Thwaites, ed., *Early Western Journals, 1748–1765*, rpt. of *Early Western Travels*, vol. 1 (1904; Lewisburg, PA: Wennawoods Publishing, 1998), 43.

21. *EAID* 2:283; *CRP* 5:666.

22. Mulkearn, *George Mercer Papers*, 476.

23. Gallup, *Céloron Expedition to the Ohio Country*, 40–45; *NYCD* 10:206.

24. *Pennsylvania Archives*, 1st ser., 2:31.

25. *EAID* 2:244, 5:111.

26. Bailey, *Ohio Company of Virginia*, 74–78; *EAID* 3:329n (Warriors' Path); Paul R. Misenick, *George Washington and the Half-King Chief Tanacharison: An Alliance That Began the French and Indian War* (Jefferson, NC: McFarland, 2014), 36–37 (Namacolin's Trail and map); Anthony F. C. Wallace, *Jefferson and the Indians: The Tragic Fate of the First Americans* (Cambridge, MA: Harvard University Press, 1999), 134 (earthwork).

27. Bailey, *Ohio Company of Virginia*, 85–100; Mulkearn, *George Mercer Papers*, 7–8, 97.

28. Mulkearn, *George Mercer Papers*, 9–10, 98–100.

29. *EAID* 3:49n; Nancy Lee Hagedorn, "'Faithful, Knowing, and Prudent': Andrew Montour as Interpreter and Cultural Broker, 1740–1772," in *Between Indian and White Worlds: The Cultural Broker*, ed. Margaret Connell Szasz (Norman: University of Oklahoma Press, 1994), 53–60; James H. Merrell, "'The Cast of His Countenance': Reading Andrew Montour," in *Through a Glass Darkly: Reflections on Personal Identity in Early America*, ed.

Ronald Hoffman, Mechal Sobel, and Fredrika J. Teute (Chapel Hill: University of North Carolina Press, 1997), 9–39; Hanna, *Wilderness Trail* 1:223–46; Tanaghrisson quote in CO 5/1327, pt. 2:270, and "The Treaty of Logg's Town, 1752," *Virginia Magazine of History and Biography* 13 (1905): 165.

30. Croghan said he was "not only very capable of doing the Business, but look'd on amongst all the Indians as one of the Chiefs" (Thwaites, *Early Western Journals*, 71). Weiser once said he thought Montour was "a Frenchman in his heart" (*EAID* 2:303), but he employed him "in sundry affairs of Consequence" and "found him faithful, knowing, & prudent" (*CRP* 5:290). Cresap said he had a good reputation "both amongst White people and Indians & very much beloved by the latter" (*CVSP* 1:245–46).

31. Mulkearn, *George Mercer Papers*, 11, 13, 101, 103.

32. Mulkearn, *George Mercer Papers*, 16, 106.

33. Mulkearn, *George Mercer Papers*, 16, 106; A. Gwynn Henderson, "The Lower Shawnee Town on Ohio: Sustaining Native Autonomy in an Indian 'Republic,'" in *The Buzzel about Kentuck: Settling the Promised Land*, ed. Craig Thompson Friend (Lexington: University Press of Kentucky, 1999), 25–55.

34. Mulkearn, *George Mercer Papers*, 19, 109.

35. Mulkearn, *George Mercer Papers*, 18, 24, 108, 114.

36. *EAID* 2:248–56; *CRP* 5:530–36; Thwaites, *Early Western Journals*, 58–69.

37. *NYCD* 7:268; *EAID* 3:198–99.

38. Mulkearn, *George Mercer Papers*, 39.

39. Mulkearn, *George Mercer Papers*, 52.

40. *EAID* 2:221–22, 244, 5:112.

41. Timothy J. Shannon, *Iroquois Diplomacy on the Early American Frontier* (New York: Penguin, 2009), 128–31; McConnell, *A Country Between*, 80–82; Hinderaker, "Declaring Independence," 108–13; Richard Aquila, *The Iroquois Restoration: Iroquois Diplomacy on the Colonial Frontier, 1701–1754* (Detroit, MI: Wayne State University Press, 1983), 204.

42. *Dinwiddie Papers* 1:6–10; Mulkearn, *George Mercer Papers*, 546; *EIAD* 5:29–33. The following paragraphs are based on C.O. 5/1327, pt. 2:263–76, rpt. in "Treaty of Logg's Town, 1752," 143–74, and Mulkearn, *George Mercer Papers*, 52–66, 127–39, 273–84.

43. Barr, *Colony Sprung from Hell*, 39.

44. CO 5/1327, pt. 2:206, 211.

45. CO 5/1327, pt. 2:267; "Treaty of Logg's Town," 160.

46. CO 5/1327, pt. 2:268; "Treaty of Logg's Town," 161.

47. CO 5/1327, pt. 2:272; "Treaty of Logg's Town," 168; Francis Jennings, *Empire of Fortune: Crowns, Colonies, and Tribes in the Seven Years War in America* (New York: Norton, 1988), 41–44, quote at 43.

48. CO 5/1327, pt. 2:274; "Treaty of Logg's Town," 171–72; Lois Mulkearn, "Half King, Seneca Diplomat of the Ohio Valley," *Western Pennsylvania Historical Magazine* 37 (Summer 1954): 71–72; David Dixon, "A High Wind Rising: George Washington, Fort Necessity, and the Ohio Country Indians," *Pennsylvania History* 74 (Summer 2007): 351n.

49. Archer Butler Hulbert and William Nathaniel Schwarze, eds., *David Zeisberger's History of the Northern American Indians* (Columbus: Ohio State Archaeological and Historical Society, 1910), 34–35; *EAID* 2:4–46; Gunlög Fur, *A Nation of Women: Gender and Colonial Encounters among the Delaware Indians* (Philadelphia: University of Pennsylvania Press, 2009); Roger M. Carpenter, "From Indian Women to English Children: The Lenni-Lenape and the Attempt to Create a New Diplomatic Identity," *Pennsylvania History* 74 (2007): 1–20.

50. Penn quoted in C. A. Weslager, *The Delaware Indians: A History* (New Brunswick, NJ: Rutgers University Press, 1972), 166; Nicholas Cresswell, *The Journal of Nicholas Cresswell, 1774–1777* (New York: Dial Press, 1924), 117, 119; Hulbert and Schwarze, *David Zeisberger's History of the North American Indians*, 92–93.

51. CO 5/1327, pt. 2:264.

52. CO 5/1327, pt. 2:271; Mulkearn, *George Mercer Papers*, 62, 512; McConnell, *A Country Between*, 98.

53. John W. Jordan, ed., "Journal of James Kenny, 1761–1763," *Pennsylvania Magazine of History and Biography* 37 (1913), 157. In the early 1760s many Delawares turned away from the peacekeeping efforts of Tamaqua in favor of more militant leaders like Netawatwees.

54. Timothy J. Shannon, ed., *The Seven Years' War in North America* (Boston: Bedford/St. Martin's, 2014), 31.

55. *CRP* 5:599–600; Michael A. McDonnell, *Masters of Empire: Great Lakes Indians and the Making of America* (New York: Hill & Wang, 2015), 152–57.

56. *JHBV, 1752–58*, 509–10; Hanna, *Wilderness Trail* 2:292–99; White, *Middle Ground*, 233–34.

57. Donald H. Kent, *The French Invasion of Western Pennsylvania, 1753* (Harrisburg: Pennsylvania Historical and Museum Commission, 1954), 1–4, 13–15; Mulkearn, "Half King," 73 (earth trembling).

58. *CRP* 5:623.

59. White, *Middle Ground*, 227–37.

60. *CRP* 5:569–70.

61. White, *Middle Ground*, 235.

62. *CRP* 5:614–16.

63. *CRP* 5:635.

64. *EAID* 5:177.

65. *EAID* 2:269–70, 284; *CRP* 5:666–67.

66. CO 5/1327, pt. 2:295; *EAID* 2:275; *CRP* 5:635.

67. Amy C. Schutt, *The Lands Would Be Entirely Theirs Again: Indians and the Seven Years' War in the Ohio Valley* (Fort Washington, PA: Eastern National, 2009), 16; Misenick, *George Washington and the Half-King Chief Tanacharison*, 64.

68. Kent, *French Invasion of Western Pennsylvania*, 47–49; *EAID* 2:277–79; CO 5/1328:11–18; *CRP* 5:667–68.

69. Kent, *French Invasion of Pennsylvania*, 49–51; Fernand Grenier, ed., *Papiers Contrecoeur et autres documents concernant le conflit Anglo-François sur l'Ohio de 1745 à 1756* (Quebec: Les Presses Universitaires Laval, 1952), 53–58 (council with the Tsonnontounans [Senecas]), 61–62 (Shawnee reluctance); *EAID* 2:280.

70. McConnell, *A Country Between*, 104; Mulkearn, "Half King," 74–75; *CRP* 5:667–68.

71. *CRP* 5:669, 684 (tears); *EAID* 2:302 ("Lyon" quote); Jennings, *Empire of Fortune*, 54.

72. *Dinwiddie Papers* 1:57 ("squeeze You to Death"), 58–84, 99, 121, 131–34; *EAID* 5:160–61, 165–80, 199–222; *JHBV, 1752–58*, 516–23; William L. McDowell Jr., ed., *The Colonial Records of South Carolina: Documents relating to Indian Affairs, 1750–1754* (1958; Columbia: South Carolina Dept. of Archives and History, 1992), 466–68, 472–74, 477–84, 522–39; William L. McDowell Jr., ed., *The Colonial Records of South Carolina: Documents relating to Indian affairs, 1754–1765* (1970; Columbia: South Carolina Department of Archives and History, 1992), xii; Jeff W. Dennis, *Patriots and Indians: Shaping Identity in Eighteenth-Century South Carolina* (Columbia: University of South Carolina Press, 2017), 33–34.

73. *CRP* 5:698.

74. Kenneth P. Bailey, ed., *The Ohio Company Papers, 1753–1817, Being Primarily Papers of the "Suffering Traders" of Pennsylvania* (Arcata, CA: Sons of the American Revolution Library, 1947), 23–24.

75. *CRP* 5:691; *WJP* 9:626, 655. A son of Anglican converts, and a staunch English ally, Jonathan Cayenquerigo was Conrad Weiser's adoptive brother and sachem of the Bear Clan at the Mohawk town of Canajoharie (*EAID* 3:46).

76. *CRP* 6:1–7, 49.

CHAPTER 3: INTO TANAGHRISSON'S WORLD

1. J. Frederick Fausz, "'Engaged in Enterprises Pregnant with Terror': George Washington's Formative Years among the Indians," in *George Washington and the Virginia Backcountry*, ed. Warren R. Hofstra (Madison, WI: Madison House, 1998), 121–22.

2. *PGW, Col.* 1:56–62.

3. Washington's instructions, the letter to the French, and Washington's journal are in CO 5/1328:45, 47, 51–60; CO 5/14, pt. 1:59, 63–70; *PGW, Col.* 1:60–61; *The Journal of Major*

George Washington: An Account of his First Official Mission, Made as Emissary from the Governor of Virginia to the Commandant of the French Forces on the Ohio, October 1753–January 1754, facsimile ed. (Williamsburg, VA: Colonial Williamsburg Foundation, 1959), 25–26; *Diaries of GW* 1:127; Lois Mulkearn, ed., *George Mercer Papers relating to the Ohio Company of Virginia* (Pittsburgh, PA: University of Pittsburgh Press, 1954), 74–75.

4. Choctaw delegates took seventy-seven days to travel from their Mississippi homeland to the Treaty of Hopewell in 1785, traveling at a deliberate and ritualistic pace, as befitted a mission they regarded as a spiritual as well as a diplomatic undertaking. Greg O'Brien, "The Conqueror Meets the Unconquered: Negotiating Cultural Boundaries on the Post-Revolutionary Southern Frontier," *Journal of Southern History* 67 (2001): 39–72.

5. CO 5/1328:47; *PGW, Col.* 1:60; *Diaries of GW* 1:128.

6. CO 5/14, pt. 1:63 and *Journal of Major George Washington,* 4 (quote); *Diaries of GW* 1:132; "Journal of Mr. Christopher Gist, who accompanied Major George Washington in his First Visit to the French Commander of the Troops in the Ohio, 1753," *Collections of the Massachusetts Historical Society,* 3rd ser., 5 (1836), 102.

7. Fausz, " 'Engaged in Enterprises Pregnant with Terror,' " 115; *PGW, Col.* 1:155 ("sense and experience").

8. CO 5/14, pt. 1:63; *Journal of Major George Washington,* 5; *Diaries of GW* 1:133.

9. CO 5/14, pt. 1:64; *Diaries of GW* 1:135–36; David Dixon, "A High Wind Rising: George Washington, Fort Necessity, and the Ohio Country Indians," *Pennsylvania History* 74 (2007): 333–37. For a detailed narrative of their subsequent relationship, see Paul R. Misencik, *George Washington and the Half-King Chief Tanacharison: An Alliance That Began the French and Indian War* (Jefferson, NC: McFarland, 2014).

10. CO 5/14, pt. 1:64; *Journal of Major George Washington,* 6–7; *Diaries of GW* 1:137.

11. Mulkearn, *George Mercer Papers,* 76.

12. CO 5/14, pt. 1:64; *Journal of Major George Washington,* 8; *Diaries of GW* 1:137–38.

13. Fred Anderson, ed., *George Washington Remembers: Reflections on the French and Indian War* (Lanham, MD: Rowman & Littlefield, 2004), 16, 31–32, 118, 137–38; David Humphreys, *"Life of General Washington," with George Washington's "Remarks,"* ed. Rosemarie Zagarri (Athens: University of Georgia Press, 1991), 10; *Diaries of GW* 1:183, 184n; *PGW, Col.* 1:87–88, 2:98 (to Montour); *PGW, Confed.* 5:516.

14. When the Delawares gave Colonel Daniel Brodhead the name Maghinga Keesoch (Great Moon) in 1779, they told him that he was expected to be of the same disposition as the original holder of the name and that he must use it in his formal dealings with all the Indian nations. Louise Phelps Kellogg, ed., *Frontier Advance on the Upper Ohio, 1778–1779* (Madison: Wisconsin State Historical Society, 1916), 282.

15. CO 5/14, pt. 1:65; *Journal of Major George Washington,* 9–10; *Diaries of GW* 1:140; Mulkearn, "Half King," 75.

16. CO 5/14, pt. 1:65–66; *Journal of Major George Washington,* 11–12; *Diaries of GW* 1:141.

17. CO 5/14, pt. 1:66; *Journal of Major George Washington,* 12.

18. CO 5/1328:28–29; Ian K. Steele, "Shawnee Origins of Their Seven Years' War," *Ethnohistory* 53 (2006): 657–87.

19. Richard S. Grimes, "We 'Now Have Taken Up the Hatchet against Them': Braddock's Defeat and the Martial Liberation of the Western Delawares," *Pennsylvania Magazine of History and Biography* 137 (2013): 227–59.

20. CO 5/14, pt. 1:66; *Journal of Major George Washington,* 12; *Diaries of GW* 1:142.

21. WJP 9:604 (no weight); Wilbur R. Jacobs, *Wilderness Politics and Indian Gifts: The Northern Colonial Frontier, 1748–1763* (Lincoln: University of Nebraska Press, 1966), chs. 6–7.

22. CO 5/14, pt. 1:66; *Journal of Major George Washington,* 13; *Diaries of GW* 1:142–43. Gist described the Indian escort as "the Half King and two old men and one young warrior"; "Journal of Christopher Gist," 103. Francis Jennings, *Empire of Fortune: Crowns, Colonies, and Tribes in the Seven Years War in America* (New York: Norton, 1988), 63; *EAID* 2:418 (Weiser's description of Belt of Wampum), 491n49–50; *CRP* 6:614. On Guyasuta, see Brady J. Crytzer, *Guyasuta and the Fall of Indian America* (Yardley, PA: Westholme, 2013).

23. CO 5/14, pt. 1:66; *Diaries of GW* 1:143.

24. CO 5/14, pt. 1:66; *Journal of Major George Washington*, 13–14; *Diaries of GW* 1:144–45.
25. CO 5/14, pt. 1:66; "Journal of Christopher Gist," 103–4; *Diaries of GW* 1:145–46.
26. CO 5/14, pt. 1:66–67; *Journal of Major George Washington*, 14–15; *Diaries of GW* 1:146.
27. CO 5/14, pt. 1:67; *Journal of Major George Washington*, 15; *Diaries of GW* 1:146.
28. CO 5/14, pt. 1:67; *Journal of Major George Washington*, 15–16; *Diaries of GW* 1:147.
29. "Journal of Christopher Gist," 104.
30. CO 5/14, pt. 1:67; *Journal of Major George Washington*, 16; *Diaries of GW* 1:147.
31. CO 5/14, pt. 1:67; *Journal of Major George Washington*, 16–17; "Journal of Christopher Gist," 104–5; *Diaries of GW* 1:148–49.
32. CO 5/14, pt. 1:68; *Journal of Major George Washington*, 17–18; *Diaries of GW* 1:150.
33. CO 5/14, pt. 1:68; *Journal of Major George Washington*, 19; *Diaries of GW* 1:151–52.
34. CO 5/14, pt. 1:68; *Journal of Major George Washington*, 19–20; *Diaries of GW* 1:152.
35. CO 5/14, pt. 1:68–69; *Journal of Major George Washington*, 20; *Diaries of GW* 1:154.
36. CO 5/14, pt. 1:69; *Journal of Major George Washington*, 21; "Journal of Christopher Gist," 105–6; *Diaries of GW* 1:154–55.
37. CO 5/14, pt. 1:69; *Journal of Major George Washington*, 21; "Journal of Christopher Gist," 106–7; *Diaries of GW* 1:155.
38. CO 5/14, pt. 1:69; *Journal of Major George Washington*, 21–22; *Diaries of GW* 1:155–56; "Journal of Christopher Gist," 107; Brady J. Crytzer, *Major Washington's Pittsburgh and the Mission to Fort Le Boeuf* (Charleston, SC: History Press, 2011), 114–15.
39. CO 5/14, pt. 1:69; *Journal of Major George Washington*, 22; *Diaries of GW* 1:156.
40. Andrew Gallup, ed., *The Céloron Expedition to the Ohio Country, 1749: The Reports of Pierre-Joseph Céloron and Father Bonnecamps* (Bowie, MD: Heritage Books, 1997), 39; Reuben G. Thwaites, ed., *Early Western Journals, 1748–1765*, rpt. of *Early Western Travels*, vol. 1 (1904; Lewisburg, PA: Wennawoods Publishing, 1998), 24 and 24n16 (Weiser and Celeron quotes); "The Treaty of Logg's Town, 1752," *Virginia Magazine of History and Biography* 13 (Oct. 1905): 157; Charles A. Hanna, *The Wilderness Trail*, 2 vols. (New York: G. P. Putnam's Sons, 1911), 1:329, 344 (Kanuksusy as spokesman).
41. CO 5/14, pt. 1:69; *Journal of Major George Washington*, 22; *Diaries of GW* 1:156; "Journal of Christopher Gist," 107.
42. CO 5/14, pt. 1:69; *Journal of Major George Washington*, 22.
43. Daniel P. Barr, *A Colony Sprung from Hell: Pittsburgh and the Struggle for Authority on the Western Pennsylvania Frontier, 1744–1794* (Kent, OH: Kent State University Press, 2014), 47.
44. CO 5/14, pt. 1:61, 69; *Journal of Major George Washington*, 27–28; *Diaries of GW* 1:158–60; *Executive Journals* 5:458–60.
45. *JHBV, 1752–58*, 175–77.
46. *Diaries of GW* 1:163.
47. *JHBV, 1752–58*, 178, 182–83, 185.
48. CO 5/1328:43, 45, 47, 51–60.
49. *Dinwiddie Papers* 1:55–57; Mulkearn, *George Mercer Papers*, 82–83; *Executive Journals* 5:460.
50. James Titus, *The Old Dominion at War: Society, Politics, and Warfare in Late Colonial Virginia* (Columbia: University of South Carolina Press, 1991), 41–45; *Dinwiddie Papers* 1:59; *PGW, Col.* 1:64–65.
51. *Dinwiddie Papers* 1:88–90, 109–11; *Executive Journals* 5:462, 499–500; Edward G. Lengel, *General George Washington: A Military Life* (New York: Random House, 2005), 21.
52. Titus, *The Old Dominion at War*, 14–23, 43–45.
53. *Dinwiddie Papers* 1:92–93, 106 (Washington's complaints and Dinwiddie reply); *PGW, Col.* 1:72–74.

CHAPTER 4: TANAGHRISSON'S WAR

1. CO 5/1328:21; *CRP* 5:734.
2. David Dixon, "A High Wind Rising: George Washington, Fort Necessity, and the Ohio Country Indians," *Pennsylvania History* 74 (2007): 341.

3. *EAID* 2:330; Richard White, *The Middle Ground: Indians, Empires, and Republics in the Great Lakes Region, 1650–1815* (Cambridge: Cambridge University Press, 1991), 238.

4. Fred Anderson, *Crucible of War: The Seven Years' War and the Fate of Empire in British North America, 1754–1766* (New York: Knopf, 2000), 32.

5. Contrecoeur's summons in CO 5/14, pt. 2:193–94, CO 5/1328:95–96, *CRP* 6:29–30, and NYCD 6:841–43. *PGW, Col.* 1:85–87; Anderson, *Crucible of War*, 46–49; Neville B. Craig, ed., *The Olden Time*, 2 vols. (Pittsburgh: J. W. Cook, 1846–48), 1:83–84; Lois Mulkearn, "Half King, Seneca Diplomat of the Ohio Valley," *Western Pennsylvania Historical Magazine* 37 (Summer 1954): 78. Edward Ward's account of events is in CO 5/14, pt. 2:195–96, CO 5/1328:101–2, and Kenneth P. Bailey, ed., *The Ohio Company Papers, 1753–1817, Being Primarily Papers of the "Suffering Traders" of Pennsylvania* (Arcata, CA: Sons of the American Revolution Library, 1947), 26–31.

6. Donald H. Kent, ed., "Contrecoeur's Copy of George Washington's Journal for 1754," *Pennsylvania History* 19 (Jan. 1952): 10; Lois Mulkearn, ed., *George Mercer Papers relating to the Ohio Company of Virginia* (Pittsburgh: University of Pittsburgh Press, 1954), 85–88; Edward G. Lengel, *General George Washington: A Military Life* (New York: Random House, 2005), 32–33.

7. Kent, "Contrecoeur's Copy of George Washington's Journal," 11–12. Another version of Tanaghrisson's speech is in CO 5/14, pt. 2:164, 189; Mulkearn, *George Mercer Papers*, 88; and *CRP* 2:321, 6:31.

8. Kent, "Contrecoeur's Copy of George Washington's Journal," 13–14; CO 5/1328:97–98; CO 5/14, pt. 2:191–92; *Diaries of GW* 1:183–84.

9. *PGW, Col.* 1:89; CO 5/1328:98.

10. CO 5/1327, pt. 2:300–301.

11. *Executive Journals* 5:468–69.

12. Kent, "Contrecoeur's Copy of George Washington's Journal," 15; *Dinwiddie Papers* 1:152.

13. Kent, "Contrecoeur's Copy of George Washington's Journal," 18; *Diaries of GW* 1:189.

14. Kent, "Contrecoeur's Copy of George Washington's Journal," 19; *Diaries of GW* 1:191–92.

15. *PGW, Col.* 1:101.

16. *Dinwiddie Papers* 1:171–73, 189; *PGW, Col.* 1:102.

17. *PGW, Col.* 1:105.

18. Kent, "Contrecoeur's Copy of George Washington's Journal," 20; *Diaries of GW* 1:193–94; Lengel, *General George Washington*, 36.

19. *Scoouwa: The Indian Captivity Narrative of James Smith* (1799; Columbus: Ohio Historical Society, 1978), 152.

20. Kent, "Contrecoeur's Copy of George Washington's Journal," 20–21; *Diaries of GW* 1:194–95; Dixon, "A High Wind Rising," 343.

21. Kent, "Contrecoeur's Copy of George Washington's Journal," 21; *Diaries of GW* 1:195–96; *PGW, Col.* 1:110; *Dinwiddie Papers* 1:179.

22. Fred Anderson, ed., *George Washington Remembers: Reflections on the French and Indian War* (Lanham, MD: Rowman & Littlefield, 2004) 17, 121.

23. "An Ohio Iroquois Warrior's Account of the Jumonville Affair, 1754," in David L. Preston, *Braddock's Defeat: The Battle of the Monongahela and the Road to Revolution* (New York: Oxford University Press, 2015), 27, 351–53.

24. Anderson, *Crucible of War*, 53–59; Dixon, "A High Wind Rising," 344. French eyewitness in *PGW, Col.* 1:114; statements of Davison and Scarouady in *CRP* 6:195; *Pennsylvania Gazette*, June 27, 1754; "An Ohio Iroquois Warrior's Account of the Jumonville Affair, 1754," 352.

25. Kent, "Contrecoeur's Copy of George Washington's Journal," 21–22; Joseph L. Peyser, trans. and ed., *Letters from New France: The Upper Country, 1686–1783* (Urbana: University of Illinois Press, 1992), 196–97.

26. Kent, "Contrecoeur's Copy of George Washington's Journal," 21–22; *Diaries of GW* 1:197–98; *GWP, Col.* 1:110–11, 116–17; *Dinwiddie Papers* 1:176–83, 225–28.

27. *PGW, Col.* 1:119; *Dinwiddie Papers* 1:186.

28. "Affidavit of John Shaw," in William L. McDowell Jr., ed., *The Colonial Records of South Carolina: Documents relating to Indian Affairs, 1754–1765* (Columbia: South Carolina Department of Archives and History, 1970), 4; Hayes Baker-Crothers and Ruth Allison Hudnut, "A Private Soldier's Account of Washington's First Battles in the West: A Study in Historical Criticism," *Journal of Southern History* 10 (1952): 24.

29. Anderson, *Crucible of War*, 57–58. Anderson notes that the deserter's name, Denis Kaninguen, suggests he may have been a Catholic Iroquois, although most Catholic Iroquois came from the mission villages on the St. Lawrence and would have been unlikely to join an English army.

30. *PGW, Col.* 1:112; *Dinwiddie Papers* 1:214 (black wampum), 216; Paul R. Misencik, *George Washington and the Half-King Chief Tanacharison: An Alliance That Began the French and Indian War* (Jefferson, NC: McFarland, 2014), 114; Dixon, "A High Wind Rising," 345.

31. Beverly McAnear, ed., "Personal Accounts of the Albany Congress of 1754," *Mississippi Valley Historical Review* 39 (1953): 742.

32. CO 5/14, pt. 2:197–98; CO 5/1328:117; *PGW, Col.* 1:114–15; *Dinwiddie Papers* 1:206; also Martin West, ed., *War for Empire in Western Pennsylvania* (Ligonier, PA: Fort Ligonier Association, 1993), 20.

33. Mulkearn, "Half King," 80.

34. *NYCD* 10:270.

35. *PGW, Col.* 1:118–19; Stephen Brumwell, *George Washington, Gentleman Warrior* (London: Quercus, 2012), 54; David A. Clary, *George Washington's First War* (New York: Simon & Schuster, 2011), 89; Ron Chernow, *Washington: A Life* (New York: Penguin, 2010), 44.

36. Anderson, *Crucible of War*, 58–59.

37. Anderson, *Crucible of War*, 60.

38. Kent, "Contrecoeur's Copy of George Washington's Journal," 23; *Diaries of GW* 1:199; *PGW, Col,* 1:122–23; *Dinwiddie Papers* 1:191.

39. *Diaries of GW* 1:199–201; *PGW, Col.* 1:125n, 135, 174; *Dinwiddie Papers* 1:148n, 222; *EIAD* 5:192; CO 5/1328:29 (Scarouady's son christened).

40. *PGW, Col.* 1:121 (wampum), 124 ("singular use"), 129–30 ("in all affairs"), 146; *Dinwiddie Papers* 1:187–90, 192, 229.

41. *Dinwiddie Papers* 1:193.

42. Kent, "Contrecoeur's Copy of George Washington's Journal," 25–30; *Diaries of GW* 1:202–4.

43. Mulkearn, "Half King," 80; Kent, "Contrecoeur's Copy of George Washington's Journal," 30; *Washington's Journal, 1754*, 78; *Diaries of GW* 1:207–8.

44. Villiers's journal of his expedition is in Fernand Grenier, ed., *Papiers Contrecoeur et autres documents concernant le conflit Anglo-François sur l'Ohio de 1745 à 1756* (Quebec: Presses Universitaires Laval, 1952), 196–202, trans. in Peyser, *Letters from New France*, 198–208; Contrecoeur's orders at 201. On the ambivalence of the Indian allies, see D. Peter MacLeod, *The Canadian Iroquois and the Seven Years' War* (Toronto: Dundurn Press, 1996), 43–44.

45. Dixon, "A High Wind Rising," 347.

46. *PGW, Col.* 1:158–64 ("Bayonets screw'd" at 161); Anderson, *Crucible of War*, 17.

47. Peyser, *Letters from New France*, 205; MacLeod, *Canadian Iroquois and the Seven Years' War*, 48; Dixon, "A High Wind Rising," 348–49; Alan Axelrod, *Blooding at Great Meadows: Young George Washington and the Battle That Shaped the Man* (Philadelphia: Running Press, 2007).

48. *PGW, Col.* 1:160–72; Grenier, *Papiers Contrecoeur et autres documents*, 202–5; Peyser, *Letters from New France*, 205–7; *CRP* 6: 52–53.

49. Writing during the Revolution, Hector St. John De Crèvecouer reflected on the irony that the murderer of Jumonville was now "the idol of the French." Henri L. Bourdin, Ralph H. Gabriel, and Stanley T. Williams, eds., *Sketches of Eighteenth Century America: More "Letters from an American Farmer" by St. John De Crèvecouer* (New Haven: Yale University Press, 1925), 176–77.

50. *Pennsylvania Journal and Weekly Advertiser*, July 25, 1754.

51. Quoted in James Thomas Flexner, *George Washington: The Forge of Experience, 1732–1775* (Boston: Little, Brown, 1965), 107.

52. *PGW, Col.* 1:167–68, 170.
53. Kent, "Contrecoeur's Copy of George Washington's Journal," 1, 3 (Duquesne quote); Axelrod, *Blooding at Great Meadows*, 242–43 (Washington quote).
54. Quoted in Willard Sterne Randall, *George Washington: A Life* (New York: Henry Holt, 1997), 105.
55. *NYCD* 6:852.
56. Clary, *George Washington's First War*, 112; Thomas Agostini, *Imperial Dilemmas*, manuscript in progress, ch. 2.
57. *CRP* 6:51; *Pennsylvania Journal and Weekly Advertiser,* July 25, 1754.
58. *Dinwiddie Papers* 1:256.
59. Francis Jennings, *Empire of Fortune: Crowns, Colonies, and Tribes in the Seven Years War in America* (New York: Norton, 1988), 67–68 (quote), 155–56.
60. Lengel, *General George Washington*, 45–46.
61. Robert J. Kapsch, *The Potomac Canal: George Washington and the Waterway West* (Morgantown: West Virginia University Press, 2007), 10–15.
62. *PGW, Col.* 1:185, 187.
63. *CRP* 6:140–41; *NYCD* 7:270; *EAID* 3:200; "Croghan's Journal," in *Early Western Journals, 1748–1765*, ed. Reuben G. Thwaites, rpt. of *Early Western Travels*, vol. 1 (1904; Lewisburg, PA: Wennawoods Publishing, 1998), 96–97.
64. *CRP* 6:145–50.
65. Anthony F. C. Wallace, *King of the Delawares: Teedyuscung, 1700–1763* (Syracuse, NY: Syracuse University Press, 1990), 58–59.
66. *EAID* 2:353; *CRP* 6:151–52; [Charles Thomson], *An Enquiry into the Causes of the Alienation of the Delaware and Shawanese Indians from the British Interest, and into the Measures Taken for Recovering Their Friendship* (London: Printed for J. Wilkie, 1759), 80–81.
67. *EAID* 2:352–60 ("high Wind" at 356); *CRP* 6:152–56.
68. "An Ohio Iroquois Warrior's Account of the Jumonville Affair, 1754," 351–53.
69. *NYCD* 6:870 (Hendrick quote); Timothy J. Shannon, *Indians and Colonists at the Crossroads of Empire: The Albany Congress of 1754* (Ithaca, NY: Cornell University Press, 2000), 168.
70. Claus quoted in Thomas Flexner, *Lord of the Mohawks* (Boston: Little, Brown, 1959), 122; *PTJ* 2:99.
71. *EAID* 2:363; *CRP* 6:180, 182–84; *Dinwiddie Papers* 1:369.
72. *EAID* 2:398; *Virginia Gazette*, Nov. 7, 1754; *CRP* 6:342 (Scarouady seems to be the speaker).
73. *Dinwiddie Papers* 1:427, 430; *WJP* 9:155–56.
74. C. Hale Sipe, *The Indian Wars of Pennsylvania* (Harrisburg, PA: Telegraph Press, 1929), 173–74.
75. *JHBV, 1752–58*, 217–18; *PGW, Col.* 1:209, 219–20.
76. *Dinwiddie Papers* 1:524.
77. Anderson, *George Washington Remembers*, 18 ("degrading"); *PGW, Col.* 1:223–27; CO 5/15, pt. 1:5.
78. *CRP* 6:186.

CHAPTER 5: BRADDOCK AND THE LIMITS OF EMPIRE

1. Thomas E. Crocker, *Braddock's March: How the Man Sent to Seize a Continent Changed American History* (Yardley, PA: Westholme, 2009), 47–56; *Dinwiddie Papers* 2:32–33, 72.
2. *Dinwiddie Papers* 2:48, 273.
3. Douglas Edward Leach, *Roots of Conflict: British Armed Forces and Colonial Americans, 1677–1763* (Chapel Hill: University of North Carolina Press, 1986), ch. 5; Douglas R. Cubbison, *On Campaign against Fort Duquesne: The Braddock and Forbes Expeditions, 1755–1758, through the Experiences of Quartermaster Sir John St. Clair* (Jefferson, NC: McFarland, 2015), ch. 3.
4. *CRP* 6:307.
5. Francis Jennings, *Empire of Fortune: Crowns, Colonies, and Tribes in the Seven Years War in America* (New York: Norton, 1988), 141–51; Louis P. Masur, ed., *The Autobiography of Benjamin Franklin with Related Documents*, 2nd ed. (Boston: Bedford/St. Martin's, 2003), 139–43.

6. Bernhard Knollenberg, *George Washington: The Virginia Period, 1732–1775* (Durham, NC: Duke University Press, 1964), 44.

7. John Ferling, *The Ascent of George Washington: The Hidden Political Genius of an American Icon* (New York: Bloomsbury, 2009), 26, 28.

8. *PGW, Col.* 1:241–49 (correspondence with Orme), 256 ("worthy of his notice").

9. Marion Tinling, ed., *The Correspondence of the Three William Byrds of Westover, Virginia, 1684–1776*, 2 vols. (Charlottesville: University of Virginia Press, 1977), 2:615.

10. *PGW, Col.* 1:277–78; Crocker, *Braddock's March,* 71–75.

11. Quoted in David Clary, *George Washington's First War* (New York: Simon & Schuster, 2010), 122.

12. Crocker, *Braddock's March,* 47–48, 56, 63.

13. Daniel P. Barr, *A Colony Sprung from Hell: Pittsburgh and the Struggle for Authority on the Western Pennsylvania Frontier, 1744–1794* (Kent, OH: Kent State University Press, 2014), 60–61.

14. *Dinwiddie Papers* 2:70, 76–77.

15. Quoted in Hugh Cleland, *George Washington in the Ohio Valley* (Pittsburgh, PA: University of Pittsburgh Press, 1955), 127–29.

16. David L. Preston, "'Make Indians of Our White Men': British Soldiers and Indian Warriors from Braddock's to Forbes's Campaign, 1755–1758," *Pennsylvania History* 74 (2007): 285–86; Clary, *George Washington's First War,* 134; Fred Anderson, *Crucible of War: The Seven Years' War and the Fate of Empire in British North America, 1754–1766* (New York: Knopf, 2000), 95.

17. Beverley Bond Jr., ed., "The Captivity of Charles Stuart, 1755–57," *Mississippi Valley Historical Review* 13 (June 1926): 63–65.

18. *Dinwiddie Papers* 2:426; Masur, *Autobiography of Benjamin Franklin,* 144.

19. *WJP* 9:171–79, 188, 191–98; Winthrop Sargent, ed., *The History of an Expedition against Fort Du Quesne in 1755; under Major-General Edward Braddock* (1856; Lewisburg, PA: Wennawoods Publishing, 1997), 309; Wilbur R. Jacobs, *Wilderness Politics and Indian Gifts: The Northern Colonial Frontier, 1748–1763* (Lincoln: University of Nebraska Press, 1966), 142–43.

20. *NYCD* 7:270; *EAID* 3:200; Charles A. Hanna, *The Wilderness Trail,* 2 vols. (New York: G. P. Putnam's Sons, 1911), 2:16.

21. Daniel P. Barr, "'This Land Is Ours and Not Yours': The Western Delawares and the Seven Years' War in the Upper Ohio Valley, 1755–1758," in *The Boundaries between Us: Natives and Newcomers along the Frontiers of the Old Northwest Territory, 1750–1850,* ed. Daniel P. Barr (Kent, OH: Kent State University Press, 2006), 28–30.

22. *WJP* 9:203–4.

23. David L. Preston, *Braddock's Defeat: The Battle of the Monongahela and the Road to Revolution* (New York: Oxford University Press, 2015), esp. 81–82, 109–18. George Yagi, *The Struggle for North America, 1754–1758: Britannia's Tarnished Laurels* (London and New York: Bloomsbury, 2016) similarly dismantles stereotypes about British arrogance and ineptitude in the early years of the war.

24. D. Peter MacLeod, *The Canadian Iroquois and the Seven Years' War* (Toronto: Dundurn Press, 1996), 50–51; Preston, *Braddock's Defeat,* 135–37; Barbara Graymont, "Atiatoharongwen," in *Dictionary of Canadian Biography,* vol. 5 (University of Toronto/Université Laval, 2003–), http://www.biographi.ca/en/bio/atiatoharongwen_5E.html (accessed April 2, 2015).

25. Anderson, *Crucible of War,* 106–7.

26. Preston, *Braddock's Defeat,* 112–13, 191, 204, 245; Francis Jennings, ed., *The History and Culture of Iroquois Diplomacy: An Interdisciplinary Guide to the Treaties of the Six Nations and Their League* (Syracuse, NY: Syracuse University Press, 1985), 240–41; 246; *EAID* 2:415, 3:45–46n, 55n; *CRP* 6:524. (C. Hale Sipe, *The Indian Wars of Pennsylvania* [Harrisburg, PA: Telegraph Press, 1929], 181, said White Thunder did not return to Braddock's army after conducting the Indian women back to Aughwick.) Newcastle died of smallpox in Philadelphia in November 1756, and Jerry was killed by British soldiers; Hanna, *Wilderness Trail* 1:79–80; *WJP* 9:566, 825; James H. Merrell, *Into the American Woods: Negotiators on the Pennsylvania Frontier* (New York: Norton, 1999), 65–66 (Kanuksusy's names).

27. Anderson, *Crucible of War,* 106.

28. Clary, *George Washington's First War*, 135–37; *PGW, Col.* 1:281–93.
29. *PGW, Col.* 1:322, quoted in Cubbison, *On Campaign against Fort Duquesne*, 86.
30. *PGW, Col.* 1:321; Crocker, *Braddock's March*, 178–82; Preston, *Braddock's Defeat*, 180–82.
31. *PGW, Col.* 1:322; Peter Way, "The Cutting Edge of Culture: British Soldiers Encounter Native Americans in the French and Indian War," in *Empire and Others: British Encounters with Indigenous Peoples, 1600–1850*, ed. Martin Daunton and Rick Halpern (Philadelphia: University of Pennsylvania Press, 1999), 123–48.
32. Crocker, *Braddock's March*, 196; Preston, *Braddock's Defeat*, 204; Sargent, *History of an Expedition against Fort Du Quesne*, 350.
33. *PGW, Col.* 1:319.
34. Cubbison, *On Campaign against Fort Duquesne*, 129–30.
35. Preston, *Braddock's Defeat*, 355; John W. Jordan, ed., "Journal of James Kenny, 1761–1763," *Pennsylvania Magazine of History and Biography* 37 (1913), 183 (no Delawares).
36. Preston, *Braddock's Defeat* is the definitive account of the battle. See also Anderson, *Crucible of War*, ch. 9; Croker, *Braddock's March*, ch. 18.
37. *CRP* 6:488. A list of the officers killed and wounded is at 489–91.
38. *PGW, Col.* 1:336, 343.
39. George Washington Parke Custis, *Recollections and Private Memoirs of Washington*, ed. Benson J. Lossing (New York: Derby & Jackson, 1860), 304 ("chief of nations"); Sipe, *Indian Wars of Pennsylvania*, 189; John Joseph Mathews, *The Osages: Children of the Middle Waters* (Norman: University of Oklahoma Press, 1961), 226–27.
40. CO 5/146, pt. 1:47–48; *PGW, Col.* 1:336–37, 339, 343; *Writings of Washington* 1:148–50.
41. "Anonymous Letter, July 25, 1755," quoted in *PGW, Col.* 1:338n.
42. Quoted in Cubbison, *On Campaign against Fort Duquesne*, 110.
43. Crocker, *Braddock's March*, 222; John Mack Faragher, *Daniel Boone, The Life and Legend of an American Pioneer* (New York: Henry Holt, 1992), 37–38.
44. Helen Hornbeck Tanner, ed., *Atlas of Great Lakes Indian History* (Norman: University of Oklahoma Press, 1987), 45.
45. Fred Anderson, ed., *George Washington Remembers: Reflections on the French and Indian War* (Lanham, MD: Rowman & Littlefield, 2004), 19; David Humphreys, *"Life of General Washington," with George Washington's "Remarks,"* ed. Rosemarie Zagarri (Athens: University of Georgia Press, 1991), 15; Knollenberg, *George Washington: The Virginia Period*, 34; Don Higginbotham, ed., *George Washington Reconsidered* (Charlottesville: University Press of Virginia, 2011), 60.
46. Anderson, *George Washington Remembers*, 20; Humphreys, *"Life of General Washington," with George Washington's "Remarks,"* 18.
47. Anderson, *George Washington Remembers*, 21. See also, *PGW, Col.* 1:298–99.
48. *CRP* 6:496, 514.
49. *PGW, Col.* 1:340, 342, 344; *JHBV, 1752–58*, 297; *Dinwiddie Papers* 2:118–20, 123, 140–49, 160, 163–64, 172–75, 181–82, 192–94, 204–10, 215–16, 221–25, 229–31, 258–59; CO 5/16, pt. 2:174, 181–85, 272–73; *CRP* 6:513, 548, 558, 563, 602; Masur, *Autobiography of Benjamin Franklin*, 145.
50. *CRP* 6:593.
51. *EAID* 2:414–17; *CRP* 6:589–91; Jennings, *Empire of Fortune*, 165–66.
52. *CRP* 6:783.
53. Barr, "'This Land Is Ours and Not Yours,'" 29–32; Richard S. Grimes, "We 'Now Have Taken Up the Hatchet against Them': Braddock's Defeat and the Martial Liberation of the Western Delawares," *Pennsylvania Magazine of History and Biography*, 137 (July 2013): 227–59; Eric Hinderaker, "Declaring Independence: The Ohio Indians and the Seven Years' War," in *Cultures in Conflict: The Seven Years' War in America*, ed. Warren R. Hofstra (Lanham, MD: Rowman & Littlefield, 2007), 105–25.
54. *PGW, Col.* 1:352.
55. *PGW, Col.* 2:114.

56. *Dinwiddie Papers* 2:184–86; *JHBV, 1752–58*, 302, 309–10, 319; *PGW, Col.* 1:356–59, 2:3–4; Clary, *George Washington's First War*, 168–70; Edward G. Lengel, *General George Washington: A Military Life* (New York: Random House, 2005), 63–64.

57. *PGW, Col.* 1:359.

58. *EAID* 3:481n (Warriors' Path).

59. *PGW, Col.* 2:17–20, 23, 27.

60. Warren R. Hofstra, " 'A Parcel of Barbarian's and an Uncouth Set of People': Settlers and Settlements of the Shenandoah Valley," in *George Washington and the Virginia Backcountry*, ed. Warren R. Hofstra (Madison, WI: Madison House, 1998), 92.

61. James Titus, *The Old Dominion at War: Society, Politics and Warfare in Late Colonial Virginia* (Columbia: University of South Carolina Press, 1992), 94–95, 102; Ian K. Steele, *Setting All the Captives Free: Capture, Adjustment, and Recollection in Allegheny Country* (Montreal: McGill-Queens University Press, 2013), 117.

62. *PGW, Col.* 2:72–73.

63. James Thomas Flexner, *George Washington: The Forge of Experience, 1732–1775* (Boston: Little, Brown, 1965), 163.

64. Peter Silver, *Our Savage Neighbors: How Indian War Transformed Early America* (New York: Norton, 2008), ch. 4; Matthew C. Ward, *Breaking the Backcountry: The Seven Years' War in Virginia and Pennsylvania, 1754–1765* (Pittsburgh: University of Pittsburgh Press, 2003), 45–58; Matthew C. Ward,, " 'The European Method of Warring Is Not Practiced Here': The Failure of British Military Policy in the Ohio Valley, 1755–1759," *War in History* 4 (1997), 247–63; Barr, " 'This Land Is Ours and Not Yours,' " 30–31; *PGW, Col.* 5:33; *NYCD* 10:413 (Vaudreuil quote); *WJP* 9:310 ("vast Tract"). French summaries of the Delaware and Shawnee raids are in *NYCD* 10:423–25, 435–37, 469–70, 481–82, 486.

65. Hinderaker, "Declaring Independence"; Ian K. Steele, "Shawnee Origins of Their Seven Years' War," *Ethnohistory* 53 (2006): 657–87; *NYCD* 10:423; *EAID* 3:445; CO 5/1328:28–29; *Bouquet Papers* 4:405.

66. *EAID* 3:2, 15, 19 ("Dogs" and "Slaves"), 148 (Teedyuscung).

67. *EAID* 3:423–25. Ackawonothio is variously identified as western Delaware or Shawnee.

68. Michael A. McDonnell, *Masters of Empire: Great Lakes Indians and the Making of America* (New York: Hill & Wang, 2015), 170–71, 177; Barr, " 'This Land Is Ours and Not Yours,' " 30–37.

69. Timothy J. Shannon, "War, Diplomacy, and Culture: The Iroquois Experience in the Seven Years' War," in Hofstra, *Cultures in Conflict: The Seven Years' War in North America*, 79–103.

70. *EAID* 3:7 ("ill Language"), 213 ("private Parts"); *WJP* 9:310 ("no longer Women").

71. Jane T. Merritt, *At the Crossroads: Indians and Empires on a Mid-Atlantic Frontier, 1700–1763* (Chapel Hill: University of North Carolina Press, 2003), ch. 5; *Bouquet Papers* 4:405 ("greatest Mischief"); Steele, *Setting All the Captives Free*, ch. 4 (Patton at 86).

72. Bond, "Captivity of Charles Stuart, 1755–57," 62.

73. Steele, *Setting All the Captives Free*, ch. 4 (figures at 115–16); James E. Seaver, ed., *A Narrative of the Life of Mrs. Mary Jemison* (Norman: University of Oklahoma Press, 1995).

74. "The Narrative of Marie le Roy and Barbara Leininger, for Three Years Captives among the Indians," *Pennsylvania Magazine of History and Biography* 29 (1905), 409. Similarly, Susanna Johnson and her family expected severe beatings when their Abenaki captors marched them through the gauntlet at Odanak in Quebec, but "each Indian only gave us a tap on the shoulder." "A Narrative of the Captivity of Mrs. Johnson," in *North Country Captives: Selected Narratives of Indian Captivity from Vermont and New Hampshire*, ed. Colin G. Calloway (Hanover, NH: University Press of New England, 1992), 66.

75. Samuel Cole Williams, ed., *Adair's History of the American Indians* (1930; New York: Promontory Press, n.d.), 172; Steele, *Setting All the Captives Free*, ch. 4.

76. Ward, *Breaking the Backcountry*, 70 (one thousand); Ward, " 'The European Method of Warring Is Not Practiced Here,' " 247–48 (casualties and territory abandoned); Ferling, *The Ascent of George Washington*, 33 (one-third); Steele, *Setting All the Captives Free*, 99 (928 farms and swath of territory).

77. Merritt, *At the Crossroads*, 184–88; Amy C. Schutt, *Peoples of the River Valleys: The Odyssey of the Delaware Indians* (Philadelphia: University of Pennsylvania Press, 2007), 114; Steele, *Setting All the Captives Free*, 95–96; Masur, *Autobiography of Benjamin Franklin*, 148; Patrick Spero, *Frontier Country: The Politics of War in Early Pennsylvania* (Philadelphia: University of Pennsylvania Press, 2016), 112–18.

78. *Scoouwa: James Smith's Indian Captivity Narrative* (1799; Columbus: Ohio Historical Society, 1978), 62.

79. Titus, *The Old Dominion at War*, 1–5, 72; Ward, *Breaking the Backcountry*, 92; *PGW, Col.* 4:90.

80. Humphreys, *"Life of General Washington," with George Washington's "Remarks,"* 20.

81. *Dinwiddie Papers* 2:116–18, 155 ("Panick").

82. *Dinwiddie Papers* 2:114, 474.

83. Titus, *The Old Dominion at War*, ch. 2; Ward, *Breaking the Backcountry*, ch. 3.

84. Titus, *Old Dominion at War*, 75–77, 142–48.

85. Anderson, *George Washington Remembers*, 21; Humphreys, *"Life of General Washington," with George Washington's "Remarks,"* xxxviii–xl.

86. *Dinwiddie Papers* 2:425–26.

87. *Dinwiddie Papers* 2:325, 355.

88. *PGW, Col.* 5:33.

89. Masur, *Autobiography of Benjamin Franklin*, 145.

90. Lengel, *General George Washington*, 61–62. Stephen Brumwell, *Redcoats: The British Soldier and War in the Americas, 1755–1763* (Cambridge: Cambridge University Press, 2002), chs. 6–7; Ward, "'The European Method of Warring Is Not Practiced Here,'" 252–57; Way, "Cutting Edge of Culture"; John W. Hall, "An Irregular Reconsideration of George Washington and the American Military Tradition," *Journal of Military History* 78 (2014): 961–93; Wayne E. Lee, *Barbarians and Brothers: Anglo-American Warfare, 1500–1865* (New York: Oxford University Press, 2011), 192.

91. Hofstra, "'A Parcel of Barbarian's,'" 88–92; *Dinwiddie Papers* 2:236–38; *PGW, Col.* 2:101–3, 3:6.

92. Warren R. Hofstra, "'And Die by Inches': George Washington and the Encounter of Cultures on the Southern Colonial Frontier," in *George Washington's South*, ed. Tamara Harvey and Greg O'Brien (Gainesville: University Press of Florida, 2004), ch. 3 (quotes at 71, 75).

93. *PGW, Col.* 2:109–10 ("not to be alarmed"); 156–60 ("more scared" at 158); Gregory Evans Dowd, *Groundless: Rumors, Legends, and Hoaxes on the Early American Frontier* (Baltimore, MD: Johns Hopkins University Press, 2015), 102–14.

94. *PGW, Col.* 2:213, 278, 290.

CHAPTER 6: FRONTIER DEFENSE AND A CHEROKEE ALLIANCE

1. Paul Kelton, "The British and Indian War: Cherokee Power and the Fate of Empire in North America," *William and Mary Quarterly*, 3rd ser., 69 (2012): 763–92; Daniel J. Tortora, *Carolina in Crisis: Cherokees, Colonists, and Slaves in the American Southeast, 1756–1763* (Chapel Hill: University of North Carolina Press, 2015), 44–46; Douglas McClure Wood, "'I Have Now Made a Path to Virginia': Outacite Ostenaco and the Cherokee-Virginia Alliance in the French and Indian War," *West Virginia History*, n.s., 2 (Fall 2008): 31–60.

2. *PGW, Col.* 2:54–56, 72, 97–99, 120, 125, 140–41, 154; *Dinwiddie Papers* 2:240, 243.

3. *EAID* 13:86–87, 133–43.

4. William L. McDowell Jr., ed., *Colonial Records of South Carolina: Documents relating to Indian Affairs, 1750–1754* (Columbia: South Carolina Archives Department, 1958), 433–34, 439; Samuel Cole Williams, ed., *Adair's History of the American Indians* (1930; New York: Promontory Press, n.d.), 255.

5. *EAID* 13:216–17, 280–302.

6. Theda Perdue, "Cherokee Relations with the Iroquois in the Eighteenth Century," in *Beyond the Covenant Chain: The Iroquois and Their Neighbors in Indian North America, 1600–1800*, ed. Daniel K. Richter and James H. Merrell (Syracuse, NY: Syracuse University Press, 1987), 135–40; Tyler Boulware, *Deconstructing the Cherokee Nation: Town, Region, and Nation among Eighteenth-Century Cherokees* (Gainesville: University Press of Florida, 2011).

7. *Dinwiddie Papers* 2:168–69, 187–89, 263, 267, 270, 280, 285–86, 289–90, 298–305, 308; William L. McDowell Jr., ed., *The Colonial Records of South Carolina: Documents relating to Indian Affairs, 1754–1765* (Columbia: South Carolina Department of Archives and History, 1970), 102, 106–8; Marion Tinling, ed., *The Correspondence of the Three William Byrds of Westover, Virginia, 1684–1776*, 2 vols. (Charlottesville: University of Virginia Press, 1977), 2:619–21; *EAID* 5:201–22 and CO5/1328:205–23 (treaty).

8. *Dinwiddie Papers* 2:292, 294–96, 313–15, 319–22, 336–37, 382 ("nothing essential"); *PGW, Col.* 2:214, 235, 278, 290, 334 ("apprehensions"), 344 ("nothing essential"); *Executive Journals* 6:673; Wood, "'I Have Now Made a Path to Virginia'" (Shawnee campaign at 39–43); Matthew C. Ward, *Breaking the Backcountry: The Seven Years' War in Virginia and Pennsylvania, 1754–1765* (Pittsburgh, PA: University of Pittsburgh Press, 2003), 104–5.

9. John E. Ferling, *The First of Men: A Life of George Washington* (New York: Oxford University Press, 2010), 43–45.

10. *PGW, Col.* 2:333, 337, 3:1, 33, 59–60; *Dinwiddie Papers* 2:383–85.

11. Robert L. Jolley, "Fort Loudon, Virginia: A French and Indian War Period Fortification Constructed by George Washington," in *The Archaeology of French and Indian War Frontier Forts*, ed. Lawrence E. Babits and Stephanie Gandulla (Gainesville: University Press of Florida, 2013), 102–21; Norman L. Baker, *Fort Loudon: Washington's Fort in Virginia* (Winchester, VA: French and Indian War Foundation, 2006); Rufus Rockwell Wilson, ed., *Burnaby's Travels through North America* (New York: A. Wessels, 1904), 74–75.

12. *PGW, Col.* 2:333–35, 338, 3:45.

13. Kristofer Ray, "Cherokees and Franco-British Confrontation in the Tennessee Corridor, 1730–1760," *Native South* 7 (2014): 33–67; *WJP* 9:569–81, 596–98 (Kerlerec's negotiations and treaty), 613 (Silver Heels).

14. Duane H. King, ed., *The Memoirs of Lt. Henry Timberlake: The Story of a Soldier, Adventurer, and Emissary to the Cherokees, 1756–1765* (Cherokee, NC: Museum of the Cherokee Indian Press, 2007), 37.

15. David H. Corkran, *The Cherokee Frontier: Conflict and Survival, 1740–62* (Norman: University of Oklahoma Press, 1962), 67 (carriage); Tortora, *Carolina in Crisis*, 30; John Oliphant, *Peace and War on the Anglo-Cherokee Frontier, 1756–1765* (Baton Rouge: Louisiana State University Press, 2001), 22 (stayed with Jeffersons).

16. CO 5/17, pt. 3:370–77; Edith Mays, ed., *Amherst Papers, 1756–1763: The Southern Sector: Dispatches from South Carolina, Virginia and His Majesty's Superintendent of Indian Affairs* (Bowie, MD: Heritage Books, 1999), 1–5; *Dinwiddie Papers* 2:389–91 (instructions to Lewis and message to Cherokees); *PGW, Col.* 3:43. On Cherokee desires for a fort and relations at Fort Loudon, see Daniel Ingram, *Indians and British Outposts in Eighteenth-Century America* (Gainesville: University Press of Florida, 2012), ch. 1.

17. CO 5/17, pt. 3:377 (Ostenaco, referred to here as Outacite); McDowell, *Colonial Records of South Carolina: Documents relating to Indian Affairs, 1754–1756*, 107–8 (Hagler), 137–38 (Attakullakulla), 277–79 (Ostenaco), 290–91 (Dinwiddie), 480 (Lyttelton).

18. On Attakullakulla's French connections, see McDowell, *Colonial Records of South Carolina: Documents relating to Indian Affairs, 1750–1754*, 71, 80, 101–2, 183, 223, 263; McDowell, *Colonial Records of South Carolina: Documents relating to Indian Affairs, 1754–1756*, 144 (Demere's assessment), 148, 200, 205, 241.

19. McDowell, *Colonial Records of South Carolina: Documents relating to Indian Affairs, 1750–1754*, 434.

20. *PGW, Col.* 3:42, 56.

21. *PGW, Col.* 3:397–98.

22. *PGW, Col,* 3:107, 444.

23. Douglas Southall Freeman, *Washington*, 1-vol. abridgement by Richard Harwell of the 7-vol. *George Washington* (New York: Simon & Schuster, 1992), 120.

24. *PGW, Col.* 3:308, 397 ("Tusks"); *Executive Journals* 6:38–39 ("heartily accepted"). On the earlier conflict, see David LaVere, *The Tuscarora War: Indians, Settlers, and the Fight for the Carolina Colonies* (Chapel Hill: University of North Carolina Press, 2014).

25. *Dinwiddie Papers* 2:442–46, 454, 484, 491, 493, 507, 539, 545, 548–50, 616, 620, 623, 625, 627, 629–33, 640–41, 657, 713.
26. *Bouquet Papers* 1:168, 173; McDowell, *Colonial Records of South Carolina: Documents relating to Indian Affairs, 1754–1756*, 434–35; Corkran, *Cherokee Frontier*, ch. 5.
27. *JHBV, 1752–58*, 320 (bounty extended); Ian K. Steele, *Setting All the Captives Free: Capture, Adjustment, and Recollection in Allegheny Country* (Montreal: McGill-Queens University Press, 2013), 264–65 (equivalent three months labor); *PGW, Col.* 3:405, 4:16, 29, 129, 163, 249; *Dinwiddie Papers* 2:605, 607, 616, 620 ("barbarous Method"), 623, 625, 656.
28. *PGW, Col.* 2:334.
29. *JHBV, 1752–58*, 473–75.
30. *EAID* 3:21, 27; *CRP* 7:88–89; C. Hale Sipe, *The Indian Wars of Pennsylvania* (Harrisburg, PA: Telegraph Press, 1929), 281–83; Daniel P. Barr, "'This Land Is Ours and Not Yours': The Western Delawares and the Seven Years' War in the Upper Ohio Valley, 1755–1758," in *The Boundaries between Us: Natives and Newcomers along the Frontiers of the Old Northwest Territory, 1750–1850*, ed. Daniel P. Barr (Kent, OH; Kent State University Press, 2006), 36; Henry J. Young, "A Note on Scalp Bounties in Pennsylvania," *Pennsylvania History* 24 (1957): 209–11; Peter Silver, *Our Savage Neighbors: How Indian War Transformed Early America* (New York: Norton, 2008), 161–68; Steele, *Setting All the Captives Free*, 102 (no women captured), 266–67.
31. Ferling, *The First of Men*, 46; John E. Ferling, *The Ascent of George Washington: The Hidden Political Genius of an American Icon* (New York: Bloomsbury, 2009), 34; "Adam Stephen's Council of War [at Fort Cumberland] and George Washington's Comments," Oct. 30, 1756, Huntington Library, Loudon Papers, box 48, #4 ("unsuitable for Defense"; thanks to Kris Ray for furnishing me a copy) and *PGW, Col.* 3:447–52; *PGW, Col.* 3:45–46, 48–51, 4:4; David Clary, *George Washington's First War* (New York: Simon & Schuster, 2010), 203–6; Bernhard Knollenberg, *George Washington: The Virginia Period, 1732–1775* (Durham, NC: Duke University Press, 1964), ch. 9.
32. Daniel P. Barr, "Victory at Kittanning? Reevaluating the Impact of Armstrong's Raid on the Seven Years' War in Pennsylvania," *Pennsylvania Magazine of History and Biography* 131 (2007): 5–32; Brady J. Crytzer, *War in the Peaceable Kingdom: The Kittanning Raid of 1756* (Yardley, PA: Westholme, 2016).
33. Helen Hornbeck Tanner, ed., *Atlas of Great Lakes Indian History* (Norman: University of Oklahoma Press, 1987), 46–47, 62; Steele, *Setting All the Captives Free*, 105; *PTJ* 2:99, 102; Michael N. McConnell, "Kuskusky Towns and Early Pennsylvania Indian History, 1748–1778," *Pennsylvania Magazine of History and Biography* 116 (Jan. 1992): 48, 50.
34. *Executive Journals* 6:20–21; *PGW, Col.* 4:50–51; Knollenberg, *George Washington: The Virginia Period*, 41–42.
35. *PGW, Col.* 4:79–90, quote at 82–83.
36. James Thomas Flexner, *George Washington: The Forge of Experience, 1732–1775* (Boston: Little, Brown, 1965), 165–75; Ferling, *The Ascent of George Washington*, 37–38 (gambling and shopping).
37. *PGW, Col.* 4:132–33.
38. *PGW, Col.* 4:136.
39. Clary, *George Washington's First War*, 196–97.
40. Wilbur R. Jacobs, *Wilderness Politics and Indian Gifts: The Northern Colonial Frontier, 1748–1763* (Lincoln: University of Nebraska Press, 1966); Gregory Evans Dowd, "'Insidious Friends': Gift Giving and the Cherokee-British Alliance in the Seven Years' War," in *Contact Points: American Frontiers from the Mohawk Valley to the Mississippi, 1750–1830*, ed. Andrew R. L. Cayton and Fredrika J. Teute (Chapel Hill: University of North Carolina Press, 1998), 114–50; Jessica Yirush Stern, *The Lives in Objects: Native Americans, British Colonists, and Cultures of Labor and Exchange in the Southeast* (Chapel Hill: University of North Carolina Press, 2017), ch. 3, esp. 100–101, 106; Corkran, *Cherokee Frontier*, 129; Ward, *Breaking the Backcountry*, 104, 141–45.
41. Jacobs, *Wilderness Politics and Indian Gifts*, 167; *Dinwiddie Papers* 2:283, 469, 605–6, 639.

42. *PGW, Col.* 4:139–41; Mays, *Amherst Papers,* 10–14.
43. *PGW, Col.* 4:163; *Dinwiddie Papers* 2:640–41.
44. *Bouquet Papers* 1:397.
45. Edward P. Hamilton, ed., *Adventure in the Wilderness: The American Journals of Louis Antoine de Bougainville, 1756–1760* (Norman: University of Oklahoma Press, 1964, 1990), 148–49 ("without cavalry"), 163–65, 170 ("necessary evil"), 169–75; Ian K. Steele, *Betrayals: Fort William Henry and the "Massacre"* (New York: Oxford University Press, 1990).
46. *NYCD* 7:782 (ensign), 10:582–84 (Vaudreuil).
47. James H. Merrell, *The Indians' New World: Catawbas and Their Neighbors from European Contact through the Era of Removal,* 2nd ed. (Chapel Hill: University of North Carolina Press, 2009), 162.
48. *Executive Journals* 6:31–33.
49. *PGW, Col.* 4:168–69; see also *Dinwiddie Papers* 2:633.
50. Wilbur R. Jacobs, ed., *The Appalachian Indian Frontier: The Edmond Atkin Report and Plan of 1755* (Lincoln: University of Nebraska Press, 1967), quotes at 3, 38.
51. *PGW, Col.* 4:154; *Dinwiddie Papers* 2:622–23.
52. *PGW, Col.* 4:171–72.
53. *PGW, Col.* 2:151.
54. *PGW, Col.* 4:175, 183–84; Mays, *Amherst Papers,* 35–46.
55. *PGW, Col.* 4:198–99.
56. *PGW, Col.* 4:200, 208–9, 215–16; Corkran, *Cherokee Frontier.*
57. *PGW, Col.* 4:225, 261, 263 ("scourge"), 271, 285, 307–8.
58. *PGW, Col.* 5:2–3, 44–45.
59. *PGW, Col.* 5:20, 52–53; *Dinwiddie Papers* 2:707–9, 715–16.
60. Flexner, *George Washington: The Forge of Experience,* 184.
61. *PGW, Col.* 5:86.
62. Edward G. Lengel, *General George Washington: A Military Life* (New York: Random House, 2005), 62, 65.
63. *PGW, Col.* 5:33.
64. *PGW, Col.* 5:10, 100–101.
65. Matthew P. Dziennik, *The Fatal Land: War, Empire, and the Highland Soldier in British America* (New Haven, CT: Yale University Press, 2015), 47.
66. John Oliphant, *John Forbes: Scotland, Flanders and the Seven Years' War, 1707–1759* (London: Bloomsbury, 2015); Douglas R. Cubbison, *The British Defeat of the French in Pennsylvania, 1758: A Military History of the Forbes Campaign against Fort Duquesne* (Jefferson, NC: McFarland, 2010), 10–14.
67. James Titus, *The Old Dominion at War: Society, Politics, and Warfare in Late Colonial Virginia* (Columbia: University of South Carolina Press, 1992), 122.
68. Fred Anderson, *Crucible of War: The Seven Years' War and the Fate of Empire in British North America, 1754–1766* (New York: Knopf, 2000), 229; Knollenberg, *George Washington: The Virginia Period,* 63.
69. *PGW, Col.* 5:117.
70. Tinling, *Correspondence of the Three William Byrds* 2:607, 638–45, 647–52 ("great difficulty" at 651), 655–57; Forbes HQ Papers, reel 1, items 43–45, 88, 158 "("haunted", "squaws," and "dream"); *Executive Journals* 6:92–93. William Byrd II's famous sexual exploits are recorded in Louis B. Wright and Marion Tinling, eds., The *Secret Diary of William Byrd of Westover, 1709–1712* (Richmond, VA: Dietz Press, 1941).
71. *Bouquet Papers* 2:304.
72. Forbes HQ Papers, reel 1, items 110, 124 ("in want"), 133–34 (return of the Southern Indians at Winchester), 135 ("everything in my power"); Alfred Proctor James, ed., *The Writings of General John Forbes relating to his service in North America* (Menasha, WI; Collegiate Press, 1938), 65, 68–71 ("turn me into a Cherokee" at 70–71), 74–75, 77–78.
73. Douglas R. Cubbison, *On Campaign against Fort Duquesne: The Braddock and Forbes Expeditions, 1755–1758, through the Experiences of Quartermaster Sir John St. Clair* (Jefferson, NC: McFarland, 2015), ch. 7.

74. Cubbison, *British Defeat of the French in Pennsylvania*, 81–85; Forbes HQ Papers, reel 2, items 163, 166, 205, 208, 229, 234, 237, 242, 247, 250.

75. "A Compilation of Indian Trade Goods Presented to the Cherokee and Catawba Warriors during the Forbes Campaign," in Cubbison, *British Defeat of the French in Pennsylvania*, 199–211.

76. *PGW, Col.* 5:117, 123n3 (numbers of Indian parties coming and going), 131, 138, 148.

77. Forbes HQ Papers, reel 1, item 132.

78. *PGW, Col.* 5:154–56.

79. Forbes HQ, reel 2, items 171 ("Cowards"), 234; James, *Writings of General John Forbes*, 83–84; *PGW, Col.* 5:165–66n, 177.

80. *PGW, Col.* 5:175–78.

81. Forbes HQ Papers, reel 2, items 336, 404; *EAID* 3:640 ("since we were created"); *EAID* 2:240 ("very Bones").

82. Anthony F. C. Wallace, *King of the Delawares: Teedyuscung, 1700–1763* (Syracuse, NY: Syracuse University Press, 1990), 93–115; *EAID* 3: ch. 3.

83. James H. Merrell, *Into the American Woods: Negotiators on the Pennsylvania Frontier* (New York: Norton, 1999), 238–42.

84. *EAID* 3:233–302 (wampum belt at 285); Wallace, *King of the Delawares*, 155–59.

85. Boulware, *Deconstructing the Cherokee Nation*, 100–101; Forbes HQ Papers, reel 1, items 97, 99 ("disgusting").

86. *EAID* 3:383.

87. *EAID* 3:386–88, 391–93.

88. James, *Writings of General John Forbes*, 91–92, 102.

89. Forbes HQ Papers, reel 2, items 232, 240, 287, 298, 303.

90. Paul Kelton, *Cherokee Medicine, Colonial Germs: An Indigenous Nation's Fight against Smallpox, 1518–1824* (Norman: University of Oklahoma Press, 2015), 110–11.

91. Forbes HQ Papers, reel 2, items 238, 239, 298.

92. Kelton, "British and Indian War," 777; Forbes HQ Papers, reel 2, item 303 (laughed at).

93. James, *Writings of General John Forbes*, 112–13, 117; *Bouquet Papers* 2:65. On relations between Highland soldiers and Indians, see Colin G. Calloway, *White People, Indians, and Highlanders: Tribal Peoples and Colonial Encounters in Scotland and America* (New York: Oxford University Press, 2008), ch. 4, and Dziennik, *Fatal Land*, ch. 3.

94. Forbes HQ, reel 2, items 234, 237, 239, 277, 303.

95. *Bouquet Papers* 2:15–16, 41, 49, 74, 95, 98–102, 143, 180, 215–17, 253, 260, 292, 313, 315, 338, 405.

96. McDowell, *Colonial Records of South Carolina: Documents relating to Indian Affairs, 1754–1762*, 471.

97. Forbes HQ Papers, reel 2, items 239, 298, 325, 326, 353; George Reese, ed., *The Official Papers of Francis Fauquier, Lieutenant Governor of Virginia, 1758–1768*, 3 vols. (Charlottesville: University Press of Virginia, 1980–83), 1:16, 18, 24, 29.

98. *PGW, Col.* 5:224–27, 354; *Writings of Washington* 2:215–16.

99. Clary, *George Washington's First War*, 244.

100. *Bouquet Papers* 2:221–22.

101. Kelton, "British and Indian War," 778; James, *Writings of General John Forbes*, 117.

102. James, *Writings of General John Forbes*, 140, 176–77; *Bouquet Papers* 2:15 (adopted).

103. James, *Writings of General John Forbes*, 142.

104. Forbes HQ Papers, reel 3, item 440.

105. Forbes HQ Papers, reel 3, items, 473, 475, 477; Reese, *Official Papers of Francis Fauquier* 1:59–60.

106. *PGW, Col.* 5:275–76, 303; Reese, *Official Papers of Francis Fauquier* 1:50–51, 53.

107. *PGW, Col.* 5:416; *Bouquet Papers* 2:416, 418; James, *Writings of General John Forbes*, 188, 192.

CHAPTER 7: FRONTIER ADVANCE AND A CHEROKEE WAR

1. Linda Baumgarten, *What Clothes Reveal: The Language of Clothing in Colonial and Federal America* (Williamsburg, VA: Colonial Williamsburg Foundation in association with Yale University Press, 2002), 68.

2. J. Frederick Fausz, "'Engaged in Enterprises Pregnant with Terror': George Washington's Formative Years among the Indians," in *George Washington and the Virginia Backcountry*, ed. Warren R. Hofstra (Madison, WI: Madison House, 1998), 132–33; *PGW, Col.* 5:152, 193, 257–59, 282, 287, 290; *Bouquet Papers* 2:159.

3. *PGW, Col.* 5:285, 290.

4. Peter E. Russell, "Redcoats in the Wilderness: British Officers and Irregular Warfare in Europe and America, 1740 to 1760," *William and Mary Quarterly*, 3rd ser., 35 (1978): 629–52; *Bouquet Papers* 2:124 ("delight"), 136 ("must comply"); Forbes HQ Papers, reel 3, item 512; Alfred Proctor James, ed., *The Writings of General John Forbes relating to His Service in North America* (Menasha, WI: Collegiate Press, 1938), 125 ("must comply"); David L. Preston, "'Make Indians of Our White Men': British Soldiers and Indian Warriors from Braddock's to Forbes's Campaigns, 1755–1758," *Pennsylvania History* 74 (2007): 291–94.

5. *Scoouwa: James Smith's Indian Captivity Narrative* (1799; Columbus: Ohio Historical Society, 1978), 118.

6. *Bouquet Papers* 2:258.

7. *Bouquet Papers* 2:206, 222 ("Irruption"), 269.

8. *Bouquet Papers* 2:263–64.

9. *Bouquet Papers* 2:134.

10. James, *Writings of General John Forbes*, 141; Douglas R. Cubbison, *The British Defeat of the French in Pennsylvania, 1758: A Military History of the Forbes Campaign against Fort Duquesne* (Jefferson, NC: McFarland, 2010), 36, 86–95.

11. *PGW, Col.* 5:324, 353–60, 376, 389, 398, 424, 432–33 (to Robinson), 439–43 (to Fauquier); George Reese, ed., *The Official Papers of Francis Fauquier, Lieutenant Governor of Virginia, 1758–1768*, 3 vols. (Charlottesville: University Press of Virginia, 1980–83), 1:57–58, 66–67, 82; *Executive Journals* 6:108; *Bouquet Papers* 2:179, 273, 277–78, 298–303, 318–19, 343, 364, 443, 615.

12. *Bouquet Papers* 2:291.

13. *Bouquet Papers* 2:344; James, *Writings of General John Forbes*, 156–57, 171 ("unguarded letter"), 173, 199 ("like a Soldier"); Forbes HQ Papers, reel 3, item 464; Bernhard Knollenberg, *George Washington: The Virginia Period, 1732–1775* (Durham, NC: Duke University Press, 1964), 65–67.

14. Cubbison, *British Defeat of the French in Pennsylvania*, 36–37.

15. *PGW, Col.* 6:41–43.

16. James, *Writings of General John Forbes*, 205; Hugh Cleland, *George Washington in the Ohio Valley* (Pittsburgh, PA: University of Pittsburgh Press, 1955), 199.

17. *CRP* 6:536, 671 (Morris).

18. *PGW, Col.* 5:109.

19. *Scoouwa: James Smith's Indian Captivity Narrative*, 117.

20. *NYCD* 10:861.

21. James, *Writings of General John Forbes*, 115; *Bouquet Papers* 2:103, 304, 461.

22. *WJP* 9:786.

23. Forbes HQ Papers, reel 2, item 405; James, *Writings of General John Forbes*, 127, 138; *WJP* 9:945–51, 956–61; Paul Kelton, "The British and Indian War: Cherokee Power and the Fate of Empire in North America," *William and Mary Quarterly* 69 (2012): 779–84.

24. James, *Writings of General John Forbes*, 165.

25. *EAID* 3:342, 346–73; Anthony F. C. Wallace, *King of the Delawares: Teedyuscung, 1700–1763* (Syracuse, NY: Syracuse University Press, 1990), 168–75; Daniel P. Barr, "'This Land Is Ours and Not Yours': The Western Delawares and the Seven Years' War in the Upper Ohio Valley, 1755–1758," in *The Boundaries between Us: Natives and Newcomers along the Frontiers of the Old Northwest Territory, 1750–1850*, ed. Daniel P. Barr (Kent, OH: Kent State University Press, 2006), 38.

26. Forbes HQ Papers, reel 2, items 176 ("terrible pannick"), 350, 351.

27. *CRP* 8:135–36; C. Hale Sipe, *The Indian Wars of Pennsylvania* (Harrisburg, PA: Telegraph Press, 1929), 358.

28. Walter T. Champion Jr., "Christian Frederick Post and the Winning of the West," *Pennsylvania Magazine of History and Biography* 104, no. 3 (1980): 308–25; James H. Merrell, *Into the American Woods: Negotiators on the Pennsylvania Frontier* (New York: Norton, 1999), 242–49. The journal of Post's first trip is in Forbes HQ Papers, reel 2, item 376. Post was born in East or Polish Prussia but a naturalized British citizen; *EAID* 3:343.

29. "The Journal of Christian Frederick Post," in *Early Western Journals, 1748–1765*, ed. Reuben G. Thwaites, rpt. of *Early Western Travels*, vol. 1 (1904; Lewisburg, PA: Wennawoods Publishing, 1998), quotes at 199, 200, 212, 214–16; *Pennsylvania Archives* 3:520–44; *EAID* 3:414–16.

30. "Journal of Christian Frederick Post," 213–14; John W. Jordan, ed., "James Kenny's 'Journal to Ye Westward,' 1758–59," *Pennsylvania Magazine of History and Biography* 37 (1913): 429; Michael N. McConnell, "Pisquetomen and Tamaqua: Mediating Peace in the Ohio Country," in *Northeastern Indian Lives, 1632–1816*, ed. Robert S. Grumet (Amherst: University of Massachusetts Press, 1996), 273–94 ("sunset" quote at 287).

31. James, *Writings of General John Forbes*, 180–81; Forbes HQ Papers, reel 3, item 477; *Bouquet Papers* 2:383. On the efforts of Forbes, Post, and the Pennsylvania Quakers to secure peace, see Francis Jennings, *Empire of Fortune: Crowns, Colonies, and Tribes in the Seven Years War in America* (New York: Norton, 1988), 375–404; Fred Anderson, *Crucible of War: The Seven Years' War and the Fate of Empire in British North America, 1754–1766* (New York: Knopf, 2000), ch. 28.

32. *Executive Journals* 6:109; James, *Writings of General John Forbes*, 203 (quote).

33. James, *Writings of General John Forbes*, 219–20, 225, 237–38; *Bouquet Papers* 2:499–504, 508–9, 517–21; *PGW, Col.* 6:38–48; *Scoouwa: James Smith's Indian Captivity Narrative*, 119.

34. C. Hale Sipe, *The Indian Chiefs of Pennsylvania* (Butler, PA: Zeigler, 1927; rpt. Lewisburg, PA: Wennawoods Publishing, 1994), 372–73; *CVSP* 1:280.

35. Cubbison, *British Defeat of the French in Pennsylvania*, 139–40, 191; *NYCD* 10:888.

36. *Bouquet Papers* 2:471–73.

37. Kelton, "British and Indian War," 787; James, *Writings of General John Forbes*, 230 (quote), 233, 235 ("consummate Dog"); *Bouquet Papers* 2:562.

38. James, *Writings of General John Forbes*, 248; *Bouquet Papers* 2:584–85.

39. James, *Writings of General John Forbes*, 221 (five hundred Indians; "God knows"); Boyd Stanley Schlenther, "Training for Resistance: Charles Thomson and Indian Affairs in Pennsylvania," *Pennsylvania History* 50 (1983): 202–3; *WJP* 3:4 ("Much Divided"); *EAID* 3:259 (507 Indians), 427–66 (list of nations at 428–29); *CRP* 8:175–223; Susan Kalter, ed., *Benjamin Franklin, Pennsylvania, and the First Nations: The Treaties of 1736–62* (Urbana: University of Illinois Press, 2006), 291–333; Matthew C. Ward, *Breaking the Backcountry: The Seven Years' War in Virginia and Pennsylvania, 1754–1765* (Pittsburgh, PA: University of Pittsburgh Press, 2003), 178–82.

40. *EAID* 3:344, 467–68.

41. James, *Writings of General John Forbes*, 251–53; *EAID* 3:467–68; Anderson, *Crucible of War*, 279–80.

42. *PGW, Col.* 6:105. Later orders added that "any Single Indians wearing a blue and red badge about their Heads as well as a Yellow one" were to be "received as friends" (6:148). Forbes likewise ordered that friendly Indians wear yellow headbands or armbands; *Bouquet Papers* 2:224; James, *Writings of General John Forbes*, 125, 149, 152.

43. *EAID* 3:345.

44. David A. Clary, *George Washington's First War* (New York: Simon & Schuster, 2012), 241.

45. Anderson, *Crucible of War*, 258.

46. *Bouquet Papers* 2:475; *Scoouwa: The Indian Captivity Narrative of James Smith*, 118; James, *Writings of General John Forbes*, 194, 239–40; *Pennsylvania Archives* 12:393; Michael A. McDonnell, *Masters of Empire: Great Lakes Indians and the Making of America* (New York: Hill & Wang, 2015), 191, 193.

47. Cubbison, *British Defeat of the French in Pennsylvania*, 150–51.

48. *PGW, Col.* 6:121n–122n; Fred Anderson, ed., *George Washington Remembers: Reflections on the French and Indian War* (Lanham, MD: Rowman & Littlefield, 2004), 23, 127; David

Humphreys, *"Life of General Washington," with George Washington's "Remarks,"* ed. Rosemarie Zagarri (Athens: University of Georgia Press, 1991), xlii–xliv, 21–22; Clary, *George Washington's First War*, 256–57; John Ferling, *The Ascent of George Washington: The Hidden Political Genius of an American Icon* (New York: Bloomsbury, 2009), 43.

49. "Journal of Christian Frederick Post," 255–56.

50. Years later Washington claimed that he commanded the leading brigade; in fact, he was given command of the third of three brigades, which Forbes moved forward by leapfrogging one ahead of the others. Humphreys, *"Life of General Washington," with George Washington's "Remarks,"* 21; Knollenberg, *George Washington: The Virginia Period*, 69; Cubbison, *British Defeat of the French in Pennsylvania*, 157–58, 163.

51. *Bouquet Papers* 2:610, 612–14.

52. *NYCD* 10:905; *Pennsylvania Archives* 8:232.

53. James, *Writings of General John Forbes*, 262–64, 267.

54. *EAID* 3:477–79; *Bouquet Papers* 2:621–26.

55. James, *Writings of General John Forbes*, 287, 291n.

56. *Bouquet Papers* 2:608, 611 (quote).

57. *Bouquet Papers* 3:164.

58. *Bouquet Papers* 3:164–65, 416–18, 470, 493, 502–3.

59. *EAID* 3: ch. 6; *Bouquet Papers* 3:27–31, 507–11.

60. *PGW, Col,* 6:158–62; Reese, *Official Papers of Francis Fauquier* 1:115–18; Cleland, *George Washington in the Ohio Valley*, 221–20.

61. *Bouquet Papers* 3:192, 4:7.

62. Brian Leigh Dunnigan, ed., *Memoirs on the Late War in North America between France and England by Pierre Pouchot* (Youngstown, NY: Old Fort Niagara Assoc., 1994), 415–16; *WJP* 10:55.

63. Anderson, *Crucible of War*, 330–38; Jennings, *Empire of Fortune*, 414–19; Timothy J. Shannon, "War, Diplomacy, and Culture: The Iroquois Experience in the Seven Years' War," in *Cultures in Conflict: The Seven Years' War in North America*, ed. Warren R. Hofstra (Lanham, MD: Rowman & Littlefield, 2007), 87–88. French accounts of the siege are in Dunnigan, *Memoirs on the Late War*, 200–231, 503–28.

64. Robert F. Dalzell Jr. and Lee Baldwin Dalzell, *George Washington's Mount Vernon: At Home in Revolutionary America* (New York: Oxford University Press, 1998), 49.

65. Jennings, *Empire of Fortune*, 410.

66. On Custis's plantations and business operations, see Lorena S. Walsh, *Motives of Honor, Pleasure, and Profit: Plantation Management in the Colonial Chesapeake, 1607–1763* (Chapel Hill: University of North Carolina Press, 2010), 440–47.

67. *JHBV, 1761–65,* 111, 117.

68. *PGW, Col.* 6:343.

69. *PGW, Col.* 6:361.

70. Dorothy Twohig, "The Making of George Washington," in Hofstra, *George Washington and the Virginia Backcountry*, 17.

71. *PGW, Col.* 7:55 ("a Story too stale"), 80 ("great Continent").

72. *Executive Journals* 6:122; Tom Hatley, *The Dividing Paths: Cherokees and South Carolinians through the Era of Revolution* (New York: Oxford University Press, 1993), 102–3; Jessica Yirush Stern, *The Lives in Objects: Native Americans, British Colonists, and Cultures of Labor and Exchange in the Southeast* (Chapel Hill: University of North Carolina Press, 2017), 106, 108.

73. Samuel Cole Williams, ed., *Adair's History of the American Indians* (1930; New York: Promontory Press, n.d.), 259–61; Preston, "'Make Indians of Our White Men,'" 299–300; James, *Writings of General John Forbes*, 256–57; CO 5/386:178; Reese, *Official Papers of Francis Fauquier* 1:89–90 (killings and repeal of scalp bounty), 292–94 (hostages); *Executive Journals* 6:94–96, 112, 124–30 ("heal all Wounds" at 125); Kelton, "British and Indian War," 789–90; Hatley, *Dividing Paths*, 100–114; David H. Corkran, *The Cherokee Frontier: Conflict and Survival, 1740–62* (Norman: University of Oklahoma Press, 1962), ch. 11.

74. *Bouquet Papers* 3:544, 4:17n.

75. James H. Merrell, *The Indians' New World: Catawbas and Their Neighbors from European Contact through the Era of Removal* (Chapel Hill: University of North Carolina Press, 2009), 192–95,

203; Daniel J. Tortora, *Carolina in Crisis: Cherokees, Colonists, and Slaves in the American Southeast, 1756–1763* (Chapel Hill: University of North Carolina Press, 205), 83–84; Paul Kelton, *Cherokee Medicine, Colonial Germs: An Indigenous Nation's Fight against Smallpox, 1518–1824* (Norman: University of Oklahoma Press, 2015), 114–17.

76. Williams, *Adair's History of the American Indians*, 266.

77. John Oliphant, *Peace and War on the Anglo-Cherokee Frontier, 1756–1763* (Baton Rouge: Louisiana State University Press, 2000); *PGW, Col.* 6:361.

78. Reese, *Official Papers of Francis Fauquier* 1:158; Marion Tinling, ed., *The Correspondence of the Three William Byrds of Westover, Virginia, 1684–1776*, 2 vols. (Charlottesville: University of Virginia Press, 1977), 2:669 (quote), 671, 717.

79. *PGW, Col.* 6:453.

80. Reese, *Official Papers of Francis Fauquier* 1:397, 409, 411.

81. Tortora, *Carolina in Crisis*, chs. 6–10; Hatley, *Dividing Paths*, ch. 10; Oliphant, *Peace and War on the Anglo-Cherokee Frontier*, chs. 4–5; Corkran, *Cherokee Frontier*, ch. 17; Kelton, *Cherokee Medicine, Colonial Germs*, 134–36; Tyler Boulware, *Deconstructing the Cherokee Nation: Town, Region, and Nation among Eighteenth-Century Cherokees* (Gainesville: University Press of Florida, 2011), ch. 6; "Journal of the March and Operations of the Troops under the Command of General Grant," Papers of James Grant of Ballindalloch, microfilm ed. at the David Library of the American Revolution, Washington Crossing, PA, reel 32, 8–21.

82. Tortora, *Carolina in Crisis*, 142, 152; Duane H. King and E. Raymond Evans, eds., "Memoirs of the Grant Expedition against the Cherokees in 1761," *Journal of Cherokee Studies*, special issue (Summer 1977): 322 (Silver Heels's drunken violence).

83. Reese, *Official Papers of Francis Fauquier* 2:578–82, 586–87, 592–94.

84. *PGW, Col.* 7:58–59, 80 ("gaping Mouths"), 96–97 ("poor Wretches").

85. *Executive Journals* 6:185, 199, 204, 206; Edith Mays, ed., *Amherst Papers, 1756–1763, The Southern Sector: Dispatches from South Carolina, Virginia and His Majesty's Superintendent of Indian Affairs* (Westminster, MD: Heritage Books, 2006), 260–62, 293–300; Tinling, *Correspondence of the Three William Byrds* 2:743–45, 748; Oliphant, *Peace and War on the Anglo-Cherokee Frontier*, ch. 6; King and Evans, "Memoirs of the Grant Expedition against the Cherokees," 280 (Attakullakulla quote); *EAID* 5:243–49; CO 5/1386:19–22; Reese, *Official Papers of Francis Fauquier* 2:685–88.

86. *JHBV, 1761–65*, xvii; Reese, *Official Papers of Francis Fauquier* 2:727.

87. *Executive Journals* 6:214–16; Oliphant, *Peace and War on the Anglo-Cherokee Frontier*, 191–93, 208.

88. *Executive Journals* 6:216–17; Reese, *Official Papers of Francis Fauquier* 2:726–31.

89. *EAID* 5:250–56; Duane H. King, ed., *The Memoirs of Lt. Henry Timberlake* (Cherokee, NC: Museum of the Cherokee Indian, 2007), 55–72; John Oliphant, "The Cherokee Embassy to London, 1762," *Journal of Imperial and Commonwealth History* 27 (1999): 1–26; Stephanie Pratt, *American Indians in British Art, 1700–1840* (Norman: University of Oklahoma Press, 2005), 51–60; Alden T. Vaughan, *Transatlantic Encounters: American Indians in Britain, 1500–1776* (Cambridge: Cambridge University Press, 2006), 165–75; Jace Weaver, *The Red Atlantic: American Indigenes and the Making of the Modern World, 1000–1927* (Chapel Hill: University of North Carolina Press, 2014), 157–63; Kate Fullagar, *The Savage Visit: New World People and Popular Imperial Culture in Britain, 1710–1795* (Berkeley: University of California Press, 2012); Coll Thrush, *Indigenous London: Native Travelers at the Heart of Empire* (New Haven, CT: Yale University Press, 2016), 84–96.

90. *EAID* 14:200–202.

91. James Titus, *The Old Dominion at War: Society, Politics, and Warfare in Late Colonial Virginia* (Columbia: University of South Carolina Press, 1992), 131.

92. Douglas Edward Leach, *Roots of Conflict: British Armed Forces and Colonial Americans, 1677–1763* (Chapel Hill: University of North Carolina Press, 1986), 164–65.

93. John E. Ferling, "School for Command: Young George Washington and the Virginia Regiment," in Hofstra, *George Washington and the Virginia Backcountry*, 195–222; Edward G. Lengel, *General George Washington: A Military Life* (New York: Random House, 2005), 77–80; Anderson, *Crucible of War*, 289–92.

94. GW to Stephen, July 20, 1776, NYPL, GW, reel 4; *PGW, Rev.* 5:408–9.

CHAPTER 8: CONFRONTING THE INDIAN BOUNDARY

1. When Lawrence Washington owned Mount Vernon, his most important rooms faced the Potomac, and beyond that the Chesapeake, the Atlantic, and England. Robert F. Dalzell Jr. and Lee Baldwin Dalzell, *George Washington's Mount Vernon: At Home in Revolutionary America* (New York: Oxford University Press, 1998), 52–53, suggest that reorienting the house to the West "symbolically may have been the most important of all the changes" Washington made at Mount Vernon.

2. Joseph Ellis, *His Excellency: George Washington* (New York: Vintage, 2005), 53.

3. *PGW, Col.* 7:236–37, 257.

4. John Ferling, *The Ascent of George Washington: The Hidden Political Genius of an American Icon* (New York: Bloomsbury, 2009), 57–59; *PGW, Col.* 6:343 ("no Stone").

5. Ferling, *Ascent of George Washington,* 136–37.

6. Bruce A. Ragsdale, "Young Washington's Virginia: Opportunity in the 'Golden Age' of Planter Society," in *George Washington and the Virginia Backcountry,* ed. Warren R. Hofstra (Madison, WI: Madison House, 1998), 50–52.

7. Bernard Bailyn, *Voyagers to the West: A Passage in the Peopling of America on the Eve of the Revolution* (New York: Knopf, 1986), 25–28; Alan Taylor, *American Revolutions: A Continental History, 1750–1804* (New York: Norton, 2016), 56.

8. Stuart Banner, *How the Indians Lost Their Land: Law and Power on the Frontier* (Cambridge, MA: Harvard University Press, 2005), 87.

9. *JHBV, 1761–65,* xii–xiii; *Bouquet Papers* 4:532–36.

10. *CRP* 8:269, 296, 389, 766–67; *Pennsylvania Archives,* ser. 1, 3:572–74; *Bouquet Papers* 2:621–22 (quote).

11. *Bouquet Papers* 3:30; "The Journal of Christian Frederick Post," in *Early Western Journals, 1748–1765,* ed. Reuben G. Thwaites, rpt. of *Early Western Travels,* vol. 1 (1904; Lewisburg, PA: Wennawoods Publishing, 1998), quotes and Croghan's refusal at 274, 278, 283.

12. John W. Jordan, ed., "James Kenny's 'Journal to Ye Westward,' 1758–59," *Pennsylvania Magazine of History and Biography* 37 (1913): 424, 433.

13. Jordan, "James Kenny's 'Journal to Ye Westward,' 1758–59," 427–29.

14. Fred Anderson, *Crucible of War: The Seven Years' War and the Fate of Empire in British North America, 1754–1766* (New York: Knopf, 2000), 284–85, 328–29; David L. Preston, *The Texture of Contact: European and Indian Settler Communities on the Frontiers of Iroquoia, 1667–1783* (Lincoln: University of Nebraska Press, 2009), 221, 245–46, 251–52.

15. Anderson, *Crucible of War,* 524–26; *Bouquet Papers* 5:355, 437, 844 (Bouquet's proclamation), 847, 6:39–40, 44–45; Lois Mulkearn, ed., *George Mercer Papers relating to the Ohio Company of Virginia* (Pittsburgh, PA: University of Pittsburgh Press, 1954), 614–15; *Executive Journals* 6:205; George Reese, ed., *The Official Papers of Francis Fauquier, Lieutenant Governor of Virginia, 1758–1768,* 3 vols. (Charlottesville: University Press of Virginia, 1980–83), 2:663–66.

16. Mulkearn, *George Mercer Papers,* 151–53.

17. Reese, *Official Papers of Francis Fauquier* 2:774–75.

18. Alfred Proctor James, ed., *The Writings of General John Forbes relating to His Service in North America* (Menasha, WI: Collegiate Press, 1938), 283, 290.

19. *WJP* 10:660 (no right); *NYCD* 7:665 ("free people").

20. John W. Jordan, ed., "Journal of James Kenny, 1761–1763," *Pennsylvania Magazine of History and Biography* 37 (1913): 187.

21. *NYCD* 10:974.

22. *EAID* 3:573–74.

23. *WJP* 10:649, 652.

24. *Bouquet Papers* 6:157 ("very Jealous"); *WJP* 10:680 ("every bad report"), 683.

25. Jordan, "Journal of James Kenny," 171–72, 175, 186, 188; Guy Soulliard Klett, ed., *Journals of Charles Beatty, 1762–1769* (University Park: Pennsylvania State University Press, 1962), 65 ("evil ways"), 69–70.

26. Jordan, "Journal of James Kenny," 169, 172, 178.

27. *WJP* 10:477–78, 964, 971; Jordan, "Journal of James Kenny," 174, 196.

28. Jordan, "Journal of James Kenny," 24 ("against ye Wall"), 25, 34, 154 (Delaware George), 158 (Shingas's kindness), 160–61, 168 ("not so Cheerful"); Michael N. McConnell, "Pisquetomen and Tamaqua: Mediating Peace in the Ohio Country," in *Northeastern Indian Lives, 1632–1816*, ed. Robert S. Grumet (Amherst: University of Massachusetts Press, 1996), 292; *WJP* 13:233, 236, 254–55.

29. Naming wars after Indian leaders—King Philip's War, the Black Hawk War, Red Cloud's War, and so on—is problematic because it implicitly attributes blame for the war to them. Historians have struggled to find a good alternative name for this one, adopting such awkward titles as "the War Called Pontiac's." Back in 1929, C. Hale Sipe used "the Pontiac and Guyasuta War," which at least diffuses the leadership role. Sipe, *The Indian Wars of Pennsylvania* (Harrisburg, PA: Telegraph Press, 1929), 427.

30. *WJP* 3:444, 456, 460–67, 521, 629–30; Anthony F. C. Wallace, *The Death and Rebirth of the Seneca* (New York: Random House, 1969), 114–15 ("under the nose").

31. *WJP* 4:95.

32. *PGW, Col.* 7:230–31, 236–37, 257–60.

33. Matthew L. Rhoades, *Long Knives and the Longhouse: Anglo-Iroquois Politics and the Expansion of Colonial Virginia* (Teaneck, NJ: Fairleigh Dickinson University Press, 2011), 159.

34. *Bouquet Papers* 6:261–63, 315 ("Execrable Race"), 333, 515 ("raging"); "Journal of William Trent," in *Pen Pictures of Early Western Pennsylvania*, ed. John W. Harpster (Pittsburgh, PA: University of Pittsburgh Press, 1938), 103–4; Elizabeth A. Fenn, "Biological Warfare in Eighteenth-Century North America: Beyond Jeffery Amherst," *Journal of American History* 86 (2000): 1552–80, invoice at 1554; Philip Ranlet, "The British, the Indians, and Smallpox: What Actually Happened at Fort Pitt in 1763?" *Pennsylvania History* 67 (2000): 427–41.

35. *Bouquet Papers* 6:338–40, 342–45 (Bushy Run). For more on the war, see Gregory Evans Dowd, *War under Heaven: Pontiac, the Indian Nations, and the British Empire* (Baltimore, MD: Johns Hopkins University Press, 2002); David Dixon, *Never Come to Peace Again: Pontiac's Uprising and the Fate of the British Empire in North America* (Norman: University of Oklahoma Press, 2005); and Richard Middleton, *Pontiac's War: Its Causes, Course and Consequences* (New York: Routledge, 2007).

36. *CRP* 9:188–92.

37. *EAID* 3:685–702; *Bouquet Papers* 6:649–50, 653–57, 660–62, 665–77, 681–83, 686–87, 690–704; Ian K. Steele, *Setting All the Captives Free: Capture, Adjustment, and Recollection in Allegheny Country* (Montreal: McGill-Queens University Press, 2013), ch. 10.

38. *Writings of Washington* 2:396–97; *PGW, Col.* 7:205–7.

39. Bruce A. Ragsdale, "George Washington, the British Tobacco Trade, and Economic Opportunity in Pre-Revolutionary Virginia," in *George Washington Reconsidered*, ed. Don Higginbotham (Charlottesville: University Press of Virginia, 2001), 67–93; T. H. Breen, *Tobacco Culture: The Mentality of the Great Tidewater Planters on the Eve of Revolution* (Princeton, NJ: Princeton University Press, 1985), 81–82, 148–50; Lorena S. Walsh, *Motives of Honor, Pleasure, and Profit: Plantation Management in the Colonial Chesapeake, 1607–1763* (Chapel Hill: University of North Carolina Press, 2010), 440 (Washington no Custis); *Writings of Washington* 2:392–96, 398, 404–6, 414–21; *PGW, Col.* 7:191–97, 201–2.

40. Anderson, *Crucible of War*, 593–94.

41. Anderson, *Crucible of War*, 592–94; *PGW, Col.* 7:219–25 (articles of association).

42. *PGW, Col.* 7:242–50 (petition to king and letter of justification).

43. Mississippi Company to Thomas Cumming, March 1, 1767, quoted in Rick Willard Sturdevant, "Quest for Eden: George Washington's Frontier Land Interests" (PhD diss., University of California, Santa Barbara, 1982), 27.

44. Thomas Perkins Abernethy, *Western Lands and the American Revolution* (New York: Russell & Russell, 1959), 47; Ferling, *Ascent of George Washington*, 61–62; Bernhard Knollenberg, *George Washington: The Virginia Period, 1732–1775* (Durham, NC: Duke University Press, 1964), 90–91.

45. *PGW, Col.* 7:269–75; Charles Royster, *The Fabulous Story of the Dismal Swamp Company* (New York: Vintage, 2004); Ellis, *His Excellency*, 54.

46. CO 5/1330:160–61; James Thomas Flexner, *George Washington: The Forge of Experience, 1732–1775* (Boston: Little, Brown, 1965), 293.

47. Colin G. Calloway, *The Scratch of a Pen: 1763 and the Transformation of North America* (New York: Oxford University Press, 2006); Michael A. McDonnell, *Masters of Empire: Great Lakes Indians and the Making of America* (New York: Hill & Wang, 2015), 230–39.

48. Douglas Edward Leach, *Roots of Conflict: British Armed Forces and Colonial Americans, 1677–1763* (Chapel Hill: University of North Carolina Press, 1986), chs. 5–6; Walter S. Dunn Jr., *The New Imperial Economy: The British Army and the American Frontier, 1764–1768* (Westport, CT: Praeger, 2001); John Shy, *Toward Lexington: The Role of the British Army in the Coming of the American Revolution* (Princeton, NJ: Princeton University Press, 1965), 45–46, 52–83; Peter D. G. Thomas, "The Cost of the British Army in North America, 1763–1775," *William and Mary Quarterly* 45 (1988): 510–16; Woody Holton, "The History of the Stamp Act Shows How Indians Led to the American Revolution," *Humanities* 36, no. 4 (July/Aug. 2015): 16–19.

49. *WJP* 2:879.

50. Secretary of State Lord Egremont, quoted in Abernethy, *Western Lands and the American Revolution*, 20.

51. Anderson, *Crucible of War*, 565.

52. The proclamation is reprinted in Adam Shortt and Arthur G. Doughty, eds., *Documents Relating to the Constitutional History of Canada, 1759–1791*, 2 vols. (Ottawa: Historical Documents Publication Board, 1918), 163–68. Terry Fenge and Jim Aldridge, eds., *Keeping Promises: The Royal Proclamation of 1763, Aboriginal Rights, and Treaties in Canada* (Montreal: McGill-Queens University Press, 2015), examine its enduring importance in Canada.

53. Banner, *How the Indians Lost Their Land*, 92–94, 108.

54. S. Max Edelson, *The New Map of Empire: How Britain Imagined America before Independence* (Cambridge, MA: Harvard University Press, 2017), ch. 4.

55. *EAID* 5:281–306 (Augusta treaty); John Borrows, "Wampum at Niagara: The Royal Proclamation, Canadian Legal History, and Self-Government," in *Aboriginal and Treaty Rights in Canada*, ed. Michael Asch (Vancouver: University of British Columbia Press, 1997), 155–72.

56. Patrick Griffin, *American Leviathan: Empire, Nation, and Revolutionary Frontier* (New York: Hill & Wang, 2007), 60.

57. Reese, *Official Papers of Francis Fauquier*, 3:1355–56, 1368–70, 1378–79, 1394, 1411–12, 1480–81; *Executive Journals* 6:602, 604–5. In May 1765, for example, colonists killed five Cherokees who were traveling with passes from the government; when two of the perpetrators were arrested, a mob broke into the jail and freed them. Fauquier feared "that the people on our Frontiers are rather desirous that we should be at War than in peace with the Indians." Reese, *Official Papers of Francis Fauquier*, 3:1234–42 (quote at 1243), 1248–49, 1253–61, 1265–69.

58. Howard H. Peckham, ed., *George Croghan's Journal of His Trip to Detroit in 1767 with His Correspondence relating Thereto* (Ann Arbor: University of Michigan Press, 1939), 23; Andrea L. Smalley, "'They Steal Our Deer and Land': Contested Hunting Grounds in the Trans-Appalachian West," *Register of the Kentucky Historical Society* 114 (2016): 303–9.

59. Mulkearn, *George Mercer Papers*, 184–85.

60. Banner, *How the Indians Lost Their Land*, 107–9; Woody Holton, *Forced Founders: Indians, Debtors, Slaves, and the Making of the American Revolution in Virginia* (Chapel Hill: University of North Carolina Press, 1999), 29–30; Woody Holton, "The Ohio Indians and the Coming of the American Revolution in Virginia," *Journal of Southern History* 60 (1994): 455.

61. Ragsdale, "Young Washington's Virginia," 55.

62. Craig Yirush, *Settlers, Liberty, and Empire: The Roots of Early American Political Theory, 1675–1775* (Cambridge: Cambridge University Press, 2011); Holton, *Forced Founders*, ch. 1; Abernethy, *Western Lands and the American Revolution*, ch. 2.

63. Breen, *Tobacco Culture*, 80–82, 181; Edward G. Lengel, *First Entrepreneur: How George Washington Built His—and the Nation's—Prosperity* (Boston: Da Capo, 2016), 60–61.

64. Ellis, *His Excellency*, 54–55.

65. Banner, *How the Indians Lost Their Land*, 101.

66. Banner, *How the Indians Lost Their Land*, 106.

67. *WJP* 5:130.

68. *PGW, Col.* 8:3 ("Field before you"), 34–37, 211–15; Charles H. Ambler, *George Washington and the West* (Chapel Hill: University of North Carolina Press, 1936), 136–37. On Posey, see Flexner, *George Washington: The Forge of Experience*, 252–53.

69. *PGW, Col.* 6:135n.

70. Consul W. Butterfield, ed., *The Washington-Crawford Letters: Being the Correspondence between George Washington and William Crawford, from 1767 to 1781, concerning Western Lands* (Cincinnati: Robert Clarke, 1877), vii; Ambler, *George Washington and the West*, 137.

71. *PGW, Col.* 8:26–29; Butterfield, *Washington-Crawford Letters*, 1–5; Ambler, *George Washington and the West*, 137–38; *Writings of Washington* 2:488–70.

72. *PGW, Col.* 8:37–40; Butterfield, *Washington-Crawford Letters*, 5–10.

73. Barnet Schecter, *George Washington's America: A Biography through His Maps* (New York: Walker, 2010), 64.

74. Butterfield, *Washington-Crawford Letters*, 11.

75. *WJP* 12:21, 337–40, 360, 456–58; *NYCD* 8:38–53.

76. *NYCD* 8:40, 47.

77. *EAID* 3:720–45, quotes at 732, 744; *CRP* 9:514–43.

78. *EAID* 5:326–32; *Executive Journals* 6:279, 287, 306.

79. Colin G. Calloway, *Pen and Ink Witchcraft: Treaties and Treaty Making in American Indian History* (New York: Oxford University Press, 2013), ch. 2; William J. Campbell, *Speculators in Empire: Iroquoia and the 1768 Treaty of Fort Stanwix* (Norman: University of Oklahoma Press, 2012).

80. Quoted in Holton, "Ohio Indians and the Coming of the American Revolution," 457.

81. Abernethy, *Western Lands and the American Revolution*, 35–38.

CHAPTER 9: "A GOOD DEAL OF LAND"

1. *PGW, Col.* 8:149–53.

2. Woody Holton, "The Ohio Indians and the Coming of the American Revolution in Virginia," *Journal of Southern History* 60 (1994): 458; Woody Holton, *Forced Founders: Indians, Debtors, Slaves, and the Making of the American Revolution in Virginia* (Chapel Hill: University of North Carolina Press, 1999), 3.

3. Thomas P. Slaughter, *Independence: The Tangled Roots of the American Revolution* (New York: Hill & Wang, 2014).

4. *DAR* 1:159, 315, 2:21–25, 28, 87, 105, 166, 169, 203–4, 253–54, 261–62, 3:43, 85, 5:135, 12:189; *WJP* 7:184, 404–8; CO 5/71:41.

5. *PGW, Col.* 8:272–80; *DAR* 2:201–3, 209; *Executive Journals* 6:337–38; John Ferling, *The Ascent of George Washington: The Hidden Political Genius of an American Icon* (New York: Bloomsbury, 2009), 63–64 ("hints"); Bernhard Knollenberg, *George Washington: The Virginia Period, 1732–1775* (Durham, NC: Duke University Press, 1964), 91–93; Thomas Perkins Abernethy, *Western Lands and the American Revolution* (New York: Russell & Russell, 1959), 70; *Writings of Washington* 2:528–32.

6. *Executive Journals* 6:311–12; Craig Thompson Friend, *Kentucke's Frontiers* (Bloomington: Indiana University Press, 2010), 39–40.

7. *EAID* 5:336–40, 346–49, 352–53; *JHBV, 1766–69*, xxvi–xxxvii, 264–65, 300–301, 335–36; Holton, *Forced Founders*, 4.

8. *DAR* 1:34; 2:28; "(adventurers")", 95 (killing deer); *JHBV, 1770–72*, xi–xiii; *Executive Journals* 6:354–57.

9. *DAR* 2:210–15, 237–38, 261–62 (land speculators: "self-interested men"); *EAID* 5:360–75; *JHBV, 1770–72*, xv–xvi; *Executive Journals* 6:360, 364–65.

10. *DAR* 5:51–53; *PTJ* 2:78–80.

11. *DAR* 6:234.

12. *PGW, Col.* 8:241.

13. CO 5/90:5 ("black clouds"), 78 ("exterminated"); also in *DAR* 3:254–55, 5:203.

14. John R. Van Atta, *Securing the West: Politics, Public Lands, and the Fate of the Old Republic, 1785–1850* (Baltimore, MD: Johns Hopkins University Press, 2014), 22–23. The population would soar to 220,000 by 1800.

15. Abernethy, *Western Lands and the American Revolution*, ch. 3 ("bought off" at 48); Jack M. Sosin, *Whitehall and the Wilderness: The Middle West in British Colonial Policy, 1760–1775* (Lincoln: University of Nebraska Press, 1961), ch. 8; Clarence W. Alvord, *The Mississippi Valley in British Politics*, 2 vols. (Cleveland: Arthur H. Clark, 1917), 2: chs. 4–6; James Donald Anderson, "Vandalia: The First West Virginia?" *West Virginia History* 40 (1979): 375–92.

16. Charles H. Ambler, *George Washington and the West* (Chapel Hill: University of North Carolina Press, 1936), 140.

17. *PGW, Col.* 8:300–303; Holton, *Forced Founders*, 11; Ron Chernow, *Washington: A Life* (New York: Penguin, 2010), 149; Ferling, *Ascent of George Washington*, 66; John E. Ferling, *The First of Men: A Life of George Washington* (New York: Oxford University Press, 2010), 72–73 ("for a pittance").

18. Washington's journal of the trip is in *Diaries of GW* 2:277–328; Hugh Cleland, *George Washington in the Ohio Valley* (Pittsburgh, PA: University of Pittsburgh Press, 1955), 240–69. Roy Bird Cook, *Washington's Western Lands* (Strasburg, VA: Shenandoah Publishing House, 1930), ch. 2, follows the movements of the travelers.

19. Franklin B. Dexter, ed., *Diary of David McClure, 1748–1820* (New York: Knickerbocker Press, 1899), 108; *The Journal of Nicholas Cresswell, 1774–1777* (New York: Dial Press, 1924), 100.

20. *Journal of Nicholas Cresswell*, 165.

21. *PGW, Col.* 8:402–4, 449–50, 513–14, 530; Consul W. Butterfield, ed., *The Washington-Crawford Letters: Being the Correspondence between George Washington and William Crawford, from 1767 to 1781, concerning Western Lands* (Cincinnati: Robert Clarke, 1877), 18–26; *Diaries of GW* 2:281–82n; Abernethy, *Western Lands and the American Revolution*, 69; Charles A. Hanna, *The Wilderness Trail*, 2 vols. (New York: G. P. Putnam's Sons, 1911), 2:66–68.

22. *Diaries of GW* 2:292–93; Cleland, *George Washington in the Ohio Valley*, 246.

23. *Diaries of GW* 2:293.

24. Abernethy, *Western Lands and the American Revolution*, 70.

25. *Diaries of GW* 2:294.

26. *Diaries of GW* 2:296–98.

27. Cleland, *George Washington in the Ohio Valley*, 243.

28. *Diaries of GW* 2:304, 310; Cleland, *George Washington in the Ohio Valley*, 258–59, 263; C. Hale Sipe, *The Indian Chiefs of Pennsylvania* (1927; Lewisburg, PA: Wennawoods Publishing, 1994), 371; Dexter, *Diary of David McClure*, 42.

29. George Washington Parke Custis, *Recollections and Private Memoirs of Washington*, ed. Benson J. Lossing (New York: Derby & Jackson, 1860), 301–5.

30. *Diaries of GW* 2:315.

31. Roger G. Kennedy, *Hidden Cities: The Discovery and Loss of Ancient North American Civilization* (New York: Penguin, 1994), 98–99, 102; *Diaries of GW* 2:310–14.

32. John G. Fitzpatrick, *George Washington, Colonial Traveler, 1732–1775* (Indianapolis: Bobbs-Merrill, 1927), 281 (Mingo Town delay); *Diaries of GW* 2:316; Cleland, *George Washington in the Ohio Valley*, 264–65.

33. Cameron B. Strang, "Michael Cresap and the Promulgation of Settler Land-Claiming Methods in the Backcountry, 1765–1774," *Virginia Magazine of History and Biography* 118 (2010): 106–35; Honor Sachs, *Home Rule: Households, Manhood, and National Expansion on the Eighteenth-Century Kentucky Frontier* (New Haven, CT: Yale University Press, 2015), 27–32.

34. *Diaries of GW* 2:316; Cleland, *George Washington in the Ohio Valley*, 265.

35. "A Narrative of the Transactions, Imprisonment, and Sufferings of John Connolly, an American Loyalist and Lieut.-Col. in His Majesty's Service," *Pennsylvania Magazine of History and Biography* 12 (1888): 311; *Diaries of GW* 2:322; Cleland, *George Washington in the Ohio Valley*, 267–68.

36. *Diaries of GW* 2:328.

37. Butterfield, *Washington-Crawford Letters*, 16.
38. *PGW, Col.* 8:396.
39. *PGW, Col.* 8:550–55 ("trifle" at 555).
40. *PGW, Col.* 8:428, 439–40. A roll of the officers in the Virginia Regiment of 1754 is at 451.
41. *Diaries of GW* 3:61n, 67–68n; *PGW, Col.* 8:534–41, 9:143–48; Ferling, *Ascent of George Washington*, 64–65; Knollenberg, *George Washington: The Virginia Period*, 94–97.
42. Chernow, *Washington*, 148.
43. James Corbett David, *Dunmore's New World* (Charlottesville: University of Virginia Press, 2013) offers a balanced depiction of Dunmore, whose historical reputation was tarnished by the writings of enemies and revolutionaries, especially after his 1775 proclamation promising freedom to the slaves of Virginia rebels.
44. Charles Royster, *The Fabulous History of the Dismal Swamp Company: A Story of George Washington's Times* (New York: Vintage, 1999), 213; Daniel P. Barr, *A Colony Sprung from Hell: Pittsburgh and the Struggle for Authority on the Western Pennsylvania Frontier, 1744–1794* (Kent, OH: Kent State University Press, 2014), 145–51; David, *Dunmore's New World*, ch. 3.
45. *PGW, Col.* 8:555.
46. Barr, *Colony Sprung from Hell*, 146.
47. *Executive Journals* 6:438–40, 513–14, 516; Rick Willard Sturdevant, "Quest for Eden: George Washington's Frontier Land Interests" (PhD diss., University of California, Santa Barbara, 1982), 39.
48. *PGW, Col.* 9:55–56.
49. Nick Bunker, *An Empire on the Edge: How Britain Came to Fight America* (New York: Knopf, 2014), 80–84, 192; Bruce A. Ragsdale, *A Planters' Republic: The Search for Economic Independence in Revolutionary Virginia* (Madison, WI: Madison House, 1990).
50. Alan Taylor, *American Revolutions: A Continental History, 1750–1804* (New York: Norton, 2016), 118–19.
51. Strang, "Michael Cresap and the Promulgation of Settler Land-Claiming Methods," 121; Barr, *Colony Sprung from Hell*, 142–44; Barbara Rasmussen, "Anarchy and Enterprise on the Imperial Frontier: Washington, Dunmore, Logan, and Land in the Eighteenth-Century Ohio Valley," *Ohio Valley History* 6 (Winter 2006): 1–26; Patrick Griffin, *American Leviathan: Empire, Nation, and Revolutionary Frontier* (New York: Hill & Wang, 2007), ch. 4.
52. *PGW, Col.* 9:118–21 ("cream of the Land" at 120); *Executive Journals* 6:510, 513–14; Knollenberg, *George Washington: The Virginia Period*, 95; Royster, *Fabulous History of the Dismal Swamp Company*, 192.
53. Royster, *Fabulous History of the Dismal Swamp Company*, 193.
54. W. W. Abbot, "George Washington, the West, and the Union," in *George Washington Reconsidered*, ed. Don Higginbotham (Charlottesville: University Press of Virginia, 2001), 202–3.
55. Ambler, *George Washington and the West*, 152.
56. Ferling, *Ascent of George Washington*, 65–66; *PGW, Col.* 9:380 ("best on the hole River"); Butterfield, *Washington-Crawford Letters*, 34–35; *Writings of Washington* 33:407; Dorothy Twohig, "The Making of George Washington," in *George Washington and the Virginia Backcountry*, ed. Warren R. Hofstra (Madison, WI: Madison House, 1998), 13.
57. Ferling, *Ascent of George Washington*, 65–66; Ferling, *First of Men*, 73; *PGW, Col.* 9:380 ("shagreend"); 460–61 (Muse); Paul R. Misencik, *George Washington and the Half-King Chief Tanacharison: An Alliance That Began the French and Indian War* (Jefferson, NC: McFarland, 2014), 169.
58. Knollenberg, *George Washington: The Virginia Period*, 98–99.
59. Knollenberg, *George Washington: The Virginia Period*, 99.
60. Douglas Southall Freeman, *Washington*, 1-vol. abridgement by Richard Harwell of the 7-vol. *George Washington* (New York: Simon & Schuster, 1992), 195.
61. Ambler, *George Washington and the West*, 150.
62. *PGW, Col.* 9:199, 204–7. This was the father of Captain James Wood, who served as commissioner at the Fort Pitt conference in 1775.

63. *PGW, Col.* 9:217–18, 322–23 ("facilitating Schemes"); Butterfield, *Washington-Crawford Letters,* 27–28.
64. Cook, *Washington's Western Lands,* 39.
65. *PGW, Col.* 9:328–32; Butterfield, *Washington-Crawford Letters,* 29–33.
66. *PGW, Col.* 9:248–49.
67. *Diaries of GW* 3:152; Stuart Banner, *How the Indians Lost Their Land: Law and Power on the Frontier* (Cambridge, MA: Harvard University Press, 2005), 102–3.
68. Sturdevant, "Quest for Eden," ch. 3, quote at 52.
69. *PGW, Col.* 9:278–79.
70. *PGW, Col.* 9:490 ("Malice, absurdity, & error"), 500–501 ("malignant disposition"); Holton, *Forced Founders,* 32.
71. Joseph Ellis, *His Excellency: George Washington* (New York: Vintage, 2005), 58.
72. Rasmussen, "Anarchy and Enterprise on the Imperial Frontier."
73. Reuben G. Thwaites and Louise Phelps Kellogg, eds., *Documentary History of Dunmore's War, 1774* (Madison: Wisconsin Historical Society, 1905), 371; *DAR* 8:253.
74. *WJP* 8:615–16 ("vast Influence"), 679, 1012, 1016, 1032, 1086; *NYCD* 8:315, 495.
75. *WJP* 12:1044–61, quotes at 1045, 1052–53.
76. *WJP* 12:1095–98; Thwaites and Kellogg, *Documentary History of Dunmore's War,* 9–19, 246; Strang, "Michael Cresap and the Promulgation of Settler Land-Claiming Methods," 125–26; Griffin, *American Leviathan,* 108–10. Reports that Cresap's men killed forty Indians appear to have been much exaggerated. On Cresap's subsequent career and reputation, see Robert G. Parkinson, "From Indian Killer to Worthy Citizen: The Revolutionary Transformation of Michael Cresap," *William and Mary Quarterly* 63 (2006): 97–122.
77. Butterfield, *Washington-Crawford Letters,* 48–51; *PGW, Col.* 10:54 ("at my house" and "Avackquated"), 93 ("unavoidable.")
78. *Pennsylvania Archives,* ser. 1, 4:569–70.
79. *WJP* 12:1098.
80. *WJP* 12:1099.
81. *WJP* 12:1060; *DAR* 8:134, 208; *Diaries of GW* 3:286n.
82. Thwaites and Kellogg, *Documentary History of Dunmore's War,* 66–67 ("scheming party"); *DAR* 8:15. In the turmoil of the Ohio Valley, writes Barbara Rasmusson, "Cresap answered to John Connolly, who answered to Dunmore, who increasingly answered to no one." Instead of a renegade act committed by rash individuals, Ramusson builds the case that the assault was "conceived by Dunmore, planned by Connolly, and led by Daniel and Nathaniel Greathouse, militia soldiers under Cresap's command." Rasmusson, "Anarchy and Enterprise," quotes at 1–2; Strang, "Michael Cresap and the Promulgation of Settler Land-Claiming Methods," 125–29; Griffin, *American Leviathan,* 104–13; Holton, *Ohio Indians,* 473; Barnet Schecter, *George Washington's America: A Biography through His Maps* (New York: Walker, 2010), 67. David, *Dunmore's New World,* 76–93, offers a more generous interpretation and argues that conjuring up a war was beyond the governor's capability. Using more Virginian sources, Glenn F. Williams, *Dunmore's War: The Last Conflict of America's Colonial Era* (Yardley, PA: Westholme, 2017) counters accounts based on Pennsylvanian sources and portrays Virginian soldiers as fighting "a defensive war against unprovoked Shawnee and Mingo attacks on the south bank of the Ohio." Dunmore resorted to offensive operations only when that seemed the most effective way to end the war and secure the frontier (xiv). It would not be the last time in American history that a governor fomented an Indian war for economic reasons; see *Report of the John Evans Study Committee,* Northwestern University, May 2014, http://www.northwestern.edu/provost/committees/equity -and-inclusion/study-committee-report.pdf (accessed Aug. 15, 2017).
83. *PGW, Col.* 10:72–73, 87.
84. Thwaites and Kellogg, *Documentary History of Dunmore's War,* 91–93.
85. Strang, "Michael Cresap and the Promulgation of Settler Land-Claiming Methods," 123–24.
86. *PGW, Col.* 10:12–16, 50–53.
87. *PGW, Col.* 10:169; Butterfield, *Washington-Crawford Letters,* 85–99.

88. Thwaites and Kellogg, *Documentary History of Dunmore's War*, 33–35.

89. *PGW, Col.* 10:96–97.

90. Butterfield, *Washington-Crawford Letters*, 52–53. Dunmore's account of the war is in *DAR* 8:257–62.

91. Hermann Wellenreuther and Carola Wessel, eds., *The Moravian Mission Diaries of David Zeisberger, 1772–1781* (University Park: Pennsylvania State University Press, 2005), 232.

92. *DAR* 8:261–62; Wellenreuther and Wessel, *Moravian Mission Diaries of David Zeisberger*, 233n527; Charles A. Stuart, ed., *Memoir of Indian Wars, and Other Occurrences, by the Late Colonel Stuart, of Greenbrier* (New York: New York Times and Arno Press rpt., 1971), 46–48; Thwaites and Kellogg, *Documentary History of Dunmore's War*, 253–96.

93. *PGW, Col.* 10:181–83; Butterfield, *Washington-Crawford Letters*, 54–57; Thwaites and Kellogg, *Documentary History of Dunmore's War*, 303–4 ("chiefly Women & Children"); Ambler, *George Washington and the West*, 156.

94. *PGW, Col.* 10:241.

95. François Furstenberg, "The Significance of the Trans-Appalachian Frontier in Atlantic History," *American Historical Review* 113 (2008): 654; Holton, *Forced Founders*, 33.

96. Knollenberg, *George Washington: The Virginia Period*, 96–98; *PGW, Col.* 10:320; Chernow, *Washington*, 176.

97. *PGW, Rev.* 2:553.

98. Ambler, *George Washington and the West*, 149–50; Schecter, *George Washington's America*, 65–66 (map). A detailed summary listing of Washington tracts—locations, acreage, when and how acquired—is provided in *PGW, Confed.* 1:93–95n.

99. Holton, *Forced Founders*, 28 ("rejected land petitions"), 37.

100. Abernethy, *Western Lands and the American Revolution*, 218; Knollenberg, *George Washington: The Virginia Period*, 97–98 (Dinwiddie claims); Friend, *Kentucke's Frontiers*, 114–15, 131; Holton, "Ohio Indians," 477–78; Holton, *Forced Founders*, 38; Sachs, *Home Rule*, 32–40.

101. Abernethy, *Western Lands and the American Revolution*, 368–69.

102. *PGW, Col.* 9:517.

103. Reuben G. Thwaites and Louise P. Kellogg, eds., *The Revolution on the Upper Ohio, 1775–1777* (Madison: Wisconsin Historical Society, 1908), 129.

104. *DAR* 12:189.

105. The treaty is in *EAID* 18:203–5; depositions regarding the treaty are in *PTJ* 2:68–110 (Dragging Canoe and "bloody ground" at 74, 87, 97, 105–6); *CVSP* 1:282–87 ("bloody Ground" at 283), 290–92, 303–11; *DAR* 9:33–34 ("moderate"); *PGW, Col.* 10:247, 298 ("Virga Gentlemen"), 312 ("neither understand"), 333.

106. *Executive Journals* 6:662–63.

107. *DAR* 9:90.

108. *DAR* 12:198–99; William L. Saunders, ed., *The Colonial Records of North Carolina*, vol. 10 (Raleigh, NC: State Printer, 1890), 764; John Stuart to Lieut. General Clinton, Aug. 29, 1776, University of Michigan, Clements Library, Clinton Mss. 18:11.

CHAPTER 10: THE QUESTION OF INDIAN ALLIES

1. *DAR* 9:105, 142; *American Archives*, ser. 4, 2:714.

2. Caroline Cox, "The Continental Army," and Stephen Conway, "The British Army and the War of Independence," in *The Oxford Handbook of the American Revolution*, ed. Edward G. Gray and Jane Kamensky (New York: Oxford University Press, 2013), chs. 9 and 10 (nothing revolutionary at 163); James Kirby Martin and Mark Edward Lender, *A Respectable Army: The Military Origins of the Republic, 1763–1789*, 2nd ed. (Wheeling, IL: Harlan Davidson, 2006), 43–44; John W. Hall, "An Irregular Reconsideration of George Washington and the American Military Tradition," *Journal of Military History* 78 (2014): 961–93.

3. *PGW, Rev.* 23:723.

4. *PGW, Rev.* 8:302–3n; "Memorial of James Smith," *Pennsylvania Archives*, 2nd ser., 1 (1874): 714; *Scoouwa: James Smith's Indian Captivity Narrative* (1799; Columbus: Ohio Historical Society, 1978), 144–46.

5. *PGW, Rev.* 10:482–83, 636 ("well acquainted"), 641–42, 11:12, 38 ("Panic Struck"). Burgoyne reckoned "the rebels are more alarmed at the report of engaging Indians than at any other measure." Quoted in Andrew Jackson O'Shaughnessy, *The Men Who Lost America: British Leadership, the American Revolution, and the Fate of the Empire* (New Haven, CT: Yale University Press, 2013), 138.

6. *PGW, Rev.* 6:249 ("to the risque"), 13:156 (St. Clair).

7. *PGW, Rev.* 20:707; Wayne Lee, *Barbarians and Brothers: Anglo-American Warfare, 1500–1865* (New York: Oxford University Press, 2011), 194.

8. *PGW, Rev.* 1:12–13 (quote), 17, 19.

9. Edward G. Lengel, *General George Washington: A Military Life* (New York: Random House, 2005), 149–50, 168; John Ferling, *The Ascent of George Washington: The Hidden Political Genius of an American Icon* (New York: Bloomsbury, 2009), 148–49.

10. Lengel, *General George Washington*, 87.

11. *PGW, Rev.* 1:37.

12. Schuyler's papers as commissioner of Indian affairs in the Northern Department during the Revolution are in NYPL, Philip Schuyler Papers, reel 7, Indian Papers.

13. Occom to John Thornton, 1776, Dartmouth College, Rauner Library, Ms. 776900.2; Joanna Brooks, ed., *The Collected Writings of Samson Occom, Mohegan* (New York: Oxford University Press, 2006), 113.

14. Colonel George Morgan Letterbooks, 1775–79, 3 vols., Carnegie Library of Pittsburgh, 2:2.

15. Robert G. Parkinson, *The Common Cause: Creating Race and Nation in the American Revolution* (Chapel Hill: University of North Carolina Press, 2016), 101; Paul H. Smith et al., eds. *Letters of Delegates to Congress, 1774–1789*, 20 vols. (Washington, DC: Library of Congress, 1976–93), 1:452 (Adams quotes).

16. *DAR* 10:182, 11:15–17, 12:15, 70–71.

17. Colin G. Calloway, *The American Revolution in Indian Country* (Cambridge: Cambridge University Press, 1995), 28, 34; Barry O'Connell, ed., *On Our Own Ground: The Complete Writings of William Apess, a Pequot* (Amherst: University of Massachusetts Press, 1992), 239–40; George Quintal Jr., *Patriots of Color: "A Peculiar Beauty and Merit": African Americans and Native Americans at Battle Road and Bunker Hill* (Boston: Boston National Historical Park, 2002), 30–31; Eric G. Grundset, ed., *Forgotten Patriots: African American and American Indian Patriots of the Revolutionary War* (Washington, DC: National Society Daughters of the American Revolution, 2008).

18. Calloway, *American Revolution in Indian Country*, 92, 94; *PCC*, reel 144, item 134, 43; *NYCD* 8:626.

19. [Joseph Merriam], "Diary of an (unknown) soldier at Cambridge, 1775," Boston Public Library, Ms. Ch. B. 12.72.

20. *DAR* 11:105.

21. Simon Schama, *Rough Crossings: Britain, the Slaves, and the American Revolution* (New York: HarperCollins, 2006), 7.

22. Alan Taylor, *American Revolutions: A Continental History, 1750–1804* (New York: Norton, 2016), 231.

23. *JCC* 3:401.

24. *JCC* 4:410–12, 415; *PGW, Rev.* 4:456, 516.

25. *PGW, Rev.* 5:59–60n; *JCC* 5:452 (rewards).

26. *PGW, Rev.* 4:538n8.

27. *JCC* 5:473; *PGW, Rev.* 5:102–3, 125; *PCC*, reel 23, item 12A, 1:194, 196.

28. *PGW, Rev.* 5:519; *PCC*, reel 166, item 152, 2:316.

29. *PGW, Rev.* 5:548; *PCC*, reel 23, item 12A, 2:14; *JCC* 5:627–28.

30. *PGW, Rev.* 5:595–95, 613, 625–26; *PCC*, reel 166, item 152, 2:363.

31. *PGW, Rev.* 6:41, 129, 157, 187.

32. *PCC*, reel 166, item 152, 2:363.

33. *PGW, Rev.* 7:381–83.

34. *American Archives*, ser. 4, 3:490.

35. Calloway, *American Revolution in Indian Country*, 96; *JCC* 9:840.

36. *PGW, Rev.* 16:448; Joseph P. Tustin, ed., *Diary of the American War: A Hessian Journal: Captain Johann Ewald, Field Jäger Corps* (New Haven, CT: Yale University Press, 1979), 144–45; J. G. Simcoe, *Simcoe's Military Journal: A History of the Operations of a Partisan Corps, Called the Queen's Rangers* (New York: Bartlett & Welford, 1844), 81, 85–86; Patrick Frazier, *The Mohicans of Stockbridge* (Lincoln: University of Nebraska Press, 1992), 221–25. A list of the Stockbridge men killed in battle during the Revolution is in Pickering Papers 62:167.

37. *Writings of Washington* 20:44–45; *PCC*, reel 170, item 152, 9:165–66.

38. Frazier, *Mohicans of Stockbridge*, 227–29; *PCC*, reel 170, item 152, 9:165–66; *PGW, Rev.* 21:184, 345–47; *Writings of Washington* 23:75, 80.

39. *PCC*, reel 50, item 41, 4:422; Pickering Papers 62:167, 167A.

40. *Writings of Washington* 27:53.

41. *JCC* 29:688–89.

42. *PGW, Rev.* 3:202–3.

43. *PGW, Rev.* 1:367–69, 2:554, 600 ("incontrovertable").

44. *PGW, Rev.* 2:27–28.

45. Calloway, *American Revolution in Indian Country*, ch. 2; Colin G. Calloway, *The Western Abenakis of Vermont, 1600–1800* (Norman: University of Oklahoma Press, 1990), ch. 11.

46. *PGW, Rev.* 1:306, 331–32; Calloway, *American Revolution in Indian Country*, 69–70; *Writings of Washington* 3:423–24, 437.

47. *PGW, Rev.* 1:229 ("totally averse" and "cherish these dispositions"); David L. Preston, *Braddock's Defeat: The Battle of the Monongahela and the Road to Revolution* (New York: Oxford University Press, 2015), 324.

48. L. H. Butterfield, ed., *Diary and Autobiography of John Adams*, 4 vols. (Cambridge, MA: Harvard University Press, 1961), 2:227.

49. *PGW, Rev.* 3:34, 112–13, 180–81, 202 ("first Man"), 218; *American Archives*, ser. 4, 4:580–82, 840–41.

50. *PGW, Rev.* 3:202–3, 223 (Indian speech), 234, 239–40 (to Schuyler); *American Archives*, ser. 4, 4:872–73, 908–9.

51. *PGW, Rev.* 3:313; *American Archives*, ser. 4, 4:1146.

52. *PGW, Rev.* 4:388.

53. Pickering Papers 33:239; GW to Schuyler, July 23, 1779 ("our friend"), GWPLC; Maryly B. Penrose, ed., *Indian Affairs Papers: American Revolution* (Franklin Park, NJ: Liberty Bell Associates, 1981), 192, 223–24, 349; *DHFFC* 7:378–80 (secretary of war's report on commissioning of Cook and other Oneidas and Tuscaroras). At Valley Forge: Anthony Gerring, "Col. Louis Cook: Operatic Abenaki, US Patriot, Devoted Catholic," *National Catholic Register*, June 18, 2017 (thanks to Rich Holschuh for this); Darren Bonaparte, "Colonel Louis at Oriskany and Valley Forge," http://www.wampumchronicles.com /oriskanyandvalleyforge.html

54. Durand Echeverria, "The Iroquois Visit Rochambeau at Newport in 1780: Excerpts from the Unpublished Journal of the Comte de Charlus," *Rhode Island History* 11 (1952): 73–81, quote at 77.

55. Elizabeth Cometti, trans. and ed., *Seeing America and Its Great Men: The Journal and Letters of Count Francesco dal Verme, 1783–1784* (Charlottesville: University of Virginia Press, 1969), 13, 107n32.

56. *PGW, Rev.* 4:87, 90, 147; *American Archives*, ser. 4, 5:989.

57. *PGW, Rev.* 2:176.

58. Colin G. Calloway, *The Indian History of an American Institution: Native Americans and Dartmouth* (Hanover, NH: University Press of New England, 2010), 38–42; *JCC* 2:176–77; Resolutions of the U.S. Continental Congress, Sept. 19, 1776, Dartmouth College, Rauner Library, Ms. 776519; Wheelock to Commissioners of Indian Affairs, Oct. 13, 1777, and May 27, 1778, Ms. 77563.1 and 778327; Wheelock to Congress, Nov. 1, 1778 and Apr. 2, 1779, Ms. 778601 and 779252.1; GW to Bayley, Mar. 15, 1780, GWPLC.

59. *PGW, Rev.* 4:413.

60. *PGW, Rev.* 18:289, 290, 512–13n.

61. Calloway, *Western Abenakis*, 216; "Muster Roll of Captain John Vincent's Company of Indian Rangers," in Frederic P. Wells, *History of Newbury, Vermont* (St. Johnsbury, VT: Caledonian, 1902), 409.

62. GW to John Wheelock and twice to Bayley, June 9, 1781, GWPLC.

63. Calloway, *American Revolution in Indian Country*, ch. 2, esp. 70–74, 81; Colin G. Calloway, "Sentinels of Revolution: Bedel's New Hampshire Rangers and the Abenaki Indians on the Upper Connecticut," *Historical New Hampshire* 45 (1990): 271–95.

64. Calloway, *American Revolution in Indian Country*, 76–78; Calloway, *Western Abenakis*, 208, 213, 218–19; *PGW, Rev.* 18:45–46 ("willing to join"), 259 (Bayley's recommendation); *PCC*, reel 24, item 14, 327; *PCC*, reel 159, item 147, 4:301; *PCC*, reel 170, item 152, 8:159; *JCC* 16:334–45; GW to Congress, Nov. 10, 1779 ("fidelity"), GWPLC; *Writings of Washington* 17:68–69, 82–83.

65. Haldimand Papers 21772:2–4.

66. Calloway, *Western Abenakis*, 210–11.

67. Neil Goodwin, *We Go as Captives: The Royalton Raid and the Shadow War on the Revolutionary Frontier* (Barre and Montpelier: Vermont Historical Society, 2010).

68. *DAR* 20:179–80, 249–50, 21:58.

69. "The Catholic Indians and the American Revolution," *The American Catholic Historical Researches*, new ser., 4 (1908): 198–201; Richard I. Hunt, "Ambroise St-Aubin," and "Pierre Tomah," *Dictionary of Canadian Biography* 4:693, 735–36.

70. Grundset, *African American and American Indian Patriots of the Revolutionary War*, 14.

71. *PGW, Rev.* 2:186, 201; *American Archives*, ser. 5, 3:802; "Catholic Indians and the American Revolution," 203.

72. *PGW, Rev.* 5:235, 266.

73. *PGW, Rev.* 5:201.

74. *PGW, Rev.* 5:270–71.

75. *American Archives*, 1:838–50, 3:800–807; *PGW., Rev.* 5:510–14n4; *PCC*, reel 166, item 152, 2:379–81; John Ferling, *Independence: The Struggle to Set America Free* (New York: Bloomsbury, 2011), 344 (Declaration read).

76. *PGW, Rev.* 6:483, 7:218–19, 361.

77. *PGW, Rev.* 7:433–34; *American Archives*, ser. 5, 3:1403–4.

78. *DAR* 15:185.

79. Hunt, "Pierre Tomah," 736.

80. British Headquarters (Sir Guy Carleton) Papers, 1747 (1777)–1783, microfilm, 30 reels (Washington, DC: Recordak, 1957), reel 5, no. 1690; reel 8, no. 2838.

81. *JCC* 7:38–39; Calloway, *American Revolution in Indian Country*, 36.

82. *PGW, Rev.* 13:402; Lengel, *General George Washington*, 313.

83. *JCC* 10:203, 220–21; *PGW, Rev.* 13:409n, 14:68, 167–68.

84. *DAR* 12:130–32, 189–208; Calloway, *American Revolution in Indian Country*, ch. 7; Nadia Dean, *A Demand of Blood: The Cherokee War of 1776* (Cherokee, NC: Valley River Press, 2012).

85. *PGW, Rev.* 8:57–58n, 249; 13:408n.

86. Calloway, *American Revolution in Indian Country*, 199–200; *EAID* 18:217–20.

87. *EAID* 18:226–55 (Corn Tassel quote at 239), 265–70.

88. Colin G. Calloway, "Declaring Independence and Rebuilding a Nation: Dragging Canoe and the Chickamauga Revolution," in *Revolutionary Founders: Rebels, Radicals, and Reformers in the Making of the Nation*, ed. Alfred F. Young, Gary B. Nash, and Ray Raphael (New York: Knopf, 2011), ch. 11.

89. *EAID* 18:241.

90. *PGW, Rev.* 15:20–21, 129–30.

91. "You were no nation then," the chiefs said, "We took pity on you then, and assisted you." *CVSP* 3:171–72, 398.

92. Parkinson, *Common Cause*, 374–84, 440–41, 474–75; Calloway, *American Revolution in Indian Country*, 292–301.
93. Lengel, *General George Washington*, 313.

CHAPTER 11: TOWN DESTROYER

1. Peter J. Hatch, *"A Rich Spot of Earth": Thomas Jefferson's Revolutionary Garden at Monticello* (New Haven, CT: Yale University Press, 2012), 83; Benjamin Henry Latrobe, *The Journal of Latrobe: Being the Notes and Sketches of an Architect, Naturalist and Traveler in the United States from 1796 to 1829* (New York: D. Appleton, 1905), 60 ("negroes").
2. A. C. Flick, ed., "New Sources on the Sullivan-Clinton Campaign in 1779: The Indian-Tory Side of the Campaign," *Quarterly Journal of the New York State Historical Association* 10 (July–Oct. 1929): 193.
3. John Ferling, *The Ascent of George Washington: The Hidden Political Genius of an American Icon* (New York: Bloomsbury, 2009), 172–73.
4. Hugh F. Rankin, ed., *Narratives of the American Revolution: As told by a young sailor, a home-sick surgeon, a French volunteer, and a German general's wife* (Chicago: R. R. Donnelley, 1976), 201.
5. Karim M. Tiro, *The People of the Standing Stone: The Oneida Nation from the Revolution through the Era of Removal* (Amherst: University of Massachusetts Press, 2011), 39–40; Joseph T. Glatthaar and James Kirby Martin, *Forgotten Allies: The Oneida Indians and the American Revolution* (New York: Hill & Wang, 2006), 203–8.
6. Joseph J. Ellis, *American Creation: Triumphs and Tragedies at the Founding of the Republic* (New York: Vintage, 2007), 61–77; Edward G. Lengel, *First Entrepreneur: How Washington Built His—and the Nation's—Prosperity* (Boston: Da Capo, 2016), 126–30; *PGW, Rev.* 13:323, 351, 447–48, 592 ("Horrid Intercource"), 683, 14:327, 352–54, 368, 476–77, 486–87, 492.
7. David L. Preston, *The Texture of Contact: European and Indian Settler Communities on the Frontiers of Iroquoia, 1667–1783* (Lincoln: University of Nebraska Press, 2009).
8. *PGW, Rev.* 1:367.
9. *PGW, Rev.* 3:349.
10. *PGW, Rev.* 4:193–94.
11. *PGW, Rev.* 4:267–68.
12. Barbara Graymont, *The Iroquois in the American Revolution* (Syracuse, NY: Syracuse University Press, 1972), 92; *PGW, Rev.* 4:388, 475, 5:517, 531; *American Archives*, ser. 4, 6:768–70.
13. *PGW, Rev.* 4:373.
14. *PGW, Rev.* 4:516.
15. *PGW, Rev.* 5:584.
16. *PGW, Rev.* 6:448–49, 531. The word "Cayugas" is rather indistinct in Washington's letter to Philip Schuyler, Oct. 10, 1776, in the *George Washington Papers* at the Library of Congress (GWPLC). Peter Force in *American Archives*, ser. 5, 2:974, identified the visiting Indians as "Caughnuagas," not Cayugas, which makes sense as James Dean, the interpreter who accompanied them, had recently returned from Canada, but Force appears to have based his transcription on that made by Richard Varick. Washington's letter book in GWPLC has "Cayugas," as does Schuyler's letter book in the New York Public Library. The editors of *PGW, Rev.* used the latter for the copytext since it is the closest available to Schuyler's received copy. Benjamin L. Huggins, associate editor, *PGW*, personal communication, July 21, 2016.
17. Colin G. Calloway, *Pen and Ink Witchcraft: Treaties and Treaty Making in American Indian History* (New York: Oxford University Press, 2013), 70–74.
18. David Levinson, "An Explanation for the Oneida-Colonist Alliance in the American Revolution, *Ethnohistory* 23 (1976): 265, 280–81; Tiro, *People of the Standing Stone*, 45–47.
19. Oneida declaration, Correspondence of Samuel Kirkland, Hamilton College, 57b, in *EAID* 18:4; David J. Norton, *Rebellious Younger Brother: Oneida Leadership and Diplomacy, 1750–1800* (DeKalb: Northern Illinois University Press, 2009), 72; Glatthaar and Martin, *Forgotten Allies*, 87–89.

20. Onondaga chief Tenhoghskweaghta at the Johnstown conference, March 10, 1776, NYPL, Schuyler Papers, box 14.

21. Kirkland to Schuyler, Mar. 11, 1776, Hamilton College, Kirkland Papers, 64b.

22. *JCC* 2:187.

23. *PGW, Rev.* 2:70.

24. On Brant and Kirkland, see Alan Taylor, *The Divided Ground: Indians, Settlers, and the Northern Borderland of the American Revolution* (New York: Knopf, 2006); Glatthaar and Martin, *Forgotten Allies*, 78–85.

25. *PGW, Rev.* 14:168.

26. Graymont, *Iroquois in the American Revolution*, 34–40.

27. Tiro, *People of the Standing Stone*, 42–43.

28. Glatthaar and Martin, *Forgotten Allies*, 95–96; *PGW, Rev.* 2:61.

29. Schuyler to GW, May 31, 1776, NYPL, GW reel 1.

30. *PGW, Rev.* 5:26.

31. Mark E. Lender and James Kirby Martin, eds., *Citizen-Soldier: The Revolutionary War Journal of Joseph Bloomfield* (Newark: New Jersey Historical Society, 1982), 90–91.

32. *PGW, Rev.* 8:517, 9:10; *Writings of Washington* 7:328–29.

33. Karim M. Tiro, "James Dean in Iroquoia," *New York History* 80 (1999): 391–422; Tiro, *People of the Standing Stone*, 44–45; Colin G. Calloway, *The Indian History of an American Institution: Native Americans and Dartmouth* (Hanover, NH: University Press of New England, 2010), 39–40; Wheelock to Trumbull, March 27, 1775, Papers of Eleazar Wheelock, Dartmouth College, Rauner Library, Ms. 775222.2; Wheelock to Trumbull, March 16, 1775, Ms. 775216.2; Wheelock to Macluer, March 20, 1775, Ms. 775220.1.

34. *PGW, Rev.* 3:193; Laura J. Murray, ed., *To Do Good to My Indian Brethren: The Writings of Joseph Johnson, 1751–1776* (Amherst: University of Massachusetts Press, 1998), 280–82.

35. From Daniel Claus, June 27, 1778, Society for the Propagation of the Gospel Archives, London, C. Mss., C/CAN/PRE, 14.

36. *PCC*, item 153, 3:43–75; item 170, 2:88–112.

37. *PGW, Rev.* 10:625; *DAR* 14:248–51; Tiro, *People of the Standing Stone*, 48–49; Colin G. Calloway, *The American Revolution in Indian Country* (Cambridge: Cambridge University Press, 1995), 13–14; Graymont, *Iroquois in the American Revolution*, ch. 6.

38. Glatthaar and Martin, *Forgotten Allies*, 194–96; *PGW, Rev.* 13:402, 14:167–68; GW to Schuyler, Mar. 13, 1778, NYPL, GW, reel 1.

39. *PGW, Rev.* 14:276–77, 15:191; Schuyler to GW, Mar. 22, Apr. 26, 1778, NYPL, GW, reel 1.

40. Glatthaar and Martin, *Forgotten Allies*, 205–16; *PGW, Rev.* 15:129–30, 390.

41. Stanley J. Idzerda, ed., *Lafayette in the Age of the American Revolution: Selected Letters and Papers, 1776–1790*, 5 vols. (Ithaca, NY: Cornell University Press, 1977–83), 2:76.

42. GW to Congress, Dec. 24, 1779, GWPLC.

43. *PGW, Rev.* 15:224–25; *Writings of Washington* 11:457; Lengel, *First Entrepreneur*, 145.

44. *DAR* 15:18–19, 36, 199, 261–63.

45. *Writings of Washington* 12:496.

46. *PGW, Rev.* 14:679.

47. Barbara Alice Mann, *George Washington's War on Native America* (Lincoln: University of Nebraska Press, 2008), 27–28.

48. *JCC* 13:251–52.

49. *JCC* 11:588–90, 720–21; *PGW, Rev.* 16:132, 182–83, 226–29; Flick, "New Sources on the Sullivan-Clinton Campaign," 210–11.

50. *PGW, Rev.* 15:359–61, 483–85n (McHenry quote), 490–91.

51. *PGW, Rev.* 16:145, 197, 275.

52. Calloway, *American Revolution in Indian Country*, ch. 4 (Butler and veteran at 124); *PGW, Rev.* 17:386, 461–62, 523 ("places of Rendezvous"), 18:37 (Brant's HQ); *Writings of Washington* 13:97–98, 111, 131; James Austin Holden et al., eds., *Public Papers of George Clinton, First Governor of New York, 1777–1795, 1801–1804*, 10 vols. (New York and Albany: State Printers, 1889–1914), 4:163–64, 222–28; *PCC*, reel 179, item 162, 213.

53. *PGW, Rev.* 17:388 ("No Man"), 18:614.

54. Ferling, *Ascent of George Washington*, 185–90; *PGW, Rev.* 18:149–51, 169.

55. Max M. Mintz, *Seeds of Empire: The American Revolutionary Conquest of the Iroquois* (New York: New York University Press, 1999), 65.

56. *PGW, Rev.* 21:185; *PTJ* 2:285, 3:5–6.

57. Louise Phelps Kellogg, ed., *Frontier Advance on the Upper Ohio, 1778–1779* (Madison: Wisconsin State Historical Society, 1916), 365.

58. Joseph R. Fischer, *A Well-Executed Failure: The Sullivan Campaign against the Iroquois, July-September 1779* (Columba: University of South Carolina Press, 1997), 173; *PGW, Rev.* 18:48, 350–52, 571, 19:xxix–xxx, 73, 114–17, 127, 176–79, 203–6, 270, 307–10, 329–30, 345–46, 353–54, 502–3, 511–14, 537–39, 555–56, 564–66, 593–94, 610–13, 646–47, 667, 676–92 (map at 685), 729–34, 20:99–100, 137–39, 243, 265–66, 305–6, 589–92, 606–7. GW to Hand, Feb. 7, Mar. 16, 1779; to Schuyler, Feb. 11, 26; to Maxwell, Mar. 25, 1779; Questions Answered…, Mar. 2, 1779, all in GWPLC. Many copies and extracts of correspondence about preparations for the campaign are in *PCC*, roll 183, item 166.

59. *PGW, Rev.* 20:xxviii.

60. *PGW, Rev.* 16:183, 19:612; GW to Knap, Apr. 27, 1779, GWPLC.

61. *PGW, Rev.* 18:571; Richard K. Showman et al., eds., *The Papers of General Nathanael Greene*, 13 vols. (Chapel Hill: University of North Carolina Press for the Rhode Island Historical Society, 1976–2005), 3:145.

62. *PGW, Rev.* 18:627.

63. Tiro, *People of the Standing Stone*, 53; *PGW, Rev.* 19:270.

64. *PGW, Rev.* 19:511–14, 610–13, 729–30; Greene to GW, Mar. 2, 1779, GWPLC.

65. *PGW, Rev.* 19:xxx, 203–6, 20:148.

66. *PGW, Rev.* 21:217.

67. *PGW, Rev.* 19:612, 20:335 ("Coin").

68. Mann, *George Washington's War*, 28; William L. Stone, *Life of Joseph Brant–Thayendanegea*, 2 vols. (New York: Alexander V. Blake, 1838), 1:407.

69. *PGW, Rev.* 20:335; Graymont, *Iroquois in the American Revolution*, 196 (Clinton warning); Mann, *George Washington's War*, 29–33; Calloway, *American Revolution in Indian Country*, 53; Haldimand Papers 21756:94, 21762:238, 21779:109–10; Flick, "New Sources on the Sullivan-Clinton Campaign," 222–23.

70. *PGW, Rev.* 20:349, 373, 403, 407, 429.

71. Schuyler to GW, June 10, 1776, NYPL, GW, reel 1; *PGW, Rev.* 4:504.

72. *PGW, Rev.* 20:307–8, 341, 658; GW to Schuyler, May 5, 28, 1779, GWPLC; GW to Commissioners for Indian Affairs, May 28, 1779, GWPLC.

73. *PGW, Rev.* 19:377–78, 388–89.

74. *PGW, Rev.* 20:90–93; Otis G. Hammond, ed., *Letters and Papers of Major-General John Sullivan*, 3 vols. (Concord: New Hampshire Historical Society, 1939), 3:1–9.

75. Hammond, *Letters and Papers of Major-General John Sullivan* 3:48–53; *PGW, Rev.* 20:717–18; Stephen Brumwell, *George Washington: Gentleman Warrior* (London: Quercus, 2012), 346–47.

76. *PGW, Rev.* 21:350.

77. Frederick Cook, ed., *Journals of the Military Expedition of Major General John Sullivan against the Six Nations of Indians in 1779* (Auburn, NY: Knapp, Peck & Thomson, 1887), 39, 64, 182, 226.

78. *PGW, Rev.* 20:606–7.

79. Fischer, *Well-Executed Failure*, ch. 5; Glenn F. Williams, *Year of the Hangman: George Washington's Campaign against the Iroquois* (Yardley, PA: Westholme, 2005), ch. 11; *PGW, Rev.* 21: xxvii, 150–51, 253, 272, 291, 300, 323–24, 426–28, 726–32, 737, 749, 22:124–29, 196–200, 205; Hammond, *Letters and Papers of Major-General John Sullivan* 3:52–54, 57–78.

80. *DAR* 17:187; Graymont, *Iroquois in the American Revolution*, 204–7; Flick, "New Sources on the Sullivan-Clinton Campaign," 279–80 (incl. Guyasuta).

81. Tiro, *People of the Standing Stone*, 54; Hammond, *Letters and Papers of Major-General John Sullivan* 3:114–15.

82. *PGW, Rev.* 21:184, 345–47.

83. Cook, *Journals*, 7–8 ("scalped immediately" and skinned), 26–27, 71–72, 88, 94–95, 126–28, 155, 172, 231–32, 244 ("Drest them for Leggins"), 279 ("Sm. Skn."); Hammond, *Letters and Papers of Major-General John Sullivan* 3:107–12; Flick, "New Sources on the Sullivan-Clinton Campaign," 282–84, 308–9, 316; *PGW, Rev.* 22:134–36, 301–4, 387, 406, 422, 537; Mintz, *Seeds of Empire*, 128. John Butler's account of the battle is in *DAR* 17:197–99.

84. Cook, *Journals*, 383; Hammond, *Letters and Papers of Major-General John Sullivan* 3:121; Flick, "New Sources on the Sullivan-Clinton Campaign," 311.

85. *PGW, Rev.* 22:528; Flick, "New Sources on the Sullivan-Clinton Campaign," 310.

86. Mann, *George Washington's War*, 88.

87. *PGW, Rev.* 22:529–30; Cook, *Journals*, 9, 12, 33, 45, 49, 57, 73, 89, 96, 100, 158, 164, 173, 176, 186, 233, 271; Hammond, *Letters and Papers of Major-General John Sullivan*, 1257; Mann, *George Washington's War*, 89–93. Susan M. S. Pearsall, "Re-Centering Women in the American Revolution," in *Why You Can't Teach United States History without American Indians*, ed. Susan Sleeper-Smith et al. (Chapel Hill: University of North Carolina Press, 2015), 57–70, discusses this incident as part of a campaign of systematic violence again indigenous women in the Revolutionary War.

88. Cook, *Journals*, 59.

89. Cook, *Journals*, 54.

90. *PGW, Rev.* 22:136.

91. Kurt A. Jordan, "Seneca Iroquois Settlement Pattern, Community Structure, and Housing, 1677–1779," *Northeast Anthropology* 67 (2004): 40–44; Mann, *George Washington's War*, 69.

92. I am grateful to William Kerrigan of Muskingum College, historian of apples in America, for this observation.

93. Cook, *Journals*, 13.

94. *PGW, Rev.* 22:531–33 ("grand Capital" at 531); Cook, *Journals*, 40, 48, 60, 75, 91, 99, 111, 142, 162–63 (piled up), 175, 188 ("beautiful flats"), 206, 235 ("Most Horrid Manner"), 301; Hammond, *Letters and Papers of Major-General John Sullivan* 3:129–32; Glatthaar and Martin, *Forgotten Allies*, 253; Mann, *George Washington's War*, 94–100.

95. Graymont, *Iroquois in the American Revolution*, 218; Glatthaar and Martin, *Forgotten Allies*, 254–55; Hammond, *Letters and Papers of Major-General John Sullivan* 3:117–19, 133–34.

96. *PGW, Rev.* 22:522–23.

97. *PGW, Rev.* 22:533; Cook, *Journals*, 303; Hammond, *Letters and Papers of Major-General John Sullivan* 3:134.

98. Jordan, "Seneca Iroquois Settlement Pattern," 40–41, lists seventeen Seneca settlements destroyed by Sullivan; Mintz, *Seeds of Empire*, 153–54; Hammond, *Letters and Papers of Major-General John Sullivan* 3:147–148, 158, 161–62, 165–67; *PGW, Rev.* 22:772; General Orders, Oct. 21, 1779, GWPLC.

99. William N. Fenton, ed., *Parker on the Iroquois* (Syracuse, NY: Syracuse University Press, 1968), 20; *PGW, Rev.* 22:433–36, 752–53; *Pennsylvania Archives*, 1st ser., 12:155–58, 165; Louise Phelps Kellogg, ed., *Frontier Retreat on the Upper Ohio* (Madison: Wisconsin Historical Society, 1917), 56–66. (In Brodhead's estimate of "30 m. Dollars" "m" stood for *mille*, meaning one thousand.)

100. GW to Gates, Oct. 16, 1779, GWPLC.

101. *PGW, Rev.* 22:669–70; Hammond, *Letters and Papers of Major-General John Sullivan* 3:143–46; Graymont, *Iroquois in the American Revolution*, 219–20. On Tiononderoga earlier in the century, see Preston, *Texture of Contact*, 85–92 (tavern at 289).

102. Mann, *George Washington's War*, 75.

103. June Namias, ed., *A Narrative of the Life of Mrs. Mary Jemison by James E. Seaver* (Norman: University of Oklahoma Press, 1992), 104–5.

104. Flick, "New Sources on the Sullivan-Clinton Campaign," 296; Haldimand Papers 21765:140.

105. Calloway, *American Revolution in Indian Country*, ch. 5.

106. *ASPIA* 1:140.

107. *PGW, Rev.* 23:57.

108. Fischer, *Well-Executed Failure.*

109. Sayengeraghta quoted in Calloway, *American Revolution in Indian Country*, 132–33.

110. Haldimand Papers 21765:141 (revenge); William T. Hutchinson et al., eds., *The Papers of James Madison*, 10 vols. (Chicago: University of Chicago Press, 162–77), 2:37; Cook, *Journals*, 101 ("nests").

111. Mintz, *Seeds of Empire*, 162; Fischer, *Well-Executed Failure*, 192–93; Peter C. Mancall, *Valley of Opportunity: Economic Culture along the Upper Susquehanna, 1700–1800* (Ithaca, NY: Cornell University Press, 1991), 139.

112. Haldimand Papers 21774:121.

113. Holden et al., *Public Papers of George Clinton* 3:458–59, 5:883–84; James Clinton to GW, Jan. 7, 1779, NYPL, GW, reel 1; *PGW, Rev.* 18:549n, 552–53, 602–3, 19:412–13.

114. Oneida chiefs to Van Dyke, June 18, 1780, GWPLC; GW to Van Schaick, June 22, 1780, GWPLC; Haldimand Papers 21764:86–87 (prisoners), 21767:91, 99, 104, 125, 129, 157; *DAR* 18:208.

115. *Writings of Washington* 21:284–85.

116. *JCC* 20:465, 25:491–92.

117. Tiro, *People of the Standing Stone*, 56–57; Glatthaar and Martin, *Forgotten Allies*, 270–80.

118. Elizabeth Cometti, trans. and ed., *Seeing America and Its Great Men: The Journal and Letters of Count Francesco dal Verme, 1783–1784* (Charlottesville: University of Virginia Press, 1969), 16, 18, 109.

119. Pickering Papers, reel 62, 157–74.

120. Flick, "New Sources on the Sullivan-Clinton Campaign," 194.

CHAPTER 12: KILLING CRAWFORD

1. Patrick Griffin, *American Leviathan: Empire, Nation, and Revolutionary Frontier* (New York: Hill & Wang, 2007); Daniel P. Barr, *A Colony Sprung from Hell: Pittsburgh and the Struggle for Authority on the Western Pennsylvania Frontier, 1744–1794* (Kent, OH: Kent State University Press, 2014), 175–93; Honor Sachs, *Home Rule: Households, Manhood, and National Expansion on the Eighteenth-Century Kentucky Frontier* (New Haven, CT: Yale University Press, 2015); Patrick Spero, *Frontier Country: The Politics of War in Early Pennsylvania* (Philadelphia: University of Pennsylvania Press, 2016), ch. 10.

2. Richard White, *The Middle Ground: Indians, Empires, and Republics in the Great Lakes Region, 1650–1815* (Cambridge: Cambridge University Press, 1991), ch. 9.

3. Hugh Cleland, *George Washington in the Ohio Valley* (Pittsburgh: University of Pittsburgh Press, 1955), 273.

4. Sachs, *Home Rule*, 29–30.

5. *JHBV, 1773–76*, 282; Robert L. Scribner, ed., *Revolutionary Virginia: The Road to Independence: A Documentary Record*, 7 vols. (Charlottesville: University Press of Virginia, 1973–83), 3:270; Reuben G. Thwaites and Louise P. Kellogg, eds., *The Revolution on the Upper Ohio, 1775–1777* (Madison: Wisconsin Historical Society, 1908), 34.

6. Barr, *Colony Sprung from Hell*, 194.

7. Scribner, *Revolutionary Virginia* 7:257–73; Thwaites and Kellogg, *Revolution on the Upper Ohio*, 35–42.

8. The conference proceedings are in Thwaites and Kellogg, *Revolution on the Upper Ohio*, 25–127.

9. Guyasuta's assurances are in Thwaites and Kellogg, *Revolution on the Upper Ohio*, 108, and *EAID* 18:107; Scribner, *Revolutionary Virginia* 4:199 (Virginia and Pennsylvania).

10. Thwaites and Kellogg, *Revolution on the Upper Ohio*, 53, 61–62; Scribner, *Revolutionary Virginia* 3:377–78 (determined on war), 389–90, 7:770.

11. Scribner, *Revolutionary Virginia* 4:113, 117–18; Thwaites and Kellogg, *Revolution on the Upper Ohio*, 27–33.

12. Scribner, *Revolutionary Virginia* 4:222.

13. Hermann Wellenreuther, "White Eyes and the Delawares' Vision of an Indian State," *Pennsylvania History* 68 (2001): 139–61; Scribner, *Revolutionary Virginia*, 3:262–65, 4:180, and Thwaites and Kellogg, *Revolution on the Upper Ohio*, 86–87 ("foolish people"); Randolph C. Downes, *Council Fires on the Upper Ohio* (Pittsburgh: University of Pittsburgh Press, 1940), 185, and Wellenreuther, "White Eyes and the Delawares' Vision of an Indian State," 149–50 (petticoat speech).

14. *JCC* 4:208, 266–70; *EAID* 18:114.

15. Wellenreuther, "White Eyes and the Delawares' Vision of an Indian State."

16. Hermann Wellenreuther and Carola Wessel, eds., *The Moravian Mission Diaries of David Zeisberger, 1772–1781* (University Park: Pennsylvania State University Press, 2005), 35–36, 319–21, 608–10.

17. Gregory Schaaf, *Wampum Belts and Peace Trees: George Morgan, Native Americans and Revolutionary Diplomacy* (Golden, CO: Fulcrum Publishing, 1990); Wellenreuther and Wessel, *Moravian Mission Diaries*, 324.

18. Morgan to Commissioners of Indian Affairs, May 16, 1776, "Letter Book of George Morgan, 1776," Pennsylvania Historical Commission, Harrisburg.

19. *American Archives*, ser. 4, 5:816.

20. "Letter Book of George Morgan, 1776," 36–39; *EAID* 18:121–22; Thwaites and Kellogg, *Revolution on the Upper Ohio*, 172; *American Archives*, ser. 5, 1:36–37.

21. *JCC* 5:621.

22. *EAID* 18:134–36.

23. *American Archives*, ser. 5, 2:512.

24. Cornstalk's speech to Congress, Nov. 7, 1776, "Letter Book of George Morgan, 1776"; *EAID* 18:147.

25. Colonel George Morgan Letterbooks, 1775–79, 3 vols., Carnegie Library of Pittsburgh, 1:57; hereafter Morgan Letterbooks.

26. John Mack Faragher, *Daniel Boone: The Life and Legend of an American Pioneer* (New York: Henry Holt, 1992), 131–40; Craig Thompson Friend, *Kentucke's Frontiers* (Bloomington: Indiana University Press, 2010), 72.

27. On Cornstalk's murder, see Charles A. Stuart, ed., *Memoir of Indian Wars and Other Occurrences, by the late Colonel Stuart, of Greenbrier* (New York: New York Times and Arno Press, 1971), 58–62; Draper Mss. 3D164–73, 2YY91–94; Reuben G. Thwaites and Louise P. Kellogg, eds., *Frontier Defense on the Upper Ohio, 1777–1778* (Madison: Wisconsin Historical Society, 1912), 126–27, 149, 157–63, 175–77, 188–89, 205–9, 258–61.

28. Thwaites and Kellogg, *Frontier Defense*, 188–89; *PGW, Rev.* 12:562–63n.

29. *PGW, Rev.* 11:238–39, 12:179–80.

30. *PGW, Rev.* 12:353, 420.

31. *PGW, Rev.* 6:350, 8:314.

32. Roy Bird Cook, *Washington's Western Lands* (Strasburg, VA: Shenandoah Publishing House, 1930), 118.

33. *PGW, Rev.* 8:376.

34. Consul W. Butterfield, ed., *Washington-Irvine Correspondence: The Official Letters Which Passed between Washington and Brig.-Gen. William Irvine and between Irvine and Others concerning Military Affairs in the West from 1781 to 1783* (Madison, WI: David Atwood, 1882), 15–16; Thwaites and Kellogg, *Frontier Defense*, 215–23; Wellenreuther and Wessel, *Moravian Mission Diaries*, 29 (son); Amy C. Schutt, *Peoples of the River Valleys: The Odyssey of the Delaware Indians* (Philadelphia: University of Pennsylvania Press, 2007), 167 (brother); White, *Middle Ground*, 385 (brother); *PGW, Rev.* 14:182.

35. *PGW, Rev.* 15:167; Louise Phelps Kellogg, ed., *Frontier Advance on the Upper Ohio, 1778–1779* (Madison: Wisconsin State Historical Society, 1916), 54 (quote), 60.

36. *PGW, Rev.* 15:204–5, 249; Kellogg, *Frontier Advance*, 59.

37. Butterfield, *Washington-Irvine Correspondence*, 116; Consul W. Butterfield, ed., *The Washington-Crawford Letters: Being the Correspondence between George Washington and William Crawford, from 1767 to 1781, concerning Western Lands* (Cincinnati: Robert Clarke, 1877), ix–x, 64–73.

38. *PGW, Rev.* 15:345, 373.
39. Wellenreuther and Wessel, *Moravian Mission Diaries*, 28–29, 388 (quote).
40. Kellogg, *Frontier Advance*, 117–18; Wellenreuther and Wessel, *Moravian Mission Diaries*, 30 (White Eyes).
41. *PGW, Rev.* 17:388.
42. *EAID* 18:161–69; *IALT*, 3–5; "Account of a Council Meeting," Sept. 12, 1778, and "Articles of Confederation between the United States and the Delaware Nation," Sept. 17, 1778, Morgan Letterbook 3.
43. Wellenreuther, "White Eyes and the Delawares' Vision of an Indian State," 160.
44. Kellogg, *Frontier Advance*, 240.
45. Barr, *Colony Sprung from Hell*, 211.
46. Kellogg, *Frontier Advance*, 178–80; Downes, *Council Fires on the Upper Ohio*, 220.
47. Kellogg, *Frontier Advance*, 20–21; Downes, *Council Fires on the Upper Ohio*, 217.
48. Morgan Letterbook 3:149–51; *EAID* 18:173–74; Kellogg, *Frontier Advance*, 203–4, 217, quoted in Downes, *Council Fires*, 216. Wellenreuther, "White Eyes and the Delawares' Vision of an Indian State" provides evidence from Zeisberger's diary to refute charges that the treaty was a betrayal or forgery.
49. Morgan Letterbook 3:136; *PCC*, reel 180, item 163, 321.
50. Morgan Letterbook 3:162–65; *PCC*, reel 183, item 166, 411–17; *EAID* 18:176–78; *PGW, Rev.* 20:405, 414–17; Kellogg, *Frontier Advance*, 313, 317–21.
51. *PGW, Rev.* 20:495; Kellogg, *Frontier Advance*, 327.
52. Kellogg, *Frontier Advance*, 303.
53. GW to Congress, May 14, 1779 ("at a loss"), GWPLC; *PGW, Rev.* 20:447–49; Kellogg, *Frontier Advance*, 322–24.
54. Ron Chernow, *Washington: A Life* (New York: Penguin, 2010), 360.
55. Martha quoted in James Thomas Flexner, *George Washington in the American Revolution* (Boston: Little, Brown, 1967), 346.
56. *PGW, Rev.* 20:461.
57. *PGW, Rev.* 20:302, 551–52; Kellogg, *Frontier Advance*, 296–98, 332.
58. Kellogg, *Frontier Advance*, 307.
59. Kellogg, *Frontier Advance*, 337–38, 354–56.
60. Kellogg, *Frontier Advance*, 340–42, 351–53; *EAID* 18:179–82.
61. *PGW, Rev.* 22:76; Butterfield, *Washington-Crawford Letters*, 73–75.
62. *PGW, Rev.* 19:7, 199, 497; Kellogg, *Frontier Advance*, 200, 238–39.
63. *PGW, Rev.* 19:451–52, 454n, 478.
64. *PGW, Rev.* 20:344.
65. *PGW, Rev.* 19:565–66.
66. *PGW, Rev.* 20:148, 412–14; Kellogg, *Frontier Advance*, 293–94, 315–17; Louise P. Kellogg, ed., *Frontier Retreat on the Upper Ohio, 1779–1781* (Madison: Wisconsin State Historical Society, 1917), 18.
67. Barr, *Colony Sprung from Hell*, 214.
68. Barr, *Colony Sprung from Hell*, 215; Butterfield, *Washington-Irvine Correspondence*, 41–42.
69. Kellogg, *Frontier Advance*, 279–80, 349.
70. Downes, *Council Fires on the Upper Ohio*, 249; Kellogg, *Frontier Advance*, 262, 371, 388.
71. Kellogg, *Frontier Retreat*, 55–66; *PGW, Rev.* 22:433–36.
72. *Pennsylvania Archives*, 1st ser., 8:167, 176, 283, 369, 393; Kellogg, *Frontier Retreat*, 183.
73. James Alton James, ed., *George Rogers Clark Papers, 1781–1784* (Springfield: Illinois State Historical Society, 1926), 144, 167, 189.
74. Milo M. Quaife, ed., *The Conquest of the Illinois by George Rogers Clark* (Chicago: R. R. Donnelley and Sons, 1920), 166–68.
75. Downes, *Council Fires on the Upper Ohio*, 229.
76. White, *Middle Ground*, 368–78; Griffin, *American Leviathan*, 141–47 (land grab at 142).
77. *DAR* 17:50 (Hamilton); Haldimand Papers 21781:74 (every day).
78. *PTJ* 3:259, 276, 27:693.

79. J. Martin West, ed., *Clark's Shawnee Campaign of 1780: Contemporary Accounts* (Springfield, OH: Clark County Historical Society, 1975).

80. *MPHC* 10:462–65.

81. Kellogg, *Frontier Retreat*, 101, 111–12, 114–15, 123–24; *Writings of Washington* 19:119–20; Butterfield, *Washington-Irvine Correspondence*, 83.

82. Kellogg, *Frontier Advance*, 371; Kellogg, *Frontier Retreat*, 314; *Writings of Washington* 21:82–83.

83. C. A. Weslager, *The Delaware Indians: A History* (New Brunswick, NJ: Rutgers University Press, 1972, 1989), 314; *Writings of Washington* 21:457; Kellogg, *Frontier Retreat*, 342–44, 352–53, 376–81, 399 (£80,000); *Pennsylvania Archives*, 1st ser., 9:161–62 (no casualties). Barbara Alice Mann, *George Washington's War on Native America* (Lincoln: University of Nebraska Press, 2008), 140–41, says the twenty prisoners were killed; C. Hale Sipe, *The Indian Wars of Pennsylvania* (Harrisburg, PA: Telegraph Press, 1929), 629, questions the evidence that the killings were carried out in cold blood.

84. Paul A. W. Wallace, ed., *Thirty Thousand Miles with John Heckewelder; or, Travels among the Indians of Pennsylvania, New York & Ohio in the 18th Century* (Lewisburg, PA: Wennawoods Publishing, 1998), 189–200; *Pennsylvania Archives*, 1st ser., 9:524–25; *PCC*, reel 73, item 59, 3:49–51: *CVSP* 3:122–24.

85. Butterfield, *Washington-Irvine Correspondence*, 99–109 (to Washington), 343–45 (to his wife).

86. *Writings of Washington* 24:273, 279.

87. Quoted in Peter Silver, *Our Savage Neighbors: How Indian War Transformed Early America* (New York: Norton, 2008), 276.

88. Haldimand Papers 21762:13–14.

89. John P. Bowes, *Land Too Good for Indians: Northern Indian Removal* (Norman: University of Oklahoma Press, 2016), ch. 3, quote at 84.

90. Haldimand Papers 21756:94, 21779:109–10.

91. Butterfield, *Washington-Irvine Correspondence*, 118n.

92. Wallace, *Thirty Thousand Miles with John Heckewelder*, 199.

93. John Heckewelder, *History, Manners, and Customs of the Indian Nations Who Once Inhabited Pennsylvania and the Neighboring States* (Philadelphia, 1876; rpt. New York: Arno, 1971), 284–89.

94. Quoted in David Andrew Nichols, *Red Gentlemen and White Savages: Indians, Federalists, and the Search for Order on the American Frontier* (Charlottesville: University of Virginia Press, 2008), 13.

95. Haldimand Papers 21762:80; Eugene Bliss, ed., *The Diary of David Zeisberger, a Moravian Missionary among the Indians of Ohio*, 2 vols. (Cincinnati: R. Clarke, 1885), 1:431 (Joseph); Wallace, *Thirty Thousand Miles with John Heckewelder*, 199; Hardin in *CVSP* 3:235.

96. Haldimand Papers 21756:94, 21779:109–10.

97. Butterfield, *Washington-Irvine Correspondence*, 125; *Writings of Washington* 24:417; *PGW, Confed.* 4:36 (Mrs. Crawford's slaves).

98. Butterfield, *Washington-Irvine Correspondence*, 126–27, 249; *CVSP* 3:235. The accounts of Knight and Slover are in Archibald Loudon, *A Selection of Some of the Most Interesting Narratives of Outrages, Committed by the Indians in Their Wars with the White People*, 2 vols. (Carlisle, PA: A. Loudon, 1808), 1:1–40.

99. Washington to Irvine, Aug. 6, 1782, GWPLC; Butterfield, *Washington-Irvine Correspondence*, 131–32; *Writings of Washington* 24:474.

100. Griffin, *American Leviathan*, 169–77.

101. Sipe, *Indian Wars of Pennsylvania*, 665–71; Butterfield, *Washington-Irvine Correspondence*, 176, 251, 381–83.

102. Haldimand Papers 21762:149–50; *DAR* 21:114–15; *CVSP* 3:275–76, 280–83, 333–34; Faragher, *Daniel Boone*, 16–25.

103. "Journal of Daniel Boone," *Ohio Archaeological and Historical Publications* 13 (1904): 276; Draper Mss. 1AA 276–77.

104. William T. Hutchinson et al., eds., *The Papers of James Madison*, 17 vols. (Chicago: University of Chicago Press, and Charlottesville: University of Virginia Press, 1962–91), 5:44, 92 (first quote, Edmund Randolph; the second, Edmund Pendleton).

105. De Peyster to McKee, Aug., 6, 1782, Claus Family Papers, National Archives of Canada, MG 19 F1, 3:147 (reel C-1478); Colonel Arent Schuyler De Peyster, *Miscellanies by an Officer, 1774–1813* (New York: A. E. Chasmer, 1888), ix–xxxv, xxxiv–xxxv; *DAR* 21:116, 155.

106. *Writings of Washington* 25:420 (Irvine), 26:283 (Congress), 305 (Carleton).

107. Silver, *Our Savage Neighbors*; Robert G. Parkinson, *The Common Cause: Creating Race and Nation in the American Revolution* (Chapel Hill: University of North Carolina Press, 2016), 534–43.

108. Haldimand Papers 21779:111–12.

109. Colin G. Calloway, *The American Revolution in Indian Country* (Cambridge: Cambridge University Press, 1995), 293–95; Parkinson, *Common Cause*, 547–51.

110. John Thomas Flexner, *George Washington in the American Revolution* (Boston: Little, Brown, 1967), 423; John E. Ferling, The *First of Men: A Life of George Washington* (New York: Oxford University Press, 2010), 295.

111. François Furstenberg, "The Significance of the Trans-Appalachian Frontier in Atlantic History," *American Historical Review* 113 (2008): 655.

112. Griffin, *American Leviathan*, 175.

113. Cameron B. Strang, "Michael Cresap and the Promulgation of Settler Land-Claiming Methods in the Backcountry, 1765-1774," *Virginia Magazine of History and Biography* 118 (2010): 127–30.

114. John Ferling, *The Ascent of George Washington: The Hidden Political Genius of an American Icon* (New York: Bloomsbury Press, 2009), 185–90, 222.

115. Mann, *George Washington's War on Native America*, 147–48.

116. Haldimand Papers 21763:42–43, 70, 86–87; Mary Beacock Fryer, *Allan Maclean, Jacobite General* (Toronto: Dundurn Press, 1987), 197–98.

117. L. H. Butterfield et al., eds., *Adams Family Correspondence* (Cambridge, MA: Harvard University Press, 1963), 2:23 (quote), 63.

118. Elizabeth A. Fenn, *Pox Americana: The Great Smallpox Epidemic of 1775–82* (New York: Hill & Wang, 2001) ("weapon of Defence" at 90); Colin G. Calloway, *One Vast Winter Count: The Native American West before Lewis and Clark* (Lincoln: University of Nebraska Press, 2003), 415–26.

CHAPTER 13: BUILDING A NATION ON INDIAN LAND

1. James H. Merrell, "Declarations of Independence: Indian-White Relations in the New Nation," in *The American Revolution: Its Character and Limits*, ed. Jack P. Greene (New York: New York University Press, 1987), 197, 201.

2. *Writings of Washington* 27:135; GW to Duane, Sept. 7, 1783, GWPLC.

3. Haldimand Papers 21756:138.

4. Kathleen DuVal, *Independence Lost: Lives on the Edge of the American Revolution* (New York: Random House, 2015), 226, 268, 313 ("imagined futures").

5. François Furstenberg, "The Significance of the Trans-Appalachian Frontier in Atlantic History," *American Historical Review* 113 (2008): 659–65; Bethel Saler, *The Settlers' Empire: Colonialism and State Formation in America's Old Northwest* (Philadelphia: University of Pennsylvania Press, 2015), ch. 1; Andro Linklater, *Measuring America: How the United States Was Shaped by the Greatest Land Sale in History* (New York: Penguin/Plume, 2002), 60; Paul Frymer, *Building an American Empire: The Era of Territorial and Political Expansion* (Princeton, NJ: Princeton University Press, 2017). W. Meinig, *The Shaping of America: A Geographical Perspective on 500 Years of History*, vol. 1, *Atlantic America, 1492–1800* (New Haven, CT: Yale University Press, 1986), 386, describes the idea of a continental republic as "a new experiment on a grand scale."

6. *JCC* 9:919.

7. Dorothy V. Jones, *License for Empire: Colonialism by Treaty in Early America* (Chicago: University of Chicago Press, 1982), 150–51, 155.

8. Joseph Ellis, *The Quartet: Orchestrating the Second American Revolution, 1783–1789* (New York: Knopf, 2015), xiv.

9. Peter Silver, *Our Savage Neighbors: How Indian War Transformed Early America* (New York: Norton, 2008) terms the uniting element in the 1760s an "anti-Indian sublime."

10. Robert G. Parkinson, *The Common Cause: Creating Race and Nation in the American Revolution* (Chapel Hill: University of North Carolina Press, 2016).

11. Eric Hinderaker, *Elusive Empires: Constructing Colonialism in the Ohio Valley, 1673–1800* (Cambridge: Cambridge University Press, 1997), 186, 270.

12. David Andrew Nichols, *Red Gentlemen and White Savages: Indians, Federalists, and the Search for Order on the American Frontier* (Charlottesville: University of Virginia Press, 2008), 10–11.

13. Carroll Smith-Rosenberg, *This Violent Empire: The Birth of an American National Identity* (Chapel Hill: University of North Carolina Press, 2010); Mark Rifkin, *Manifesting America: The Imperial Construction of U.S. National Space* (New York: Oxford University Press, 2009), 8–10, 38; Saler, *Settlers' Empire;* Patrick Wolfe, "Settler Colonialism and the Elimination of the Native," *Journal of Genocide Research* 8 (2006): 387–409; Lisa Ford, *Settler Sovereignty: Jurisdiction and Indigenous People in America and Australia, 1788–1836* (Cambridge, MA: Harvard University Press, 2010).

14. Franklin had long urged agricultural expansion into the vast lands of the interior as the basis for extending empire, first British and then American. Carla J. Mulford, *Benjamin Franklin and the Ends of Empire* (New York: Oxford University Press, 2015), 95–96, 143–44, 174 ("easily prevail'd on to part with Portions of Territory").

15. Gregory Evans Dowd, *A Spirited Resistance: The North American Indian Struggle for Unity, 1745–1815* (Baltimore, MD: Johns Hopkins University Press, 1992).

16. Ezra Stiles, *The United States Elevated to Glory and Honor* (New Haven, CT: Thomas and Samuel Green, 1783), quotes at 8–9, 10, 16, 36–37; Joshua 6:1–27 (quote at verse 21). I am grateful to Catherine Brekus of Harvard Divinity School for pointing me to this depiction of Washington as genocidal Joshua.

17. Mulford, *Benjamin Franklin and the Ends of Empire*, 172–75.

18. *PGW, Confed.* 1:199.

19. John Rhodehamel, *George Washington: The Wonder of the Age* (New Haven, CT: Yale University Pres, 2017), 170 (quote), 189–90; "Circular to the States," June 8, 1783, in *Writings of Washington* 26:483–96; Peter Onuf and Nicholas Onuf, *Federal Union, Modern World: The Law of Nations in an Age of Revolutions, 1776–1814* (Madison, WI: Madison House, 1993), 102, 123–28.

20. Terry Bouton, "The Trials of the Confederation," in *The Oxford Handbook of the American Revolution*, ed. Edward G. Gray and Jane Kamensky (New York: Oxford University Press, 2013), ch. 20; *PGW, Confed.* 4:318–19.

21. *PGW, Confed.* 4:483.

22. Haldimand Papers 21763:168, 179.

23. Cf. Jeffrey Ostler, "'To Extirpate the Indians': An Indigenous Consciousness of Genocide in the Ohio Valley and Lower Great Lakes, 1750s–1810," *William and Mary Quarterly* 72 (2015): 621; Michael Mann, *The Dark Side of Democracy: Explaining Ethnic Cleansing* (Cambridge: Cambridge University Press, 2005), 89–90.

24. David S. Shields, "George Washington: Publicity, Probity, and Power," in *George Washington's South*, ed. Tamara Harvey and Greg O'Brien (Gainesville: University Press of Florida, 2004), 151.

25. Adams quoted in David O. Stewart, *Madison's Gift: Five Partnerships That Built America* (New York: Simon & Schuster, 2015), 75; Jefferson quoted in James Thomas Flexner, *George Washington and the New Nation, 1783–1793* (Boston: Little, Brown, 1969), 86.

26. Rick Willard Sturdevant, "Quest for Eden: George Washington's Frontier Land Interests" (PhD diss., University of California, Santa Barbara, 1982), ch. 5.

27. Edward J. Larson, *The Return of George Washington: Uniting the States, 1783–1789* (New York: HarperCollins, 2014), 33.

28. Louis B. Wright and Marion Tinling, eds., *Quebec to Carolina in 1785–86: Being the Travel Diary and Observations of Robert Hunter, Jr., a Young Merchant of London* (San Marino, CA: Huntington Library, 1943), 193–94.

29. Charles H. Ambler, *George Washington and the West* (Chapel Hill: University of North Carolina Press, 1936), 173; *PGW, Confed.* 1:93n–95n.

30. John Ferling, *The First of Men: A Life of George Washington* (New York: Oxford University Press, 2010), 335.

31. Ferling, *The First of Men*, 398.

32. *PGW, Confed.* 4:213.

33. Larson, *Return of George Washington*; Edward J. Larson, *George Washington, Nationalist* (Charlottesville: University of Virginia Press, 2016); Richard H. Kohn, *Eagle and Sword: The Federalists and the Creation of the Military Establishment in America, 1783–1802* (New York: Free Press, 1975), chs. 3–4.

34. Quoted in Barnet Schecter, *George Washington's America: A Biography through His Maps* (New York: Walker, 2010), 200.

35. Joseph Ellis, *His Excellency: George Washington* (New York: Vintage, 2005), 145; *Writings of Washington* 27:185–90.

36. Philander D. Chase, "A Stake in the West: George Washington as Backcountry Surveyor and Landholder," in *George Washington and the Virginia Backcountry*, ed. Warren R. Hofstra (Madison, WI: Madison House, 1998), 184–85.

37. James Thomas Flexner, *George Washington in the American Revolution* (Boston: Little Brown, 1967), 422–23.

38. Flexner, *George Washington in the American Revolution*, 518; Roy Bird Cook, *Washington's Western Lands* (Strasburg, VA: Shenandoah Publishing House, 1930), 139 (6,000 acres and 1793 sale).

39. Dorothy Twohig, "The Making of George Washington," in Hofstra, *George Washington and the Virginia Backcountry*, 32n41.

40. Kohn, *Eagle and Sword*, 2–6; *Writings of Washington* 26:376; James Kirby Martin and Mark Edward Lender, *A Respectable Army: The Military Origins of the Republic, 1763–1789*, 2nd ed. (Wheeling, IL: Harlan Davidson, 2006), 201–3.

41. *Writings of Washington* 27:17–18.

42. Reginald Horsman, *Expansion and American Indian Policy, 1783–1812* (Norman: University of Oklahoma Press, 1992), 6–7.

43. *Writings of Washington* 27:133–140; GW to Duane, Sept. 7, 1783, GWPLC.

44. Ambler, *Washington and the West*, 172–73; Horsman, *Expansion and American Indian Policy*, 10–12. The committee's report is in *JCC* 25:680–95 and *Pennsylvania Archives*, 1st ser., 10:119–25.

45. Stuart Banner, *How the Indians Lost Their Land: Law and Power on the Frontier* (Cambridge, MA: Harvard University Press, 2005), 118

46. *JCC* 24:503.

47. *JCC* 25:602.

48. *PGW, Confed.* 1:91–92, 95–97, 107–9 ("deranged"), 117 ("handsome"), 123–24, 141, 153–54, 312–314, 2:340.

49. Consul W. Butterfield, ed., *The Washington-Crawford Letters: Being the Correspondence between George Washington and William Crawford, from 1767 to 1781, concerning Western Lands* (Cincinnati: Robert Clarke, 1877), 77–78; *PGW, Confed.* 1:197–98.

50. *PGW, Confed.* 1:201–4n; Cook, *Washington's Western Lands*, 123.

51. *PGW, Confed.* 1:225.

52. *PGW, Confed.* 1:492.

53. *Diaries of GW* 4:2–3, 14–15; Cook, *Washington's Western Lands*, 69; Ron Chernow, *Washington: A Life* (New York: Penguin, 2010), 479.

54. *Diaries of GW* 4:4, 6, 54–55.

55. Lawrence Kinnaird, ed., *Spain in the Mississippi Valley, 1765–1794: Translations of Materials from the Spanish Archives in the Bancroft Library*, 3 pts., vols. 2–4 of *Annual Report of the American Historical Association for 1945*, 4 vols. (Washington, DC: Government Printing Office, 1946–49), vol. 3, pt. 2, 117.

56. *PGW, Confed.* 2:119–20; *Writings of Washington* 27:486.

57. *Diaries of GW* 4:25, 32–33; *PGW, Confed.* 1:117–18, 315–17, 2:68 ("respectable people"), 78–80 (instructions to Freeman), 489, 3:43–45, 158, 308–10; Butterfield, *Washington-Crawford Letters*, 79–81.

58. *PGW, Confed.* 3:127, 4:63–66, 5:446–47, 6:41–44.

59. *Diaries of GW* 4:21–31; *PGW, Confed.* 2:340–56, 442–46, 3:121–25, 245–46, 365–69, 438–39 ("Sinners"), 4:172–73, 255–61, 339–43, 405–7, 5:39–41, 327–28, 472; 6:91–92; Flexner, *George Washington and the New Nation*, 57–62; Ellis, *His Excellency*, 156–57; John Ferling, *The Ascent of George Washington: The Hidden Political Genius of an American Icon* (New York: Bloomsbury, 2009), 249; Chernow, *Washington*, 480–81.

60. *Diaries of GW* 4:57.

61. *PGW, Confed.* 5:505–8; *PGW, Pres.* 1:15–16, 110–11, 133, 168.

62. Warren R. Hofstra, "'And Die by Inches': George Washington and the Encounter of Cultures on the Southern Colonial Frontier," in Harvey and O'Brien, *George Washington's South*, 83.

63. Honor Sachs, *Home Rule: Households, Manhood, and National Expansion on the Eighteenth-Century Kentucky Frontier* (New Haven, CT: Yale University Press, 2015), 32, 37–38, 43–45, 75–78; Daniel Blake Smith, "'This Idea in Heaven': Image and Reality on the Kentucky Frontier," in *The Buzzel about Kentuck: Settling the Promised Land*, ed. Craig Thompson Friend (Lexington: University of Kentucky Press, 1999), 77–98; Stephen Aron, *How the West Was Lost: The Transformation of Kentucky from Daniel Boone to Henry Clay* (Baltimore, MD: Johns Hopkins University Press, 1996), 79 (two-thirds and quote).

64. *Diaries of GW* 4:19, 21; *PGW, Confed.* 2:116, 119–20, 170.

65. *Writings of Washington* 27:485.

66. Joel Achenbach, *The Grand Idea: George Washington's Potomac and the Race to the West* (New York: Simon & Schuster, 2004), 202.

67. *Diaries of GW* 4:57.

68. Larson, *Return of George Washington*, quotes at 39, 47.

69. *Diaries of GW* 4:58–68 (quotes at 58, 59), 670; *PGW, Confed.* 2:86–99, 102–3, 106–9, 122, 126–33, 282–84; Achenbach, *Grand Idea*; Robert J. Kapsch, *The Potomac Canal: George Washington and the Waterway West* (Morgantown: West Virginia University Press, 2007); Sturdevant, "Quest for Eden," chs. 4, 6–7; Charles Royster, *The Fabulous Story of the Dismal Swamp Company* (New York: Vintage, 2000) 294–95; Schecter, *George Washington's America*, 16, 65; Ferling, *Ascent of George Washington*, 250–55.

70. Stewart, *Madison's Gift*, 78–79.

71. *PGW, Confed.* 1:176, 215–18, 237–40; *PGW, Pres.* 2:258.

72. L. Scott Philyaw, *Virginia's Western Visions: Political and Cultural Expansion on an Early American Frontier* (Knoxville: University of Tennessee Press, 2004), 113–14.

73. *Diaries of GW* 4:66–67; *PGW, Confed.* 2:92.

74. Craig Thompson Friend, *Kentucke's Frontiers* (Bloomington: Indiana University Press, 127–33, 140–41 (Washington quoted at 141); Sachs, *Home Rule*; David Hackett Fischer and James C. Kelly, *Bound Away: Virginia and the Westward Movement* (Charlottesville: University Press of Virginia, 2000), 155–58; Aron, *How the West Was Lost*.

75. Samuel Cole Williams, *History of the Lost State of Franklin*, rev. ed. (New York: Press of the Pioneers, 1933); Kevin Barksdale, *The Lost State of Franklin: America's First Secession* (Lexington: University Press of Kentucky, 2009); Kristofer Ray, "Leadership, Loyalty, and Sovereignty in the Revolutionary American Southwest: The State of Franklin as a Test Case," *North Carolina Historical Review* 92 (2015): 123–44 (Martin quoted at 137); Kristofer Ray, *Middle Tennessee, 1775–1825: Progress and Popular Democracy on the Southwestern Frontier* (Knoxville: University of Tennessee Press, 2007), ch. 1; William T. Hutchinson et al., eds., *The Papers of James Madison*, 17 vols. (Chicago: University of Chicago Press and Charlottesville: University of Virginia Press, 1962–91), 10:271 (Stephen quote).

76. *PGW, Confed.* 6:491.

77. Ellis, *His Excellency*, 54.

78. Peter S. Onuf, *The Origins of the Federal Republic: Jurisdictional Controversies in the United States, 1775–1787* (Philadelphia: University of Pennsylvania Press, 1983); Deborah A. Rosen, *American Indians and State Law: Sovereignty, Race, and Citizenship, 1790–1880* (Lincoln: University of Nebraska Press, 2007), chs. 1–2; Frymer, *Building an American Empire*, ch. 2.

79. Haldimand Papers 21779:147–48.

80. *JCC* 25:68–84, 27:456.

81. A Council with the Chiefs and Warriors of the Six Nations, July 2, 1783, NYPL, Schuyler Papers, reel 7, box 14.

82. Haldimand Papers 21772:223–24.

83. David Lehman, "The End of the Iroquois Mystique: The Oneida Land Cession Treaties of the 1780s," *William and Mary Quarterly* 47 (1990): 529–30, 540–41.

84. *EAID* 18:301; Michael Leroy Oberg, *Peacemakers: The Iroquois, the United States, and the Treaty of Canandaigua, 1794* (New York: Oxford University Press, 2015), 29–30.

85. *EAID* 18:299–301.

86. *EAID* 18:301–12; James Austin Holden et al., eds., *Public Papers of George Clinton, First Governor of New York, 1777–1795, 1801–1804*, 10 vols. (New York and Albany: State Printers, 1889–1914), 8:349–78.

87. *EAID* 18:308.

88. *EAID* 18:313–27.

89. *PGW, Confed.* 2:181–83.

90. *St. Clair Papers* 2:7; Consul W. Butterfield, ed., *Journal of Captain Jonathan Heart... to which is added the Dickinson-Harmar Correspondence of 1785–86* (Albany, NY: Joel Munsell's Sons, 1885), 77–78.

91. *PGW, Confed.* 2:36.

92. Saler, *Settlers' Empire*, 13; Hutchinson et al., *Papers of James Madison* 8:119–20, 140, 156–57; Jacob T. Levy, "Indians in Madison's Constitutional Order," in *James Madison and the Future of Limited Government*, ed. John Samples (Washington, DC: Cato Institute, 2002), 121–33 (quotes at 124).

93. Woody Holton, *Unruly Americans and the Origins of the Constitution* (New York: Hill & Wang, 2007), 24 ("very spot"); Lehman, "End of the Iroquois Mystique," 528; Hutchinson et al., *Papers of James Madison* 8:497; Dean R. Snow, Charles T. Gehring, and William A. Starna, eds., *In Mohawk Country: Early Narratives about a Native People* (Syracuse, NY: Syracuse University Press, 1996), 305, 319 ("most fertile on our globe").

94. *PGW, Confed.* 2:171–72 (GW to Knox), 181, 301–2 (Knox quotes), 3:198 (GW to McHenry).

95. *JCC* 24:491–91; *IALT*, 5.

96. Joseph T. Glatthaar and James Kirby Martin, *Forgotten Allies: The Oneida Indians and the American Revolution* (New York: Hill & Wang, 2006), ch. 13; Alan Taylor, *The Divided Ground: Indians, Settlers, and the Northern Borderland of the American Revolution* (New York: Knopf, 2006), ch. 5; Lehman, "End of the Iroquois Mystique," 523–47; Franklin B. Hough, ed., *Proceedings of the Commissioners of Indian Affairs appointed by law for the Extinguishment of Indian Titles in the State of New York*, 2 vols. (Albany, NY: Joel Munsell, 1861), 1:84–108 (Herkimer Treaty), 122–24 (Livingston lease), 241–46 (Fort Schuyler Treaty); *EAID* 18:332–38, 472–74.

97. *EAID* 18:468–70, 472–74, 500–503; Francis G. Hutchins, *Tribes and the American Constitution* (Brookline, MA: Amarta Press, 2000), 112–13, 158.

98. Pickering Papers 60:121–22.

99. Glatthaar and Martin, *Forgotten Allies*, 310; *IALT*, 37–39.

100. Laurence M. Hauptman, *Conspiracy of Interests: Iroquois Dispossession and the Rise of New York State* (Syracuse, NY: Syracuse University Press, 1999), ch. 4; Pickering Papers 62:103 ("a very trifle").

101. Glatthaar and Martin, *Forgotten Allies*, 2–5, 315–16; Auguste Levasseur, *Lafayette in America in 1824 and 1825: Journal of a Voyage to the United States*, trans. Alan R. Hoffman (Manchester, NH: Lafayette Press, 2006), 482–83 (quotes).

102. *ASPIA* 1:38–44; *EAID* 18:405–8; *IALT*, 8–11; *DHFCC* 2:169–80, 5:1072–92.

103. *ASPIA* 1:44; *EAID* 18:402–4 (Blount), 428 (Caswell); Florette Henri, *The Southern Indians and Benjamin Hawkins, 1796–1816* (Norman: University of Oklahoma Press, 1986), 43, 45, 48.

104. Edmund C. Burnett, ed., *Letters of Members of the Continental Congress*, 8 vols. (Washington, DC: Carnegie Institution of Washington, 1921–36), 8:343–44.

105. CO 5/81:139–41 (Chickasaw message); Colin G. Calloway, *The American Revolution in Indian Country* (Cambridge: Cambridge University Press, 1995), ch. 8; James R. Atkinson, *Splendid Land, Splendid People: The Chickasaw Indians to Removal* (Tuscaloosa: University of Alabama Press, 2004), ch. 8.

106. *CVSP* 3:278–79, 297–300, 356–58.

107. *EAID* 18:370–71; *CVSP* 3:515–17; *PCC*, reel 104, item 78, 24:445–49.

108. *EAID* 18:374–76; *CVSP* 3:548.

109. *EAID* 18:424; *DHFFC* 5:1111–16; *IALT*, 15–16.

110. John Walton Caughey, *McGillivray of the Creeks* (Norman: University of Oklahoma Press, 1938), 239; Atkinson, *Splendid Land, Splendid People*, 134, 146.

111. Richard White, *The Roots of Dependency: Subsistence, Environment, and Social Change among the Choctaws, Pawnees, and Navajos* (Lincoln: University of Nebraska Press, 1983), chs. 4–5.

112. Greg O'Brien, *Choctaws in a Revolutionary Age, 1750–1830* (Lincoln: University of Nebraska Press, 2002), ch. 4 ("great civility" at 66); *CVSP* 4:268; Diary of Stephen Minor in Charles A. Weeks, *Paths to a Middle Ground: The Diplomacy of Natchez, Boukfouka, Nogales and San Fernando de las Barrancas, 1791–1795* (Tuscaloosa: University of Alabama Press, 2005), Washington portrait at 175.

113. Calloway, *Revolution in Indian Country*, 234.

114. *ASPIA* 1:43; *CVSP* 4:306.

115. Hinderaker, *Elusive Empires*, 268.

116. *Territorial Papers* 2:6–9; Archer Butler Hulbert, ed., *The Records of the Original Proceedings of the Ohio Company*, 2 vols. (Marietta, OH: Marietta Historical Commission, 1917), 1:xvii–xviii; John R. Van Atta, *Securing the West: Politics, Public Lands, and the Fate of the Old Republic, 1785–1850* (Baltimore, MD: Johns Hopkins University Press, 2014), 29–32; Frymer, *Building an Empire* (patterns of settlement).

117. Andrew R. L. Cayton, *The Frontier Republic: Ideology and Politics in the Ohio Country, 1780–1825* (Kent, OH: Kent State University Press, 1986), ch. 1; Andrew R. L. Cayton, "Radicals in the 'Western World': The Federalist Conquest of Trans-Appalachian North America," in *Federalists Reconsidered*, ed. Doron Ben-Atar and Barbara B. Oberg (Charlottesville: University of Virginia Press, 1998), 79–80; Van Atta, *Securing the West*, ch. 1; Peter S. Onuf, *Statehood and Union: A History of the Northwest Ordinance* (Bloomington: Indiana University Press, 1987), chs. 1–2; Timothy J. Shannon, "'This Unpleasant Business': The Transformation of Land Speculation in the Ohio Country, 1787–1820," in *The Pursuit of Public Power: Political Culture in Ohio, 1787–1861*, ed. Jeffrey P. Brown and Andrew L. Cayton (Kent, OH: Kent State University Press, 1994), 20; Richard White, *Railroaded: The Transcontinentals and the Making of Modern America* (New York: Norton, 2011).

118. Philyaw, *Virginia's Western Visions*, 98.

119. Linklater, *Measuring America*, 69–71; Patrick Griffin, *American Leviathan: Empire, Nation, and Revolutionary Frontier* (New York: Hill & Wang, 2007), ch. 7.

120. *PGW, Confed.* 2:440 (Williamson), 3:63 (Knox); *Writings of Washington* 28:108; also in William Parker and Julia Perkins Cutler, eds., *Life, Journals and Correspondence of Rev. Manasseh Cutler, LL.D.*, 2 vols (Cincinnati: Robert Clarke, 1888), 1:131–32.

121. Larson, *Return of George Washington*, 49.

122. "Land Ordinance of 1785," in *Territorial Papers* 2:12–18; Linklater, *Measuring America*; Onuf, *Statehood and Union*, ch. 2.

123. *PGW, Confed.* 3:69–70.

124. *PGW, Confed.* 3:152–53.

125. R. Douglas Hurt, *The Ohio Frontier: Crucible of the Old Northwest, 1720–1830* (Bloomington: Indiana University Press, 1996), 144–48.

126. Horsman, *Expansion and American Indian Policy*, 20.

127. *GWP, Confed.* 2:437.

128. *A Narrative of a Revolutionary Soldier: Some of the Adventures, Dangers, and Sufferings of Joseph Plumb Martin* (New York: Penguin/Signet Classics, 2010), 118.

129. The negotiations at Fort Finney are described in *The Military Journal of Major Ebenezer Denny* (Philadelphia: J. B. Lippincott, 1859), 63ff., and "Journal of General Richard Butler at the Treaty of Fort Finney," in *The Olden Time*, ed. Neville B. Craig, 2 vols. (Pittsburgh: J. W. Cook, 1846–48), 2:510–31. Excerpts from Butler's journal and the treaty itself are reprinted in *EAID* 18:340–51. The treaty is also in *IALT*, 16–18.

130. CO 42/49:21–22 ("soldiers at your Backs").

131. *CVSP* 4:202, 204, 212, 258–59; *PCC*, reel 85, item 7, 2:471; Haldimand Papers 21736:262–63; *St. Clair Papers* 2:19.

132. CO 42/67:177–82.

133. *PGW, Confed.* 4:398–400, 5:456–64 (vocabulary, etc.).

134. *PGW, Confed.* 6:29–32n; Henry P. Johnston, ed., *The Correspondence and Public Papers of John Jay*, 4 vols. (New York: G. P. Putnam's Sons, 1890–93), 3:320.

135. *Collections of the Massachusetts Historical Society*, 3rd ser., 5 (1836): 286–87.

136. *PGW, Confed.* 6:26–27. Washington sent the same requests for information to William Irvine; 6:34–35.

137. Cutler, *Life, Journals and Correspondence* 1:180–87; "Articles of Association by the Name of the Ohio Company," Winthrop Sargent Papers, Massachusetts Historical Society, reel 2, 652–58; Hulbert, *Records of the Original Proceedings of the Ohio Company* 1:4–12; Hurt, *Ohio Frontier*, 155–57.

138. Hulbert, *Records of the Original Proceedings of the Ohio Company* 1:12; Cutler, *Life, Journals and Correspondence* 1:191–92.

139. Linklater, *Measuring America*, 51–53; Rowena Buell, ed., *The Memoirs of Rufus Putnam and Certain Official Papers and Correspondence* (Boston: Houghton Mifflin, 1903), 217, 223; Cutler, *Life, Journals and Correspondence* 1:168, 174; *PGW, Confed.* 1:263–65n, 421–22.

140. Cutler, *Life, Journals and Correspondence* 1:192–95.

141. Nichols, *Red Gentlemen and White Savages*, 89.

142. *PGW, Confed.* 4:35.

143. Cutler, *Life, Journals and Correspondence* 1:137–45; *PGW, Pres.* 1:16; *Writings of Washington* 27:17.

144. *JCC* 31:891–92.

145. The speech of the united Indians is in *ASPIA* 1:8–9; CO 42/50:70–73, 87:324–26; *EAID* 18:356–58; and *DHFFC* 2:146–48.

146. Holton, *Unruly Americans and the Origins of the Constitution*, 144.

147. *JCC* 33:399–401, 427–30; *Territorial Papers* 2:52–57.

148. Cutler, *Life, Journals and Correspondence* 1:296.

149. Cutler, *Life, Journals and Correspondence* 1:305; Sargent Papers, reel 2, 703–4; Cayton, *Frontier Republic*, 24–25.

150. "At a Meeting of the Directors and Agents of the OHIO COMPANY, held at the Bunch of Grapes Tavern in Boston, Aug. 29, 1787," Early American Imprints, scr. 1, no. 20602; Cutler, *Life, Journals and Correspondence* 1:319–22; Butler, *Records of the Original Proceedings of the Ohio Company* 1:13–17.

151. Hurt, *Ohio Frontier*, 157; Linklater, *Measuring America*, 80–81, estimates twelve cents an acre.

152. Cutler, *Life, Journals and Correspondence* 1:326. The company's contract is in Hulbert, *Records of the Original Proceedings of the Ohio Company* 1:29–37.

153. Kohn, *Eagle and Sword*, 100.

154. "Ordinance of 1787," in *Territorial Papers* 2:39–50; Onuf, *Statehood and Union*, ch. 3.

155. *EAID* 18:451–53, 455–58; *ASPIA* 1:16; *JCC* 32:328, 33:388–90, 477–81 ("politic and just" at 480).

156. Saler, *Settlers' Empire*, 26–29.

157. Patrick Wolfe, "Against the Intentional Fallacy: Legocentrism and Continuity in the Rhetoric of Indian Dispossession," *American Indian Culture and Research Journal* 36 (2012): 3–45; Jeffrey Ostler, "'Just and Lawful War' as Genocidal War in the (United States) Northwest Ordinance and Northwest Territory, 1787–1832," *Journal of Genocide Research* 18 (2016): 1–20.

158. Arthur St. Clair, *A Narrative of the Manner in which the Campaign against the Indians, in the Year One Thousand Seven Hundred and Ninety-one, was Conducted, under the Command of Major General Arthur St. Clair* (Philadelphia: n.p., 1812), 39.

159. *PGW, Confed.* 6:340–41.

160. Ferling, *First of Men,* 364.

161. Samuel Kirkland Papers, 1764–1837, Dartmouth College, Rauner Library, MS-867, file #5, 19–20.

CHAPTER 14: AN INDIAN POLICY FOR THE NEW NATION

1. Cécile R. Ganteaume, *Officially Indian: Symbols That Define the United States* (Washington, DC: Smithsonian Institution, 2017).

2. 100th Congress, 2nd Session, H. Con. Res. 331.

3. Iris Marion Young, "Hybrid Democracy: Iroquois Federalism and the Postcolonial Project," in *Political Theory and the Rights of Indigenous Peoples,* ed. Duncan Ivinson, Paul Patton, and Will Sanders (Cambridge: Cambridge University Press, 2000), 237–58. For different positions in the debate, see Elisabeth Tooker, "The United States Constitution and the Iroquois League," *Ethnohistory* 35 (1988): 305–36; Bruce E. Johansen, "American Societies and the Evolution of Democracy in America, 1600–1800," and Elisabeth Tooker, "Rejoinder to Johansen," *Ethnohistory* 37 (1990), 279–90, 291–297; Donald A. Grinde and Bruce E. Johansen, *Exemplar of Liberty: Native America and the Evolution of Democracy* (Los Angeles: American Indian Studies Center, University of California, 1991); Forum, "The 'Iroquois Influence' Thesis—Con and Pro," *William and Mary Quarterly* 53 (1996): 587–636.

4. Woody Holton, *Unruly Americans and the Origins of the Constitution* (New York: Hill & Wang, 2007), 244–49; Richard H. Kohn, *Eagle and Sword: The Federalists and the Creation of the Military Establishment in America, 1783–1802* (New York: Free Press, 1975), ch. 5; Gregory Ablavsky, "Savage Constitution," *Duke Law Journal* 63 (2014): 1067–71.

5. Ablavsky, "Savage Constitution," 999–1089; Gregory Ablavsky, "Beyond the Indian Commerce Clause," *Yale Law Journal* 124 (2014–15): 1012–90, quote at 1056; Jacob T. Levy, "Indians in Madison's Constitutional Order," in *James Madison and the Future of Limited Government,* ed. John Samples (Washington, DC: Cato Institute, 2002), 121–33; K. Tsianina Lomawaima, "Federalism: Native, Federal, and State Sovereignty," in *Why You Can't Teach United States History without American Indians,* ed. Susan Sleeper-Smith et al. (Chapel Hill: University of North Carolina Press, 2015), 273–83

6. Michael J. Klarman, *The Framers' Coup: The Making of the United States Constitution* (New York: Oxford University Press, 2016); Fergus M. Bordewich, *The First Congress: How James Madison, George Washington, and a Group of Extraordinary Men Invented the Government* (New York: Simon & Schuster, 2016), Madison quote at 5.

7. A "correct Copy of the Constitution" was prefixed to *Acts Passed at a First Congress of the United States of America, 1789.* Washington's annotated copy is housed at the Fred W. Smith Library in Mount Vernon. *PGW, Pres.* 18:441 ("never can abandon"); Akhil Reed Amar, *America's Unwritten Constitution: The Precedents and Principles We Live By* (New York: Basic Books, 2012), 309–10.

8. William T. Hutchinson et al., eds., *The Papers of James Madison,* 17 vols. (Chicago: University of Chicago Press and Charlottesville: University of Virginia Press, 1962–91), 12:398–99.

9. T. H. Breen, *George Washington's Journey: The President Forges a New Nation* (New York: Simon & Schuster, 2016).

10. Woody Holton, *Unruly Americans and the Origins of the Constitution* (New York: Hill & Wang, 2007).

11. Francis Paul Prucha, *The Great Father: The United States Government and the American Indians*, 2 vols. (Lincoln: University of Nebraska Press, 1984), 1:33, 50–51; Francis Paul Prucha, *American Indian Policy in the Formative Years: The Indian Trade and Intercourse Acts, 1790–1834* (Lincoln: University of Nebraska Press, 1970), 43–45; Ablavsky, "Beyond the Indian Commerce Clause," 1019–22; Francis G. Hutchins, *Tribes and the American Constitution* (Brookline, MA: Amarta Press, 2000), ch. 4.

12. Hutchinson et al., *Papers of James Madison* 11:45–46, 12:139, 444–45.

13. *St. Clair Papers* 2:64.

14. Hutchinson et al., *Papers of James Madison,* 12:192.

15. Dorothy V. Jones, *License for Empire: Colonialism by Treaty in Early America* (Chicago: University of Chicago Press, 1982), 169.

16. Eliga H. Gould, *Among the Powers of the Earth: The American Revolution and the Making of a New World Empire* (Cambridge, MA: Harvard University Press, 2012); Leonard J. Sadosky, *Revolutionary Negotiations: Indians, Empires, and Diplomats in the Founding of America* (Charlottesville: University Press of Virginia, 2009), Franklin quoted at 78; Benjamin H. Irvin, *Clothed in Robes of Sovereignty: The Continental Congress and the People Out of Doors* (New York: Oxford University Press, 2011), 177–92; Peter Onuf and Nicholas Onuf, *Federal Union, Modern World: The Law of Nations in an Age of Revolutions, 1776–1814* (Madison, WI: Madison House, 1993). Apparently, Washington neglected to return *The Law of Nations*. When the staff of the Washington museum at Mount Vernon heard about the overdue book, they were unable to locate it but purchased a second, identical copy, which was ceremoniously "returned" on May 20, 2010, 221 years late. The library waived the late fees. "George Washington's 221-Year-Overdue Library Book: A Timeline," *The Week*, May 21, 2010, http://theweek.com/articles/494173/george-washingtons-221year-overdue-library-book-timeline (accessed May 8, 2017).

17. Ablavsky, "Beyond the Indian Commerce Clause," 1061–63, 1067–70; Onuf, *Federal Union, Modern World*, 108; S. James Anaya, *Indigenous Peoples in International Law*, 2nd ed. (New York: Oxford University Press, 2004), 21–23.

18. Ian Hunter, "Vattel in Revolutionary America: From the Rules of War to the Rule of Law," in *Between Indigenous and Settler Governance*, ed. Lisa Ford and Tim Rowse (New York: Routledge, 2013), 12–22.

19. Ablavsky, "Beyond the Indian Commerce Clause," 1087; *CVSP* 3:488 (Clark).

20. Ablavsky, "Savage Constitution," 1059.

21. Harold C. Syrett et al., eds., *The Papers of Alexander Hamilton*, 27 vols. (Charlottesville: University of Virginia Press, 1961–87), 4:422.

22. Max M. Edling, *A Hercules in the Cradle: War, Money, and the American State, 1783–1867* (Chicago: University of Chicago Press, 2014), chs. 1–3. Ablavsky, in "The Savage Constitution," argues that whereas Madison wanted a strengthened federal government to protect Indians and states alike, Hamilton wanted to create a "fiscal-military state that would possess the means to dominate the borderlands at the Indians' expense" (quote at 1007).

23. Stephen F. Knott and Tony Williams, *Washington and Hamilton: The Alliance That Forged America* (Naperville, IL: Sourcebooks, 2015).

24. John E. Ferling, *The First of Men: A Life of George Washington* (New York: Oxford University Press, 2010), 420. On these and other differences between the president and his secretary of state, see Thomas H. Fleming, *The Great Divide: The Conflict between Washington and Jefferson That Defined a Nation* (New York: Da Capo/Perseus, 2015). On Washington's drive to build a national army, see William Hogeland, *Autumn of the Black Snake: The Creation of the U.S. Army and the Invasion That Opened the West* (New York: Farrar, Straus & Giroux, 2017).

25. Alan Taylor, *The Divided Ground: Indians, Settlers, and the Northern Borderland of the American Revolution* (New York: Knopf, 2006), 281.

26. Isaac Weld Jr., *Travels through the States of North America, and the Provinces of Upper and Lower Canada, during the years 1795, 1796, and 1797* (London: J. Stockdale, 1799), 12.

27. Reginald Horsman, *Expansion and American Indian Policy, 1783–1812* (Norman: University of Oklahoma Press, 1992), 30–46; *EAID* 18:458–59; *Territorial Papers* 2:78–79, 117; *St. Clair Papers* 2:37; *ASPIA* 1:9; *JCC* 33:711–12; *DHFFC* 2:148–49.

28. *DHFFC* 2:149–50; *Territorial Papers* 2:104–5, 117–18.

29. *Territorial Papers* 2:166.

30. *EAID* 18:481–97; *ASPIA* 1:5–10; *St. Clair Papers* 2:111–13; *DHFFC* 2:150–63; *Territorial Papers* 2:174–86, 192–93; *Military Journal of Major Ebenezer Denny: An Officer in the Revolutionary and Indian Wars* (Philadelphia: J. B. Lippincott, 1859), 127–30; *PGW, Pres.* 2:196–98.

31. *PGW, Pres.* 3:580–89, quote at 585.

32. CO 42/65:59.

33. *St. Clair Papers* 2:124.

34. *ASPIA* 1:13.

35. *St. Clair Papers* 2:126.

36. Gould, *Among the Powers of the Earth*; *JPP*, 73.

37. Horsman, *Expansion and American Indian Policy*, 53; *PGW, Pres.* 4:529, 5:76, 79; Knox Papers 53:164.

38. *DHFFC* 21:613–15.

39. Robert F. Berkhofer Jr., *The White Man's Indian: Images of the American Indian from Columbus to the Present* (New York: Knopf, 1978), 145.

40. *DHFFC* 18:266–67.

41. *DHFFC* 19:1137, 1549, 1669.

42. Carla J. Mulford, *Benjamin Franklin and the Ends of Empire* (New York: Oxford University Press, 2015), 312.

43. Berkhofer, *White Man's Indian*, 33–69; Theda Perdue, "George Washington and the 'Civilization' of the Southern Indians," in *George Washington's South*, ed. Tamara Harvey and Greg O'Brien (Gainesville: University Press of Florida, 2004), 313–15.

44. *PGW, Confed.* 2:198–222, 291–93, 392–396 (quote at 392), 3:92–93.

45. Edward G. Lengel, *First Entrepreneur: How George Washington Built His—and the Nation's—Prosperity* (Boston: Da Capo, 2016), 164–65.

46. Joseph J. Ellis, *American Creation: Triumphs and Tragedies at the Founding of the Republic* (New York: Random House, 2007), 138.

47. Horsman, *Expansion and American Indian Policy*, 56–59; *PGW, Pres.* 2:490–94, 3:134–41; *EAID* 18:521–24, 526–30; *ASPIA* 1:12–14, 52–54; *DHFFC* 5:1003–7, 1116–21.

48. Horsman, *Expansion and American Indian Policy*, 58.

49. *ASPIA* 1:54; Francis Paul Prucha, *Indian Peace Medals in American History* (Norman: University of Oklahoma Press, 1994), 3–11, 73–87; George J. Fuld, "Washington Oval Peace Medals," in *Peace Medals: Negotiating Power in Early America*, ed. Robert B. Pickering (Tulsa, OK: Gilcrease Museum, 2011), 49–62.

50. *PGW, Pres.* 3:398; *DHFFC* 3:138; *ASPIA* 1:12.

51. *PGW, Pres.* 4:51; *ASPIA* 1:58.

52. *PGW, Pres.* 4:543–45; *Writings of Washington* 30:491–94.

53. Ablavsky, "Beyond the Indian Commerce Clause," 1041–42; *PGW, Pres.* 3:134–40 (Knox), 6:396 (GW to Mifflin), 11:272–73 (Randolph); *ASPIA* 1:231–32 (Knox).

54. David Andrew Nichols, *Red Gentlemen and White Savages: Indians, Federalists, and the Search for Order on the American Frontier* (Charlottesville: University of Virginia Press, 2008).

55. *DHFFC* 19:1549.

56. *PGW, Pres.* 8:35.

57. D. W. Meinig, *The Shaping of America: A Geographical Perspective on 500 Years of History*, vol. 1, *Atlantic America, 1492–1800* (New Haven, CT: Yale University Press, 1986), 408–9.

58. *PGW, Pres.* 3:316; Kohn, *Eagle and Sword*, 2–6; Robert Wooster, *The American Military Frontiers: The United States Army in the West, 1783–1900* (Albuquerque: University of New Mexico Press, 2010), xii.

59. Quoted in Gordon S. Wood, *Empire of Liberty: A History of the Early Republic, 1789–1815* (New York: Oxford University Press, 2009), 111.

60. William H. Guthman, *March to Massacre: A History of the First Seven Years of the United States Army, 1784–1791* (New York: McGraw-Hill, 1970), 174; James Ripley Jacobs, *The Beginning of the U. S. Army, 1783–1812* (Princeton: Princeton University Press, 1947), 50; Russell F. Weigley, *History of the United States Army* (Bloomington: Indiana University Press, 1984), 90. Knox's plan for organization of the militia is in *American State Papers: Documents, Legislative and Executive, of the Congress of the United States, Class 5: Military Affairs*, ed. Walter Lowrie and Matthew St. Clair Clarke, 7 vols. (Washington: Gales & Seaton, 1832), 1:6–13 (quotes at 7).

61. Wood, *Empire of Liberty*, 95–103.

62. Terry Bouton, "The Trials of the Confederation," in *The Oxford Handbook of the American Revolution*, ed. Edward G. Gray and Jane Kamensky (New York: Oxford University Press, 2013), 375; *The Diary of William Maclay and Other Notes on Senate Debates*, in *DHFFC* 9:346.

63. Wood, *Empire of Liberty*, 140–43; Joseph J. Ellis, *Founding Brothers: The Revolutionary Generation* (New York: Random House, 2000), ch. 2.

64. Wood, *Empire of liberty*, 143–45.

65. Ellis, *Founding Brothers*, ch. 3.

66. *ASPIA* 1:47–48.

67. *PGW, Pres.* 2:325–28; *CVSP* 4:619; *DHFFC* 2:185–88.

68. *PGW, Pres.* 2:328, 388. It has been suggested that the Rising Fawn of Great Highwassa was also known as Standing Turkey; *PGW, Pres.* 2:388n.

69. *PGW, Pres.* 3:516–17.

70. *PGW, Pres.* 3:137.

71. *PGW, Pres.* 3:521–22.

72. *PGW, Pres.* 3:561, 4:468–69.

73. William S. Coker and Thomas D. Watson, *Indian Traders of the Southeastern Spanish Borderlands: Panton, Leslie & Company and John Forbes & Company, 1783–1847* (Pensacola: University of West Florida Press, 1986), 160; Kristofer Ray, *Middle Tennessee, 1775–1825: Progress and Popular Democracy on the Southwestern Frontier* (Knoxville: University of Tennessee Press, 2007), 19–21.

74. *Territorial Papers* 4:24.

75. Alice Barnwell Keith et al., eds., *The John Gray Blount Papers*, 3 vols. (Raleigh, NC: State Department of Archives and History, 1959–65), 2:118.

76. Keith, *John Gray Blount Papers* 2:131.

77. Horsman, *Expansion and American Indian Policy*, 71.

78. *PGW, Ret.* 2:598; Pickering Papers 23:134.

79. *PGW, Pres.* 7:151; *Territorial Papers* 4:41.

80. James Thomas Flexner, *George Washington and the New Nation, 1783–1793* (Boston: Little, Brown, 1969), 261.

81. *DHFFC* 5:988–90; N. Bruce Duthu, *American Indians and the Law* (New York: Viking/Penguin, 2008), 66–67.

82. *PGW, Pres.* 9:68–69.

83. Ray, *Middle Tennessee*, 21.

84. *PGW, Pres.* 9:110–16; Prucha, *American Indian Policy in the Formative Years*, 46.

85. *PGW, Pres.* 11:342 48; quote at 344–45.

86. Prucha, *American Indian Policy in the Formative Years*, 47, 53.

87. Paul A. W. Wallace, ed., *Thirty Thousand Miles with John Heckewelder; or, Travels amoung the Indians of Pennsylvania, New York & Ohio in the 18th Century* (Lewisburg, PA: Wennawoods Publishing, 1998), 227.

88. Margaret Connell Szasz, *Indian Education in the American Colonies, 1607–1783* (Albuquerque: University of New Mexico Press, 1988); James Axtell, "Dr. Wheelock's Little Red School," in *The European and the Indian: Essays in the Ethnohistory of Colonial North America* (New York: Oxford University Press, 1981), 87–109; Colin G. Calloway, *The Indian History of an American Institution: Native Americans and Dartmouth* (Hanover, NH: University Press of New England, 2010).

89. Varnum Lansing Collins, "Indian Wards at Princeton," *Princeton University Bulletin* 13 (1902): 101–6; C. A. Weslager, *The Delaware Indians: A History* (New Brunswick, NJ: Rutgers University Press, 1972), 309–11, 365 (Osage war party); *JCC* 28:411 (congressional

committee), 468; Stephen Decatur Jr., *Private Affairs of George Washington: From the Records and Accounts of Tobias Lear, Esquire, his Secretary* (Boston: Houghton Mifflin, 1933), 57, 92; Knox Papers 26:129 (Congress funds in 1790); *PGW, Pres.* 2:433–35, 3:152, 403–4 (White Eyes letters), 4:215; *Simcoe Correspondence* 3:288–89 ("mischief").

90. *PGW, Pres.* 9:281.

91. For example, *PGW, Pres.* 3:466, 573.

92. *PGW, Pres.* 7:257.

93. David McCullough, *John Adams* (New York: Simon & Schuster, 2011), 472.

94. David McLean, *Timothy Pickering and the Age of the American Revolution* (New York: Arno Press, 1982), 318–28, 345–46; Pickering Papers 61:164–65, 168; *PGW, Pres.* 7:204–6.

95. As would Jefferson: Daniel H. Usner, "Iroquois Livelihood and Jeffersonian Agrarianism," in *Native Americans and the Early Republic*, ed. Frederick E. Hoxie, Ronald Hoffman, and Peter J. Albert (Charlottesville: University Press of Virginia, 1999), 201.

CHAPTER 15: COURTING MCGILLIVRAY

1. A Spanish census in 1793 listed thirty-one Upper Creek towns, twenty-five Lower Creek towns, and several smaller Seminole towns, and a total population of 15,160; Lawrence Kinnaird, ed., *Spain in the Mississippi Valley, 1765–1794: Translations of Materials from the Spanish Archives in the Bancroft Library*, 3 pts., vols. 2–4 of *Annual Report of the American Historical Association for 1945* (Washington, DC: Government Printing Office, 1946–49), vol. 4, pt. 3, 231–32; John Walton Caughey, *McGillivray of the Creeks* (Norman: University of Oklahoma Press, 1938). 6.

2. Robbie Ethridge, "Creeks and Americans in the Age of Washington," in *George Washington's South*, ed. Tamara Harvey and Greg O'Brien (Gainesville: University Press of Florida, 2004), 278–79; Angela Pulley Hudson, *Creek Paths and Federal Roads: Indians, Settlers, and Slaves and the Making of the American South* (Chapel Hill: University of North Carolina Press, 2010), 3–4.

3. Colin G. Calloway, *The American Revolution in Indian Country: Crisis and Diversity in Native American Communities* (Cambridge: Cambridge University Press, 1995), ch. 9.

4. Lawrence Kinnaird, "International Rivalry in the Creek Country: Part I. The Ascendency of Alexander McGillivray, 1783–1789," *Florida Historical Society Quarterly* 10 (Oct. 1931): 59; Kenneth Coleman, "Federal Indian Relations in the South, 1781–1789," *Chronicles of Oklahoma* 35 (1957–58): 436; warrior estimates at *PGW, Rev.* 12:103; *PGW, Pres.* 3:124, 4:475, 530; Knox Papers 53:164 (estimates at p. 10 of letter); "behoves" at *PGW, Rev.* 13:221–22; Joseph J. Ellis, *American Creation: Triumphs and Tragedies at the Founding of the Republic* (New York: Random House, 2007), 144

5. Claudio Saunt, *A New Order of Things: Property, Power, and the Transformation of the Creek Indians, 1733–1816* (Cambridge: Cambridge University Press, 1999), esp. ch. 3; Andrew K. Frank, *Creeks and Southerners: Biculturalism on the Early American Frontier* (Lincoln: University of Nebraska Press, 2005).

6. Edward J. Cashin, *Lachlan McGillivray, Indian Trader: The Shaping of the Southern Colonial Frontier* (Athens: University of Georgia Press, 1992).

7. John Pope, *A Tour through the Southern and Western Territories of the United States of North America* (Richmond, VA: John Dixon, 1792), 48.

8. Caughey, *McGillivray of the Creeks*, 13–17; Saunt, *New Order of Things*, ch. 3 and 188–89; J. Leitch Wright Jr., "Creek-American Treaty of 1790: Alexander McGillivray and the Diplomacy of the Old Southwest," *Georgia Historical Quarterly* 51 (Dec. 1967): 382. On McGillivray and the Creeks in the Revolution, see also Kathleen DuVal, *Independence Lost: Lives on the Edge of the American Revolution* (New York: Random House, 2015), 24–34, 75–90, 177–82, 205–6, 246–55.

9. *PGW, Pres.* 2:254.

10. Caughey, *McGillivray of the Creeks*, 62.

11. *DAR* 17:184.

12. CO 5/82:368 ("Virginia Lie"), 372–73, 405, 432; CO 5/110:70–71; CO 5/560:71–74; Caughey, *McGillivray of the Creeks*, 73–74, 90–93.

13. Caughey, *McGillivray of the Creeks*, 70.

14. Wright, "Creek-American Treaty," 380, 383; Coleman, "Federal Indian Relations in the South," 437.

15. Caughey, *McGillivray of the Creeks*, 73–74.

16. *PGW, Pres.* 3:519.

17. Kinnaird, "International Rivalry in the Creek Country," 59.

18. William S. Coker and Thomas D. Watson, *Indian Traders of the Southeastern Spanish Borderlands: Panton, Leslie & Company and John Forbes & Company, 1783–1847* (Pensacola: University of West Florida Press, 1986); Saunt, *New Order of Things*, 75–79; Kathryn E. Holland Braund, *Deerskins and Duffels: The Creek Indian Trade with Anglo-America, 1685–1815* (Lincoln: University of Nebraska Press, 1993), ch. 9.

19. David A. Nichols, "Land, Republicanism, and Indians: Power and Policy in Early National Georgia, 1780–1825," *Georgia Historical Quarterly* 85 (2001): 206–7.

20. DuVal, *Independence Lost*, 253.

21. "Letters of Benjamin Hawkins," in H. Thomas Foster, ed., *The Collected Works of Benjamin Hawkins, 1796–1810* (Tuscaloosa: University of Alabama Press, 2003), 250, 252.

22. *PGW, Confed.* 6:45–46 ("insanity"); Francis Paul Prucha, *American Indian Treaties: The History of a Political Anomaly* (Berkeley: University of California Press, 1994), 59; Randolph C. Downes, "Creek-American Relations, 1782–1790," *Georgia Historical Quarterly* 21 (June 1937): 144.

23. Caughey, *McGillivray of the Creeks*, 65, 72.

24. Walter Lowrie and Matthew St. Clair Clarke, eds., *American State Papers: Foreign Relations*, 6 vols. (Washington, DC: Gales & Seaton, 1832), 1:278–79; Caughey, *McGillivray of the Creeks*, 25, 75–76; Saunt, *New Order of Things*, 78.

25. Saunt, *New Order of Things*, 68.

26. *DHFFC* 2:165–67; *EAID* 18:372–73; James F. Doster, *The Creek Indians and Their Florida Lands, 1740–1823* (New York: Garland Publishing, 1974), 71.

27. Caughey, *McGillivray of the Creeks*, 103 ("beggar"); *PGW, Pres.* 13:226 (Willett).

28. DuVal, *Independence Lost*, 251, 255, 303.

29. Caughey, *McGillivray of the Creeks*, 105; Wright, "Creek-American Treaty," 383–84; Downes, "Creek-American Relations," 145.

30. *ASPIA* 1:18.

31. *JCC* 27:454.

32. *JCC* 27:456–457.

33. Caughey, *McGillivray of the Creeks*, 96.

34. *ASPIA* 1:17–18; *DHFFC* 5:1020–22.

35. Caughey, *McGillivray of the Creeks*, 97–98.

36. Coleman, "Federal Indian Relations in the South," 440–41.

37. Caughey, *McGillivray of the Creeks*, 103.

38. Downes, "Creek-American Relations," 147.

39. Florette Henri, *The Southern Indians and Benjamin Hawkins, 1796–1816* (Norman: University of Oklahoma Press, 1986), 42.

40. *JCC* 29:691.

41. Henri, *Southern Indians and Benjamin Hawkins*, 42.

42. *ASPIA* 1:49; *DHFFC* 5:1019; Caughey, *McGillivray of the Creeks*, 103 ("ridiculous").

43. Saunt, *New Order of Things*, 80; *ASPIA* 1:16–17; *PGW, Pres.* 3:124–25; *DHFFC* 2:167–69, 5:1017–18; *EAID* 18:390–91.

44. "Questions to the Tallisee King," Aug. 6, 1790, Knox Papers 26:120.

45. Downes, "Creek-American Relations," 152.

46. Caughey, *McGillivray of the Creeks*, 103–4.

47. Downes, "Creek-American Relations," 160.

48. Caughey, *McGillivray of the Creeks*, 31.

49. Caughey, *McGillivray of the Creeks*, 31.

50. Saunt, *New Order of Things*, 80; "Questions to the Tallisee King," Knox Papers 26:120; *DHFFC* 2:180–83; *EAID* 18:433–36.

51. Caughey, *McGillivray of the Creeks*, 139; *ASPIA* 1:18 ("Cincinnatus"); *DHFFC* 5:1022–24.

52. Caughey, *McGillivray of the Creeks*, 33; *ASPIA* 1:23 ("our life"); *DHFFC* 5:1037.

53. William T. Hutchinson et al., eds., *The Papers of James Madison*, 17 vols. (Chicago: University of Chicago Press and Charlottesville: University of Virginia Press, 1962–91), 9:348.

54. Caughey, *McGillivray of the Creeks*, 184.

55. Caughey, *McGillivray of the Creeks*, 239.

56. Kathleen Bartoloni-Tuazon, *For Fear of an Elective King: George Washington and the Presidential Title Controversy of 1789* (Ithaca, NY: Cornell University Press, 2014).

57. *ASPIA* 1:15–16; *PGW, Pres.* 3: 23–38; *DHFFC* 5:1011–15.

58. *ASPIA* 1:59–63; *DHFFC* 5:1117–18; *PGW, Pres.* 3:135.

59. Prucha, *American Indian Treaties*, 76–77.

60. The Blount brothers were "among the greatest speculators in American history," along with men like Patrick Henry, Robert Morris, Timothy Pickering, and, of course, George Washington; Alice Barnwell Keith et al., eds., *The John Gray Blount Papers*, 3 vols. (Raleigh, NC: State Department of Archives and History, 1952–65), 1:xxiii (quote), 499–501 (Williamson letter); *DHFFC* 16:1256–57.

61. Prucha, *American Indian Treaties*, 69–70.

62. *DHFFC* 1:120–27, 725, 5:998–1001, 1122–23, 11:1188–207, 1301–8.

63. Prucha, *American Indian Treaties*, 74–75; *PGW, Pres.* 3:515; *DHFFC* 2:30.

64. Prucha, *American Indian Treaties*, 77; *PGW, Pres.* 3:521–25; *ASPIA* 1:54–55.

65. *DHFFC* 2:31–35.

66. *The Diary of William Maclay and Other Notes on Senate Debates*, in *DHFFC* 9:8 ("greatest Man"), 321 ("in the hands of Hamilton the Dishclout of every dirty Speculation, as his name Goes to Wipe away blame and Silence all Murmuring"), 432 (war services).

67. *Diary of William Maclay*, 128–33; *The Journal of William Maclay, United States Senator from Pennsylvania, 1789–1791* (New York: Albert and Charles Boni, 1927), 125–30; *DHFFC* 2:35–36; *PGW, Pres.* 3:525–27; John Quincy Adams and Charles Francis Adams, *Memoirs of John Quincy Adams, Comprising Portions of his Diary from 1795 to 1848*, vol. 6 (Philadelphia: J. B. Lippincott, 1874), 427.

68. James Thomas Flexner, *George Washington and the New Nation, 1783–1793* (Boston: Little, Brown, 1969), 215–17; Mark J. Rozell, William D. Pederson, and Frank J. Williams, eds., *George Washington and the Origins of the Modern Presidency* (Westport, CT: Praeger, 2000), ix; Akhil Reed Amar, *America's Unwritten Constitution: The Precedents and Principles We Live By* (New York: Basic Books, 2012), 329 (cabinet as sounding board); Harlow Giles Unger, *"Mr. President": George Washington and the Making of the Nation's Highest Office* (New York: Da Capo, 2013), 84–89 (setting foreign policy); Ron Chernow, *Washington: A Life* (New York: Penguin, 2010), 592 ("bookshelf").

69. *ASPIA* 1:31.

70. *PGW, Pres.* 3:551–64; *ASPIA* 1:65–68; *DHFFC* 2:202–10.

71. *ASPIA* 1:69–70; *DHFFC* 2:213–15.

72. *DHFFC* 2:211–12, 219; *ASPIA* 1:69–72.

73. *ASPIA* 1:72; *PGW, Pres.* 4:86 ("white wing").

74. *ASPIA* 1:72; *DHFFC* 2:220.

75. Caughey, *McGillivray of the Creeks*, 244.

76. *ASPIA* 1:73–74; *PGW, Pres.* 4:86–88; *DHFFC* 2:222–26; Frank Landon Humphreys, *Life and Times of David Humphreys*, 2 vols. (New York: G. P. Putnam's Sons, 1917), 2:6–8.

77. Caughey, *McGillivray of the Creeks*, 251–54, 260; *DHFFC* 2:226–27; Lucia Burk Kinnaird, "The Rock Landing Conference of 1789," *North Carolina Historical Review* 9 (1932): 349–65.

78. Hutchinson et al., *Papers of James Madison*, 12:437.

79. *ASPIA* 1:75–77; *DHFFC* 2:229–30.

80. *PGW, Pres.* 4:91–94; Humphreys, *Life and Times of David Humphreys* 2:9–13.

81. *PGW, Pres.* 4:88; Humphreys, *Life and Times of David Humphreys* 2:8.

82. Humphreys, *Life and Times of David Humphreys* 2:4–6, 15; Franklin Bowditch Dexter, ed., *The Literary Diary of Ezra Stiles*, 3 vols. (New York: Scribner's, 1901), 3:373.

83. *ASPIA* 1:78–79; *DHFFC* 2:236–40; *Diaries of GW* 5:499–500.

84. *PGW, Pres.* 4:471, 475–76.

85. *PGW, Pres.* 5:140–43.

86. *PGW, Pres.* 5:207–8.

87. *DHFFC* 19:1550.

88. *PGW, Pres.* 5:208n; *Diaries of GW* 6:42; Caughey, *McGillivray of the Creeks*, 257–58.

89. Caughey, *McGillivray of the Creeks*, 41.

90. Wright, "Creek-American Treaty," 384; Nichols, "Land, Republicanism, and Indians," 208 (four-fifths of a cent); Ellis, *American Creation*, 149–50, 156. In an "Opinion on Certain Georgia Land Grants," Jefferson argued that Georgia could not convey Indian lands to the Yazoo companies because the states had ceded the power to make war and treaties to the federal government; *PTJ* 16:406–8. Georgia could not convey to the companies a right it did not possess, explained Henry Knox; Knox to Wayne, Apr. 10, 1790, Knox Papers.

91. J. Leitch Wright Jr., *William Augustus Bowles, Director General of the Creek Nation* (Athens: University of Georgia Press, 1967); Wright, "Creek-American Treaty," 385.

92. Wright, "Creek-American Treaty," 385–86.

93. Gary L. Roberts, "The Chief of State and the Chief," *American Heritage* 26 (Oct. 1975): 28–33, 86–89; Caughey, *McGillivray of the Creeks*, 261–62.

94. Caughey, *McGillivray of the Creeks*, 268.

95. Caughey, *McGillivray of the Creeks*, 263.

96. Caughey, *McGillivray of the Creeks*, 265–67.

97. Carolyn Thomas Foreman, "Alexander McGillivray, Emperor of the Creeks," *Chronicles of Oklahoma* 7 (Mar. 1929): 114; William Marinus Willett, *A Narrative of the Military Actions of Colonel Marinus Willett, Taken Chiefly from His Own Manuscript* (New York: G. & C. & H. Carvill, 1831), 110.

98. Roberts, "Chief of State and the Chief," 86; Caughey, *McGillivray of the Creeks*, 262. The Creeks' Seminole relatives clearly had no fear of the sea, paddling large canoes made of cypress trunks to Cuba, the Florida Keys, and the Bahamas, and trading deerskins, honey, and dried fish for coffee, rum, tobacco, and sugar. William Bartram, *Travels through North and South Carolina, Georgia, East and West Florida* (London, 1792; fac. rpt. Charlottesville: University Press of Virginia, 1980), 184; Calloway, *American Revolution in Indian Country*, 254.

99. Caughey, *McGillivray of the Creeks*, 43.

100. *Diaries of GW* 6:85.

101. *DHFFC* 20:2068.

102. *PGW, Pres.* 6:35; Caughey, *McGillivray of the Creeks*, 43; Ellis, *American Creation*, 151–52; Roberts, "Chief of State and the Chief," 86–87; Willett, *Narrative*, 112.

103. Caughey, *McGillivray of the Creeks*, 279.

104. Wright, "Creek-American Treaty," 379.

105. *DHFFC* 22:1149–53; *New York Daily Gazette*, July 22, 1790, 695; Philip J. Deloria, *Playing Indian* (New Haven, CT: Yale University Press, 1998), 54–56; Carole Smith-Rosenberg, *This Violent Empire: The Birth of an American National Identity* (Chapel Hill: University of North Carolina Press, 2010), 191–206; Cécile R. Ganteaume, *Officially Indian: Symbols That Define the United States* (Washington, DC: Smithsonian Institution, 2017).

106. *PTJ* 17:269, 271.

107. *DHFFC* 22:1131, 1165; Stewart Mitchell, ed., "New Letters of Abigail Adams, 1788–1801," *Proceedings of the American Antiquarian Society* 55 (1947): 168–69.

108. *Diaries of GW* 6:80, 82; Wright, "Creek-American Treaty," 389.

109. Caughey, *McGillivray of the Creeks*, 282.

110. Wright, "Creek-American Treaty," 389.

111. Wright, "Creek-American Treaty," 390.

112. FO 4/12:1, 76; *DHFFC* 21:1021.

113. *ASPIA* 2:599 (Fusatchee Mico); *DHFFC* 22:1172 ("patched up").

114. John Trumbull, *The Autobiography of Colonel John Trumbull, Patriot-Artist, 1765–1843*, ed. Theodore Sizer (New Haven, CT: Yale University Press, 1953), 166–67; Virginia Pounds Brown and Linda McNair Cohen, *Drawing by Stealth: John Trumbull and the Creek Indians* (Montgomery, AL: NewSouth Books, 2016).

115. *PGW, Pres.* 6:188; *DHFFC* 2:86–87; Wright, "Creek-American Treaty," 386.

116. *PGW, Pres.* 6:188–96; Knox Papers 53:178; *ASPIA* 1:80; *DHFFC* 2:87, 22:1154–56; Wright, "Creek-American Treaty," 386–88. The draft of the secret article is in Harold C. Syrett et al., eds., *The Papers of Alexander Hamilton*, 27 vols. (Charlottesville: University of Virginia Press, 1961–87), 26:548–49. Jefferson wrote an opinion on McGillivray's monopoly of commerce with the Creek Indians; *PTJ* 17:288–89.

117. Knox Papers 26:129, 27:70.

118. *ASPIA* 1:81–82; *IALT*, 25–28; *DHFFC* 2:241–48.

119. Knox Papers 26:126, 129–30; *PGW, Pres.* 6:206–9; *DHFFC* 2:241–18.

120. *PGW, Pres.* 6:191–92; Knox Papers 26:129–30, 53:178; *DHFFC* 2:248–49.

121. Caughey, *McGillivray of the Creeks*, 273–76.

122. *PGW, Pres.* 6:213–14; *DHFFC* 2:90–91; *ASPIA* 1:81.

123. *DHFFC* 20:2411; Wright, "Creek-American Treaty," 394.

124. *DHFFC* 20:2412–20 (account and quotes of eyewitness Judith Sargent Murray at 2412–14); *PGW, Pres.* 6:249; Caughey, *McGillivray of the Creeks*, 278.

125. *PGW, Pres.* 6:248. The treaty was published in the *Gazette of the United States*, Aug. 14, 1790, 559; *Columbian Centinel*, Aug. 25, 1790, 194; *Connecticut Courant*, Aug. 23, 1790, 4; *Hampshire Chronicle*, Aug. 25, 1790, 1; *Daily Advertiser* (New York), Aug. 14, 1790, 2; *New-York Journal, & Patriotic Register*, Aug. 17, 1790, 2; and many other papers.

126. Wright, "Creek-American Treaty," 395; Knox Papers 53:171.

127. *DHFFC* 20:2372.

128. Quoted in Wright, *William Augustus Bowles*, 47.

129. Joshua Piker, *Okfuskee: A Creek Indian Town in Colonial America* (Cambridge, MA: Harvard University Press, 2004), 199; Suzan Shown Harjo, ed., *Nation to Nation: Treaties between the United States and American Indian Nations* (Washington, DC: Smithsonian Books, 2014), 139.

130. *PGW, Pres.* 6:234.

131. Knox Papers 26:128.

132. Wright, "Creek-American Treaty," 395–96.

133. DuVal, *Independence Lost*, 342.

134. *DHCC* 22:1169–1228; Caughey, *McGillivray of the Creeks*, 45; Nichols, "Land, Republicanism, and Indians," 216–17; cf. *PGW, Pres.* 10:1–2.

135. *Diaries of GW* 6:158.

136. *PGW, Pres.* 6:237–38.

137. *PGW, Pres.* 6:342; Caughey, *McGillivray of the Creeks*, 275; *Diaries of GW* 6:70 (McGillivray quote); Flexner, *George Washington and the New Nation*, 262; *Territorial Papers* 4:34; Knox Papers 53:50.

138. Nichols, "Land, Republicanism, and Indians," 208.

139. *ASPIA* 1:125.

140. Wright, "Creek-American Treaty," 392–93.

141. *Gazette of the United States* (New York), July 24, 1790.

142. *IALT* 28–29.

143. *PGW, Pres.* 6:206.

144. Saunt, *New Order of Things*, 81.

145. John Francis McDermott, ed., *Memoir; or, A Cursory Glance at My Different Travels & My Sojourn in the Creek Nation*, trans. Geraldine De Courcy (Chicago: R. R. Donnelley & Sons, 1956), 100.

146. *ASPIA* 2:602.

147. Wright, "Creek-American Treaty," 395; Caughey, *McGillivray of the Creeks*, 45, 284–85.

148. Caughey, *McGillivray of the Creeks*, 45; *DHFFC* 14:15–16 ("caressed"), 21–23 ("Caligula" at 22), 35, 21:162, 183; Keith, *John Gray Blount Papers* 2:94–95 (Williamson).

149. Prucha, *American Indian Treaties*, 84.

150. Wright, *William Augustus Bowles*, 47–55, 73–78; FO 4/8:410–12, 9:5–17, 69–74, 81–82, 11:181–82, 208, 14:295–300, 24:423–49; CO 42/68:279–304; *ASPIA* 1:246–51, 255; (London) *Times*, Mar. 17, 1791, p. 3., col. 2 (dined with Spanish ambassador).

151. *ASPIA* 1:364; *PGW, Pres.* 11:167.

152. Pope, *Tour through the Southern Western Territories*, 47, 51.

153. Kinnaird, *Spain in the Mississippi Valley*, pt. 3, 22, 57–58; Caughey, *McGillivray of the Creeks*, 332, 337.

154. *ASPIA* 1:257, 259.

155. *PGW, Pres.* 10:306–8, 519–23, 577–81 ("in his heart" at 579); *ASPIA* 1:296, 306.

156. *PGW, Pres.* 11:20.

157. *PGW, Pres.* 12:335–37; *ASPIA* 1:310–11.

158. *PGW, Pres.* 12:416.

159. *ASPIA* 1:378; *Gentleman's Magazine* 61 (1786): 1083, 62 (1792): 567–77, 63 (1793): 767.

160. *ASPIA* 1:366–67. Washington owned a copy of William Bartram's *Travels through North and South Carolina*, published in 1791, and he signed his name on the page opposite the picture of the Seminole chief Mico Chlucco or Long Warrior.

161. Prucha, *American Indian Treaties*, 76–77, 84.

162. James Thomas Flexner, *George Washington: Anguish and Farewell, 1793–1799* (Boston: Little, Brown, 1969), 268; *Writings of Washington* 34:140, 218; *PGW, Pres.* 18:262–63.

163. *Diaries of GW* 6:149–50n; GW to Secretary of War, July 18, 1796, GWPLC; James H. Merrell, *The Indians' New World: Catawbas and Their Neighbors from European Contact through the Era of Removal*, 2nd ed. (Chapel Hill: University of North Carolina Press, 2009), 278–81.

CHAPTER 16: THE GREATEST INDIAN VICTORY

1. *St. Clair Papers* 2:126; *PGW, Pres.* 4:141.

2. *PGW, Pres.* 4:532; 5:77 (quote). For fuller studies of the ensuing campaigns, see Wiley Sword, *President Washington's Indian War: The Struggle for the Old Northwest, 1790–1795* (Norman: University of Oklahoma Press, 1985); Colin G. Calloway, *The Victory with No Name: The Native American Defeat of the First American Army* (New York: Oxford University Press, 2015); and William Hogeland, *Autumn of the Black Snake: The Creation of the U.S. Army and the Invasion That Opened the West* (New York: Farrar, Straus & Giroux, 2017).

3. *PGW, Pres.* 7:46, 149; *CVSP* 5:193–94 ("incorrigible").

4. Jeffrey Ostler, "'To Extirpate the Indians': An Indigenous Consciousness of Genocide in the Ohio Valley and Lower Great Lakes, 1750s–1810," *William and Mary Quarterly* 72 (2015): 606–14.

5. *Times* (London), Aug. 22, 1791, p. 2, col. 2; *Simcoe Correspondence* 2:42; Isaac Weld Jr., *Travels through the States of North America, and the Provinces of Upper and Lower Canada, during the years 1795, 1796, and 1797*, 2nd ed., 2 vols. (London: John Stockdale, 1799), 2:201–3.

6. *PGW, Pres.* 9:554–55.

7. *St. Clair Papers* 2:303–4.

8. Helen Hornbeck Tanner, "The Glaize in 1792: A Composite Indian Community," *Ethnohistory* 25 (Winter 1978): 16; Helen Hornbeck Tanner, ed., *Atlas of Great Lakes Indian History* (Norman: University of Oklahoma Press, 1987), map 18; Harvey Lewis Carter, *The Life and Times of Little Turtle* (Urbana: University of Illinois Press, 1987), 75–77; Milo M. Quaife, ed., "Henry Hay's Journal from Detroit to the Miami River," *Proceedings of the Wisconsin Historical Society for 1914* (Madison: WHS, 1915), 221–42.

9. Ebenezer Denny, *Military Journal of Ebenezer Denny: An Officer in the Revolutionary and Indian Wars* (Philadelphia: J. B. Lippincott, 1859), 145.

10. Sargent to St. Clair, Aug. 17, 1790, Ohio State Library, Arthur St. Clair Papers, 1788–1815 (hereafter Arthur St. Clair Papers, OSL); *Territorial Papers* 2:301.

11. Richard White, *The Middle Ground: Indians, Empires, and Republics in the Great Lakes Region, 1650–1815* (Cambridge: Cambridge University Press, 1991), 435, 441; Leroy V. Eid, "'National' War among Indians of Northeastern North America," *Canadian Review of American Studies* 16 (Summer 1985): 145; Leroy V. Eid, "American Indian Military Leadership: St. Clair's 1791 Defeat," *Journal of Military History* 57 (Jan. 1993): 71–88.

12. Carl F. Klinck and James J. Talman, eds., *The Journal of Major John Norton, 1816* (Toronto: Champlain Society, 1970), 281–82; White, *Middle Ground*, 455; Draper Mss. 23U:66–74.

13. Klinck and Talman, *Journal of John Norton*, 176; *Territorial Papers* 2:362; *St. Clair Papers* 2:95–96; CO 42/83:181 ("unreasonable").

14. Donald L. Fixico, "The Alliance of the Three Fires in Trade and War, 1630–1812," *Michigan Historical Review* 20 (Fall 1994): 11.

15. *St. Clair Papers* 2:132, 155–62; *ASPIA* 1:93–94.

16. *St. Clair Papers* 2:147, 181–82; *ASPIA* 1:97, 100.

17. Celia Barnes, *Native American Power in the United States, 1783–1795* (Teaneck, NJ: Fairleigh Dickinson University Press, 2003), 130–31.

18. Draper Mss. 2W:324–26 ("convivial glass").

19. *The Proceedings of a Court of Inquiry, Held at the Special Request of Brigadier General Josiah Harmar, to Investigate his Conduct as Commanding Officer of the Expedition against the Miami Indians, 1790* (Philadelphia: John Fenno, 1791), 2; also in *American State Papers: Documents, Legislative and Executive, of the Congress of the United States, Class 5: Military Affairs*, ed. Walter Lowrie and Matthew St. Clair Clarke, 7 vols. (Washington, DC: Gales & Seaton, 1832) vol. 1; Denny's report, Jan. 1, 1791, Arthur St. Clair Papers, OSL, card 22.

20. Woody Holton, *Unruly Americans and the Origins of the Constitution* (New York: Hill & Wang, 2007), 268.

21. "Indian History from the Manuscript of Mr. William Wells," *Western Review and Miscellaneous Magazine*, May 1820, 202.

22. *ASPIA* 1:94; Carter, *Life and Times of Little Turtle*, 44–45, 66–81.

23. John Sugden, *Blue Jacket, Warrior of the Shawnees* (Lincoln: University of Nebraska Press, 2000); Milo M. Quaife, ed., *The Indian Captivity of O. M. Spencer* (New York: Citadel Press, 1968), 89–92.

24. Paul A. W. Wallace, ed., *Thirty Thousand Miles with John Heckewelder; or, Travels amoung the Indians of Pennsylvania, New York & Ohio in the Eighteenth Century* (Lewisburg, PA: Wennawoods Publishing, 1998), 165–68 ("long knives"); Rev. John Heckewelder, *History, Manners, and Customs of the Indian Nations Who Once Inhabited Pennsylvania and the Neighbouring States* (Philadelphia: Historical Society of Pennsylvania, 1876; rpt. New York: Arno Press, 1971), 81 ("good white men"); White, *Middle Ground*, 495 (Washington comparison quote).

25. *St. Clair Papers* 2:186–87; CO 42/72:77, 79, 81; *MPHC* 24 (1895): 99–100, 102–3; *PTJ* 17:131–34, 20:107–8 (Beckwith).

26. Carter, *Life and Times of Little Turtle*, 91; Gayle Thornborough, ed., *Outpost on the Wabash, 1787–1791: Letters of Brigadier General Josiah Harmar and Major John Francis Hamtramck and Other Letters and Documents Selected from the Harmar Papers in the William L. Clements Library* (Indianapolis: Indiana Historical Society, 1957), 266. George Rogers Clark said burying grain was a regular practice and the Indians did so "very usually with success"; Harold C. Syrett et al., eds., *The Papers of Alexander Hamilton*, 27 vols. (Charlottesville: University of Virginia Press, 1961–87), 7:113.

27. Denny, *Military Journal*, 145, 147; Denny's report, Jan. 1, 1791, Arthur St. Clair Papers, OSL, card 22; "Journal of Harmar's Campaign," Draper Mss. 2W:335–48, Kekionga and Chillicothe at 340–41.

28. *PGW, Pres.* 7:70–77; Draper Mss. 2W:340–42; Denny, *Military Journal*, 146–149; Denny's report, Jan. 1, 1791, Arthur St. Clair Papers, OSL, card 22; St. Clair to Knox, Oct. 29 and Nov. 6, 1790, Arthur St. Clair Papers, OSL, card 21 and *St. Clair Papers* 2:188, 190; *Territorial Papers* 2:309–10, 313; *DHFFC* 21:181–84, 235–36, 272, 685, 711–12; Leroy V. Eid, "'The Slaughter Was Reciprocal': Josiah Harmar's Two Defeats, 1790," *Northwest Ohio Quarterly* 65 (Spring 1993): 51–67.

29. *PGW, Pres.* 6:615.

30. *PGW, Pres.* 6:668; *Writings of Washington* 31:156; *Territorial Papers* 2:310.

31. John Ferling, *The Ascent of George Washington: The Hidden Political Genius of an American Icon* (New York: Bloomsbury, 2009), 319.

32. *The Proceedings of a Court of Inquiry, Held at the Special Request of Brigadier General Josiah Harmar,* in *American State Papers, Military Affairs,* 1:20–30; Draper Mss. 2W:402–6, 419–26, 4U:19–64.

33. Draper Mss. 2W:395.

34. *The Journal of William Maclay, United States Senator from Pennsylvania, 1789–1791* (New York: Albert and Charles Boni, 1927), 339–40, 384; *The Diary of William Maclay and Other Notes on Senate Debates,* in *DHFFC* 9:340, 342, 379, 385 (pretext).

35. *PTJ* 19:440–42, 521 (quote).

36. *PGW, Pres.* 7:55–56.

37. Symmes Papers, Draper Mss. 3WW:79–81; Beverley W. Bond Jr., ed., *The Correspondence of John Cleves Symmes* (New York: Macmillan, 1926), 134, 136.

38. *PGW, Pres.* 7:100–101, 208–9, 470–72; *ASPIA* 1:121–22; Archer Butler Hulbert, ed., *The Records of the Original Proceedings of the Ohio Company,* 2 vols. (Marietta, OH: Marietta Historical Commission, 1917), 2:68; *Territorial Papers* 2:338–39.

39. *PGW, Pres.* 7:262–68, 402–13.

40. *PGW, Pres.* 8:115; *PTJ* 20:145, 214.

41. *ASPIA* 1:112–13.

42. *PGW, Pres.* 7:510; *St. Clair Papers* 2:283; Richard H. Kohn, *Eagle and Sword: The Federalists and the Creation of the Military Establishment in America, 1783–1802* (New York: Free Press, 1975), 110–11.

43. *ASPIA* 1:112, 171–74.

44. *PGW, Pres.* 7:550–52.

45. CO 42/73:35–37, 39–41; rpt. in "Information of Blue Jacket," *MPHC* 24:135–38.

46. *ASPIA* 1:129–33 (list of Indian prisoners at 133); Susan Sleeper-Smith, "George Washington and the Kidnapping of Indian Women in the Wabash River Valley," paper presented at the Native American and Indigenous Studies Conference, Washington, DC, June 4, 2015.

47. William T. Hutchinson et al., eds., *The Papers of James Madison,* 17 vols. (Chicago: University of Chicago Press, and Charlottesville: University of Virginia Press, 1962–91), 14:32–33.

48. Cutler to Sargent, Aug. 27, 1791, Winthrop Sargent Papers, Massachusetts Historical Society, reel 3, 256.

49. Wilkinson's report in *ASPIA* 1:133–35, and *St. Clair Papers* 2:233–39; *PGW, Pres.* 8:535; 9:121.

50. *American State Papers, Military Affairs* 1:36, 42.

51. *PTJ* 19:442–52, 461–64; Patrick J. Furlong, "Problems of Frontier Logistics in St. Clair's 1791 Campaign," in *Selected Papers from the 1983 and 1984 George Rogers Clark Trans-Appalachian Frontier History Conferences* (Vincennes, IN: National Park Service and University of Vincennes, 1985), available online at http://npshistory.com/series/symposia/george_rogers_clark/1983-1984/sec6.htm (accessed July 31, 2017).

52. William H. Guthman, *March to Massacre: A History of the First Seven Years of the United States Army, 1784–1791* (New York: McGraw-Hill, 1970), 207; *ASPIA* 1:188; *American State Papers, Military Affairs* 1:36–39; Knox to Butler, June 9, 1791, Arthur St. Clair Papers, OSL, card 26; Ferguson to St. Clair, June 25, 1791, and Knox to Butler, June 23, 1791, Arthur St. Clair Papers, OSL, card 28; *St. Clair Papers* 2:216–17, 223.

53. Furlong, "Problems of Frontier Logistics"; *St. Clair Papers* 2:216, 241; *American State Papers, Military Affairs* 1:37.

54. Knox Papers 28:144.

55. Knox to Butler, July 21, Aug. 4, Aug. 11, Aug. 25, 1791, Arthur St. Clair Papers, OSL, cards 30, 31, 32, 33; *St. Clair Papers* 2:232, 241.

56. "Winthrop Sargent's Diary While with General Arthur St. Clair's Expedition against the Indians," *Ohio Archaeological and Historical Society Publications* 33 (1924): 241.

57. *CVSP* 5:370; *St. Clair Papers* 2:124; *Territorial Papers* 2:216.

58. "Winthrop Sargent's Diary," 242; Denny, *Military Journal,* 170; St. Clair to Knox, Aug. 3, 1791, Knox Papers, 29:17.

59. Arthur St. Clair, *A Narrative of the Manner in which the Campaign against the Indians, in the Year One Thousand Seven Hundred and Ninety-one, was Conducted, under the Command of Major General Arthur St. Clair* (Philadelphia: n.p., 1812), 5, 26.

60. *American State Papers, Military Affairs* 1:36–39.

61. St. Clair to Knox, Sept. 18, 1791, Arthur St. Clair Papers, OSL, card 34; *St. Clair Papers* 2:240–41.

62. *PGW, Pres.* 9:38.

63. St. Clair to Ludlow, Aug. 6, 1791, Arthur St. Clair Papers, OSL, card 31; *St. Clair Papers* 2:246, 248.

64. Denny, *Military Journal,* 154–64; "Winthrop Sargent's Diary," 240–53; Milo M. Quaife, ed., "A Picture of the First United States Army: The Journal of Captain Samuel Newman," *Wisconsin Magazine of History* 2 (Sept. 1918): 60–73; *St. Clair Papers* 2:249–59; Frazer E. Wilson, ed., *Journal of Capt. Daniel Bradley* (Greenville, OH: Frank H. Jobes & Son, 1935), 19–28.

65. Denny, *Military Journal,* 171.

66. *St. Clair Papers* 2:263; St. Clair, *Narrative,* 111.

67. "Winthrop Sargent's Diary," 249, 255; St. Clair to Knox, Nov. 1, 1791, Knox Papers, 29:91.

68. *MPHC* 24:246–47, 262.

69. *Diaries of GW* 2:294.

70. Consul Willshire Butterfield, *History of the Girtys* (Cincinnati: Robert Clarke, 1890), 193.

71. Cary Miller, *Ogimaag: Anishinaabbeg Leadership, 1760–1845* (Lincoln: University of Nebraska Press, 2010), 119; Klinck and Talman, *Journal of John Norton,* 177; CO 42/89:35; *MPHC* 24:329–30.

72. CO 42/89:195; Klinck and Talman, *Journal of John Norton,* 178.

73. *St. Clair Papers* 2:263; "Winthrop Sargent's Diary," 258; Winthrop Sargent Papers, Massachusetts Historical Society, reel 1, 360; "Extract from a letter from a Gentleman...," Nov. 8, 1791," *Columbian Centinel,* Dec. 28, 1791, 3; "St. Clair's Defeat: Robert Bradshaw's Narrative," Draper Mss. 4U:143.

74. Frazer E. Wilson, ed., "St. Clair's Defeat, as Told by an Eye-Witness," *Ohio Archaeological and Historical Society Publications* 10 (1901–2): 379–80; Draper Mss. 4U:13; "Winthrop Sargent's Diary," 259; *St. Clair Papers* 2:266; Denny, *Military Journal,* 165–66; Wilson, *Journal of Capt. Daniel Bradley,* 29.

75. *St. Clair Papers* 2:263; Denny, *Military Journal,* 166; Quaife, *Captivity of O. M. Spencer,* 25; "Winthrop Sargent's Journal," 260.

76. "Robert Bradshaw's Narrative," Draper Mss. 4U:143.

77. Testimony of Captain Slough in "Testimonies of the Committee of Inquiry," Arthur St. Clair Papers, OSL, card 39; Klinck and Talman, *Journal of Major John Norton,* 178; Quaife, *Captivity of O. M. Spencer,* 25; Sword, *President Washington's Indian War,* 191.

78. Denny, *Military Journal,* 167–68; "Winthrop Sargent's Journal," 261–62; Draper Mss. 4U:13; Darke to Washington, Nov. 9, 1791, Knox Papers, 30:12, and *PGW, Pres.* 9:158–65 ("Mob at a fair" at 161); Beverley W. Bond Jr., ed., "Memoirs of Benjamin Van Cleve," *Quarterly Publication of the Historical and Philosophical Society of Ohio* 17 (Jan.–June 1922): 26–27.

79. "Winthrop Sargent's Diary," 265; Winthrop Sargent Papers, reel 3, 276–77, 284.

80. Denny, *Military Journal,* 171–74; Winthrop Sargent Papers, reel 3, 274, 282; Quaife, *Captivity of O. M. Spencer,* 27; "Winthrop Sargent's Diary," 269; Darke to Washington, Nov. 9, 1791, Knox Papers, 30:12, and *PGW, Pres.* 9:163.

81. CO 42/89:193; *MPHC* 24:336; Klinck and Talman, *Journal of John Norton,* 178; "Winthrop Sargent's Diary," 262, 272; Winthrop Sargent Papers, reel 3, 306; *Territorial Papers* 2:382; Draper Mss. 4U:166; "Indian Account, Of the unfortunate action of the 4th Nov. received via Pittsburgh." *New-Hampshire Gazette and General Advertiser,* March 7, 1791; "Story of George Ash," *Cincinnati Chronicle and Literary Gazette,* Nov. 7, 1829.

82. Winthrop Sargent Papers, reel 1, 417.
83. Lear's account appears in Richard Rush, *Washington in Domestic Life* (Philadelphia: J. B. Lippincott, 1857), 65–69, George Washington Parke Custis, *Recollections and Private Memoirs of Washington*, ed. Benson J. Lossing (New York: Derby & Jackson, 1860), 416–19, and Benson Lossing, *The Pictorial Field Book of the War of 1812* (New York: Harper's, 1868), 49–50.
84. *PGW, Pres.* 9:275; *CVSP* 5:399–400; Draper Mss. 4U:153–54, 166; *PTJ* 22:362–63, 384.
85. *PTJ* 22:389–90.
86. Denny, *Military Journal*, 175–77.
87. *PGW, Pres.* 9:274; *ASPIA* 1:136.
88. *PGW, Pres.* 9:276.
89. William Patrick Walsh, "The Defeat of Major General Arthur St. Clair, November 4, 1791: A Study of the Nation's Response, 1791–1793" (PhD diss., Loyola University of Chicago, 1977), 122.
90. Darke to Washington, Nov. 9, 1791, Knox Papers, 30:12; *PGW, Pres.* 9:158–65.
91. *PGW, Pres.* 10:156–57.
92. Hutchinson et al., *Papers of James Madison* 14:213.
93. *CVSP* 6:145–53, 155–57; *PGW, Pres.* 10:1–2 (quote).
94. *Boston Gazette*, Jan. 2, 1792, 2.
95. *PGW, Pres.* 10:558.
96. *PGW, Pres.* 9:575–77.
97. *PGW, Pres.* 9:291–92.
98. *PGW, Pres.* 9:556.
99. *PGW, Pres.* 10:93–94.
100. *PGW, Pres.* 10:97–98, 102–5.
101. Walsh, "The Defeat of Major General Arthur St. Clair," chs. 4–5; for example, the *Boston Gazette*, Feb. 13, 1792, 102.
102. Hutchinson et al., *Papers of James Madison* 14:213.
103. *PGW, Pres.* 9:505.
104. St. Clair to Washington, March 26, 1792, Feb. 24 (draft), March 26 (formal letter), March 31, 1792, Arthur St. Clair Papers, OSL, card 38; St. Clair to Washington, Apr. 7, 1792, Arthur St. Clair Papers, OSL, card 40; *St. Clair Papers* 2:279, 283–86; *PGW, Pres.* 10:155–56, 172–73, 218, 226–27; *Connecticut Courant*, Apr. 23, 1792, 1; *American Museum, or Universal Magazine*, June 3, 1792, 85–88.
105. *PTJ* 23:241–42.
106. George C. Chalou, "St. Clair's Defeat, 1792," in *Congress Investigates, 1792–1974*, ed. Arthur M. Schlesinger Jr. and Roger Burns (New York: Chelsea House, 1975), 1–18; James T. Currie, "The First Congressional Investigation: St. Clair's Military Disaster of 1791," *Parameters: US Army War College Quarterly* 20 (Dec. 1990): 95–102.
107. Knox to St. Clair, Dec. 23, 1791, Arthur St. Clair Papers, OSL, card 36; St. Clair to Fitzsimmons, Jan. 23, 1792, Arthur St. Clair Papers, OSL, card 37, and *St. Clair Papers* 2:278–79.
108. *PGW, Pres.* 10:168–69; Mark J. Rozell, "George Washington and the Origins of Executive Privilege," in *George Washington and the Origins of the Modern Presidency*, ed. Mark J. Rozell, William D. Pederson, and Frank J. Williams (Westport, CT: Praeger, 2000), 147–48. Jefferson's notes on the cabinet discussion of the question are in *PTJ* 23:261–62.
109. The testimonies of the committee of inquiry are in Arthur St. Clair Papers, OSL, cards 38–40. The committee's report is in *American State Papers: Military Affairs*, 1:36–39, St. Clair, *Narrative*, 59–79, and, with extracts from testimonies, *St. Clair Papers* 2:286–99.
110. *PTJ* 19:468; *American State Papers, Military Affairs* 1:39, 41–44; also rpt. in St. Clair, *Narrative*, 155–73.
111. St. Clair, *Narrative*
112. Patrick Griffin, *American Leviathan: Empire, Nation, and Revolutionary Frontier* (New York: Hill & Wang, 2007), 216.

113. CO 42/89:193; *MPHC* 24:336–37.
114. *Simcoe Correspondence* 1:29–30, 67, 100–101, 114, 151, 170, 173–74; CO 42/89:47–50.
115. *PGW, Pres.* 9:274, 10:85–86, 129.

CHAPTER 17: PHILADELPHIA INDIAN DIPLOMACY

1. Sandra M. Gustafson, "Historical Introduction to Hendrick Aupaumut's *Short Narration*," in *Early Native Literacies in New England: A Documentary and Critical Anthology*, ed. Kristina Bross and Hilary E. Wyss (Amherst: University of Massachusetts Press, 2008), 237.
2. Anthony F. C. Wallace, *The Death and Rebirth of the Seneca* (New York: Random House, 1969), 173.
3. *PGW, Pres.* 8:11.
4. Alyssa Mt. Pleasant, "Independence for Whom? Expansion and Conflict in the Northeast and Northwest," in *The World of the Revolutionary American Republic: Land, Labor, and the Conflict for a Continent*, ed. Andrew Shankman (New York: Routledge, 2014), 116–33.
5. *PGW, Pres.* 6:393–96, 401–2, 8:433; Pickering Papers 61:6, 10, 14; Michael Leroy Oberg, *Peacemakers: The Iroquois, the United States, and the Treaty of Canandaigua, 1794* (New York: Oxford University Press, 2015), 48–52.
6. *PGW, Pres.* 7:112.
7. *PGW, Pres.* 7:27–29; Pickering Papers 61:108.
8. Pickering Papers 61:119.
9. Christopher Densmore, *Red Jacket: Iroquois Diplomat and Orator* (Syracuse, NY: Syracuse University Press, 1999); Quaker at the Newtown conference quoted in David McLean, *Timothy Pickering and the Age of the American Revolution* (New York: Arno Press, 1982), 315.
10. Mt. Pleasant, "Independence for Whom?"
11. Granville Ganter, ed., *The Collected Speeches of Sagoyewatha, or Red Jacket* (Syracuse, NY: Syracuse University Press, 2006), 1–15; *PGW, Pres.* 7:114n2, 157–58 ("entire approbation"), 234–35 (declines); Pickering Papers 61:69–122 (Red Jacket's speeches at 62, 71, 82–83, 93–94 ["the mind of yr. broths"]); 61:113A (ambition).
12. Thomas S. Abler, *Cornplanter: Chief Warrior of the Allegany Senecas* (Syracuse, NY: Syracuse University Press, 2007), 16, 22. Abler finds "no convincing evidence" to support the notion that Cornplanter's mother was Queen Aliquippa, whom Washington had met in 1753.
13. Barbara Graymont, *The Iroquois in the American Revolution* (Syracuse, NY: Syracuse University Press, 1972), 123.
14. Archer Butler Hulbert, ed., *The Records of the Original Proceedings of the Ohio Company*, 2 vols. (Marietta, OH: Marietta Historical Commission, 1917), 1:82.
15. Abler, *Cornplanter*, 72–74 (visit to New York), 78 (Harmar treaty); Alan Taylor, *The Divided Ground: Indians, Settlers, and the Northern Borderland of the American Revolution* (New York: Knopf, 2005), 246–48.
16. Guyasuta and Cornplanter quoted in Daniel K. Richter, *Trade, Land, Power: The Struggle for Eastern North America* (Philadelphia: University of Pennsylvania Press, 2013), 222.
17. Samuel Kirkland Papers, 1764–1837, Dartmouth College, Rauner Library, MS-867, file #7, 33–39; Walter Pilkington, ed., *The Journals of Samuel Kirkland: 18th-century Missionary to the Iroquois, Government Agent, Father of Hamilton College* (Clinton, NY: Hamilton College, 1980), 208–9.
18. CO 42/82:316–38.
19. *ASPIA* 1:140–42; *PGW, Pres.* 7:7–15; Thomas A. Abler, ed., *Chainbreaker: The Revolutionary War Memoirs of Governor Blacksnake as told to Benjamin Williams* (Lincoln: University of Nebraska Press, 1989), 160–61, 176–77, 238–46. In 1786 the state of Massachusetts sold the right of preemption to lands it claimed in New York to Phelps and Gorham, who in 1788 persuaded Cornplanter and other Six Nations chiefs to sell them more than 2.5 million acres for $5,000 and an additional annuity of $500.
20. Franklin B. Hough, ed., *Proceedings of the Commissioners of Indian Affairs Appointed by Law for the Extinguishment of Indian Titles in the State of New York*, 2 vols. (Albany, NY: Joel Munsell, 1861), 2:465–66.

21. *PGW, Pres.* 7:121–27.

22. *PGW, Pres.* 7:146–50; *ASPIA* 1:142–43; Abler, *Chainbreaker,* 177–79, 246–50.

23. *PGW, Pres.* 7:218–21, 252–53, 322–23; *ASPIA* 1:143–44; Abler, *Chainbreaker,* 250–55.

24. *PGW, Pres.* 7:221; *ASPIA* 1:144–45; Abler, *Chainbreaker,* 254; Wallace, *Death and Rebirth of the Seneca,* 203–4.

25. Arthur St. Clair Papers, Ohio State Library (OSL): Knox to St. Clair, March 23, 1791, card 23; St. Clair to Knox, April 19, 1791, card 24; "Indian Goods for Col. Timothy Pickering for Treaty to be held with the Six Nations, May 16, 1791, card 24.

26. *ASPIA* 1:145–47; 149–65 (Proctor's narrative); CO 42/73:175–87; *PGW, Pres.* 8:258 (Knox quote).

27. *PGW, Pres.* 8:58.

28. *CVSP* 5:315 ("as fast as they can"), 318; *PGW, Pres.* 8:360. Others echoed Washington's sentiments. A visiting Englishman thought "it would be impossible to find any jury in the back parts of America, who would bring any one in guilty of murder, for causing the death of an Indian." Francis Baily, *Journal of a Tour in Unsettled Parts of North America in 1796 and 1797,* ed. Jack D. L. Holmes (Carbondale: Southern Illinois University Press, 1969), 106.

29. Ganter, *Collected Speeches of Sagoyewatha,* 22–32; Pickering Papers 60:69–112 (Red Jacket's speeches at 92, 96,105, 110); Taylor, *Divided Ground,* 250–53.

30. Taylor, *Divided Ground,* 253.

31. *PGW, Pres.* 10:141; Pickering to Knox, Aug. 10, 1791, Pickering Papers 60:115–16 ("corrupt"; "splendor"); Jacques Pierre Brissot de Warville, *On America: New Travels in the United States of America Performed in 1788,* 2 vols. (1792; New York: Augustus M. Kelley, 1970) 1:312–13.

32. Herman J. Viola, *Diplomats in Buckskins: A History of Indian Delegations in Washington City* (Washington, D.C: Smithsonian Institution Press, 1981).

33. *Simcoe Correspondence* 2:68–69, 86, 99–100, 102, 105.

34. *ASPIA* 1:226, 228–29, 245, 249.

35. Harold C. Syrett et al., eds., *The Papers of Alexander Hamilton,* 27 vols. (Charlottesville: University of Virginia Press, 1961–87), 11:375.

36. *ASPIA* 1:229; Taylor, *Divided Ground,* 271 (quoting Kirkland to Knox, Jan. 5, 1791). According to a note from the War Department to Tobias Lear, "the names of the Indians who are invited to dine with the President on Monday next, are, The Farmer's Brother; the Young King; China Breast Plate; the Infant; Solomon & John, young warriors; and Hendrick Aupamat & Solomon, his brother"; Stephen Decatur Jr., *Private Affairs of George Washington: From the Records and Accounts of Tobias Lear, Esquire, His Secretary* (Boston: Houghton Mifflin, 1933), 324. A portrait of the Infant painted by John Trumbull while he was in Philadelphia is in the Yale University Art Gallery.

37. Laura Auricchio, *The Marquis: Lafayette Reconsidered* (New York: Knopf, 2014), 137–39; Dean R. Snow, Charles T. Gehring, and William A. Starna, eds., *In Mohawk Country: Early Narratives about a Native People* (Syracuse. NY: Syracuse University Press, 1996), 337 (Watson); *PGW, Pres.* 10:317.

38. *PGW, Pres.* 10:142–43; Pickering Papers 62:11; Syrett et al., *Papers of Alexander Hamilton* 11:375–77.

39. *PGW, Pres.* 10:148–49, 151–52; *ASPIA* 1:229–33; Abler, *Chainbreaker,* 190–91, 260–65.

40. Pilkington, *Journals of Samuel Kirkland,* 130, 231.

41. Ganter, *Collected Speeches of Sagoyewatha,* 33–44; *PGW, Pres.* 10:190–94 (Red Jacket's speech).

42. Densmore, *Red Jacket,* 37–38.

43. Thomas S. Abler, "Governor Blacksnake as a Young Man? Speculation on the Identity of Trumbull's *The Young Sachem,*" *Ethnohistory* 34 (1987): 329–51.

44. *PGW, Pres.* 10:310, 316–17.

45. Syrett et al., *Papers of Alexander Hamilton* 11:373–74.

46. Haldimand Papers 21756:330 (pension), 21763:99 (quote), 108, 21882:29 (captain), 21785:36–38, 52, 70–71.

47. Hough, *Proceedings of the Commissioners of Indian Affairs* 2:465.

48. Hough, *Proceedings of the Commissioners of Indian Affairs* 2:470.

49. *Writings of Washington* 15:173.

50. Isabel Thompson Kelsay, *Joseph Brant, 1743–1807: Man of Two Worlds* (Syracuse, NY: Syracuse University Press, 1984), 459–63; Taylor, *Divided Ground*, 253–65, 275; William L. Stone, *Life of Joseph Brant–Thayendanegea*, 2 vols. (New York: George Dearborn, 1838), 2:319–26; *ASPIA* 1:228 "("such eminence"); *PGW, Pres.* 9:588–89, 10:310–12.

51. CO 42/90:196–97.

52. *PGW, Pres.* 10:491.

53. *PTJ* 24:106.

54. Isaac Weld Jr., *Travels through the States of North America, and the Provinces of Upper and Lower Canada, during the years 1795, 1796, and 1797*, 2nd ed., 2 vols. (London: John Stockdale, 1799), 2:279–80.

55. *ASPIA* 1:236–37; *Simcoe Correspondence* 5:18–19.

56. Kelsay, *Joseph Brant*, 470–74; Taylor, *Divided Ground*, 275–77; *PTJ* 24:133 ("best dispositions"); Stone, *Life of Joseph Brant* 2:328 (refused offers); FO 4/16:33–35 (Brant and Hammond). I am grateful to Paul Williams for suggesting the possibility of a private agreement between two Masons. On Brant as a Mason, see Joy Porter, *Native American Freemasonry: Associationalism and Performance in America* (Lincoln: University of Nebraska Press, 2011), 194–206.

57. Mary Quayle Innis, ed., *Mrs. Simcoe's Diary* (Toronto: Macmillan, 1965), 82–83.

58. Hammond's secretary said Jefferson made clear his hatred and malevolence toward Britain; he thought Washington polite but reserved: "a man of great but secret ambition, and has, sometimes, I think condescended to use little arts, and those too very shallow ones, to secure the object of his ambition." S. W. Jackman, ed., "A Young Englishman Reports on the New Nation: Edward Thornton to James Bland Burges, 1791–1793," *William and Mary Quarterly*, 3rd ser., 18 (1961): 95–97 (Jefferson), 104 (Washington).

59. FO 4/11:249–51, 255–59, 14:253–55, 15:313–14, 16:1–4, 272–74; FO 5/1:29–30, 50–51; CO 42/73:15–16, 83:134–37, 89:47–50; William Pitt, 1st Earl of Chatham, Papers, UK National Archives, formerly PRO 30/8/344:47–53; *Simcoe Correspondence* 1:58–59, 66–68, 130–31, 151, 173–76, 208–9, 233, 267–68; Syrett et al., *Papers of Alexander Hamilton* 10:373–74; 11:347, 446–48; 13:213–14; Charles R. Ritcheson, *Aftermath of Revolution: British Policy toward the United States, 1783–1795* (New York: Norton, 1971), chs. 12–13; Robert F. Berkhofer Jr., "Barrier to Settlement: British Indian Policy in the Old Northwest, 1783–1794," in *The Frontier in American Development*, ed. David M. Ellis (Ithaca, NY: Cornell University Press, 1969), 249–76. On British-Indian policy more generally at this time, see Colin G. Calloway, *Crown and Calumet: British-Indian Relations, 1783–1815* (Norman: University of Oklahoma Press, 1987), and Timothy D. Willig, *Restoring the Chain of Friendship: British Policy and the Indians of the Great Lakes, 1783–1815* (Lincoln: University of Nebraska Press, 2008).

60. *PTJ* 20:109–13, 140–41, 23:240.

61. *PGW, Pres.* 10:490.

62. *PTJ* 24:29–31, 717–21, 728–30; *Simcoe Correspondence* 1:267–68.

63. *Simcoe Correspondence* 1:142.

64. *Simcoe Correspondence* 1:142, 202 (quotes); S. F. Wise, "The Indian Diplomacy of John Graves Simcoe," *Annual Report of the Canadian Historical Association* (1953): 41.

65. *ASPIA* 1:227.

66. *ASPIA* 1:230; *PGW, Pres.* 10:187–89.

67. William T. Hutchinson et al., eds., *The Papers of James Madison*, 17 vols. (Chicago: University of Chicago Press, and Charlottesville: University of Virginia Press, 1962–1991), 14:297–98.

68. *ASPIA* 1:229–30, 243; Jacob Burnet, *Notes on the Early Settlement of the North-Western Territory* (Cincinnati: Derby, Bradley, 1847), 129–31.

69. *ASPIA* 1:337.

70. *PGW, Pres.* 10:653.

71. *PTJ* 23:240.

72. *PGW, Pres.* 10:635.

73. *PGW, Pres.* 11:29; *PTJ* 24:316.

74. *Simcoe Correspondence* 5:34 ("yanky Indian"); Alan Taylor, "Captain Hendrick Aupaumut: The Dilemmas of an Intercultural Broker," *Ethnohistory* 43 (1996): 431–57; Rachel Wheeler, "Hendrick Aupaumut: Christian-Mahican Prophet," *Journal of the Early Republic* 25 (2005): 187–220 ("front door" quote at 209).

75. B. H. Coates, ed., "A Narrative of an Embassy to the Western Indians from the Original Manuscript of Hendrick Aupaumut," *Memoirs of the Historical Society of Pennsylvania* 2, pt. 1 (1827): 76, 78.

76. Wheeler, "Hendrick Aupaumut," 205 (consent of the governed); Coates, "Narrative of an Embassy to the Western Indians," 128 ("Yorkers").

77. Richard White, *The Middle Ground: Indians, Empires, and Republics in the Great Lakes Region, 1650–1815* (Cambridge: Cambridge University Press, 1991), 458–59.

78. *PGW, Pres.* 10:338–42, 12:141–42; Taylor, *Divided Ground*, 173, 182–84, 217, 222–25, 345–56. Cook's complaint against Brant is in Pickering Papers 59:50.

79. *PGW, Pres.* 12:186.

80. *PGW, Pres.* 12:422–23; *ASPIA* 1:123 (Knox declines).

81. *PGW, Pres.* 11:85, 115–16 (quote), 124, 150.

82. Pilkington, *Journal of the Rev. Samuel Kirkland*, 231.

83. *ASPIA* 1:233–36 ("foot of their land" at 234); Rowena Buell, ed., *The Memoirs of Rufus Putnam and Certain Official Papers and Correspondence* (Boston: Houghton Mifflin, 1903), 118–20, 257–67.

84. *PGW, Pres.* 10:653.

85. Paul A. W. Wallace, ed., *Thirty Thousand Miles with John Heckewelder; or, Travels amoung the Indians of Pennsylvania, New York & Ohio in the 18th Century* (Lewisburg, PA.: Wennawoods Publishing, 1998), 258–93. On Wells, see William Heath, *William Wells and the Struggle for the Old Northwest* (Norman: University of Oklahoma Press, 2015).

86. The treaty and proceedings are in *ASPIA* 1:338–40; Buell, *Memoirs of Rufus Putnam*, 335–67; R. David Edmunds, "'Nothing Has Been Effected': The Vincennes Treaty of 1792," *Indiana Magazine of History* 74 (March 1978): 23–35; *JPP*, 66.

87. Decatur, *Private Affairs of George Washington*, 325–26; *PGW, Pres.* 11:368–70. On DuCoigne's earlier visit, see *PTJ* 6:43, 60–64n.

88. *JPP*, 11.

89. *PGW, Pres.* 15:7n. On January 6, 1793, Tobias Lear and "the other gentlemen of the family" represented the president at the funeral of one of the chiefs who died; Decatur, *Private Affairs of George Washington*, 325.

90. *JPP*, 40, 42–43; *PGW, Pres.* 12:79–80, 82–90 (quotes at 82, 83, 89); *PTJ* 25:112–18.

91. *PGW, Pres.* 12:551–53; *JPP*, 45 (pipes to War Office).

92. *PGW, Pres.* 12:137–39, 15:6–7 (Knox quote); *ASPIA* 1:470; *JPP*, 44.

93. Richard C. Knopf, ed., *Anthony Wayne: A Name in Arms: The Wayne-Knox-Pickering-McHenry Correspondence* (Pittsburgh: University of Pittsburgh Press, 1960), 84.

94. *ASPIA* 1:243; Consul Willshire Butterfield, *History of the Girtys* (Cincinnati: Robert Clarke, 1890), 203 ("can not tell the names").

95. The following discussion of the negotiations at the Glaize council is based on the account in *Simcoe Correspondence* 1:218–29; see also Coates, "Narrative of an Embassy to the Western Indians," 118; *JPP*, 3–4, 66.

96. Coates, "Narrative of an Embassy to the Western Indians," 113.

97. *ASPIA* 1:337.

98. *Simcoe Correspondence* 1:243.

99. *Simcoe Correspondence* 1:258.

100. *PGW, Pres.* 12:41–42, 57–60, 74, 246; *PTJ* 25:88–89, 229.

101. *JPP*, 31.

102. *PGW, Pres.* 12:130–31; *JPP*, 49–50.

103. *PGW, Pres.* 12:153–55, 292–93, 354–55, 457, 13:37–40; GW to cabinet (Circular), Mar. 22, 1793, GWPLC; *PTJ* 25:220–22, 258–59 (first written cabinet opinions at 259n), 271–73, 354–56 (Jefferson's report on treaties and boundaries), 424.

104. *ASPIA* 1:340–42 ("explicitly" at 341).

105. *PTJ* 25:272.
106. *ASPIA* 1:343.
107. *Simcoe Correspondence* 5:31.
108. *Simcoe Correspondence* 1:354–55, 400 (quote).
109. *Simcoe Correspondence* 5:47.
110. *Simcoe Correspondence* 1:355.
111. *ASPIA* 2:478; Brant to ——, Mar. 23, 1793, National Archives of Canada, Claus Family Papers, MG 19, 1F, 5:95–96, and reel C-1479 (quote).
112. *Simcoe Correspondence* 5:29.
113. On the Sandusky negotiations, see *Simcoe Correspondence* 2:1–35 (Brant's journal of the council at 5–17; Indian proposal at 17–20); General Benjamin Lincoln, "Journal of a Treaty held in 1793, with the Indian Tribes North-west of the Ohio, by Commissioners of the United States," *Collections of the Massachusetts Historical Society*, 3rd ser., 5 (1836): 109–76 ("express authority" at 149; Wyandot chief at 150); *ASPIA* 1:340–60 ("Great chief" at 350; Wyandot and Girty at 354); Wallace, *Thirty Thousand Miles with John Heckewelder*, 312–20; *PGW, Pres.* 14:143–47 (Beverley Randolph's report to Washington); *JPP*, 236–37; Pickering Papers 60:158, 160, 170, 175–79; and Reginald Horsman, "The British Indian Department and the Abortive Treaty of Lower Sandusky, 1793," *Ohio Historical Quarterly* 70 (1961): 189–213.
114. *ASPIA* 1:350.
115. *Simcoe Correspondence* 2:17–20; Lincoln, "Journal of a Treaty," 164–67; *ASPIA* 1:356–57; Wallace, *Thirty Thousand Miles with John Heckewelder*, 319 ("impertinent").
116. *ASPIA* 1:359; Pickering Papers 60:179.
117. CO 42/97:147; *Simcoe Correspondence* 2:68–69, 102–3.
118. *Simcoe Correspondence* 2:35.
119. *Simcoe Correspondence* 2:49, 59–60 (quote at 59), 101–2.
120. *Simcoe Correspondence* 2:102, 116, 3:239, 5:45.
121. Knopf, *Anthony Wayne*, 271.
122. *PTJ* 26:287, 393, 27:450 (quote).
123. *PGW, Pres.* 14:465.

CHAPTER 18: ACHIEVING EMPIRE

1. *PGW, Pres.* 9:519; Kevin Kokomoor, "Creeks, Federalists, and the Idea of Coexistence in the Early Republic," *Journal of Southern History* 81 (2015): 803–42.
2. Peter H. Wood, "George Washington, Dragging Canoe, and Southern Indian Resistance," in *George Washington's South*, ed. Tamara Harvey and Greg O'Brien (Gainesville: University Press of Florida, 2004), 259–77; Jon W. Parmenter, "Dragging Canoe (Tsí yu-gûnsí ni), Chickamauga Cherokee Patriot," in *The Human Tradition in the American Revolution*, ed. Nancy L. Rhoden and Ian K. Steele (Wilmington, DE: Scholarly Resources, 1999), 117–37; Colin G. Calloway, "Declaring Independence and Rebuilding a Nation: Dragging Canoe and the Chickamauga Revolution," in *Revolutionary Founders: Rebels, Radicals, and Reformers in the Making of the Nation*, ed. Alfred F. Young, Gary B. Nash, and Ray Raphael (New York: Knopf, 2011), 185–98, draws less explicit parallels between Chickamauga and American struggles for independence.
3. *PGW, Pres.* 11:343.
4. *ASPIA* 1:255 ("friendly half breed"), 263, 271.
5. *IALT*, 29–32; *ASPIA* 1:124–25 (treaty), 203–4 (Bloody Fellow quote); *Territorial Papers* 4:60–68; Alice Barnwell Keith et al., eds., *The John Gray Blount Papers*, 3 vols. (Raleigh, NC: State Department of Archives and History, 1959–65), 2:170–71 (Blount quote); David Andrew Nichols, *Red Gentlemen and White Savages: Indians, Federalists, and the Search for Order on the American Frontier* (Charlottesville: University of Virginia Press, 2008), 151–53.
6. *PGW, Pres.* 9:178–80; *Territorial Papers* 4:60–68.
7. *PGW, Pres.* 9:447–52; *Territorial Papers* 4:111–17, 120–21; *ASPIA* 1:203–6 (Bloody Fellow quotes at 204–5; common hunting ground at 204 and 273).

8. *PGW, Pres.* 9:470, 519 ("of a nature"); *ASPIA* 1:203, 247 (Shaw appointed); *IALT,* 32–33 (treaty amendment).
9. *ASPIA* 1:268 ("honorable name"); Stanley W. Hoig, *The Cherokees and Their Chiefs: In the Wake of Empire* (Fayetteville: University of Arkansas Press, 1998), 76; Charles A. Weeks, *Paths to a Middle Ground: The Diplomacy of Natchez, Boukfouka, Nogales and San Fernando de las Barrancas, 1791–1795* (Tuscaloosa: University of Alabama Press, 2005), 85–86.
10. *ASPIA* 1:271. Hugh Williamson said the Cherokees appeared to be "in a very good Temper" when they left; Keith et al., *John Gray Blount Papers* 2:183.
11. *PGW, Pres.* 14:150.
12. Weeks, *Paths to a Middle Ground,* 24, 85–86, 89, 203–6; William S. Coker and Thomas D. Watson, *Indian Traders of the Southeastern Spanish Borderlands: Panton, Leslie & Company and John Forbes & Company, 1783–1847* (Pensacola: University of West Florida Press, 1986), 162, 166; *ASPIA* 1:288–91; Lawrence Kinnaird, ed., *Spain in the Mississippi Valley, 1765–1794: Translations of Materials from the Spanish Archives in the Bancroft Library,* 3 pts., vols. 2–4 of *Annual Report of the American Historical Association for 1945* (Washington, DC: Government Printing Office, 1946–49), vol. 4, pt. 3, 96, 101; *PTJ* 26:316 (Cherokee speech to Carondelet).
13. Kinnaird, *Spain in the Mississippi Valley,* pt. 3, 164, 176.
14. Gilbert C. Din and Abraham P. Nasatir, *The Imperial Osages: Spanish-Indian Diplomacy in the Mississippi Valley* (Norman: University of Oklahoma Press, 1983); Willard H. Rollings, *The Osage: An Ethnohistorical Study of Hegemony on the Prairie-Plains* (Columbia: University of Missouri Press, 1992); Kathleen DuVal, *The Native Ground: Indians and Colonists in the Heart of the Continent* (Philadelphia: University of Pennsylvania Press, 2006), 102–27, 164–78; Kinnaird, *Spain in the Mississippi Valley,* pt. 3, 94, 119 (Chickasaw chief quote), 143–46, 148–49, 155, 299–300, 321.
15. *ASPIA* 1:205.
16. *PGW, Pres.* 9:451; *Territorial Papers* 4:114.
17. *ASPIA* 1:248–49; Kinnaird, *Spain in the Mississippi Valley,* pt. 3, 4–5; James R. Atkinson, *Splendid Land, Splendid People: The Chickasaw Indians to Removal* (Tuscaloosa: University of Alabama Press, 2004), 152–54, identifies the two other chiefs as William and George Colbert.
18. *PGW, Pres.* 9:519.
19. Keith et al., *John Gray Blount Papers* 2:195; the proceedings of the Nashville conference are in *ASPIA* 1:284–88; *PTJ* 26:265 ("evil eyes").
20. *ASPIA* 1:465.
21. Kinnaird, *Spain in the Mississippi Valley,* pt. 3, 104.
22. Kinnaird, *Spain in the Mississippi Valley,* pt. 3, 140–43, 164–67, 223–27 (Treaty of Nogales); Weeks, *Paths to a Middle Ground,* 230–32.
23. *ASPIA* 1:458, 468.
24. L. H. Butterfield et al., eds., *Adams Family Correspondence,* 10 vols. (Cambridge, MA: Harvard University Press, 1963–2011), 10:209 ("assisted in smoking"); John Quincy Adams diary 20, July 11, 1794, 5–6, in *The Diaries of John Quincy Adams: A Digital Collection* (Boston: Massachusetts Historical Society, 2004), http://www.masshist.org/jqadiaries; *PGW, Pres.* 16:383, 402 (commissions); 332–33; 424; *Territorial Papers* 4:349–50; Richard Green, "Chickasaws Visit President Washington (1794)," *Chickasaw Times,* July 2009; Atkinson, *Splendid Land, Splendid People,* 164–66; Kinnaird, *Spain in the Mississippi Valley,* pt. 3, 326 (document).
    In 1956, street construction disturbed what is believed to have been Piominko's grave. The grave contained the peace medal Washington had given him in 1792. It also contained a map displaying the boundaries of the Chickasaw nation. Piominko esteemed his relationship with Washington, but he knew he needed to be vigilant in protecting Chickasaw land. (Atkinson, *Splendid Land, Splendid People,* 154. I am grateful to Rick Thompson for the information on the map.) The sculptural/maritime artist William Rush asked Piominko to pose for the figurehead on a "state of the art" merchant ship, the

William Penn, launched in Philadelphia the year after his initial visit. Using Piominko as the model may have been a significant gesture to an important ally. I am grateful to Ed Hamilton of Corinth, Maine, for bringing the *William Penn*'s figurehead and Piominko's role as model to my attention.

25. Kinnaird, *Spain in the Mississippi Valley*, pt. 3, 313–14.

26. *PGW, Pres.* 10:614.

27. *PGW, Pres.* 11:509–10.

28. *PGW, Pres.* 12:124–25; *ASPIA* 1:429, 431, 449, 452, 457; *JPP*, 46; *Territorial Papers* 4:237–38, 248–51, 255–56, 260; Keith et al., *John Gray Blount Papers* 2:231, 244, 277.

29. *CVSP* 6:409–10, 412–13, 418, 435–36, 460; *ASPIA* 1:459. Hanging Maw's wife later petitioned Congress for compensation (unsuccessfully); *ASPIA* 2:621.

30. *ASPIA* 1:459–60; Kinnaird, *Spain in the Mississippi Valley*, pt. 3, 198–99.

31. *ASPIA* 1:468, 2:622; *CVSP* 6:575; Charles H. Faulkner, *Massacre at Cavett's Station: Frontier Tennessee during the Cherokee Wars* (Knoxville: University of Tennessee Press, 2013).

32. Weeks, *Paths to a Middle Ground*, 216.

33. *ASPIA* 1:431.

34. *Territorial Papers* 4:282 (Smith); *ASPIA* 1:408 (Seagrove), 464; *JPP*, 154–55, 171–75, 178–80.

35. *ASPIA* 1:418.

36. *Territorial Papers* 4:274, 303 ("yellow Brethren" quotes); Keith et al., *John Gray Blount Papers* 2:212, 221.

37. *PGW, Pres.* 13:170–71.

38. *PGW, Pres.* 13:213–14, 281–84, 290–91, 309, 340, 357–61, 440–41; *Territorial Papers* 4:283–89, 291–98.

39. Jeff W. Dennis describes Pickens as "a backcountry George Washington"; Dennis, *Patriots and Indians: Shaping Identity in Eighteenth-Century South Carolina* (Columbia: University of South Carolina Press, 2017), ch. 5.

40. *PGW, Pres.* 13:360.

41. *PGW, Pres.* 13:226–27.

42. *PGW, Pres.* 13:3–4; *Territorial Papers* 4:266–67; *PTJ* 26:156–57 (cabinet split).

43. *PGW, Pres.* 13:588–89; *ASPIA* 1:365–66; *JPP*, 137, 140, 166 ("disagreeable"); *PTJ* 27:32 (cabinet); Harold C. Syrett et al., eds., *The Papers of Alexander Hamilton*, 27 vols. (Charlottesville: University of Virginia Press, 1961–87), 14:507–8 (cabinet).

44. Kinnaird, *Spain in the Mississippi Valley*, pt. 3, 223–27.

45. *PGW, Pres.* 16:222–23; *JPP*, 309–10; *Territorial Papers* 4:346–48; *AISP* 2:543; *IALT*, 33–34.

46. Keith et al., *John Gray Blount Papers* 2:414, 421.

47. *ASPIA* 2:529–30, 535, 632 (quote); Kinnaird, *Spain in the Mississippi Valley*, pt. 3, 344–45.

48. *Territorial Papers* 4:360–61.

49. *ASPIA* 2:534, 537.

50. *Territorial Papers* 4:380–81.

51. *Territorial Papers* 4:386–92 (quotes at 387, 389).

52. *PGW, Pres.* 18:270, 295–96, 554–55, 559, 576–78 (speech); A. L. Crabb, "George Washington and the Chickasaw Nation, 1795," *Mississippi Valley Historical Review* 19 (1932): 404; Atkinson, *Splendid Land, Splendid People*, 175–76; Keith et al., *John Gray Blount Papers* 2:594. The text of his talk to the first delegation has not been found.

53. *PGW, Pres.* 18:698, 704; GW to Pickering, Sept. 16, 1795, GWPLC.

54. *PGW, Pres.* 18:662–64.

55. *PGW, Pres.* 17:391–402, 19:221–22.

56. *ASPIA* 2:501–2; Kokomoor, "Creeks, Federalists, and the Idea of Coexistence in the Early Republic," 829–30.

57. *ASPIA* 2:551–55; David A. Nichols, "Land, Republicanism, and Indians: Power and Policy in Early National Georgia, 1780–1825," *Georgia Historical Quarterly* 85 (2001): 210–11, 213.

58. *PGW, Pres.* 18:xxvi; GW to Senate, June 25, 1795, GWPLC.

59. "Journal of the Proceedings of the Commissioners Appointed to Ascertain and Mark the Boundary Lines Agreeably to the Treaties between the Indian Nations and the United

States," in *The Collected Works of Benjamin Hawkins, 1796–1810*, ed. H. Thomas Foster (Tuscaloosa: University of Alabama Press, 2003), 138–62; *ASPIA*, 586–616 (terms at 586–87; Fusatchee Mico at 608); *PGW, Pres.* 18:661; Leonard J. Sadosky, *Revolutionary Negotiations: Indians, Empires, and Diplomats in the Founding of America* (Charlottesville: University of Virginia Press 2009), 165–75; Kokomoor, "Creeks, Federalists, and the Idea of Coexistence in the Early Republic," 831–37.

60. Keith et al., *John Gray Blount Papers* 3:107–8.

61. William Hogeland, *Autumn of the Black Snake: The Creation of the U.S. Army and the Invasion That Opened the West* (New York: Farrar, Straus & Giroux, 2017); *ASPIA* 1:199; "Organization of the Army in 1792," in *American State Papers: Documents, Legislative and Executive, of the Congress of the United States, Class 5: Military Affairs*, selected and ed. Walter Lowrie and Matthew St. Clair Clarke, 7 vols. (Washington: Gales & Seaton, 1832), 1:40–41; Richard H. Kohn, *Eagle and Sword: The Federalists and the Creation of the Military Establishment in America, 1783–1802* (New York: Free Press, 1975), 123–27; Russell F. Weigley, *History of the United States Army* (Bloomington: Indiana University Press, 1984), 92; Francis Paul Prucha, *The Sword of the Republic: The United States Army on the Frontier, 1783–1846* (Bloomington: Indiana University Press, 1969), 28; William H. Bergmann, *The American National State and the Early West* (Cambridge: Cambridge University Press, 2012), 53–55.

62. Kohn, *Eagle and Sword*, ch. 7; Harlow Giles Unger, *"Mr. President": George Washington and the Making of the Nation's Highest Office* (New York: Da Capo, 2013), 138–39, 237.

63. *PGW, Pres.* 10:71, 74–79 (Washington quote at 74); *PTJ* 23:242 (Jefferson quote).

64. *Simcoe Correspondence* 1:131–32.

65. *DHFFC* 16:702, 747, 786 (quote).

66. Alan D. Gaff, *Bayonets in the Wilderness: Anthony Wayne's Legion in the Old Northwest* (Norman: University of Oklahoma Press, 2004), 23–24; *PGW, Pres.* 10:186.

67. *PGW, Pres.* 10:266–68, 273–74.

68. Richard C. Knopf, ed., *Anthony Wayne: A Name in Arms: The Wayne-Knox-Pickering-McHenry Correspondence* (Pittsburgh: University of Pittsburgh Press, 1960), 28, 67.

69. Gaff, *Bayonets in the Wilderness*, 71.

70. Knopf, *Anthony Wayne*, 61, 66, 71–72, 77.

71. Knopf, *Anthony Wayne*, 97, 122, 223, 230; *JPP*, 105, 289.

72. *PGW, Pres.* 11:26.

73. *ASPIA* 1:255.

74. Kinnaird, *Spain in the Mississippi Valley*, pt. 3, 280 (quote), 284, 297.

75. *PGW, Pres.* 14:96.

76. *PGW, Pres.* 14:465.

77. *PGW, Pres.* 15:14–15.

78. Henry Howe, *Historical Collections of Ohio*, 2 vols. (Cincinnati: C. J. Krehbiel, 1908), 2:232.

79. Dorchester's speech is in CO 42/98:104–5; *Simcoe Correspondence* 2:149–50; *PGW, Pres.* 15:417–19 (Cook and Clinton), 474–75, 512, 527–28.

80. Knopf, *Anthony Wayne*, 253–54, 255–56, 319, 335, 337–38.

81. Reginald Horsman, "The British Indian Department and the Resistance to General Anthony Wayne," *Mississippi Valley Historical Review* 49 (1962–63): 269–90; *Simcoe Correspondence* 2:249–45, 357; McKee Papers, National Archives of Canada, MG19, F16, 2–3.

82. Richard White, *The Middle Ground: Indians, Empires, and Republics in the Great Lakes Region, 1650–1815* (Cambridge: Cambridge University Press, 1991), 462.

83. *Simcoe Correspondence* 2:334.

84. Dresden W. H. Howard, "The Battle of Fallen Timbers as Told by Chief Kin-Jo-I-No," *Northwest Ohio Quarterly* 20 (1948): 39.

85. Knopf, *Anthony Wayne*, 350.

86. *ASPIA* 2:491 (Wayne's report to Knox); Carl F. Klinck and James J. Talman, eds., *The Journal of Major John Norton, 1816* (Toronto: Champlain Society, 1970), 186.

87. *ASPIA* 2:493–94; John C. Kotruch, "The Battle of Fallen Timbers: An Assertion of U.S. Sovereignty in the Atlantic World along the Banks of the Maumee River," in *Between*

Sovereignty and Anarchy: The Politics of Violence in the American Revolutionary Era, ed. Patrick Griffin, Robert G. Ingram, Peter S. Onuf, and Brian Schoen (Charlottesville: University of Virginia Press, 2015), 263–83; Hogeland, *Autumn of the Black Snake.*

88. *ASPIA* 2:490–91; Knopf, *Anthony Wayne*, 354–55, 357.

89. "William Clark's Journal of General Wayne's Campaign," *Mississippi Valley Historical Review* 1 (Dec. 1914): 432.

90. *Simcoe Correspondence* 3:7–8.

91. *PGW, Pres,* 16:750.

92. *PGW, Pres.* 17:11–12.

93. *PGW, Pres.* 17:xxiii, 181–88.

94. François Furstenberg, "The Significance of the Trans-Appalachian Frontier in Atlantic History," *American Historical Review* 113 (2008): 666.

95. John E. Ferling, *The First of Men: A Life of George Washington* (New York: Oxford University Press, 2010), 452.

96. Thomas P. Slaughter, *The Whiskey Rebellion* (New York: Oxford University Press, 1986); William Hogeland, *The Whiskey Rebellion: George Washington, Alexander Hamilton, and the Frontier Rebels Who Challenged America's Newfound Sovereignty* (New York: Scribner, 2006).

97. William T. Hutchinson et al., eds., *The Papers of James Madison*, 17 vols. (Chicago: University of Chicago Press, and Charlottesville: University of Virginia Press, 1962–91), 15:393.

98. Andrew R. L. Cayton, "Radicals in the 'Western World': The Federalist Conquest of Trans-Appalachian North America," in *Federalists Reconsidered*, ed. Doron Ben-Atar and Barbara B. Oberg (Charlottesville: University of Virginia Press, 1998), 88.

99. *PGW, Pres.* 17:360.

100. *PGW, Pres.* 15:512.

101. *PGW, Pres.* 16:xxii, 119–21, 219, 227–31, 353–54, 373–75, 412–13, 17:187, 360.

102. *PGW, Pres.* 16:360–61; *ASPIA* 2:522–23.

103. *PGW, Pres.* 17:171.

104. Michael Leroy Oberg, *Peacemakers: The Iroquois, the United States, and the Treaty of Canandaigua, 1794* (New York: Oxford University Press, 2015); Jack Campisi and William A. Starna, "On the Road to Canandaigua: The Treaty of 1794," *American Indian Quarterly* 19 (1995): 467–90. Pickering's journal of the treaty proceedings is in Pickering Papers 60:198–241. Other journals were kept by Quaker observers: "The Savery Journal: The Canandaigua Treaty Excerpt," in *Treaty of Canandaigua, 1794: 200 Years of Treaty Relations between the Iroquois Confederacy and the United States*, ed. G. Peter Jemison and Anna M. Schein (Santa Fe: Clear Light Publishers, 2000), 260–93; William N. Fenton, ed., "The Journal of James Emlen Kept on a Trip to Canandaigua, New York, September 15 to October 30, 1794, to Attend the Treaty between the United States and the Six Nations," *Ethnohistory* 12 (1965): 279–342.

105. *PGW, Pres.* 17:39n.

106. *Simcoe Correspondence* 3:154 (Cornplanter to Brant); *Treaty of Canandaigua, 1794*, 276, 281–82, 285.

107. Pickering Papers 60:221–22, 224–25; Laurence M. Hauptman, *Conspiracy of Interests: Iroquois Dispossession and the Rise of New York State* (Syracuse, NY: Syracuse University Press, 1999), 74 (Oneida land-loss figures).

108. *PGW, Pres.* 17:33–34, 36.

109. Pickering Papers 60:207–8. The treaty is in *IALT*, 34–37.

110. *IALT*, 37–39.

111. Richard W. Hill Sr., "Linking Arms and Brightening the Chain: Building Relations through Treaties," in *Nation to Nation: Treaties between the United States and American Indian Nations*, ed. Susan Shown Harjo (Washington, DC: Smithsonian Books, 2014), 56. William N. Fenton, *The Great Law and the Longhouse: A Political History of the Iroquois Confederacy* (Norman: University of Oklahoma Press, 1988), 237, thought Congress commissioned the belt in 1775 or 1789, when thirteen rather than fifteen figures

represented the states in the Union, but it may have been given to the delegates in Philadelphia in 1792.

112. Oberg, *Peacemakers*, 132, 138, 144, 160–63; Jemison and Schein, *Treaty of Canandaigua, 1794* (John Mohawk quote at 62).

113. Hauptman, *Conspiracy of Interests*, 74, 80.

114. *PGW, Pres.* 17:425–26.

115. *PGW, Pres.* 18:41n–44n.

116. Thomas S. Abler, *Cornplanter: Chief Warrior of the Allegany Senecas* (Syracuse, NY: Syracuse University Press, 2007), 99.

117. *IALT*, 39–45 (signatories at 44). The negotiations are in *ASPIA* 2:562–82.

118. *ASPIA* 2:564 (New Corn), 577 (Little Turtle), 580 (Tarhe), 582 (Wayne).

119. White, *Middle Ground*, 472–73.

120. *PGW, Pres.* 18:727 (quote and queries), 744, 745 (more land than expected).

121. *PGW, Pres.* 19:28.

122. *PGW, Pres.* 16:613–15; Henry P. Johnston, ed., *The Correspondence and Public Papers of John Jay*, 4 vols. (New York: G. P. Putnam's Sons, 1890–93), 4:55–56.

123. *PGW, Pres.* 18:337–39; Syrett et al., *Papers of Alexander Hamilton* 18:461–64.

124. Johnston, *Correspondence and Public Papers of John Jay* 4:139; Todd Estes, *The Jay Treaty Debate, Public Opinion, and the Evolution of Early American Political Culture* (Amherst: University of Massachusetts Press, 2006).

125. CO 42/100:109–13.

126. *PGW, Pres.* 18:146.

127. *PGW, Pres.* 19:488–89.

128. John Adams to Abigail, Jan. 9, 1794, and Feb. 8, 1796, John Adams to John Quincy Adams, May 5, 1796, *The Adams Papers Digital Edition*, ed. C. James Taylor (Charlottesville: University of Virginia Press, 2008–16).

129. Weeks, *Paths to a Middle Ground*, 3–4, 140–41, 233–35; Charles A. Weeks, "Of Rattlesnakes, Wolves, and Tigers: A Harangue at the Chickasaw Bluffs, 1796," *William and Mary Quarterly* 67 (2010): 487–518; Colin G. Calloway, The *American Revolution in Indian Country* (Cambridge: Cambridge University Press, 1995), 241–42; "Talk of the Chickasaw Chiefs at Silver Bluffs, represented by Wolf's Friend… [1797]," University of Michigan, Clements Library, McHenry Papers.

130. *Writings of Washington* 34:399–400.

131. Slaughter, *Whiskey Rebellion*, 194; Alan Taylor, *The Divided Ground: Indians, Settlers, and the Northern Borderland of the American Revolution* (New York: Knopf, 2006), 238; Woody Holton, *Unruly Americans and the Origins of the Constitution* (New York: Hill & Wang, 2007), 268–69.

132. D. W. Meinig, *The Shaping of America: A Geographical Perspective on 500 Years of History*, vol. 1, *Atlantic America, 1492–1800* (New Haven, CT: Yale University Press, 1986), 417–18.

133. *PGW, Pres.* 19:223.

134. *PGW, Pres.* 17:425.

135. *PGW, Pres.* 19:15–16, 540 ("almost incredible"), 569; Craig Thompson Friend, *Kentucke's Frontiers* (Bloomington: Indiana University Press, 2010), 176–77.

136. Cayton, "Radicals in the 'Western World,'" 88; Andrew R. L. Cayton, "'Separate Interests' and the Nation-State: The Washington Administration and the Origins of Regionalism in the Trans-Appalachian West," *Journal of American History* 79 (1992): 39–67.

137. Sven Beckert, *Empire of Cotton: A Global History* (New York: Vintage/Penguin, 2014), ch. 5 ("infinite consequence" at 100; figures at 104; fabulously profitable at 177); Adam Rothman, *Slave Country: American Expansion and the Origins of the Deep South* (Cambridge, MA: Harvard University Press, 2005).

138. Roger G. Kennedy, *Mr. Jefferson's Lost Cause: Land, Farmers, Slavery, and the Louisiana Purchase* (New York: Oxford University Press, 2003), 14, termed it the path of "migrant agricultural capitalism."

139. *PGW, Pres.* 17:63, 206–7, and GW to Spotswood, Nov. 23, 1794, NYPL, GW, reel 2, typescript.

140. *PGW, Pres.* 12:499.

141. Joel Achenbach, *The Grand Idea: Washington's Potomac and the Race to the West* (New York: Simon & Schuster, 2004), 192.

142. Philander D. Chase, "A Stake in the West: George Washington as Backcountry Surveyor and Landholder," in George *Washington and the Virginia Backcountry*, ed. Warren R. Hofstra (Madison, WI: Madison House, 1998), 183; Consul W. Butterfield, ed., *The Washington-Crawford Letters: Being the Correspondence between George Washington and William Crawford, from 1767 to 1781, concerning Western Lands* (Cincinnati: Robert Clarke, 1877), 81–83 ("cream" and "perplexities" quotes); *PGW, Pres.* 16:25–26 (to Lear), 129–35 ("Memorandum" at 131–34), 208, 237–38 ("cream" and "perplexities" quotes); 17:404–7 ("plague than profit" at 405); *Writings of Washington* 34:222 (ditto).

143. *PGW, Pres.* 18:199–200, 267–68, 505 ($2,693), 572–75; Ferling, *First of Men,* 489.

144. *Writings of Washington* 34:173–74, 438–41; *PGW, Pres.* 18:37–39.

145. *PGW, Pres.* 19:414–22, 462; *PGW, Ret.* 1:56–57; Roy Bird Cook, *Washington's Western Lands* (Strasburg, VA: Shenandoah Publishing House, 1930), 126–28.

146. *PGW, Pres.* 19:458, 462.

147. *Writings of Washington* 35:393.

148. *PGW, Ret.* 1:484–85, 507–8.

149. Rick Willard Sturdevant, "Quest for Eden: George Washington's Frontier Land Interests" (PhD diss., University of California, Santa Barbara, 1982), 306, 328.

CHAPTER 19: TRANSFORMING INDIAN LIVES

1. Rev. John Heckewelder, *History, Manners, and Customs of the Indian Nations Who Once Inhabited Pennsylvania and the Neighbouring States* (Philadelphia: Historical Society of Pennsylvania, 1876), 145, 188–89.

2. I am grateful to David Silverman for pushing my thinking on this point.

3. Richard White, *The Middle Ground: Indians, Empires, and Republics in the Great Lakes Region, 1650–1815* (Cambridge: Cambridge University Press, 1991), 474, calls the policy "imperial benevolence."

4. Knox to GW, Dec. 29, 1794, GWPLC; *PGW, Pres.* 17:328–32; *ASPIA* 2:543–44.

5. *PGW, Pres.* 9:110–16; *Writings of Washington* 31:397–98.

6. James Thomas Flexner, *George Washington and the New Nation, 1783–1793* (Boston: Little, Brown, 1969), 300; *Writings of Washington* 21:199; 32:10, 20.

7. *PGW, Pres.* 14:466; *Writings of Washington* 34:391–92.

8. Alan Taylor, *The Divided Ground: Indians, Settlers, and the Northern Borderland of the American Revolution* (New York: Knopf, 2006), 239.

9. Francis Paul Prucha, ed., *Documents of United States Indian Policy* (Lincoln: University of Nebraska Press, 1975), 16–17; Francis Paul Prucha, *American Indian Policy in the Formative Years: The Indian Trade and Intercourse Acts, 1790–1834* (1962; Lincoln: University of Nebraska Press, 1970), 86–87, 146; David Andrew Nichols, *Red Gentlemen and White Savages: Indians, Federalists, and the Search for Order on the American Frontier* (Charlottesville: University of Virginia Press, 2008), 176–78; David Andrew Nichols, *Engines of Diplomacy: Indian Trading Factories and the Negotiation of American Empire* (Chapel Hill: University of North Carolina Press, 2016); William S. Coker and Thomas D. Watson, *Indian Traders of the Southeastern Spanish Borderlands: Panton, Leslie & Company and John Forbes & Company, 1783–1847* (Pensacola: University of West Florida Press, 1986), 195; *ASPIA* 2:583–84 (awaiting goods).

10. William Cronon, *Changes in the Land: Indians, Colonists, and the Ecology of New England* (New York: Hill & Wang, 1983), 147.

11. Theda Perdue, "George Washington and the 'Civilization' of the Southern Indians," in *George Washington's South*, ed. Tamara Harvey and Greg O'Brien (Gainesville: University Press of Florida, 2004), 313–25.

12. Daniel K. Richter, *Trade, Land, Power: The Struggle for Eastern North America* (Philadelphia: University of Pennsylvania Press, 2013), 229; Anthony F. C. Wallace, *The Death and Rebirth of the Seneca* (New York: Random House, 1969), 220–21.

13. Wallace, *Death and Rebirth of the Seneca,* 221–28; Thomas S. Abler, *Cornplanter: Chief Warrior of the Allegany Senecas* (Syracuse, NY: Syracuse University Press, 2007), 138–40.

14. *Iroquois Indians: A Documentary History of the Diplomacy of the Six Nations and Their League,* ed. Francis Jennings et al., 50 reels (Woodbridge, CT: 1985), reel 44 (1797), Feb. 28, quoted in Abler, *Cornplanter,* 122.

15. Isabel Thompson Kelsay, *Joseph Brant, 1743–1807: Man of Two Worlds* (Syracuse, NY: Syracuse University Press, 1984), 576–77.

16. *IALT,* 37; Knox to GW, Nov. 14, 1795, GWPLC; *PGW, Pres.* 19:151–52.

17. June Namias, ed., *A Narrative of the Life of Mrs. Mary Jemison by James E. Seaver* (Norman: University of Oklahoma Press, 1992), 84–85.

18. Granville Ganter, ed., *The Collected Speeches of Sagoyewatha, or Red Jacket* (Syracuse, NY: Syracuse University Press, 2006), 41, 138–48.

19. Archer Butler Hulbert and William N. Schwarz, *David Zeisberger's History of the North American Indians* (Columbus: Ohio State Archaeological and Historical Society, 1910), 121–22.

20. Leonard W. Labaree, ed., *The Papers of Benjamin Franklin,* 39 vols. (New Haven, CT: Yale University Press, 1959), 4:481–83; Henri L. Bourdin, Ralph H. Gabriel, and Stanley T. Williams, eds., *Sketches of Eighteenth Century America: More "Letters from an American Farmer" by St. John de Crèvecoeur* (New Haven, CT: Yale University Press, 1925), 193–95; Adolph B. Benson, ed., *Peter Kalm's Travels in North America: The English Version of 1770,* 2 vols. (New York: Wilson-Erickson, 1937), 2:457; Francis Baily, *Journal of a Tour in Unsettled Parts of North America in 1796 and 1797,* ed. Jack D. L. Holmes (Carbondale: University of Southern Illinois Press, 1969), 212.

21. Louise Phelps Kellogg, ed., *Frontier Advance on the Upper Ohio, 1778–1779* (Madison: Wisconsin State Historical Society, 1916), 168; Gregory Evans Dowd, *A Spirited Resistance: The North American Indian Struggle for Unity, 1745–1815* (Baltimore, MD: John Hopkins University Press, 1992), 77–78.

22. Hermann Wellenreuther and Carola Wessel, eds., *The Moravian Mission Diaries of David Zeisberger, 1772–1781* (University Park: Pennsylvania State University Press, 2005), 11 (tavern), 18–19; Guy S. Klett, ed., *Journals of Charles Beatty, 1762–1769* (University Park: Pennsylvania State University Press, 1962), 46 (tavern); Hermann Wellenreuther, "White Eyes and the Delawares' Vision of an Indian State," *Pennsylvania History* 68 (2001): 139–61.

23. *The Journal of Nicholas Cresswell* (New York: Dial), 106.

24. Rachel Wheeler, "Hendrick Aupaumut: Christian-Mahican Prophet," *Journal of the Early Republic* 25 (2005): 187–220 (quote at 205–6).

25. John Sugden, *Blue Jacket, Warrior of the Shawnees* (Lincoln: University of Nebraska Press, 2000), 54.

26. *ASPIA* 2:579; Sugden, *Blue Jacket,* 213; "Letters of Colonel John Francis Hamtramck," *MPHC* 34 (1904), 739 (quote).

27. Richard C. Knopf, ed., *Anthony Wayne: A Name in Arms: The Wayne-Knox-Pickering-McHenry Correspondence* (Pittsburgh: University of Pittsburgh Press, 1960), 532.

28. Sugden, *Blue Jacket,* 214–15.

29. *Writings of Washington* 35:299–302, GW's speech, Nov. 29, 1796, GWPLC.

30. Sugden, *Blue Jacket,* 215.

31. John to Abigail Adams, Dec. 4, 1796, C. James Taylor et al., eds., *The Adams Papers: Adams Family Correspondence* 11:430, http://rotunda.upress.virginia.edu/

32. Sugden, *Blue Jacket,* 216–17.

33. Colin G. Calloway, *The Shawnees and the War for America* (New York: Viking/Penguin, 2007), ch. 7. Stephen Warren, *The Shawnees and Their Neighbors, 1795–1870* (Urbana: University of Illinois Press, 2005) examines subsequent Shawnee responses and sociopolitical adjustments to American cultural assault.

34. Knopf, *Anthony Wayne,* 532.

35. *PGW, Ret.* 1:534.

36. Harvey Lewis Carter, *The Life and Times of Little Turtle* (Urbana: University of Illinois Press, 1987, 158; Donald H. Gaff, "Three Men from Three Rivers: Navigating between Native

and American Identity in the Old Northwest Territory," in *The Boundaries between Us: Natives and Newcomers along the Frontiers of the Old Northwest Territory, 1750–1850*, ed. Daniel P. Barr (Kent, OH: Kent State University Press, 2006), 148.

37. George W. Corner, ed., *The Autobiography of Benjamin Rush* (Princeton, NJ: Princeton University Press, 1948), 240–41.

38. Carter, *Life and Times of Little Turtle*, 4–6.

39. Adams to James Wilkinson, Feb. 4, 1798, *Founders Online,* National Archives, http://founders.archives.gov/documents/Adams/99-02-02-2321 (last modified July 12, 2016).

40. Harold C. Syrett et al., eds., *The Papers of Alexander Hamilton,* 27 vols. (Charlottesville: University of Virginia Press, 1961–87), 23:231.

41. *PTJ* 36:274–90; Paul Kelton, *Cherokee Medicine, Colonial Germs: An Indigenous Nation's Fight against Smallpox, 1518–1824* (Norman: University of Oklahoma Press, 2015), 176.

42. William Heath, *William Wells and the Struggle for the Old Northwest* (Norman: University of Oklahoma Press, 2015), ch. 8; Gaff, "Three Men from Three Rivers," 149.

43. *ASPIA* 2:551.

44. *IALT,* 31.

45. William G. McLoughlin, *Cherokee Renascence in the New Republic* (Princeton, NJ: Princeton University Press, 1983), quotes at xv, 3, 34; Theda Perdue and Michael D. Green, eds., *The Cherokee Removal: A Brief History with Documents,* 2nd ed. (Boston: Bedford/St. Martin's, 2005), 7, 13 ("new Cherokee world").

46. *Writings of Washington* 35:193–98.

47. Perdue, "George Washington and the 'Civilization' of the Southern Indians," 319–20; Theda Perdue, *Cherokee Women: Gender and Culture Change, 1700–1835* (Lincoln: University of Nebraska Press, 1998), 109–12, 115–20.

48. *ASPIA* 1:247; McLoughlin, *Cherokee Renascence in the New Republic,* 39–42.

49. *Writings of Washington* 35:196; Dinsmoor's account of his public service [undated], Dinsmoor Papers, Dartmouth College, Rauner Library, Ms. 40, box 4, miscellaneous file (hereafter DP40/4), and Ms. 797118.1 (spinning wheel).

50. McLoughlin, *Cherokee Renascence in the New Republic,* 43.

51. Silas Dinsmoor Alumni File, 1791, Dartmouth College, Rauner Library, "Genealogies: Col. Silas Dinsmoor," 453–55.

52. Dinsmoor's account of his public service, DP40/4.

53. Charles A. Weeks, *Paths to a Middle Ground: The Diplomacy of Natchez, Boukfouka, Nogales and San Fernando de las Barrancas, 1791–1795* (Tuscaloosa: University of Alabama Press, 2005), 205–6.

54. Dinsmoor's account of his public service, DP40/4.

55. Quoted in McLoughlin, *Cherokee Renascence in the New Republic,* 43.

56. GW to 1st Session of the 4th Congress, Feb. 2, 1796, GWPLC.

57. GW to Secretary of State, July 17, 1796, GWPLC; *Writings of Washington* 35:112 (quote), 146, 149.

58. H. Thomas Foster, ed., *The Collected Works of Benjamin Hawkins, 1796–1810* (Tuscaloosa: University of Alabama Press, 2003), 160–64.

59. Baily, *Journal of a Tour in Unsettled Parts of North America,* 245, 262.

60. *ASPIA* 2:637–40 (quotes); *IALT,* 51–54; Alice Barnwell Keith et al., eds., *The John Gray Blount Papers,* 3 vols. (Raleigh, NC: State Department of Archives and History, 1959–65), 3:197–98, 205, 249.

61. "Genealogies: Col. Silas Dinsmoor," 452.

62. *PGW, Ret.* 3:177; "Genealogies: Col. Silas Dinsmoor," 455; Silas Dinsmoor Vertical File, Fred W. Smith National Library for the Study of George Washington, Mount Vernon, VA.

63. Florette Henri, *The Southern Indians and Benjamin Hawkins, 1796–1816* (Norman: University of Oklahoma Press, 1986), 205.

64. Dinsmoor's account of his public service, DP40/4; War Department instructions to Dinsmoor, May 8, 1802, DP40/4.

65. McLoughlin, *Cherokee Renascence in the New Republic,* 44–45; John Phillip Reid, *A Law of Blood: The Primitive Law of the Cherokee Nation* (New York: New York University Press, 1970).

66. Mark Rifkin, *Manifesting America: The Imperial Construction of U.S. National Space* (New York: Oxford University Press, 2009), 40–41.

67. McLoughlin, *Cherokee Renascence in the New Republic*, 57; Daniel Heath Justice, *Our Fire Survives the Storm: A Cherokee Literary History* (Minneapolis: University of Minnesota Press, 2006), 75–76.

68. Gary E. Moulton, ed., *The Papers of Chief John Ross, 1807–1866*, 2 vols. (Norman: University of Oklahoma Press, 1985), 1:155, 322, 2:276–77; Gary E. Moulton, *John Ross, Cherokee Chief* (Athens: University of Georgia Press, 1978), 13. Ross was not the last southern Indian leader to name a son for the first president. For example, George Washington Grayson, a Creek warrior, rancher, and politician, who fought for the Confederacy during the Civil War, served as Creek chief from 1917–20 and led the Creeks during the dissolution of Indian Territory to make way for Oklahoma statehood. W. David Baird, ed., *A Creek Warrior for the Confederacy: The Autobiography of Chief G. W. Grayson* (Norman: University of Oklahoma Press, 1988); Mary Jane Warde, *George Washington Grayson and the Creek Nation, 1843–1920* (Norman: University of Oklahoma Press, 1999).

69. *Writings of Washington* 35:195; Joel W. Martin, *Sacred Revolt: The Muskogees' Struggle for a New World* (Boston: Beacon Press, 1991), 87–88; Robbie Ethridge, *Creek Country: The Creek Indians and Their World* (Chapel Hill: University of North Carolina Press, 2003), 17–18. Ethridge thinks Hawkins was "probably fluent in Muskoghean."

70. Letters of Benjamin Hawkins, in Foster, *Collected Works*, 56.

71. Martin, *Sacred Revolt*, 92.

72. Henri, *Southern Indians and Benjamin Hawkins*, 94–96.

73. Kathryn E. Holland Braund, *Deerskins and Duffels: The Creek Indian Trade with Anglo-America, 1685–1815*, 2nd ed. (Lincoln: University of Nebraska Press, 2008). On broader patterns of exchange in the colonial era, see Daniel H. Usner Jr., *Indians, Settlers, and Slaves in a Frontier Exchange Economy: The Lower Mississippi Valley before 1783* (Chapel Hill: University of North Carolina Press, 1992); on the consequences and collapse of the deerskin trade among the Choctaws, see Richard White, *The Roots of Dependency: Subsistence, Environment, and Social Change among the Choctaws, Pawnees, and Navajos* (Lincoln: University of Nebraska Press, 1983), chs. 4–5.

74. Angela Pulley Hudson, *Creek Paths and Federal Roads: Indians, Settlers, and Slaves and the Making of the American South* (Chapel Hill: University of North Carolina Press, 2010).

75. Ethridge, *Creek Country*, 111; Hudson, *Creek Paths and Federal Roads*, 5.

76. *Writings of Washington* 35:157–58, 311, 350–51; Ethridge, *Creek Country*, 176–94, 215–28; Robbie Ethridge, "Creeks and Americans in the Age of Washington," in *George Washington's South*, ed. Tamara Harvey and Greg O'Brien (Gainesville: University Press of Florida, 2004), 284–85, 290. Hudson, *Creek Paths and Federal Roads*, ch. 2, examines the ongoing issue of the Creek boundary, and its porous nature.

77. Ethridge, *Creek Country*, 9, 158–74; Ethridge, "Creeks and Americans in the Age of Washington," 281–82; Hudson, *Creek Paths and Federal Roads*, 34–35; Coker and Watson, *Indian Traders of the Southeastern Spanish Borderlands*, 202.

78. American Philosophical Society, Philadelphia (hereafter APS), Benjamin Hawkins, "A Sketch of the Creek Country in the Years 1798, 1799"; Benjamin Hawkins, "A Sketch of the Creek Country," in Foster, *Collected Works*, 115, 126–28; Claudio Saunt, *A New Order of Things: Property, Power, and the Transformation of the Creek Indians, 1733–1816* (Cambridge: Cambridge University Press, 1999), 171–73.

79. Ethridge, *Creek Country*, 99; Letters of Benjamin Hawkins, in Foster, *Collected Works*, 20–21.

80. Saunt, *New Order of Things*, ch. 6; Ethridge, *Creek Country*, 113; Letters of Benjamin Hawkins, in Foster, *Collected Works*, 47–48, 83–85 (quote).

81. APS, Hawkins, "A Sketch of the Creek Country," 19; Hawkins, "A Sketch of the Creek Country," in Foster, *Collected Works*, 24s–25s; Ethridge, *Creek Country*, 29, 31.

82. Ethridge, *Creek Country*, 92, 181; Saunt, *New Order of Things*.

83. Hawkins, "A Sketch of the Creek Country," in Foster, *Collected Works*, 44s. On the Grierson family, see Claudio Saunt, *Black, White, and Indian: Race and the Unmaking of an American Family* (New York: Oxford University Press, 2005).

84. *ASPIA* 1:384 ("first man"); APS, Hawkins, "A Sketch of the Creek Country," 23–24, 31–32; Hawkins, "A Sketch of the Creek Country," in Foster, *Collected Works*, 27s, 30s.

85. APS, Hawkins, "A Sketch of the Creek Country," 111–12.

86. *ASPIA* 2:602. Cussetah Mico's observation echoes that of the Onondaga orator Canasatego at the Treaty of Lancaster in 1744; Colin G. Calloway, ed., *The World Turned Upside Down: Indian Voices from Early America* (Boston: Bedford/St. Martins, 1994), 101–4, and as elaborated by Benjamin Franklin, Leonard W. Labaree et al., eds., *The Papers of Benjamin Franklin*. 41 vols. to date (New Haven, CT: Yale University Press, 1959–), 4:483.

87. APS, Hawkins, "A Sketch of the Creek Country," 133–35; Ethridge, *Creek Country*, 105–7; Saunt, *New Order of Things*, 179–80; Letters of Benjamin Hawkins, in Foster, *Collected Works*, 57 ("Indispensable"); Evan Nooe, "Common Justice: Vengeance and Retribution in Creek Country," *Ethnohistory* 62 (2015): 241–61.

88. Saunt, *New Order of Things*.

89. Barbara Krauthamer, *Black Slaves, Indian Masters: Slavery Emancipation and Citizenship in the Native American South* (Chapel Hill: University of North Carolina Press, 2013); Saunt, *Black, White, and Indian*.

90. *Writings of Washington* 35:311.

91. Letters of Benjamin Hawkins, in Foster, *Collected Works*, 252.

92. Letters of Benjamin Hawkins, in Foster, *Collected Works*, 316–17.

93. *PGW, Ret.* 1:178–80.

94. Douglas Southall Freeman, *Washington*, 1-vol. abridgement by Richard Harwell of the 7-vol. *George Washington* (New York: Simon & Schuster, 1992), 714–15.

95. Letters of Benjamin Hawkins, in Foster, *Collected Works*, 252.

96. *PTJ* 31:335.

97. Ethridge, *Creek Country*, 20–21, 238–41; Saunt, *New Order of Things*, chs. 10–12; Martin, *Sacred Revolt*, 135 (Hoboithle Mico); J. Leitch Wright Jr., *Creeks and Seminoles: Destruction and Regeneration of the Muscogulge People* (Lincoln: University of Nebraska Press, 1986), 118, 150, 175 (Hoboithle Mico's letter and death); Kathryn E. Holland Braund, ed., *Tohopeka: Rethinking the Creek War and the War of 1812* (Tuscaloosa: University of Alabama Press, 2012); Joshua Piker, *Okfuskee: A Creek Indian Town in Colonial America* (Cambridge: Harvard University Press, 2004), 196–204 (Nuyukv).

98. William Strickland, *Journal of a Tour in the United States of America, 1794–1795*, ed. Rev. J. E. Strickland (New York: New-York Historical Society, 1971), 168.

CHAPTER 20: A DEATH AND A NON-DEATH

1. Rick Willard Sturdevant, "Quest for Eden: George Washington's Frontier Land Interests" (PhD diss., University of California, Santa Barbara, 1982), ch. 9.

2. *PGW, Ret.* 1:391.

3. *PGW, Pres.* 19:154–55; *PGW, Ret.* 1:66–68, 247–48.

4. Joseph J. Ellis, *His Excellency: George Washington* (New York: Knopf, 2004), 262.

5. *PGW, Ret.* 2:70.

6. *PGW, Ret.* 1:438–39, 451–54, 459–60, 470–73, 2:606–7.

7. *PGW, Ret.* 1:483, 490–91, 493, 507–9, 511–14, 2:34–35, 508, 3:92–93, 470–71 (quotes), 4:76, 90; Sturdevant, "Quest for Eden," 353–59, 362–66.

8. *PGW, Pres.* 18:199, 267–68, 505–6; *PGW, Ret.* 2:265–66, 3:66–68, 3:275–76, 314–15.

9. *PGW, Ret.* 2:364–65, 492–94, 4:514; John E. Ferling, *The First of Men: A Life of George Washington* (New York: Oxford University Press, 2010), 489–90; Sturdevant, "Quest for Eden," 348–50; Roy Bird Cook, *Washington's Western Lands* (Strasburg, VA: Shenandoah Publishing House, 1930), 94–97 ("legal difficulties"), 130.

10. *PGW, Ret.* 4:344–45 (quote), 351–53, 403–4, 519–20.

11. *PGW, Ret.* 2:27–29; Cook, *Washington's Western Lands*, 70–71.

12. *PGW, Ret.* 2:53–54, 4:422; *Writings of Washington* 36:142–43, 251–52.

13. *PGW, Ret.* 3:349–50.

14. *PGW, Ret.* 4:407–9 ("futile").

15. *PGW, Ret.* 4:456n–477 (quote at 457n); Sturdevant, "Quest for Eden," 371.

16. *PGW, Ret.* 2:1; Edward G. Lengel, *First Entrepreneur: How George Washington Built His—and the Nation's—Prosperity* (Boston: Da Capo, 2016), 204–6; Sturdevant, "Quest for Eden," 371–80.

17. Sturdevant, "Quest for Eden," x.

18. James Thomas Flexner, *George Washington: Anguish and Farewell, 1793–1799* (Boston: Little, Brown, 1969), 372–73; *Writings of Washington* 36:256–57, 295–300.

19. *PGW, Ret.* 4:477–512; Philander D. Chase, "A Stake in the West: George Washington as Backcountry Surveyor and Landholder," in *George Washington and the Virginia Backcountry*, ed. Warren R. Hofstra (Madison, WI: Madison House, 1998), 184.

20. *PGW, Ret.* 4:512–19.

21. *PGW, Ret.* 4:514–16.

22. Lengel, *First Entrepreneur*, 246.

23. *PGW, Ret.* 3:175–76, 474–76, 4:74–75.

24. Lengel, *First Entrepreneur*, 148–56, 196–200; *PGW, Ret.* 1:255.

25. *PGW, Pres.* 10:359.

26. Richard Parkinson, *A Tour in America in 1798, 1799, and 1800, Exhibiting Sketches of Society and Manners and a Particular Account of the American System of Agriculture with Its Recent Improvements*, 2 vols. in 1 (London: J. Hardy & J. Murray, 1805), 1:5 (12,000 acres); 88–117 (narratives), 154 ("dangerous").

27. Roger G. Kennedy, *Mr. Jefferson's Lost Cause: Land, Farmers, Slavery, and the Louisiana Purchase* (New York: Oxford University Press, 2003), 2, 17 ("constant cultivation").

28. *PGW, Ret.* 1:254–55.

29. *PGW, Pres.* 17:63, 206–7, and GW to Spotswood, Nov. 23, 1794, NYPL, GW, reel 2, typescript.

30. Ron Chernow, *Washington: A Life* (New York: Penguin, 2010), 750.

31. Michael A. McDonnell, *The Politics of War: Race, Class, and Conflict in Revolutionary Virginia* (Chapel Hill: University of North Carolina Press, 2007), 485.

32. François Furstenberg, *In the Name of the Father: Washington's Legacy, Slavery, and the Making of a Nation* (New York: Penguin, 2006), 83.

33. Jacques Pierre Brissot de Warville, *New Travels in the United States of America performed in 1788*, 2 vols. (London, 1792), 1:281, 290. Andrew Burnaby, an Englishman who had visited Mount Vernon in 1759, made similar observations about how slavery shaped the character of Virginians; Rufus Rockwell Wilson, ed., *Burnaby's Travels through North America* (New York: A. Wessels, 1904), 53–55.

34. Susan P. Schoelwer, ed., *Lives Bound Together: Slavery at George Washington's Mount Vernon* (Mount Vernon Ladies Association, 2016); Philip D. Morgan and Michael L. Nicholls, "Slave Flight: Mount Vernon, Virginia, and the Wider Atlantic World," in *George Washington's South*, ed. Tamara Harvey and Greg O'Brien (Gainesville: University Press of Florida, 2004), 197–222.

35. *PGW, Ret.* 4:288.

36. Ellis, *His Excellency*, 237; John Avlon, *Washington's Farewell: The Founding Father's Warning to Future Generations* (New York: Simon & Schuster, 2017).

37. *PGW, Ret.* 4:527–40.

38. *PGW, Ret.* 4:256.

39. Henry Wiencek, *An Imperfect God: George Washington, His Slaves, and the Creation of America* (New York: Farrar, Straus & Giroux, 2003) provides an overview of Washington's changing attitudes toward slavery.

40. Furstenberg, *In the Name of the Father*, 30.

41. Bethel Saler, *The Settlers' Empire: Colonialism and State Formation in America's Old Northwest* (Philadelphia: University of Pennsylvania Press, 2015), 29. On "big government," see Stephen J. Rockwell, *Indian Affairs and the Administrative State in the Nineteenth Century* (Cambridge: Cambridge University Press, 2010); on the army, see William Hogeland, *Autumn of the Black Snake: The Creation of the U.S. Army and the Invasion That Opened the West*

(New York: Farrar, Straus & Giroux, 2017); on the role of the federal government in regulating settlement patterns to shape the contours of national expansion, see Paul Frymer, *Building an American Empire: The Era of Territorial and Political Expansion* (Princeton, NJ: Princeton University Press, 2017).

42. James Belich, *Replenishing the Earth: The Settler Revolution and the Rise of the Anglo-World, 1783–1939* (New York: Oxford University Press, 2009); Gregory Evans Dowd, "Indigenous Peoples without the Republic," *Journal of American History* 104 (June 2017): 19–41.

43. Gregory Ablavsky, "Beyond the Indian Commerce Clause," *Yale Law Journal* 124 (2014–15): 1012–90, esp. 1021, 1067, 1075–81, 1083–84, 1089–90; Francis G. Hutchins, *Tribes and the American Constitution* (Brookline, MA: Amarta Press, 2000), 103–6.

44. Anthony F. C. Wallace, *Jefferson and the Indians: The Tragic Fate of the First Americans* (Cambridge, MA: Harvard University Press, 1999), 337.

45. Julian P. Boyd et al., eds., *The Papers of Thomas Jefferson*, 42 vols. to date (Princeton, NJ: Princeton University Press, 1950–), 38:209–10, 39:590–91.

46. In reality, the United States acquired only the right of preemption and then had to pay many times the purchase price of $15 million to buy the land from the Indian nations who inhabited and held it. Robert Lee, "Accounting for Conquest: The Price of the Louisiana Purchase of Indian Country," *Journal of American History*, 103 (2017), 921–42.

47. Alexis de Tocqueville, *Democracy in America*, ed. J. P. Mayer (New York: Doubleday/Anchor, 1969), 334, 337.

48. *PGW, Pres.* 19:225; *Writings of Washington* 35:214–38.

49. D. W. Meinig, *The Shaping of America: A Geographical Perspective on 500 Years of History*, vol. 1, *Atlantic America, 1492–1800* (New Haven, CT: Yale University Press, 1986), 370. The relationship of Indian people with Washington, DC, in subsequent years was in fact quite complex; C. Joseph Genetin-Pilawa, "The Indians' Capital City: Diplomatic Visits, Place, and Two-Worlds Discourse in Nineteenth-Century Washington, DC," in *Beyond Two Worlds: Critical Conversations on Language and Power in Native North Ameica*, ed. James Joseph Buss and C. Joseph Genetin-Pilawa (Albany: SUNY Press, 2014), 117–35.

50. Gerald E. Kahler, *The Long Farewell: Americans Mourn the Death of George Washington* (Charlottesville: University of Virginia Press, 2008), 18; *Columbian Mirror and Alexandria Gazette*, Mar. 20, 1800, p. 3.

51. *ASPIA* 2:660–62, 672, 679 (Efau Hadjo quote).

52. Thomas S. Abler, *Cornplanter: Chief Warrior of the Allegany Senecas* (Syracuse: Syracuse University Press, 2007), 185; Arthur C. Parker, *The History of the Seneca Indians* (Port Washington, NY: J. Friedman, 1926), 132.

53. Gary E. Moulton, ed., *The Papers of Chief John Ross, 1807–1866*, 2 vols. (Norman: University of Oklahoma Press, 1985), 1:155, 187–88, 227, 322, 453, 481, 524, 2:85, 105, 145, 276–77.

54. Matthew Dennis, *Seneca Possessed: Indians, Witchcraft, and Power in the Early American Republic* (Philadelphia: University of Pennsylvania Press, 2010); Anthony F. C. Wallace, *The Death and Rebirth of the Seneca* (New York: Vintage, 1970), 239–49.

55. Wallace, *Death and Rebirth of the Seneca*, 183.

56. Lewis Henry Morgan, *League of the Iroquois* (1851; Secaucus, NJ: Citadel Press, 1972), 178–79, 256–57; Parker, *History of the Seneca Indians*, 132.

57. Quoted in Francis Paul Prucha, *Indian Peace Medals in American History* (Norman University of Oklahoma Press, 1994), 9.

58. Wallace, *Death and Rebirth of the Seneca*, 303.

59. *PGW, Pres.* 19:431–33, 579–80; *ASPIA* 2:617–18 (quotes).

60. *PGW, Pres.* 19:608.

61. Colin G. Calloway, "My Grandfather's Axe: Living with a Native American Past," in *Reflections on American Indian History: Honoring the Past, Building a Future*, ed. Albert L. Hurtado (Norman: University of Oklahoma Press, 2008), 3–31; Charles F. Wilkinson, *Blood Struggle: The Rise of Modern Indian Nations* (New York: Norton, 2005); N. Bruce Duthu, *American Indians and the Law* (New York: Viking/Penguin, 2008).

INDEX

Note: An 'f' or 'm' following a page number indicates a figure or a map, respectively. A plate is indicated by 'pl.'

A

Abeel, Henry, 456

Abenakis, 21m, 51, 53, 76, 94, 222–23, 225–27, 228, 514n74. *See also* Cook, Louis; Gill, Joseph Louis; Swashan

Abercromby, James, 121, 141, 152

Ablavsky, Gregory, 322, 551n22

Achenbach, Joel, 297

Achiout. *See* Half Town (Seneca)

Ackawonothio (Shawnee or Western Delaware), 117

Ada-gal'kala. *See* Attakullakulla (Cherokee)

Adair, James, 42, 119, 125, 163, 164

Adams, Abigail, 288, 367

Adams, John, 218, 223, 281, 326, 332, 357, 358, 359, 460, 461, 466, 467

Adams, John Quincy, 427

African Americans (blacks), 218, 237. *See also* Atiatoharongwen *and other African Americans;* enslaved African Americans

Agashawa. *See* Egushawa (Ottawa)

agriculture. *See also* "civilization"; corn; cotton; settlers (colonials, farmers, frontiersmen, squatters); tobacco
> Cornplanter and, 401, 404
> East against West and, 337
> English, 23, 480
> Federal Indian policies and, 341–45
> gender and, 454–55, 462
> Guyasuta and, 263
> Handsome Lake and, 489, 490
> Indian, 22, 23, 31, 345
> Mount Vernon and, 480, 481
> Pickering and, 405, 406–7
> plantation system of, 172
> Red Jacket and, 399–400
> soil depletion and, 31–32, 78, 448

Treaty of New York and, 369, 372, 373
> Virginia and, 25, 31–32
> Western Indians and, 412
> westward expansion and, 36

Agushaway. *See* Egushawa (Ottawa)

Agwerondongwas. *See* Good Peter (Oneida)

Akiatonharónkwen. *See* Cook, Louis (Abenaki–African American–Kahnawake Mohawk)

Akwesasnes, 437, 490–91

Alabama, 27, 285, 346, 364, 471. *See also* Creeks; Yazoo Companies

Albany, 21m, 90

Albany conference (1776), 238

Albany Congress (1754), 100, 107, 117–18, 578n86

Albany Plan (1754), 98–99

Algonquians, 21m, 263, 444. *See also* Abenakis *and other Algonquians*

Algonquins, 21m, 94

Alien and Sedition Acts, 497n13

Aliquippa, Queen, 79, 91, 92, 100

Allan, John, 228, 231

Allegheny Mountains, 36, 43, 55, 115, 195. *See also* roads

Allegheny River, 5, 51, 61, 67, 79, 82m, 132, 248, 250–51, 255, 257, 263, 271, 272, 296m

Allegheny Senecas, 455. *See also* Cornplanter; Guyasuta

Allen, Ethan, 215

Allerton, Isaac, 25

Alumapees (Delaware), 60

Ambler, Charles, 202

Ambridge (Pennsylvania), 53

American Archives (Force), 535n16

American history, 3–5, 13–14

American identity, 12, 285, 367, 544n9

American Revolution. *See also* Allen, Ethan
and other leaders; Oneidas *and other*
Indian allies and enemies; Peace of Paris
(1783); Revolutionary War in the West;
Stamp Act; veterans, Revolutionary
British land policies and, 6, 12
Chickasaws and, 305
corn and, 235–37, 243, 245, 246
Creeks and, 347
Indian identity and, 347
Indian land and, 6, 12, 212, 234
Indians and, 217–21
Indian ways of fighting and, 215–16, 231
Iroquois and, 220–21, 230, 235, 237–39,
240, 242–45, 258
McGillivray and, 348
McGillivray's father and, 347
Mi'kmaqs and, 231
Oneidas and, 235, 236–37, 239–43,
258–59, 458
Pontiac's War and, 177
Royal Proclamation of 1763 and, 184
Somerset v. Stewart (1772) and, 201
speculators and, 212
strategies, offensive *versus* defensive, 216–17
Virginia independence and, 212
war debt and, 327
Washington and, 5–6, 167, 245–46,
259, 386
Washington and Indians and, 5–6, 14,
216–17, 218–34, 245–46
Washington's Indian land acquisitions
and, 234, 243–44, 289
white racial consciousness and, 285
Amherst, Jeffery, 174, 176
Anderson, Fred, 89, 108, 157, 167, 510n29
Anglo-Cherokee War, 6. *See also* frontier
advance and Cherokee war
Anglo-French rivalry. *See also* Braddock's
defeat (Battle of the Monongahela);
Canada; Fort Duquesne; French, the;
"French and Indian War"; frontier
defense and Cherokee alliance; Ohio
country; Seven Years' War;
Tanaghrisson's war; Treaty of Paris
(1763)
American neutrality and, 397
Cherokees and, 126, 127
Delawares and, 116–17
Dinwiddie and, 65, 67, 80–81
Forks of the Ohio and, 68, 80
forts and, 80, 117
French and Indian War and, 148
Great Lakes Indians and, 135
Indian land and, 154–55

Indians and, 136, 152, 175
Iroquois and, 49–53, 53–54, 61, 74, 98,
144, 161
Logstown Treaty and, 59
Ohio country and, 260
Ohio country forts and, 61–62, 65, 84
Ohio Indians and, 58, 62, 63, 72, 73, 81,
93, 94–95, 97–98, 99, 107
Saint-Pierre and, 80–81
Scarouady and, 100, 108
Shawnees and, 116–17
Shingas and, 106, 107
Tanaghrisson and, 62–65, 67, 68–71,
90–91
Washington and, 82m
Anishinaabeg, 72. *See also* Ojibwas; Ottawas;
Potawatomis
Annosanah. *See* Gist, Christopher
Apess, William (Pequot), 218
Apotheosis of Washington (Commemoration of
Washington), pl13
Appalachian Mountains, 45, 181, 182, 284
Armstrong, John, 132
Arnold, Benedict, 222, 228, 229
Aroas (Silver Heels) (Seneca), 7, 87, 108,
113, 128, 165, 175, 262
Assarigoa (Howard Effingham), 30
assimilation, 488. *See also* "civilization"
Astiarix (Seneca), 244–45
Atiatoharongwen (Atayataghronghta).
See Cook, Louis (Abenaki–African
American–Kahnawake Mohawk)
Atkin, Edmond, 136–37, 138, 143
Atkinson, James R., 569n17
Atlantic exchange system, 32–33, 42, 255, 347
Attakullakulla (Ada-gal'kala) (Little
Carpenter) (Ouconecaw) (Overhill
Cherokee chief)
American Revolution and, 232
British and, 43, 125, 129
Dinwiddie and Glen and, 128–29
Forbes and, 140, 145, 146, 156, 163
frontier defense and, 130
peace and, 166
Royal Proclamation of 1763 negotiations
and (1768), 188
Treaty of Long Island of Holston (1777)
and, 232–33
Treaty of Sycamore Shoals and, 213
Virginia and, 43, 164
Auglaize River, 438, 439
Aupaumut, Hendrick (Stockbridge
Mahican), 1, 406, 412–13, 414, 416,
418, 458, 565n36
Aupaumut, Solomon, 565n36

B
Bacon, Nathaniel and his rebellion,
    25–26, 43
Baily, Francis, 457, 466
Baird (Beard), John, 428
Ballew, Bennet, 338
Baptiste, Jean. *See* Ogaghsagighte
    (Kahnawake Mohawk)
Barbary powers, 446, 467
Barr, Daniel, 272
Barralet, John James, pl 13
Bartoli, F., pl 6
Battle of Barren Hill (1778), 243
Battle of Fallen Timbers (1794), 379m,
    438, 442, 454
Battle of Fort Necessity (1754)
    described, 94–96
    Indians and, 92–95, 96, 97–98
    map, 296m
    surrender terms and, 104
    Washington and, 91, 100, 103–4, 114,
        168, 172, 449
    Washington's Indian land acquisitions
        and, 199
    withdrawal from, 96–97
Battle of Horseshoe Bend or Tohopeka
    (1814), 475
Battle of Indian Field (1778), 220
Battle of the Monongahela. *See* Braddock's
    defeat
Battle of Newtown, 251
Battle of Oriskany, 242
Battle of Point Pleasant, 210
Battle of Tohopeka or Horseshoe Bend
    (1814), 475
Bayley, Jacob, 223, 226
Beard (Baird), John, 428
Beaujeu, Daniel-Hyacinthe-Marie
    Liénard de, 110
Beauséjour fort (Nova Scotia), 102
Beaver. *See* Tamaqua (Delaware)
Beaver Creek, 51, 70, 132, 157
Beaver River, 154
Beaver Town (Sawcunk) (Shingas's
    Town), 160
Beckwith, George, 384, 411
Bedel, Timothy, 224, 225–26
Belt of Wampum (the Belt)
    (Kaghswaghtaniunt)
    (Tohashwughtonionty) (White
    Thunder) (Seneca), 57, 73, 108, 155,
    498n30, 512n26
Berkeley, William, 25, 26–27
Berkin, Carol, 497n13
Beverly, Robert, 22, 26, 28

Beverly, William, 34
Big Knives, 413
Big Tree (Great Tree) (Karontowanen)
    (Kiandochgowa) (Seneca), 401,
    402, 406
Billouart, Louis, chevalier de Kerlerec, 127
Birch, William, pl 11
Bird Tail King. *See* Fusatchee Mico (Creek)
Black Hoof (Shawnee), 443, 461
Blair, John, 138
Bloody Fellow (Nenetuah) (Nenetooyah)
    (General Eskaqua) (General Iskagua)
    (Cherokee), 7, 423, 424–25, 426, 430,
    465, 466, 487. *See also* Treaty of Tellico
    (1798)
Bloody Fellow Swan (Cherokee), 465
Bloomfield, Joseph, 241
Blount, John Gray, 356–57, 556n60
Blount, Thomas, 356, 556n60
Blount, William. *See also* Treaty of
    Holston (1791)
    British and, 474
    Cherokees and, 425, 430, 464
    Chickasaws and, 426
    Indian land acquisitions and, 305, 339,
        356, 424
    on McGillivray, 366
    southern Indians and, 429, 430–31
    speculation and, 556n60
    Treaty of Hopewell and, 305
Blue Jacket (Waweyapiersenwaw) (Pekowi
    Shawnee), 7, 381, 387, 391, 437, 443,
    458–59, 460. *See also* Treaty of
    Greenville (1795)
Blue Licks attack, 278
Blue Ridge Mountains, 29, 30, 33–34
    Washington and, 37–38, 115, 171, 296m
Boone, Daniel, 109, 112, 149, 264–65, 278
Boone, Israel, 278
Bosomworth, Abraham, 134, 141, 142, 144
Boston, 210, 219, 223, 226, 231, 238, 281
Boston Tea Party, 206
Botetourt, Governor, 189, 192, 199
Bougainville, Louis Antoine de, 135
boundaries. *See also* frontier advance and
    Cherokee war; Hawkins, Benjamin;
    Royal Proclamation of 1763; Treaty of
    Fort Stanwix (1768) *and other treaties;*
    westward expansion
    British and, 437
    Canada-US, 411
    Chickasaws and, 569n24
    Creek-Georgia, 355
    DuCoigne and, 415
    W. Johnson on, 5

boundaries (*continued*)
McGillivray and, 362
national unity and, 283–85, 284–85,
290, 292
Piominko and, 426
Red Jacket and, 416–17
southern Indians and, 353
Spain and, 338
speculators and, 324
treaties and, 186m
US-Canada, 437
Washington on, 292
Bouquet, Henry, 139, 148, 149–51, 155,
159, 160, 161, 162, 173, 174, 177
Bowdoin, John, 229–30
Bowles, William Augustus, 365, 374–75, 376
Bowman, John, 246
Boyd, Thomas, 254
Braddock's defeat (Battle of the
Monongahela), 107. *See also* "French
and Indian War"
aftermath, 116–17, 118
British and, 512n23
British army and, 102, 105, 108–9, 110,
111–13, 120, 122
Indians and, 105–8, 109, 110, 113–14,
135, 512n26
Indian ways of fighting and, 112–13,
121–22
strategy of, 102–3
Washington and, 6, 13, 103–4, 108,
109–11, 112, 114–15, 121–23, 145,
150, 168, 197, 385
Braddock's Defeat (Preston), 513n36
Bradstreet, John, 151
Brant, Joseph (Thayendanegea) (Mohawk).
See also Philadelphia Indian diplomacy
attacks by, 244, 245, 248, 257, 258, 304
Aupaumut and, 413
background of, 240, 242, 408
black servants and, 410
British and, 242, 402, 408, 410, 421
Cook and, 413
Cornplanter and, 400, 402
Indian unity and, 317–18
Northwestern Confederacy and, 381,
408–9, 417
Ohio River as boundary and, 406
Philadelphia diplomacy and, 409–10,
411–12, 412–13, 414, 420
portrait, pl 5
Sandusky conference and, 420–21
on Schuyler, 300
Simcoe and, 411–12, 420–21

on St. Clair's defeat, 391
Sullivan's campaign and, 251, 252, 255
Treaty of Fort Stanwix (1784) and, 400
Washington and, 7, 244, 245, 248, 410,
416, 441, 455–56
Wayne and, 440
Brant, Molly (Mary), 408
Brent, Giles, 25
Bright Lightning, 498n30
Britain and the British. *See also* American
Revolution; Anglo-French rivalry;
Atlantic exchange system; Braddock's
defeat (Battle of the Monongahela);
Brant, Joseph *and other Indians;*
Canada; frontier advance and
Cherokee war; Jay Treaty (1794);
Johnson, William *and other British
people;* law of nations; Logstown
(Ohio country); Pennsylvania;
Philadelphia Indian diplomacy;
Royal Proclamation of 1763; settlers
(colonials, farmers, frontiersmen,
squatters); Treaty of Fort Stanwix
(1768) *and other treaties;* Virginia
and other British colonies
after Fort Duquesne, 173, 175
American national unity and, 288
on American policy, 380
American trading posts and, 453–54
Aupaumut and, 413
W. Blount and, 474
Brant and, 242, 402, 408, 410, 421
Cherokees and, 65, 125–26, 130,
143–44, 165–66
Cornstalk and, 265
Delawares and, 268
Efau Hadjo and, 472
French and, 411, 438, 445
gifts and, 133–34, 160, 175, 177
Hoboithle Mico and, 475
Indian allies of, 56
Indian land and, 20, 22, 182, 213, 237
Indians and, 4, 56, 167, 173, 176,
265, 446
Indigenous peoples and, 484
Iroquois and, 98, 237–39, 405, 440
Logstown Treaty and, 59
McGillivray and, 347–48, 350
Miamis and, 56
North American population of
(1700-1775), 172
Northwestern Confederacy war and,
380, 397
Northwest Territory and, 396

Ohio Company and, 47–48, 174
Ohio country and, 49–53, 53–54
Old Briton and, 61
Oneidas and, 258
Ostenaco and, 166
Philadelphia diplomacy and, 401, 409,
    410–13, 414
plantation system of agriculture and, 172
Proctor and, 404
Sandusky conference and, 420
Scarouady and, 100
Senecas and, 263–64
Shawnees and, 173, 175, 311
Silver Heels and, 175
smallpox and, 281
Spain and, 365
St. Clair, Arthur and, 383
Tanaghrisson and, 58, 59, 99
trade and, 177–78, 305, 470
treaties and, 285
Washington and, 95, 213, 437, 444–45
Washington's tobacco trade and, 177–78
Wayne and, 437, 438, 439
westward expansion and, 172–73,
    179–81, 328
British army (regulars), 89, 103, 104, 122,
    167, 173, 179–80, 510n29. *See also*
    Braddock's defeat *and other battles and*
    campaigns
Brodhead, Daniel, 248, 250–51, 255,
    257, 267, 271–72, 273–74, 507n14,
    541n48
Brown, John (Chickasaw), 431
Bryan's Station attack, 278
Buchanan, George, 33
Buckongahelas (Pachgantschihilas)
    (Delaware), 263, 383, 391, 443
Bucksinosa. *See* Paxinosa (eastern Shawnee)
Bullen, James (Jimmy) (Catawba), 146
Bullitt, Thomas, 158, 178, 204
Bullskin Creek, 38
Burgoyne, John, 216, 220, 227, 242, 243,
    532n5
Burnaby, Andrew, 28–29, 579n33
Burr, Aaron, 393
Burwell, Lewis, 50
Butler, Jane, 26
Butler, John, 244, 251, 257
Butler, Richard, 8, 208, 310–12, 389,
    391. *See also* Treaty of Fort Finney
    (1786)
Butler, Walter, 244
Butler, William, 245
Byrd II, William, 29, 42, 518n70

Byrd III, William, 126, 139, 140, 144, 146,
    164, 165
Byrds of Westover, 25

C
California, 281
calumet pipe of peace, 1, 2, 370, 414, 415,
    427, 430
Calusas, 21m
Cameron, Alexander, 193
Campbell, Arthur, 348, 350
Campbell, John. *See* Loudon, Earl of
Campfield, Jabez, 253
Canachquasy. *See* Kanuksusy (Seneca)
Canada and Canadians. *See also* New France;
    Quebec; Quebec Act; Simcoe, John
    Graves *and others*
    Battle of Monongahela and, 107
    boundary with US and, 411
    French and, 116, 163, 246
    Gnadenhütten massacre and, 275
    invasion of, 139, 246, 280
    Iroquois and, 99, 488
    Villiers and, 94
    Washington on, 164
    westward expansion and, 396
Canadian Indians, 219–20, 221–25, 228,
    241, 282, 416. *See also* Seven Nations of
    Canada; St. Lawrence Indians
Canasatego (Onondaga), 321, 578n86
Captain Abeel. *See* Cornplanter (Allegheny
    Seneca)
Captain Jacobs (Tewea) (Delaware), 113,
    119, 132
Captain Lewis. *See* Vincent, Lewis (Huron)
Captain Pipe. *See* Pipe (Delaware)
Captain Solomon. *See* Hendricks, Solomon
    (Stockbridge)
Captian Oppamylucah (Delaware), 57
Carey, James, 474
Carleton, Guy. *See* Dorchester, Lord
Carolina, 27
Carondelet, Baron, 425, 426–27
Carroll, Charles, 418
Carroll, Daniel, 293
Carter, Robert "King," 31, 36
Carter family, 34–35
Cassiowea. *See* Kanuksusy (Seneca)
Caswell, Richard, 305
Catawbas. *See also* Hagler *and other Catawbas*
    Braddock and, 105
    British and, 144
    Dinwiddie and, 65
    Forbes and, 141, 143

Catawbas (*continued*)
    frontier war and, 124, 135
    Iroquois and, 30, 143
    map, 21m
    Mingoes and, 126
    Ohio Company and, 49
    Shawnees and, 72, 126
    smallpox and, 164
    Tanaghrisson's war and, 86
    Virginia and, 30, 124, 135–36
    Washington and, 129, 146, 377
Catherine the Great of Russia, 8, 311–12
Caughnawagas (Caughnuagas).
    See Kahnawakes
Cavagnial, Pierre de Rigaud de Vaudreuil
    de, 115
Cavelier, René-Robert (sieur de La Salle), 49
Cayenquerigo, Jonathan (Mohawk), 65,
    506n75
Cayugas, 21m, 30, 51, 239, 249, 254, 406,
    535n16. *See also* Iroquois
    (Haudenosaunee) and their
    confederacy; Jeskakake (Déjiquéqué)
    and other Cayugas; Mingoes; Treaty of
    Canandaigua (1794); Treaty of Fort
    Schuyler (1788)
Cayuhoga River, 132
Céleron de Blainville, Pierre-Joseph, 49–50,
    53–54, 61, 79
Chapin, Israel, 440
Chapin council (1794), 440–41
Charles II, 31
Chenussio (Genessee Castle), 254
Chequalaga. *See* Doublehead (Cherokee)
Chernow, Ron, 199, 294–95, 360, 481
Cherokees (*Ani-Yunwiya). See also* Bloody
    Fellow *and other Cherokees;* Lower
    Cherokees; southern Indians; Treaty
    of Long Island of Holston (1777);
    Treaty of Fort Stanwix (1768);
    Treaty of Hard Labor (1768);
    Treaty of Holston (1791); Treaty
    of Hopewell (1785-86); Treaty of
    Lochaber (1770)
    American Revolution and, 230–31,
        231–32, 234, 534n91
    ancient lands and, 9
    W. Blount and, 474
    Braddock and, 105
    British and, 65, 125–26, 130, 143–44,
        165–66
    "civilization" and, 473
    colonists and, 164, 427–28, 526n57
    Delawares and, 153

Dinwiddie and, 65, 126–27, 130
Forbes' campaign and, 140–41, 143–45,
    146–47, 163
Franklin (state) and, 299
French and, 65, 126, 133, 146
gun trade and, 27
Iroquois and, 30, 143, 153
Knox and, 424–25, 427–28, 429–30
map, 21m
Mississippi Company and, 179
Northwestern Confederacy and, 416
Ohio Indians and, 144
Philadelphia diplomacy and, 2
Revolutionary War in the West and,
    246, 264–65
Royal Proclamation of 1763 negotiations
    and (1768), 188
scalped by colonists, 163–64
Shawnees and, 126–27, 128, 213–14
smallpox and, 164, 281
South Carolina trade and, 42–43
Spain and, 425
Tanaghrisson's war and, 86
US Senate and, 358
Virginia's alliance with (1755-1758),
    124–26, 128–29, 130, 133–34, 137–38,
    140–41, 142–47
Virginia's Indian country and, 20, 30
Washington and, 3, 136, 143, 145–46,
    163, 165–66, 179, 337–39, 427–28,
    430, 431, 462, 465–66, 468, 487
Winchester and, 115
Cherokee war, 163–66
Chickahominies, 19
Chickamauga Cherokees, 246, 281, 423,
    430, 460, 568n2
Chickasaws. *See also* Piominko *and other
    Chickasaws;* Treaty of French Lick
    (1784); Treaty of Hopewell (1785-86)
    American Revolution and, 305
    boundaries and, 569n24
    "civilization" and, 427
    Creeks and, 426, 429
    map, 21m
    Philadelphia yellow fever and, 2
    Pickens and W. Blount and, 429
    Spain and, 305–6, 425, 426–27,
        431–32, 446
    St. Clair's army and, 390
    Tanaghrisson's war and, 86
    trade and, 27, 470
    US Senate and, 358
    Washington and, 3, 339–40, 425,
        426–27, 431–32

Wayne and, 436
westward expansion and, 425
chickens, 11
Chillicothe division of Shawnees, 51, 246
China Breast Plate, 565n36
Chincanacina. *See* Dragging Canoe
  (Chickamauga Cherokee)
Choctaws, 21m, 306–7, 358, 425, 426–27,
  429, 436, 446, 470, 473, 507n4.
  See also Franchimastabé; southern
  Indians; Taboca *and other Choctaws;*
  Treaty of Mobile (1784); Treaty of
  Hopewell (1785-86)
Chota, 128, 186m, 213–14, 232, 337,
  349m, 463
Chouteau, Auguste and Pierre, 425
Christian, William, 233
Christianity. *See* religion
Chuquilatague. *See* Doublehead (Cherokee)
Chutloh (Tsu-la) (Kingfisher) (Cherokee),
  423
"civilization." *See also* education; religion
  agriculture and, 331, 332f, 454–55
  assimilation and, 488
  Brant and, 455–56
  Cherokees and, 462–68, 473
  Chickasaws and, 427, 473
  Cornplanter on, 401
  Creeks and, 461, 468–75
  Franklin and, 329
  Indian agents and trading posts and,
    453–54
  Indian land and, 375
  Indian reactions to, 456–59, 472,
    473, 475
  Indians and, 45, 412
  Knox on, 402–3
  Pickering and, 343–44
  private property and, 451, 458–59
  Sullivan's campaign and, 250
  Treaty of Greenville (1795) and, 459–61
  Treaty of New York (1790) and, 369
  Washington and, 205, 330, 332f, 341,
    387, 427, 451–53, 454, 458, 461–62,
    472–73, 473–74, 475–76, 484–85
  westward expansion and, 331
Clark, George Rogers, 272–73, 278, 280,
  326, 329, 414, 560n26. *See also* Treaty
  of Fort Finney (1786); Treaty of Fort
  McIntosh (1785)
Clark, William, 439
Clarke, Elijah, 432, 433
Claus, Daniel, 99, 242, 257–58
Cleveland (Ohio), 51

Clinton, George, 244, 245, 249, 290, 301,
  303, 304, 366, 402, 405, 407, 408, 437
Clinton, James, 247, 250, 251, 259, 272
Clymer, George, 432
Cognaawagas. *See* Kahnawakes
Cohama. *See* McGillivray, William
  (Chickasaw)
Colbert, George (Tootematubbe)
  (Chickasaw), 426, 460, 569n17
Colbert, William (Cooshemataha)
  (Chickasaw), 426, 431, 569n17
Colesquo. *See* Cornstalk (Mekoche
  Shawnee)
College of William and Mary, 28, 37, 192
Colonel Louis. *See* Cook, Louis
  (Abenaki–African
  American–Kahnawake Mohawk)
colonialism and imperialism, 44, 485–86.
  See also "civilization"
colonials. *See* elites; settlers (colonials,
  farmers, frontiersmen, squatters)
Common Disturber. *See* Teesteke
  (Cherokee)
communal ethic, Indian, 41
confederations of Indians, 374. *See also*
  Iroquois (Haudenosaunee) and their
  confederacy (Five Nations)
  (Six Nations); Northwestern
  Confederacy war
Connecticut, 307–8, 336
Connesauty, 400. *See also* Pickering,
  Timothy
Connolly, John, 199, 204–5, 209, 530n82
Conoghquieson (Kanaghquaesa) (Oneida),
  188, 241
Conotocarious. *See* Town Destroyer
Conoys, 43, 156–57, 390, 416
conquest, fiction of, 34, 48, 99, 300, 316,
  327, 330, 484
conscription bounties, 121, 139
Continental Congress, 218, 219–20, 244,
  261, 283, 308
Contrecoeur, Claude-Pierre Pécaudy, 61,
  85, 87, 89, 90–91, 94, 95
conventional warfare, 121, 122. *See also*
  Indian ways of fighting
Cook, Louis or Lewis (Colonel Louis)
  (Atiatoharongwen
  (Akiatonharónkwen)
  Atayataghronghta) (Abenaki–African
  American–Kahnawake Mohawk), 1,
  107, 223, 224, 412–13, 418, 437,
  490–91, 492, pl 4
Cooper, James Fenimore, 96

Cooper, Polly, 235
Cooshemataha. *See* Colbert, William
  (Chickasaw)
corn
  American Revolution and, 235–36, 245,
    246, 248
  Brodhead and, 255
  Butler's destruction of, 245
  Cherokee grievances and, 338
  Maumee River villages and, 380
  Northwestern Confederacy war and, 384
  Revolutionary War in the West and, 273,
    278, 280
  Shelby's destruction of, 246
  Sullivan's campaign and, 251
  tobacco *versus*, 23
  Washington and, 235–37, 243
  Wayne and, 438–39
  Wyandots and British and, 274
Cornplanter (Kayenthwahkeh) (Ki-on-
    twog-ky) (Obeal) (Captain Abeel)
    (Allegheny Seneca). *See also* Chapin
    council (1794); Treaties of Fort
    Harmar (1789); Treaty of Fort
    Stanwix (1784)
  education and, 341
  Iroquois and, 441
  land sales by, 564n19
  Northwestern Confederacy and, 416
  Philadelphia diplomacy and, 406
  portrait of, pl 6
  raids led by, 257
  on scalpings and roads, 412
  Senecas and, 412–13
  Washington and, 7, 400–404, 407, 440,
    441, 487
  Wayne and, 436
Cornstalk (Colesquo) (Mekoche Shawnee),
    210, 264, 265, 273, 274, 278, 279
Corn Tassel (Tassel) (Old Tassel)
    (Utsi'dsata) (Cherokee), 232, 233,
    307, 338
Cornwallis, Charles, 258, 261
Coshocton, 274
cotton, 337, 448, 462, 465, 470, 471,
    472, 473
council fires, 53
Covenant Chain, 30, 61, 98
Cowass, 223, 226
Coweta. *See* Hallowing King (Creek)
Cowkiller. *See* Red Jacket (Seneca)
Craik, James, 85, 138, 195, 197, 203,
    294, 483
Crane, the (Tarhe) (Wyandot), 443

Crawford, Valentine, 209–10
Crawford, William
  Dunmore and, 204, 210
  Indian lands and, 261
  Koonay's baby and, 208
  Revolutionary War in the West and,
    265–66
  Sandusky campaign of, 276–78
  torture and death of, 276–78, 278–79,
    481
  Virginia war with Shawnees
    and, 210
  Washington and, 185, 277
  Washington's Indian land acquisitions
    and, 85, 187–88, 192, 195–96, 199,
    200, 201, 202, 203, 204, 206, 208,
    211, 212, 271
Crawford, William (nephew), 276, 277
credit and debt, 308, 313, 485. *See also*
  national debt
Creeks. *See also* Lower Creeks; McGillivray,
    Alexander *and other Creeks;* Treaty of
    Fort Jackson (1814); Treaty of Colerain
    (1796); Treaty of Galphinton (1785);
    Treaty of New York (1790);
    Upper Creeks
  agriculture and, 372
  army of, 356
  W. Blount and, 474
  Cherokees and, 126
  Chickasaws and, 422–32, 426, 429
  "civilization" and, 473, 475
  Georgia and, 322, 350, 353, 355,
    429, 432–33
  maps, 21m
  McGillivray and, 351–52, 353
  Northwestern Confederacy
    and, 416
  Peace of Paris and, 348
  smallpox and, 281
  Spain and, 355–56, 358, 362, 369, 374,
    431–32
  speculators and, 30, 356–57
  US Senate and, 360–61
  Washington and, 3, 347, 355–56, 370,
    429, 431–32
  Wayne and, 435
  West Indies trade and, 557n98
Cresap, Michael, 207
Cresap, Thomas, 38, 47, 48, 54, 55, 66,
    199–200, 530nn76,82
Cresswell, Nicholas, 195–96, 458
Crèvecoeur, Hector St. John de, 457,
    510n49

Croghan, George
  Anglo-French rivalry and, 84, 160
  Braddock and, 106–7, 110
  at Fort Cumberland, 105
  Fort Pitt council and, 173
  French ensign interrogation and, 135
  Gist's expedition and, 55, 56
  Logstown Treaty and, 57, 59
  on Montour, 55, 505n30
  Ohio Indian land and, 58
  Pennsylvania and, 56
  Pine Creek meeting and, 62
  Royal Proclamation of 1763 and, 185,
    188–89
  smuggled information and, 96
  "Suffering Traders" and, 194
  on Tanaghrisson, 99
  trading post of, 97
  Treaty of Easton (1758) and, 156, 173
  Treaty of Fort Stanwix (1768) and, 189
  Washington and, 66, 92, 96–97
  Washington's Indian land
    acquisitions and, 196
Croghan, William, 275
Crown Point fort, 102
cultures, hybrid, 11–12
Cumberland, Duke of, 49, 54, 103, 104
Cuming, Alexander, 125
Cunne Shote (Stalking Turkey)
  (Cherokee), 166
Currin, Barnaby, 67, 76
Cussetah or Cussitah King. *See* Eneah
  or Neah Mico (Creek)
Custaloga (Delaware), 71, 75
Custis, Daniel Parke, 178
Custis, George Washington Parke, 197
Custis, Martha "Patsy," 204
Cutler, Manasseh, 313, 314, 499n40
Cuyahoga River, 51, 266

D
Dane, Nathan, 314
Darke, William, 391–92, 393
Dartmouth, Lord, 206, 211
Dartmouth College, 225, 226, 242, 464
David, James Corbett, 529n43, 530n82
Davison, John, 67, 68, 70, 75, 87, 88
Dean, James, 224, 241–42, 248, 251, 258,
  303, 535n16
Deanaghrison. *See* Tanaghrisson (Seneca)
Death of General Montgomery, The (painting),
  pl 3
deerskin trade, 25, 26, 27, 42, 306, 462,
  470, 557n98, 577n73

Déjiquéqué (Jeskakake) (Cayuga), 61, 72
DeLancey, James, 95
Delaware George (Nenatcheehunt)
  (Nenatchehan) (Delaware), 154,
  160, 176
Delawares (Lenni Lenapee). *See also* Fort
  Laurens council; Fort Pitt meeting
  (1775); Gnadenhütten massacre;
  Northwestern Confederacy war; Ohio
  Indians; Shingas; Treaties of Fort
  Harmar (1789); Treaty of Fort Pitt
  (1778)
  agriculture and, 263
  alliance with, 267
  American Revolution and, 230
  Anglo-French rivalry and, 65, 72, 107,
    114, 116–17, 117–18, 152
  Beaujeu and, 110
  Braddock and, 107
  Brant and, 417
  British and, 56, 173
  captives and, 118, 119, 177
  Cherokees and, 153
  Christian education and, 342
  "civilization" and, 456, 457–58
  Clark and, 272–73
  Congressional meeting and, 269–70
  Forbes and, 152–53, 160
  Forks of the Ohio fort and, 84
  Fort Duquesne smuggled information
    and, 96
  French and, 63, 155, 270–71
  French and Indian War and, 148
  frontier war and, 124
  Gist and, 57
  Iroquois and, 117–18, 260
  Mahicans and, 413
  map, 46m
  mixing of peoples and, 43
  Moravianism and, 274–75
  Morgan and, 263, 269, 271
  Ohio country and, 53
  Pennsylvania and, 99, 131, 132
  Post and, 153–54
  Revolutionary War in the West and,
    266–71, 273, 278
  Sandusky campaign and, 276
  Sandusky conference and, 420
  scalpings and, 273
  settlers and, 198
  Six Nations and, 60–61
  Tamaqua and, 506n53
  Tanaghrisson and, 64, 70, 90, 97, 98
  Tanaghrisson's war and, 92

Delawares (*continued*)
Treaty of Easton (1758) and, 156–57
Treaty of Logstown and, 59
Virginia war with Shawnees and, 210
vocabulary of, 312
wampum belt and, 70–73
war losses of, 162
Washington and, 71–72, 96, 146, 269–70, 459
Wayne and, 436
western migrations of, 51
Demere, Paul, 165
Demere, Raymond, 129
Dennis, Jeff W., 570n39
Denny, Ebenezer, 383
Denny, William, 144, 153
Devourer of Villages (Town Destroyer) (Conotocarious) (J. Washington), 7, 13, 69–70, 86, 125
Dinsmoor, Silas, 464–65, 464f, 466–67
Dinsmoor, Silas (John Ross's son), 468
Dinwiddie, Robert. *See also* Fort Duquesne; frontier defense and Cherokee alliance; land grants and land bounties
Anglo-French rivalry and, 65, 66–67, 69
Braddock and, 102, 103, 106
on conventional warfare, 121
Dunbar and, 113
frontier defense and Cherokee alliance and, 125, 126–27, 128–29, 130, 131, 132–33, 134, 136–37, 138
Gist and, 56
Indians and, 65, 96, 99, 105
on Lewis' attack, 126
Ohio Company and, 50, 65, 66
Saint-Pierre and, 66–68, 80–81
scalping parties and, 130–31
Tanaghrisson and, 70, 89, 90, 92, 99
Treaty of Logstown and, 54, 58
on Virginians, 120
Virginia Regiment and, 81, 83
Washington and, 40, 66–68, 69–70, 86, 89, 100, 143
"Dinwiddie" ("Head of Everything"), 92
diplomacy. *See also* gifts; Philadelphia Indian diplomacy; treaties; wampum belts; war *versus* negotiation
Braddock and, 106
Delawares and, 154–55
Forbes and, 152–53, 157, 159, 167
French and Indian War and, 6
Indian land and, 7
Indian mourning for Washington and, 487
Indian practices of, 397

Jumonville's death and, 89
roads and, 412, 417
Tangaghrisson and, 68
war *versus*, 328–29
Washington and, 67, 68, 397
Washington's status and, 66
women and, 80
diseases. *See* smallpox and other diseases
Dixon, David, 90, 94
Doegs, 25
Donelson, John, 186m, 193
Dorchester, Lord (Guy Carleton), 311, 411, 437
Doublehead (Chequalaga) (Chuquilatague) (Cherokee), 349m, 423, 430
Dowd, Gregory, 457
Downs, Lavinia (perhaps Creek), 8
Dragging Canoe (Tsí-yu-gûnsí-ni) (Tsi'yu-gûnsi'ni) (Chincanacina) (Overhill/Chickamauga Cherokee), 213, 232, 233, 423, 568n2
Duane, James, 301
DuCoigne, Jean Baptiste (Kaskaskia), 7, 414–15
Duer, William, 313, 314, 315, 388, 394, 395
Dunbar, Thomas, 102, 109, 112, 113
Dunmore, Earl of (John Murray). *See also* Treaty of Camp Charlotte
British and, 211, 213
enslaved African Americans and, 529n43
Henderson's land deals and, 213
reputation of, 529n43, 530n82
Royal Proclamation and, 201, 529n43
Virginia land-dealing gentry and, 207, 211
Virginia war with Shawnees and, 208–11, 530n82
Washington's land acquisitions and, 202, 203, 204, 206, 211, 294
westward expansion and, 199, 200
Duquesne, marquis, 61, 80, 90–91, 95

E
economic policy, 326, 335–37. *See also* trade
education, 28, 341–44, 369, 404, 484, 488–89. *See also* "civilization"; religion
Edwards, Timothy, 220
Eel clan. *See* Good Peter
Eel River, 459
Efau Hadjo (Mad Dog) (Creek), 363, 376, 472, 474, 487
Effingham, Howard (Assarigoa), 30
Eghnisara. *See* Montour, Andrew

Egushawa (Egushewa) (Agushaway)
(Agashawa) (Negushwa) (Ottawa), 443
Elbert, Samuel, 347
elites. *See also* Jefferson, Thomas *and other elites;* speculators
frontier, 24
Indian raids and, 120–21
Ohio country and, 47
Royal Proclamation of 1763 and, 183–84
Scottish, 33
settlers and, 26, 194–95, 198–99, 260–61, 280, 334
westward expansion and, 179
Elliott, Matthew, 390
Ellis, Joseph, 171, 184, 206, 285, 482
empire. *See* westward expansion
Eneah or Neah Mico, (Cussetah Mico) (Cussetah or Cussitah King) (Fat King or Fat King of Cussitah) (Creek), 352, 353, 355, 361, 363, 373, 472–73, 578n86. *See also* Rock Landing meeting; Treaty of Galphinton (1785); Treaty of Shoulderbone Creek (1786)
enlistment bounties, 121, 139
enslaved African Americans
American identity and, 12
American Revolution and, 211, 219
Carter and, 36
cotton and, 448
Dinwiddie and, 120
Dunmore and, 529n43
Efau Hadjo and, 472
federal authority and, 337
Indians compared, 4
land companies and, 179
McGillivray and, 347, 375
Northwest Ordinance (1787) and, 315
Somerset v. Stewart (1772) and, 201
southern Indians and, 473
tobacco and, 32, 33, 202
Virginia and, 25, 26–27, 28, 121, 481–82, 579n33
Washington and, 10–11, 29, 177, 178, 209, 236, 289, 294, 478, 481–83, 491, 579n39
enslaved Indians, 25, 26–27, 28
environment, 10, 32
Eries, 27
Eskaqua. *See* Bloody Fellow (Cherokee)
ethnic cleansing, 488
Ethridge, Robbie, 577n69
Euchees, 363
executive privilege, 395

F
Fairfax. *See* Kanuksusy (Seneca)
Fairfax, George William, 37, 80, 209
Fairfax, Sally, 38, 80
Fairfax, Thomas, 31, 38
Fall Line, 29
Farewell Address (Washington), 482, 486
Farmer's Brother (Honanyawas) (Honeyewus) (Ogh-ne-wi-ge-was) (Buffalo Creek Seneca), 399–400, 402, 406, 416–17, 565n36
Fat King or Fat King of Cussetah. *See* Eneah or Neah Mico (Creek)
Fauquier, Francis, 131, 163, 164, 166, 182–83, 526n57
Fausz, J. Frederick, 24
federal authority *versus* states' power (national unity). *See also* Georgia; Treaty of Fort Stanwix (1784); US Constitution
boundaries and, 283–85, 292
Confederation Congress and, 284–85
federal authority and, 284–86
Indian land and, 4, 100, 285–86, 288, 290–93, 307–17, 403
Indians and, 305–7, 314, 317
Indian unity and, 286, 317–18
Jefferson on, 557n90
land rush and, 293–94
national debt and, 336
Northwest *versus* Southwest Territories and, 422
Potomac River and, 298–99
religion and, 286–87
settlers and, 284, 285–86, 292–93, 293–94
speculators and, 291–92
statehood and, 293
states and, 283–84, 284–85, 299–305, 307–8, 405, 431, 442
St. Clair's defeat and, 395, 396
taxes, 314
Treaty of Hopewell and, 338–39
US Army and, 291, 439–40
US Constitution and, 321–24
Washington and, 287–93, 316, 317, 323–25, 333–37, 340–41, 431, 479, 483, 485, 486, 492
Washington's Indian land acquisitions and, 294–98, 296m
Washington's Indian policies and, 4
westward expansion and, 290, 307–18, 323, 446–47

federal budget, 7. *See also* national debt
Federalist Papers, The (Hamilton), 326
Ferling, John, 172, 236, 280, 317, 385
Ferry Farm, 40
Few, William, 354
"First of Council," 92
Fitzhugh, William, 40
Fitzhugh family, 34–35, 178
Five Lower Towns (Chickamauga
    Cherokees), 423
Five Nations. *See* Iroquois
    (Haudenosaunee) and their
    confederacy
Fletcher, Thomas, 230
Flick, A. C., 259
Florida, 21m, 180, 181, 201, 203–4, 306,
    348, 367–68, 374, 474. *See also*
    Seminoles; Treaty of San Lorenzo
    (1795)
Forbes, John, and his campaign. *See also*
    "French and Indian War"; roads; Treaty
    of Easton (1758)
  army of, 145, 152
  background of, 139
  British army and, 145
  Cherokees and, 140–41, 143–45,
    146–47, 163
  colonials and, 151–52
  death of, 159, 174
  Indians and, 140–46, 152–57, 158, 159,
    160, 163, 174, 521n42
  Indian ways of fighting and, 149
  victory of, 157–58, 159, 160, 161,
    163, 167
  Washington and, 6, 140, 141, 142–43,
    145–47, 148–49, 149–50, 151, 157,
    158, 159, 160, 162, 167, 246, 522n50
Force, Peter, 535n16
"foreign" Indians, 20, 26
Forks of the Ohio, 6, 47, 48, 49, 67, 68, 80,
    81, 82m, 83, 102, 199, 202. *See also*
    Dinwiddie, Robert; Fort Duquesne;
    Treaty of Logstown (1752)
Fort Ancient Culture, 51
Fort Chartres, 202
Fort Cumberland, 104, 106, 115, 131, 132
Fort Defiance, 438, 443
Fort Dunmore, 261
Fort Duquesne. *See also* Forbes, John, and
    his campaign; Fort Pitt
  Braddock and, 103
  building of, 65, 80, 84–85
  French and Indian allies and, 65, 66,
    107, 116

reinforcements, 94
smuggled information about, 96
Washington and, 87, 91, 115, 132,
    133, 139
Fort Frederick, 115
Fort Frontenac, 151, 158
Fort Greenville, 436
Fort Hamilton, 379m
Fort Laurens council, 268
Fort LeBoeuf, 63, 67, 74, 75, 76, 162
Fort Loudon (at Winchester, Virginia), 127,
    131, 136, 140–42
Fort Loudon (on Little Tennessee River),
    128–29, 134, 165
Fort Machault, 63
Fort McIntosh, 266
Fort Miamis, 437
Fort Necessity. *See* Battle of Fort Necessity
Fort Niagara, 21m, 61, 102, 103, 161
Fort Oswego, 61, 63
Fort Pitt, 160, 161, 173–74, 175, 176–77,
    196, 202, 207, 248, 271–72. *See also*
    Fort Duquesne; Treaty of Fort Pitt
    (1778)
Fort Pitt conference (1775), 261–63,
    529n62
Fort Pitt conference (1776), 263–64
Fort Presque Isle, 46m, 61, 63, 76, 162
Fort Randolph, 273
Fort Recovery, 436, 437
forts. *See also* Fort Duquesne *and other forts*
  Anglo-French rivalry and, 80, 117
  Berkeley and, 25
  Cherokees and, 127
  French, 61, 68, 158
  frontier defense and, 132
  Georgia and, 432
  Indian return of, 177
  Ohio Company and, 48, 67
  Ohio country, 61–62, 63, 65, 178
  Royal Proclamation of 1763
    negotiations and (1768), 188–89
  settlers and, 120
  Treaty of Greenville and, 443
  Virginia and Pennsylvania and, 84
Fort Schuyler, 290
Fort Stanwix, 242. *See also* Treaty of Fort
    Stanwix (1768); Treaty of Fort
    Stanwix (1784)
Fort Ticonderoga, 152, 317
Fort Venango, 46m, 162
Fort Wayne, 439, 443
Fort William Henry, siege and surrender of,
    95–96, 135

Fowler, Theodosius, 388
Foxes (Mesquakies), 416
Franchimastabé (Choctaw), 306
Franklin (state), 299
Franklin, Benjamin, 90, 98–99, 103, 106,
    122, 194, 267, 286, 321, 325, 329,
    457, 544n14
Fraser (Frazier), John and his cabin, 63,
    73, 79
freedom, Cook and, 491
Freeman, Douglas Southall, 129, 203,
    499n45
Freeman, Thomas, 295
French, the. *See also* Anglo-French rivalry;
    Beaujeu, Daniel-Hyacinthe-Marie
    Liénard de *and other French people;*
    Canada; Fort Duquesne; "French
    and Indian War"; French Revolution;
    law of nations; Ohio country;
    Quebec; Tanaghrisson's war; Treaty
    of Easton (1758); Treaty of Montreal
    (1701); Treaty of Paris (1763);
    Venango
    American Revolution and, 233–34,
        243, 267
    Britain and, 411, 438, 445
    Cherokees and, 43, 133, 146
    Delawares and, 63, 155, 270–71
    Dinwiddie and, 66
    Efau Hadjo and, 472
    England and, 30
    forts and, 61, 68, 158, 161
    gifts and, 134–35
    Indian dress and, 121
    Indians and, 62, 116, 157–58, 158–59,
        175, 218
    intermarriage and, 28
    retreat of, 162
    Tanaghrisson and, 510n49
"French and Indian War." *See also*
    Braddock's defeat; Forbes, John,
    and his campaign; Fort Duquesne;
    Fort Pitt; frontier advance and
    Cherokee war; frontier defense and
    Cherokee alliance; Tanaghrisson;
    Tanaghrisson's war; Treaty of
    Easton (1758)
    American Revolution and, 12
    Forbes and, 139
    Indian land and, 171, 290, 450
    Indians and, 6, 12, 114, 115–17, 148,
        152, 157, 161, 218, 232, 234, 377
    Washington and, 6, 166–67, 216, 217,
        232, 234, 288, 290, 386, 450

French Creek, 63
French Indians, 222
French Revolution, 3, 483
French speakers, 10
frontier. *See* long knives; settlers (colonials,
    farmers, frontiersmen, squatters);
    westward expansion
frontier advance and Cherokee war,
    148–49, 163–66. *See also* Forbes, John,
    and his campaign
frontier defense and Cherokee alliance.
    See also Dinwiddie, Robert; Forbes,
    John, and his campaign; settlers
    (colonials, farmers, frontiersmen,
    squatters)
    Catawbas and, 129, 130, 135–36, 141,
        142, 143–44, 146
    Cherokees and, 125–27, 129, 130,
        133–34, 137–38, 140–41, 142
    Indian objectives and, 128, 133–34
    Indian raids and, 130–31, 135, 138–39
    Loudon's snub and, 132–33
    Pennsylvania and, 131, 132, 143–44, 145
    Six Nations and, 142–43
    South Carolina and, 125, 126, 128,
        129, 137
    Washington and, 124–25, 127–28,
        129–30, 131–33, 134–39, 139–40,
        141–42, 145, 146–47
fruit trees, 254, 538n92
Fry, Joshua, 49, 58, 81, 83, 85, 92
Frymer, Paul, 580n41
Furstenberg, François, 483
Fusatchee Mico (White Bird King) (Bird
    Tail King) (Creek), 363, 368, 433

G
Gage, Thomas, 110
Gahgeote. *See* Half Town (Seneca)
Gahickdodon (Johnny) (Seneca), 108
Ganiodaio (Handsome Lake) (Seneca),
    441, 488–89, 490
Gansevoort, Peter, 255–56
Gates, Horatio, 102, 216, 220, 249
Gayoso de Lemos, Manuel Luis, 428
Gelemend (John Killbuck) (Kaylelamund)
    (Delaware), 263
gender, 23, 42, 452, 454, 462, 463, 464,
    471, 484. *See also* women, Indian;
    women, non-Indian
General Eskaqua (General Iskagua).
    See Bloody Fellow (Cherokee)
Genesee Company of Adventurers,
    301, 304

Genet Affair, 497n13
genocide, 484–85
George II (Britain), 47, 48, 91, 92
George III (Britain), 166, 180–81
Georgia. *See also* Creeks; Treaty of Colerain
    (1796); Treaty of Galphinton (1785);
    Treaty of Hopewell (1785-86); Treaty
    of Long Island of Holston (1777);
    Treaty of New York (1790)
    Cherokees' land and, 233
    Chickasaws and, 305
    "civilization" of Indians and, 453
    deerskin trade and, 42
    federal authority *versus* states' and, 354,
      355, 432–33, 557n90
    forts and, 432
    Muskogeans and, 27
    national debt and, 336
    Peace of Paris and, 348
    US Constitution and, 322, 350–51, 364
    Washington on, 351
German Flatts meeting (1776), 238,
    239, 241
Germans, 121, 172, 206, 207
German-speaking peoples, 29, 38
Gibson, John, 208, 266, 274
Gideon. *See* Teedyuscung (eastern Delaware)
gifts, diplomatic. *See also* tobacco;
    wampum belts
    American Revolution and, 233
    British and, 133–34, 160, 175, 177
    corn as, 23
    Forbes' campaign and, 141, 145, 150
    Indians, British and French and, 133–35
    murdered Senecas and, 398
    Niagara meeting and, 182
    Queen Aliquippa and, 80
    Rock Landing meeting and, 360
    Tanaghrisson and, 53
    Treaty of Holston and, 424
    Ugulayacabe to Blount, 426
    Washington on, 86, 141
    Washington to Indians, 228, 307, 375
Gill, Joseph Louis (White Chief of the
    Abenakis), 226–27
Gilman, Andrew, 230
Girty, Simon, 277, 390
Gist, Christopher (Annosanah)
    Atkin and, 136–37, 138
    Cherokees and, 143
    death of, 164
    Forbes' attack and, 156
    Fort LeBoeuf to Frazier's cabin journey
      and, 78–79

    Fort Loudon council and, 142
    Indian allies and, 125
    Indian land surveys and, 5
    Logstown Treaty and, 59, 68
    Ohio country travels of, 54–56, 57–58, 67
    Shingas and, 68
    status of, 66
    Tanaghrisson and, 70, 87, 507n22
    Treaty of Logstown and, 58–59
    Washington and, 67, 70, 72–73, 74, 75,
      114, 136–37
Gist, Nathaniel, 172, 232, 233
Gist, Thomas, 156
Gist's settlement, 93
Gladwin, Henry, 176
Glaize, 387, 390
Glen, James, 43, 65, 125, 129
Gnadenhütten massacre, 275–76,
    277–79, 383
Gooch, William, 31, 33, 47, 48, 49, 50
Good Child King. *See* Hoboithle or
    Hopoithle or Opothle Mico (Creek)
Good Peter (Agwerondongwas)
    (Agwrondougwas) (Gwedelhes)
    (Oneida), 303, 304, 406, 414,
      458, pl 8
Gorham, Nathaniel, 402, 564n19
grain burying, 384, 560n26
Grand Ohio Company (Walpole Company),
    194
Grant, James, 155, 165
Grayson, George Washington (Creek),
    577n68
Greathouse, Daniel, 207, 530n82
Greathouse, Nathaniel, 530n82
Great Indian Warpath, 30
Great Lakes, 103
Great Lakes Indians, 72, 107, 135, 158.
    See also Northwestern Confederacy war;
    Ojibwas *and other Great Lakes Indians*
Great Law of Peace (Iroquois), 399
Great Meadows, 87, 88–91, 199, 480.
    See also Battle of Fort Necessity
Great Moon (Maghinga Keesoch), 507n14.
    See also Brodhead, Daniel
Great Plains Indians, 281–82
Great Tree. *See* Big Tree (Seneca)
Greenbrier Company, 47, 193
Greene, Nathaneal, 216, 246, 247, 248
Grenada, 181
Grierson, Robert, 472
Griffin, Cyrus, 360
guerrilla warfare, 123. *See also* Indian ways
    of fighting/dress

Gunter, Edmund and Gunter's chain, 36
Guyasuta (Kayashuta) (Kayasota)
  (Quiashuta) (the Hunter)
  (Allegheny Seneca)
  Bouquet and, 177
  British and, 251
  Cornplanter and, 400
  death of, 443
  Fort Pitt meeting and, 262, 263–64, 268
  W. Johnson and, 207
  Pontiac's War and, 176
  Revolutionary War in the West and, 265,
    278, 279
  Royal Proclamation of 1763 negotiations
    and (1768), 188–89
  Washington and, 7, 73, 78, 197, 208, 401
  Wayne and, 435–36
Gwedelhes. *See* Good Peter (Oneida)

H
Hagler (King Hagler) (Nopkehe)
  (Catawba), 128–29, 135
Haiti, 483
Haldimand, Governor, 258
Half King, the. *See* Tanaghrisson (Seneca)
Half Town (Gahgeote) (Achiout) (Seneca),
  341, 401
Halifax, Lord, 180
Halkett, Francis, 142
Halkett, Peter, 102, 110
Halkett's son, 110
Hallowing King (Creek), 355, 361, 363
Hamilton, Alexander. *See also* whiskey tax
  and rebellion
  Beckwith and, 368
  British and, 384, 411
  Cherokee meeting and, 430
  Creek-Chickasaw war and, 429
  Duer and, 313
  federal authority *versus* states' and,
    551n22
  Federal Indian policies and, 326
  Hammond and, 411
  Jefferson and, 3
  Maclay and, 359
  national bank and, 337
  national debt and, 394
  Philadelphia diplomacy and, 2
  St. Clair's defeat and, 394, 395
  US armed forces and, 290–91, 326–27,
    335–36, 551n22
  Washington's Farewell Address and, 482
  westward expansion and, 326–27, 398
  Whiskey Rebellion and, 439–40

  yellow fever and, 2
Hamilton, Henry, 212, 272, 273
Hamilton, James, 49, 52, 62, 97, 131
Hammond, George, 410–11, 434, 566n58
Hamtramck, John Francis and his
  expedition, 384, 390, 459
Hanbury, John, 47, 104
Hancock, John, 219–20, 228, 239
Hand, Edward, 265, 266, 434
Handsome Lake (Ganiodaio) (Seneca),
  441, 488–89, 490
Hanging Maw (Uskwa'li-gu'ta) (Scolaguta)
  (Cherokee), 264, 427, 430, 570n29
Hannastown attack (1782), 278
Hanyerry (Hanyost) (Oneida).
  See Thaosagwat (Oneida)
Hardin, John, 328, 384, 412
Harjo, Suzan Shown, 371
Harmar, Josiah and his expedition, 276–77,
  302, 324, 379m, 382–85, 409, 439
Harris, John, 99
Harrison, Benjamin, 298–99
Harrison, William, 276, 277, 480
Harrison, William Henry, 332
Harvard, 344
Haudenosaunees, 488, 490. *See also*
  Iroquois (Haudenosaunee) and their
  confederacy
Hawkins, Benjamin. *See also* Treaty of
  Holston (1791); Treaty of Hopewell
  (1785-86)
  background of, 8
  W. Blount and, 474
  boundaries and, 304–5, 305–6, 324, 353,
    432–33, 466
  Creeks and, 468–72, 472–73, 474, 475
  Dinsmoor and, 467
  Hoboithle Mico and, 475
  Indian agriculture and, 469–70,
    470–72, 475
  Indian land acquisitions and, 380,
    468–69, 475
  McGillivray and, 364
  Muskogee language and, 8, 577n69
  peace and, 393
  portrait, 469f
  statehood committee and, 293
  St. Clair's defeat and, 393
  suspicion of, 474
  vocabulary of southern Indians by, 312
Heath, William, 221, 230
Heckewelder, John, 4, 276, 277, 341, 383,
  414, 451
Hector, Francisco Luis, 374

Henderson, Richard, 213
Hendrick, (Theyanoguin) (Mohawk), 90,
    98, 99
Hendricks, Solomon (Uhhaunauwaunmut)
    (Captain Solomon) (Stockbridge),
    219, 220–21, 565n36
Henry, Patrick, 184, 265, 556n60
Herkimer, Nicholas, 242
Hillsborough, Earl of, 180. *See also* Royal
    Proclamation of 1763
historians, 3, 4, 5, 13
History and Present State of Virginia, The
    (Beverley), 22
*History of the Dividing Line betwixt Virginia
    and North Carolina* (Byrd II), 42
Hoag, Peter, 85, 115
Hobocan. *See* Pipe (Delaware)
Hoboithle or Hopoithle or Opothle Mico,
    (the Tame King) (Tallassee King)
    (Good Child King) (Creek), 352, 352f,
    363, 366, 373, 472, 475. *See also* Rock
    Landing meeting; Treaty of
    Shoulderbone Creek (1786)
Hodgdon, Samuel and William, 388–89, 395
Hofstra, Warren, 122
Holton, Woody, 206, 211–12
Honanyawas (Honeyewus). *See* Farmer's
    Brother (Buffalo Creek Seneca)
Hopocan. *See* Pipe (Delaware)
Howard, Carlos, 373
Hudson Bay Indians, 182
Humphreys, David, 69, 88, 158, 360, 361,
    362, 363
Hunter, the. *See* Guyasuta (Allegheny
    Seneca)
Huntingdon, Countess of, 330
Huron confederacy, 51
Hurons, 70, 94. *See also* Vincent, Lewis
    (Louis Vincent) (Captain Lewis)
    (Sawantanan) (Sawatanen)
Hurons (Wyandots), 112
Hutchins, Thomas, 309

I
Illinois, 178, 268, 305, 315
imperialism and colonialism, 44, 485–86
indentured servants, 26, 237
Indiana, 178, 315
Indian agents, 452. *See also* Dinsmoor and
    other agents
Indiana Grant, 194
Indian country. *See* Indian land; Ohio
    country; Virginia's Indian country;
    westward expansion

Indian identity, 8, 24, 44, 286, 347, 367,
    489. *See also* "civilization"
Indian land, 5, 117, 118, 285–86. *See also*
    American Revolution; boundaries;
    Indian sovereignty; land grants and
    land bounties; law of nations; right of
    conquest; speculators; treaties;
    Washington's Indian land acquisitions;
    Washington's Indian policies; westward
    expansion
Indian life and culture. *See also* agriculture;
    "civilization"; gifts; Indian mounds;
    Indian ways of fighting/dress
    British sailor's description of, 105
    colonials and, 237
    communal ethic, 41, 451, 458
    hybrid cultures, 11–12
    material culture and, 259
    pressures of colonial settlers and, 43
    Virginia's Indian country and, 22
    Washington and, 7, 9–11, 11–12, 83,
        86–87, 92, 96, 198, 483–84, 490
Indian mounds, 198, 205
Indian populations, 4–5, 19–20, 22, 24, 26,
    27–28, 28–29, 286–87
Indian power, 9, 12
Indians, enslaved, 20, 25, 26, 27, 383
Indian sovereignty, 9, 325–26, 442, 484,
    485
    Knox and Washington and, 484
    Logstown and, 53
Indian Trade and Intercourse Act (US),
    368
Indian unity, 317–18. *See also* Northwestern
    Confederacy war
Indian ways of fighting/dress, 121–22, 123,
    127–28, 148–49, 167, 215–16, 231,
    249, 250, 272, 391, 392. *See also*
    uniforms, traditional
India opinion (Pratt and Yorke), 205
Indigenous peoples elsewhere, 484
Infant, the (Iroquois), 565n36
"Instructions for the good Government
    of the Indian Department"
    (Carleton), 311
"intentional fallacies," 316
intermarriage , 28
Intolerable Acts (Britain), 206
invasive species, 11, 32
Irish, the, 172, 206. *See also* Scotch-Irish
Iroquois (Haudenosaunee) and their
    confederacy (Five Nations) (Six
    Nations). *See also* Cayugas; Fort Pitt
    meeting (1775); Mingoes; Mohawks

(Kanienkehaka); Northwestern
Confederacy war; Ohio Indians;
Oneidas; Onondagas; Senecas;
Sullivan's campaign; Tanaghrisson
and other Iroquois; Treaties of Fort
Harmar (1789); Treaty of
Canandaigua (1794); Treaty of Fort
Stanwix (1768); Treaty of Fort
Stanwix (1784); Tuscaroras
American Revolution and, 220–21, 230,
235, 237–39, 240, 242–45, 258
Anglo-French rivalry and, 65, 72, 144,
152, 161
Anishinaabeg and, 72
Beaujeu and, 110
Braddock and, 108
British and, 237–38, 405
Catawbas and, 143
Cherokees and, 143, 153
Delawares and, 56, 60–61, 114,
117–18
Fort Necessity defeat and, 99
Great Law of Peace of, 399–400
history of, 30
Indian land and, 99
Indian unity and, 318
W. Johnson and, 100
Jumonville deserter, 510n29
land sales by chiefs of, 564n19
Logstown negotiations and, 56–57
migrations and mixing of peoples and,
44, 51
Mississippi Land Company settlements
and, 179
New York and, 301–4, 407
Northwestern Confederacy and, 416,
440–41
Ohio Company and, 48
Ohio country and, 50, 51–53
Ohio Indians and, 58
Ohio Valley defense and, 81
peace *versus* war and, 300–301
Pennsylvania and, 52, 440, 504n17
Philadelphia diplomacy and, 1, 398–99,
406, 407–8, 418
Proctor and, 404
reservations and, 488
Revolutionary War in the West and,
246–59
Royal Proclamation of 1763 negotiations
and (1768), 188–89
Sandusky conference and, 420
Senecas and, 413
Shawnees and, 84, 117–18

southern Indians and, 86
Tanaghrisson and, 64, 84, 91–92, 97
Tanaghrisson's war and, 86, 94
Teedyuscung and, 144, 156
"Town Destroyer" and, 69–70,
256–57
Treaty of Easton (1758) and, 155,
156–57
Treaty of Lancaster and, 49, 54
Tuscaroras and, 130
US Constitution and, 321–22
Virginia's Indian country and, 20, 29–31,
33–34
Virginia war with Shawnees (1774)
and, 208
wampum received by, 131
Washington and, 98, 196, 238, 244,
398, 489
Winchester and, 115
irregular warfare. *See* Indian ways of
fighting
Irvine, William, 275, 276, 277, 362
Iskagua. *See* Bloody Fellow (Cherokee)

J
Jackson, Andrew, 329, 475
Jackson, James, 354, 374
James River, 22, 25
Jay Treaty (1794), 444–45
Jean Baptist. *See* Ogaghsagighte
(Kahnawake Mohawk)
Jefferson, Peter, 49, 58
Jefferson, Thomas. *See also* US Declaration
of Independence
on American liberty, 288–89
British and, 566n58
Cherokees and, 430
"civilization" and, 485
corn and, 236
Creek-Chickasaw relations and, 429
Dinsmoor and, 467
DuCoigne and, 414
on federal authority *versus* states',
557n90
Federal Indian policies and, 323–24,
329–30
Hamilton and, 3
Hammond and, 410, 411
Indian culture and, 9
Indian land acquisitions and, 184, 191
Indian policies of, 485
Jay Treaty and, 445
Little Turtle and, 461
murder of Indians reported by, 208

Jefferson, Thomas (*continued*)
  Northwestern Confederacy war and, 386
  Ostenaco and, 128
  Philadelphia diplomacy and, 1, 2, 418
  Potomac River and, 298
  Shawnees and, 273
  St. Clair's defeat and, 392
  on Tennessee River expedition, 246
  Treaty of New York and, 367, 369
  US Army and, 385
  Virginia's Indian country and, 19
  westward expansion and, 308
  yellow fever and, 2
Jemison, Mary, 118–19, 256, 456
Jenkins, William, 67
Jennings, Francis, 59, 73, 162
Jerry. *See* Skowonidous
Jeskakake (Déjiquéqué) (Cayuga), 72, 73
Johnny. *See* Gahickdodon (Seneca)
Johnson, Guy, 208, 217, 565n36
Johnson, John, 238–39
Johnson, Joseph (Mohegan), 175, 242
Johnson, Mary or Molly (Brant), 408
Johnson, Susanna, 514n74
Johnson, William
  on boundaries, 5
  death of, 208
  on Fort Pitt, 161
  on French and Indians, 107
  Guyasuta and, 207
  Indian ways and, 149
  Iroquois and, 100, 153
  Royal Proclamation of 1763 and, 185
  Royal Proclamation of 1763 negotiations
    and (1768), 188–89
  settlement restriction and, 180
  "Suffering Traders" and, 194
  as superintendent in North, 136
  Treaty of Easton (1758) and, 155
  Treaty of Fort Stanwix (1768), 189
  on Washington, 95
Johonerissa. *See* Tanaghrisson (Seneca)
Joncaire, Philippe-Thomas Chabert de
  (French-Seneca), 56–57, 71, 73–74,
  75, 78
Joseph (Moravian), 277
Judd's Friend. *See* Ostenaco (Cherokee)
Jumonville, Joseph Coulon de Villiers, sieur
  de, 87, 88, 89–90, 94, 95, 98, 114, 167,
  510n29

K
Kaghswaghtaniunt. *See* Belt of Wampum
  (Seneca)

Kahnawake, 413, 490–91
Kahnawakes (Caughnawagas)
  (Caughnuagas) (Cognaawagas), 215,
  222–25, 239, 371, 535n16. *See also*
  Vincent, John
Kanaghorait. *See* White Mingo (Seneca)
Kanaghquaesa. *See* Conoghquieson
  (Oneida)
Kanagita. *See* Little Turkey (Cherokee)
Kanawha River and valley
  as boundary, 189, 193, 209
  A. Lewis and, 127, 210
  petroglyphs, 9
  Virginia land grants and, 47
  Virginia war with Shawnees and, 210
  Washington's Indian land acquisitions
    and, 192, 195, 196–99, 200, 202–3,
    205, 449, 450, 478–79, 480
Kaninguen, Dennis, 510n29
Kanitta. *See* Little Turkey (Cherokee)
Kanonwalohale, 258, 304
Kanuksusy (Canachquasy) (Cassiowea)
  (Newcastle) (Fairfax) (Seneca), 7,
  79–80, 92, 108, 144, 512n26
Karontowanen. *See* Big Tree (Seneca)
Kaskaskias, 1, 414, 459. *See also* DuCoigne,
  Jean Baptiste
Kayashuta (Kayasota). *See* Guyasuta
  (Allegheny Seneca)
Kayenquarachton (Kayinguaraghtoh). *See*
  Sayengeraghta (Seneca)
Kayenthwahkeh. *See* Cornplanter
  (Allegheny Seneca)
Kaylelamund (John Killbuck) (Gelemend)
  (Delaware), 263
Keehteetah (Keenettehet) (Kenotetah)
  (Rising Fawn) (Cherokee), 338
Keekyuscung (Ketiuscund) (Delaware),
  153, 173
Keenaguna (Lying Fawn) (Cherokee), 430
Keenettehet. *See* Keehteetah (Cherokee)
"Keeps Them Awake." *See* Red Jacket
  (Seneca)
Keetakeuskah. *See* Kithagusta (Cherokee)
Kekionga, 380, 382, 384, 386, 439
Kennedy, Quentin, 165
Kennedy, Roger, 198
Kenny, James, 155, 175
Kenotetah. *See* Keehteetah (Cherokee)
Kentucky
  boundaries and, 193
  Cherokees and, 430
  DuCoigne on, 415
  Indian raids and, 328

landless settlers and, 297
map, 39m
Northwestern Confederacy war and, 382, 385, 387, 389, 391
Revolutionary War in the West and, 246, 278
Royal Proclamation of 1763 and, 183
separatism and, 299
settlers and, 268, 297
Shawnees and, 265
Spain and, 434
Treaty of Greenville and, 447
Treaty of Hard Labor and, 189
Treaty of Paris and, 178
Vandalia and, 194
Virginia and, 212, 262, 285, 299
Walker and, 49
Washington and, 204
Washington's Indian land acquisitions and, 449, 480
Wayne and, 436
white population of, 194, 262
Kentucky bluegrass, 11
Kentucky River, 193
Keowee, 134, 140. *See also* Ostenaco (Cherokee); Wawhatchee
Kerelrec, Louis Billouart, chevalier de, 127
Ketagusta. *See* Kithagusta (Cherokee)
Ketiuscund (Keekyuscung) (Delaware), 153, 173
Kiandochgowa. *See* Big Tree (Seneca)
Kickapoos, 51, 436, 459. *See also* Northwestern Confederacy war
Killbuck, John (Gelemend) (Kaylelamund) (Delaware), 263, 267, 268–69, 270, 274, 312
Killbuck, John, Jr. (Delaware), 269, 342
Killbuck, Thomas (Delaware), 269, 342
Kingfisher. *See* Chutloh (Cherokee)
King George's War, 52
King Hagler. *See* Hagler (Catawba)
"kings," 60
Ki-on-twog-ky. *See* Cornplanter (Allegheny Seneca)
Kirkland, Samuel, 3, 240–41, 242, 248, 258, 303, 343, 401, 406, 407, 408, 409, 414
Kispoko division of Shawnees, 51, 207
Kithagusta (Kitegisky) (Ketagusta) (Keetakeuskah) (the Prince) (Cherokee), 423
Kittanning, 51
Knight, John, 276, 277

Knollenberg, Bernhard, 203
Knox, Henry
Brant and, 409, 416
Cherokees and, 424–25, 429–30
chiefs and, 427
"civilization" and, 464
Cornplanter and, 402–3, 403–4
Creeks and, 356–57, 363, 376, 429, 432, 557n90
diplomacy and, 424
employing Indians against Indians and, 429–30
Federal Indian policies and, 340
final report of, 452
Indian lives and, 9, 452–53, 456, 464
Indian policies and, 9, 323–24, 328, 329–32, 334, 340, 394
on Indians, 2
Indian sovereignty and, 484
on Kunoskeskie, 423
law of nations and, 484
McGillivray and, 348, 356, 366, 373, 375, 436
Northwestern Confederacy and, 414
Northwestern Confederacy war and, 382, 383, 385–86, 388, 389, 392, 394–95, 412
on *one Nation*, 303
Philadelphia diplomacy and, 1, 2, 405, 407, 408, 409, 410, 411, 412, 413, 414, 415, 416, 418
Pickering and, 408
Piominko and, 426, 427
portrait of, pl 7
Sandusky conference and, 42, 418, 420
southern Indians and, 356, 358–59, 363, 366, 367, 369, 374–75, 376, 422
St. Clair and, 383–84, 395
St. Clair's defeat and, 394
teaching agricultural skills and, 404
treaties and, 338, 358, 359, 368, 369, 371, 372, 373
treaties *versus* wars and, 316, 327, 328, 333–34, 378
Treaty of New York and, 369, 371, 375
on US armed forces, 335
US Army and, 335, 394, 433, 553n60
war *versus* peace and, 452
Wayne and, 421, 435, 436, 437, 452
westward expansion and, 333, 486
Koonay (Mingo), 208
Koquethagechton. *See* White Eyes (Delaware)

Kunoskeskie. *See* Watts, John (Chickamauga
  Cherokee)
Kuskuski, 51, 132, 154, 160

L
Lafayette, marquis de, 243, 246, 304,
  311–312, 406. *See also* Treaty of Fort
  Stanwix (1784)
La Galissonière, comte de, 49
Lake Champlain, 102, 139
Lakotas, 41
land. *See* Indian land
land companies, 191. *See also* Ohio
  Company of Virginia *and other land
  companies;* speculators
land grants and land bounties. *See also* right
  of preemption; Treaty of Fort Stanwix
  (1768) *and other treaties*
  boundaries and, 292
  Continental Congress and, 283, 308
  Cornplanter and, 404
  Crawford and, 187
  Croghan and, 58
  federal authority *versus* states' and,
    365–66, 415
  Indian resistance to, 283
  land rushes and, 283
  Ohio Company of Virginia and, 47–49,
    54, 174, 315
  Pennsylvania and, 103, 185, 404
  Royal Proclamation of 1763 and, 181,
    191, 206
  surveyors and, 36–37
  veterans and, 83, 181, 192–93, 195, 292,
    314, 350
  Virginia and, 20, 26, 31, 34, 212, 307
  Washington and, 292
  Washington's Indian land acquisitions
    and, 171–72, 174, 179, 184, 185,
    191–93, 195, 199–206, 211,
    294, 400
  westward expansion and, 99, 181–84,
    308
land patents, 202
land prices, 184, 315, 433, 446, 447, 449,
  478, 580n46
land rushes, 283, 295, 308
land warrants, 350
Langlade, Charles-Michel Mouet de, 61
La Salle, sieur de, René-Robert
  Cavelier, 74
Last of the Mohicans, The (Cooper), 96
law of nations, 325, 326, 484, 491
Law of Nations, The (Vattel), 325, 551n16

League of the Iroquois, The (L. H. Morgan),
  489
Lear, Tobias, 342–43, 370, 392, 393,
  567n89
Lee, Arthur, 184, 191, 293. *See also* Treaty of
  Fort McIntosh (1785); Treaty of Fort
  Stanwix (1784)
Lee, Charles, 8, 498n30
Lee, Richard, 25
Lee, Thomas, 34, 47, 48, 49, 50, 54
Lee brothers, 178
Lee family, 34–35, 47
Legardeur de Repentigny, Pierre
  ("Reparti"), 76
Legardeur de Saint-Pierre, Jacques, 75,
  76–77, 80–81
Lengel, Edward, 87, 166, 217, 480
Leninger, Barbara, 119
Leutze, Emanuel, 14
Lewis, Andrew, 92, 115, 126–27, 134, 156,
  162, 174, 176, 189, 193, 210, 261,
  267, 268
Lewis, Thomas, 192, 267, 268, 297
Lichtenau, 267
Lignery, François-Marie Le Marchand de,
  157, 158
Lincoln, Benjamin, 360, 362, 418, 420
Linklater, Andro, 36
Little Carpenter. *See* Attakullakulla
  (Cherokee)
Little Miami River, 449, 450
Little Turkey (Kanitta) (Kanagita)
  (Cherokee), 428, 466. *See also* Treaty of
  Tellico (1798)
Little Turtle (Mishikinaakwa) (Miami), 7,
  381, 382f, 383, 391, 437, 443, 459,
  460, 461
Livingston, John, 304
Livingston leasing scheme, 402
Logan, Benjamin, 311
Logan, James, 29
Logan, John (Tachnechdorus) (Mingo),
  207–8, 209
Logstown (Ohio country), 53, 54, 55,
  56–57, 58–61, 63, 68–70. *See also*
  Treaty of Logstown (1752)
Lomax, Lunford, 58
Longhouse religion, 489
long knives, 30
Loudon, Earl of (John Campbell), 132–33,
  139, 140
Louis (King of France), 91
Louisiana, 49, 127. *See also* Hector,
  Francisco Luis; New Orleans

Louisiana Territory, 485
Lower Cherokees, 165, 233
Lower Creeks, 21m, 346–47, 373, 376,
    471–72, 474, 554n1
Lower Town Cherokees, 134
Loyal Land Company, 49, 191, 193
Lydius, Henry, 99
Lying Fawn. *See* Keenaguna (Cherokee)
Lyttelton, William Henry, 129, 165

M
Mackay, James, 92, 95
Maclay, William, 336, 358–59, 359–60, 385
Maclean, Allan, 281, 408
MacQuire, John, 67
Mad Dog. *See* Efau Hadjo (Creek)
Madison, James, 257, 298, 302, 303, 322,
    324, 336–37, 355, 445, 551n22
Maghinga Keesoch (Great Moon), 507n14.
    See also Brodhead, Daniel
Mahicans, 51, 220, 274, 413, 416. *See also*
    Aupaumut, Hendrick
Malgue, Pierre Paul de la (sieur de Marin),
    61, 63, 64, 65, 68–69, 75
Maliseets, 21m, 228, 231. *See also* Treaty of
    Watertown (1776)
Mankiller of Keowee. *See* Ostenaco
    (Cherokee)
Mannahoacs, 19
Mansfield, Chief Justice Lord, 201
Marchand, Sehoy (Creek), 347
Marchand de Lignery, François-Marie Le,
    116
Martin, Alexander, 299
Martin, Joel, 469
Martin, Joseph, 337
Maryland. *See also* Fort Frederick; Treaty of
    Lancaster (1744)
    Braddock and, 108–9
    Fort Duquesne and, 85
    Indian lands and, 194
    Indian raids and, 120
    Indians and, 30, 34, 143, 366
    national debt and, 336
    national unity and, 290, 307–18
    Ohio Company and, 47
    Virginia and, 24, 29
    wampum and, 100
Mascoutens, 1, 51, 414
Mason, George, 25, 183, 213
Massachusetts, 564n19. *See also* Shirley,
    William *and other Massachusettians*
    Indians and, 227–28, 228–31
    national debt and, 336

New York and, 301
Stockbridges' land and, 221
Mattaponis, 19, 25
Matthews, John Joseph, 111
Maumaltee (Delaware), 176–77
Maumee River villages, 380, 439. *See also*
    Fort Defiance; Fort Miamis
McCarty, Daniel, 478
McClure, David, 195, 197
McCullough, David, 343
McDonald, John, 425
McGillivray, Alexander (Creek). *See also*
    Rock Landing meeting; Treaty of
    Galphinton (1785); Treaty of New York
    (1790)
    background of, 347–48
    confederacy and, 346–47, 350
    Creek army of, 347
    Creeks and, 353
    death of, 376
    Knox and, 348, 356, 366, 373, 375, 436
    Piominko and, 306
    Spain and, 306, 348–50, 349m, 351–52,
        352–53, 354–55, 355–56, 363, 364–65,
        374, 375
    speculators and, 364
    Washington and, 7, 355, 363–69,
        365–66, 375
    Willett and, 435
McGillivray, Lachlan, 347
McGillivray, William (Coahama) (Red
    Coat) (Chickasaw), 431
McHenry, James, 244, 460, 466
McIntosh, Lachlan, 248, 266, 267, 268,
    269–70, 271, 353, 434
McIntosh's expedition (1778), 268
McKee, Alexander, 196–99, 208, 390, 418,
    420, 439
McLoughlin, William, 462
Measuring America (Linklater), 36
medals, 331–32, 332f, 408, 414, 415, 426,
    443–44, 489–90, 569n24
medicinal plants, indigenous, 499n40
Meherrins, 130
Meinig, D. W., 447, 487
Mekoche division of Shawnees, 51, 310,
    459. *See also* Cornstalk
Melonthe. *See* Moluntha (Mekoche
    Shawnee)
Memeskia (Old Briton) (Piankashaw), 61,
    435
"Memoranda on Indian Affairs"
    (Washington), 363
Menneville, Ange de, 61

Mercer, George, 92, 115, 134, 158, 162,
      172, 194, 199
Mercer, Hugh, 160
Merrell, James, 12, 153–54, 377
Messquakenoe. *See* Painted Pole
      (Red Pole) (Shawnee), 416
Mexico, 281
Miami River council (1792), 414
Miamis. *See also* Little Turtle *and other
      Miamis;* Northwestern Confederacy war
   Anglo-French rivalry and, 65
   British and, 384
   Cornplanter and, 403
   French and Indian attacks on, 61, 62
   Gist's report and, 56
   Iroquois confederacy and, 160, 381
   Mahicans and, 413
   map, 21m, 46m, 186m
   migrations and mixings of peoples and,
      51
   Sandusky conference and, 420
   trade and, 461
   Washington and, 459
   Wayne and, 436
Miami towns, 381
Miami Valley, 51
Michigan, 293, 315, 382
Michilimackinac fort, 178
Middle Cherokee towns, 165
Mifflin, Thomas, 334
migrations and mixing of peoples, 43,
      44–45, 51, 107, 467. *See also* westward
      expansion
Mi'kmaqs, 228, 231. *See also* Treaty of
      Watertown (1776)
Milford, Louis LeClerc de, 373
military warrants, 308, 315
militias, 120, 121, 434
Miller's Run, 265–66, 449
Mingoes. *See also* Cayugas; Logan, John *and
      other Mingoes;* Senecas; Tanaghrisson
   Anglo-French rivalry and, 65
   Beaujeu and, 110
   Braddock and, 105
   Brodhead and, 248, 272
   Cherokees and, 126
   Dunmore and, 530n82
   Forbes and, 153
   Iroquois and, 51, 52
   map, 46m
   Post and, 154
   settlers and, 198
   Tanaghrisson and, 70, 87
   violence against, 194

Virginia war with Shawnees and (1774),
      208
Minnesota, 382
Minor, Stephen, 307
Miró, Estevan, 355, 373
Mishikinaakwa. *See* Little Turtle (Miami)
missionaries, 28, 263, 303. *See also* Kirkland,
      Samuel *and other missionaries;*
      Moravians; Quakers
Mississaugua Objibwas, 408
Mississippi Indians, 107, 182. *See also* Creeks
Mississippi Land Company, 178–79, 191,
      211
Mississippi River and Valley, 21m, 27, 49,
      54–55, 130, 178, 337. *See also*
      Chickasaws; Spain; Treaty of San
      Lorenzo (1795)
mixing of peoples, 43, 44–45, 51, 107, 470
M'kmaqs, 21m
Mohawk, John, 442
Mohawks (Kanienkehaka), 3, 21m, 30, 51,
      53, 222, 237, 238–39, 242–43, 248,
      256, 390. *See also* Atiatoharongwen;
      Battle of Oriskany; Brant, Joseph *and
      other Mohawks;* Kahnawake Indians
Mohawk Valley, 303
Mohegans, 218. *See also* Johnson, Joseph;
      Occom, Samson
Moluntha (Melonthe) (Mekoche Shawnee),
      311
Monacans, 19
Monacatootha. *See* (Scarouady) (Oneida)
Monongahela River, 54, 82m, 110–12, 114,
      185, 187, 192, 199. *See also* Braddock's
      defeat
Monroe, James, 302, 303, 315
Montcalm, Marquis de, 95–96, 135, 152
Montgomery, Archibald, 164
Monticello, 31
Montour, Andrew (Satellihu) (Eghnisara)
      (Oneida-French intermediary), 58
   Anglo-French rivalry and, 63
   background of, 55
   Croghan on, 55, 505n30
   at Fort Cumberland, 105
   Fort Pitt council and, 173
   Hamilton and, 131
   Indian allies and, 124–25
   Logstown Treaty and, 58, 59
   Pennsylvania and, 56
   refusal to translate British and, 173
   Treaty of Easton (1758) and, 156
   Treaty of Fort Stanwix (1768), 189
   Washington and, 7, 92, 96–97

Montour, Isabelle ("Madame" Montour), 55
Montreal, 21m, 222, 256
Montreal treaties, 30, 52
Moravians, 263, 267, 273–74, 274–75, 276, 277, 458. *See also* Gnadenhütten massacre; Zeisberger *and other Moravians*
Morgan, Daniel, 109, 112, 216, 271, 295, 434
Morgan, George, 263, 265, 268, 269–70, 271, 278, 312, 342
Morgan, Lewis Henry, 489
Morris, Gouverneur, 271
Morris, Robert Hunter, 97, 101, 103, 112–13, 116, 137, 152, 556n60
Mountain Leader. *See* Piominko (Chickasaw)
Mount Vernon. *See also* agriculture; tobacco
 agriculture and, 480, 481
 enslaved African Americans and, 289, 410, 482
 history/descriptions of, 25, 33, 40, 104, 524n1
 Indian land and, 25
 Indians and, 3, 9, 377
 lease of, 450
 map, 21m, 46m, 186m, 296m
 offer to lease, 450
 Potomac River and, 300, 524n1
 Washington and, 161–62, 165, 171, 266, 288, 289
"mourning" wars, 30
mulattoes, 20, 28
Munsees, 250–51
Murray, John. *See* Dunmore, Earl of
Murray, Patrick, 384
Muscle Shoals, 425, 432
Muse, George, 203
Muskingum River and Valley, 51, 132, 381
Muskogean peoples, 27
Muskogee language, 8

N
Namacolin (Delaware), 54
Nanticokes, 21m, 43, 156–57, 390, 416
Nash, Gary B., 568n2
Nashville conference (1792), 426
national bank, 337
national debt, 293, 327, 336, 385, 394, 446
nationalism, American, 497n13. *See also* federal authority *versus* states' power (national unity)
national unity. *See* federal authority *versus* states' power

nation-building, 7, 12, 13–14. *See also* federal authority *versus* states' power (national unity); westward expansion
nation-to-nation relations, 12
Neah Mico. *See* Eneah or Neah Mico (Creek)
Neetotehelemy (Netawatwees) (Newcomer) (Delaware), 61, 174
Negushwa. *See* Egushawa (Ottawa)
Nenatcheehunt (Nenatchehan). *See* Delaware George (Delaware)
Nenetooyah (Nenetuah). *See* Bloody Fellow (Cherokee)
Neolin (Delaware), 175
Netawatwees. *See* Neetotehelemy (Delaware)
Nevins, Allan, 499n45
New Arrow (Seneca), 401
Newcastle. *See* Kanuksusy (Seneca)
New Castle (Pennsylvania), 51
Newcomer. *See* Neetotehelemy (Delaware)
New Corn (Potawatomi), 443
New England Indians, 21m, 218, 221–22, 228, 458. *See also* Abenakis *and others*
New France, 49–50, 57, 90, 115–16. *See also* Canada; Menneville, Ange de
New Mexico, 281
New Orleans, 284, 298, 299, 354–55. *See also* Miró, Estevan; Treaty of San Lorenzo (1795)
Newtown Point meeting (1791), 404, 405
New York. *See also* Dunmore, Earl of (John Murray) *and other New Yorkians;* Sullivan, John and his campaign; Treaty of Albany (1701); Treaty of Canandaigua (1794); Treaty of Fort Stanwix (1768); Treaty of Fort Stanwix (1784)
 Aupaumut and, 413
 federal government *versus* 301–4, 404, 405, 407, 442
 Fort Duquesne and, 85
 French and, 116
 Iroquois and, 30, 244, 245, 301–4, 404, 407, 413
 refugees from, 222
 Senecas and, 488
 Stockbridges and, 220
 Washington and, 85, 246
 Washington's Indian land acquisitions and, 40, 290, 480
New York Indians, 21m, 236, 416, 437, 455. *See also* Oneidas *and others*
Niagara, 176, 251, 256
Niagara meeting (1764), 182

Nicholas, George, 324, 387, 393, 394, 412, 440
Nicholson, Joseph, 196
Nimham, Abraham (Stockbridge), 220
Nimwha (Shawnee), 188
Nipissings, 53, 94
Nontuaka (the Northward) (the North Nation) (Cherokee), 423, 424–25, 429–30
Nootka Sound Crisis, 365, 367
Nopkehe. *See* Hagler (Catawba)
North Carolina, 85, 108–9, 145, 164, 193, 233, 285, 299–300, 338–39, 348, 425. *See also* Blount, William; Catawbas; Franklin (state); Transylvania Company; Treaty of Hopewell (1785-86); Treaty of Tellico (1798); Tuscaroras
Northern Neck (Virginia), 25, 34–36, 35m
Northward, the (the North Nation). *See* Nontuaka (Cherokee)
Northwest Coast Indians, 282
Northwestern Confederacy wars. *See also* Hamtramck, John Francis; Harmar, Josiah; Philadelphia Indian diplomacy; Scott, Charles; St. Clair, Arthur; Treaty of Greenville (1795); Wayne, Anthony; Wilkinson, James
  Brant and, 408–9, 410
  Cherokees and, 422–23
  Cornplanter and, 404
  costs of, 446
  described, 381–82
  Indian resistance and, 378, 379m, 380, 382, 385, 387, 390–91
  Philadelphia Indian diplomacy and, 403, 405–6, 407–8, 412–14
  Simcoe and, 420–21
  southern Indians and, 429, 432–33
  war *versus* negotiation and, 397–98, 404, 416
  Washington and, 3, 378, 380, 386–87, 416–17, 433–42
Northwest Ordinance (1785), 309–10
Northwest Ordinance (1787), 314–16
Northwest Territory, 293, 314, 316–17, 327–28, 396, 421. *See also* Northwestern Confederacy war
Notes on the State of Virginia (Jefferson), 19, 208
Nottaways, 19, 124, 129–30
Nova Scotia Indians and settlers, 102, 180, 182, 201, 221, 227, 228, 230, 231. *See also* Beauséjour fort

O
Obeal. *See* Cornplanter (Allegheny Seneca)
Occaneechis, 27
Occom, Samson (Mohegan), 218, 458
Oconees, 373
Oconostota (Overhill Cherokee), 166, 193, 213, 232–33
Odanak, 222–23, 225–27, 226–27, 514n74
Ogaghsagighte (Jean Baptiste) (Kahnawake Mohawk), 223, 224
Ogh-ne-wi-ge-was. *See* Farmer's Brother (Buffalo Creek Seneca)
Ohio, 178, 293, 315. *See also* Northwest Ordinance (1785) *and* (1787)
Ohio Company of Associates (New England), 312–13, 314–15, 317, 388, 400
Ohio Company of Virginia
  Braddock and, 104
  Braddock's road and, 150–51
  British and, 47–48, 174
  Dinwiddie and, 50, 65, 66
  Duke of Cumberland and, 104
  forts and, 48, 67, 80
  Indian allies and, 108
  Indian land and, 47–49, 174
  Logstown and, 54
  Mercer and, 194
  Mississippi Land Company and, 178, 179
  Ohio country trade and, 54–55, 57
  Ohio Indians and, 160–61
  Pennsylvania and, 194
  Royal Proclamation of 1763 and, 183, 184–85
  Vandalia and, 194
  Virginia and, 81, 83, 120
  Washington and, 48, 104, 108
Ohio country. *See also* Anglo-French rivalry; Belt of Wampum (the Belt) (Kaghswaghtaniunt) (Tohashwughtonionty) (White Thunder) (Seneca); Braddock's defeat *and other battles and campaigns;* forts; Indian land; Indian mounds; land bounties; Logstown Treaty *and other treaties;* Northwestern Confederacy war; Ohio Company of Associates; Ohio Company of Virginia; Ohio Indians; Revolutionary War in the West; Royal Proclamation of 1763; Tanaghrisson; Tanaghrisson's war; Treaty of Fort Stanwix (1784); Treaty of Greenville (1795); Treaty of Lancaster (1744); Washington's Indian land acquisitions; westward expansion

Delaware diplomacy and, 155
French and, 45, 48, 49–50, 51–52,
    51–53, 53–54, 61, 74
map, 46m
migrations and mixings of peoples
    and, 51
Peace of Paris (1783) and, 280, 281
Potomac River and, 34, 36
Quebec and, 280
Thomson on, 8
trade and, 49, 61, 160–61
Treaty of Lancaster and, 34, 45–47, 49
Virginians and, 41–44, 49
Washington and, 6, 45, 259, 260,
    311–12
Washington's 1753 trip to, 81, 82m
Washington's diplomatic expedition to
    (1753), 6, 66–83, 82m
Washington's military expedition to
    (Tanaghrisson's War) (1754), 6,
    81–101
Ohio Indians. *See also* Indian land; Jay
    Treaty (1794); Northwestern
    Confederacy war; Pontiac's War;
    Shawnees *and other Ohio Indians;* Treaty
    of Easton (1758); Treaties of Fort
    Harmar (1789); Treaty of Fort
    McIntosh (1785)
Anglo-French rivalry and, 58, 62, 73, 84,
    94–95, 107
Braddock and, 108
British sailor's description of, 105
Cherokees and, 144
Denny and, 153
Forbes' campaign and, 153, 157
history of, 50–51
informant on Washington/Tanaghrisson
    ambush, 88
Iroquois and, 51–52, 161
Logstown negotiations and, 58
map, 21m
peace negations (1759 and 1761), 160
Tanaghrisson and, 59
Tanaghrisson's war and, 93, 94, 96
trade and, 160–61
Virginia and, 49
Washington and, 93, 96–97
westward expansion and, 54
Ohio River. *See also* Forks of the Ohio
as boundary, 194, 263, 264, 311, 381–82,
    406, 409, 417
Cherokees and, 130
forts, 61, 67–68
French and, 49
land for militia and, 83

map, 21m
Shawnee raids and, 273
Tanaghrisson and, 63–64
Treaty of Fort Stanwix (1768) and, 189
Virginia war with Shawnees and, 210
Washington and, 204
Washington's Indian land acquisitions
    and, 178, 449, 450
Ojekheta. *See* Otsequette (Oneida)
Ojibwas, 21m, 51, 70, 72, 86, 110, 160,
    178, 264, 282, 459. *See also*
    Northwestern Confederacy war;
    Pickawillany attack
Okfuskee. *See* White Lieutenant (Creek)
Old Briton. *See* Memeskia (Piankashaw)
Old Smoke. *See* Sayengeraghta (Seneca)
Old Tassel. *See* Corn Tassel (Cherokee)
Oneidas. *See also* Battle of Oriskany; Good
    Peter *and other Oneidas;* Iroquois
    (Haudenosaunee) and their
    confederacy (Five Nations) (Six
    Nations); Kanaghquaesa
    (Conoghquieson) (Oneida); Treaty of
    Canandaigua (1794); Treaty of Fort
    Schuyler (1788)
American Revolution and, 235, 236–37,
    239–42, 239–43, 244–45, 258–59, 458
British and, 258
colonials and, 237
corn and, 236–37
Indian clothing and, 216
Iroquois and, 258
map and locations, 21m, 51
Mohawks and, 242–43
Philadelphia diplomacy and, 406
Revolutionary War in the West and,
    258–59
Senecas and, 243, 258
smallpox and, 281
Sullivan's campaign and, 248, 251,
    254, 255
treaties and, 303–4
Washington and, 3, 240, 241, 243, 258
O'Neill, Arturo, 348, 353
Onondagas. *See also* Canasatego *and other
    Onondagas;* Iroquois (Haudenosaunee)
    and their confederacy (Five Nations)
    (Six Nations); Treaty of Canandaigua
    (1794)
American attacks and, 276
American Revolution and, 240
Anglo-French rivalry and, 63, 72
Braddock and, 113
Canachquasy and, 79–80
Croghan on, 84

Onondagas (*continued*)
  Iroquois league and, 51, 52–53, 58, 63, 240
  Logstown Treaty and, 58, 59
  map, 21m
  neutrality and, 72, 80
  Ohio Indians and, 58, 93
  Philadelphia diplomacy and, 406
  Revolutionary War in the West and, 248–49
  smallpox and, 281
  Sullivan's campaign and, 248–49
  Tanaghrisson and, 57, 59, 63–64, 84, 90
  Treaty of Lancaster and, 54
  Virginia and, 54, 100
Onontio, 57, 89
Opechancanough (Powhatan), 23–24
Opoia Mutaha. *See* Piominko (Chickasaw)
Oppamylucah, Captain (Delaware), 57
Oquaga (New York), 245
Ore, James, 430
Orme, Robert, 103–4, 109, 110
Orono, Joseph (Penobscot), 231
Osages, 110, 111, 343, 425, 426
Ostenaco (Ustenaka) (Judd's Friend)
    (Outacite) (Outacity) (Outassite)
    (Skiagusta) (Mankiller of Keowee)
    (Cherokee), 126–27, 128–29, 137,
    164, 165, 166, 193, pl 2
Otchikeita. *See* Otsequette (Oneida)
Otos, 110
Otsequette (Otsiquette, Peter) (Ojekheta)
    (Otchikeita) (Oneida), 406
Ottawas. *See also* Egushawa; Northwestern
    Confederacy war; Pickawillany attack;
    Pontiac's War
  alleged scalping and, 79
  Anglo-French rivalry and, 72
  Beaujeu and, 110
  Fort Pitt meeting and, 262
  Fort Recovery and, 437
  Iroquois and, 160
  map and locations, 21m, 51
  Ohio country and, 53
  Pickawillany attack by, 61
  Post and, 154
  Tanaghrisson and, 70
  Tanaghrisson's war and, 86, 94
  Washington and, 459
  Wyandots and, 56
Otto, Louis Guilllaume, 334, 363–64
Ouconecaw. *See* Attakullakulla
    (Cherokee)
Ouiatenon, 387, 388

Outacite (Outacity) (Outassite).
    See Ostenaco (Cherokee)
Overhill Cherokees, 43, 126, 127, 232.
    See also Attakullakulla *and other Overhill
    Cherokees*

P
Pachgantschihilas. *See* Buckongahelas
    (Delaware)
Pacific Northwest, 365
Painted Pole (Red Pole) (Messquakenoe)
    (Shawnee), 311, 416, 443, 459, 460
Pamunkeys, 19, 25, 28
Panton, Leslie & Company, 364–65,
    374–75, 470
Panton, William, 425
Papers of George Washington, 7
Parker, Arthur C. (Seneca), 255, 487
Parker, Ely S. (Seneca), 489–90
Parker, Hugh, 48
Parkinson, Richard, 480–81
Parsons, Samuel, 312–13
Passamaquoddies, 21m, 228, 230, 231, 232
paths, 67
Patton, James, 47, 58, 118
Paxinosa (Bucksinosa) (eastern Shawnee),
    144
Peace of Paris (1783), 280, 281, 283,
    348, 437
Peale, Charles Willson, 10, pl 1,7,9,10
Pekowi division of Shawnees, 51, 459
Pemberton, Israel, 152
Penn, Thomas, 103
Penn, William, 60
Pennsylvania. *See also* Anglo-French rivalry;
    frontier defense and Cherokee
    alliance; Morris, Robert Hunter *and
    other Pennsylvanians;* Sullivan's
    campaign; Treaty of Easton (1758);
    Treaty of Fort Stanwix (1768); Treaty
    of Fort Stanwix (1784); Treaty of
    Lancaster (1744); Walking Purchase
  Braddock and, 103, 104
  Braddock's road and, 150–51, 157
  Connecticut and, 307
  Creeks and, 366
  Croghan and Montour and, 56, 57
  Delawares and, 99, 131, 132
  Forbes' road and, 150–51
  forts and, 80, 84
  French and Indians and, 63, 100, 120
  Indian trade and, 162
  Iroquois and, 143, 237, 244
  Kanuksusy and, 108

land grants and, 187
Logstown Treaty and, 59
migrations and mixing of peoples
 and, 51
Montour and, 55
Northwestern Confederacy wars and, 446
Ohio Company and, 47–48, 57
Ohio country and, 45, 49, 61, 65
Ohio Indians and, 97, 157
Onondagas and, 52, 63
scalp bounties and, 131, 177, 272
Scarouady and, 113
Senecas and, 401, 402, 404
Shawnees and, 62, 209, 265
Shingas attacks and, 114
Virginia and, 29, 199, 202, 209, 260, 262
wampum and, 100
Washington and, 114
Washington's Indian land acquisitions
 and, 480
Penobscots, 21m, 228, 229–30, 231.
 See also Treaty of Watertown (1776)
Peorias, 1, 414
Pequots, 218
Perkins, Thomas, 212
Peters, Richard, 100, 293
petroglyphs, 9
Pheasant, the, 196, 197–98
Phelps, Oliver, 402, 564n19
Philadelphia, 281, 337, 405, pl 11
Philadelphia Indian diplomacy. *See also*
 Sandusky conference (1793);
 Treaty of Vincennes; Treaty of
 Vincennes (1792)
Brant and, 408–10, 411–12, 413, 417
British and, 401, 409, 410–13, 414
Cook and, 413
DuCoigne and, 414
Indian disunity and, 405–6, 412–13,
 413–14, 416
Indian land and, 416–17, 418
Iroquois and, 1, 407–8
Logstown council fire and, 53
Northwestern Confederacy and, 403,
 405–6, 407–8, 412–14
Ohio country and, 52
Pickering and, 398–400, 404–5
Putnam and, 414
Red Jacket and, 416–17
Senecas and, 398–404
war *versus* negotiation and, 397–98
Washington and, 1–3, 406–8, 411–12,
 415, 567n89
Philadelphia meeting (1796), 459–61

Piankashaws, 1, 51, 61, 314, 328, 384, 414,
 459. *See also* Memeskia (Old Briton);
 Miamis
Pickawillany attack, 61, 72
Pickens, Andrew, 353, 429, 432, 466,
 570n39
Pickering, Timothy. *See also* Sandusky
 conference (1793)
Brant and, 409
Cherokees and, 430
Cornplanter and, 440–41
Iroquois and, 398–400, 404–5, 441–42
Jay Treaty and, 445
Oneidas and, 304
Philadelphia diplomacy and, 2, 406–7
portrait of, pl 10
Quakers and, 455
Senecas and, 398–99, 408
southern Indians and, 430–31
as speculator, 556n60
Treaty of Canandaigua (1794) and, 443
Treaty of Greenville and, 444
Washington's Indian policy and,
 343–45, 406–7
Piedmont area, 21m, 27, 31, 36
Pigeon (Woyi) (Pouting Pigeon), 166
Pinckney, Charles, 434. *See also* Treaty of
 San Lorenzo (1795)
Pine Creek meeting, 62
Piominko (Piomingo) (Opoia Mutaha)
 (Mountain Leader) (Chickasaw), 7,
 305, 306, 390, 425–26, 427, 436, 460,
 569n24
Pipe (Hobocan) (Hopocan) (Captain Pipe)
 (Delaware), 263, 267, 268, 271,
 276–77, 278. *See also* Treaties of Fort
 Harmar (1789); Treaty of Fort Pitt
 (1778)
pipes, 2, 331
Piqua division of Shawnees, 207, 273
Piscataways, 22, 25
Pisquetomen (Delaware), 153–55, 156,
 157, 173, 176
Pitt, William, 139–40, 152
Pittsburgh (Pennsylvania), 159, 162, 262.
 See also Fort Pitt
plats, 36
Pocahontas, 23, 28
Pond, Peter, 412
Pontiac's War, 6, 176–77, 179, 180–81, 262,
 525n29
Pope, John, 375
population estimates of Indians, 19, 28, 283
Portsmouth (Ohio), 56

Posey, John, 185
Post, Christian Frederick, 153–54, 157, 173, 521n28
Potawatomis, 1, 21m, 72, 112, 160, 414, 443, 459. *See also* Northwestern Confederacy war; Pickawillany attack; Treaties of Fort Harmar (1789)
Potomac River and Valley
  agriculture and, 23
  Iroquois and, 34
  map, 21m
  Mount Vernon and, 25
  national unity and, 289, 297–98, 298–99
  Ohio Company and, 54
  Powhatans and, 22
  Washington and, 96, 179, 290, 298–300, 479
  Washington's Indian land acquisitions and, 298–99
  westward expansion and, 36, 48, 96
Pouchot, Pierre, 161
Pouting Pigeon (Woyi) (Pigeon), 166
Powhatan (Wahunsonacock) (Powhatan), 22–23
Powhatans, 19, 22–25
Pratt, Charles, 205
Preston, David, 513n36
Preston, William, 209
Prince, the. *See* Kithagusta (Cherokee)
private property and property rights, 23, 380, 454, 458, 471, 472
Proctor, Thomas, 404
promissory notes, 336
Putnam, Rufus, 313, 380, 385, 414, 434, 450

Q
Quakers, 8, 62, 103, 115, 121, 155, 393, 418, 424, 455, 456, 488, 490, 572n104. *See also* Pemberton, Israel
Quebec, 21m, 181, 221, 222, 280. *See also* Dorchester, Lord; Haldimand, Governor; Quebec Act
Quebec Act, 211, 212
Quebec meeting (1790), 374
Queen Aliquippa (Seneca), 79, 91, 92, 100
Quequedegatha. *See* White Eyes (Delaware)

R
race, 12, 28, 464. *See also* enslaved African Americans; enslaved Indians; Indian identity; mulattoes; white identity
Randolph, Beverly, 366, 418, 420, 429
Randolph, Edmund, 1, 340, 395, 439

Randolph, Peter, 126
Randolph, Peyton, 202
Raphael, Ray, 568n2
Rappahannock River, 22, 31, 34, 40
Rasmusson, Barbara, 530n82
Raven of Chota (Savanukah) (Cherokee), 213, xiii
Raven Warrior of Hiwassee (Cherokee), 142, 143, xiii
Read, Jacob, 302
Red Coat. *See* McGillivray, William (Chickasaw)
Red Jacket (Sagoyewatha) ("Keeps Them Awake") (Cowkiller) (Seneca)
  boundaries and, 416–17
  "civilization" and, 456
  Cornplanter compared, 402
  medal and, 332f, 489–90
  Philadelphia diplomacy and, 407
  Pickering and, 399–400, 404–5, 441
  portrait of, pl 12
  Sandusky conference and, 417
  Senecas and, 412–13
  Shawnees and, 417
  Washington and, 7, 406, 408, 416–17
Red King (Chickasaw), 306
Red Pole. *See* Painted Pole (Messquakenoe) (Shawnee)
Redstone Creek, 54, 199
Reed, Joseph, 247
refugee crisis, 256, 258
religion. *See also* missionaries; Moravians; Quakers
  British sailor and, 105
  Cornplanter and, 401
  Indian identity and, 489
  land rights and, 23
  Oquaga and, 245
  Red Jacket and, 456
  Washington and, 10, 287, 341, 458, 544n14
  Washington's Indian policies and, 270, 341–44
  westward expansion and, 286–87, 330
Revolutionary War in the West. *See also* Sullivan, John; Town Destroyer; Van Schaick, Goose
  British and, 279, 281
  Brodhead and, 271–72, 273–74
  Clark and, 272–73
  corn and, 251, 278, 280
  Crawford and, 265–66
  Delawares and, 266–71
  Fort Pitt meetings and, 261–65

frontierspeople *versus* elites, 260–61
Gnadenhütten massacre and, 275–76,
277–79, 278–79
Indian land and, 269, 279, 280
McIntosh and, 266
Oneidas and, 258
Onondagas and, 248–49
Sandusky expedition and, 276–79
smallpox and, 281–82
Washington and, 7, 245–46, 246–47,
249–50, 279, 280
Reynolds, Joshua, 166, pl 2
right of conquest, 34, 48, 99, 300, 316,
327, 330, 484
right of preemption, 181, 212, 325, 334,
405, 407, 564n19, 580n46
right of purchase, 420
Rising Fawn. *See* Keehteetah (Cherokee);
Treaty of Tellico (1798)
Ritchie, Matthew, 449
roads
Braddock's, 46m, 104, 108–9, 110,
150–51, 157, 160, 173
Creek country and, 470
diplomacy and, 412, 417
Forbes', 46m, 150–51, 157, 160, 173–74
St. Clair's, 390
Robert Cary and Company, 165, 178
Robertson, James, 425, 426
Robinson, Sr., John, 47
Rochambeau, General, 224
Rock Landing meeting, 361–63
Rogers's Rangers, 222
Rolfe, John, 23, 28
Ross, James, 478
Ross, John (Cherokee), 468, 487
Round Bottom, 39m, 478
Roy, Marie le, 119
Royal Proclamation of 1763
boundaries and, 186m, 190
British and, 180–85
Dunmore and, 201, 529n43
India opinion and, 205
Peace of Paris and, 293
Trade and Intercourse Act compared,
340, 403
Treaty of Fort Stanwix (1768) and, 191
US and, 293
Virginia and, 212
Washington on, 292
Washington's Indian land acquisitions
and, 187–88, 190, 192, 195, 201, 202,
203–4, 206, 211, 294
Rush, William, 569n24

Russell, William, 266

S
Sagoyewatha. *See* Red Jacket (Seneca)
Saint-Aubin, Ambroise (Maliseet),
228, 229
Saint-Pierre, Jacques Legardeur de, 75,
76–77, 80–81
Salt Lick Town, 210
Sandusky (Ohio), 51, 275–76, 276–78,
379m, 417–18, 436. *See also* Wyandots
(Wendats)
Sandusky conference (1793), 417–21
Sandusky Wyandots, 443
Saponis, 30, 130
Saratoga (1777), 220, 224, 243
Sargent, Winthrop, 313, 392
Satellihu. *See* Montour, Andrew
Sauks, 416
Saunt, Claudio, 351
Savanukah. *See* Raven of Chota
(Cherokee)
Sawantanan (Sawatanen). *See* Vincent,
Lewis (Huron)
Sawcunk (Beaver Town) (Shingas's
Town), 160
Sayengeraghta (Sayenqueraghta)
(Kayenquarachton) (Kayinguaraghtoh)
(Old Smoke) (Vanishing Smoke) (the
Seneca King) (Seneca), 257
scalp bounties, 130–31, 163, 177,
261, 272
scalpings
Brodhead and, 274
of Crawford, 277
"French and Indian War" and, 218
of Hardin and Trueman, 412
Kentucky militia and, 328
Ottawas and, 79
Sullivan's campaign and, 251, 254
Washington and, 130–31, 146
Wayne and, 439
Scarouady (Scaroyady) (Monacatootha)
(Monacatoocha) (Oneida)
Anglo-French rivalry and, 58, 62, 63, 64,
65, 100, 105
background of, 53
Braddock and, 105–6, 108, 110, 113
"Dinwiddie" and, 92
Hamilton and, 131
smallpox and, 152
Tanaghrisson and, 70, 97, 100
Treaty of Logstown and, 57, 91
Washington and, 67, 68, 71, 87, 88, 92

Scarouady's son, 108, 109
Schuyler, Philip
  Cayugas and, 535n16
  Indians and, 222, 224–25
  Iroquois and, 238, 239, 243, 300, 442
  G. Johnson and, 217
  New York and, 301
  Oneidas and, 241, 258
  Revolutionary War in the West and,
    246, 249
  on Sullivan's campaign, 248
  Sullivan's campaign and, 247
  Tuscaroras and, 258
  on westward expansion, 291
  on white enlistees, 219
Scioto Company, 314, 315, 388
Scioto River and Valley, 51, 56, 126,
  204–5, 210
Scolaguta. *See* Hanging Maw (Cherokee)
Scotch-Irish, 29, 121, 182, 206, 207, 237,
  295–96
Scots, 33, 139, 144, 172, 177, 206, 297,
  347, 472, 480. *See also* Scotch-Irish;
  Stephen, Adam *and other Scots*
Scott, Charles and his expedition, 379m,
  387, 434, 436
Seagrove, James, 375–76, 428, 429
Seminoles, 347, 363, 471, 474, 554n1
Seneca King, the. *See* Sayengeraghta
  (Seneca)
Senecas. *See also* Battle of Oriskany;
  Cornplanter *and other Senecas;* Iroquois
  (Haudenosaunee) and their
  confederacy; Mingoes; Ohio Indians;
  Treaty of Fort Stanwix (1784)
  American Revolution and, 244–45
  British and, 263–64
  Brodhead and, 272
  "civilization" and, 341, 455–56
  Cook and, 413
  Fort Niagara and, 161
  Indian unity and, 318
  Iroquois and, 413
  land losses of, 488
  map, 21m, 46m
  migrations and mixing of peoples and, 51
  murders of, 398, 404
  Oneidas and, 258
  Oneidas/Tuscaroras and, 243
  peace league and, 30
  Philadelphia Indian diplomacy and,
    398–404
  Revolutionary War in the West and, 249,
    250–51, 265

Sullivan's campaign and, 248, 254, 256
Washington and, 3, 146, 244–45, 246,
  406, 489–90
settlers (colonials, farmers, frontiersmen,
  squatters). *See also* agriculture;
  boundaries; frontier defense and
  Cherokee alliance; land rushes;
  national security; Northwest Ordinance
  (1785) *and* (17787); Revolutionary
  War in the West; Royal Proclamation of
  1763; Swiss, the *and other settlers;*
  westward expansion
  American Revolution and, 237
  Aupaumut on, 413
  Bouquet and, 174
  Braddock's road and, 151, 173
  Cherokees and, 164, 427–28, 526n57
  Creeks and, 350, 432
  elites and, 26, 194–95, 198–99, 260–61,
    280, 334
  federal authority *versus* states' and, 324,
    580n41
  forts and, 115, 120
  French and Indian allies and, 116
  hunters *versus*, 286
  Indians and, 179–80, 260, 452
  Iroquois and, 237–38
  Kentucky and, 268, 297
  Mississippi Land Company and, 179
  murder juries and, 565n28
  national unity and, 284, 285–86, 288
  Northwestern Confederacy war
    and, 380
  plantation economy and, 172
  Pontiac's War and, 180
  Rock Landing meeting and, 360
  Sandusky conference and, 420
  scalpings by, 163–64
  Shawnees' land and, 207
  Spain and, 324
  speculators and, 37, 172, 202, 212,
    309, 427
  St. Clair's defeat and, 393, 396
  Treaty of Fort Pitt and, 268
  Treaty of Holston and, 425, 430
  Treaty of Hopewell and, 430
  Treaty of Paris and, 174
  Virginia and, 193
  Virginia Regiment and, 121
  Virginia's Indian country and, 28
  war with Shawnees and, 209
  Washington and, 7, 122–23, 178,
    198–99, 201, 261, 279, 285–86, 291,
    334, 447, 483

Washington's Indian land acquisitions
and, 294–95, 330
Seven Nations of Canada, 222, 416, 437,
490–91. *See also* St. Lawrence Indians
Seven Ranges, 309
Seven Years' War, 90, 124. *See also* "French
and Indian War"; Tanaghrisson's war
Sevier, John, 299, 339
Shamokin Daniel (Delaware), 154
Shanango River, 51
Shannopin, 5
Shaw, Francis, 230
Shaw, John, 89
Shaw, Leonard, 424, 462–63
Shawnee River, 49
Shawnees. *See also* Blue Jacket *and other
Shawnees;* Chillicothe division of
Shawnees; Fort Pitt meeting (1775);
Northwestern Confederacy war; Ohio
Indians; Scioto River and Valley;
Shawnees' land; Treaty of Camp
Charlotte; Treaty of Fort Finney (1786)
American Revolution and, 230
ancient, 9
Anglo-French rivalry and, 65, 72, 73,
116–17, 152
Beaujeu and, 110
Brant and, 409, 417
British and, 173, 175, 311
Brodhead and, 272
R. Butler and, 8, 312
captives and, 118–19
Catawbas and, 72, 126
Cherokees and, 126–27, 128, 213–14
"civilization" and, 575n33
Clark and, 273
Dunmore and, 208–9, 530n82
Forbes and, 153
frontier war and, 124
history/divisions of, 51
Iroquois and, 84, 117–18
Logstown Treaty and, 59
Mahicans and, 413
map, 46m
migration and mixing of peoples and, 43,
44, 460–61
Ohio country and, 50–51, 53
Pennsylvania and, 62, 99, 209, 265
Post and, 154
Red Jacket and, 417
Revolutionary War in the West and, 278
Sandusky conference and, 420
scalpings and, 273
settlers and, 198

Tanaghrisson and, 64, 70, 71, 97, 98
Tanaghrisson's war and, 92
Treaty of Fort McIntosh and, 310
Treaty of Fort Stanwix (1768) and,
193, 207
Treaty of Lancaster and, 52
Virginia's Indian country and, 20
wampum and, 71–72
war losses of, 162
war with Virginia (1774) and, 207–11
Washington and, 71–72, 146, 204–5,
310, 459
Washington's Indian land acquisitions
and, 204–5, 210, 211, 264–65
Wayne and, 436
Westos and, 27
Shay's Rebellion, 288
Shelby, Evan, 246
Shenandoah Valley, 21m, 29, 30, 31, 33–34,
38–40, 39m, 115
Shenango River, 51
Shingas (Delaware)
Anglo-French rivalry and, 93
Braddock and, 105–6, 107
Forbes and, 157
at Fort Pitt, 177
Fort Pitt council and, 173
French and, 113–14, 116
Logstown Treaty and, 60, 61
peace and, 175–76
Post and, 154
raids by, 116, 123
Stuart and, 118
Tanaghrisson and, 90
Tanaghrisson's council and, 97
Teedyuscung and, 153
Treaty of Logstown and, 60
wampum and, 72
Washington and, 7, 68, 71, 93, 123
Shingas's Town (Sawcunk) (Beaver
Town), 160
Shirley, William, 127
Shirley's son ("Poor Shirley"), 110, 112–13
Shreve, Israel, 449, 478
sieur de La Salle. *See* Cavelier, René-Robert
sieur de Marin. *See* Malgue, Pierre Paul de
la (sieur de Marin)
Silver, Peter, 544n9
Silver Heels (Aroas) (Seneca), 7, 87, 108,
113, 127, 128, 165, 175, 262
Simcoe, John Graves, 380, 410, 411,
418–19, 420–21
Simpson, Gilbert, 295
Sipe, C. Hale, 512n26, 525n29

Six Nations. *See* Iroquois (Haudenosaunee) and their confederacy
Skenandoah (John Skenandon) (Oneida), 235, 241, 406
"Sketch of the Creek Country" (Hawkins), 471
Skiagusta. *See* Ostenaco (Cherokee)
Skowonidous (Jerry), 108, 512n26
slavery. *See* enslaved African Americans; enslaved Indians
Sleeper-Smith, Susan, 387
Slover, John, 276, 277
smallpox and other diseases
    blankets and, 176–77
    Cherokee population and, 42, 164
    Fort Pitt and, 176
    Indian land and, 282
    Indian populations and, 19, 27, 158
    Newcastle and, 144, 512n26
    Onondaga and, 242
    path of, 27
    Philadelphia diplomacy and, 2, 415
    Scarouady and, 152
    Southeast and, 164
    vaccinations and, 461
    Virginia's Indian country and, 24
    Washington and, 11, 40
    westward expansion and, 281–82
Smith, Daniel, 428–29
Smith, James, 87–88, 120, 149, 156, 216
Smith, John, 23
Smith, William, 371
Solomon (Iroquois), 565n36
Somerset v. Stewart (1772), 201
South Carolina, 42–43, 72, 85, 92, 117, 127, 163–64, 166, 233, 336, 429. *See also* Catawbas; Glen, James; Treaty of Hopewell (1785-86); Treaty of Long Island of Holston (1777); Yazoo Companies
southern colonies, 182
southern Indians, 99, 164, 306–7, 346–47, 349m, 350, 353, 422–23, 432–33, 474. *See also* Cherokees, Creeks *and other southern Indians;* Georgia *and other southern states;* Treaty of Hopewell (1785-86) *and other treaties*
Southwest Territory, 339, 474
sovereignty. *See* Indian sovereignty; US sovereignty
Spain and the Spanish. *See also* Chickasaws; Creeks; Florida; law of nations; McGillivray, Alexander (Creek); Treaty of Mobile (1784); Treaty of New York

(1790); Treaty of Pensacola (1784); Treaty of San Lorenzo (1795)
    boundaries and, 338
    Britain and, 365
    Jay Treaty and, 445
    Northwestern Confederacy war and, 397
    Peace of Paris (1783) and, 348
    Potomac River gateway and, 298
    settlers and, 324
    southern Indians and, 3, 306–7, 346, 422, 425–27, 426–27, 428, 429, 431–32, 446
    treaties and, 285
    Treaty of New York and, 374–75
    Treaty of Paris (1763) and, 174
    Washington and, 3, 246, 375–76, 429, 431
    Wilkinson and, 434
speculators. *See also* elites; Indiana Grant; Ohio Company of Virginia *and other land companies;* Washington's Indian land acquisitions; individual speculators
    boundaries and, 193, 324
    Braddock's road and, 151
    Cherokees and, 425
    "civilization" and, 475–76
    Creeks and, 350, 356–57
    federal authority and, 442
    Federal Indian policies and, 339, 340
    financial crisis and, 201
    forts and, 80
    Indian ownership and, 5
    Iroquois and, 404
    McGillivray and, 364, 373
    national unity and, 291–92
    Northwestern Confederacy war and, 385–86, 393, 396
    Ohio country and, 45, 48–49
    profits of, 477–78
    promissory notes and, 336
    Royal Proclamation of 1763 and, 183, 184, 185–88, 187m
    Schuyler and, 217
    Senecas and, 402
    settlers and, 37, 172, 202, 212, 309, 427
    states *versus* federal authority and, 324, 334
    surveying and, 36–38
    tobacco agriculture and, 202
    Treaty of Fort Pitt and, 268
    Treaty of Lancaster and, 34

Virginia war with Shawnees and, 209
Washington's Indian land acquisitions and, 297
westward expansion and, 173, 308
spirits, 30, 41, 111, 469
spiritual power, 44, 507n4
Spotswood, Alexander, 28, 30–31
squatters. *See* settlers (colonials, farmers, frontiersmen, squatters)
"squaw campaign," 266
Stalking Turkey. *See* Cunne Shote (Cherokee)
Stamp Act, 180
standing armies, 6, 291
Standing Bear, Luther (Lakota), 41
Stark, John, 245
statehood, 293, 297, 308–9, 315, 324
states. *See also* federal authority *versus* states' power (national unity); Virginia *and other states*
St. Clair, Arthur. *See also* Fort Recovery
background of, 316–17
British and, 383
Cherokees and, 144
Indian allies of, 425–26
Indian victory over, 379m, 405–6, 409, 411, 423–24, 434, 435, 439, 446, 459
Iroquois and, 404
Northwestern Confederacy victory over, 379m, 387–96
Northwest Territory and, 327–28
Ohio Company of Associates and, 313
Philadelphia diplomacy and, 1, 418
portrait of, pl 9
on strategy, 216
war *versus* negotiation and, 382
Washington and, 378, 386, 389, 392, 393, 394, 395
St. Clair, John, 103, 111–12, 141, 144
Steedman, William, 412
Stephen, Adam, 85, 115, 123, 124, 149, 165, 172, 174, 176, 178, 210, 261, 299, 323
Steward, Henry, 67
Stewart, Robert, 162, 164, 172
Stiles, Ezra, 286–87
St. Lawrence Indians, 107, 222–23, 242
St. Lawrence River, 139
St. Leger, Barry, 242
Stobo, Robert, 96, 199
Stockbridges, 219–21, 251, 406, 413, 442, 458, 533n36. *See also* Hendricks, Solomon *and other Stockbridges;*

Mahicans; Treaty of Canandaigua (1794)
Stone, William, 248
"Stranger Indians," 27
Strickland, William, 475
Stuart, Charles, 105–6, 118
Stuart, Gilbert, 461, pl 5
Stuart, John, 182, 185, 189, 213. *See also* Treaty of Hard Labor
"Suffering Traders," 194
Sugden, John, 459
Sullivan, John
Albany conference and, 238
Brodhead and, 271, 272
campaign of, 247–59
Indian land and, 259
map, 252m
Onondagas and, 248–49
Washington and, 247–48, 254–55, 257, 271, 272
surveyors and surveying, 5, 36–38, 37–41, 38–39, 39m, 41, 45, 48, 286, 334. *See also* Gist, Christopher *and other surveyors;* Northwest Ordinance (1785) *and* (1787)
Susquehannah Delawares, 143–44
Susquehannah towns and tribes, 113, 131
Susquehannah Valley, 22, 26, 43, 51, 99, 257
Susquehannocks, 22, 24, 25, 43, 69
Swashan (Abenaki), 223, 226
Swiss, the, 29. *See also* Bouquet, Henry; Vattel, Emer de

T
Taboca (Choctaw), 306–7
Tachanoontia (Onondaga), 34
Tachnechdorus. *See* Logan, John (Mingo)
Taken Out of the Water. *See* Tekakiska (Cherokee)
Tallassee King. *See* Hoboithle or Hopoithle or Opothle Mico (Creek)
Tall King (Creek), 363
Tamaqua (Beaver) (Delaware), 57, 60–61, 153, 154–55, 157, 159, 160, 173, 176, 177, 188, 506n53
Tame King. *See* Hoboithle or Hopoithle or Opothle Mico (Creek)
Tanaghrisson (Tanachrisson) (Thanayieson) (Johonerissa) (Deanaghrison) (the Half King) (Seneca), 72. *See also* Tanaghrisson's war
Anglo-French rivalry and, 62–65, 67, 68–72, 93, 105

Tanaghrisson (*continued*)
  background of, 53
  death of, 99–100
  described, 68
  Dinwiddie and, 70, 90, 92
  English and, 90–91, 58, 99
  Forks of the Ohio fort and, 84, 85
  French and, 90–91, 510n49
  Gist and, 507n22
  Logstown negotiation and, 54, 57, 60
  Logstown Treaty and, 58–59
  on Montour, 55
  Pennsylvania council of, 97–98
  Saint-Pierre and, 76–77
  Shingas and, 61
  Six Nations and, 64–65, 91–92
  Venango meeting and, 75
  Washington and, 6, 67, 68–71, 72–78,
    85–86, 87–89, 92, 93, 97–98, 100–101
Tanaghrisson's war, 81–101. *See also* Battle
    of Fort Necessity
  British and, 92
  Contrecoeur and, 87
  Great Meadows ambush and, 88–91
  Jumonville death and, 88, 89–90
  Washington and, 85–87, 87–88, 91–92,
    93–94
Tarhe (the Crane) (Wyandot), 443
Tassel. *See* Corn Tassel (Cherokee)
Tawalooth (Mohawk), 416
taxes, 6, 180, 293. *See also* whiskey tax and
    rebellion
Taylor, Alan, 327, 400
Teedyuscung (Gideon) (eastern Delaware),
    8, 117, 143–44, 153, 156
Teesteke (Toostaka) (Common Disturber)
    (the Waker) (Cherokee), 423
Tekakiska (Tekakisskee) (Taken Out of the
    Water) (Cherokee), 430
Telfair, Edward, 354
Tennessee, 27, 233, 285, 338, 339, 428.
    See also Treaty of San Lorenzo (1795);
    Treaty of Tellico (1798); Yazoo
    Companies; Yazoo Company
Tennessee River, 21m, 189, 246, 305, 430
Tewea. *See* Captain Jacobs (Delaware)
Texas, 281
Thanayieson. *See* Tanaghrisson (Seneca)
Thaosagwat, Hanyerry (Hanyost) (Oneida),
    251, 254
Thatcher, George, 329
Thawekila division of Shawnees, 51
Thayendanegea. *See* Brant, Joseph
    (Mohawk)

Thomas, George, 52
Thomson, Charles, 8, 144, 153, 156, 418
Three Fires, 381. *See also* Northwestern
    Confederacy war
Ticonderoga, 152, 317
Tidewater region (Virginia), 20, 26, 27, 28,
    31, 33
Timberlake, Henry, 128, 166
Tioga Point meeting (1790), 398–99, 402
Tiononderoga (Lower Mohawk Castle), 256
tobacco
  Atlantic exchange system and, 32–33,
    177–78
  boom-and-bust cycles and, 172, 177–78,
    201
  as diplomatic gift, 68, 80, 370, 390
  enslaved African Americans and, 32, 33
  financial crisis and, 201
  single-crop agriculture and, 31–32
  slavery and, 26, 473
  speculators and, 202
  Washington and, 177–78, 184
  West Indies trade and, 557n98
  westward expansion and, 202
Tocqueville, Alexis de, 485
Tohashwughtonionty. *See* Belt of Wampum
    (Seneca)
Tomah, Pierre (Maliseet), 228, 231
Toostaka. *See* Teesteke (Cherokee)
Tootematubbe. *See* Colbert, George
    (Chickasaw)
Town Destroyer (Conotocarious) (Devourer
    of Villages) (J. and G. Washington), 7,
    13, 25, 69–70, 86, 125, 256–57, 401
trade. *See also* Anglo-French rivalry; Atlantic
    exchange system; Logstown (Ohio
    country); Lydius, Henry *and other
    traders;* Ohio Company of Virginia;
    Ohio country; "Suffering Traders";
    tobacco; Treaty of San Lorenzo (1795)
  Braddock's road and, 151
  British, 445
  Cherokees and, 42
  Creeks and, 470
  Creek-West Indies, 368, 557n98
  Declaration of Independence
    and, 284
  deerskin, 25, 26, 27, 42, 306, 462, 470,
    557n98, 577n73
  East against West and, 337
  federal authority and, 442
  Federal Indian policy and, 324
  global, 10
  Indian land and, 327

Logstown Treaty and, 59
McGillivray/Spain and, 364–65, 371
Niagara and, 161
Ohio country and, 49, 61, 160–61
Revolutionary War in the West and,
    255–56
Royal Proclamation of 1763 and, 181
Royal Proclamation of 1763 negotiations
    and (1768), 188–89
southeastern, 350
Treaty of Easton (1758) and, 157
Treaty of Lancaster and, 54
Treaty of Pensacola and, 351–52
Treaty of Westminster and, 125
Virginia's Indian country and, 23, 24,
    25, 27, 31, 33
war *versus*, 226
Washington on, 160–61, 452–54, 479
West Indies and, 557n98
westward expansion and, 36
Trade and Intercourse Act (1790), 339–40,
    341, 399, 403
trading posts, 452–53, 461
Transylvania Company, 213
treaties. *See also* boundaries; diplomacy;
    Federal Indian policies; Treaty of New
    York (1790) *and other treaties;* war *versus*
    negotiation
    Confederation Congress and, 327
    federal authority and, 284–85
    Federal Indian policies and, 331
    Iroquois and, 30
    Jefferson and, 418
    land and, 307
    law of nations and, 325
    national unity and, 314
    Oneida land and, 303–4
    Thomson on, 8
    US Constitution and, 323
    Virginia and, 213
    Washington and, 7, 324, 325, 333,
        357–60, 442–43, 465–66, 483, 492
Treaty, Jay (1794), 444–45
Treaty of Albany (1701), 52, 157
Treaty of Albany (1722), 33, 52
Treaty of Albany (Albany Congress) (1754),
    98–99, 107, 118, 157, 321
Treaty of Augusta (1783), 352, 355, 356,
    358, 360, 368
Treaty of Camp Charlotte (1774), 210, 261
Treaty of Canandaigua (1794), 441–42, 456
Treaty of Colerain (1796), 432–33
Treaty of Easton (1758), 152–53, 155,
    156–58, 160, 173

Treaty of Fort Finney (1786), 310–11, 314
Treaties of Fort Harmar (1789), 327–28,
    400, 403
Treaty of Fort Jackson (1814), 107
Treaty of Fort McIntosh (1785), 310,
    313, 314
Treaty of Fort Pitt (1778), 264, 267–69,
    271, 277, 278
Treaty of Fort Schuyler (1788), 304
Treaty of Fort Stanwix (1768)
    boundaries and, 189–90, 193–95, 213
    Dunmore and, 201, 207, 211
    Shawnees' lands and, 21, 198, 207
    speculators and, 189, 191–92, 194, 207
    Washington's Indian land acquisitions
        and, 191–92, 194
Treaty of Fort Stanwix (1784), 301–3, 314,
    400, 401–2, 403
Treaty of French Lick (1784), 306
Treaty of Galphinton (1785), 353–55, 356,
    358, 360, 368, 372
Treaty of Greenville (1795), 443–44, 447,
    459–60
Treaty of Hard Labor (1768), 189,
    192–93, 213
Treaty of Herkimer (1785), 252m, 303
Treaty of Holston (1791), 423–25, 430,
    462, 465–66
Treaty of Hopewell (1785-86), 304–5, 306,
    307, 337–39, 339–40, 372, 423, 430,
    507n4
Treaty of Lancaster (1744)
    Dinwiddie on, 58
    Logstown Treaty and, 59
    Ohio Company and, 48, 49
    Ohio country and, 34, 45–46, 47, 54
    Six Nations and, 52
    Tanaghrisson and, 59
    terms of, 33–34
Treaty of Lochaber (1770), 186m, 193
Treaty of Logstown (1752), 46m, 54, 57,
    58–61, 69, 80, 118
Treaty of Long Island of Holston (1777),
    186m, 232–33
Treaty of Mobile (1784), 306, 307
Treaty of Montreal (1701), 52
Treaty of New York (1790), 366–77, 393,
    432, 433, 469–70
    secret articles of, 369–70, 371, 374, 375
Treaty of New York (1796), 490–91
Treaty of Nogales (1793), 427, 429
Treaty of Paris (1763), 174, 178
Treaty of Paris (1783), 280–81, 283,
    348, 437

Treaty of Pensacola (1784), 351–52, 353, 373
Treaty of Sandusky, 436
Treaty of San Lorenzo (1795), 445–46
Treaty of Shoulderbone Creek (1786), 355, 356, 358, 360, 368, 372
Treaty of 1646 (Anglo-Powhatan), 24
Treaty of Sycamore Shoals (1775), 213
Treaty of Tellico (1798), 466
Treaty of Tellico Blockhouse (1794), 349m, 430
Treaty of Vincennes (1792), 415–16, 437
Treaty of Watertown (1776), 229–30
Treaty of Westminster (1730), 125
Trent, William, 62, 65, 81, 85, 176–77
"tribal map," 43
tributary Indians (Virginia), 20, 30
Trueman, Alexander, 412
Truman, Thomas, 25
Trumbull, John, 352f, 368, 408, pl 3,4,8
Tsu-la. *See* Chutloh (Cherokee)
Tuckabatchee, 349m, 352, 355, 363
Turtle Clan (Delawares), xiii
Turtle Clan (Senecas), 263, 398, 400
Turtle Heart (Delaware), 176–77
Tuscaroras, 21m, 33, 43–44, 124, 129–30, 243, 244–45, 252m, 258, 303, 442, 533n53. *See also* Treaty of Canandaigua (1794)
Tutelos, 156–57
Twightwees, 62. *See also* Miamis

U
Ucahula (Cherokee), 142–43
Ugulayacabe (Wolf's Friend) (Chickasaw), 306, 426–27, 431
Uhhaunauwaunmut. *See* Hendricks, Solomon (Stockbridge)
uniforms, traditional, 83, 114, 148–49, 370, 426, 427, pl 1. *See also* Indian ways of fighting/dress
union, colonial, 99–100
United States, 9. *See also* American Revolution; national debt; Revolutionary War in the West; *individual Americans*
US Army. *See also* Wayne, Anthony *and other leaders*
"civilization" and, 475
Creeks and, 356
federal authority and, 439–40, 442
Federal Indian policies and, 333, 335–36
Indian destruction of (1791), 391–92, 497n13

national unity and, 291, 322
Northwestern Confederacy war and, 385, 386
St. Clair's defeat and, 391–92, 394, 396
US Congress and, 386, 433
US sovereignty and, 438
Washington and, 289, 291–92, 333, 433–34, 486
westward expansion and, 327
US Congress
Cornplanter and, 400
Creek land acquisitions and, 357
meeting with Delawares, 269
Red Jacket and, 404–5
southern Indians and, 353
St. Clair's defeat and, 392–93, 394–95
trading posts and, 453–54
US armed forces and, 386, 433
US Constitution, 100, 317, 321–25, 357–60, 376, 550n7
US Declaration of Independence, 218–19, 229, 279, 284
US Senate
Blount and, 474
Cherokees and, 424
Creeks and, 357–60, 368, 369–70
Iroquois and, 321, 407
Jay Treaty and, 445
St. Clair and, 385, 392
treaties and, 323, 333, 346, 357–60, 368, 369–70
Treaty of New York and, 376–77
Treaty of Vincennes and, 415–16
US sovereignty, 9, 325–26, 345, 438. *See also* federal authority *versus* states' power (national unity)
Upper Canada, 408. *See also* Simcoe, John Graves
Upper Creeks, 21m, 318, 346, 347, 363, 365–66, 373, 376, 474, 554n1. *See also* Treaty of Mobile (1784)
Uskwa'li-gu'ta. *See* Hanging Maw (Cherokee)
Ustenaka. *See* Ostenaco (Cherokee)
Utsi'dsata. *See* Corn Tassel (Cherokee)

V
Valley Forge (1778), 224, 236, 243
Van Braam, Jacob, 67, 76, 95, 96, 199
Vandalia scheme, 194, 199–200, 209
Vanishing Smoke. *See* Sayengeraghta (Seneca)
Van Schaick, Goose, 248–49
Vattel, Emer de, 325

Vaudreuil de Cavagnial, Pierre de Rigaud
de, 115–16, 135
Venango, 51, 63, 68, 71, 76, 78, 124
Venango, Fort, 46m, 162
Venango meeting (1753), 73–75
Vermont, 299, 301
veterans, Revolutionary, 291, 292, 309,
313–14, 315, 336, 380, 442. *See also*
land grants and land bounties; Ohio
Company of Associates
"Vices of the Political System of the United
States" (Madison), 355
Villiers, Louis Coulon de, 93–94, 94–95
Vincennes, 414. *See also* Treaty of Vincennes
(1792)
Vincent, John (Kahnawake Mohawk), 226
Vincent, Lewis (Louis Vincent) (Captain
Lewis) (Sawantanan) (Sawatanen)
(Huron), 226
Virginia. *See also* Anglo-French rivalry;
Dinwiddie, Robert *and other Virginians*;
Fort Duquesne; Fort Pitt meeting
(1775); frontier defense and Cherokee
alliance; land grants and land bounties;
Ohio Company of Virginia *and other
Virginian companies*; Potomac River;
Revolutionary War; Treaty of Fort
Stanwix (1768); Treaty of French Lick
(1784); Treaty of Lancaster (1744);
Treaty of Logstown (1752); Virginia
Regiment; westward expansion
backcountry of, 122
Braddock and, 103, 104, 108
captives and, 118
Catawbas and, 30, 124, 135–36
Cherokee alliance with (1755-1758),
124–26, 128–29, 130, 133–34, 137–38,
140–41, 142–47
Cherokees and, 164
Chickasaws and, 305, 306
Creeks and, 366
defense of Ohio country and, 81
enlistment bounty and, 139
enslaved African Americans and, 25,
26–27, 28, 121, 481–82, 579n33
federal authority and, 285, 307, 336–37
Fort Necessity and, 100
forts and, 115
French and Indians and, 120
Hendrick on, 99
Indian land and, 194, 212–13, 233, 307
Indian trade and, 24, 162
Joncaire and, 73–74
Kentucky and, 212, 262, 285, 299

Logstown Treaty and, 59
maps, 35m, 39m
Northwestern Confederacy wars
and, 446
Oconostota and, 166
Ohio country and, 45, 62, 65, 80
Ohio Indians and, 58
Overhill Cherokees and, 127
Pennsylvania and, 29, 199, 202, 209,
260, 262
Revolutionary War in the West
and, 278
Royal Proclamation of 1763 and, 182–83
Saint-Pierre's letter and, 81
scalpings and, 131, 163
Shawnees and, 208–11, 265
Shingas attacks and, 114
Tanaghrisson and, 59, 68–69
Treaty of Hard Labor and, 189
Washington and, 81, 99, 114, 115, 120
Virginia Company, 22, 24
Virginia Military District, 307
Virginia Regiment. *See also* Byrd III,
William; Crawford, William; land
grants and land bounties; Stephen,
Adam; Tanaghrisson's war
attacks on Shawnee towns (1756),
126–27
Byrd III and, 164, 165
Cherokee war and, 165
composition of, 83
Dinwiddie and, 81, 100
disbanded, 166
Forbes' campaign and, 149–50
Fort Duquesne and, 85
Fort Necessity withdrawal and, 96
French and Indian War and, 6
Indian land bounties and, 199–203
land bounties and, 191–92
"lesser sort" and, 121
Montour and, 124
roll of officers (1754), 529n40
Tanaghrisson's War and, 81, 85, 89
uniforms and, 148–49
Washington and, 83, 92, 100, 111,
114–15, 123, 138, 139–40, 167
Virginia Regiment, 2nd, 13, 139, 140
Virginia's Indian country
Indian land and, 20–26, 30–31
Indian populations and, 4–5, 19–20,
28–29
Ohio country and, 41–44
slavery, gun trade and disease and, 25,
26–27, 26–28

Virginia's Indian country (*continued*)
surveying/speculation and, 37–41, 39m
westward expansion and, 5, 29–37, 35m,
41–44
vocabularies, 312, 464

W
Wabash Indians, 328, 386, 403, 414, 459.
See also Northwestern Confederacy war
Wabash Valley, 51, 387
Wahunsonacock (Powhatan), 22–23
Waker, the. *See* Teesteke (Cherokee)
Waldo, Albigence, 236
Walker, John, 261
Walker, Thomas, 49, 109, 189, 191, 193,
261
Walking Purchase, 60
Wallace, Anthony, 397, 485
Walpole Company (Grand Ohio Company),
194, 199–200
wampum belts. *See also* gifts, diplomatic
Braddock and, 106
Cherokees receiving, 232
Cherokees to Denny, 153
Clark and, 272
Delawares refusing, 117
Denny to Ohio Indians, 153
Dinwiddie and, 92
diplomacy and, 72–73
Efau Hadjo to Washington, 474
Forbes to Ohio Indians, 157
Fort Pitt meeting and, 262, 263
Guyasuta and, 176
Hamilton sending, 131
Joncaire and, 56–57
Jumonville's death and, 90
Lignery to Indians, 158–59
Logstown negotiations and, 57
Morris receiving, 113
New York and, 301
Niagara meeting and, 182
Northwestern Confederacy and, 413, 416
Onondaga receiving, 100
Philadelphia diplomacy and, 407
rejection of, 69
Sandusky conference and, 418
Scarouady giving, 117
Tanaghrisson and, 70, 71, 72, 75, 85, 92
Teedyuscung receiving, 144
Treaty of Easton (1758) and, 155
Treaty of Fort Finney and, 311
Treaty of Fort Pitt and, 267
Treaty of Greenville and, 459
war belts, 175

Washington and, 1, 2, 68, 70, 72–73, 85,
92, 93, 129–30, 196, 426, 442,
572n111
Wawhatchee and, 134
writing *versus*, 269
Ward, Edward, 85
War in the West. *See* Revolutionary War in
the West
Warriors' Path, 30, 44, 54, 115, 188
war *versus* negotiation. *See also* diplomacy;
right of conquest
British and, 380, 396
federal power *versus* states and, 300
Indian raids and, 328
Jefferson and, 485
Northwestern Confederacy and, 397–98,
404, 416
Philadelphia diplomacy and, 397–98,
415
Pickering and, 405
Sandusky conference and, 420
trade and, 226
Treaty of New York (1790) and, 371–72,
376–77
US Senate and, 358
Washington and, 316, 333, 378, 387,
393–94, 396, 397–98, 403, 411, 412,
418, 421, 485–86
Warville, Jacques-Pierre Brissot de, 405, 481
Washington, Anne (sister-in-law), 40
Washington, Augustine (father), 26, 32, 40
Washington, Bushrod (nephew), 294
Washington, Charles (brother), 195
Washington, D.C., 336–37
Washington, George. *See also* American
Revolution *and other wars and battles;*
Dinwiddie, Robert *and other non-Indian
contacts;* diplomacy; Ohio country;
Philadelphia Indian diplomacy;
speculators; Tanaghrisson *and other
Indian contacts;* Town Destroyer
(Conotocarious) (Devourer of
Villages); Virginia Regiment;
Washington's Indian land acquisitions;
Washington's Indian policies
Assembly seat and, 172
as biblical figure, 287, 544n14
birth of, 26
death of, 482–83, 487
diseases and, 2, 40
House of Burgesses seat and, 162, 261
ignorance of history of, 130
Indian prisoner and, 78–79
inexperience of, 87–88, 91, 92

journal of expedition of, 95
legacy of, 6–7, 483–92
lying and, 93
marriage of, 164, 177
military career of, 40, 103, 104, 499n45
overview, 1–15, 499n45
paintings of, 14, pl 1, 13
retirement concerns, 477–83
scapegoating by, 172
Washington/Indian allies and, 221–31
wealth and social status and, 32
will of, 479–80, 482
young, 7, 37–41, 499n45
Washington, George (Delaware), 8
Washington, John (great-grandfather), 25, 26
Washington, John Augustine (Jack) (brother), 104, 178
Washington, Jr., Augustine (half-brother), 47
Washington, Lawrence (grandfather), 26
Washington, Lawrence (half-brother), 40, 47, 50, 104, 524n1
Washington, Sarah (niece), 40
Washington Crossing the Delaware (painting), 14
Washington's Bottom, 198, 295, 296m, 297, 449
Washington's Indian land acquisitions. *See also* Kanawha River and valley; Mississippi Land Company; Ohio Company of Virginia; Royal Proclamation of 1763; westward expansion
acreage of, 7, 39m, 478, 531n98
American Revolution and, 234, 243–44, 283, 294
Cornstalk on, 264
Crawford and, 85, 187–88, 192, 195–96, 199, 200, 201, 202, 203, 204, 206, 208, 211, 212, 271, 479
Dunmore and, 202, 203, 204, 206, 211, 294
Fort Stanwix Treaty land rush and, 211
his birthplace as, 26
Johnson's Pennsylvania boundary and, 185
land grants and bounties and, 171–72, 174, 179, 184, 191–92, 191–93, 195–203, 199–206, 211, 292, 294, 400
land rush and, 285–86
liquidation of, 449–50
Mohawk Valley and, 303
national unity and, 294–98, 296m
Ohio Company of Associates and, 313–14
Potomac River and, 290

Revolutionary War in the West and, 250–51, 261, 266, 271, 280
settlers and, 205–6, 285–86, 295–97, 296m, 330
surveying/speculation and, 37–40, 39m, 48, 286
Virginia war with Shawnees and, 209–10, 211
Washington's policy and, 3–6, 14
Washington's retirement and, 477–79
Washington's travels in Ohio country and, 75–76, 161, 163, 294–98, 296m
westward expansion and, 171–72, 448–50
Yorktown and, 280
Washington's Indian policies. *See also* "civilization"; federal authority *versus* states' power (national unity); war *versus* negotiation; westward expansion
Cherokees and, 128, 468
Cherokees and Chickasaws and, 337–40
Christian education and, 342–43
Hammond on, 566n58
humanitarian, 328–32, 343, 377, 380, 417, 485, 489
Indian freedom and, 321–22
Indian land and, 3, 5, 6–7, 328–29, 414, 415, 417, 418
Indian sovereignty and, 325–26, 329
influences on, 324–25, 326–27, 343–44
Iroquois and, 321–22
war debt and, 327
Waterford (Pennsylvania), 63
Watson, Ekanah, 406
Watts, John (Kunoskeskie) (Young Tassel) (Chickamauga Cherokee), 423, 430, 460
Waweyapiersenwaw. *See* Blue Jacket (Pekowi Shawnee)
Wawhatchee (Cherokee), 134–35, 137
Wayne, Anthony and his expeditions, 343, 379m, 418, 421, 434–39, 443–44, 447, 459, 461
Weas, 51, 314, 328, 387, 459
Weiser, Conrad, 53, 55, 73, 79, 97–98, 505n30
Welch, James, 478, 480
Wellenreuther, Hermann, 541n48
Wells, William, 414, 461
Wendats. *See* Wyandots (Wendats)
werowance, 23
Western Indians. *See* Northwestern Confederacy war
"western land," 4. *See also* Indian land
Western Reserve, 308

West Indies, 350, 557n98
Westos, 27
West Virginia, 194, 196–97, 478
westward expansion. *See also* boundaries;
    Indian land; land grants and land
    bounties; Northwestern Confederacy
    war; Northwest Ordinance (1785) *and*
    (1787); Ohio country; settlers
    (colonials, farmers, frontiersmen,
    squatters); speculators; surveyors;
    treaties
Albany Plan and, 98–99
big government and, 483
Britain and, 179–81, 328, 396
British and Spanish and, 444–46
"civilization" and, 331
civilization for land and, 330
Dunmore and, 200
enslaved African Americans and, 448,
    449, 482
farmers and, 193
federal authority *versus* states' power and,
    290, 307–18, 323, 446–47
Federal Indian policies and, 326–27,
    333–34
federal power and, 422
Franklin and, 544n14
Indian identity and, 286
Indian sovereignty and, 9
justice and, 486
Mt. Vernon reorientation and, 524n1
national identity and, 12
national unity (federal authority *versus*
    states' power) and, 327, 333–34
Northwestern Confederacy and, 433–44,
    446–47
Pickens and, 429
Pickering on, 344–45
Potomac River and, 36, 48, 96
religion and, 286–87
Royal Proclamation of 1763 and, 182
smallpox and, 281–82
St. Clair on, 328
tobacco and, 202
Treaty of Paris and, 174
Virginia and, 115
Virginia's Indian country and, 5, 29–37,
    35m, 41–44
war in the North and, 422, 433–47
war in the South and, 423–33
Washington and, 3, 6–7, 163, 171, 179,
    193–94, 290–91, 308, 309, 323,
    326–27, 329, 447, 450, 486, 524n1
Washington's Indian land acquisitions
    and, 171–72, 448–50

white racial consciousness and, 285
Wheelock, Eleazar, 225, 240, 241–42, 344
whiskey tax and rebellion, 336, 337, 382,
    439–40, 497n13
White Bird King. *See* Fusatchee Mico (Creek)
White Chief of the Abenakis. *See* Gill,
    Joseph Louis
White Eyes (George Morgan) (son of White
    Eyes), 342–43
White Eyes (Quequedegatha)
    (Koquethagechton) (Delaware),
    262–63, 267, 268, 274, 278, 279, 457
white identity, 12, 285
White Lieutenant (Creek), 363, 376
White Mingo (Kanaghorait) (Seneca), 196,
    262, 264, 265
White Thunder. *See* Belt of Wampum
    (Seneca)
Wiencek, Henry, 579n39
"wilderness," 5, 11, 13
"wild" Indians, 38, 41–42
Wilkinson, James and his expedition, 379m,
    388, 434, 461
Willett, Marinus, 352, 364, 365–66,
    429, 435
William, George, 38
William Penn's figurehead, 570n24
Williams, Glenn F., 530n82
Williamsburg talks, 233
Williamson, David, 274–75, 276, 277
Williamson, Hugh, 356–57, 374
Wills Creek, 54, 80
Winchester (Virginia), 65, 115, 132, 137.
    See also Fort Loudon
Wingenund (Delaware), 276, 327
Wisconsin, 315, 382
Wolcott, Oliver, 301
Wolcott Jr., Oliver, 492
Wolfe, Patrick, 316
Wolf's Friend. *See* Ugulayacabe (Chickasaw)
women, Indian, 10, 60, 105, 140, 198, 387.
    See also Queen Aliquippa
women, non-Indian, 119
Wood, James, 203–4, 261, 529n62
Wood's River Company, 47
Woyi (Pigeon) (Pouting Pigeon), 166
Wyandots (Wendats). *See also* Northwestern
    Confederacy war; Ohio Indians; Tarhe
    (the Crane); Treaties of Fort Harmar
    (1789)
Battle of Fallen Timbers and, 443
boundaries and, 420
Braddock's defeat and, 110, 112
Brodhead and, 248
Delawares and, 132, 263, 267, 274

diplomacy and, 160, 416, 443
Fort Pitt meeting and, 262
French *versus* English and, 56, 116
Iroquois and, 262
maps and locations of, 21m, 46m, 51
Sandusky campaign and, 274, 276, 443
St. Clair's defeat and, 390, 391
Virginia war with Shawnees and, 210
Washington and, 248, 459
Wyatt, Francis, 24
Wyllys, John, 384
Wyoming River Valley, 99, 117

X
XYZ Affair, 497n13

Y
Yazoo Companies, 340, 363, 373, 432, 557n90
yellow fever, 2, 427, 436
Yorke, Charles, 205
Yorktown surrender, 261
Youghiogheny River, 195, 449
Young, Alfred F, 568n2
Young King, 565n36
Young Tassel. *See* Kunoskeskie (Chickamauga Cherokee)

Z
Zeisberger, David, 60, 267, 269, 275, 312, 456, 541n48